The Dragon in the West

The Dragon in the West

From Ancient Myth to Modern Legend

DANIEL OGDEN

OXFORD

UNIVERSITY PRESS

OXFORD
UNIVERSITY PRESS

Great Clarendon Street, Oxford, OX2 6DP,
United Kingdom

Oxford University Press is a department of the University of Oxford.
It furthers the University's objective of excellence in research, scholarship,
and education by publishing worldwide. Oxford is a registered trade mark of
Oxford University Press in the UK and in certain other countries

First Edition published in 2021

Impression: 1

Published in the United States of America by Oxford University Press
198 Madison Avenue, New York, NY 10016, United States of America

British Library Cataloguing in Publication Data
Data available

Library of Congress Control Number: 2021933413

ISBN 978-0-19-883018-4

Printed and bound by
CPI Group (UK) Ltd, Croydon, CR0 4YY

わが最愛の妻
江里子に

Acknowledgements

This book has two principal catalysts: first, an inspirational conference devoted to the dragon in comparative perspective organized by Joseph Nagy (now of Harvard) at UCLA in 2015; and, second, the suggestion of Charlotte Loveridge at the Press that I turn my thoughts from an augmented edition of *Drakōn* to a new volume instead. A number of scholars have been generous with references and support, not least Barbara Borg (Exeter), Joanna Bowring (Librarian of Exeter College, Oxford), Rolf Bremmer (Leiden), Christian Djurslev (Aarhus), Debbie Felton (Massachusetts at Amherst), Rui Carlos Fonseca (Lisbon), David Horrell (Exeter), Levente Nagy (Pécs), Daniel Riaño Rufilanchas (Universidad Autónoma de Madrid), Gina Salapata (Massey), and, above all, Jan Bremmer (Groningen). My PhD student Ryan Denson has been an inexhaustible source of citations on sea-monsters, hippocamps, and allied creatures: the profound thanks offered here replaces countless local expressions of gratitude in the footnotes. The Exeter Inter-Library Loans librarians have fought indefatigably to retrieve the most recalcitrant items for me. Once again, I salute the OUP editorial team: in addition to Ms Loveridge, Karen Raith and Georgina Leighton.

Iidabashi, 2020

Contents

Appendices

List of Abbreviations

AASS	*Acta Sanctorum* 1643–1940
ANET[3]	Pritchard 1969
ANRW	*Aufstieg und Niedergang der römischen Welt* 1972–
ATU	Uther 2004
CIL	*Corpus inscriptionum Latinarum* 1863–
CPG	Leutsch and Schneidewin 1839–51
BHG	Halkin 1957
BHL	*Bibliotheca Hagiographica Latina* 1898–1901
BHO	Peeters 1910
BNJ	Worthington 2012–
CTA	Herdner 1963
CTH	Laroche 1971
DSS	Ogden 2013b
DW	*The Dragon in the West* (this volume)
EMI	LiDonnici 1995
FGrH	Jacoby et al. 1923–
GL	Keil and Heinrich 1857–80
IG	*Inscriptiones Graecae* 1903–
IGROM	*Inscriptiones Graecae ad res Romanas pertinentes* 1906–27
K-A	Kassel and Austin 1983–2001
KTU	Dietrich et al. 1995
LCI	Kirschbaum et al. 1968
LIMC	Kahil et al. 1981–99
MGH	*Monumenta Germaniae historica* 1826–
NEB	*New English Bible* 1961
PG	Migne 1857–1904
PGM	Preisendanz and Henrichs 1973–4
PL	Migne 1884–1904
RAC	*Reallexikon für Antike und Christentum* 1950–
RE	Pauly, Wissowa, and Kroll 1893–
SEG	*Supplementum Epigraphicum Graecum* 1923–
SGD	Jordan 1985
TLG	*Thesaurus linguae Graecae* (online resource)
TrGF	Snell et al. 1971–2004
TUAT	*Texte aus der Umwelt des Alten Testaments*

List of Figures

List of Tables

Note on Orthography

As usual, I have leaned towards Latinization in the rendering of Greek names, the friendlier way to handle them in English. I give titles of ancient works in English when they are more familiar in that form, or when it is helpful to do so. Following convention, Old Norse names have been rendered more accessible, other than in the titles of works as specified in the footnotes. With limited exceptions, the following principles are adopted: lengthening acutes are omitted; ǫ is modernized to ö; þ is printed as 'th'; ð as 'd'. I confess to little consistency in the retention and omission of the inflectional -r, preferring Sigurd to Sigurdr and Ragnar to Ragnarr but Valr to Val. Our dragons are sometimes 'it' and sometimes 'he' (occasionally 'she'); 'it' usefully distinguishes the creatures from their human antagonists in blizzards of fast-moving pronouns, but when a dragon is given a name or otherwise strongly personalized 'he' becomes unavoidable.

Introduction

Wer hât mich guoter ûf getan? 'What good person has opened me?' No matter: all of us in the modern West have a strong and clear idea of what a dragon looks like and of the sorts of stories it inhabits. One does not have to be a particular devotee of the fantasies of J. R. R. Tolkien, J. K. Rowling, or George R. R. Martin to do so. In physical form dragons are broadly serpentine, but have animalian heads, thick central bodies, wings, and clawed legs (as illustrated, for example in Fig. 0.1). In their stories they live in caves, lie on treasure, maraud, and burn; they are extraordinarily powerful, but even so ultimately worsted in their battles with humans. Despite the inestimable success of this physical form and of this broad story-type, there is nothing obvious, inevitable, or natural about them. Rather, both are complex and artificial constructs. Where do they come from?

The object of this book is to answer these questions. In 2013 I published two substantial volumes on the dragon of the Greek and Roman worlds, *Drakōn* (2013a) and *Dragons, Serpents, and Slayers* (2013b), in which I offered an account of its physical form—in essence just that of a massive snake, a great worm, albeit many qualifications are needed—as well as of the story-types and of the motifs in which it was engaged in that era. Since the appearance of those publications I have come to wonder about the joining of the dots. How did we get from there to here, to the modern notions of dragondom? I was frustrated by the fact that there existed no serious or systematic attempt, in any language, to follow this path and address this question, of such foundational importance and self-evident interest.[1] And so it has been that, not for the first time, I have attempted to create myself the book I longed to read but could not find. My training and experience in scholarship is almost exclusively in the field of Greek and Latin Classics, and it is with some trepidation that I venture so deeply into the full chronological span of the hagiographical tradition, and it is with even greater trepidation that I venture into the world of Old Norse and Medieval Germanic literature. I trespass in these fields not in a spirit of arrogance but one of despair: if no one else will attempt the book the world awaits, it falls to me to do so. If the inadequacies and infelicities of my account provoke the practiced experts of those fields at last to tell the story properly, with greater authority, closer accuracy, finer sensitivity, and subtler

---

[1] This is not the goal of Rauer's *Beowulf and the Dragon* (2000), but this outstanding book marshals much information of interest for the question.

Fig. 0.1 Winged, four-legged dragon. German, engraving, Athanasius Kircher: Kircher 1678: ii.96. Cornell University Library. Public domain (Artstor).

nuance than I have been able to do myself, then this volume may yet provide a worthwhile service after all, in the greater scheme of things: material to burn.

This book will, then, attempt to trace the development of the dragon in the West both in its physical form and also in its narrative contexts. All Gaul: three Parts, which differ considerably in their structures and their flavours.[2] Part I looks primarily at the evolution in the dragon's physical form between the eighth century BC, the beginning of the classical era, and the ninth century AD, by which time a recognizably modern dragon has been developed. Part II surveys the structures and motifs of the dragon tales of the hagiographical tradition, Greek and especially Latin, from the second century AD until the fifteenth century AD: the timespan is vast and the tales are unnumbered, but the tradition's remarkable conservatism renders the project viable. Part III considers the form of the dragon and the shape of its tales in Germanic literature produced between the eighth and fifteenth centuries AD, although the bulk of the attention must go to the brilliant flowering of Norse literature in the thirteenth and fourteenth centuries.

The breakdown of chapters in more detail now. In Part I, Chapter 1 needs to re-establish the baseline of our investigation by presenting a model of the classical dragon, the *drakōn*, in both its form and its narrative contexts. This model

---

[2] The titles of these three parts are admittedly meretricious. In an ancient context the term 'hero' properly refers to a dead man in receipt of cult, a status not possessed by all of the dragon-fighters discussed in this part. The status of 'saint' is less problematic, though it is curious that it should have been conferred upon the archangel Michael, and sad that, as of 1969, Margaret should have been stripped of it. A 'viking' is properly a sea-borne adventurer; only a handful of the dragon-fighters in our third part could properly be so described.

inevitably draws heavily on my two previous volumes on the subject. For efficiency here the reader will normally be referred for further evidence and discussions back to these, although some supplementary bibliography is also supplied. In course, new points of substance are made on: (1) definitional issues; (2) the origin of the dragon's beard; and (3) the form of Typhon. The next two chapters approach the classical material again to address fully for the first time a rather fundamental pair of questions: What was the difference between a Greek dragon and a Roman one? And what was the difference between a male dragon and a female one? As to the former question, the dragon culture espoused by the Greeks and the Romans was a coherent and continuous one, and so it made sense to treat Greek and Roman evidence together in those earlier books. However, this does raise the issue as to whether there was indeed anything distinctive about the reflex of the dragon in Latin culture specifically, the *draco*, and that is the question we now attempt to address in Chapter 2. It is argued that there was a certain tendency for the Romans to take a greater interest in the figure of the dragon and its perspective, and therefore to personalize it and anthropomorphize it. A simpler way of putting this would be to say that the Romans loved dragons rather more than the Greeks did. As to the latter question, Chapter 3 asks more particularly what the significance was of the term *drakaina*, the female-denoting reflex of the term *drakōn*. Here it is contended that, whilst the term could indeed be applied to a creature that resembled a pure-serpent *drakōn* in all respects, save for being female, the concept it more typically evoked was that of a female anguipede, a creature with the lower half of a serpent and the upper half of a woman.[3] Chapter 4 does the heavy lifting in terms of addressing the first part of our all-important focal question, namely: How did the classical dragon, essentially just a massive snake in form, a worm, evolve, in early Christian culture, into the very particular and distinctive fantasy creature we know as a 'dragon' today in the West? Here it is argued, in short, that the dragon acquired its animalian head and more bulbous central body from another well-established creature of classical fantasy, the ancient sea-monster (*kētos*), this by virtue of the fact that, whilst dragon and sea-monster had remained largely distinct creatures in classical culture, they had been confounded by the Septuagint. Its wings, however, and probably too in effect its two legs (the latter placed in the position of the sea-monster's front flippers), it derived rather from demons and the Devil, the latter being associated with snakes already in the Old Testament, and then spectacularly so in the New Testament's Revelation. By the ninth century AD these two developments had crystallized in the wyvern-type dragon. The dragon had to wait some centuries more to acquire a second pair of legs on a regular basis, a development that fully crystallized at the turn of the fifteenth century.[4]

---

[3] The substance of this chapter was first put together for an (unpublished) conference on underworld deities hosted by Maciej Paprocki at the Ludwig-Maximilians-Universität in 2017.

[4] The material in this chapter is partly based on Ogden (forthcoming a), to be published in the proceedings of a 2015 UCLA conference, edited by Joseph Nagy.

Parts II and III, on the dragon in the hagiographical (saintly) tradition and the dragon in medieval Germanic culture respectively, retain some attention upon the physical form of the dragon, but take rather more interest now in the types of narrative in which the dragon is engaged in those cultures. Hagiographical culture is so deeply conservative that the dragon's physical evolution in the Christian world outside it has relatively little impact on it, and for the most part the hagiographical dragon remains worm-style in form ('vermiform'), as we shall see in Chapter 5. The Christian winged dragon had a rather greater impact, surprisingly, on the physical evolution of the dragon in Germanic culture, as we shall see subsequently in Chapter 10. Germanic dragon traditions give us both vermiform dragons, presumed to reflect a creature-type indigenous to Germanic mythology (but, for reasons given, the influence of Latin hagiography here cannot be ruled out), and also, in greater quantities, winged-and-legged dragons of a sort comfortingly familiar to the modern audience. A significant number of Germanic texts, however, seem, interestingly, to be stranded between the two conceptions, in that they give us dragons that are described as flying or actually as winged, or are indicated to be so, but which don't leave the ground when they ought to, as if the role of a vermiform dragon in a traditional story has been superficially and cosmetically recast with its winged cousin, without any further adaptations being made to showcase the new star's more distinctive abilities.

But the bulk of these two Parts is, as said, devoted rather to the story-types in which the dragons are now engaged. Part II, on the hagiographical dragon fight, is dominated by a substantial and unfortunately indivisible Chapter 6 in which we survey, on the basis of some two hundred examples, the motifs that make up the principal narrative course of such dragon fights. Attention is given both to what is most typical, of course, but also to the more interesting and creative variations upon the typical. The themes reviewed here include the dragon's inhabiting of caves, wells, and tombs; its monopolization of springs, its marauding, its production of pestilential breath, its fieriness; the saint's spiritual preparations for battle, his deployment of prayers, of the sign of the cross, and of his stole against it; his exorcistic banishment of it, in the fashion of a demon, beyond water, to the wilderness, or to the abyss; otherwise, his killing of it and his disposal of its carcass; his conversion of the local community, and his memorial construction of a church or monastery. This survey is preceded by the preparatory Chapter 5, in which we look not only at the physical form of the dragon in hagiographical literature, as indicated, but also, importantly, at the biblical jumping-off points for many of the motifs in this principal narrative course. Chapter 7 then looks at a number of elaborate and recurring sets of motifs with greater independence from the principal narrative course, here dubbed 'major subroutines', including the dragon's brood, human sacrifices to the dragon, and the revivification of the dragon's final victim.

Chapter 8 dips back in time to look at the archaeology of the hagiographical dragon fight, as attested by a remarkable pagan parody of the story-type roughly contemporary with the earliest extant example of it (in proper form, at any rate), this parody being found in Lucian's *Philopseudes* of around the AD 170s. The parody indirectly attests the prior existence of a number of motifs in the tradition not actually documented within it until some centuries later. Chapter 9 looks to the two major military saints heavily associated with dragon fights. Some of the Theodore Tyron tales align in intriguing ways with secular Byzantine dragon-slaying traditions, whilst the iconography of George, familiar and thriving still today, can be shown to have its roots in the very earliest classical art.

We turn to the Germanic dragon in Part III. Whilst Chapter 10 looks at its physical form, Chapter 11 begins by considering how it was imagined first to have come across that form. As part of this investigation we must also consider the Germanic dragon's propensity to lie on treasure. The chapter then proceeds to review the remainder of what might be termed 'the principal narrative course' for the Germanic dragon, together with some subroutines, although the former treatment feels somewhat looser than its hagiographical counterpart. The themes considered here include: the dragon's weaponry, its slayer's weaponry, not least the named sword, the dragon's path between its cave and its river, the dragon's blood, and the dragon's brood once again.

This book is devoted to a (fairly vast) series of semi-continuous western traditions, but it is not an attempt to explain the dragon, or humankind's obsession with it, at any universal level, psychological or other. However, I note that universal, so-called 'sociobiological' explanations of the dragon have a better chance of being made to stick when they focus on its rootedness in the world of actual snakes as opposed to focusing on any of its abstract or compound characteristics. Mundkur may elicit a modicum of sympathy when he contends that, 'Sensitivity to the serpent's form and sinuous motion was fixed in man's psyche during anthropogenesis and is reflected in extraordinary ways in his animal behaviour, which is inseparable from his social behaviour and religious beliefs involving the serpent. These overt expressions are rooted in the complex long-term physiological effects of fear, which subsumes anxiety and stress—including their psychological repercussions.' For Mundkur, this accounts for humankind's obsessive fascination with the serpent, and consequently for the serpent's rich role in symbologies and 'primitive religions' (he imagines that serpent cults are more ancient and more widespread than those of any other animal).[5] By contrast, Jones elicits rather less

---

[5] Mundkur 1983 (the quote from p. xvi); the book merited a tolerant review from the heroic Fontenrose (1983). Charlesworth 2010:44-57 charts thirty-two ways (some of them dubious) in which the snake is distinctive in its physiology and behaviour and thereby lends itself to symbolic thought. Khalifa-Gueta 2018 now offers another universal, sociobiological, and perhaps also cognitive account of the dragon similarly grounded in the snake.

sympathy when he contends that humans retain deep in their brains from monkey days (!) an all-purpose admonitory image of a predator, accordingly a composite image of snake, cat, and raptor, an image that expresses itself to the consciousness in the form of a dragon. He is, of course, attempting to universalize the very particular and *contingent* features of the modern western dragon. Other objections aside, the dragon of (pagan) classical antiquity was bereft of feline elements and almost completely bereft of avian ones too.[6]

[6] Jones 2000 passim, esp. 60–2; cf. Ogden 2013a:24–5. Blust 2000 finds the origin of a universal dragon rather in the human response to rainbows.

PART I
HEROES

1

Drakōn

The Classical Dragon

1.1 *Drakōn*: The Semantic Field

The Greek term *drakōn* (plural: *drakontes*), taken up into Latin as *draco* (plural: *dracones*), signified a large, often gargantuan, snake 'and something more', that is to say, a snake with a supernatural quality or affinity, and often too with additional or exceptional physical or behavioural attributes.[1] In archaic and classical Greek literature the term is applied to snakes in the following (overlapping) categories: snakes in the service of a god, be they resident in his temple, handled in his rites, or entrusted with a more particular task, such as guardianship; snakes participating in or conveying omens, including in dreams; snakes participating in metamorphosis; snakes decorating arms, especially shields, where they exercise a talismanic function; and snakes in poetic similes, where they are anthropomorphized.[2] In the Hellenistic age the term was expanded to embrace also the miraculous snakes of remote lands, including the Indian serpents whose brains crystallized upon death into precious jewels.[3] Unsurprisingly, the more general Greek term for snake, *ophis*, could also be applied to all these creatures.

---

[1] For studies of the *drakōn* in the ancient world, see Fontenrose 1959; Merkelbach 1959; Mitropoulou 1977; Sancassano 1997; Grabow 1998; Rodríguez Pérez 2008; Charlesworth 2010:125–87; Ogden 2013a, 2013b.

[2] See Ogden 2013a:2–4, where the evidence is collated. When compiling these pages I was unaware of Daniel Riaño Rufilanchas' excellent 1999 investigation into the significance of the term ('Δράκων', published in a Festschrift for Conchita Serrano), and I am grateful to have the opportunity to draw attention to it here. Our general findings are in close accord: on the basis of a more broadly based survey than my own (my survey ended *c*.400 BC; he takes his down to the mid-ii BC Nicander), he defines *drakōn* as signifying a serpent in the aspect of a 'portentous, sacred, miraculous, and terrible creature' (esp. 174).

[3] Pliny *Natural History* 37.158; Philostratus *Life of Apollonius* 3.6–9; Solinus *De mirabilibus mundi* 30.15–18 (Pliny and Solinus cite Sotacus). See also Posidippus at *Greek Anthology* Appendix 3.79 (= Posidippus no. 15 Austin-Bastianini); Lucan *Pharsalia* 6.677–8, *Cyranides* 4.65; Tertullian *De cultu feminarum* 1.6; Isidore of Seville *Etymologies* 16.14.7. For the possibility that the Greek traditions of the massive and miraculous serpents of India originated in the indigenous Nagas, see Karttunen 1989:190–12, 216, 1997:227. Cf. Ptolemy Chennus' fantastical claim in his *Strange History* (at Photius *Bibliotheca* cod. 190, 153b), where we are told of a Pan-fish that contains a stone that catches fire when exposed to the sunlight. The folkloric theme of the serpent that contains a precious stone within its body is widely distributed. For example, the medieval Welsh tale of *Peredur vab Efrawc* tells of a *pryf du*, a 'black worm' that dwells in a lake and carries a stone in its tail. Whoever holds this in one hand is able to acquire as much gold as he desires in the other one; see Minard 2007:124–7. Armenian tradition holds that the king of the mountain snakes bears a crown-like, sun-like gem on his head,

1.2 The Great Dragons of Myth: Dragon-Fights

The greatest *drakontes* of the Greek imaginaire belonged either to the realm of myth or to that of cult. The former tended to find themselves in opposition to mankind or god-kind, and it was their destiny ever to be killed or overcome in terrible battles with heroes or gods. The latter, by contrast, were the most benign of deities, kindly disbursers of health and wealth. Let us begin by reviewing some of the more prominent examples amongst the great *drakontes* of myth.[4]

1.2.1 The Dragon of Ares

The Dragon of Ares, first attested in the earlier sixth century BC, was set by the god to guard the virgin spring of Dirce or Thebe, at the site of the future city of Thebes. When Phoenician Cadmus, charged with founding the city, needed its water, he faced the serpent and killed it, according to the most canonical version, with a rock. Cadmus sowed its teeth in the earth to produce a crop of ready-armed warriors (he was credited with the first discovery of metal: perhaps this was how), and these became the originating ancestors of the city's noble families. Ares initially punished Cadmus for killing his serpent, though he was later given the god's daughter Harmonia in marriage. But in due course, and under obscure circumstances, the couple were transformed into a pair of *drakontes* in turn and ended their lives in this form. Ovid's superb account of the fight is given in Chapter 2 (§2.2), but for now Apollodorus' (i–ii AD) account, which builds on earlier accounts by Pherecydes (*fl.* 454 BC) and Hellanicus (later V BC), will suffice:

> Apollo told Cadmus…to follow a cow that would show him the way, and to found a city wherever it fell down tired. Having received the oracle, he made his way through the land of the Phocians, and then encountered a cow amongst the herds of Pelagon. He followed behind it. Passing through Boeotia, it lay down at the point where the city of Thebes is now. Wishing to sacrifice the cow to Athena, he sent some of his men to get water from the spring of Ares. A *drakōn* guarding the spring, which some said was born of Ares, killed the majority of those sent.

possession of which can confer wisdom or the power of sorcery: Abeghian 1899:76. Note also the close involvement of serpents with magical gemstones in the xiv AD *Konrad's Saga*: Chapter 11, §11.4.2.

[4] All the creatures reviewed here are referred to as *drakontes* or *dracones*, although not always in the specific passages quoted. The examples are given in an order convenient for exposition. If we were to give them rather in the order of their attestation (which is not, of course, necessarily the order in which they came into existence), the progression would be as follows: (1) Hydra, (2) Ladon, (3) Dragon of Ares, (4) Python, (5) Dragon of Colchis, and (6) Dragon of Nemea. While not attested first, Typhon (§1.6 and Appendix A) is likely to be in effect the oldest of them all.

Cadmus became angry and slew the *drakōn* and, on Athena's advice, sowed its teeth. When the teeth had been sown, men rose up from the ground under arms, whom they called the Spartoi ['Sown Men']. These men killed each other, some in the course of arguments, knowing what they were doing, and others without realizing it. Pherecydes says that Cadmus, seeing the armed men growing up out of the earth, threw stones at them, and they, thinking that they were being attacked by each other, fell to fighting. But five remained over, Echion, Oudaios, Chthonios, Hyperenor, and Peloros. In return for his killing, Cadmus was indentured to Ares for a long year. For a year at that time was equal to eight modern ones. After his period of service Athena bestowed a kingdom upon him, and Zeus gave him Harmonia to wife, the daughter of Aphrodite and Ares.... Cadmus left Thebes with Harmonia and went to the Encheleans ['Eel people']. The Illyrians were making war on them, but the god prophesied that they would beat them if they had Cadmus and Harmonia as their leaders. The Encheleans were persuaded and so made them their leaders against the Illyrians, and conquered them. Cadmus became king of the Illyrians. After this Cadmus turned into a *drakōn*, together with Harmonia, and was sent by Zeus to the Elysian fields.

Apollodorus *Bibliotheca* 3.4.1–2, 3.5.4
(incorporating Hellanicus F51 Fowler and Pherecydes F22a Fowler)[5]

The teeth of the Dragon of Ares also found their way to Colchis (see §1.2.4), where Aeetes used them to produce another crop of sown men for Jason to do battle with, prior to his engagement with the local dragon there. According to Apollonius of Rhodes (*c*.270–245 BC), it was Athena that divided the teeth between Cadmus and Aeetes;[6] according to the *Orphic Argonautica* (iv AD or later), Phrixus brought half of them to Colchis as a bride-price for Medea's sister Chalciope.[7]

1.2.2 The Dragon of Nemea

The Dragon of Nemea, first attested in the earlier fifth century BC, served as the guardian of the spring of Langia for Zeus in his sacred grove at Nemea (Fig 1.1). Hypsipyle, the slave-nurse to baby Opheltes, put him down in the grass to fetch water for the Seven against Thebes as they passed through, whereupon he was

---

[5] Further principal texts: Euripides *Bacchae* 1330–9, 1355–60, *Phoenissae* 638–48, 657–75, 818–21, 931–41, 1006–12, 1060–6, F930 *TrGF*; Palaephatus 3; Ovid *Metamorphoses* 3.28–98 (quoted below); Philostratus *Imagines* 1.18; Nonnus *Dionysiaca* 4.348–463. Iconography: *LIMC* Kadmos i 7–47. For more sources and discussions, see Ogden 2013a:48–54, 2013b:109–18, to which add Rodríguez Pérez 2008:183–215.

[6] Apollonius *Argonautica* 3.1176–90.   [7] *Orphic Argonautica* 873.

Fig. 1.1 The Dragon of Nemea constricts Opheltes. Roman, red jasper intaglio, *c*.i BC–iii AD. Metropolitan Museum, New York, Gift of John Taylor Johnston, 1881, 81.6.110. Public domain.

killed by the serpent, either deliberately or accidentally, with a flick of its gigantic tail. The Seven slew the serpent to avenge the child and established the Nemean Games in the boy's memory. Here is the central part of Statius' expansive description of the episode:

In the meantime a serpent [*serpens*], born of the Earth, the sacred terror of the Achaean grove, rose up in the fields, and with a loose drawing motion now drove its monstrous self forwards, now left its back behind it. There was a bluish fire in its eyes. The green foam of its swollen venom was poised in its mouth. Three tongues flickered. There were three ranks of barbed teeth. A splendid but cruel crest projected from its gilded forehead. The peasants said that it was sacred to Jupiter the Thunderer, who presided over the place and received the meagre offerings made on forest altars. Now the serpent twined around the temples of the gods, gliding with wandering coil, now it wore away the oaks of the wretched forest and smashed enormous ash trees in its coils. Often it stretched itself out across rivers, lying on both raised banks at once, and the river, bisected by its scales, seethed up. But at other times, when all the land was gasping at the behest of Ogygian Dionysus, and the trembling nymphs [i.e. the naiad springs] lay hidden in the dust, it twisted its winding frame backward on the ground more savagely and curved its sides around, and raged dangerously with the fire of its parched venom. It rolled over ponds, dry lakes and failing springs, and wandered in empty riverbeds. Tentatively, it now lifted back its mouth and licked at the liquid air, and now, facing downwards as it grated over the groaning fields, it cleaved to the earth, in case the green plants should exude any moisture. But, wherever it applied its mouth, the grasses, stricken by the hot blasts of its breath, collapsed, and the field died before its hissing. It was as large as the Snake that separates the ether from the Artic Plough and extends to the South and the foreign sky. It was as big as that snake too [i.e. Python] that twisted round the twin peaks of sacred Parnassus with its coils, until, transfixed by you, Delian

Apollo, it carried with it a forest of arrows, with a hundred wounds. Little boy, what god allotted to you so weighty a fate? Did you already lie dead before this foe, when scarcely at the very threshold of life? Was it all so that you might die in a fashion worthy of such a great tomb, and become sacred for the peoples of Greece throughout the centuries? You died, boy, when grazed by the lashing tip of the serpent's tail (it knew it not), and at once sleep fled from your limbs, and your eyes opened only into death. But when your shocked, dying cry was released into the breezes, and then fell silent in your mouth, your complaints broken short, just as utterances go unfinished when people dream, Hypsipyle heard, and, lifeless herself, snatched along her sickened knees which baulked at the easy course. She was already sure of disaster, foreboding it in her mind, and she scanned everything with hasty gaze, searching over the ground and repeating in vain the words known to the small child. He was nowhere to be seen, and the meadows had already lost his fresh tracks. The sluggish enemy slumbered in the greensward, gathered into a spiral, and occupied broad acres, its neck laid out upon its slanting belly. The unfortunate woman shuddered at the sight and fired the deep grove with her long cry. The serpent was not disturbed; it merely continued to lie there. The tearful howls reached the ears of the Argives. As soon as they were alerted, on the leader's nod, the Arcadian knight Parthenopaeus, burning with eagerness, sped to find the cause and brought back the explanation. Then, finally, the fierce creature stirred its scaly neck in response to the glinting of the arms and the cries of the men. With a huge exertion Hippomedon snatched up a rock, with which a field had been marked off, and, raising himself aloft, drove it through the empty air. It whirled with the motion of the stones hurled against gates barred in war. The leader's valour was fruitless: the snake had already swung its pliable neck backwards and it defused the blow as it made contact. The earth reverberated and the densely entwined foliage was torn apart throughout the pathless groves. Capaneus came up to challenge the snake with an ash-wood spear, and cried out, 'But you will never escape the wounds I deal you, whether you are the wild inhabitant of a trembling grove, or a source of pleasure granted to the gods (and would that you were). You would not do so even if you were to carry on this back of yours a giant to join battle with me.' The trembling spear flew and entered the monster's gaping mouth. It cut the wild bonds of the three-furrowed tongue. Then it shot out through the standing crests that decorated its flashing head. Coated with the gore of the black brain, it lodged itself deeply in the ground. The agony had hardly coursed through the entirety of the snake's frame, but, rolling itself up swiftly, it encompassed the weapon, tore it out and fled back with it into the hidden temple of the god. There it stretched out its great bulk over the ground and hissed out its life in supplication at its master's altars. You mourned for him, indignant marsh of akin Lerna [home of the Hydra], Nymphs accustomed to sprinkle the snake with spring

Fig. 1.2 Heracles, the Hesperids, and Ladon. Red-figure terracotta vase, attributed to the Hesperides Painter, early iv BC. Metropolitan Museum, New York, Fletcher Fund, 1924, 24.97.5. Public domain.

flowers, the fields of Nemea it crawled over, and the wood-dwelling fauns of every grove, with your pan pipes. Zeus himself had called for his weapons from the height of the ether, and clouds and storms were gathering. But his anger was too small, and Capaneus was held not to deserve the greater weapon. However, the draft of the launched thunderbolt caught the top of his helmet crest.

Statius Thebaid 5.505–87[8]

1.2.3 Ladon, the Dragon of the Hesperides

Ladon was the unsleeping guardian of the golden apples of the Hesperides (Fig. 1.2). When we first glimpse him, in Hesiod's early seventh-century BC *Theogony*, he is brooding over the apples, in a cave-lair inside the Earth, in the manner of Fafnir and other Germanic dragons (see Chapter 11, §11.2):

Ceto made love with Phorcys and bore her youngest child, a terrible snake [*ophis*] which guards all-gold apples within its great coils in its lair in the dark Earth. This is the family of Ceto and Phorcys.   Hesiod *Theogony* 333–6

---

[8] Further principal sources: Bacchylides *Epinicians* 9.10–14 (earlier v BC); Euripides *Hypsipyle* FF754a, 757 *TrGF*; Hyginus *Fabulae* 74; Pausanias 2.15.2–3. Iconography: *LIMC* Archemoros *passim*, Hypsipyle i 2–9, Nemea 13–15, Septem 12–20. For more sources and discussions, see Ogden 2013a:54–8, 2013b:119–24.

Subsequently, in art, Ladon is shown hanging with the apples in their parent tree, where he is fed from a phiale, a shallow bowl, by the Hesperid maidens. Heracles was tasked with taking some of the apples as one of his Labours. By one tradition, Heracles clubbed him to death to take them. By another, one of the maidens, as it seems, fell in love with the hero, enabling him to prevail upon the sisters to get the apples for him whilst drugging the unsleeping serpent (here immortal) or distracting him with food.[9]

1.2.4 The Dragon of Colchis

Like Ladon, the unsleeping Dragon of Colchis too hung in a tree to guard a golden treasure, in this case the golden fleece (cf. Figs 1.3 and 4.17). Like Ladon too, this dragon was tended by a maiden, Medea, daughter of the fleece's owner, Aeetes, and she too drugged it so that the hero with whom she had fallen in love, Jason, could steal its treasure. Valerius Flaccus' rich account of the taking of the fleece will be quoted in Chapter 2 (§2.2), but here is Apollonius of Rhodes' influential version (*c.*270–245 BC):

Fig. 1.3 Jason and the Dragon of Colchis. Greek, terracotta column-krater, *c.*470–460 BC. Metropolitan Museum, New York, Harris Brisbane Dick Fund, 1934, 34.11.7. Public domain.

---

[9] Unfortunately, no single text in itself provides a satisfactory, let alone expansive, account of either of these episodes. Nonetheless, the principal sources, such as they are, are: Panyassis *Heraclea* F10 Davies/F11 Bernabé/F15 West; Pherecydes F16c Fowler; Apollonius *Argonautica* 4.1396–1407; [Eratosthenes] *Catasterismi* 1.4; Virgil *Aeneid* 4.480–6; Seneca *Hercules Furens* 524–32; Apollodorus *Bibliotheca* 2.5.11; Hyginus *Astronomica* 2.6.1; Solinus 24.4. Iconography: *LIMC* Herakles 1697–1761, 2676–787, Ladon i. More sources and discussions at Ogden 2013a:33–40and 2013b:57–62, to which add Verbanck-Piérard and Gilis 1998 (a comparison between the traditions, literary and iconographic, of Heracles' Ladon Labour and his Hydra Labour); Rodríguez Pérez 2008:101–47; and now Salapata 2021 (an insightful essay with a strong challenge to the way in which I have read the tradition myself). The name 'Ladon' is only found at Apollonius *Argonautica* 4.1396 (late, derivative sources aside).

Jason and Medea came down the path to the sacred grove in search of the giant oak, over which the fleece had been cast, like a cloud that glows red under the fiery rays of the rising sun. But the snake [*ophis*], watching out with its sleepless eyes, stretched out its long neck to meet them as they came and gave out a monstrous hiss. The long riverbanks and the vast grove reverberated around them. This was heard by the inhabitants of the Colchian land who lived a long way from Titanian Aea [i.e. Colchis itself], by the debouch of the Lycus, which splits off from the roaring river Araxes and mixes its sacred stream with the Phasis. They combine their streams into one and debouch into the Caucasian sea. New mothers woke in fear and, distressed, threw their hands round their baby children, who were sleeping in the crooks of their arms, and who shook at the hiss. As above smouldering wood unnumbered circles of sooty smoke coil upwards and one ever rises quickly on top of another, ascending from below in spirals, so then did that huge creature gather its unnumbered coils, covered over with dry scales. The girl came before its eyes as it coiled. In a sweet voice she invoked Sleep, highest of the gods, to help her in bewitching the monster. She cried out to the night-wandering queen, the underworld goddess [Hecate, patron of witches], to look kindly upon her project. The son of Aeson [Jason] followed her, scared, but the snake was already bewitched by her song and was unfolding its long, spiralling spine and straightening its countless circles, just as a black wave, silent and without noise, rolls over a calm sea. Even so, it raised its terrible head aloft and was eager to enfold the pair of them in its ruinous jaws. But she sprinkled its eyes with a fresh-cut sprig of juniper, dipping this pure herb into her potion to the accompaniment of her incantations. The intense smell of the drug cast sleep round about. The snake laid down its jaw and rested it just where it was. Its endless coils were unfurled a long way behind through the wood of many trees. Then, as the girl instructed him, he seized the golden fleece from the oak. But she stood her ground and smeared the head of the creature with her drug, until Jason himself bade her return to his ship, and she left the shady grove of Ares.   Apollonius *Argonautica* 4.123–66[10]

The first attestation of the Colchis *drakōn* comes on the *c*.480–470 BC Duris Cup (Fig. 1.4), which is also the most magnificent portrait of any *drakōn* to survive from antiquity. The interesting image suggests that the *drakōn* had initially succeeded in swallowing Jason, but had to regurgitate him, perhaps because Medea's lotion of invincibility had rendered him indigestible.[11]

---

[10] Further principal sources: Pindar *Pythians* 4.242–50 (462 BC); Euripides *Medea* 480–2; Valerius Flaccus *Argonautica* 8.54–121 (quoted below, Chapter 2, §2.2); Orphic *Argonautica* 887–1021; Tzetzes on Lycophron *Alexandra* 615, incorporating Lycus *FGrH* 570 F3 and Timaeus *FGrH* 566 F53. Iconography: *LIMC* Argonautai 20–1, Iason 22–54, Medeia 2–4. More sources and discussions: Ogden 2013a:58–63, 2013b:125–33; to which add Rutherford 2001:24–9; Bremmer 2008:317–20 (arguing that the episode refracts the Hittite myth of Illuyanka); and Rodríguez Pérez 2008:149–82.

[11] *LIMC* Iason 32.

Fig. 1.4 The Colchis Dragon regurgitates Jason before the golden fleece; Athena attends. The Duris Cup, Attic red-figure cylix, *c*.480–470 BC. Vatican, Museo Gregoriano 16545. © Vatican Museums and Galleries, Vatican City/ Bridgeman Images.

1.2.5 Python (or Delphyne), the Dragon of Delphi

The *drakōn* of Delphi, owner of the Delphic oracle, is found in both a female variant, Delphyne, first attested *c*.590 BC, and a more common male one, Python (Figs 1.5, 1.6). It is told of Python that, after receiving a (self-fulfilling) oracle to the effect that Apollo, the son Leto was expecting, was destined to kill him and take the shrine, he harried the goddess in her pregnant state. In revenge, Apollo, once born, shot him with arrows from his mother's arms. Delphi acquired the by-name of Pytho from the pestilential rotting (*pythein*) of his gargantuan carcass (an over-determined aetiology). Here is Euripides' account of the central episode (*c*.412 BC):

> Lovely is the offspring of Leto [Apollo], whom once she bore in the fruit-bearing hollows of Delos, the golden-haired one, skilled in the lyre, and who delights in the good aim of the bow. She, his mother, brought him from the sea-ridge and the glorious place of birth to the peak of Parnassus that revels with Dionysus,

Fig. 1.5 Python challenges Leto, with babies Apollo and Artemis. Apulian, lost red-figure neck amphora, earlier iv BC. Recoloured print by J. H. W. Tischbein, after Hamilton and Tischbein 1791–5:iii, fig. 4. Property of the author.

Fig. 1.6 Apollo of Cyrene with Python. Roman, marble statue, ii AD. British Museum 1861,0725.1. Photo: Daniel Ogden.

Parnassus of flooding waters. There the mottled-backed dark-eyed *drakōn* occupied a grove, well shaded with leafy laurel, a huge monster of the Earth, and tended the chthonic oracle. Phoebus [Apollo], though still a baby, though still playing in your mother's arms, you killed him, and succeeded to his place in charge of the divine oracle. You sit on the golden tripod, on an unlying throne, disbursing prophecies to men from your divine inner sanctum, neighbour of the streams of Castalia, occupying a hall at the centre of the world.

Euripides *Iphigenia in Tauris* 1234–57[12]

1.2.6 The Hydra, the Dragon of Lerna

The Hydra (first attested *c.*700 BC) was the multi-headed *drakōn* of the Lernaean marsh (Fig. 1.7). Her proper name—or perhaps it is merely a designation or title—consists of the standard word for a common or garden 'water-snake'. Another of Heracles' Labours tasked him with killing the serpent, and he did so with the help of his companion Iolaus, whilst a crab (!) came to the aid of the Hydra. In the canonical version of the fight, whenever Heracles chopped off one of the serpent's heads with his sickle, a weapon well adapted to her standing crop of necks, the Hydra would instantaneously grow two more to replace them. Heracles eventually defeated the creature by having Iolaus sear the remaining stump as soon as each head was lopped off. For all the fame of this myth, it is poorly served in the extant literary tradition. The fullest of the straightforward accounts of it is provided by Apollodorus (i–ii AD):

> The second Labour he [Eurystheus] assigned to him was to kill the Lernaean Hydra. This was reared in the swamp of Lerna and used to venture forth onto the plain and plunder the cattle and the land. The Hydra had a huge body, and nine heads, eight of them mortal, but the middle one was immortal. Heracles

Fig. 1.7 Heracles, Iolaus, and the Hydra. Caeretan terracotta hydria attributed to the Eagle Painter, *c.*520–510 BC. The J. Paul Getty Museum, 83.AE.346. Public domain.

---

[12] Further principal sources: *Homeric Hymn* (3) *to Apollo* 300–9, 349–73 (*c.*590 BC; quoted, in part, in Chapter 3, §3.3.2); Ephorus *FGrH* 70 F31b; Plutarch *Moralia* 414b and 417f–18c (*Failure of Oracles*); Hyginus *Fabulae* 140; Menander Rhetor *Peri epideiktikōn* 3.17 pp. 441–2 Spengel. Iconography: *LIMC* Apollon 39f, 39n, 79, 81a, 200i, 215, 209, 222, 224, 238, 261a, 371, 373, 602, 993–1002, Apollon/Apollo 38–40a, 52, 54l, 56a, 61k, 197, 356, 375a, 482, 499a, 519, 551, Python 1–7. For more sources and discussions, see Ogden 2013a:40–8, 2013b:39–44; to which add Miller 1986 esp. 70–91; Rodríguez Pérez 2008:69–100.

mounted his chariot, with Iolaus as his driver, arrived at Lerna, and brought his horses to a halt. He caught sight of the Hydra on a hill beside the springs of Amymone, where she had her lair. He pelted her with lighted arrows and compelled her to come out. As she came out, he overpowered her and kept tight hold of her. The Hydra attached herself to one of his feet and wound herself around it. He beat her heads with his club, but he was not able to achieve anything. When he had beaten one head, two new ones grew up. A huge crab came to help the Hydra, biting his foot. Therefore, when he had killed it, he himself too called in Iolaus, who, setting light to part of the nearby wood, seared off the stumps of the Hydra's heads with brands and prevented them from rising up. Having overcome the re-growing heads in this way, he cut off the immortal one, buried it, and placed a heavy rock on top, beside the road through Lerna that leads to Elaeus. He sliced up the body of the Hydra and dipped his arrows in the venom. But Eurystheus claimed that this Labour should not be counted amongst the ten, for Heracles had not overcome the Hydra alone but with the help of Iolaus.

Apollodorus *Bibliotheca* 2.5.2[13]

The name or designation 'Hydra' usually usurps the term *drakōn* in the source tradition, but the latter is at least applied to the creature by (probably) all three of the Tragedians.[14] We shall say something of the Hydra's identity as a female entity in Chapter 3, §3.2.

1.3 The Dragons of Cult, Great and Small

The following are the more prominent examples of great *drakontes* of cult.

1.3.1 Healing Gods: Asclepius and Amphiaraus

The folkloric association between snakes and healing extends far beyond the confines of the classical world.[15] Within it, the ancients would on occasion point to

---

[13] Further principal sources: Pisander *Heraclea* F3 Davies/F2 Bernabé/F2 West (vii–vi BC); Panyassis *Heraclea* F3 Davies/F6 Bernabé/F8 West; Sophocles *Trachiniae* 831–8; Euripides *Heracles* 1274–5; Palaephatus 38; Diodorus 4.36 and 38; Heraclitus *De incredibilibus* 18; Ptolemy Chennus *Strange History* at Photius *Bibliotheca* cod. 190, 147b22–8, incorporating Aristonicus of Tarentum *FGrH*/*BNJ* 57 F2 and Alexander of Myndus *FGrH*/*BNJ* 25 F5; Pausanias 2.37; Servius on Virgil *Aeneid* 6.287; schol. Plato *Phaedo* 89c, incorporating Hellanicus F103 Fowler and Herodorus of Heraclea F23 Fowler. We rely on Aristonicus (i AD?) for the exquisite detail that the Hydra's middle head was golden: did this author exist, or was he a figment of the fantasist Ptolemy Chennus' imagination? Cameron 2004:202 considers him imaginary, but Dowden (*BNJ* ad loc.) continues to believe. Iconography: *LIMC* Herakles 1697–1761, 1990–2092. For more sources and discussions, see Ogden 2013a:26–33, 2013b:50–6. Mundkur 1983:74–5 finds in the Hydra's vitality after decapitation a refraction of the fact that both halves of a bisected snake can remain strikingly vigorous for some fifteen minutes.

[14] Aeschylus F123 *TrGF* (probably); Sophocles *Trachiniae* 834; Euripides *Phoenissae* 1134–8.

[15] e.g. ATU 612; the type-tale is Grimm no. 16, 'The Three Snake Leaves'.

the seemingly regenerative power of a snake's sloughing.[16] The great healing god Asclepius is typically represented in avuncular, bearded, humanoid form, with a smallish *drakōn* coiling around his staff (Fig. 1.8): alter ego, avatar, symbol, servant, or pet?—seemingly all of these.[17] But the mythical narratives of his journeys to new cult centres reveal that his base-form was actually that of a giant *drakōn*. We shall look at Ovid's superb account of his journey from Epidaurus to Rome in this form in the following chapter (§2.3). Asclepius' cult came to prominence only in the fifth century BC (and he is first attested with a *drakōn*-association *c*.420 BC), but it spread rapidly in the Hellenistic period and he became one of the Roman empire's most popular gods: over nine hundred of his shrines have been identified.[18]

It is in the context of the cults of healing gods like Asclepius, which were based on incubation, that we encounter ancient *drakontes* in their most tangible form; for actual, sacred snakes—'*drakontes*'—were maintained in their shrines as avatars of the gods themselves. A miracle inscription from Epidaurus shows how the

Fig. 1.8 Asclepius with his serpent staff. Roman, plasma intaglio, i BC–iii AD. Metropolitan Museum, New York, Gift of John Taylor Johnson, 1881, 81.6.92. Public domain.

---

[16] Above all see Apollodorus of Athens *FGrH* 244 F138a; cf. also Cornutus *Theologiae Graecae compendium* 33, Artemidorus *Oneirocritica* 2. 13, Eusebius *Praeparatio evangelica* 3.11.26, Macrobius *Saturnalia* 1.20.1–4; Theodoret *Graecarum affectionum curatio* 8.23; Cosmas on Gregory of Nazianz *Carmen* 52; schol. Aristophanes *Wealth* 733.

[17] In modern medical imagery Asclepius' staff with its single serpent coiling around it has been erroneously supplanted by the more elaborate rod of Hermes, the caduceus, around which a pair of snakes entwines symmetrically, these snakes sometimes also being winged. This is because Churchill, the British publisher of the medical textbooks that circulated in the United States in the 1840s, printed the caduceus on its title pages. For the press itself the image was merely a traditional printers' device that had been in use since the early 1500s, a device that celebrated the affinity between their work and that of the messenger of the gods. See Cavanaugh 2018:7–17.

[18] Sources for Asclepius: Edelstein and Edelstein 1945, a vast collection; LiDonnici 1995 (for the Epidaurian miracle inscriptions). Iconography: *LIMC* Asklepios passim. For the shrines, see the monumental Riethmüller 2005; for incubation in his sanctuaries, see now Renberg 2017 esp. i, 115–270, 634–49, 689–713. For Asclepius' serpentine affinities and the possible reasons for them (sloughing aside), see Ogden 2013a:310–17, 342–6, with earlier bibliography.

god could work simultaneously in both an (ethereal) humanoid manifestation and a more tangible serpentine one (iv BC):

> A man had his toe cured by a snake [*ophis*]. This man was in a bad way, with a nasty ulcer on his toe. During the day he was carried out by the attendants and seated on a bench. Sleep took hold of him, and during this sleep a *drakōn* came out of the dormitory and cured his toe with its tongue, and after doing this went back into the dormitory. When he woke from his sleep and was well, he said he had seen a vision, and that he had seen a young man of beautiful form sprinkle a drug over his toe.   *EMI* (A) 17

A similar story was told in visual form by Archinus, who had been healed in the shrine of the Asclepian-style god (or hero) Amphiaraus at Oropus (early iv BC). The image on the relief plaque he dedicated there consists of three overlapping planes. In the foreground Archinus stands before the humanoid Amphiaraus himself, whose divinity is marked out by his larger-than-human size; he makes some sort of application to Archinus' bad shoulder; presumably this represents a dream. In the middle ground the same Archinus lies abed whilst a large snake loops up over the side of his couch and applies itself to the same errant shoulder; this will represent his real-world incubation. In the background the healthy Archinus expresses his gratitude by dedicating the plaque at which we are looking, in a nice *mise en abyme*. The message that the god acts through his *drakōn*-avatar could not be clearer.[19]

But the snakes of an Asclepieion could be deployed in a more structured or ritual way too. As petitioning patients spent the night in the god's shrine, they would be tended to by practitioners of scientific medicine, but, more germanely for us, they would also be visited by members of the shrine's staff brandishing *drakontes*, which they would apply to the area of concern for a lick or a gentle bite, to pass the god's healing power directly into it. The richest literary account of this practice is provided by Aristophanes in his 388 BC comedy *Wealth*. Here the god's own daughters, Iaso and Panacea ('Healing' and 'Cure-All') take on the role of temple staff in the new Athenian Asclepieion. After the reclining patients have received their herbal applications, the girls do their rounds of them, as they incubate, covering their compromised body parts over with a scarlet cloth, and then slipping the god's *drakontes* under the cloth to lick them.[20] Perhaps the

---

[19] *LIMC* Amphiaraos 63. Discussions: Sineux 2007; Ogden 2013a:347–71 (with sources and scholarship); Renberg 2017:310–15, 650–3.

[20] Aristophanes *Wealth* 633–747; on this play see now Barrenechea 2018. In the seventeenth century the 'grotta dei serpenti', 'snake grotto', a small thermal cave near the summit of Monte delle fate at Sasso in Cerveteri, was celebrated for its healing properties, not least in relation to scurvy, leprosy, palsy, and gout. Patients would, we are told, be laid out naked to sweat in the cave's humid (34°C) atmosphere. The resident snakes would emerge from their holes to lick their skin dry, thereby

snake-wranglers in Asclepius' shrines were indeed typically female. Asclepius' most familiar daughter-personification, Hygieia, 'Health', curiously does not feature here: she is mythless, but in her copious iconography she feeds her own serpent-avatar from a phiale or shallow dish: the serpent winds around her body when she stands and coils in her lap when she sits (Fig. 1.9).[21]

What varieties of snakes were so deployed? The ancient descriptions and representations of the healing snakes are vague, but the best candidate amongst the snakes we know to have existed in ancient Greece, based on its adult length, its non-venomous nature, its coloration (to a certain extent), its placidity, and its phlegmatic attitude to being mauled by humans, is a variety of rat-snake, the four-lined snake (Elaphe quatuorlineata), the snake that currently features in the remarkable serpent-handling *Serpari* festival dedicated to St Dominic Sora at

Fig. 1.9 Hygieia. Roman, marble statue. i–ii A D. Metropolitan Museum, New York, Gift of Mrs Frederick F. Thompson, 1903, 03.12.11a. Public domain.

extracting the corrupted humours. The cave formed the subject of a number of learned treatises in that century, in which Asclepian comparanda were adduced. See Gambari 2017.

[21] *LIMC* Hygieia, Salus, *passim*; discussion at Ogden 2013a:317–21.

Cucullo (Cocullo) in Italian Abruzzo.[22] So, if one wishes to lay eyes upon a real-life *drakōn* today, that is the label to look out for in the Reptile House![23]

1.3.2 Gods of Good Fortune and Wealth: Zeus Meilichios and Agathos Daimon

The *drakōn* gods that protected the wealth and good fortune of the household have the look of originating in projections into the divine sphere of the earthly 'house-snake', the snake encouraged to live in or under a house, its storeroom especially, to eat and deter rodents—a phenomenon once widespread in the world—and thereby to protect and to preserve the house's food-stores, i.e. its wealth, and indeed its good fortune. A good example is provided by Zeus Meilichios ('Gentle Zeus'), first attested with a *drakōn*-association *c.*400 BC, the dedicatee of a series of superb relief stelae from fourth-century BC Athens: on these the god is portrayed as a huge, rampant, vertically coiling serpent towering benignly over his grateful petitioners, who approach him as a nuclear family, parents and children.[24]

Another god of household wealth and good luck was Agathos Daimon ('Good Spirit'), first attested with a *drakōn*-association from the late fourth century BC (Figs 1.10, 1.11). He was recognized as a patron deity of Alexandria, alongside Alexander the Great himself, from soon after the city's foundation in 330 BC. The *Alexander Romance* (in its earliest available recension, from the early third century AD) preserves an aetiological myth for the house-snakes in the city. In this frankly under-explained story a *drakōn* attacks the workmen as they are attempting to build the city's first houses. It is killed but then transformed, on the one

---

[22] For which, see Ogden 2013a:379; and now Gambari 2017:77–83.

[23] When I wrote on this subject in 2013 (Ogden 2013a:372–8, with prior scholarship, to which add Riaño Rufilanchas 1999:175–8; and Rodríguez Pérez 2008:231–52), I identified the four-lined snake as the best candidate amongst the snakes found in the Greece of today. I focused on the snakes of the present as opposed to those that stalked the country in the past because (1) so far as the literary record is concerned, it is difficult to match up ancient snake categories with modern ones, and (2) so far as the archaeological record is concerned, it is—usually—impossible to identify snake bones in it. All this whilst conceding, of course, that we had no right to assume that the land's herpetological ecology had remained stable since antiquity. However, in the same year a remarkable article appeared documenting the discovery of a unique assemblage of cut and burned animal bones deposited in a disused cistern in the sanctuary of Poseidon at Calauria on Poros shortly after 50 BC: Mylona 2013 (I thank Gina Salapata for drawing my attention to the piece). Amongst these there survive, after all, no fewer than 2,720 snake bones. Those diagnostic for species were found to derive from: the Montpellier snake, the Balkan whip snake, the grass snake (or the dice snake), the horned viper and, gratifyingly indeed, the four-lined snake. The find, incidentally, raises the prospect of something we would not otherwise have suspected, namely the existence of snake-sacrifice on a large scale in the ancient world, a phenomenon barely attested in the literary record.

[24] For the stelae, see Lalonde 2006. For further sources and scholarship, see Ogden 2013a:272–83.

Fig. 1.10 Agathos Daimon (flanked by Isis and Sarapis). Delos, marble naiskos, Hellenistic. Delos Archaeological Museum A 3195. Photo: *BCH* 31 (1907) 526 fig. 24.

hand, into a presiding hero or god for the new city, and also, on the other hand, into a host of smaller snakes that does the job of protecting the city's individual constituent houses on a one-to-one basis:

> They began to build Alexandria.... A *drakōn* which was in the habit of presenting itself to people in the area kept frightening the workmen, and they would break off their work upon the creature's arrival. News of this was given to Alexander. He gave the order that on the following day the serpent should be killed wherever it was caught. On receipt of this permission, they got the better of the beast when it presented itself at the place now called the Stoa and killed it. Alexander gave the order that it should have a precinct there, and buried the serpent. And he gave the command that the neighbourhood should be garlanded in memory of the sighting of Agathos Daimon.... When he had laid the foundations for most of the city and measured it out, he inscribed [sc. on a stela] five letters, alpha, beta, gamma, delta, epsilon: alpha for 'Alexander', Beta for 'king', gamma for 'scion', delta for 'of Zeus', and epsilon for 'founded this unforgettable city'.... When the foundations of the heroon ['hero-shrine', sc. for the slain Agathos Daimon serpent] had been laid down <he set it [sc. the stela on which he had inscribed the letters] on a pillar>. There leaped out from it a large host <of snakes>, and, crawling off, they ran into the four [?] houses that were already there. Alexander, who was still present, founded the city and the heroon itself on the 25th Tybi. From that point the doorkeepers admitted these snakes [*opheis*] to the houses as *agathoi daimones* ['good spirits']. These snakes are not

Fig. 1.11 Agathos Daimon (far left),
Isis-Tyche, Aphrodite, and Thermouthis.
Roman, gold bracelet. i BC–i AD.
Metropolitan Museum, New York,
Rogers Fund, 1923, 23.2.1.
Public domain.

venomous, but they do ward off those snakes that do seem to be venomous,
and sacrifices are given to the hero himself <, as snake-born>.... Alexander
ordered that the guardians of the houses be given wheat. They took it and
milled it and made porridge [?] and gave it to the snakes in the houses. The
Alexandrians preserve this custom until today. On the 25th of Tybi they...
make sacrifice to the *agathoi daimones* that look after their houses and make
them gifts of porridge.   *Alexander Romance* (A) 1.32.10–13 ≈ (Arm.) §§ 86–8[25]

Byzantium too had a culture of friendly snakes, its citizens being bidden not to
destroy snakes caught inside the city, because they were 'benefactors' (*euergetai*).
Hesychius Illustrius (*c.* AD 500) preserves the explanatory myth in this case:
when, in its early days, the city was under siege from the Scythian king Odryses,
Phidaleia (cf. *ophidion*, 'little snake'?), wife of the founder Byzas, had gathered
together all the snakes in the city and then suddenly appeared before the enemy,
sending the snakes against them like missiles and darts, destroying many of them
and raising the siege.[26]

---

[25] For commentaries on the A text, see Stoneman 2007 and now Nawotka 2017. More sources and
discussions at Ogden 2013a:286–308; to which add Barbantani 2014:228–32; Djurslev and Ogden
2018; Dunand 1969 is of particular importance.

[26] Hesychius Illustrius *Patria Constantinopoleos* 18–19 (cf. 34). But Tzetzes *Chiliades* 2 no. 60
(xii AD) has a tale of Byzantium that reworks the same theme in a light less flattering to the snakes. He
tells that in the age of Nero the barbarians attacked the city when its ruler was away. His wife collected
the city's snakes into pots and distributed them amongst the citizens to sling out at the enemy army.
The snakes attacked the enemy and routed them, but after that they turned back against the Byzantines,
killing them with their venomous bites. The snakes were attacked in turn by an army of storks, but
these just dropped the snakes into the city's cisterns, poisoning the water supply, and thereby killing
even more of the citizens. The sage Apollonius of Tyana saved the day by setting up some talismanic
stone storks to avert the real ones. Cf. Faraone 1992:40.

1.4 '... and something more' (1): *Drakontes* with Additional Physical Attributes

We have already noted additional physical attributes in the case of the Hydra: her multiple (and pullulating) heads. The early iconographic tradition for Ladon, the *drakōn* of the Hesperides, also gives him multiple heads, either two or three. Fans of Ray Harryhausen's 1963 stop-motion movie *Jason and the Argonauts* may suppose that the Colchis *drakōn* was also multi-headed. In fact Harryhausen simply replaced the Colchis *drakōn* with the better-known and more crowd-pleasing Hydra (the creature is explicitly so named). But Harryhausen's myth-bending may have been prescient, for in 1990 a *c.*660–640 BC Caeretan amphora was discovered bearing a crude image of a woman tending or petting a massive three-headed serpent. The standard lexicon for ancient mythical iconography, the so-called *LIMC*, boldly classifies the image under 'Medea', and accordingly reads it precisely as an illustration of the Colchis *drakōn*.[27] This is an interesting possibility, but given that Ladon, tended by the Hesperid maidens, is otherwise attested as multi-headed, whilst the Colchis *drakōn*, tended by Medea, is not, Occam's Razor invites us to suppose that the image represents rather Ladon with a Hesperid. However, it remains possible that the image represents neither of these things, or neither of these things specifically. If Greek myth knew of two (groups of) *drakōn*-tending maidens, then it may well have known of more. And indeed we do hear of supposedly historical examples of sacred *drakontes* (usually suspiciously unseen ones) tended and maintained by priestesses, virgin or otherwise. The most famous example is that of the *oikouros ophis* ('temple-watching snake') that lived on the Athenian acropolis and was maintained by the priestess of Athena Polias. The 480 BC sack of the city by the Persians was foretold when the serpent declined to eat its ritual offering of honey-cakes.[28]

Multi-headed serpents consist of the addition to a snake of supplementary body-parts, albeit body-parts of the same creature-type. To this extent they constitute an important conceptual and perhaps even justificatory bridge to the more diverse composite forms we shall consider next. However, striking and otherworldly though the concept of a multi-headed serpent may appear to be, they are not uncommon in nature. Unlike the forlorn two-headed lambs one finds pickled yellow in university storerooms, two-headed snakes are essentially viable and, furthermore, both heads can be fully active; captive examples happily gobble down pairs of freeze-dried mice in tandem. (In the wild, however, the life-spans of such creatures can often be shortened as one head can attempt to eat the other if it smells food on it.)

---

[27] Amsterdam, Allard-Pierson Collection, 10.188 = *LIMC* Medeia, 2.
[28] *Oikouros ophis*: Herodotus 8.41; but snakes can't eat honey-cakes.... *Drakōn*-tending virgins more generally: Ogden 2013a:201–6, 347–50.

From *c.*675 to 650 BC we find *drakontes* sporting beards in the iconographic record, with the first examples being the *drakontes* sprouting from the (oddly cauldron-shaped) heads of the Gorgons on one of the earliest surviving representations of these creatures in full body.[29] The *general* significance of this beard can only coincide with the significance we have reconstructed for the term *drakōn* itself, which is to say that it signifies that the snake in question is one with a supernatural affinity: in short, it may be said, the beard turns the common or garden snake into a *drakōn*. (The signifier is an optional one, it should be stressed: there is no reason to think that painters ever attempt to deny *drakōn* status by withholding a beard.) What was the origin of these beards? The unexpected answer seems to be Egypt. In Egyptian art beards act as transferable signifiers of divinity and (the same thing in Egyptian terms) royalty, with the result that even the female Pharaoh Hatshepsut boasts one in her iconography. Bearded snakes are first referenced in Egyptian literature as far back as the Middle Kingdom: a gold and lapis-lazuli serpent thirty cubits long with a beard of two cubits already appears in the *Story of the Shipwrecked Sailor* of *c.*2200 BC. They are often found in papyri, with a notable example in the *Papyrus of Dirpu* of the Twenty-First Dynasty (*c.*1113–949 BC), and they become frequent in them during the Late Period (*c.*712–332 BC).[30] By *c.*400 BC our Greek *drakontes* can also acquire crests above their heads to balance their beards.[31] Where did these in turn derive from? It is just possible that the Egyptian fount was revisited and that the crest was inspired by the crown that occasionally balanced the beards of Egyptian serpents.[32] But it remains likelier that the *drakontes* acquired these in the course of their curious (and unexplained) association with crested and wattled cocks on archaic Greek vases, this from *c.*550 BC, the broad comparability of beard and wattle creating a bridge that allowed the snakes to share the cock's upper adornments as well as their lower ones.[33] (We shall consider in Chapter 3, §3.2, the limited degree to which beards can serve alternatively as a marker of sex in serpent images.)

---

[29] *LIMC* Perseus 151 = Grabow 1998 K2. If I am wrong to read beards into this image (the projections from the snake-heads could otherwise represent flickering tongues) then the earliest attested bearded snakes will derive from vases of *c.*625 BC: Grabow 1998 K12 (a large bearded serpent rears up between the heads of two grazing horses) and Lane 1933–4 pl. 32a (a fragment with series of rearing, bearded snakes, also with flickering tongues—or it is the Hydra?).

[30] Guralnick 1974 esp. 183–6; and Skuse 2015 ch. 5, from which I have learned much. On the basis of these studies, I am less tentative than I was at Ogden 2013a:155–61 about the Egyptian-origin hypothesis. *Story of the Shipwrecked Sailor*: Lichtheim 1973–80:i, 211–15.

[31] Some of the earliest examples (*c.*400 BC): *LIMC* Medeia 35–6; cf. Ogden 2013a:157–8.

[32] As Skuse has suggested. He points to the wooden funerary stela of Djeddjehutyiuefankh of the Third Intermediate Period (*c.*770–12 BC; Ashmolean Museum) and to the wooden funerary stela of Neskhonsu (*c.*700–650 BC; Museo Egizio, Turin, no. 1596).

[33] An early example of a serpent paired with wattled cock: Grabow 1998:46–58, with K27–35. Cf. Aelian *Nature of Animals* 11.26. Discussion at Ogden 2013a:158–61.

1.5 '...and something more' (2): The Tails That Wag their Dogs

We pass on now to a series of mythical monsters that incorporated *drakontes* in their form without ever being described as *drakontes* in their entirety. They claim our attention because their *drakōn* elements, whilst constituting only a small proportion of their physical being, evidently lay nonetheless at the heart of their nature and, more especially, their armoury.

Casual readers of Greek mythology may be surprised to learn that Cerberus, the three-headed dog that kept the ghosts confined in the underworld, incorporated *drakontes* in his form (he is first attested as doing so from *c.*590 BC).[34] Indeed there is little mention of the *drakontes* in literary texts, though Hecataeus (early V BC), in seeking to rationalize Cerberus' myth, suggested that it had originated in a historical tale of a *drakōn* terrorizing Tainaron, supposed home to a prominent underworld entrance.[35] But his iconography tells a different story. He is characteristically portrayed as sporting a *drakōn*-headed tail, and in earlier art he can be shown with tiny *drakontes* sprouting from all over his body, sometimes like locks of matted hair.[36] These *drakontes* were more than decorative: Cerberus was thoroughly pervaded by a *drakōn* nature. First, the possession of multiple (canine) heads can itself be seen as a trait borrowed from pure *drakontes* like Ladon and the Hydra. Second, *drakontes* are, as we have seen, particularly strongly associated in Greek myth with the role of guarding, as much so as is any dog. Third, a minor episode of Cerberus' myth tells of the poor dog's terror when Heracles dragged him out of the underworld through another entrance at Heraclea Pontica (the modern Eregli, on the Turkish coast of the Black Sea, where tourists can visit the cave from which he emerged). He had never seen daylight before, and vomited or slavered in reaction to it. The liquid fell upon a hitherto harmless plant of the region, the aconite, rendering it deadly poisonous. There is no reason to think that Cerberus vomited or drooled from his serpent-heads as opposed to his dog-heads, but his poisonousness can only be construed as emanating from his *drakōn* nature.[37]

[34] For the principal sources for Cerberus, see Hesiod *Theogony* 767–74 (vii BC); Euripides *Heracles* 610–19; Critias *Pirithous, TrGF* 43 F1 lines 10–14; Euphorion F71 Lightfoot; Diodorus 4.25.1, 4.26.1; Virgil *Aeneid* 6.417–25; Apollodorus *Bibliotheca* 2.5.12; Hyginus *Astronomica* 2.14; Lucian *Dialogues of the Dead* 4; Pausanias 3.25.4–6, incorporating Hecataeus *FGrH* 1 F27; Hesychius s.v. ἐλεύθερον ὕδωρ; schol. Homer *Iliad* 5.395–7. More sources and discussions at Ogden 2013a:104–15, 2013b:63–74.

[35] Hecataeus *FGrH* 1 F27.

[36] See in particular *LIMC* Herakles 2553 (*c.*590–80 BC), 2554, 2560, 2571, 2579, 2581, 2586, 2588, 2595, 2600, 2603–6, 2610–11, 2614, 2616, 2621, 2628.

[37] For the venomous slaver or vomit, see Herodorus of Heraclea *FGrH* 31 F31 = F31 Fowler (*c.*400 BC); Xenophon *Anabasis* 6.2.2; Theophrastus *Historia plantarum* 9.16.4–7; Euphorion *Xenios* F41a Lightfoot; Nicander *Alexipharmaca* 13–15 with schol. 13b; Diodorus 14.31.3; Ovid *Metamorphoses* 7.404–19; Pomponius Mela 1.92; Seneca *Agamemnon* 859–61, *Hercules Furens* 46–62, 782–829; Dionysius Periegetes 787–92, with schol. and Eustathius ad loc.

The curious Chimaera ('She-goat'), first attested in the earlier seventh century BC, is described as a lion in front, a goat in the middle, and a *drakōn* behind (Figs 1.12, 1.13, 9.4). In art the bulk of the creature is typically a lion, but she has the head or forepart of a goat sprouting up from the middle of her back, and her tail is *drakōn*-headed in just the same way as is Cerberus'. This marauding creature ranged over Lycia and Phrygia, burning up the land with her fiery breath. Eventually she was destroyed by the hero Bellerophon who, flying on the winged horse Pegasus, speared her from the air. This is Apollodorus' account (i–ii AD):

> Iobates read the letter and ordered Bellerophon to kill the Chimaera in the belief that he would be destroyed by the beast. It was not easy for many men, let alone just one, to catch her. Her forepart consisted of a lion, her tail of a *drakōn*, and she had a third head in the middle, that of a goat, through which she sent forth fire. She laid waste to the land and plundered the cattle. For although she was a single creature, she had the power of three beasts. It is said also that this Chimaera was reared by Amisodarus, as Homer too has said, and she was spawned by Typhon and Echidna, as Hesiod relates. Bellerophon mounted himself on Pegasus, the winged horse he had that was born of Medusa and Poseidon. He flew high into the air and shot the Chimaera from the back of him.
>
> Apollodorus *Bibliotheca* 2.3.2[38]

Fig. 1.12 The Chimaera (black-figure). Greek, black-figure kylix, 550–540 BC. Metropolitan Museum, New York, Fletcher Fund, 1927, 27.122.27. Public domain.

[38] For further principal sources, see Homer *Iliad* 6.152–95, 16.328–9 (earlier vii BC); Hesiod *Theogony* 319-25; Pindar *Olympians* 13.60–6 and 84–90; Strabo C665; Pliny *Natural History* 2.236; Heraclitus *De incredibilibus* 15; Tzetzes on Lycophron *Alexandra* 17; schol. Homer *Iliad* 6.181. Iconography: *LIMC* Chimaira, Chimaira in Etruria, Pegasos. More sources and discussions at Ogden 2013a:98–104, 2013b:75–81.

Fig. 1.13 Bellerophon fights the Chimaera from the back of Pegasus (terracotta). Melos, terracotta plaque, *c.*490–470 BC. British Museum 1842,0728.1135. Photo: Daniel Ogden.

The signal and terrible power of this physically quite comical monster was her fire-breathing, and this is a capacity she can only have derived from her *drakōn* element. Fieriness of mouth and eye is a frequently noticed feature of most of the great *drakontes* of myth (see §1.7), and it is an understandable extrapolation of the burning sensation caused by viper venom, a phenomenon of which the ancients were keenly aware.[39] Apollodorus tells that the Chimaera breathed her

---

[39] Nicander (mid-ii BC) on vipers: *Theriaca* 245 (πυρπολέουσα) and 364 (πυρπολέοντα). More particularly, Nicander tells that the dipsad ('thirst snake') variety of viper inflames the hearts of its victims to the point where they drink water maniacally until their navels burst (334–58; ἐμφλέγεται, 338). Lucan's similar take on the dipsad is discussed below (9.734–60; *ignis edax*, 742; Chapter 2, §2.1). For Lucian the dipsad 'burns and corrupts and sets alight, and people scream out as if lying on a pyre' (ἐκκαίει, σήπει, πίμπρασθαι ποιεῖ, *Dipsads* 4). Isidore of Seville *Etymologies* 12.4.40 explains that snakes are cold because their venom draws the heat of their bodies into itself. See Gow and Scholfield 1953:176; and Jacques 2002:118–20. Already before this at Sophocles *Trachiniae* 831–8 (468–406 BC) the venom of the Hydra is identified as the active ingredient in the burning substance with which Deianeira imbues Heracles' tunic. Then in the early iv BC Ctesias (*FGrH* 688 F45r = Aelian *Nature of Animals* 5.3; cf. F45.46) speaks of the seven-cubit long Indian *skōlēx* snake producing a napalm-like burning oil from its body. For the actual natural history of vipers and the effects of their venoms, see Thorpe et al. 1997.

fire through her goat head—perhaps thereby seeking to explain the choice of her name, or otherwise to bring the head's terribleness into line with that of the other two—but in general the literary sources tend to be vague as to which mouth the Chimaera breathed her fire from, implying by default that it was her frontal lion mouth, and the iconography, which occasionally makes the effort to represent her fire, tends to agree. Once again, the relatively small *drakōn* element seems to dominate and confer its essence upon the whole. (We should, however, note one late Roman mosaic, from the excavations at Mertola, the ancient Myrtilis, in which flames proudly proceed from all three of the creature's heads: here at least we have a rare illustration of the phenomenon fairly common in the literature: a fire-breathing *drakōn*-head.[40]) Some readers may continue to find the Chimaera's *drakōn*-credentials unimpressive; she will, nonetheless, come to play a significant role in the archaeology of the medieval dragon in the West, as we shall see in Chapter 9, §9.2.

In Medusa, decapitated by Perseus with his sickle, and her Gorgon sisters (first attested with a *drakōn*-association *c.*675 BC, as we have seen) we once again have monsters only a relatively small part of whose form is made up of *drakontes* (Figs 1.14, 1.15). As is well known, in their canonical form the Gorgons had humanoid female bodies with serpents for hair. In the earlier tradition they occasionally had serpents growing rather from the sides of their necks, or entwining around their waists. Sometimes they were winged. Their terrible power is also well known: they could turn people (animals and objects also) to stone with their gaze.[41] This power too can only have derived from their *drakōn* element. It is a widely held folk belief that snakes can hypnotize their prey to freeze it before seizing.[42] The notion is erroneous, but proceeds understandably from observable phenomena: the fact that snakes have no eyelids and cannot close their eyes, which lends them the appearance of a peculiarly concentrated and penetrating stare; and the fact that some animals freeze themselves upon a snake's approach, in fear or for camouflage. It is surely this notion that underpins the Gorgon's weaponry. Once again, the *drakōn*, though constituting a relatively small part of

---

[40] Mosaic, Museu de Mertola, Portugal.

[41] I gloss over some complications here. For the principal sources see [Hesiod] *Shield* 216–37 (vi BC); Pherecydes F11 Fowler; Pindar *Pythians* 12.6–26; Palaephatus 31; Ovid *Metamorphoses* 4.617–20, 772–803; Lucan *Pharsalia* 9.619–99; Pausanias 2.21.5–7, incorporating Procles of Carthage *FHG* iv pp. 483–4 F1; John Malalas *Chronicle* 2.11 Thurn. More sources and discussions at Ogden 2013a:92–8, 2013b:82–96; to which add Topper 2007. The Gorgons' mythology and natural history continued to develop in lively and distinctive ways during the central medieval period. The *Physiologus* (second, 'Byzantine' recension) 23 (v–xi AD?) explains how sorcerers hunt Gorgons. The Gorgon exploits the mating season to call out to all animals in their own languages, but when they approach and see her, they die. When she calls to the sorcerer in his own language, he calls back that he will come to her if she digs a pit and sticks her head in it. This she does, permitting the hunter to decapitate her harmlessly, whereupon he puts her head in a vessel, to use for his own ends. The account concludes by noting, in lapidary fashion, that Alexander the Great had such a Gorgon head.

[42] For an explicit expression of the notion in (late) antiquity, see Isidore of Seville *Etymologies* 12.4.19: the scytale captures its prey by mesmerism (*miraculo sui stupentes capit*).

Fig. 1.14 Gorgoneion. South Italian, painted terracotta antefix, *c.*540 BC. Metropolitan Museum, New York, Harris Brisbane Dick Fund, 1939, 39.11.9. Public domain.

the creature as a whole, dominates it and provides the key to its nature. The Greeks and Romans certainly seem to have found significance in a *drakōn*'s eyes: their etymologists hypothesized that the term derived from the verb *derkomai*, 'look at' (which has the aorist participle form *drakōn*). Modern philologists are inclined to think that this is no mere folk etymology, and that the two words were indeed historically cognate, though the present author remains dubious.[43] It is noteworthy too that the ancients associated the projection of fire with *drakontes'* eyes even more often than they did with their mouths (see §1.7 below).

---

[43] Festus *De verborum significatu* 67 M, 110 M; Porphyry *De abstinentia* 3.8; Macrobius *Saturnalia* 1.20.1–4; schol. Aristophanes *Wealth* 733; *Etymologicum Gudianum* s.v. δράκων; *Etymologicum parvum* s.v. δράκων; *Etymologicum magnum* s.v. δράκων. The etymology may already be implicit at Hesiod *Theogony* 828, quoted below. Discussions and bibliography at Ogden 2013a:173 (to which add Wild 1962:2 and Riaño Rufilanchas 1999:172, who also accept the ancient etymology). The summary of Ptolemy Chennus' fantastical *Strange History* salutes the fabled keenness of the dragon's vision when it attributes Candaules' wife's exceptional sight to the fact that she possessed both double pupils and a 'dragon stone' (δρακοντίτην...λίθον; Photius *Bibliotheca* cod. 190, 150b).

Fig. 1.15 Perseus confronting Phineus with the head of Medusa. Italian, painting, Sebastiano Ricci, *c.* A D 1705–10. The J. Paul Getty Museum, 86.PA.591. Public domain.

1.6 '… and something more' (3): Anguipedes, and Some Deep History

A particularly popular variety of compound-*drakōn* was the anguipede, that is to say, a creature with a humanoid upper half and a serpentine lower half. These came in male and female varieties. We will devote a separate chapter (Chapter 3) to the interesting female variety, but say a few words about the male one here. A good example of a (benign) male anguipede is provided by the figure of Cecrops: born of the Earth, he was the first king of Attica, which he named Cecropia after himself; he helped Athena to become the city's patron goddess; and he was the city's first lawgiver. It was no coincidence, then, that the city's first historical law-giver ('legendary' might be more accurate), working in the 39th Olympiad,

624–621 BC, acquired the name of *Drakōn* ('Draco').[44] Less benign were the Giants (Gigantes), the Earthborn race that made war on the gods, who acquired anguipedes amongst their number in the course of the fourth century BC. These were, furthermore, of a distinctive type: they were humanoid down to their thighs, whereupon each leg gave way to separate serpent bodies that terminated not in tails, but in heads.[45]

But the greatest of the male anguipedes and the most terrible monster of any kind faced by men or gods in the world of Greek myth was the similarly Earthborn Typhon (first attested in the late eighth or earlier seventh century BC). Like his brother Giants, Typhon battled Zeus himself for control of heaven, unsuccessfully of course, and did so with his fiery breath. In art he is most typically depicted with the usual serpentine lower body, whilst his humanoid upper body also sports a pair of wings.[46] Literary descriptions tend to be much more complex, giving him large numbers of snake heads in addition and even the heads of other animals too in an overall form that is difficult to imagine as a physical possibility in 3D space. Here is Hesiod's (vii BC) account of Typhon and his great battle:

But when Zeus had expelled the Titans from heaven, the massive Earth brought forth her youngest child, Typhon, after making love with Tartarus, through the agency of golden Aphrodite [goddess of love]. He accomplished his deeds by the might of his hands. The feet of the powerful god did not grow tired.[47] From his shoulders grew the hundred heads of a snake [*ophis*], a terrible *drakōn*, and these flickered with dark tongues. Fire flashed forth from the eyes under the brows of his awesome heads. And from all his heads as he gazed [*derkomenoio*] fire burned. And there were voices in all his terrible heads that sent forth every kind of unspeakable sound. Sometimes they spoke in such a way that the gods could understand, sometimes they spoke with the voice of a loud-bellowing bull, unrestrainable in might, proud in voice, and sometimes with the voice of a lion with shameless heart. At other times his voice resembled that of puppies, a

---

[44] The principal source for Cecrops is Apollodorus *Bibliotheca* 3.14–15 (i–ii AD); see *LIMC* Kekrops for the iconography. For further sources and discussions, see Gourmelen 2004; Ogden 2013a:259–63 (and cf. 263–7 on Ericthonius). The principal source for Draco is [Aristotle] *Athenaiōn politeia* 4.1, 7.1, 41.2 (late iv BC).

[45] Principal texts: Diodorus 3.70.3–6 (= Dionysius Scytobrachion *FGrH* 32 F85), 71.2–6; Horace *Odes* 3.4.49–80; Ovid *Metamorphoses* 1.151–62; Ptolemy Chennus *Strange History* at Photius *Bibliotheca* cod. 190, 147b (a fire-breathing Giant, *si credere dignum est*); Apollodorus *Bibliotheca* 1.6.1–3; Claudian 53 Hall (*Gigantomachia*). Iconography: *LIMC* Gigantes. Further sources and discussions: Ogden 2013a:82–6.

[46] *LIMC* Typhon *passim*.

[47] What kind of feet, one wonders?

wonder to hear, at other times again he would hiss, and the high mountains would reverberate. Indeed there would have been on that day an achievement no one could have done anything about, and he would have ruled over mortals and immortals, if the father of gods and men had not quickly realized what was happening. He thundered hard and loud and the Earth resounded around about in terrible fashion, and so did the broad heaven above and the sea and the streams of Ocean and Tartarus beneath the Earth. Great Olympus quaked beneath the immortal feet of the lord as he roused himself. And the Earth groaned in response. The heat that they both generated took hold of the dark blue sea, the heat of the thunder and the lightning, and of the fire from the monster, and of the burning winds and the burning thunderbolt. The entire Earth boiled, and so did the fire and the sea. The long waves beat about the shores at the violence of the immortals and an unquenchable shaking arose. Hades trembled as he ruled over the dead below, and so did the Titans under Tartarus, those who live with Cronus, because of the unquenchable noise and the dread battle. When Zeus had raised high his might and taken up his weapons, thunder, lightning, and the flashing thunderbolt, he struck him, leaping from Olympus. And he burned all the heads of the terrible monster on all sides. But when he had beaten him with blows and conquered him, Typhon crashed down lamed, and the massive Earth groaned. A flame flashed forth from that lord, smitten and struck with the thunderbolt in the obscure dells of the craggy mountain. The massive Earth was burned over a wide expanse by an awesome vapour, and it melted like tin when smelted by strong craftsmen in well-drilled crucibles, or iron, which is the strongest substance. It is subdued in the dells of a mountain with burning fire, and it melts in the divine Earth by the hands of Hephaestus. In this way then the Earth melted in the gleam of flashing fire. Grieving in heart he cast him down into broad Tartarus. From Typhon is the wet might of the blowing winds, except for Notus [South Wind], Boreas [North Wind], and brightening Zephyr [West Wind]. For these are of the race of the gods, and they are a boon to mortals. But the others blow at random over the sea. Some fall upon the misty sea, a great bane to mortals, and rage in an evil storm. They blow from different directions at different times, scattering ships and destroying sailors. There is no defence against this evil for the men who encounter them on the sea. Other winds, blowing over the limitless, blooming Earth, destroy the lovely works of the men that live upon it, filling them full of dust and harsh tumult.

Hesiod *Theogony* 820–80[48]

---

[48] Further principal sources: Apollodorus *Bibliotheca* 1.6.1–3; Pindar *Pythians* 1.15–28; Strabo C750–1; Pausanias of Antioch *FGrH/BNJ* 854 F9 (= John Malalas *Chronicle* 2.12 Thurn); Nonnus *Dionysiaca* 1–2 *passim*. More sources and discussions at Ogden 2013a:69–80, 2013b:20–38; to which

The literary sources can nonetheless reveal, more clearly than most of the art, that it was the *drakōn* element that was the most fundamental to his nature. Thus Hesiod, despite his complex and contrived physical description, does seem to assert that he was at heart a *drakōn*.[49] And when, according to Strabo, Typhon squirmed into the Syrian earth to escape Zeus' (reciprocally fiery) thunderbolts, thereby creating a meandering, serpentine riverbed, the ensuing river took both the name of 'Typhon' and the name of 'Drakon' (subsequently becoming the 'Orontes').[50]

'Than *most* of the art': however, the case for Typhon's fundamental identity as a *drakōn* has received a fillip from the important 2012 publication of a Corinthian alabastron vase of c.575–550 BC by Anna Arvanitaki. On this a bearded male figure wields a thunderbolt, which he holds up and behind himself with his right hand, in the so-called 'smiting pose', ready to hurl it or dash it against a large, *pure* serpent, which he grasps by the throat with his left. The latter must be a simplified and quintessential Typhon, because only Zeus wields the thunderbolt, and Typhon is his only known anguiform opponent. The form of the thunderbolt is of particular interest: it consists not of the clutch of lightning-flashes that familiarly represents thunderbolts in Greek art, but rather of a tool-haft from which lightning flashes project. As such, the image harks back to the rich Near Eastern traditions of battles between storm-gods and great serpents, in which the storm-gods' thunderbolts are more directly represented as clubs or axes. Thus, in the fourteenth-century Ugaritic-Canaanite tale of the storm god Baal-Sapon's fight against the serpent Litan, the god's thunderbolts are conceptualized as throwing-clubs made for him by the smith-god Kothar. A ninth-century BC Assyrian relief in the Aleppo Archaeological Museum (or formerly so) depicts the storm-god Adad fighting a serpent: the god strides forward; with his left hand he grasps the large, hanging serpent by the throat; with his right he holds up and behind him an axe, ready to strike. The alabastron also helps us make sense of a curious Cyprian oinochoe of the eighth or seventh century BC on which a man similarly grasps a large, hanging serpent with his left hand, whilst holding up and behind him a small double axe with his right, ready to strike. This too, we can now see, must represent what is in Greek terms Zeus' battle with Typhon. Zeus is not bearded, but his chin is

---

add Rodríguez Pérez 2008:23–68; Goslin 2010; Stephenson 2016:48–53; and the items cited in Appendix A.

[49] Hesiod *Theogony* 820–80. NB 825: 'there projected from his shoulders a hundred heads of *a* snake, *a* terrible *drakōn* [sing.]'.

[50] Strabo C750–1; so too Pausanias of Antioch *FGrH/BNJ* 854 F9 (= John Malalas *Chronicle* 2.12 Thurn).

stubbled: the battle is apparently seen here as the coming-of-age exploit of a youthful god.[51]

Our task in this book is to tell the story of the evolution of the dragon in form and narrative from the beginning of the western tradition in ancient Greece until the late medieval period, by which point we arrive at the fully developed dragon we all recognize today. But the Typhon narratives at any rate belong to a story-type that has a deep context both in inherited Indo-European mythology and in the borrowed mythologies of the Near Eastern peoples (Indo-European and non-Indo-European alike) with which the Greeks were in contact in both prehistoric and historical times (it is not possible to disentangle these two streams of influence satisfactorily). The reconstructed story-type is summarized in Appendix A, where we also catalogue the source-texts from which it is derived, and provide a detailed tabulation of its constituent motifs. We shall speak of the Hebrew version of the story-type in Chapter 4, §4.4, and the Norse one in Chapter 10, §10.1.

1.7 Six Core Narrative Motifs

The second and third Parts of this book will be devoted chiefly to the establishment of an ideal narrative course or courses that underlie the dragon-fight traditions of hagiography and the Germanic world. It is not necessary to do the same in a comprehensive way for the Greek and Roman culture, which is more diffuse and varied in its story-types than the subsequent cultures,[52] but it will be worthwhile to draw brief attention to six core motifs that the ancient world shares with both hagiography and the Germanic material alike.

1. Marauding: depredations against the local crops, sheep, cattle, and people. We have already noted the marauding nature of the Chimaera.[53] The motif is attached to other ancient dragons too: the Hydra,[54] the Delphic dragon in

---

[51] Arvanitaki 2012. The Corinthian alabastron: Athens, NM 703–4, illustrated at Arvanitaki 2012:173. Baal-Sapon's fight against Litan: *KTU* 1.1–2 (= *CTA* 1–2), *KTU* 1.3 (= *CTA* 3) iii 35–52 and 1.5 (= *CTA* 5) i2•–3; for the text, see Smith 1994; for English translations thereof, Coogan 1978; Gibson 1978. The Assyrian relief: illustrated at Moortgat 1967:125, fig. 254; Arvanitaki 2012:176. The Cyprian oinoche: illustrated at Grabow 1998 K1; Arvanitaki 2012:176.

[52] However, I offer an attempt at such an analysis, in schematic form, for Graeco-Roman dragon-fight narratives at Ogden 2013b:xix–xxiii.

[53] Note in particular Pliny *Natural History* 2.236; Apollodorus *Bibliotheca* 2.3.2.

[54] Apollodorus *Bibliotheca* 2.5.2.

both male and female forms,[55] the Dragon of Thespiae,[56] the Dragon of the river Sagaris in Lydia,[57] the Dragon of the river Bagrada in Libya (see Chapter 2, §2.1),[58] the Dragon of the river Hermus in Ionia,[59] the Lamia sent against Argos,[60] and the Lamia-Sybaris that attacked Delphi[61] (for these last three cases see Chapter 3, §§3.2, 3.4.1).

2. Fieriness of mouth or eye. We have already noted the fire-breathing attributed to the Chimaera (§1.5)[62] and Typhon (§1.6).[63] It is also attributed to the Dragon of Nemea[64] and the Bagrada Dragon.[65] More often, surprisingly, classical sources associate the projection of fire rather with the dragon's eyes. The motif is given to: Typhon again,[66] the Dragon of Ares,[67] the Dragon of Nemea,[68] the Colchis Dragon,[69] the serpent-pair sent by Hera against baby Heracles,[70] the serpent-pair sent against Laocoon and his sons (see Chapter 4, §4.3.3),[71] Cerberus,[72] the Bagrada Dragon again,[73] and even the benign Asclepius.[74]

3. The production of pestilential breath and bad winds. We have already seen this motif in the case of Typhon.[75] The motif is further attached to the Dragon of Ares,[76] the Dragon of Nemea,[77] and the Dragon of the river Bagrada.[78] The carcass of the slain dragon can subsequently present a similar air-infecting pestilential hazard, as in the cases of Ladon,[79] the Delphic dragon,[80] the Lamia sent against Argos,[81] and the Dragon of the river Bagrada again.[82]

---

[55] Note in particular *Homeric Hymn* (3) *to Apollo* 300–9; Plutarch *Failure of Oracles, Moralia* 414b; Menander Rhetor *Peri epideiktikōn* 3.17 pp. 441–2 Spengel.

[56] Pausanias 9.26.7–8.

[57] Hyginus *Astronomica* 2.14.   [58] Silius Italicus *Punica* 6.140–293.

[59] Nonnus *Dionysiaca* 25.451–552.   [60] Statius *Thebaid* 1.562–669.

[61] Antoninus Liberalis *Metamorphoses* 8.

[62] Homer *Iliad* 6.152–95; Pindar *Olympians* 13.84–90; Pliny *Natural History* 2.236; Apollodorus *Bibliotheca* 2.3.2; Schol. Homer *Iliad* 6.181; Tzetzes on Lycophron *Alexandra* 17.

[63] Hesiod *Theogony* 828, 845; Pindar *Pythians* 1.15–28.   [64] Statius *Thebaid* 5.521.

[65] Silius Italicus *Punica* 6.219.   [66] Hesiod *Theogony* 826–7; Apollodorus *Bibliotheca* 1.6.3.

[67] Ovid *Metamorphoses* 3.33.   [68] Statius *Thebaid* 5.508.

[69] Valerius Flaccus 8.60.   [70] Theocritus 24.18.

[71] Virgil *Aeneid* 2.199–231; Petronius *Satyricon* 89.   [72] Euphorion F71 Lightfoot.

[73] Silius Italicus *Punica* 6.220.

[74] Ovid *Metamorphoses* 15.674. For the fieriness of the classical dragon in general, see Ogden 2013a:218–32.

[75] Hesiod *Theogony* 820–80; Apollodorus *Bibliotheca* 1.6.3; Nonnus *Dionysiaca* 1–2 passim.

[76] Ovid *Metamorphoses* 3.28–98.   [77] Statius *Thebaid* 5.505–87.

[78] Valerius Maximus 1.8 ext 19; Silius Italicus *Punica* 6.140–293.

[79] Apollonius *Argonautica* 4.1396–1407.   [80] *Homeric Hymn* (3) *to Apollo* 349–73.

[81] Statius *Thebaid* 1.562–669.   [82] Valerius Maximus 1.8 ext 19.

4. The dragon's cave-lair. The motif of the dragon's cave lair, the snake's hole writ large, is found in the cases of the Echidna,[83] Ladon,[84] Typhon,[85] the Lamia-Sybaris sent against Delphi,[86] the Dragon of Ares,[87] the serpent-pair sent against Laocoon,[88] and the Dragon of the river Bagrada.[89] In art at any rate the motif is also associated with the Delphic dragon (Fig. 1.5 again).[90]

5. The dragon's monopolization and control of a water-source. We have already seen this motif in the case of the Dragon of Ares, guardian of the spring of Dirce,[91] and the Dragon of Nemea, guardian of the spring of Langia.[92] The motif probably lurks also behind the Hydra's ('Water Snake's') traditional association with the springs of Amymone,[93] and the Delphic Delphyne's association with a nearby sweetly flowing spring.[94] Lamia-Sybaris actually metamorphoses into a spring.[95] River guardians are found in the cases of the Dragon of the river Bagrada,[96] the dragon-pair that presides over the source of the Styx,[97] the Dragon of the river Hermus,[98] and probably too in the case of the serpent killed by Heracles on the banks of the river Sagaris.[99]

6. The generation of the dragon from a corpse. Exposition of this interesting motif is deferred to Chapter 11, where the classical material will be given a common treatment with the hagiographical and the Germanic.

1.8 Conclusion

Such then is our survey of the classical dragon, its form and its principal associations in mythical narrative and in cult. We trust to have made the case that the ancient *drakōn* should, in general, be conceptualized as 'a snake and something more'. We have not concerned ourselves with the search for a universal definition for the dragon. Were we do to so, we might suggest that this same formulation is as good a contender for it as any.[100] Before we begin to consider how the dragon's

---

[83] Hesiod *Theogony* 295–318.   [84] Hesiod *Theogony* 333–6.
[85] Apollodorus *Bibliotheca* 1.6.1–3; Nonnus *Dionysiaca* 1–2 *passim*.
[86] Antoninus Liberalis *Metamorphoses* 8.
[87] Euripides *Phoenissae* 1006–12; Ovid *Metamorphoses* 3.28–98.
[88] Quintus Smyrnaeus *Posthomerica* 12.444–97.   [89] Silius Italicus *Punica* 6.140–293.
[90] Lost red-figure neck amphora, earlier iv BC: drawing at Hamilton and Tischbein 1791–5:iii, fig. 4.
[91] Euripides *Phoenissae* 658–61; Apollodorus *Bibliotheca* 3.4.1–2, 3.5.4, etc.; cf. Ogden 2013a:166–8.
[92] Euripides F754a *TrGF* = F18 Bond; cf. also Tiiia *TrGF*; cf. Ogden 2013:168–9.
[93] Apollodorus *Bibliotheca* 2.5.2; Pausanias 2. 37. 4; cf. Ogden 2013a:169–71.
[94] *Homeric Hymn* (3) *to Apollo* 300: see Chapter 3, §3.3.2.
[95] Antoninus Liberalis *Metamorphoses* 8.   [96] Silius Italicus *Punica* 6.140–293.
[97] Apuleius *Metamorphoses* 6.14-15: Zeus' eagle is able to evade them in order to fill a jar for Psyche; for the association of dragons and serpents with the underworld, see Ogden 2015.
[98] Nonnus *Dionysiaca* 25.451–552.   [99] Hyginus *Astronomica* 2.14.
[100] At any rate, it seems to encompass the dragons of all the cultures discussed in the collection of essays in Nagy (forthcoming).

classical form began to mutate in late antiquity and the early medieval era, let us pursue two more particular questions about the creature in its ancient context. First, did the Roman take on the dragon differ in any significant way from the Greek one (Chapter 2)? Secondly, was there anything distinctive about the conceptualization of female dragons in the ancient world (Chapter 3)? As we shall see, the answer in both cases is a qualified affirmative.

2
Draco
The Roman Dragon

By the time that Latin culture becomes accessible to us through its literature, Greek culture had been deeply integrated into it for centuries already, and Greek ideas about dragons were certainly included in this integration. Accordingly, the dragon known to the Romans in the period of the late republic and early empire exhibited no categorical differences from its Greek predecessor. But there were, nonetheless, some distinctive tendencies in the ways in which the Romans liked to represent dragons, and these will form the principal subject of this short chapter. In brief, the Romans loved their dragons. The Romans' narratives of the great dragon fights of Greek myth are normally more expansive, more detailed, and simply richer than any earlier accounts on the Greek side itself (of course we can only speak here of what is extant), though a few Greek accounts of the imperial era exhibit similar traits. These Roman narratives typically focalize large parts of their accounts of the fights through the figure of the dragon itself—perhaps, accordingly, we should say 'himself'. It follows from this that the dragon is often anthropomorphized; that he is endowed with a personality (a feisty one, of course); that he is endowed with the dignity and nobility of a warrior, to match that of his human(oid) opponent; and that he is treated with a certain degree of sympathy. Given the Romans' enthusiasm for dragons and dragon-fight stories, it is a remarkable, indeed inexplicable, fact that they had so little interest in developing new dragon-traditions of their own. The single significant exception to this rule, and it is a striking one, is the tale of the Dragon of the river Bagrada, which is, gratifyingly, defeated by distinctively Roman means—the army with its ballistas.

Latin culture's dependence on Greek culture for its dragons is eloquently conveyed in its direct borrowing, as we have already noted, of the Greek word *drakōn* in its own term *draco* (plural: *dracones*). But Latin did deploy its indigenous vocabulary for the concept too, *serpens* ('serpent') in particular. Where Greek would have simply given us a *drakōn*, Latin, not least in such contexts as retellings of Greek dragon-fight myths, gives us a *draco* in perhaps 50 per cent of cases, and a *serpens* in the other 50 per cent. And just as Greek can also use broader 'snake' terms to define dragons, such as *ophis*, so too Latin can also apply to them its own more general 'snake' terms, *anguis* and *coluber*.[1]

---

[1] Bile 2000:130–1 sees *draco* as more prominent in poetry than in prose in classical Latin; this may simply be a function of the fact that dragon stories are more likely to be found in verse texts anyway.

2.1 The Bagrada Dragon and its Libyan Context

Let us begin with this single, significant exception. The story of the Bagrada Dragon goes back, so far as we can trace it, to the mid-first-century BC work of the historian Q. Aelius Tubero. Tubero's lost account is summarized by Aulus Gellius, and it probably underlay Livy's account too, which is also lost, but summarized by Valerius Maximus. The historical setting of the story is 256/5 BC during the First Punic War. A massive serpent (*serpens*) denies Regulus and his army access to the river Bagrada (Medjerda) in Libya. It devours many of his soldiers and crushes others with its tail. Its skin is impenetrable to javelins, but the army eventually prevails over it by hurling stone missiles at it from their then new-fangled ballistas. The creature is flayed and its 120-foot-long skin sent back to Rome. But its corpse renders the region pestilential, and so Regulus has to move his army on.[2] Silius Italicus was subsequently to give the tale the epic treatment it called for, and in his *Punica* (c. AD 83–103) he fully integrates the serpent into the landscape it stalks. It inhabits a cave in a grove beside the river, a cave that seemingly descends to the underworld. As it is finally killed, a bellow bursts forth from the sad river itself and mutterings pour forth from its lowest depths. The grove, the cave, and the riverbanks resound in response. It is revealed that the serpent had been the servant of the river's naiads, and that they had nurtured it themselves in the warm waters. In revenge for the killing the naiads place a curse on Regulus and his army, a curse destined to come to fruition in the army's destruction at the battle of Tunis and in Regulus' torture and execution by the Carthaginians.[3] Here is the central part of the narrative of the great battle. Marus speaks:

> The murky Bagrada cuts though dry sands with slow pace. No other river in the Libyan land extends its muddy waves further or envelops the wide plains with its still depths. Here, desperate for water, which the land does not supply in plenty, we happily established our camp in those wild regions. Nearby was a motionless grove that kept itself in colourless shade, Styx-like and unpenetrated by the sun. From it there burst forth into the air a thick exhalation that gave off a foul smell. Within lay a dreadful home, a huge cave twisting beneath the earth, and dismal darkness without light. I shudder again as I remember it. A deadly monster, produced by the earth's anger, the like of which hardly any age of men will have seen, a serpent [*serpens*] extending over a hundred ells, dwelled on that lethal

---

[2] Valerius Maximus 1.8 ext. 19 = Livy F9 W-M (cf. periocha 18); Aulus Gellius 7.3, incorporating Tubero F8 Peter = F11 Cornell. Further Latin sources: Seneca *Letters* 82.24; Pliny *Natural History* 8.37 (a mere 80 feet long); Silius Italicus *Punica* 6.140–293; Florus 1.18.20; Orosius 4.8.10–14. Cassius Dio refers to the creature as a *drakōn* (F42.23 = Zonaras 8.13.2 = ii p. 209 Dindorf; cf. John Damascene *De draconibus et strygibus* 1 p. 472a–b = *PG* 94, 1600). The Valerius Maximus and Silius passages are translated at Ogden 2013b:141–5. Discussion at Basset 1955; Spaltenstein 1986 (on Silius ad loc.); Cornell 2013 (on Tubero F11); Ogden 2013a:66–7, with further scholarship.

[3] For the fate of Regulus and his army, see Polybius 1.26–34 (battle of Tunis); Aulus Gellius 7.4; Augustine *City of God* 1.15; [Aurelius Victor] *De viris illustribus* 40 (torture and execution of Regulus).

riverbank and in those Avernian groves. Lions caught at the spring used to sate the voraciousness of its huge stomach and venom-pregnant belly, or herds driven to the river by the heat of the searing sun, or birds drawn to it down through the air by the foul heaviness and corruption of its breath. Half-eaten bones lay on the ground, bones which it had vomited up in its black cave after laying waste to flocks and sating itself to the point of dyspepsia on its horrible feast. When it wanted to assuage the burning produced by its fervid eating in the river's fast-flowing swell and the foaming waves, it was already laying its head on the edge of the opposite bank before it had plunged the entirety of its body into the stream.... The serpent was bigger than those with which the Giants were armed when they attacked heaven. It was bigger than the one that made Heracles weary in the waters of Lerna. It resembled the snake of Juno [i.e. Ladon] that guarded the branches clothed in gold. That was the size of the snake that burst forth from the earth, raising its head aloft. It scattered its first slaver into the clouds and befouled heaven with its gape. We fled in different directions and, breathless with fear, tried to raise a cry of alarm in vain. For the hissing filled the entire grove. Avens, blinded by sudden fear, and reprehensible for doing it (but he was compelled by fate), hid himself in the huge trunk of an ancient oak in the hope that he could evade the unspeakable monster. I myself can hardly believe it. It dragged up the bulk of the lofty tree with its huge coils, tore it up from its base and roots and overturned it. Then it snatched him up as he trembled and called upon his comrades with his final words and, sucking him down with its black throat (I saw it as I looked back), it put him away in its hideous belly. The hapless Aquinus had entrusted himself to the river and the tumbling waves and was swimming in speedy flight. It attacked him in the middle of the stream and fed upon his limbs, after bringing them back to the bank (what an unspeakable variety of death!).... A band armed with shields hurriedly followed at Regulus' command, bringing up heavy ballistas, torsion catapults for use against walls and the huge-pointed spear used to shatter lofty towers. And now when the horses' hooves, leaping over the grassy plain, surrounded its deadly habitat with a resounding noise, the serpent, aroused by the whinnying, slid out of its cave and hissed forth Stygian heats from its smoking mouth. A terrible fire flashed forth from its twin eyes. The height of its raised crest exceeded that of the grove and the high treetops of the wood. Its tongue flickered and flashed through the air with a three-forked movement and leaped up and licked the ether. But when the trumpets blasted, it was alarmed, reared up its huge body, then, settling back, grouped together the rest of its bulk under its breast in twisting coils. From that stance it darted into dread war and, quickly unravelling its twisted coils, extended its full bulk with straightened body and at once reached to the faces of those far distant from it. All the horses snorted in dismay at the serpent. They did not respond to the light rein and breathed out frequent fires from their noses. Rearing up, the snake nodded its high head from side to side on its swol-len neck. Then, goaded by anger, it now snatched some men up aloft, now delighted in crushing them down beneath its great weight. Then it would suck down the black gore, breaking their bones, and, with blood flowing from its mouth, agape, it would change its victim and abandon half-eaten limbs. The ranks of soldiers were giving way before it, and the victorious snake was over-whelming with its pestilential breath squadrons that had ridden far back... with-out fear Regulus hurled his swift spear through the air with thunderbolt-arm. The hurl was successful, and the point lodged directly in its forehead, aided in the force of its impact by the fact that the creature was rushing against it with ardour, and it settled in its head, quivering. The men raised a shout to the stars and their voices, suddenly poured forth, reached to the ethereal halls. Immediately the earth-born monster raged with anger. It scorned flight and the experience of pain was new to it. Then for the first time in its long life did it experience iron. The swift attack the creature made, goaded by pain, would not have been in vain, had not Regulus, with his skill in riding, turned away his horse and evaded it as it darted forwards. When it continued the pursuit of the wheeling horse by twisting its flexible back, Regulus swiftly evaded it by yanking the rein with his left hand. But I, Marus, was no mere spectator amid such events, and my right hand was not inactive. My spear was the second in the monster's massive body. At any point now it would have been licking the hind-quarters of the horse, tired from the struggle, with its three-forked tongue. I hurled my weapon and at once directed the cruel snake's war lust towards myself. Hence the soldiers followed my lead and competitively threw their spears with their right hands and diverted the wild creature to other focuses for its anger, until a ballista stopped it short with a blow designed for walls. From that point, finally, its strength was broken. It could no longer raise its damaged spine in the rigid fashion it used to for making its attack, nor could it raise its head into the clouds as it was in the habit of doing. We pressed upon it more vigorously, and now a *falarica* bolt was plunged deep into its belly and lodged there, and swift arrows stole away the sight from both its eyes. As a result of the deep wound, the black cave of its mouth breathed forth a noxious slaver, its jaws gaping. Now the end of its tail was pinned to the ground because of the javelins heaped onto it and the weight of the poles. Now at last it threatened with only a tired gape. Finally a beam, driven from a torsion catapult with a screech, broke its head apart with a great crack. The snake unravelled itself along the rampart of the riverbank and finally breathed out into the breezes the dark cloud of venom that escaped from its mouth.... Silius Italicus *Punica* 6.140–282 (with omissions)

The landscape in which the Bagrada Dragon lives is significant. The Greeks had already known that the land of Libya had a prime role to play in the genesis of the world's most terrible serpents.[4] Apollonius of Rhodes (*c.*270s BC) is the first to tell us about this, in amplifying his account of Mopsus' death after a snake strikes him from the sands there. As Perseus flew over the land of Libya on his winged sandals, escaping from the remote home of the Gorgons with the freshly decapitated head of Medusa and taking it back to Polydectes on Seriphos, drops of its dark blood had fallen to earth and generated the brood.[5] But it was the Romans, and the poet Lucan above all, in his *Pharsalia* (AD 65), that seized upon this notion and ran with it.[6] Lucan's narration of Cato the Younger's forced march east through the Libyan desert from Cyrene to Leptis Magna and the kingdom of Juba I during the later part of the Civil War in 48 BC is prefaced by an elaborate retelling of Perseus' beheading of Medusa.[7] The land the drops of blood had then fallen upon was barren, resistant to the production of anything good, but it eagerly drank in the 'dire dew', which was then incubated in the hot sand.[8] His catalogue of the terrible serpents thereby produced resembles a Roman-Gothic version, of just the sort one would expect from Lucan, of the serpent-bestiaries of Nicander's (mid-ii BC) *Theriaca* and Philumenus' (ii AD) *On Venomous Creatures and the Antidotes to Them*.[9] We hear, for example, of the *chelydrus*, a snake so hot and fiery that it leaves a smoky trail behind it. But it is the *draco* itself that quite properly occupies the climactic position in this catalogue of terror, for all that it is not venomous: this Libyan variety sucks down birds as it breathes, it constricts even elephants, and it kills bulls with a flick of its tail.[10] The highlight of the ensuing narrative of the march itself, indeed one might say of the poem as a whole, is the

---

[4]   This paragraph draws on Ogden 2018b.

[5]   Apollonius *Argonautica* 4.1502–17 and F4 Powell (= schol. Nicander *Theriaca* 12a; this is a fragment of his lost *Foundation of Alexandria*, discussed with much learning and speculation at Barbantani 2014). A case could be made for including the Gorgons themselves amongst the serpentine terrors of Libya, since, from Aeschylus onwards, this was the most traditional of their locations (amongst a great many others): see Aeschylus *Phorcides* (*TrGF*); Herodotus 2.91; Pausanias 3.17.3; discussion at Ogden 2008:47–50.

[6]   See Ovid *Metamorphoses* 4.616–19; Silius Italicus *Punica* 3.314–16; Solinus 27.28 ('Africa is so fertile in serpents that it has the strongest claim to win the palm-prize for this evil').

[7]   Lucan *Pharsalia* 9.607–95. For a detailed and dutiful commentary on Lucan's snake episode, see Raschle 2001; note also Lausberg 1990; Wick 2009. At the beginning of this section (607–18) Cato's troops discover a spring in Libya which they fear is poisoned by all the serpents around it, but Cato shows them that the water is safe by drinking it, and explains that serpents' venom is only dangerous when mixed with blood, not with water.

[8]   Lucan *Pharsalia* 9.696–9.

[9]   And to a lesser extent in survey works of broader compass, such as Aelian's *Nature of Animals* (passim); Pliny's *Natural History* (esp. 8–11); and Isidore of Seville's *Etymologies* (12.4); cf. Jacques 2002:xx–xxv for a conspectus of (partly) extant ancient works of herpetological interest. For Philumenus, see Wellman 1908. For commentaries on Nicander, see Gow and Scholfield 1953; Scarborough 1977; Jacques 2002 (particularly strong on the ancient herpetological tradition); and Overduin 2015 (cf. also 2005, 2012, 2014); note also Leitz 1997. For Lucan's serpent excursus in Nicandrian context specifically, see Cazzaniga 1957. It is probable that Lucan's most direct inspiration, however, was the lost *Theriaca* of the Augustan poet Aemilius Macer (*Commenta Bernensia* on Lucan 9.701 = Macer F9 Büchner).

[10]   Lucan *Pharsalia* 9.700–33, esp. 711 (*chelydrus*), 727–33 (*draco*).

series of scenes in which various soldiers are picked off one at a time by the differ-ent snakes. Aulus is bitten by a *dipsas* ('dipsad', 'thirst snake'). At first he feels nothing, but the venom slowly dries up his internal organs, and he is suffused with the sensation of burning and beset by an unquenchable thirst. In despair he gulps down the briny sea at the Syrtis and, when that falls short (!), opens his veins in order to drink his own blood. Sabellus is bitten on the leg by a tiny *seps* ('putrefaction snake'). At once the skin shrinks back from the wound and his entire body, bones and all, dissolves into a pool of gloop. Nasidius is bitten by a *prester* ('hurricane snake') and experiences an opposite kind of fate. His face turns red and swells to the point at which all his features are eliminated. His body fol-lows suit, and eventually he is distended into a single shapeless, tumid blob. The army can only abandon his body, swelling still. Tullus is bitten by a *haemorrhois* ('blood-flow snake'). His blood is projected forth at once through every bodily orifice, including his sweat glands, until his whole body becomes a single wound. Laevus is killed by a *Niliaca serpens* ('Nilotic snake') the venom of which instantly solidifies his blood and stops his heart. Paulus is killed by a *iaculus* ('javelin snake'). The name explains the technique: the serpent kills him, without venom, simply by launching itself from a tree and hurling itself, faster than an arrow, straight through his temples, to emerge on the far side before escaping. Murrus is killed by a basilisk. He drives his own spear (without provocation) into the snake, whereupon its venom shoots up the shaft of the spear and directly into his hand. With great presence of mind he draws his sword with his other hand and lops the infected arm off at the shoulder before the venom can travel further into his body.[11] Cato's men are eventually spared further danger by the advent of men of the Psylli, that magical Libyan race that is congenitally proof against all snake-bites. By night they deter the snakes from his camp with circuit purifications, and by day they suck the venom out of anyone attacked on the march.[12] (Dio Chrysostom's *c.* AD 100 Greek account of the *lamias* of Libya offers a further per-spective on that region's terrible herpetology, as we shall see in Chapter 3, §3.4.1.)

2.2 Focalization and Anthropomorphization

One of the distinctive features of the Latin accounts of mythical dragon-fights, their fullness and richness aside, is their tendency to focus much of the narrative upon the dragon itself, even, to some extent, to focalize the narrative through it, and thereby to personalize it, to anthropomorphize it, and accordingly to present

---

[11] Lucan *Pharsalia* 9.737–60 (*dipsas*), 762–88 (*seps*), 789–804 (*prester*), 805–14 (*haemorrhois*), 815–21 (*Niliaca serpens*), 822–7 (*iaculus*), 828–39 (*basiliscus*).
[12] Lucan *Pharsalia* 9.890–937.

it with a degree of understanding and sympathy.[13] This is abundantly clear in Silius' account of the Bagrada Dragon (above), and in Statius' account of the Dragon of Nemea, quoted in Chapter 1, §1.2.2. Let us consider two further passages. In these, which we must inevitably quote at length, the portions of text that focus on the dragon are rendered in bold font, the modest remainder in roman (a similar exercise could be profitably performed with the Silius and Statius texts). First, Ovid on the battle between Cadmus and the Dragon of Ares (AD 8):

An old wood stood violated by no axe. In its midst was a cave covered over thickly with twigs and withies, making a low arch with its structure of stones. It was fertile in rich waters. **Buried in this cave was a snake [*anguis*] of Mars [Ares], remarkable for his golden crest. His eyes flickered with fire, his whole body swelled with venom. Three tongues flickered, his teeth were arranged in three rows.** The Tyrians [i.e. Cadmus and his Phoenician companions], with luckless step, stopped at this grove on their journey. The jar, lowered down to the waters, made a noise, **and the dark blue serpent [*serpens*] lifted his head out of the length of his cave and gave out a terrible hiss.** The jars fell from their hands, the blood left their bodies, and a sudden trembling seized their stricken limbs. **The serpent rolled his scaly coils in rounded gatherings and threw them up into huge arcs. With more than half of his body lifted high into the gentle breezes, he looked down over the entire grove. His body was as great as the one you would see if you gazed upon the full length of the serpent that separates the twin Bear constellations. Without delay he snatched up the Phoenicians, whether they were pulling out their weapons, whether they were making to escape, or whether terror was preventing them from doing either. Some he killed with his bite, others with the embrace of his extensive coils, others again with the blast of his venom, deadly with corruption.** Now the sun, at its highest point in the sky, reduced the shadows to their minimum. Cadmus, born of Agenor, wondered what was delaying his comrades and followed their tracks. His shield was a hide torn from a lion, his weapons a spear of shining iron and a javelin and a spirit superior to every weapon. On entering the grove, he saw the slaughtered bodies and the victorious enemy, with his massive body, hanging over them, licking their wretched limbs with a bloody tongue. 'Bodies most loyal to me, I shall either be the avenger of your death, or your companion in it', said Cadmus. So he spoke and with his right hand he picked up a huge rock, the size of a millstone, and hurled it, with great exertion. Lofty walls and their high towers would have been damaged by its impact, **but the serpent**

---

[13] This is a matter of a tendency rather than of any categorical difference with the preceding Greek tradition. Typhon of course receives a degree of personalization in Hesiod's account of Zeus' great battle with him (quoted above in Chapter 1, §1.6), but given his humanoid upper half (there), he is rather an exception proving a rule.

remained unwounded. He was protected by his scales as if by a breastplate, and he repelled the violent blow from his skin by the hardness of his black hide. But this hardness did not overcome the javelin as well. This lodged, fixed in the middle of the curve of his twisting back and the entirety of its iron point penetrated into his guts. The wild creature twisted back his head towards his back, saw the wound and bit onto the shaft that was fixed there. When, with much force, he had loosened the shaft on all sides, he eventually managed to rip it out of his back. But even so the iron point remained stuck in his bones. That was the point at which, this new cause being added to his normal rage, his throat swelled with full veins, and white foam splashed over his deadly snarl. The earth resounded as he scraped over it with his scales, and he infected the corrupted air with a black breath of the sort that issues from a Stygian mouth. Now he would coil round and fashion a monstrous circle from his coils; now he would stand up rampant, straighter than a tall beam, now he would surge forward with huge force like a river made violent by rains and crush down with his breast the woods that lay in his way. The son of Agenor conceded a little ground, deflected his attack with his lion-prize shield and frustrated the mouth that pressed upon him by defending himself with his spear. The serpent raged and vainly attempted to deal wounds to the hard iron. He fixed his teeth around the point. Now it was that the blood began to flow forth from his venomous palate and bespatter the green grass. But the wound was just a superficial one, because he dragged himself back from the blow and drew his damaged neck backwards. By giving ground he tried to prevent Cadmus' blow from striking home or penetrating more deeply. But at the same time the son of Agenor, relentlessly following the serpent, drove on the iron he had lodged in his throat **until an oak tree blocked his way as he went backwards and his neck became pinned to the wood. The tree bowed under the serpent's weight and bewailed the fact that its trunk was being lashed by the tip of his tail.** As the victor contemplated the bulk of the enemy he had overcome, a voice was suddenly heard (it was difficult to tell whence it emanated, but nonetheless, heard it was): 'Why, son of Agenor, do you gaze at the serpent you have killed? You too will be gazed at in the form of a serpent.'

Ovid *Metamorphoses* 3.28–98

Second, something a little different: Valerius Flaccus' account of the battle—if such it can be called—between Jason and the Dragon of Colchis, in which the animal is presented as a pet subjected to reluctant cruelty by his keeper Medea:

So Medea said and with rapid step made her way along the pathless course. Jason stuck close by her side and was feeling sorry for her in her journey, when suddenly he saw a huge flame in the midst of the clouds, and the darkness shimmering with a cruel light. 'What is that redness in the sky? Which star shines so dismally?' he said. The maiden answered, as he trembled, 'See, you are looking at the eyes and the wild stare of the dragon [*draco*] himself. He shakes those thunderbolts from his crest. I am the only one that he looks upon with fear. He has the habit of calling me by choice, and he asks me for food with a fawning tongue. Come, tell me now, would you prefer to carry off the spoils from him whilst he is awake and sees you, his enemy, or should I rather plunge his eyes in sleep and give you a tamed snake [*anguis*]?' He remained silent, so forcibly was he gripped by awe for the maiden. And now the Colchian stretched up her hands and wand to the stars, pouring out spells with a barbarian metre, and she began to rouse you up, father Sleep: 'All-powerful Sleep, I, the Colchian, bid you now come from all over the world and enter this dragon alone. Relying on your horn, I have often overcome the waves, the clouds, the thunderbolts and whatever flashes throughout the heaven. But now, now, come to me in greater force, most like your brother Death. **For you too** [this is addressed to the dragon], **most faithful guardian of the Phrixean sheep** [i.e. the golden fleece], **it is at last time to turn away your eyes from your object of concern. What trick do you fear whilst I am standing by you? I myself will look after the grove for a brief while. In the meantime you lay aside your long toil.'** He could not abide, though tired, to abandon the Aeolian gold, nor to give his eyes over to the rest he had been permitted, much as he would have liked to. Struck by a cloud of initial drowsiness, he shivered and shook the sweet sleep from his body. But on the other side the Colchian maiden continued to foam with Tartarean spells and shake about all the silences of her bough of Lethe [forgetfulness]. **She overwhelmed his struggling eyes with an incantation against them, and with tongue and hand she tried all her Stygian power, until sleep was in control of his blazing anger. Now his lofty crests sank down.** His head, under compulsion, and his huge neck nodded down from the fleece, like the Po in backward flow or the Nile dispersed into seven rivers or the Alpheos as it arrives in the Hesperian world. Medea herself, when she saw the head of her dear dragon on the ground, threw herself upon him and put her arms around him, and wept for herself and for her nursling, to whom she was being so cruel. 'This was not how you looked when, late at night, I brought you offerings and feasts, nor was I like this when I put honey-cakes in your gaping mouth and faithfully nourished you with my poisons [*venena*]. How heavy your bulk as you lie! How slowly you breathe as you lie there motionless! At least, unfortunate one, I have not killed you! Alas, you are destined to experience a cruel daylight! Soon you will see no fleece, no shining offering under your shade. So withdraw, and pass your old age in other groves, and forget me, I beg you. Nor let your hostile hissing drive me forth over all the sea. But you, son of Aeson [Jason], dispel all delays, seize the fleece and flee! With my drugs I extinguished my father's bulls and I gave the Earth-born warriors over to death. **See, you have** the body of the dragon sprawling before you, and now at last, I trust, I have finished my crimes.' Then the hero asked her by what route he should carry himself up to the top of the gold-bearing tree. 'There', she said, 'come, climb over the *draco* himself and press your steps into his back before you.' There was no delay. The descendent of Cretheus [Jason] put his trust in her words, scaled his way up to the top of the ash tree, high as it was, the branches of which were still protecting the ruddy skin, the like of illuminated clouds or Iris [the Rainbow] when she undoes her dress and glides to meet blazing Apollo. Jason snatched up the prize he had longed for, his final labour. Only reluctantly did the tree surrender the memento of Phrixus' flight, which it had borne through long years. It groaned, and dismal darkness surrounded it. They left....

Valerius Flaccus Argonautica 8.54–121

Examples of this kind of approach in early imperial Latin poetic texts could be multiplied.[14]

2.3 Kindly Dragon Deities at Rome: Asclepius and Friends

As much as Rome embraced the hostile dragons of the Greek tradition, so it embraced, with perhaps greater enthusiasm still, its kindly dragon-related deities, and in doing so rather occluded a grimmer variety of serpent-wielding deity that had previously flourished in the Italian peninsula, as found in Aita, the Etruscan Hades.[15] Indeed from the beginning of the third century BC the kindliest of them all, Asclepius, had been given a privileged home in the heart of the city. The god's arrival in the city in 292 or 291 BC in response to a plague is spoken of in a wide

---

[14] Consider also, for example, Seneca's detailed description of the battle between Heracles and Cerberus at *Hercules Furens* 782–829 (a stepping-stone, of a kind, to the Greek satirist Lucian's presentation of a talking Cerberus at *Dialogues of the Dead* 4: rational, matter-of-fact, and even cod-philosophical) and Statius' description of the depredations of the Lamia sent against Argos at *Thebaid* 1.597–626 (quoted in Chapter 3, §3.4.1). The same approach is found in narratives of heroic battles against the dragons' marine cousins, the sea-monsters, *kētē* or *ceti* (see Chapter 4, §4.3, for the nature of the relationship between these two creatures): thus, the descriptions of Perseus' battle against the Ketos of Ethiopia or Joppa at Ovid *Metamorphoses* 4.663–739 and Manilius *Astronomica* 5.538–618, and of Heracles' battle against the *Kētos* of Troy at Valerius Flaccus *Argonautica* 2.451–578.
[15] On a *c.*350–325 BC stamnos two snakes project from Aita's hair over his forehead (Museo Gregoriano Etrusco Vaticano 14963 = *LIMC* Aita/Calu 1). In a fresco from the *c.*340–320 BC Orcus II tomb at Corneto Aita brandishes a black snake, poised to hurl it at Geryon; his companion Persephone has her hair bound in a diadem of snakes (*LIMC* Aita/Calu 6). Attention may be drawn also to three images on fourth-century BC vases from Orvieto: on one Aita brandishes a snake-sceptre (Orvieto, Museo Faina 20 [2646] = *LIMC* Aita/Calu 14); on the other two Persephone's chariot is drawn by large birds of prey with serpent heads and tails, whilst the ground below is infested with serpents (Museo Faina, Orvieto 19 [2645 = *LIMC* Aita/Calu 9] and 21 [= 2647]); see further Chapter 4, §4.2, for these last two vases.

range of texts, appropriately to its lasting importance to the city.[16] But the richest and most glorious account is that supplied by Ovid in the final book of his *Metamorphoses*.[17] His story proceeds as follows. The city sends a delegation of sacred ambassadors to Apollo at Delphi to ask how they might obtain release from the plague gripping the city. Apollo sends them on to his son, Asclepius, in his central shrine at Epidaurus. The ambassadors ask the Epidaurian officials to give them the god to take back to Rome, but they are naturally hesitant to surrender both the god and the wealth that his shrine generates for their community (they do not yet appreciate his remarkable ability to travel to a new home whilst paradoxically remaining firmly ensconced in his original one).[18] However, during the following night the god reveals himself to the ambassadors in their dreams, taking the humanoid form famous from his statues. He undertakes to come to Rome with them and draws their attention to the serpent that winds around his staff. This is the form in which he will appear to them, albeit on a much larger scale, as befits a celestial deity.

Dawn the next day had dismissed the fiery stars. The officials remained unsure still as to what they should do as they came together in the richly wrought temple of the god the Romans had asked for. They asked him to indicate in which location he wished to stay by making a sign in the heaven. They had scarcely finished their prayer when the golden god, manifest in the form of a serpent [*serpens*] with a lofty crest, gave forth a hiss to alert them to his imminent arrival. As he came he caused everything to shake: the statue, the altars, the temple doors, the marble floor, and the golden pediment. He came to a halt in the middle of the temple and raised his head up to be level with their breasts. He looked about him, his eyes flashing with fire. The terrified crowd trembled, but the priest, his holy locks bound in a white fillet, recognized the god and said, 'Lo, the god! It is the god! All present be silent of tongue and reverent of mind. Most beautiful one, be propitious to us in your manifestation and succour the people that observe your rites!' All present worshipped the god as commanded and repeated the priest's words. The Romans worshipped him with mind and voice.

[16] In addition to the Ovid and Valerius Maximus texts discussed here, see Livy periocha 11 and 29.11.1; Pliny *Natural History* 29.72; Q. Serenus Sammonicus *Liber medicinalis* prooemium 6–8; Lactantius *Divinae institutiones* 2.7.13, 2.16.11; Arnobius *Against the Gentiles* 7.44–8; [Aurelius Victor] *De viris illustribus* 22.1–3; Orosius *Histories against the Pagans* 3.22.5; Claudian *On the Consulship of Stilicho* 3.171–3; Augustine *City of God* 3.17; Sidonius Apollinaris *Letters* 1.17.12; *Latin Anthology* 1.2.719e.3–4 (T614 Edelstein). See Edelstein and Edelstein 1945:ii, 252–4; Riethmüller 2005:i, 86, 233–6, ii, 431 (with images of medallions of the age of Antoninus showing the serpent-god arriving on his ship); Ogden 2013a:310–17.

[17] Ovid *Metamorphoses* 15.622–744.

[18] For further examples of episodes in which Asclepius travelled from Epidaurus in the form of a snake to found new temples, whilst somehow remaining at home all along, see Ogden 2013a:312–17 (the cases of Athens, Halieis, Sicyon, Epidaurus Limera, Cos).

The god nodded to them, his crest waving, in a token of his firm guarantee, and emitted three hisses with his flickering tongue. Then he slid down his shining steps. Turning his head around, he looked back at the ancient altars as he was to leave them behind, and bade farewell to his accustomed home and the temple in which he had lived. From there the huge serpent slithered over the ground that was covered here and there with flowers, flexing his coils. He made his way through the middle of the city to the harbour that was fortified with a curving rampart. Here he came to a halt and seemed, with gentle look, to send home the host of devotees that had dutifully followed him. He laid his body on the Italian ship. The boat felt the load of his godhead, and the hull sank down under his weight.   Ovid *Metamorphoses* 15.665–94

The delighted ambassadors set off for home with the serpent. Ovid discreetly obscures the matter, but seems to imply that the serpent, who rests his bulk on the stern (home of the rudder) whilst staring out over the sea, actually takes responsibility for steering the ship. Stormy weather compels the party to seek safety by putting in at Antium. As they come to land, the serpent slithers aground to be hosted in his father Apollo's temple, situated there on the shore. When calm is restored, the serpent returns to the ship, gliding up its rudder, and takes up position again on the stern. As the ship sails up the Tiber into Rome, the citizens crowd the riverbanks to welcome it. The serpent now rests his head on the top of the mast, so as to be able to scan from side to side to find a suitable new home. He chooses the Tiber Island, disembarks there, resumes his heavenly form (*specie caeleste resumpta*), in other words disappears, and thenceforth suffuses the city with his powers of good health.[19]

The anthropomorphism of this serpent could not be clearer. The god first appears in fully humanoid form to declare that the serpent about to appear will be himself. The serpent's own human touches are varied and winning: the discreet warning hiss as he arrives, in an awareness of the alarm his form can cause; the raising of his head to human chest level, the better to communicate (albeit silently); the nod to indicate assent; the wistful final glance back at his old home; the assumption of the role of helmsman; the visit, en route, to the house of his father. Ovid is not the only Latin author to recall the arrival of Asclepius in terms of this sort—terms that must have been well established in the city's memory. The Tiberian Valerius Maximus speaks of the serpent slithering slowly around the city of Epidaurus for three days with a gentle look (*mitibus oculis*), whilst— initially paradoxically—showing himself eager to head for Rome the while. The

---

[19] From the earlier first century BC onwards, this tale had been promulgated in the fabric of the Tiber Island. Naturally ship-like in shape, a stone prow was built for it and an obelisk erected in its middle to resemble a mast: Besnier 1902; Schouten 1967:18–20; Riethmüller 2005:i, 235–6.

contradiction is seemingly resolved when we then learn that he also spends three days at Antium. Evidently, the three-day period has a sacred significance. But it remains possible too to infer that the serpent is conflicted as he prepares to leave his original city.[20]

Asclepius brings us to another type of divine manifestation at Rome in which dragon and human meet: the siring of an emperor (or an emperor *avant la lettre*) by a god in dragon form.[21] This phenomenon too is first found in the Greek world, where the dragon-sire in question is always identified with or aligned with Asclepius himself. A (iv BC) miracle inscription from his Epidaurian shrine records how the childless Nicasibula had incubated there, whereupon the god visited her in her dreams and his serpent avatar penetrated her, siring two sons for her.[22] A (iii–ii BC) inscribed offertory base from the same shrine tells us that the offertory it once held was in the form of a dragon, to salute the form in which the god had sired Aratus of Sicyon.[23] The earliest record of Alexander the Great's dragon sire, a passing reference in Cicero's *On Divination*, associates the sire with a healing serpent that subsequently manifested itself in a dream to Alexander at Harmatela in India, showing him the herb he needed to find in order to heal his general Ptolemy, who was dying from the effects of a (venomous) poison arrow.[24] A (*c*. AD 160) inscription of Caesarea Troketta tells that Miletus, the priest of Apollo Soter, had been sired by the god's son, the 'Paphlagonian Glycon', which is

---

[20] Valerius Maximus 1.8.2. Valerius more patriotically makes the initial consultation one of Rome's own Sibylline Oracles, rather than of Delphic Apollo. There is no steering of the ship this time; rather, the serpent coils around the shipboard tent of Ogulnius, the head of the sacred embassy. It is his own (Asclepian) temple that the serpent visits for three days at Antium, winding himself around a lofty (and presumably staff-like) palm-tree in its forecourt in the meantime. When he arrives in Rome, he finds a temple already built for him on Tiber Island and waiting to receive him, and swims across the river to reach it (for the construction of a temple in advance in anticipation of Asclepius' arrival, see also Lucian *Alexander* 10–14).

[21] See Ogden 2013a:330–42.

[22] *EMI* B 42 = *IG* iv² 122.42 = Edelstein and Edelstein 1945 no. 423.

[23] *IG* iv² 622; so too Pausanias 2.10.3 and 4.14.7.

[24] Cicero *On Divination* 2.135; cf. Diodorus 17.103 and Curtius 9.8.22—8. I have resiled from the view (Ogden 2010:42–52) that Alexander's serpent-sire was held to be a manifestation of Zeus Meilichios. As I now see it, there obtained two originally discrete legendary traditions about the siring of Alexander. According to the first of these, he was sired by a manifestation of Zeus or Ammon: Ephorus *FGrH* 70 F217; Callisthenes *FGrH* 124 F14 (apud Strabo C814); Diodorus 17.51; Justin 11.11 (i.e. Trogus); Curtius 4.7.8.25–7; Plutarch *Alexander* 27; Lucian *Dialogues of the Dead* 13. According to the second tradition, he was sired by a divine serpent with, for reasons given, Asclepian characteristics: Cicero (as cited); Livy 26.19.7–8; Justin 11.11 (i.e. Trogus); Ptolemy Chennus apud Photius cod. 190, §148a; Aulus Gellius 6.1.1; Lucian *Dialogues of the Dead* 13; Solinus 9.18. The confusion arises because five ancient sources contaminated these two traditions: Antipater of Thessalonica at *Greek Anthology* 9.241 ('the famous Ammon was a snake', Ἄμμων δ' ὠμφιβόητος ὄφις); Plutarch *Alexander* 2–3; Alexandrian choliambic epitaph at Fraser 1972:ii, 950; Pausanias 4.14.7; *Alexander Romance* (A) 1.6–8, 10, 12, 14, 24, 30, 35, 2.13, 21, 3.33. The full version of this argument will be laid out in Ogden (forthcoming b).

to say the serpentine manifestation of the 'New Asclepius' promoted by the prophet Alexander of Abonouteichos.[25]

As the phenomenon of the serpent sire moved into the Roman world, the focus broadened a little from Asclepius himself. Caius Oppius (43–33 BC) and others after him tell that Scipio Africanus, victor over Hannibal, had been sired on his mother Pomponia by Jupiter in the form of a serpent.[26] The (earlier iv AD) *De viris illustribus urbis Romanae* ascribed to Aurelius Victor records that the serpent had subsequently been found coiling around the baby's neck.[27] Asclepiades of Mendes (late i BC) and others after him tell that Octavian-Augustus was sired on his mother Atia by Apollo in the form of a serpent, as she incubated overnight in his temple (it is noteworthy here that the context of the siring—temple incubation—remains strongly Asclepian, despite the featured god being rather Asclepius' father, Apollo).[28] The (post-iv AD) *Epitome de Caesaribus* also ascribed to Aurelius Victor tells of the emperor Galerius' boast that he had been sired upon his mother by a dragon, though the identity of the god remains unspecified.[29] Two further emperors should probably be added to the list. Tacitus and Suetonius (both *c.* AD 120) and others report the tradition that the baby Nero was protected by a guardian *draco* (or perhaps two), and that this had chased away an assassin sent against him by Messalina. The serpent had left a piece of slough around the child's neck, which his mother Agrippina enclosed in a protective golden bracelet for him. And, similarly, the (*c.* AD 400?) *Historia Augusta* tells that a serpent was found coiling around the head of the (presumably adult) Septimius Severus as he slept in a pub.[30]

2.4 Dragons, Dragons Everywhere: *Genii Loci*

Glorious dragon murals are a prominent feature of a series of shrines frozen in time in the Pompeii and Herculaneum of AD 79, and we presume that similar

---

[25] *IGROM* iv.1498 (cf. Lucian *Alexander* 42). In a final example from the Greek world, Pausanias 4.14.7 uniquely tells us that the legendary hero of the archaic Messenian resistance against Sparta, Aristomenes of Messene, had been sired by a serpent, but he declines to identify the god in question.

[26] Aulus Gellius 6.1.1 (citing Caius Oppius and Julius Hyginus); Livy 26.19.7–8; Silius Italicus *Punica* 13.634–49; Cassius Dio 16.7.39 (cf. 17.57.63).

[27] [Aurelius Victor] *De viris illustribus urbis Romanae* 49.1.

[28] Suetonius *Augustus* 94 (citing Asclepiades of Mendes *FGrH* 617 F2); Cassius Dio 45.1.2–3; Sidonius Apollinaris *Carmina* 2.121–6.

[29] [Aurelius Victor] *Epitome de Caesaribus* 40.17.

[30] Scriptores *Historiae Augustae*, Septimius Severus 1.10. The same text tells that Alexander Severus' mother had dreamed before his birth that she was about to produce a purple dragonlet (Alexander Severus 14.1: *purpureum dracunculum*).

shrines were once to be found throughout the Roman world.[31] These shrines are located inside the richer homes and at street corners (there are nine of the latter), and one is found in the Temple of Isis. Sometimes a single serpent winds around a round altar, but more usually a balancing pair of serpents squiggles from left and right towards a central altar. Sometimes, by no means always, they are differentiated into male and female, with the male serpent sporting a beard in contrast to the female and being slightly larger and darker than she is. The setting is a lush and verdant garden. On the altar sit offerings for the serpents (the object of their interest), eggs, or pine cones, sometimes separate ones for each of the pair. These painted scenes often sit in a separate band beneath paintings featuring more humanoid gods, a pair of dancing Lares (whom the serpent pair can balance in turn) and a householder's personal (humanoid) *genius*.[32]

The literary sources tell us little of these magnificent murals, but Isidore of Seville (*c.* AD 600) makes a valuable observation as he gives sense to a line of Persius' obscurantist *Satires* (AD 62): 'Snakes were always held to be spirits of *place* [*genii locorum*] amongst the pagans, which is why Persius says, "Paint a pair of snakes, boys: the place is sacred".'[33] A clue to their significance is also to be found in the record of a lost mural of *c.* AD 45–79 from Herculaneum. In this a single serpent, coiling around its round altar in its garden, and tucking into its offerings of a pair of eggs and a pair of pinecones, was accompanied by an integrated inscription that had originally read '*genius* of this mountain' (*genius huius montis*).[34] We are put in mind of the passage of Virgil's *Aeneid* in which Aeneas famously encounters a serpent at the tomb of his father Anchises, which takes some food from the altar on which he is making offerings to him, whereupon he wonders whether it is a servant of his father's ghost or a 'genius of the place' (*geniumne loci*).[35] Commenting on the passage, Servius (iv AD) observes that 'no place is without its *genius*, and this is commonly manifest in the form of a snake',[36] whilst elsewhere he informs us that *genii* is the Roman term for the Greek Agathoi Daimones, and that they 'rejoice in houses'.[37] Servius is evidently right that the

---

[31] See now the treatment of these within Flower's monumental study of the *Lares*, 2017, esp. 63–75, which I largely follow. See also Boyce 1942, Tinh 1992, and Charlesworth 2010:461–8.

[32] Pairs of serpents: *LIMC* Lar, Lares 33, 37–8, 63, 65, 68, 70–2, 74. Single serpents: 34–6, 39, 64, 67, 69, 75–6, 78, 79–80; cf. 81 (Rome, relief of i AD, serpent coils around altar). Good illustrations and reconstructions of many of these shrines are also provided at Flower 2017:64, 68, and colour pll. 6–8, 11–15, 19–20.

[33] Isidore of Seville *Etymologies* 12.4.1, incorporating Persius *Satires* 1.113: *angues autem apud gentiles pro geniis locorum erant habiti semper, unde Persius; 'Pinge duos angues, pueri: sacer est locus.'* See further Kißel 1990:259–60.

[34] *CIL* viii.14588; see Flower 2017:65–6, with illustration at 68 (fig. i.6).

[35] Virgil *Aeneid* 5.84–96. Indeed the word *loci* appears to have been inserted after the fact into the Herculaneum inscription (Flower 2017:65–6), presumably in tribute to Virgil, to produce the rather awkward *genius huius <loci> montis* ('genius of this place, the mountain').

[36] Servius on Virgil *Aeneid* 5.84: *nullus locus sine genio est qui per anguem plerumque ostenditur.*

[37] Servius on Virgil *Georgics* 3.417: *gaudet tectis ut sunt ἀγαθοὶ δαίμονες quos Latini genios vocant.*

origin of these protective serpents lay in the Graeco-Egyptian culture of the house-protecting Agathos Daimon and Agathe Tyche serpents: their association with the Temple of Isis and the fact that some of them sport the pshent (the double crown of the two Egypts) proclaim this.[38] These painted serpents were, then, the protective deities of the places in which their shrines were erected, and their connection to physical place in general is presumably celebrated in the garden setting in which they are shown.

Given that we are told by several ancient authorities that a female *genius* was a *iuno*, we might wonder whether the serpents differentiated out as female would have been so termed.[39] However, it is possible that the female term was applied only in the case of the humanoid protective *genii* of (female) householders, and not in the case of the serpentine protective *genii* of place.[40]

It is self-evident that, just like the Greek Agathoi Daimones, these protective deities must have been regarded as a friendly and supportive presence. This in itself perhaps speaks of a degree of anthropomorphism in their conceptualization. Their frequent alignment with the humanoid Lares and personal *genii* tends to make the same point.

2.5 Conclusion

We may speculate about the roots of the Romans' approach towards the representation of the *draco*. (1) Did it lie in the influence of the all-but-lost dragon-slaying tradition of Hellenistic Greek literature?[41] (2) Did it lie simply in the propensity of Latin authors to inflate and build out the type-scenes they found both in their Greek models and also in the writings of their Roman rivals, often on a quite manifestly competitive basis? If a dragon-fight narrative was to be expanded, then the bestowal of extra screen-time on the dragon itself was an obvious way to go about this. (3) Did it lie in the authors' experiences of watching beast-fights in the arena, where fights between man and animal were presented in parallel with fights between man and man? The Romans' taste for the arena might certainly account for the significant increase in the goriness of their literary dragon-fights.

---

[38] Like *genius*, the term ἀγαθὸς δαίμων could define both a protective spirit of a place and a protective spirit of individual people, i.e. the *Di Manes*: Ganschinietz 1918:46–7 collates evidence for the latter significance.

[39] [Tibullus] 312.1; Seneca *Letters* 110.1; Petronius *Satyricon* 25.4; Pliny *Natural History* 2.16; *CIL* 11.944.

[40] See Flower 2017:59–60. In the past scholars have tended to confound these two varieties of *genius*: Wissowa 1912:176–7; Otto 1910:1162; Kunckel 1974:18; Ogden 2013a:308–9 (!).

[41] The only significant dragon-fights in extant Hellenistic literature are Apollonius of Rhodes' account of the Colchis Dragon (*Argonautica* 4.123–66, quoted in Chapter 1, §1.2.4) and Theocritus' account of baby Heracles' battle against the pair of serpents sent against him by Hera (Theocritus *Idylls* 24.10–33, 56–9, 82–100).

(4) Or did it lie in that transformative moment in Roman history when the great, kindly, serpentine god, Asclepius, at once man and serpent, was imported into the city and took up residence in its very heart, on the Tiber Island? Whatever the cause—and perhaps it is better to think in terms of sympathetic contexts rather than in terms of causes as such—the dragon with a personality, the anthropo-morphized dragon, can be seen as a stepping stone (not the only one) to the dragon of early Christian culture, which, typically identified with demons, was often shown to exhibit human traits (see Chapter 6, §6.5.1).

3

Drakaina

The She-Dragon

What is a *drakaina*?[1] In the most basic sense the word is the feminine and female-denoting reflex of the familiar masculine term *drakōn*, 'dragon' (the plural is *drakainai*). Whilst many uses of it seem to signify a creature of more or less pure serpentine form *in the first instance*, in practice it was almost always imbued, in some way, with a notion of the female humanoid form too. Sometimes it was specifically deployed for metaphors for or comparanda for human or humanoid women. But sometimes too it was more particularly applied to female anguipedes, creatures that consisted primarily of a humanoid upper half and a serpentine lower half, in the fashion of Melusine, and more immediately in the manner of Typhon and Cecrops, whom we looked at in Chapter 1, §1.6, and to whom the simple term *drakōn* could correspondingly be applied.[2] It is probable, indeed, that the female anguipede was the image that the word most commonly summoned to the ancient mind.

3.1 The Grammarians

The term *drakaina* is relatively rare: the standard database of ancient and medieval Greek texts (*TLG*) knows of only 103 uses prior to the fall of Constantinople, and that too with a certain amount of double-counting for book fragments. An indication of the word's obscurity is the fact that the context in which it is most commonly found is the works of the grammarians. From the second century AD onwards, at least, scholars took an interest in its morphological relationship with its masculine counterpart *drak-ōn*, and in the analogy of this relationship with relationships between a list of further pairs of masculine/feminine, male-denoting/female-denoting nouns, especially *le-ōn/le-aina* ('lion', 'lioness'), *therap-ōn/therap-aina* ('servant', 'servant-woman') and *Lak-ōn/Lak-aina* ('Spartan man',

---

[1] Biles's definition of the term (2000:128–9) makes appeal only to Delphyne.
[2] Melusine: Jean d'Arras *Roman de Mélusine* (AD 1392–4), etc.

'Spartan woman').[3] The *drakaina~leaina* jangle was a compelling one for Greek authors, with a number of them bringing the terms together in various contexts.[4] The term was also taken up into Latin in the expected transcription *dracaena*, but in this language it appears *exclusively* (and therefore fruitlessly for us) in the works of its grammarians. From the fourth century AD onwards these Latin grammarians incorporate it into similar lists of pairs, albeit with Greek and Latin words now side by side (as e.g. in Donatus: *draco/dracaena, leo/leaena, gallus/gallina, rex/regina*). As in the Greek grammarians, the dragon-pair example remains strongly yoked to that of the lion-pair.[5]

3.2 Pure-Serpent *Drakainai*, Tout Court

The use of the term *drakaina* to indicate a pure serpent without any sort of humanoid context is rare. The most important text here is Philostratus' description of the terrible snakes of India. He has this to say of the marsh *drakontes*:

> The ones that live in the marshes are slow and have a length of thirty cubits. They have no crest standing up, but they resemble *drakainai*. Their backs are very black and they are less scaly than the others.
>
> Philostratus *Life of Apollonius* 3.6.2

This text seems to assume that the observable physical difference between *drakontes* in general and *drakainai* in general consists (solely) in the matter of the

---

[3] Aelius Herodianus *De prosodia catholica* iii.1 p. 250 line 10 Lentz, Περὶ ὀρθογραφίας iii.2 p. 425 line 15 Lentz, Περὶ κλίσεως ὀνομάτων iii.2 p. 726 line 23 Lentz, Περὶ κλίσεως ὀνομάτων iii.2 p. 733 line 13 Lentz, Περὶ παρωνύμων iii.2 p. 856 line 10 Lentz, *Partitiones* p. 218 lines 3–8 Boissonade (ii AD); Apollonius Dyscolus *De adverbiis* at ii.1.1 p. 142 line 22 Schneider (ii AD); [Arcadius] *De accentibus* p. 109 Schmidt (iv AD); Theodosius of Alexandria *Canones isagogici de flexione nominum* 4.2 p. 20 Hilgard, Περὶ κλίσεως τῶν εἰς ων βαρυτόνων p. 20 Hilgard; [Theodosius of Alexandria] Περὶ γραμματικῆς p. 120 Götling (iv–v AD); Theognostus *Canones sive De orthographia* 583 (ix AD); George Choeroboscus *Prolegomena et scholia in Theodosii Alexandrini canones isagogicos de flexione nominum* p. 275 Hilgard, *Epimerismi in Psalmos* p. 121 Gaisford and Περὶ ποσότητος (e cod. Barocc. 50) p. 316 Cramer (ix AD); *Epimerismi Homerici* μ 36 Dyck (ix AD?); *Lexica Segueriana, Anonymous Antatticista* s.v. δράκαινα (x AD); *Etymologicum Gudianum* s.v. μέλαινα (xi AD); Eustathius on Homer *Iliad* ii p. 51 line 8 van der Valk (xii AD), on Homer *Odyssey* i p. 302 Stallbaum; *Etymologicum Symeonis* s.v. ἀμφιμέλαιναι (xii AD); Gennadius Scholarius *Grammatica* 1 p. 363 Jugie-Petit-Siderides (xv AD); cf. also *Suda* s.v. δράκαινα (x AD), a blank entry.

[4] See below (§3.3) on Anaxilas, Oppian of Apamea, the *Greek Anthology*, Ephraem Syrus (etc.), and Manuel Philes.

[5] Donatus *Ars grammatica* 3.5, *GL* iv p. 376 Keil (iv AD); Diomedes *Ars grammatica, GL* i p. 328 Keil (iv AD); Consentius *De nomine et verbo, GL* v p. 346 Keil (iv–v AD); Servius Auctus on Virgil *Eclogues* 2.63, 3.245 (v AD); Pompeius *Commentum artis Donati, GL* v p.164 Keil (v AD); Cledonius *Ars grammatica, GL* v p. 41 Keil (v AD?); Priscian *Institutiones grammaticae* book 5, *GL* ii p. 146, book 6, *GL* ii p. 209 Hertz-Keil, *Partitiones XII uersuum Aeneidos principalium* on Virgil *Aeneid* 4.1, *GL* iii p. 478 Keil (vi AD); *Ars Bernensis, GL Suppl.* pp. 101, 124 Hagen (viii AD); Remigius Autissiodorensis *Commentum Einsidlense in Donati artem maiorem, GL Suppl.* p. 238 Hagen (ix AD).

crest. This is a distinction that might make some sense in a more domestic or quasi-domestic Roman context. There is seemingly sometimes an attempt to make an iconographical distinction between pure *drakontes* and pure *drakainai* in images of the house-protecting *genii loci* serpents (discussed in Chapter 2, §2.4). In some of the Pompeian murals we find pairs in which one snake is larger and darker than the other and is bearded and crested whilst the other is not, or at any rate sports only a reduced crest; this last configuration might fit with Philostratus' words particularly well.[6] Occasionally we find the same sort of differentiation by beard specifically made in bas-reliefs, as in the case of a relief from Ostia's Piccolo Mercato.[7] However, this is not a distinction that could be made to stick across the full range of the Graeco-Roman iconographic record. *Genius loci* images uniquely flout the rule that otherwise seems to obtain for *drakōn* iconography, to the effect that the beard (and like it the balancing crest) serves not as a marker of gender but as an optional marker of a supernatural affinity, as we have seen (Chapter 1, §1.4): we should note that the distinctively female Hydra, of whom more anon, often sports beards.[8]

A pair of similarly (but confusingly) worded accounts of the topography of the Forum Amastrianum in Constantinople written between the eighth and tenth centuries A D seem to indicate that it was decorated with, inter alia, turtles, birds, and sixteen *drakainai*. The medium of the art is unclear (sculpture?). Given that the accounts specify *drakainai* as opposed to simply *drakontes*, one is moved to ask whether there was some observable marker of femaleness in the images. One thinks again of crests (and beards), but the withholding of these would not have been such a clear marker in the absence of differentiated male *drakontes* retaining them. Must we think of a more dramatic kind of marking-out? Were these *drakainai* anguipedes, even?[9]

The scholia to Euripides' *Phoenissae* tell us that the Sphinx had a *drakaina* for a tail (I suppose we may regard the tail in itself as a pure serpent, even if it is attached to a variety of other forms). Why not a *drakōn* tail? Presumably because the Sphinx herself is a (distinctively) female creature as a whole and the gender of her tail is accordingly assimilated.[10]

Finally, let us look at the other side of the coin, and note two texts in particular that almost ostentatiously avoid deploying the word *drakaina* for an emphatically female dragon of pure serpent form. It is important to be clear that the

---

[6] E.g. Flower 2017 pll. 6, 7, 15.

[7] There are many imperial-period reliefs in which Agathos Daimon (assimilated to Sarapis) sports a beard whilst his consort Agathe Tyche (assimilated to Isis-Thermouthis) does not, but these are not relevant to our case because in these reliefs Agathe Tyche no longer takes the form of *drakōn* of any kind, but of a cobra: e.g. *LIMC* Agathodaimon 10, 13–15, 17, 20, and our Fig. 1.11 again.

[8] See e.g. *LIMC* Herakles 2003, 2007, 2012–16, 2033, 2038.

[9] Παραστάσεις σύντομοι χρονικαί 41 Preger (viii–ix A D); [Codinus] *Patria Constantinopoleos* 2.52 Preger (x A D). Janin's discussion of the forum (1964:68–9) can shed no light on the problem, alas.

[10] Schol. Euripides *Phoenissae* 1760.

pure-anguiform (albeit multi-headed) Hydra is indeed a creature of female sex, and not merely a grammatically feminine one: she is classified in a group of distinctively and significantly female monsters in a fragment of Anaxilas (mid-iv BC), to which we shall turn in the next section.[11] Now, in speaking of the agony caused by the Hydra's venom that drives Heracles to his suicide, Sophocles deploys the phrase 'the venom, which Death sired, and to which the darting *drakōn* gave birth'. Here the Hydra is strikingly designated by the masculine form, even as she is (metaphorically) presented in the role of a birthing mother.[12]

Second, in drawing a most elaborate picture for us of a pure-dragon couple Nonnus (*c.* AD 400) applies the term *drakōn* to the husband repeatedly, but fails to apply the term *drakaina* to the wife, designating her rather by the slightly prosaic phrase 'female snake' (*thēlys ophis*). The episode in question, narrated in the ecphrasis of the Shield of Olympus, concerns the marauding, 5,000-feet-long, cobra-hooded *Drakōn* of the river Hermus. The dragon seizes, mangles, and kills Tylus as he walks by its river. His sister Moria, having witnessed the attack from afar, begs the Giant Damasen for help, and he obliges. He overwhelms the dragon, despite it directing a jet of toxic green foam into his face. Uprooting a tree, he dashes it down behind the dragon's head, whereupon it re-roots itself in the earth, garrotting him to death. At this point the dragon's consort presents herself. Finding her husband dead, she plucks a 'flower of Zeus' in her 'viperish' (*echidnēenti*) jaws and applies it to her husband's nostril. He is restored to life and disappears into his hole. Moria, having observed this, applies the same flower to Tylus' nose too and brings him back to life in turn.[13]

---

[11] Anaxilas *Neottis* F22 K-A, apud Athenaeus 558a–b. Her general designation as 'the *H/hydra*', we should point out, whilst grammatically feminine, does not in itself entail her actual femaleness, since it merely consists of the standard word for a 'water snake', which is of course equally applicable to water snakes of both sexes.

[12] Sophocles *Trachiniae* 833–4: ἰού, / ὃν τέκετο θάνατος, ἔτεκε δ' αἰόλος δράκων. Note that in the aorist the active voice of τίκτω is characteristically reserved for the female role, the middle for the male (LSJ s.v. τίκτω I.2–4). Lobeck's arbitrary emendation of the manuscripts' ἔτεκε to ἔτρεφε ('reared'), accepted by Easterling but rejected by Davies, may be disregarded. The term *drakōn* is also applied (indirectly) to the Hydra at Euripides *Phoenissae* 1134–40 and possibly at Aeschylus F123 *TrGF* (cf. Chapter 1, §1.2.6).

[13] Nonnus *Dionysiaca* 25.451–552. The term *drakōn*: 457, 501, and 521; cf. also 453, *drakontophonos*. He is 50 *pelethra* in length, a *pelethron* being 100 feet: 504. His cobra-hood, a unique attribute for a *drakōn*: 457, πλατὺν αὐχένα τείνας. The toxic jet: 511. *Thēlys ophis*: 522. Her viperish jaws: 527. A slightly different version of the story is attributed in a brief note to (the v BC) Xanthus of Lydia at Pliny *Natural History* 25.14 = *FGrH*/*BNJ* 765 F3a (where Paradiso's superb commentary adduces some fascinating numismatic material). The narrative is an example of a well-established folktale, ATU 612, of which the type-tale is Grimm no. 16 ('The Three Snake Leaves'). In ancient contexts analogues are also to be found in the tale of Polyidus and Glaucus (Apollodorus *Bibliotheca* 3.3.1–2; Hyginus *Fabulae* 136, etc.) and, in refracted form, the tale of Alexander the Great and Ptolemy at Harmatela (Diodorus 17.103.4–8; Curtius 9.8.22–8—i.e. Clitarchus?) and Apuleius' tale of the Thelyphrons (*Metamorphoses* 2.21–30); the last deploys weasels in the role of the snakes, as do Marie de France's lai *Eliduc* (AD 1160–78) and the *Völsunga saga*'s tale of Sigmund and Sinfjötli (§8, xiii AD); see the discussion at Ogden 2021:49–52.

Why would Sophocles and Nonnus withhold the term *drakaina* in these cases? Perhaps because they both felt that it tended to *connote* something other than a pure female *drakōn*.

3.3 The *Drakaina* as a Female Anguipede

In a substantial group of the references to *drakainai*, a pure-form *drakaina* is seemingly invoked, but the context is ever one in which the creature is adduced specifically to serve as a comparison, association, or elucidation for a human (or humanoid) female:

- A ruinous courtesan, who is also compared to a slew of distinctively female monsters, the fire-breathing Chimaera, Charybdis, Scylla of the three heads, a female 'sea dog' (*pontia kuōn*), the Sphinx, the Hydra, the Lioness (*Leaina*), the Echidna, and the winged race of the Harpies (Anaxilas, mid-iv BC).[14]
- Circe, the archetypal witch, she of the herbal poisons (Lycophron *Alexandra*, *c.*200 BC),[15] and thereafter witches more generally (Psellus, xi AD;[16] Constantine Manasses, xii AD).[17]

---

[14] Anaxilas *Neottis* F22 K-A, apud Athenaeus 558a–b; cf. Eustathius on Homer *Odyssey* ii p. 13 l.30 Stallbaum. The nature of the Lioness in this list remains obscure, but we note the propensity of the *leaina* to sit side by side with the *drakaina* in the jangling lists of the grammarians.

[15] Lycophron *Alexandra* 673–5; cf. schol. ad loc. For Circe's evil *poisons*, see Homer *Odyssey* 10.213, 236, 276, 290, 317, 326–7, 392–4. Serpents were believed to feed on poisonous herbs in order to generate their venom (Homer *Iliad* 22.93–4; Virgil *Aeneid* 2.471; Pliny *Natural History* 8.139; Oppian of Apamea *Cynegetica* 3.223–4; Aelian *Nature of Animals* 6.4), and indeed Valerius Flaccus *Argonautica* 8.97 brings the notion of a serpent's venom and witches' poisons together by having Medea feed the Dragon of Colchis, her pet, with her own magical cuttings, as we saw in Chapter 2, §2.2. We should also note here the congruence between the myth that Perseus created the terrible serpents of Libya by flying over the land with the Gorgon's head, with the drips of blood falling from it giving birth to the snakes in the sand (Apollonius *Argonautica* 4.1513–17; Lucan *Pharsalia* 9.619–95; cf. Chapter 2, §2.1), and the myth that Medea created the poisonous herbs of Thessaly (and concomitantly the culture of witchcraft there) by casting a box of her evil cuttings out of her serpent-chariot as she flew over the land (schol. vet. Aristophanes *Clouds* 749a).

[16] Michael Psellus *Poems* 21 lines 177–84: 'O venomous *drakaina* [or witch-*drakaina*: *pharmakis drakaina*], bitter beast, dread murry-eel and sea-stingray, bull's blood, striking, destroying, beast teeming with poison, trickery and gall, blister-beetle, leech [?] or chameleon, o crone-Erinys, cause of disasters, night-tomb-witch [*nuktitumbas*], secret witch [*pharmakis*], filling houses with smoke and despair...' For a helpful discussion of this poem and its context, see Bernard 2014:280–90. Psellus' words are built upon in a brief poem by Manuel Philes, *Immediate Response to the Great Emperor's Speech on Envy, Poems* 3.29, lines 8–16 (xiii–xiv AD). The central part of the poem consists of a sustained comparison of envy with snakes and other reptiles: 'It is an enemy living with one, a *drakōn* gobbling down everything, a snake unravelling its coils for the kill, an ancient lizard pallid from disease, a chameleon openly changed of colour (for it becomes a mother-killing viper [*echidna*], which makes a bitter meal of its parent in travail), a lioness [*leaina*] and *drakaina* and all-consuming fire, and a basilisk that comes from a blood-staining asp, a sudden thunderbolt from hidden clouds.' The familiar pairing of *drakaina* with *leaina* here is all the more striking for the anomalousness of the lioness within the list otherwise: all other terms relate to reptiles or their fiery venom. One wonders whether the author imagines that the term *leaina* can also refer to a kind of reptile.

[17] Constantine Manasses *Breviarum chronicum* 3199–203: 'Envy, intractable beast, robber, murderer, pursuer, scorpion of ten thousand stings, man-eating tiger, venomous *drakaina* [or *drakaina*-witch:

- The wicked Clytemnestra, described specifically as a *drakaina*-dipsad (Lycophron *Alexandra, c.*200 BC;[18] a poem of the *Greek Anthology* undated).[19]
- The goddess Rhea-Demeter (Athenagoras, AD 176–80, reporting an Orphic myth).[20]
- The goddess Athena (Orphic hymn, ii–iii AD?).[21]
- A human mother threatened with the loss of her child (Oppian of Apamea, early iii AD).[22]
- A human mother searching for her lost child (Sophronius, vi–vii AD).[23]

---

drakaina pharmakeutria], deadly plant, ironless dart, most piercing of all spears, what sort of evils you perpetrate, what terrible sorts of thing you contrive!'

[18] Lycophron *Alexandra* 1113–17; cf. Hornblower 2015 ad loc.; the term is recycled at schol. Lycophron *Alexandra* 1108, 1114. John Apocaucus subsequently appears to borrow this phrase in an unreflecting way when he compares a thirsty *man* to a '*drakaina* dipsad' (*Notitiae et epistulae* 78 Bees, xii–xiii AD). In terms of the history of Greek, the portmanteau entails a category mistake, the *drakōn* and the 'thirst-viper' dipsad normally being conceived of as different species, rather than the former denoting an umbrella category beneath which the latter sits. See Nicander *Theriaca* esp. 334–58, 438–57 (cf. Jacques 2002; and Overduin 2015 ad loc.); Lucan *Pharsalia* 9.587–949 esp. 718, 728 (cf. Raschle 2001 ad loc.); Philumenus *On Venomous Animals* 20, 30; Isidore of Seville *Etymologies* 12.4.4, 21.4.13.

[19] *Greek Anthology*, Appendix, Epigrammata demonstrativa 198 Cougny: 'The avenger [Orestes] of his father [Agamemnon], fulfilling the oracle of the most powerful god, triumphed in killing the lioness [*leaina*] or the *drakaina* [Clytemnestra], not his mother, and the husband with which she lived [Aegisthus], the killer of his father, when she was alone and unprepared, with the result that in dying, before she died, she saw fulfilment come to her ancient dreams. But his full sister [Electra], full of joy, let go her bitter grief, together with a gushing tear.'

[20] Athenagoras *Legatio* 20.3. Zeus-Sabazius pursues his own mother Rhea-Demeter. To evade his advances she transforms herself into a *drakaina*, whereupon Zeus-Sabazius then transforms himself into a *drakōn*, and has sex with her in a 'knot of Heracles', thereby siring Persephone, whom he goes on to rape, again in the form of a *drakōn*, thereby siring Dionysus-Zagreus in the form of a bull.

[21] *Orphic Hymns* 32 line 11 Quandt: Athena is addressed as *drakaina* in the midst of a blizzard of perplexing epithets.

[22] Oppian of Apamea *Cynegetica* 3.223–4. Oppian imagines the anthropomorphic plea of a female wild ass as she attempts to stop her husband from destroying their male offspring (as the creature is supposedly wont to do, for fear of competition). She protests that the baby ass is 'not the poison-herb-devouring offspring of a completely implacable *drakaina*, nor the lawless cub of a mountain-wandering lioness [*leaina*]'. Cf. also Eutecnius *Paraphrasis in Oppiani* Cynegetica p. 33 Tüselmann (iii–v AD).

[23] Sophronius *Narratio miraculorum sanctorum Cyri et Joannis* 34.10. Sophronius tells the engaging tale of one Dorothea's pilgrimage to the church of the two martyr-saints at Menuthis. En route, her young son Callimachus finds a snake's egg beneath a tree (it had been put there for him to find by the Devil), and gulps it down. As they reach the shrine the egg hatches within him and the baby serpent begins to devour his guts; he collapses and rolls about in agony. His distraught mother makes appeal to the saints, who accordingly appear to her in a dream and tell her that, at an appointed time, she should carry her son out of the shrine and lay him apart on the open ground outside and await a God-sent miracle. His mother and the assembled crowd duly witness the arrival of the *drakaina* that had laid the egg in the first place, calling out for her lost offspring. The *drakaina* whispers down to her offspring through Callimachus' ears and mouth. The baby snake responds and shoots up and out through Callimachus' mouth again. The joyful mother-snake collects her child up in her own mouth and 'skips' joyfully back to her hole with it. Callimachus is immediately restored to health. Dorothea and the onlooking crowd rejoice and sing the praises of God and the martyr-saints. The sustained (and unrealistic) comparison of the creature to a human mother searching for her lost child is striking: 'When a short half-hour had elapsed from the laying out of Callimachus there, and with a great crowd standing by, waiting to observe the outcome, lo! the *drakaina* that had produced that egg arrived, searching for it, crawling and hissing and calling out to it in just the way in which a woman,

- Wives, all too likely as they are to destroy their husbands ([Basil of Caesarea], iv AD?).[24]
- The wicked Delilah (Ephraem Syrus, iv AD; [John Chrysostom], v or vi AD; John Damascene, vii–viii AD).[25]
- The wicked Salome (Chrysippus of Jerusalem, v AD).[26]
- The young woman Chrysorrhoe, mistakenly believed to be the daughter of a wicked *drakōn* (*Callimachus and Chrysorrhoe*, xiv AD or before).[27]

Otherwise the term *drakaina* appears to be applied to entities that combine *drakōn* and humanoid female in a more direct and physical way, that is, to female anguipedes.

3.3.1 Echidna

The first of our great anguipedes is the Echidna (lit. 'Viper'), who manifests herself in diverse ways—at least three—in diverse texts. She arrives first in the *Theogony*, where her anguipede form is clearly described:

And she [probably Ceto] bore another irresistible monster, nothing like mortal men or the immortal gods, in a hollow cave, the divine, strong-minded Echidna, who in half of her body is a nymph with rolling eyes and fair cheeks, but in the other half is a monstrous snake [*ophis*], terrible and great, darting, eating raw flesh [*ōmēstēs*], deep in hidden lairs in the sacred earth. There is her cave, down below, under a hollow rock, far from the immortal gods and mortal men. There the gods allocated to her a glorious home in which to dwell. And the baleful

---

calling out to a lost infant son with wailing and lamentation, is wont to make her search for the longed-for child.'

[24] [Basil of Caesarea] *Sermo de contubernalibus*, PG 30, 820. The author warns against the dangers of a man taking a wife with a comparison from the natural world: 'For the *drakōn*, in making a common life with the *drakaina*, receives death as his reward for the cohabitation, the female beast having such a nature' (ὁ γὰρ δράκων τῇ δρακαίνῃ συγγινόμενος, θάνατον λαμβάνει τὸν μισθὸν τῆς συμβιώσεως, τοιαύτης φύσεως τυγχάνοντος τοῦ θήλεος θηρίου).

[25] Ephraem Syrus *Aduersus improbas mulieres* p. 203 Phrantzoles (iv AD); [John Chrysostom] *On the Beheading of St John*, PG 59, 488; John Damascene *Sacra parallela*, PG 95, 1328. We have the same outpouring of outrage in all three texts: 'Tell me, what kind of wild beast ever yet contrived things of this sort against her own male? What *drakaina* wishes to destroy her own husband? What kind of lioness [*leaina*] hands over her own male for slaughter?' This rhetorical flourish is less innocent than at first appears, and the claim may be knowingly tendentious. As we have just seen, [Basil] was rather noting the specific propensity of *drakainai* to kill their male consorts after sex.

[26] Chryisppus *Encomium on John the Baptist* 1 p. 44 Sigalas. In the transmitted text Chrysippus describes Salome's mother Herodias as an *echidna* (viper), and then Salome herself as she comes before Herod as 'the daughter of the venomous *echidna*, the new *drakaina*' and also as 'that unclean *drakaina*' (θυγάτηρ τῆς ἐχίδνης τῆς ἰοβόλου, ἡ νέα δράκαινα...τῆς δὲ ἐχίδνης ἐκείνης καὶ δρακαίνης...τῆς ἀκαθάρτου δρακαίνης ἐκείνης). The editor Sigalas regards these phrases as interpolations, but this does not make much difference for the current argument.

[27] *Callimachus and Chrysorrhoe* 1515, 1539–40, and 1587. The context is explained in Chapter 9, §9.1.3.

Echidna keeps watch under the earth in Arima, an immortal nymph, unaging all her days. They say that Typhon was joined with her in love, the terrible, violent, and lawless creature with the nymph of rolling eyes. She conceived and bore strong-minded children.   Hesiod *Theogony* 295–308

Hesiod goes on to list the monstrous offspring, partly anguiform, that this broodmother bears to Typhon: Orthus, Cerberus, Hydra, Chimaera, Sphinx, and the Nemean Lion.[28] Apollodorus tells that this Echidna was slain in her sleep by the all-seeing Argus.[29]

In the *Frogs* (405 BC) Aristophanes has Aeacus threaten Dionysus, masquerading as Heracles, with a number of underworld terrors, including 'hundred-headed Echidna, who will tear your guts apart'. Is this supposed to be the same Echidna as Hesiod's, or roughly so? Probably. The detail of the hundred heads is strongly reminiscent of Hesiod's description of his Echidna's consort Typhon, who has a humanoid torso with his hundred snake-heads branching from his shoulders (Chapter 1, §1.6).[30] Accordingly, we may be invited to construe Aristophanes' Echidna's overall form on the same model as his.

Secondly, Herodotus (c.425 BC) gives us an Echidna encountered by Heracles in Scythia. She steals his horses and will only return them to him when she has slept with him (thereby acquiring three children from him: the brood-mother motif again). Herodotus describes her as 'a half-maiden, an *echidna* of double form, whose parts above the buttocks were those of a woman, and those below a snake'.[31]

Third, we have the Echidna that presides over the gloriously overwrought serpentine horrors of Ophiorhyme, 'Snake-Town' (i.e. the Phrygian Hierapolis, modern Pammukale), and its environs in the *Acts of Philip* (c. AD 400). She recalls her more classical forebears, those of Hesiod and Aristophanes at least, in her eventual fate, which is to be swallowed up into the underworld abyss (this in response to the saint's prayers). Unlike her forebears, however, this Echidna is given no explicit physical description, but she is explicitly defined as a *drakaina*. Not only that, she is also described as 'the mother of snakes' in yet another occurrence of the brood-mother motif.[32] The desert that Philip must cross en route to Ophiorhyme is described as 'a desert of *drakainai*'.[33] Why so? It may be

---

[28] Hesiod *Theogony* 309–27; cf. West 1966 ad loc.   [29] Apollodorus *Bibliotheca* 2.1.2.
[30] Aristophanes *Frogs* 473–4. Typhon: Hesiod *Theogony* 824–6.
[31] Herodotus 4.8–10. See Visintin 2000; Ustinova 2005; P'yankov 2006; and Asheri, Lloyd, and Corcella 2007 ad loc.
[32] *Acts of Philip* 8.4 (G); τῆς δρακαίνης μητρὸς τῶν ὄφεων. For the *Acts of Philip*, which will feature prominently in Part II, see Bovon 1988; Amsler 1996; Amsler et al. 1996, 1999; Rutherford 2007; Bovon and Matthews 2012; Huttner 2013:355–71; Ogden 2013b:207–20; Bremmer 2017a:37–40. I confess that hasty editing left the distinction between Phrygian Hierapolis (Pammukale) and Syrian Hierapolis (Bambyce) less lucid than it should have been at Ogden 2013a:422. However, in relation to the arguments put forth at that point, it is reassuring to find now that Bremmer 2017a:40 is also (independently) dismissive of any connection between the Echidna and the Cybele of Phrygian Hierapolis.
[33] *Acts of Philip* 8.16 (V): τὴν ἔρημον τῶν δρακαινῶν.

because the author wishes to put before us the dreadful prospect of yet more brood-mothers; here it may be significant that the great dragon Philip encounters in the desert, whilst identified by the masculine/male term *drakōn*, is nonetheless accompanied by a host of smaller snakes.[34] Or it may simply be that the term is used merely as a result of attraction or assimilation to the term used for the greatest serpent of them all.

Indeed, the association of the terms *drakaina* and *echidna* is a common one. We will see the terms brought together by Euripides in his description of the Erinyes; and we have already seen them brought together by Chrysippus in his characterization of Herodias and her daughter Salome (n. 26), and by Manuel Philes in his words on envy (n. 16). The scholia to Lycophron remark that the poet refers to Clytemnestra as a *drakaina* 'in place of the word *echidna*.' They go on to explain that after mating the *echidna* proceeds to kill her husband, just as Clytemnestra kills Agamemnon, which precisely replicates Basil's notion of the mating habits of the *drakaina* (see above).[35] We shall return to this association in Chapter 8, §8.3.4

One might briefly speculate here about the Orphic reflex of Echidna, Eurynome, the consort of Typhon's Orphic reflex, Ophion or Ophioneus ('Snake-man'). The couple was already known to Pherecydes of Syrus in the vi BC.[36] Whilst Origen, after Pherecydes, makes it fairly clear that Ophion himself had a serpentine form, what form did Eurynome possess, and did it parallel Echidna's? No source describes it, but Pausanias knew of a goddess also called Eurynome worshipped in Phigalia. Was she the same, or similar? He tells that she was an aspect of Artemis and that she was a maiden above and a fish below. Not then an anguipede or an anguiform in the strict sense, but a creature of a broadly similar configuration. Perhaps, more specifically, her lower half was that of a sea-monster (cf. Scylla in her canonical form; see Chapter 4, §4.3.3).[37]

3.3.2 Delphyne

The earliest recorded use of the term *drakaina* comes in the *Homeric Hymn* (3) *to Apollo* (shortly after 590 BC):[38]

---

[34] *Acts of Philp* 8.9 (V).

[35] Schol. Lycophron *Alexandra* 1114: ἀντὶ τοῦ ἔχιδνα/ἀντὶ ἐχίδνης.

[36] For Eurynome and Ophion, see Pherecydes of Syrus FF73, 78–80 Schibli; Apollonius *Argonautica* 1.496–511; Lycophron *Alexandra* 1191–7, with scholl. at 1191, 1196; Philo of Byblos apud Eusebius *Praeparatio evangelica* 1.10.50; Lucian *Podagra* 99–105; Maximus of Tyre *Philosophoumena* 4.4.5–8; Origen *Contra Celsum* 6.42–3; [Clement of Rome] *Recognitions* 10.23; Nonnus 2.572–4, 8.158–61; schol. Homer *Iliad* 8.479; First Vatican Mythographer 3.1.1.

[37] Pausanias 8.41.

[38] For the dating of the 'Pythian' portion of the hymn, see West 2003:10. For the Delphic dragoness more generally, see Ogden 2013a:40–2.

Nearby was the sweetly flowing spring, where Lord Apollo, the son of Zeus, killed the *drakaina*, shooting from his stout bow. She was fat and huge, a wild monster, who did much harm to people on the earth, much harm to people themselves and much to slender-footed sheep, for she was a blood-reeking bane. And once she received from Hera of the golden throne the terrible, harsh Typhon, and reared him, a bane to mortals. Hera bore him when she was angry with father Zeus, when the son of Cronus produced glorious Athena from the top of his head.   *Homeric Hymn to Apollo* 300–9[39]

According first to third-century BC sources, Callimachus and Maeandrius, this Delphic *drakaina*, the mythical alternate to the (eventually more famous) *drakōn* Python, was called Delphyne.[40] More to the point, according to Apollodorus, this *drakaina* Delphyne was an anguipede:

Similarly, he [Typhon] put away the sinews [of Zeus] there, hiding them in the skin of a bear, and he set the *drakaina* Delphyne as guard over them. The maiden was a half-beast [*hēmithēr*].   Apollodorus *Bibliotheca* 1.6.3

Was Delphyne an anguipede already for the *Homeric Hymn to Apollo*? It is hard to say. The description 'fat and huge' might be thought to fit a pure serpent form slightly better, but the point is hardly a decisive one. Already in the poem she has an association with Typhon as his former nurse, which makes us think of the other great female serpent associated with Typhon in early poetry, the Echidna we have just discussed, his explicitly anguipede consort in the *Theogony*.[41]

3.3.3 Harmonia

Towards the end of their lives Cadmus and Harmonia were transformed into serpents, perhaps as a form of (further) compensation for Cadmus' slaying of the Dragon of Ares, as we saw in Chapter 1, §1.2.1. A number of sources refer to this transformation with frustrating brevity.[42] Can we be a little more precise about it?

---

[39]   Reference is made to the *drakaina* of Delphi also at Plutarch *Failure of Oracles* 8 = *Moralia* 4141b.

[40]   Schol. Apollonius *Argonautica* 2.706, incorporating Callimachus F88 Pfeiffer (cf. Harder 2012 ad loc.) and Maendrius *FHG* ii pp. 334–8 F10 = *BNJ* 293 F14a (not in *FGrH*; possibly rather 'Leandrius'). Delphyne is also defined as a *drakaina* at schol. Aristophanes *Wealth* 213.

[41]   Discussions: Fontenrose 1959:13–14, 44, 59, 68, 72–3, 94–7, 118, 207, 243–5, 256, 366, 371–4, 377, 390–2, 409, 411, 468, 546–8; Sourvinou-Inwood 1987; Gantz 1993:38, 88–9; Watkins 1995:461–2; Gourmelen 2004:377–80; Ogden 2013a:40–8.

[42]   Hyginus *Fabulae* 6: 'were turned into snakes in the region of Illyria'. Apollodorus *Bibliotheca* 3.5.4: 'Cadmus left Thebes with Harmonia and went to the Encheleis. The Illyrians were making war on them, but the god prophesied that they would beat them if they had Cadmus and Harmonia as their leaders. The Encheleis were persuaded and so made them their leaders against the Illyrians, and conquered them. Cadmus became king of the Illyrians. After this Cadmus turned into a *drakōn*,

At the end of Euripides' *Bacchae* Cadmus foresees his own and his wife's eventual fate, to be turned into serpents themselves (possibly in further compensation for the slaying):

> I will lead my wife Harmonia, the daughter of Ares, against Greek altars and tombs....I will be a *drakōn*; she will have the form of a wild *drakaina*....
>
> Euripides *Bacchae* 1357–9

There is a fair case that both Cadmus and Harmonia were conceptualized as being transformed not into pure serpents but into anguipedes. Philostratus gives us an *ecphrasis* of a fantasy painting of the final scene of the *Bacchae*, which includes the final transformation foreshadowed by Euripides as a decorative detail:

> And there [sc. on Mt. Cithaeron] are Harmonia and Cadmus, but they are not as they were. For they are becoming *drakontes* up to their thighs and they are already covered in scales. Gone are their feet, gone are their buttocks, and the transformation of their form is creeping up their bodies. They are astonished and embrace each other as if trying to hold onto what remains of their bodies, so as not to be deprived of them.   Philostratus *Imagines* 1.18

It is not clear, and perhaps Philostratus leaves it deliberately vague, whether the transformation will continue to progress up the entirety of their bodies, or whether they will be left as anguipedes. Also relevant here is a fragment from an unidentified tragedy of Euripides, which describes a similar sort of transformation, and almost certainly refers to Cadmus again: 'Alas, half of me becomes a *drakōn*, child. Embrace what is left of your father!'[43]

3.3.4 Hecate, Hecate Ereschigal, Artemis

In her earliest identifiable portrait, that of an Attic black-figure lekythos of *c.*470 BC, Hecate is shown as an anguipede with, additionally, a pair of dogs projecting forth from her midriff, winningly engaged in the tearing apart of a human soul between them.[44] An Aristophanes fragment then speaks of 'Hecate of the earth

---

together with Harmonia, and was sent by Zeus to the Elysian field.' Cf. Callimachus F11 Pfeiffer; [Scylax] *Periplus* 24; Nonnus *Dionysiaca* 4.416–20, 5.135–89, 44.107–18; schol. Pindar *Pythian* 3.88–91; First Vatican Mythographer 2.49. For discussion, see Ogden 2013a:52–4.

[43] Euripides F930 *TrGF*; cf. Seaford 1996 on 1330–2. Note also Ovid *Metamorphoses* 3.98: 'You too will be gazed at in the form of a serpent [*serpens*].'

[44] National Museum 19765 = *LIMC* Hekate 95 = Erinys 7. For discussion of Hecate in general, see Heckenbach 1912; Küster 1913:112–15; Kraus 1960; Nouveau-Piobb 1961; Boedeker 1983; Johnston 1990; Sarian 1992; West 1995:189–292; Sauzeau 2000; Lautwein 2009; Ogden 2013a:254–9; Bortolani 2016:219–336.

[*chthonia*] rolling coils of snakes', which similarly seems to describe an anguipede.[45] But the most striking literary description of an anguipede Hecate comes to us in Lucian's *Philopseudes*:

> I saw a fearsome woman approaching me, almost half a stadium's length high. In her left hand she held a torch and in her right a sword twenty cubits long. Below the waist she was snake-footed [*ophiopous*]; above it she resembled a Gorgon, so far as concerns the look in her eyes and her terrible appearance, I mean. Instead of hair, writhing snakes fell down in curls around her neck, and some of them coiled over her shoulders.... [The goddess' dogs] were taller than Indian elephants... similarly black and shaggy, with dirty, matted hair. Anyway, when I saw her, I came to a halt and at the same time turned back the seal-ring that the Arab had given me to the inside of my finger. Hecate stamped on the ground with her dragon foot [*drakonteiōi podi*] and created a huge chasm, as deep as Tartarus. Presently she jumped into it and was gone. I steeled myself and bent over it, after taking hold of a tree that was growing near the hole, to stop myself falling into it headlong from vertigo. Then I saw everything in Hades, Pyriphlegethon, the lake, Cerberus and the dead, whom I could see so clearly that I even recognized some of them. I got a good view of my father, still dressed in the clothes in which we had buried him.   Lucian *Philopseudes* 22[46]

The hair aside, this Hecate is a perfect match for the lekythos. But as to the hair, a Sophocles fragment had previously spoken of Hecate as 'garlanded with oak and the twisted coils of savage *drakontes*'.[47] Sophocles may already be speaking of Gorgonian snaky hair, as found in Lucian's words here; alternatively, he may have been thinking literally in terms of a head-band made from snakes (as sported by certain versions of the Erinyes, for which see next). Hecate could be associated with snakes in other configurations too. A first-century AD curse tablet of the prayers-for-justice variety includes a confusing image seemingly of a three-bodied Hecate. One of her three pairs of arms consists simply of serpents.[48] Imperial-period statuettes show the three-bodied Hecate in the round, and in these one or two of her figures brandish (separate) snakes.[49]

So far so good, but what of Hecate as a *drakaina*? In the *Hymn to Hecate-Selene* in the Great Magical Papyrus in Paris (iv AD), the goddess is given the epithet *drakaina* amongst a blizzard of others, in immediate context 'horse, maiden

---

[45] Aristophanes F515 K-A.
[46] For general discussion of this episode, see Ebner et al. 2001 ad loc.; Ogden 2007:161–70.
[47] Sophocles F535 *TrGF*.
[48] *SEG* xxx no. 326 = *SGD* no. 21 (with important emendations) = Gager 1992 no. 84, with illustration at p. 181. See the discussions at Elderkin 1937; Jordan 1980; and Gager 1992 ad loc.
[49] *LIMC* Hekate 95.

[korē], drakaina, torch, lightning-bolt, star, lion [leōn], she-wolf'.[50] Similarly in the magical recipe detailed in another of the Greek Magical Papyri (iii–iv AD) the spell-maker is told to address Hecate-Ereschigal in the following terms: 'Ereschigal, virgin, drakaina, garland, key, herald-staff, golden sandal of the Tartarus-holder'.[51] In both cases the latter part of the list becomes a little surreal, but the first two terms of virgin and drakaina fit Hecate(-Ereschigal) well enough. Michael Italicus (xii AD) discusses a piece of Chaldaean obscurantism in correspondingly obscure terms: at least it can be said that in the course of it he appropriately associates Hecate with a drakaina (and again we have the Sophoclean-Lucianian conceit that Hecate also sports snaky hair, à la Gorgon).[52] The short Encomium on St John pseudonymously attributed to John Chrysostom reminds the saint that he 'shattered the drakaina Artemis, fighting in single combat, with the trophy of the cross'. The author may have had Artemis in her aspect of Hecate in mind here, but this was not necessarily the case: the term may be deployed in a more generalized way simply to demonize the pagan goddess (cf. also on Eurynome-Artemis above).[53]

3.3.5 Erinyes (Furies)

The term drakaina is applied at a much earlier stage to Hecate's close associates, the Erinyes or Furies. In Aeschylus' Eumenides (458 BC) the ghost of Clytemnestra observes that the work of the Furies pursuing Orestes has been undermined by weariness: 'sleep and labour... have exhausted the might of the dread drakaina'.[54] The ghost also notes that they resemble Gorgons and that their cry resembles that of hunting dogs.[55] These details evoke an image similar to that of the early angui-pede Hecate of the lekythos (in which, as it happens, the Erinyes appear alongside her, albeit in fully humanoid form, in what is also their first appearance in the iconographic record), and more particularly the Lucianian Hecate, who also sports

[50] PGM IV 2242–347 = Magical Hymns 17 Preisendanz (= 11 Bortolani) line 58; cf. Bortolani 2016 ad loc.

[51] PGM LXX.10–12.

[52] Michael Italicus Letters 28 p. 190 Gautier: Τί δ' εἰ λέγοιμι περὶ τῶν τῆς Ἑκάτης χαιτῶν καὶ τῶν κροτάφων καὶ τῶν λαγόνων αὐτῆς καὶ τῶν περικρανίων πηγῶν καὶ ζωστήρων, εἰς ἀλλόκοτα γὰρ ὡς εἰκὸς ἐξαγάγω τὸν λόγον καὶ πράγματα καὶ νοήματα, λέγω δὴ τὴν πυριπλῆτιν πηγὴν καὶ τὴν μετ' ἐκείνην δράκαιναν καὶ δρακοντόζωνον, ἣν καὶ σπειροδρακοντόζωνον ἄλλοι παρασυνθέτως προσαγορεύουσι, καὶ τὴν ἐπ' αὐταῖς λεοντοῦχον. 'What am I to say of the locks and temples of Hecate, and her flanks and the "founts" and "girdles" that surround her head, to bring the discussion to matters and notions that are weird? I speak of the fiery fount and the one after it, the drakaina and the drakōn-girt one, to which others apply the compound term "coil-of-drakōn-girt", and after them the lion-holding one.' Cf. Gautier 1972:189–90, ad loc.

[53] [John Chrysostom] Encomium on St John, PG 61,719: τὴν μονομάχον δράκαιναν Ἄρτεμιν τῷ τροπαίῳ τοῦ σταυροῦ κατήραξας.

[54] Aeschylus Eumenides 127–8.

[55] Aeschylus Eumenides 46–56, 132–3; for the Gorgon comparison, see also Choephoroe 1048.

snake-hair. In Euripides' *Iphigenia in Tauris* (414–412 BC) Orestes is quoted as describing an attack of the Erinyes to Pylades in the following terms: 'Pylades, have you seen this woman? Do you not see how this *drakaina* of Hades, edged/fringed [*estomōmenē*] with dread *echidnai*, wants to kill me? Beside her another one beats her wings, breathing fire and blood...'[56] Compatibly, in the *Orestes* Euripides describes the Erinyes as 'bloody-faced serpent-like maidens [*drakontōdeis korai*]'.[57]

However, the anguipede configuration was not the most popular one for the Erinyes. In the *Choephoroe* Aeschylus affirms that their bodies are thickly entwined with *drakontes*.[58] This seems to imply that the Erinyes are fully human-oid females with attendant serpents coiling round them. Similarly, in Euripides' *Electra* we are told that Athena will ward off the Erinyes, with their *drakontes*, and also that they have snakes twining around their arms (*cheirodrakontes*).[59] A nice aetiology of the name of Mt Cithaeron preserved in a fragment of Leon of Byzantium (iv BC) tells how the Erinys Tisiphone fell in love with Cithaeron, a shepherd-boy on the then Mt Asterium, but he scorned her for her repulsive appearance, whereupon she drew one of the *drakontes* out of her hair and threw it at him. It constricted him to death, and the gods renamed the mountain in his honour.[60]

And this is the way in which the Erinyes were predominantly to be represented in art. The second iconographic document of the Erinyes is another Attic leky-thos, this one dated to *c*.460–450 BC. On this an elegant winged humanoid Erinys runs, holding her serpent-entwined arms out in front of her, with a third serpent coiling around her head. The vase's legend has been read as *estheton* and con-strued as a dual imperative addressed by the humanoid maiden to the pair of ser-pents she holds out before her, 'Devour!'[61] For the remainder of antiquity the iconography of the Erinyes was to portray them as women with serpents similarly entwining around the head and the arms, either together or separately.[62] In the *Aeneid* Virgil explicitly compares the Fury (Erinys) Allecto to a Gorgon; she car-ries venomous snakes in her hair, one of which she detaches and throws upon or even into Amata in order to madden her and to sow discord: Virgil is perhaps making knowing play here with the established conundrum as to whether the snakes on a Fury's head are integral or detachable.[63]

So much then, for entities to which the term *drakaina* is directly applied.[64]

---

[56] Euripides *Iphigenia in Tauris* 285–9: Πυλάδη, δέδορκας τήνδε; τήνδε δ' οὐχ ὁρᾷς / Ἅιδου δράκαιναν ὥς με βούλεται κτανεῖν / δειναῖς ἐχίδναις εἰς ἔμ' ἐστομωμένη;/ἡ 'κ γειτόνων δὲ πῦρ πνέουσα καὶ φόνον / πτεροῖς ἐρέσσει....

[57] Euripides *Orestes* 256.   [58] Aeschylus *Choephoroe* 1049–50.

[59] Euripides *Electra* 1256, 1345.   [60] Leon of Byzantium *FGrH/BNJ* no. 132 F3.

[61] *LIMC* Erinys 1; discussion at Sarian 1986:841. One might rather have expected *esthieton*.

[62] See *LIMC* Erinys *passim*.   [63] Virgil *Aeneid* 6.555–672, 7.323–72, 12.845–8.

[64] Our survey attempts to encompass all extant uses of the term *drakaina* prior to the fall of Byzantium. For the sake of completeness, let us mop up here the straggler and anomalous uses undeserving of attention in the main text:

3.4 Further Female Anguipedes Not Explicitly Designated by the Term *Drakaina*

We turn now to two important further examples of female anguipedes, to whom, however, the term *drakaina* is not found explicitly applied.

3.4.1 Lamia

The Lamias are slippery creatures.[65] The bulk of the ancient source tradition builds the following picture: Lamia had once been a beautiful Libyan queen, a daughter of Belos (i.e. Bel, Baal), and she was seduced by Zeus; an envious Hera killed the children she bore, whereupon she was somehow transformed in turn, through her own envy, into a child-killing, sometimes child-devouring, demon,

---

- Fish. *Drakaina* was also the name of a fish. The anonymous medical text *De alimentis* tells that it is amongst the thicker of the soft-fleshed fishes (75 Ideler). In the *Panarion* (iv AD) Epiphanius twice speaks of triumphing over a metaphorical sea of troubles stocked by a series of variously dangerous fish. Here the *drakaina* takes its place alongside the stingray, the shark, the murry-eel, and the scorpion-fish, *skorpaina* (*Panarion* i p. 382, ii p. 62 Holl). Paul of Aegina (vii AD) records the properties of some healing foodstuffs; amongst these he notes that the red mullet, filleted and applied raw to the wound, cures the bite of 'the sea *drakōn*, the scorpion, and the *drakaina*' (*Epitomae medicae libri septem* 7.3.19); context suggests that he has a fish in mind here (and in any case, why would he specify that the mullet cures the bite of a serpent-*drakaina* as opposed to a serpent-*drakōn*?). In this usage *drakaina* served as an alternate to the term *drakainis*, which only signified a fish, and which is referred to by Ephippus and Mnesimachus, both of whom are quoted by Athenaeus (Ephippus *Cydon* F12 K-A = Athenaeus 322e; Mnesimachus *Hippotrophos* F4 K-A = Athenaeus 403c; cf. Athenaeus *Deipnosophistae* Epitome ii.1 p. 149 Peppink).
- Whip. Hesychius (v AD) tells us that Aristophanes used the word *drakaina* to mean a whip (s.v. δράκαιναν = Aristophanes F808 K-A). This aligns with the broader Greek propensity for naming instruments of torture whimsically after animals: there was also a 'mouse' (μῦς, 'gag'; cf. μύω), a crab (καρκίνος, 'pincers'), and a 'wolf' (λύκος, 'flesh-hook'); cf. Headlam 1922 on Herodas 3.85. Why should a whip be a *drakaina* as opposed to a *drakōn*? Perhaps simply because the standard Greek words for 'whip' were also feminine (Hesychius glosses the Aristophanic *drakaina* with the two feminines ὑστριχίς and μάστιξ); accordingly, another sort of assimilation may be in play here.
- Non-diagnostic references. Finally there are some passing references to *drakainai* from which we can derive little. A fragment of a lyric poem from a ii–iii AD papyrus seemingly refers to the 'strike of a *drakaina*' (τύπον δρακαίνης), but there is little useable context (Fragmenta Adespota 13b *PMG*). Nor can we tell much from an obscurantist theological pronouncement of the ix–x AD Leo Choerosphactes, *Chiliostichos theologia* 36.27–30 (lines 1040–4): 'Show yourself to adore this thing [God, in somewhat Platonic aspect] and lavish worship upon it. In vain do the foolish sophist and the shabby writer long to persuade their audience without being persuasive, alas, and set up their cheerful *drakaina* (ἄφρων σοφιστὴς καὶ πένης λογογράφος / πείθειν ἀπειθῶς, φεῦ, ποθοῦσι τοὺς πέλας / δράκαιναν εὐφρόσυνον ἱστῶντες μάτην). In his baffled commentary on the lines Vassis 2002:195–6 deliberates whether Choerosphactes is making reference to just any female snake or more specifically to the Delphic dragoness. Neither suggestion seems plausible, and one wonders whether the term is perhaps just an arbitrary substitution for the masculine *drakōn*, soubriquet of the Devil.

[65] On Lamias and their form, see Lawson 1910:173–9; Schwenn 1924; Rohde 1925:590–3; Fontenrose 1959:44–5, 100–4, 119–20, 1968:81–3; Vermeule 1977; Scobie 1983:21–30; Boardman 1992; Burkert 1992:82–7; Leinweber 1994; Johnston 1995, 1999:161–202; Hansen 2002:128–30; Resnick and Kitchell 2007; Viltanioti 2012; Felton 2013; Ingemark and Ingemark 2013; Ogden 2013a:86–92, 2013b:97–108 (nos. 68–74); Patera 2015:1–105 esp. 27–34 (a detailed study); Björklund 2017a.

with the ability to remove her own unsleeping eyes; it is sometimes indicated that there was not merely one Lamia demon, but many; singular or plural, Lamias were used as bogies by mothers to frighten their children and keep them in line.[66]

But I wish here to draw attention to the rather neglected sometime serpentine aspects of this creature. In this regard, we have four striking case studies, all of them, alas, problematic: in one pair of cases we have explicit descriptions of an anguipede form, but lack the direct application of the name Lamia; in the other pair of cases we have the direct application of the name Lamia, but not the explicit description of an anguipede form.

First, in Statius' expansive account of Coroebus of Argos and the foundation of Tripodisci (c. AD 92), Delphic Apollo punishes Argos for the death of his lover Psamathe and their son Linus by sending a terrible monster against the city; Coroebus kills the monster and is instructed by the god to found the city in recompense. Here is the central part of Statius' narrative:

All too late, Phoebus, did you recall your love and contrive a consolation for her sad death: a monster conceived in the deepest part of the Acheron, in the Furies' unspeakable halls. The monster had the face and breast of a girl but from her head there rose a snake [*anguis*], hissing continuously, parting her ruddy forehead. Then this dread blight slid into rooms by night with scaly gait, snatched new-born souls from the bosoms of their nurses, devoured them with bloody bite and grew fat on the grief of the land. But Coroebus, outstanding in arms and spirit, could not tolerate this and chose to confront the monster with a band of picked youths, the foremost in strength and keen to enhance their repute, even at the expense of their lives. She was on her way after raiding another set of homes and at the gateway between two roads. The bodies of two small children hung by her side, and already her hooked hand was fast in their guts and her iron-shod talons were growing warm in their soft hearts. He confronted her, with his ring of men pressing close on every side, and buried his huge iron sword deep in her hard breast. He searched out the deepest hiding-places of her soul with his flashing blade and at last returned his monster to the Jupiter of the depths [Hades] to keep. It is a joy to go and examine closely her eyes, black in death, the unspeakable spillage of her womb and her breast filthy with congealed gore. This was the monster that had taken the lives of our people. The young men of Argos stared in amazement. After the tears, the rejoicing was great but

---

[66] Crates F20 K-A; Euripides F472m *TrGF* (= 922 Nauck); Aristophanes *Wasps* 1035, repeated verbatim at *Peace* 758 (bizarre); Duris of Samos *FGrH* 76 F17; Diodorus 20.41.3–6 (incorporating the Euripides fragment); Horace *Ars Poetica* 340; Dionysius of Halicarnassus *On Thucydides* 6; Plutarch *Moralia* 398c (*On the Pythian Oracles*); Pausanias 10.12.1; Heraclitus *De incredibilibus* 34; Clement of Alexandria *Stromateis* 1.15.70; Hesychius s.vv. Λάμια, λάμιαι, Μομμώ; Isidore of Seville *Etymologies* 8.11.102; Photius *Bibliotheca* s.v. Λάμια; Suda s.v. Λάμια; schol. Aristophanes *Peace* 758; schol. Aristides *Panathenaicus* 102, 5 (iii p. 42 Dindorf); Apostolius at *CPG* ii.497–8.

remained muted. By way of empty consolation for their grief they pounded her lifeless limbs with hard staves and knocked the rough teeth from her jaws. But, do what they might, they could not satisfy their anger. The birds circled her corpse by night with clamour, but they abandoned it uneaten, and they tell that the ever-active dogs left it hungry, whilst the wolves gaped in terror at the body with mouths dry.   Statius *Thebaid* 1.597–626

The monster is explicitly described as an anguipede, with maiden torso and snaky bottom half, but she also has a serpent head rising out of the top of her humanoid one. In addition to this, she has claw-like hands with talons on which she skewers the babies of the Argives.[67] A creature of precisely this form, standing before an Apollo seated on the *omphalos* with his lyre, is illustrated on a lekythos wrongly identified by the standard ancient-iconographical lexicon (*LIMC*) as depicting Python (Fig. 3.1).[68] Statius does not apply the term *lamia* to the creature, but she is eventually described in this way by the First Vatican Mythographer, *si credere dignum est*.[69]

Second, in his fifth oration Dio Chrysostom (*c.* AD 100) speaks of a marvellous race of creatures infesting the Libyan Syrtes. They have the upper halves of maidens and the bottom halves of serpents, with these bottom halves culminating not in serpent tails but in serpent heads.[70] Like Statius' monster, they have great claw-like hands. Dio describes their delightful modus operandi in the following terms:

This was the nature and appearance of their bodies: they had the female face of a beautiful woman, and exceptionally beautiful breasts, chest and neck. No mortal girl or bride at the peak of her loveliness could possess such beautiful attributes, nor could a sculptor or a painter represent them. Their skin shone brightly, and the souls of all who looked into their eyes were gripped with love and desire. But the remainder of their body was hard and armoured with scales, and the lower part was all snake [*ophis*]. At the very end was the snake's shameless head. These beasts are not said to have been winged, like sphinxes, nor, like them, are they said to have conversed, but they just made a high-pitched hiss, like *drakontes*. They

---

[67] Statius *Thebaid* 1.562–669.

[68] Musée du Louvre, CA1915 = *LIMC* Python 1 = Apollon 998; cf. Ogden 2013a:86–8. Though the image is crudely drawn, it is conceptually sophisticated: comparison with an image of the pharaoh Busiris on a vase fragment by the Heidelberg Painter (*c.*565 BC; Palermo, Museo Archaeologico Regionale, no. 1986, illustrated at Miller 2000 fig. 16.2) indicates that the artist has conceived of her snake-head in the form of a uraeus-crown. See Skuse 2015 ch. 5, superseding Ogden 2013a:88 n. 106. Meanwhile, there is no plausible case for any of the images gathered under the heading 'Lamia' in the *LIMC* lexicon actually representing a creature of this name.

[69] First Vatican Mythographer 2.66. In the Greek sources for this tale we find the monster described by the terms *kēr* ('death-demon'; *Greek Anthology* 7.154) and *Poinē* ('Punishment'; Pausanias 1.43.7–8, 2.9.8).

[70] As if they were one-legged anguipede Gigantes: *LIMC* Gigantes 389, etc.; cf. Ogden 2013a:82–6.

Fig. 3.1 The anguipede Lamia with Apollo at Delphi. Attic, white-ground lekythos, *c.*475–450 BC. Musée du Louvre, CA1915. Redrawn by Eriko Ogden.

were the fastest of all land animals, so that no one could ever escape them. They relied on their strength to catch other animals, but deceit to catch people. They would reveal their chests and breasts and enchant men just by looking at them, inflicting upon them a terrible longing for sex. Men would approach them as if they were women. They would remain still and repeatedly cast their eyes down in imitation of a decent woman. But when the man had come close they would snatch him up. For they also had beast-like hands, which they would keep concealed up until this point. Anyway, the snake would bite them at once and kill them with its venom. And then the snake and the remainder of the beast would both alike devour the corpse.[71]   Dio Chrysostom *Orations* 5.12–15

As Dio proceeds to tell, the remains of bodies so attacked are left highly toxic, and to touch them can be fatal. Again there is no use of the term Lamia here, but

[71] The hunting technique outlined broadly resembles that of the spider-tailed Persian horned viper. Camouflaging its speckled grey body against rock, it wiggles a spider-like tassel on the end of its tail, the imitation of movement being uncannier than that of form. When birds approach to take the spider, the snake-head on the other end wheels around.

scholars generally agree that the creature deserves the name. I would identify three justifications for it: (1) the Libyan setting, which is strongly associated with the myth of the supposedly original Lamia, such as it is; (2) the overall congruence in configuration with Statius' monster; (3) the monsters' taste for devouring young men, which is strongly congruent with the Lamias, explicitly so named, of the following two case studies.[72]

Third, Antoninus Liberalis (ii AD) derives a fascinating tale from the (mid-ii BC) *Heteroioumena* of Nicander, according to which the Delphians were subject to random marauding attacks from a monster called Lamia or Sybaris that lived on Mt Cirphis:

> Beside the foothills of Mt Parnassus, on the south side, there is a mountain which is called Cirphis, near Crisa. On it there is still now a gigantic cave in which a huge and overweening beast used to live, and some called her Lamia, others Sybaris. This beast would venture abroad on a daily basis and snatch up flocks and people from the fields. The Delphians had been deliberating about moving their city and consulted the oracle as to what land they should turn to. The god indicated that they would be delivered from their misfortune if they had the heart to stay where they were and expose beside the cave a citizen lad. They did just as the god said. Lots were drawn and it fell to Alcyoneus the son of Diomus and Meganira. He was his father's only child, and fair both to look at and in the nature of his personality. The priests garlanded Alcyoneus and took him off to the cave of Sybaris. As a god would have it, Eurybatus, the son of Euphemius and descendant of the river Axius, a young but noble-minded man on his return from Curetis, happened upon the boy as he was being led off. He was smitten with love and asked the purpose of their journey. He thought it terrible that they should not resist the beast by force, but should stand by and watch the boy be slain in pitiful fashion. He took the garlands from Alcyoneus' head, put them on his own and bade them take him off in the boy's place. When the priests had taken him off, he ran up and snatched Sybaris from her lair. He brought her forth to where all could see and hurled her from the rocks. As she was carried down, she struck her head against the foothills of Crisa and the creature herself, thus wounded, disappeared from view, but a spring emerged from that rock, and the locals call it Sybaris. And it was in the name of this spring that the Locrians too founded the city of Sybaris in Italy.

> Antoninus Liberalis *Metamorphoses* 8[73]

---

[72] Dio Chrysostom *Orations* 5. See Ogden 2013a:89; and now Hunter 2017 (who pursues interests very different to my own).

[73] Cf. Ogden 2013a:88–9.

Evidently, the monster was first and foremost a Lamia, with the additional name Sybaris serving only the purposes of aetiology. But what form did she take? Antoninus says nothing, but one clue is provided by her cave-dwelling and another by Pausanias' closely congruent story of Menestratus. This tells how the city of Thespiae was similarly beset by a marauding *drakōn*. Apollo advised that the beast could be brought under a certain degree of control if an ephebe (an adolescent male, perhaps between 18 and 20), chosen by lot, was sacrificed to it every year. One year the lot fell upon Cleostratus and so his lover Menestratus devised a plan. He had a bronze breastplate made covered in fish hooks and fed himself to the creature in Cleostratus' place. On being devoured, he twisted and turned and so ripped the creature apart from the inside, albeit dying himself too in the process.[74] This comparison makes it likely that the Cirphis Lamia was indeed some sort of serpent at least, though admittedly it cannot be proven that she was anguipede.

Fourth, Philostratus tells the well-known tale of Apollonius of Tyana's encounter in Corinth with a creature defined as a Lamia, an *empousa*, and a *phasma*, the episode serving as a model for John Keats' major poem *Lamia* (1820), and through it also for some fine Edwardian paintings, by John Waterhouse (1905, 1909), Anna Lea Merritt (1906), Herbert Draper (1909), and others:

Among these [the pupils directed towards Apollonius] was the Lycian Menippus, twenty-five years of age, quite sensible enough, and with a body so finely toned that he gave the appearance of being a beautiful gentleman athlete. Many thought that a foreign woman was in love with him, a woman who in turn seemed beautiful and quite gentle. She also claimed to be rich. But all this was completely false, a complete deception. When he had been walking unaccompanied down the road to Cenchreae, an apparition [*phasma*] met him, materialized in the form of a woman, clung to his hand and claimed that she had been in love with him for a long time, that she was Phoenician and that she lived in one of the Corinthian suburbs, using the name of one or other of them. 'When you arrive there during the evening', she said, 'I will be singing a song for you, and I'll give you wine, the like of which you have never drunk before. There will be no competitor for my love to give you any trouble, but I shall live with you, a beautiful woman with a beautiful man.' The young man was enticed by these words. He was strong in all other aspects of the philosophical life, but could not resist sex. So he went to see her in the evening and thenceforth paid constant visits to her, as if to a catamite, not yet perceiving that she was an apparition. Apollonius eyed up Menippus as a sculptor would do, drew a sketch of him, watched him, and came to a conclusion about him. 'You are a beautiful man, and you are

[74] Pausanias 9.26.7–8.

pursued by beautiful women, but you are warming a snake [ophis] on your bosom, and it is a snake that warms you.' Menippus was taken aback. 'Because your woman', Apollonius continued, 'is not a wife. And why? Do you believe that she loves you?' 'Yes, by Zeus', he said, 'since she behaves towards me like a woman in love.' 'Would you marry her?' 'Yes, for it is a delightful thing to marry a woman who loves you.' So Apollonius asked, 'When's the wedding?' 'I'm burning to do it', he said, '—perhaps tomorrow.' So Apollonius waited for the drinking party, and then stood over the guests once they had come, saying, 'Where is the gentle lady for whose sake you have come?' 'Here', said Menippus, and began to rise from his couch with a blush. 'To which of the two of you does the silver and the gold and all the other finery with which the drinking room has been decorated belong?' 'To the woman', said Menippus, 'for this is all I own', and he pointed to his rough philosopher's garment. Do you know about the gardens of Tantalus', said Apollonius, 'which exist and do not exist at the same time?' 'Yes, we know about them from Homer',[75] they replied, 'for we have yet to go down to Hades.' 'You must believe these decorations too to be such, for they are not substantial, but merely appear to be so.' So that you may accept what I say, the good bride is one of the empousas, which many consider to be Lamias and bogies [mormolykeia]. These female creatures fall in love, and they crave sex, but most of all human flesh, and they use sex to ensnare the men upon whom they wish to feed.' 'Shut up', she said, 'and get out.' She pretended to be repulsed by what she heard, and I supposed she jeered at the philosophers, to the effect that they were always talking rubbish. But then the golden cups and the pretended silver were shown to be made of air, everything flew from sight, and the wine-pourers and the cooks and all the servants disappeared after their unmasking by Apollonius. The apparition pretended to cry and asked him not to subject her to torture or to compel her to admit what she was. However, Apollonius was insistent and would not release her. She admitted that she was an empousa and that she was feeding Menippus fat with pleasures as a prelude to eating his body. For it was her practice to feed upon beautiful young bodies, since their blood was pure. I have had to tell this story at length because it happens to be the best known of all the Apollonius stories, for a great many people are familiar with it, inasmuch as it occurred in the middle of the Greek mainland. However, they have only had access to a summary version, to the effect that he once captured a Lamia in Corinth, but they do not yet know what her purpose was and that he acted to protect Menippus. My version of the story comes from Damis and his writings.

Philostratus Life of Apollonius 4.25[76]

---

[75] Homer Odyssey 11.582–92.

[76] For discussion of this text, see Ogden 2013a:89–90; to which add Stannish and Doran 2017. We find a dim but intriguing refraction of this episode in Nizami's (c. AD 1200) Iskandarnama (§xxxii; for a translation, see Wilberforce Clarke 1881; I thank Haila Manteghi for first bringing this passage to my attention). As Alexander ranges over the Persian empire, he destroys its Zoroastrian fire-temples. In

Clearly the creature concerned contrives to combine woman with serpent somehow or other. It could be, since she is able to cast hallucinations upon people (as with the splendidly decorated wedding hall), that we should think that she is in reality a pure serpent with the power to project herself as a humanoid woman; such an interpretation might suit the application of the word *phasma*, 'apparition', to her.[77] Another alternative is that she is a pure serpent with the power to transform herself fully into humanoid form; a model for such a transformation is provided by Apuleius' marvellous story of the massive old serpent that is able to transform himself into an appropriately crook-backed old man in order to trick a runaway slave into accompanying him to a place where he can revert to his default form and devour him (discussed in Chapter 8, §8.3.1).[78] But it is also well possible that the creature is supposed to be an anguipede. The application of the further term *empousa* to the creature might invite us to think so: the *Suda* uses this word to gloss the entry 'snake-footed woman' and also preserves an ancient folk-etymology deriving it from *hen* and *pous*, 'one-foot' (cf. here Lucian's description of his anguipede Hecate as going on 'a dragon foot', *drakonteiōi podi*).[79] We are also invited to think of her as an anguipede by a potential congruence of the narrative with Dio's material: both sets of creatures seduce desirable young men with their attractive female humanoid aspects, before devouring them. Might Philostratus' creature conceal her serpentine lower-half beneath her skirts, in the fashion of Melusine?[80]

Let us note the variability, durability, and longevity of the Lamias. It is clear that the entity derives from the ancient Mesopotamian child-killing demoness

Azerbaijan he comes across a fire-temple in the care of a girl-sorceress, Azarhumayun, who tends it accordance with the Zoroastrian religion and the customs of the Magi. She turns into a dragon to protect the temple. Alexander asks his chief minister for a spell to defeat the dragon, who is able to hurl back all the sorcery directed against her, but he is told that only Balinas (= Apollonius of Tyana), 'the master of sorcery', can produce an effective one. Balinas is brought forth and orders that a handful of rue seed be cast upon the dragon. It immediately quells her as water quenches fire, and he overcomes her deception. Now that the priestess is returned to the form of a beautiful girl, Balinas falls in love with her, and prevents Alexander's men from killing her. He presents her as a gift to Alexander, who in turn bestows her back upon Balinas to be his wife. Balinas learns all sorts of further sorceries from her, and so becomes known as 'Balinas the Magician'. In comparison with the Philostratus story, the Balinas figure combines the roles of both Apollonius and Menippus, whilst the female antagonist transforms into a serpent from a humanoid base-form, instead of possibly, changing into humanoid from a serpentine base-form. In a fascinating study, Ting 1966 draws attention to a tight Chinese analogue for Philostratus' tale, 'Madame White Snake', seemingly first recorded by Feng Menglong (xvii AD), and constructs a folkloric stemma to unite the two (190); cf. also Lai 1992.

[77] Cf. Ogden 2013a:89–90, where I favoured this line of interpretation. For the semantic field of the word *phasma*, see now Beneventano della Corte 2017.

[78] Apuleius *Metamorphoses* 8.19–21.

[79] Schol. Aristophanes *Frogs* 293; *Suda* s.vv. ἔμπουσα and ὀφιόπους γυνή (cf. also *Etymologicum magnum* s.v. ἔμπουσα). For discussion of *empousai*, see Waser 1905; Herter 1950; Brown 1991; Johnston 1999:131–8; Patera 2015:249–78.

[80] Philostratus *Life of Apollonius* 4.25.

Lamashtu, of whom, for example, the Akkadian 'Lamashtu text' (first millennium BC) has the following to say:

> ...the snatcher-demon.... The *l.*-demon will seize children.... Daughter of Anu.... Goddess whose face is fearful go away, remove yourself and fly away from the body of this child.' [This is an incantation to] 'drive out the heat and fever of Lamashtu.... Anu's daughter is furious.... her face is formed (like) the face of a ferocious lion, her flanks are spotted like those of a panther.... [go] away to the mountain range.... Anu's daughter went to Bel, her father.... she sweeps the innards of pregnant women, violently she tears the child out of the pregnant.... Her head is a lion-head, a donkey-shape is her shape... she roars like a lion, she howls like a wolf.... serpents in the hands.... Great is Anu's daughter, who torments the little ones.   (West trans.)

Another Akkadian text tells of her penetration of a house to kill a child: 'She enters through the door of the house, she slips in past the door-pivot, she has slipped in past the door-pivot, she kills the little ones; she has given it (the child) a seizure in its abdomen seven times' (West trans.).[81] These texts serve to show that Lamia's serpentine affinity was there from the first: Lamashtu is able to penetrate a house by gliding like a serpent, or else she is a brandisher of serpents. And it is in precisely the latter form that she is shown in Mesopotamian art. On the famous engraved stone amulet from Carchemish (*c.*800–500 BC) in the British Museum she: sports a lion head; has a female humanoid torso, with wild animals (a boar and a jackal) hanging from her breasts; has bird legs, with which she stands on a donkey that symbolically carries her off to a place she can do no harm; and in her humanoid arms brandishes a pair of snakes.[82]

---

[81] For both of these texts and others like them, see the collection at West 1995:250–9, 276–7. For Lamashtu and her relationship to Lamia, see Farber 1983; Burkert 1992:82–7, 197 n. 3; West 1995 esp. 292–303.

[82] London, British Museum no. 117759; illustrated at e.g. Burkert 1992 fig. 5. A further dim refraction of the Carchemish imagery, beyond the snakes, may have found its way into the Greek world. In a typically surreal Aristophanic episode in the *Frogs* (405 BC) an *empousa* is said to have one leg made of brass (*chalkoun*) and another made of dung, and to be able to shape-shift into a mule (*oreus*), inter alia (lines 289–96). Ancient commentators and lexicographers explain this reference—insofar as they do—by glossing the term *empousa* with *onoskelis*, 'donkey-legged' (schol. Aristophanes *Frogs* 293, 295c; schol. Aristophanes *Ecclesiazusae* 1048, 1056; Photius *Lexicon* s.v. Ἔμπουσα; *Lexicon artis grammaticae* 83.10; so too commentators on other texts: schol. Aelius Aristides *Panathenaicus* 102.5; Theodoret on Isaiah 5.197, 10.351; Eustathius on Homer *Odyssey* i, 442 Stallbaum). In the (i–v AD) *Testament of Solomon* 4.1–2 one *Onoskelis* (here a proper name) is described as having a female humanoid upper half and the legs of a donkey. It seems that such an *empousa-onoskelis* is to be found on three (imperial-era) magical gems, on one of which, a gem from Baghdad now in the Cabinet de Medailles, we have a demon with the tail of a bird, one bird's leg, and one donkey's leg (de Ridder 1911 no. 3470; Mastrocinque 2011:115–18). This is suggestive in the light of the Carchemish relief, on which a bird-legged Lamashtu is carried off on the back of a donkey. For discussion of the term *onoskelis*, see Patera 2015:249–90; Björklund 2017a:24–7 = 2017b:β, 3–5.

3.4.2 Campe

Apollodorus tells (after the Eumelian *Titanomachy*, supposedly of the eighth century BC) that Campe was a monster deployed to keep guard over the Cyclopes imprisoned in Tartarus; Zeus slew her to release them when he needed them to manufacture thunderbolts for him for his fight against the Titans.[83] Her life in Tartarus is perhaps reminiscent of that of the Hesiodic Echidna. Diodorus tells that she was an earthborn monster that terrorized the Libyan city of Zabirna (cf. the Libyan Lamia) and that she was slain by Dionysus, again in some sort of loose association with the fight against the Titans.[84] It is not until Nonnus that we get a full-blown physical description of her, and she is revealed as an anguipede: here we learn that she is of vast size; her principal head and torso are those of a woman, with the scales of a *kētos* (sea-monster) from the chest down; her hair consists of venomous *drakontes*; her legs consist of a thousand coiling vipers; fifty animal heads project from around her neck, including those of lions, boars, and dogs, inviting comparison with both the Sphinx and Scylla; her arms end in curving talons; a scorpion-tail arches over her head; she is a 'black-winged nymph of Tartarus' and rouses storms with her wings; she shoots fire from her eyes.[85] It is unclear whether the name Campe should be taken to signify 'sea-monster' on the one hand, or 'caterpillar' or 'silkworm' on the other; the first would appropriately salute her scales; the latter would appropriately salute her anguiform element, albeit by way of ironic litotes (see Chapter 4, §4.3.5).

Finally in this sub-section, let us briefly advert to another creature that broadly resembles an anguipede in configuration, with a maiden upper half and a serpentine lower half, and even resembles the Hecate of the lekythos and of Lucian in having dogs projecting forth from her midriff: Scylla (in her post-Homeric manifestation at any rate). However, she does not fall formally within our purview here, because, as in the case of Eurynome, her serpentine bottom half ends in a fish-tail and is that of a *kētos*, not a snake; we shall return to her, accordingly, in the next chapter (§4.3.3).

3.5 Conclusion: Occlusion

The term *drakaina* did not plainly and simply define the female equivalent of the *drakōn*. On occasion the word could indeed fulfil such a function, but it more usually connoted a female serpent in some sort of association with a woman or a humanoid female. In particular, it seems to have served as a specialized term for

---

[83] Apollodorus *Bibliotheca* 1.2.1 = Eumelus *Titanomachy* F6 West. For general discussion of Campe, see Fontenrose 1959:243–4; Mayor 2000:150–1; Ogden 2013a:85–6.
[84] Diodorus 3.72.   [85] Nonnus *Dionysiaca* 18.236–67.

female anguipedes. The female anguipedes, for all their numbers and their lurking continuity, never seem to have occupied the centre-ground of Greek mythology, but ever to have been somewhat occluded. The greatest act of occlusion comes in the iconographic realm. To the best of my knowledge there are only two extant images of female anguipedes in ancient art: the Hecate lekythos and the Lamia lekythos, the latter further occluded by the world of scholarship that has conspired to mislabel her a Python. There is occlusion too in the mythographic realm, with the tradition of the female anguipede of Delphi, Delphyne, being almost entirely smothered by the rival tradition of the male serpent Python. And the female anguipedes also suffer from a curious phenomenon that I am tempted to term 'diffraction'. This is particularly visible in the cases of Echidna and Lamia. An Echidna of anguipede form manifests herself in at least three different contexts in ancient tradition, in such a way as to leave us wondering whether we are dealing with one creature or three. Is Herodotus' broody Scythian Echidna to be identified with Hesiod's underworld brood-mother? And what of the *Acts of Philip*'s 'mother of snakes' Echidna?

Lamia presents an even more complex case. Even the broader category to which she belongs is unstable: Is she one or many? Is she a mythical heroine, like the other lovers of Zeus? Is she an apparition? Is she a child-killing demon? Is she a voracious flesh-and-blood monster? Does she attack babies? Does she attack handsome young men? Then again, amongst the specifically anguiform Lamias we seem to lack fixed ground. What is the relationship between the anguipede Lamia that attacked Argos, and was killed by Coroebus, and the Lamia, probably also anguipede, that attacked Delphi and was killed by Eurybatus? Despite the fact that both die in their own stories, are they one or the same? What is the relationship between both of these and the Lamia unmasked in Corinth by Apollonius of Tyana? Was she an anguipede too, or was she rather a serpent with the power to mutate her form into a humanoid one when convenient, or, given that she is described as a *phasma*, was she rather a serpent with the power to project a humanoid hallucination? And what was the relationship between all three of these individual Lamias and the quasi-wild-animal race of Lamias living in Libya, of which Dio Chrysostom speaks so entertainingly in a sort of natural-historical mode?

4

From Worm to Wyvern

The Evolution of the Western Dragon

4.1 Introduction: The Romanesque Dragon

Paul Acker helpfully extrapolates an ideal dragon-type from Northern European illustrated manuscripts made between AD 900 and AD 1450, and christens this the 'Romanesque (and Gothic) dragon':

> It has the scaly body of a serpent, devolving into a mass of coils, the feathery wings of a bird, the head, ears, and teeth of a predator (often a wolf), and two front legs of a mammal or bird of prey.[1]

Such a creature is well exemplified in the British Library's (*c.* AD 1255–65) Harley Manuscript (Fig. 4.1; cf. Fig. 4.19, lower left);[2] as a two-legged dragon, it might also be termed a 'wyvern' (cf. also Figs 4.2–3). It is the direct antecedent of the modern western dragon, differing from it only in the number of legs, two becoming four. By what process did the ancient *drakōn* we have so far described mutate into this Christian creature and, in particular, how did it get its wings? This is a difficult question to address for two reasons. First, the substantial literary and iconographic evidence for dragons in Europe over the first nine Christian centuries remains uncollated: accordingly, one cannot with any confidence venture to identify the *first* examples of developments; one can only point tentatively to *early* examples of them. Second, art of the early medieval West pullulated with Mischwesen, often of an experimental nature. Against such a background, it is hard to keep track of the dragon, which, as 'a snake and something more', was itself ever liable to creative elaboration. What is offered here is not a comprehensive or authoritative account of the question, but rather a provocation to those better versed than I am in the requisite early medieval materials to refine the claims advanced.

This, in brief, is the hypothesis offered. The Romanesque dragon is fundamentally the product of the attraction of the pure-serpent form of the classical *drakōn* towards two other forms of close significance for it: first, that of the sea-monster or *kētos*, the distinctively different creature from which the *drakōn* had yet struggled to remain distinct throughout classical antiquity; second, that of the (usually)

---

[1] Acker 2013:53.
[2] British Library, MS Harley 3244, fol. 39v (*c.* AD 1255–65), also illustrated at Bovey 2002:23.

Fig. 4.1 Wyvern (with elephant). Illustration in the *Liber de natura bestiarum, c.* AD 1236–50. British Library, MS Harley 3244, fol. 39v. © British Library Board / Bridgeman Images.

Fig. 4.2 The Dragon of Revelation (with a serpent-head tail) giving the sceptre of power to the Beast. English, illustrated manuscript, *c.* AD 1255–60. The J. Paul Getty Museum, MS Ludwig III 1 (83.MC.72), fol. 23v. Public domain.

humanoid winged demon. From the *kētos* the Romanesque dragon took its over-all body-shape, with its relatively stout central section and its coiling tail (whilst retaining the tail's culmination in the *drakōn's* point rather than the *kētos'* fish-tail), the positioning of its two legs, which occupied the position of the *kētos'* frontal flippers, and its animalian head with its spiky ears. From the demon it took its

Fig. 4.3 Wyvern (multicoloured). Franco-Flemish, illustrated manuscript, *c.* AD 1270. The J. Paul Getty Museum, MS Ludwig XV 3 (83.MR.173), fol. 89. Public domain.

wings and perhaps the form of its two legs, which could be animalian or avian (talons matching the wings in the latter case). The winged dragons occasionally found in classical culture may have made a small contribution to the new form, but they were surely not sufficient to sustain it in themselves.

4.2 Misleading Anticipations

Ancient artists loved to play around in creative ways with combinations of forms. The law of averages accordingly requires that, in the midst of all their centuries of Dr Moreau-like experimentation, they will occasionally have produced forms that seem in retrospect to anticipate that of the Romanesque dragon without the creatures in question being able to make any claim to being direct or significant ancestors of it. Let us consider two images, exempli gratia. First, a late V BC Boeotian black-figure vase gives us Heracles, with raised club and lion-skin, challenging a curious monster that most modern children of the West would not hesitate to identify as a dragon: it has a lion-like body, prominent, eagle-like wings, and a head that is broadly crocodilian, for all its prominent ears. The bulbous ending of its tail is compatible with a snake-head, without being particularly suggestive of it. But the creature is almost certainly correctly identified by Boardman as a griffin, i.e. as a snakeless blend of eagle and lion only.[3]

Second, we may look at two fourth-century BC Etruscan red-figure neck-amphorae in the Claudio Faina Etruscan museum in Orvieto. These give us underworld scenes (snakes infest the ground) in which Persephone sits in a chariot dawn by two short, fat-bodied, elaborately winged, bird-legged, crested serpents—creatures, once again, that any western child would easily recognize as modern dragons. It is above all the fatness of the bodies that tends to give these creatures a Romanesque look avant la lettre. The bird-legs are, however, sited too low down on the body for a strictly Romanesque configuration, though they do end in nice talons. These creatures would seem to be an anomalous, cul-de-sac development of the sorts of winged serpents that are otherwise found drawing the chariots of Triptolemus and Medea (which, as we will see, can be assimilated to birds in other ways too on the Italian peninsula).[4]

4.3 Classical Sea-Monsters (*Kētē*)

Before moving forwards towards the Romanesque dragon, we must first take a step back and give consideration to another classical creature, the sea-monster or *kētos* (pl. *kētē*; Latin *cetus*, pl. *ceti*). Just as the term *drakōn* had a semantic field that extended from the fantastical creatures of myth to real-world snakes, so too the term *kētos* had a semantic field that extended from fantastical sea-monsters to real-world whales.[5] At the real-world ends of these concepts there could be no confusion between the two classes of creature—snakes do not much resemble whales—but at the fantastical ends they could be drawn remarkably close, even though we seldom find the two terms applied to the same individual creature.[6]

---

[3] *LIMC* Herakles 2840, with Boardman 1990 ad loc.; cf. *LIMC* Gryps *passim*, with Leventopoulou 1997 ad loc.

[4] Museo Claudio Faina, Orvieto, 19 (= 2645) and 21 (= 2647); for an illustration, see *LIMC* Aita/Calu 9.

[5] For *kētē* in general, see Boardman's standard 1987 article, 'Very like a whale'; cf. also Boardman 1986; Papadopoulos 2016 is interesting but unpersuasive. For an expansive treatment of the (more-or-less) real-world *kētos*, the whale, in the ancient world, see Oppian of Corycus *Halieutica* 5.62–349 (ii AD); discussion at Kneebone 2020:345-87. This describes the progress of a whale-hunt in which inflated skins are attached to harpoons, to keep the whale close to the surface and trackable (cf. the use of flotation barrels in the movie version of *Jaws*, dir. Spielberg, 1975). For a somewhat cursory survey of the folklore of the whale in the West, see Waugh 1961.

[6] Two exceptions: the *Kētos* of Joppa is indirectly compared to a *draco* at Ovid *Metamorphoses* 4.715; and the obscure tradition for Campe may have represented her variously as a *drakōn* and a *kētos* (see Chapter 3, §3.4.2).

4.3.1 The Form of the *Kētos*

For the form of the fantastical *kētos* we depend overwhelmingly on ancient art, the creature featuring prominently, for example, in elaborate scenes with marine deities. Nereids often ride them in the fashion of horses, as, for example, when they are helping Thetis carry Achilles' new arms. Fantastical *kētē* shared with *drakontes* the fundamental similarity of a serpentine body (Figs 4.4–6). However, these bodies were often stouter in the forepart, and embellished with spines, a fish-tail, and a pair of frontal fins or flippers, whilst their heads were given quite an elaborate animalian quality, often canine or boar-like, but perhaps originally specifically leonine, and spiky ears.[7] Like *drakontes*, they could be bearded, but, unlike them, for perhaps obvious reasons, they were not usually fiery. A good standard example is provided by the appealing green sea-monster shown in a (iii BC) mosaic from Caulonia. Some classical images of sea-monsters often, curiously, have an air of a Romanesque dragon about them by virtue of sporting generous flippers, which can accordingly come to evoke wings.[8] We may point, in this instance, to the spiny flippers of the sea-monster on the *c*.450–400 BC chalcedony scaraboid seal in the Metropolitan Museum (Fig. 4.5 again),[9] or to the floppy flippers of the wonderful sea-monster on the Tellus panel of the Augustan Ara Pacis in Rome.[10]

Our current task is to trace the role of the *kētos* in the evolution of the form of the *western* dragon. Boardman, however, has recently formulated the challenging suggestion that it should be seen as contributing to the evolution of the form of the Chinese 'Han' dragon (via India and Central Asia)[11]—challenging not least in view of the clam-shell mosaic of what appears to be an all-but fully formed, mature Chinese dragon in the Neolithic (*c*.3000 BC?), grave of a Henan Province 'cosmo-priest'.[12]

---

[7] Leonine: on this point see Boardman 1987:80–2. A poorly preserved Mycenean seal in the Heraklion Museum *may* suggest that the Greeks of that age already knew of dog-headed sea-monsters: see the illustrations at Studniczka 1906:50, Marinatos 1926:58, Hopman 2013:58.

[8] But it is important to bear in mind that the *kētos'* fore-flippers were to evolve into the Romanesque dragon's legs, not its wings.

[9] Metropolitan Museum 41.160.437.   [10] Illustrated at, e.g., *LIMC* Aurai 4.

[11] Boardman's succinct formulation (2015:116; cf. also 2007:20–4) merits direct quotation: 'The relevant feature is its head, with a long snout, bridged nose, pointed ears and often horns, beard and leafy (acanthoid) excrescences. These all become features of the Chinese dragon as it begins to be depicted in the early Han period (ii–i BC). Before, their dragon had been rather fish-like or feline; now it is reptilian with clawed feet, but its head appears suddenly quite transformed and more like that of the Greek ketos than anything that had appeared before in Chinese or Asian art. Given its success in Central Asia and India it is perhaps not surprising that it should have been noticed also by Chinese artists, and with long-lasting effects.' Cf. also Boardman 2003:134–6.

[12] Grave §45 at the Xishuipo Puyang site. The creature's identity is seemingly confirmed by the fact that it appears in a meaningful zodiacal arrangement with a balancing clam-shell tiger: Pankenier 2013:38–80, esp. 38–40. For what it is worth, the most ancient Chinese writings on the subject, those prior to AD 300, for the most part consider their dragon (龍, *long*; 蛟, *jiao*, etc.) to combine the physical forms of serpent and horse and to exhibit associations with these creatures: see the sources most helpfully collected in Diény 1987, esp. 19–26, 47–51, 70–4, 78, 81, 91, 94, 116–17, 123, 149–52,

Fig. 4.4 Sea-monster (terracotta). Greek, Cretan, or South Italian terracotta vase, second half of the seventh century BC. Metropolitan Museum, New York, Gift of Ariel Herrmann, in memory of Brian T. Aitken, 2009, 2009.529. Public domain.

4.3.2 The *Kētos'* Narrative Type

Sea-monsters had much in common with *drakontes* too in their narrative contexts. Surprisingly, the ancient world knew only two substantial traditions of heroic *kētos*-slaying, and they resemble each other strongly.[13] The story of the *Kētos* of Troy is first attested in the earlier seventh century BC.[14] According to this, King Laomedon had cheated the gods Poseidon and Apollo of their promised pay

---

199–203, 214, 233–4, 244–6, 250–1. Chinese dragons are fundamentally water-spirits and water-guardians, with particular affinities to rivers and clouds (on which they ride), benign to man and his works: see the ancient sources collected in Diény 1987 (esp. 27–45, 60–4, 67–9, 72–3, 75–80, 91–5, 97–100, 103–4, 116–18, 124–9, 132, 139–73, 181–2, 222–3, 226, 232–6, 240–2, 245, 249) and the majority of the more recent tales in the engaging but, alas, under-documented anthology of Shouquan 1989. Further on the Chinese dragon, see de Visser 1913:35–134; Rawson 1984:93–9; Hay 1994; Bates 2002, 2007; and Yang and An 2005:100–10.

[13] A minor tradition recorded at Aelian *Nature of Animals* 15.23 also deserves mention, if only because the *kētos* here for once gets its meal: when the fisherman Epopeus consumed some of the pilot-fish that were sacred to Poseidon, the god sent a *kētos* to attack his boat; it devoured him as his son looked on.

[14] The principal references: Homer *Iliad* 20.144–8 (earlier vii BC) with scholl.; Palaephatus 37; Lycophron *Alexandra* 31–6 and 470–8, 951–5, with Tzetzes ad loc.; Valerius Flaccus *Argonautica* 2.451–578; Apollodorus *Bibliotheca* 2.5.9. More texts and discussions at Ogden 2013a:118–23, 2013b:153–61, to which add Wathelet 1998.

Fig. 4.5 Sea-monster (seal). Greek, chalcedony scaraboid seal, *c.*450–400 BC. Metropolitan Museum, New York, Bequest of W. Gedney Beatty, 1941, 41.160.437. Public domain.

Fig. 4.6 Sea-monster (red-figure). Etruscan, kantharos, late fourth century BC. Metropolitan Museum, New York, Rogers Fund, 1964, 64.11.6. Public domain.

for building the walls of Troy for him. So Poseidon sent a sea-monster to ravage the Trojan coast. This could only be placated by the sacrifice of Laomedon's virgin daughter Hesione to it, and she was duly pinned out on a cliff named 'Marriageless' for it to devour.[15] When Heracles happened by, Laomedon prevailed upon him to rescue the girl from the monster for the price of his immortal horses. Heracles substituted himself for the girl, even borrowing her dress, and allowed the sea-monster to swallow him so that he could attack it from within. He hacked at its liver for five days and eventually cut his way out of the carcass. Upon emerging he found that the steam of the monster's belly had dissolved his hair.[16]

Second, the story of the *Kētos* of Ethiopia, subsequently relocated to Joppa, is first attested c.575–550 BC (Figs 4.7–8). This is Apollodorus' (i–ii AD) account of the episode:

> When Perseus had arrived in Ethiopia, over which Cepheus was king, he found his daughter Andromeda laid out as food for a *kētos* of the deep. For Cassiepeia the wife of Cepheus had competed with the Nereids in beauty and had boasted that she was better than all of them. As a result of this the Nereids became angry and Poseidon, becoming angry alongside them, sent a flood-tide against their land, and the *kētos* too. Ammon gave a prophecy of deliverance from the misfortune, if Andromeda, the daughter of Cassiepeia, was given to the monster to eat. Cepheus did this under compulsion from the Ethiopians, and bound his daughter to a rock. Perseus, seeing her and falling in love with her, promised to kill the monster for Cepheus, if he would give him the girl to wife, once he had saved her. Oaths were sworn to this effect, and Perseus faced the monster, killed it, and released Andromeda. But Phineus plotted against him. He was Cepheus' brother, and formerly had had Andromeda betrothed to him. Perseus discovered the plot, showed him and his fellow conspirators the head of the Gorgon and turned him to stone in an instant.   Apollodorus *Bibliotheca* 2.4.3

---

[15] The 'Marriageless' cliff: Hellanicus F108 Fowler (later v BC).

[16] The motif of the emerging Heracles' steam-induced baldness is found first at Lycophron *Alexandra* 37 (whence it is taken up briefly in both the old and the Tzetzian scholia ad loc.). The interesting nugget found its way into the commentary tradition for the book of Jonah (perhaps first at Cyril of Alexandria *Commentary on the Twelve Minor Prophets* p. 578 Pusey, early v AD). In due course, in the Latin west, the motif was transferred to Jonah himself. This had probably happened already by the time of Létald de Micy's entertaining 208-line hexameter poem of c. AD 1000, commonly known as *Within Piscator* and more formally as *De quodam piscatore quem ballena absorbuit* (text at Bertini 1995). This tells how the Rochester fisherman Within loses all his hair after being swallowed by and emerging from a whale (166, 200), whilst describing him as a second Jonah (185). It had certainly happened by c. AD 1140, when the Admont (Gebhardt) Bible was painted in Salzburg, with its illustration of a bald Jonah emerging from the whale's mouth (MS Vienna, National Library ser. nov. 2701 fol. 243v). See the discussions of Ziolkowski 1984 (arguing for a folkloric context for the motif; cf., more generally, ATU 1889G) and Friedman 1988 (with the Admont Bible image at fig. 4). Létald de Micy is also the author of the *Life* of Julian of le Mans to which we will have cause to refer in Part II.

Fig. 4.7 Perseus and Andromeda with sea-monster. Roman, fresco from the imperial villa at Boscotrecase, last decade of the first century BC. Metropolitan Museum, New York, Rogers Fund, 1920, 20.192.16. Public domain.

Fig. 4.8 Perseus and Andromeda with sea-monster: detail. Roman, fresco from the imperial villa at Boscotrecase, last decade of the first century BC. Metropolitan Museum, New York, Rogers Fund, 1920, 20.192.16. Public domain.

Other accounts of this episode specify that Perseus killed the monster either with the sickle with which he had already decapitated Medusa, or actually by using the super-weapon he now had to hand, Medusa's head itself, to petrify it.[17]

These two narratives have much in common, in turn, with an established variety of *drakōn*-slaying narrative that we encountered in the previous chapter, that in which a hero delivers a boy he desires who has been put out for a *drakōn*. In the key example of this type, Pausanias (later ii AD), as we have seen (Chapter 3, §3.4), tells that a *drakōn* once marauded the city of Thespiae in Boeotia. An oracle told the citizens that they could limit the damage if they chose a lad to sacrifice to the

---

[17] Further principal sources: Euripides *Andromeda* Testimonium iii.a (a) and FF114–29a, 136, 145, 146 *TrGF* (412 BC); Aristophanes *Thesmophoriazusae* 1009–1135; Lycophron *Alexandra* 834–46; Conon *FGrH* 26 F apud Photius *Bibliotheca* cod. 186; Ovid *Metamorphoses* 4.663–739; Manilius *Astronomica* 5.538–618; Achilles Tatius *Leucippe and Clitophon* 3.6.3–3.7.9; Lucian *Dialogues in the Sea* 14 and *The Hall* 22; Philostratus *Imagines* 1.29. More sources and discussions at Ogden 2013a:123–9, 2013b:162–78.

beast every year. When the lot fell upon Cleostratus, his lover Menestratus determined to save him. He made a special breastplate covered in fish-hooks and fed himself to the *drakōn*, killing it by tearing it apart from within. Unlike Heracles at Troy, Menestratus died before he could emerge.[18] Antoninus' tale of the Lamia-Sybaris monster of Mt Cirphis follows along similar lines (ii AD, after a mid-ii BC original by Nicander).[19]

4.3.3 Further Aspects of the Partial Assimilation of *Drakōn* and *Kētos* in Classical Literature

Furthermore, some major classical traditions appear to merge *drakōn* and *kētos* in various ways. First, according to a late-preserved but apparently most ancient tradition, the *drakōn* Typhon may once have lived in the sea. Oppian of Corycus (ii AD) tells how Pan tricked Typhon out of his deep pit (*berethron*) to come to the sea-shore for a fish dinner, so that Zeus could strike him with his thunderbolt, once exposed. The meeting place suggests that Typhon himself comes from the depths of the sea (or had done so in earlier tellings). The possibility becomes stronger when we bear in mind one of the Typhon tale's Near Eastern forbears, the Hurrian-Hittite one (*c.*1250 BC or older). According to this, the goddess Sauska helped her brother, the storm-god Teshub, kill the sea-monster Hedammu by luring him from the safety of the sea-depths to the sea-shore with sex and beer (see Appendix A).[20]

Second, the Scylla that came to thrive in ancient art (from the mid-v BC) and in later literary texts had a form broadly comparable to that of the Hecate described in Chapter 3, §3.3.4: she had the upper body of a maiden joined to a serpentine tail, with dog-heads projecting forth at the join (Figs 4.9–10). However, as the art makes clear, Scylla's serpentine lower half is very definitely that of a *kētos*, not a *drakōn*, and accordingly ends in a fish-tail (sometimes two). A nice story was developed to account for her origin: she was once simply a fair maiden, but became the victim of the witch Circe, who was a rival for the love of Glaucus. Circe poured her evil potions into the pool in which Scylla came to bathe each day, and she duly waded into it up to waist-level before she realized the transformations that were taking place in the waters below.[21] But when we first

---

[18] Pausanias 9.26.7–8; cf. Ogden 2013a:65–6, 2013b:147.

[19] Antoninus Liberalis *Metamorphoses* 8.

[20] Oppian *Halieutica* 3.15–25. *Berethron* can signify a *watery* pit: Theophrastus uses it of underground river courses (*History of Plants* 3.1.2, etc.). However, the scholium ad loc., for the little it is worth, explicitly understands Typhon's pit to be in the land. Hedammu: *CTH* 348, esp. F11.1–3, F12.1–2, F14, F16.1–3.

[21] As described in glorious detail at Ovid *Metamorphoses* 14.8–74.

Fig. 4.9 Scylla (red-figure). Apulian, fragment of a red-figure terracotta bell krater, c.375–350 BC, by the Black Fury Group. The J. Paul Getty Museum, 86.AE.417. Public domain.

encounter Scylla in Homer's *Odyssey* (earlier VII BC), she evidently takes a very different form, as Circe herself tells Odysseus:

Of the two crags, the one reaches to wide heaven with its sharp peak, and is shrouded in lowering cloud. The cloud never dissipates, nor is the sky around the peak ever clear from the beginning to the end of summer. No mortal man could climb it or reach its top, not even if he had twenty hands and feet. For the rock is smooth, as if polished. In the middle of the crag is a murky cave, facing west, towards Erebus. You and your men must direct your ship past this, glorious Odysseus. Nor could even a man of great vigour shoot an arrow from the ship and reach the hollow cave with it. That is where Scylla lives, with her dread bark. Indeed, her voice is only as loud as that of a newborn puppy [*skylax*], but she herself is a wicked monster. No one could take joy in seeing her, not even if it were a god that were meeting her. She has twelve feet, all *aōroi*,[22] and six very

---

[22] The meaning of this adjective is unknown.

Fig. 4.10　Scylla (marble). Roman, marble table base, ii AD. National Archaeological Museum, Naples, 6672. Photo: Daniel Ogden.

long necks. On each neck there is a terrible head, and in each of them three rows of close-packed teeth, full of black death. Half of her body's length remains in the hollow cave, but she projects her heads forth from the dread hole and fishes from it. She scans around the crag in hopes of catching dolphins, sea-dogs, or even a substantial *kētos* [!], the creatures that the resounding sea rears in vast numbers. There are no sailors yet that can claim to have fled past her with their ship and emerged unharmed. For with each of her heads she carries away a man, snatching him up from his dark-prowed ship.　Homer *Odyssey* 12.73–100[23]

This cave-dwelling monster is clearly not a *kētos*: rather, with her elongated body and her elongated necks, she broadly shares the form of the Hydra, albeit being six- rather than nine-headed, and possessing feet of some sort. (We should not be misled by her 'puppy' voice into imagining that she already has dog-heads for Homer: the puppy, *skylax*, is only evoked to provide an etymology, possibly a joking one for her name. But evidently the subsequent tradition, the iconographic one in

---

[23] Cf., more fully, Homer *Odyssey* 12.73–126, 234–9.

the first instance, seized upon this term and ran with it.) Scylla's *drakōn* nature at this early stage in the Greek tradition may also be indicated by the fact that Stesichorus (*c.*600 BC) makes her mother Lamia, whose serpentine affinities we have investigated in Chapter 3, §3.4.1.[24] So here we have a monster seemingly evolving over the course of her tradition from a *drakōn* into a *kētos*.[25]

Third, in its original form, the myth of Laocoon ran as follows. He violated the sanctity of the temple of Apollo Thymbraeus on the Trojan plain by having sex with his wife in it. Accordingly, the god punished him by sending a pair of (otherwise benign) sacred *drakontes* from the temple to devour either his sons or Laocoon himself.[26] Over time this myth mutated into a tale of the type found in Virgil's *Aeneid*, from where it is now best known. Here the pair of *drakontes* arrive on the coast of Troy to complete their task after breasting their way across the sea from a nearby island. In other words, they have adopted the modus operandi of sea-monsters, and more particularly that of Hesione's sea-monster, which attacked precisely the same Trojan coast. A similar sea-breasting *drakōn* appears in the foundation myth of Nicomedia in Bithynia. The city was created between 265 and 260 BC; the myth may have been developed soon afterwards, but it is only recorded for us in the mid-fourth century AD by Libanius.[27]

4.3.4 The Partial Assimilation of *Drakōn* and *Kētos* in Classical Art

There was also a minor but striking trend in art to draw *drakontes* and *kētē* close. Three examples may be given. First, a marvellous red-figure *stamnos* fragment of *c.*500–450 BC shows the metamorphosizing goddess Thetis pullulating with animal forms as Peleus attempts to rape her: by her legs are a *drakōn* and a *kētos*; they are of similar size; their coils mirror each other's, the *kētos*' body being entirely serpentine save for its distinctive head and fish-tail; and they sport the same

---

[24] Occasionally later sources describe her lower half as that of an *ophis*: Palaephatus 20, *Suda* s.v. Σκύλλα.

[25] Stesichorus F182a–b Davies-Finglass (= F220 *PMG*/Campbell), with commentary ad loc. For further sources and scholarship on Scylla, see Boosen 1986:5–63; Andreae and Conticello 1987; Buitron-Oliver 1992:136–53; Jentel 1997; Andreae 1999; Aguirre Castro 2002, Hopman 2013; Ogden 2013a:129–35, 2013b:179–84.

[26] Principal sources for the Laocoon episode: Arctinus *Iliou Persis*, as summarized by Proclus *Chrestomathia*; Sophocles *Laocoon* FF370–7 *TrGF*; Lycophron *Alexandra* 344–7, with Tzetzes ad loc.; Virgil *Aeneid* 2.199–231, with Servius on 2.201, incorporating Bacchylides F9 Maehler and Euphorion F95 Lightfoot; Petronius *Satyricon* 89; Apollodorus *Epitome* 5.17; Hyginus *Fabulae* 135; Quintus Smyrnaeus *Posthomerica* 12.449–97. Iconography: *LIMC* Laokoon. For the otherwise benign nature of the pair of *drakontes*, see Tzetzes on Lycophron *Alexandra* introduction (partly rationalized) and scholl. Homer *Iliad* 6.76a, 7.44 (= Anticlides *FGrH* 140 F17), where they lick out the ears of the babies Helenus and Cassandra, thereby bestowing the gift of prophecy upon them. For further sources and discussions, see Ogden 2013a:135–46.

[27] Libanius *Orations* 61.4 ('Monody on Nicomedia Destroyed by an Earthquake').

spotted pattern.[28] Second, the notorious Portland vase, supposedly of the Augustan age, on the most influential (but still controversial) reading, portrays Apollo, embodied in the form of a *drakōn* avatar, impregnating Atia with the future emperor Augustus. The creature, rising up from Atia's lap, is entirely serpentine but for a distinctive *kētos*-head (its tail is hidden).[29] And, third, a superb relief panel from Antoninus Pius, Hadrianeum of AD 145, now in the Capitoline Museum, shows a captured Dacian standard of the sort Ammianus Marcellinus terms a *draco*. It is embellished with a windsock or *koinobori* in the form of a creature with an appropriately serpentine body and without a fish-tail; but the head is emphatically that of a *kētos*, with distinctive spiky ears.[30]

For these reasons, it is hard to make an absolute separation between *kētē* and *drakontes*. The proximity between them continued beyond antiquity, and *kētē* were to exert an important impact, certainly in their form and possibly too in their associated narrative-type, upon the development of the dragon in the medieval West, as we shall see.

4.3.5 The *Kētos* Acquires Legs and Wings

The *kētos'* front flippers would eventually develop into—or provide the positioning for—the fully evolved Romanesque dragon's legs. The transition was perhaps initially eased by the long career in classical art of the hippocamp, first attested in the late seventh century BC.[31] This charming creature (Fig. 4.11), compounded from the forepart of a horse and the rear part of a *kētos*, typically sports its two legs in the position in which a pure *kētos* exhibits its fore-flippers; very occasionally it can also sport a pair of Pegasean wings.[32] The hippocamp is primarily a creature of artistic marine fantasies, where it often serves, like the *kētos* itself, as a mount for Nereids, and such impact at it leaves on classical literature tends, accordingly, to be ecphrastic.[33] The Hellenistic period further elaborated upon

---

[28] Art Museum, Worcester (MA), 1953.92.

[29] For the tale of the siring *draco*, see Suetonius *Augustus* 94 = Asclepiades of Mendes, *FGrH* 617 F2. For the interpretation of the vase, see Simon 1957; and Ogden 2013a:337–8 (where I was more cautious than I need have been about the significance of the *kētos*-head).

[30] Ammianus Marcellinus describes the *draco*-standards at 16.10.7, at which point they had been adopted by the Roman army: they are purple and the wind makes them 'hiss'. They also appear frequently on Trajan's column, where, however, their heads rather resemble those of wolves. See Coulston 1991.

[31] For the hippocamp, see Lamer 1913; Shepard 1940 esp. 25–8; Boosen 1986:135–82; and, above all, Icard-Gianolio 1997. The earliest example of a hippocamp in art is *LIMC* Hippokampos 9, a late vii BC terracotta relief from Thasos. Boardman 1986:448 actually goes so far as to suggest that the canonical form of the *kētos*—presumably including the positioning of the fore-flippers—is actually influenced from the first by that of the hippocamp.

[32] For winged hippocamps, see, e.g., *LIMC* Hippokampos 14 (Syracusan coins produced between 410 and 317 BC) and 29a (Roman intaglios).

[33] Menander F720 Körte (a hippocamp in the ether); Laevius F21 Courtney (drawing a sea-chariot), Strabo C215 (a bronze statue of Poseidon holding a hippocamp; cf. *LIMC* Hippokampos 17); Virgil *Georgics* 4.387–9 (Proteus' sea-chariot drawn by 'two-footed horses'; cf. *Ciris* 295); Pliny *Natural*

Fig. 4.11 Hippocamp (below), with a Siren and a sphinx. The hippocamp appears to have a left fore-flipper and a right foreleg. Etruscan gold signet ring, 550–500 BC. The J. Paul Getty Museum, Villa Collection, Malibu, California. 85.AM.268. Open access.

the theme of the hippocamp by combining the foreparts of other quadrupeds with fish-tails to create a series of allied Mischwesen: lions, panthers, bulls, rams, goats, boars, and centaurs; of these only the semi-bulls and semi-centaurs appear to have acquired technical names with any purchase in English—'taurocamps' and 'ichthyocentaurs'.[34] It is a matter for debate whether our fantastical hippocamp (*hippokampos, hippocampus*) derived its name, together with the inspiration for its form, from that of the true seahorse, the familiar tiny creature of the Syngnathidae family,[35] or whether the term 'hippocamp' in origin signified 'horse-cum-sea-monster', with this term then being applied reflexively and archly, as it were, to the true seahorse.[36]

History 32.149, 36.26 (Rome's temple of Neptune decorated with Nereids riding dolphins, *kētē*, and hippocamps); Valerius Flaccus 2.507 (Neptune's sea-chariot drawn by 'two-footed horses'); Statius *Thebaid* 2.45–7 and *Achilleid* 1.56–60 (Neptune's sea-chariot drawn by horses with hooves and tails); Pausanias 2.1.9 (Corinth's temple of Poseidon is decorated with a ἵππος εἰκασμένος κήτει τὰ μετὰ τὸ στέρνον—'a horse made to resemble a *kētos* below its breast'); Philostratus *Imagines* 1.8 (a vase decorated with Poseidon's chariot, drawn over the sea by blue-eyed hippocamps) and *Heroicus* 45.2–3.

[34] See e.g. *LIMC* Nereides 110, 112; Shepard 1940:78. Aelian *Nature of Animals* 16.18 tells that the sea surrounding Taprobane (Sri Lanka) is full of *kētē* with the heads of lions, leopards, wolves, and rams.

[35] For the true seahorse as ἱππόκαμπος/*hippocampus* see Dioscorides Medicus 2.3; Pliny *Natural History* 32.149; Aelian *Nature of Animals* 14.20.

[36] There is vestigial evidence for the *kamp-* root signifying 'sea-monster.' Hesychius tells that Epicharmus (*c.* 500 BC) used the term *kampē* to signify *kētos* (κάμπη· κῆτος παρὰ Ἐπιχάρμῳ;

Fig. 4.12   Fresco fragment with winged sea-monsters. Roman, Boscoreale, AD 50–79.
The J. Paul Getty Museum, Villa Collection, Malibu, California. 72.AG.78.5.
Open access.

On occasion the animalian legs of the hippocamp and these allied forms could
migrate across to replace the fore-flippers of otherwise pure *kētē*. The *c.*100 BC
altar of Domitius Ahenobarbus, attributed to Scopas and now in the Munich
Glyptothek, gives us a coiling sea-monster with a fish-tail, spines, and a crest but
also two prominent lion paws in the place of its fore-flippers. It carries a Triton
and two Nereids on its back. Also on this altar we have hippocamps, a taurocamp,
and a further creature resembling the sea-monster, again with lion paws, but
sporting a humanoid upper-half in place of its sea-monster head.[37] Then in the
following century *kētē* similarly configured with lion-paws are found decorating a
series of libation trays from the extreme east of the Graeco-Roman world,
Gandhara in Pakistan. They are ridden by Nereids and cupids.[38]

Epicharmus F192 K-A = F194 Kaibel); the fragment may or may not be a genuine one, but the usage
presumably is. Similarly, the term κάμπος (*kampos*), a *hapax*, seems to denote a sea-monster or a
whale at Lycophron *Alexandra* 414; cf. Hornblower 2015 ad loc., with some linguistic notes.
Otherwise, however, the term *kampē* denoted a caterpillar, a creature better suiting a true seahorse in
its size, and perhaps too its segmentation: was the true seahorse from the first, then, a 'horse-
caterpillar'? A similar term, differing only in accentuation (καμπή), compatibly denoted a curve, flex-
ion, or winding (as of a river); see LSJ *s.vv.* Note again our discussion of the monstrous Campe in
Chapter 3 (§3.4.2).

[37]   *LIMC* Nereides 42, illustrated at Pons 2011:157 figs 5–7 (esp. 7).
[38]   See Boardman 1987 esp. 451–3; Falk 2010; and Pons 2011 esp. 155–6, with illustrations.

In a further development, which brings us quite close to the overall form of the Romanesque dragon (for all that there is no element of *drakōn* in it), a pair of actual wings—no doubt inspired by the tradition of wing-like flippers—could be added to a legged *kētos*. Such we find in the case of a fine pair of mirroring sea-monsters found on a fresco fragment from Boscoreale and now in the Getty, dated to the last three decades before Vesuvius' eruption (AD 50–79). But these are admittedly strange creatures indeed, their heads resembling not those of normal *kētē*, but rather of gryphons (Fig. 4.12).[39]

4.4 The Early Christian *Kētos* in Art and Thought

4.4.1 Art

The classical form of the *kētos* continued to thrive in early Christian art,[40] specifically in the context of the immensely popular Jonah scenes that served to anticipate the resurrection of Christ and the human soul alike.[41] These images take their cue from the fact that the Jonah-swallowing creature is explicitly described as 'a big *kētos*' in the Greek of the third- to second-century BC Septuagint (where it translates the Hebrew *dag gadol*, literally 'big fish').[42] They show Jonah variously either disappearing inside the creature headfirst, his legs alone remaining visible, or emerging from it headfirst, his torso projecting. Noteworthy examples are found already in catacomb frescos from the late second century AD. The following two centuries find these scenes represented also on some fine-relief sarcophagi, amongst other media. The creatures depicted are mostly pure classical *kētē* in form: they are broad-bodied, with a coiling tail, culminating in a fish-tail; they have foreleg-like fore-flippers; and they have animalian heads with spiky ears (Fig. 4.13).[43] Had this iconographic tradition not become established at the early

[39] Getty Museum, 72.AG.78.5.

[40] For introductions to early Christian art, see Beck and Bol 1983; Jensen 2000; and Spier 2007 with further bibliography.

[41] The three nights Jonah spends inside the creature are compared to the three days Christ himself would spend in the belly of the earth before his own resurrection at Matthew 12:40. Discussion at Narkiss 1979; Davis 2000; and Dresken-Weiland 2010:96–100, 111–15; Noegel 2015:237. On Jonah, note also Louden 2011:164–79.

[42] Jonah 1:17 (דָּ֣ג גָּד֔וֹל, κήτει μεγάλῳ), 2:1–2, 11. Noegel 2015 demonstrates that the Hebrew account is shot through with the imagery of Leviathan and the Hebrew Bible's more generic sea-monsters, the *tanninim*; cf. also Dyssel 2019. The book is thought to have been composed originally in the Persian period: Noegel 2015:257; Bracht 2020:533.

[43] These are some key images. (1) The frescos of the Cubicula of the Sacraments, chambers A3, A5, and A6, in the late ii AD Catacaomb of Callixtus, illustrated in part at Spier 2007:174, item 3b. (2) The British Museum Jonah sarcophagus, probably from Italy in origin, *c.* AD 260–300, British Museum P&E MLA 1957.10–11.1. (3) The iii AD Jonah sarcophagus in Santa Maria Antiqua, Rome, illustrated at Spier 2007:102. (4) The iii AD tombstone of Beratios Nicatoras from the Hypogeum Campana in Rome (the *kētos* here is misleadingly classified as a 'dragon' at Palli 1968:520–1). (5) An early iv AD Roman marble table base in the Metropolitan Museum (Fig. 4.13). (6) A superb iv AD mosaic from the

Fig. 4.13 Jonah swallowed and disgorged by the sea-monster (table base). Roman, marble, early iv AD. Metropolitan Museum, New York, Gift of John Todd Edgar, 1877, 77.7. Public domain.

date it did, things might have been different, for when Jerome came to publish his Latin (Vulgate) version of the Bible in AD 405, he avoided the term *cetus*, the Latin reflex of *kētos*, and, with a scrupulous eye on the Hebrew, designated the swallowing creature more properly as a *piscis grandis*, 'a big fish'.[44]

But Christian art did also continue the Mischwesen-experimentation with the form of the *kētos* that classical art had begun (§4.3.5). A group of *c*. AD 280–90 Jonah marbles, thought to have originated in Phrygia (on the basis of analysis of

Patriarchal Basilica at Aquileia, in which the crested and bearded sea-monster disgorging Jonah spirals vertically in the manner of the best classical *drakontes* and sports two large fore-fins (rather than flippers), which consequently exhibit quite a wing-like appearance. (7) Frescos of the iv AD in the catacombs of Peter and Marcellinus and of Priscilla (Cubiculum V), the latter illustrated at Spier 2007:71 and 177, fig. 52 and item 6. (8) The magnificent iv AD Jonah sarcophagus ('*the* Jonah sarcophagus') formerly in the Lateran Museum and now in the Vatican's Museo Pio Cristiano, in which the coiling *kētos* is shown twice in adjacent scenes, both swallowing and regurgitating Jonah, Vatican Museums no. 31448, illustrated at Paul 1968:415, fig. 1; Beck and Bol 1983:318, fig. 133, pp. 611–12, no. 203 (cf. pp. 615–16, no. 207); and Spier 2007:207, item 39. (9) The crude but engaging scenes on a iv AD engraved glass bowl found at Podgoritza in Montenegro and now in the Hermitage, illustrated at Spier 2007:9, fig. 4. (10) A gilt glass medallion of the later iv AD similarly shows Jonah entering the *kētos* with just his legs sticking out, Louvre, Dept. of Greek, Etruscan and Roman Antiquities 1731, illustrated at Spier 2007:186, item 14 (cf. also 185, item 13a). (11) The late iv AD ivory reliquary chest from Milan, now in the Museo Civico dell'Eta Cristiana, Brescia, again with parallel scenes of swallowing and regurgitation, illustrated at Spier 2007:17, fig. 9. See, in general, Steffen 1963 (with care—and his 1984 even more so); Paul 1968; Narkiss 1979; Sichtermann 1983; Noegel 2015; and esp. Davis 2000.

[44] However, Jerome does actually qualify his reversion to 'big fish' in his commentary on Jonah: *Commentariorum in Jonam prophetam liber unus*, PL xxv, 1131 [404], on Jonah 2:1. Although, as he explains, 'big fish' is the more literal translation, nonetheless 'it cannot be doubted that [sc. the Hebrew phrase] means *cetus*'.

the marble) and now in the Cleveland Museum of Art, gives us the *kētos* swallowing Jonah and the *kētos* regurgitating him, head-first in both cases. These superbly realized creatures, their tails coiling back over their heads, rest on strong animalian forepaws, these once again occupying the fore-flipper position. But they are also endowed with a pair of distinctly wing-like vertically rising flippers too, in just the sort of position in which the Romanesque dragon will eventually sport its wings proper (Fig. 4.14).[45] Looking ahead to the point at which we approach the birth of our Romanesque dragon, our attention is claimed by the Lombardic sarcophagus of the Abbess Theodota of the Monastery of Santa Maria della Pusterla in Pavia, who died in AD 720, now in the Musei Civici del Castello Visconteo, Pavia. This is decorated with a winning pair of creatures in the mirror arrangement. Fundamentally, they appear to be lion-cum-*kētos* Mischwesen of the sort calqued on the hippocamp. But the creatures also sport a fine pair of

Fig. 4.14 Jonah disgorged by the sea-monster (statuette). Marble, Phrygia, AD 280–90. Cleveland Museum of Art. John L. Severance Fund 1965.238. Open access.

[45] Cleveland Museum of Art, John L. Severance Fund 1965:237–8; both marbles are illustrated at Spier 2007:191 figs 1–2.

wings sprouting up from their fore-leg shoulder joints. Both these pairs of creatures, with animalian heads, a pair of legs, a broad then tapering body, and wing-like flippers or actual wings—bring us very close indeed to the form of the Romanesque dragon, for all that they possess no *drakōn* element whatsoever.

4.4.2 Thought

If Christian art was not initially ready to merge the *kētos* with the dragon, such a merging had taken place in the realms of thought and text long before, where the *kētos* was confounded with the *drakōn* from the first. This was principally because of the Septuagint's handling of the Hebrew Bible's sea-monsters, its generic *tanninim* (sing., *tannin*) on the one hand, and the two great, named, cosmic ones on the other, the multi-headed and 'twisting' Leviathan and Rahab, both destroyed by God, and probably to be identified with each other. In due course, Jerome's Latin Vulgate would go on to confound the terms *cetus* and *draco* in its own handling of the terms too, albeit differently and whilst bringing a wider range of vocabulary into the mix.[46] Thus, the Septuagint renders *tannin* with *kētos* in Genesis, but elsewhere with *drakōn*, on five occasions;[47] the Vulgate renders it with *cetus* on three occasions, with *coluber* (merely 'snake') twice in Exodus and even with *lamia* once in Lamentations.[48] The Septuagint eliminates the proper name Leviathan completely, replacing it with *kētos* on two occasions, with *drakōn* on two more and once, in Isaiah, with the more elaborate *drakōn ophis skolios* ('twisting dragon-snake');[49] the Vulgate retains the name Leviathan on four occasions, glossing it with both *serpens tortuosus* ('twisting serpent') and *cetus* in the same passage of Isaiah, and replaces it with *draco* twice in the Psalms.[50] The Septuagint retains the proper name Rahab once in the Psalms, replaces it with *kētos* twice in Job and on other occasions with more abstract terms connoting

---

[46] *Tannin*: תַּנִּין (plural *tanninim*: תַּנִּינִים); discussion of the term at Vogels 2011. Leviathan (*Livyatan*): לִוְיָתָן. Rahab: רַהַב. For the Septuagint's and the Vulgate's broader deployment of the terms *drakōn* and *draco* in rendering a range of Hebrew terms, see Wild 1962:5–7; Kiessling 1970 (esp. the useful tables at 176–7); and Delcor 1977:143–53. For the Septuagint more generally, see Gooding 1963; Collins 2000; Fernández Marcos 2000; Rajak 2011; for a complete English translation, Pietersma and Wright 2007.

[47] *Kētos*: Genesis 1:21. *Drakōn*: Exodus 7:9, 7:10; Job 7:12; Isaiah 27:1; Lamentations 4:3.

[48] *Cetus*: Genesis 1:21; Job 7:12; Isaiah 27:1. *Coluber*: Exodus 7:9, 7:10. *Lamia*: Lamentations 4:3; for the term *lamia*, see Chapter 3, §3.4.1.

[49] *Kētos*: Job 3:6 (τὸ μέγα κῆτος). *Drakōn*: Job 40:25; Psalms 73:13–14 (= Hebrew Bible 74:13–14; Leviathan is here said to be multi-headed); Psalms 103:25–6 (= Hebrew Bible 104:25-6); Isaiah 27:1 (δράκοντα ὄφιν σκολιόν). The designation of Leviathan as 'twisting' here, already in the original Hebrew, salutes the fact that the name in itself seemingly derives from a root signifying this: so Noegel 2015:247.

[50] Leviathan: Job 3:8, 40:25; Isaiah 27:1 (*Leviathan serpentem tortuosum...cetum*). *Draco*: Psalms 73:14, 103:26. The *Vetus Latina* Bible, the antecedent to Jerome's translation, had deployed the term *draco* at Job 40:25: Firmicus Maternus *De errore profanarum religionum* 22 (*PL* xii, 1030).

arrogance.[51] Jerome's Vulgate similarly retains the name Rahab in the Psalms, but replaces it with terms connoting arrogance everywhere else.[52] Here, then, long before the age of Christianity itself, was a strong manifesto for the eventual confounding also of the physical forms of the *kētos* and the *drakōn* in the Christian tradition.

The licence to confound *kētē* with *drakontes* bestowed by the Septuagint was indulged already in an early Christian text of *c.* AD 130–50, *The Shepherd of Hermas*. Here Hermas relates how his faith was tested by a terrible vision as he was walking along the Campanian Road: a monster charged towards him whipping up a great dust-cloud, from which it emerged, a hundred feet long, and spitting fiery locusts from its mouth. But Hermas remembered his faith and the creature came to stop, stretched itself out on the ground, and just stuck out its tongue. He later learned that its mouth had been bound by the angel Thegri. The creature had four colours on its head, and the symbolism of these was duly explained to Hermas by a vision of the Church, manifest in the form of a woman. The land-based setting, the charge, the fiery breath, and the tongue speak of a *drakōn*, as indeed do the incorporation of symbolism into the creature's head and the association with the Church manifest in the form of a woman, both of which remind us of the *drakōn* of Revelation (at any rate in the light of the terms in which this obscure text is traditionally interpreted). But Hermas does not call the creature a *drakōn*; he calls it 'a very great beast (*thērion*) resembling a *kētos*'.[53] Subsequently the Church Fathers could treat *kētos* and *drakōn* interchangeably, even explicitly so on occasion.[54]

4.5 *Drakontes*, Legs, and Wings in the Classical World

As we have seen, the classical world had already known compound creatures that combined a *drakōn* element with animalian legs, notably Cerberus and the Chimaera (Chapter 1, §1.5). However, it is unlikely that there was any significant continuity between these and the Romanesque dragon when it eventually appeared: their overall configuration was too far removed from that of the pure *drakōn* to have influenced its development into its Romanesque form. And besides, they had the wrong number of legs, four instead of two.

---

[51] *Raab*: Psalms 87:4. *Kētos*: Job 9:13, 26:12. Arrogance: Job 26:12; Psalms 40:5, 89:11; Isaiah 30:7, 51:9.

[52] Rahab: Psalms 87:4. Arrogance: Job 9:13, 26:12 (twice); Psalms 40:5, 89:11; Isaiah 30:7, 51:9.

[53] *Shepherd of Hermas* vision 4 (4.1–3): θηρίον μέγιστον ὡσεὶ κῆτός τι. For this text, see Quasten 1949–60:i, 92–105; Peterson 1954; Lipsett 2011; and now Harkins 2020.

[54] E.g. Didymus the Blind *In Genesim* p. 45 Doutreleau-Nautin (iv AD), where *kētos*, *drakōn*, and indeed *diabolos* (devil) are said to be equivalent terms. Basil delightfully abuses Demosthenes, the troublesome Vicar of Pontus, as a 'corpulent sea-monster' (τοῦ κήτους τοῦ πολυσάρκου) at *Letters* 231 (AD 375; cf. 225).

Of wings there is more to say. Others among the mythical compound creatures we have considered in Chapter 1 could on occasion combine *drakōn* elements with wings. Such was the case with Typhon and the Gorgons, who, in both cases, had their wings attached, angel-style, to their humanoid backs.[55]

But the classical world could also attach wings more directly to the backs of pure snakes too, in its ethnological and in effect cryptozoological literature. Herodotus famously tells of the flying snakes of Arabia. These are tiny creatures, and as such the more general word for snake, *ophis*, not *drakōn*, is applied to them. They are similar in body to water-snakes, variegated, and have bat-like wings. In mating the female seizes her mate by the neck and decapitates him; she herself dies in turn when her young are born by gnawing their way out of her womb. They guard frankincense trees. When the Arabians wish to harvest the spice, they drive them off by burning acrid *storax* gum. At the beginning of spring, these snakes take flight, en masse, for Egypt, into which they seek to fly through a narrow mountain pass near Buto. But there they are met by black ibises that kill them and leave their bones littering the floor of the pass, for which reason the Egyptians give great honour to the birds. Herodotus claims to have seen the skeletons with his own eyes.[56] Perhaps the traditions of Egyptian-associated flying snakes influenced the decorative scheme of the *tablinum* (archive room) of Pompeii's Villa of the Mysteries, which is dated to *c.*27–14 BC. The fresco incorporates a superb image of a friendly, vertically coiling serpent, with a fleur-de-lis-style crest and a fine pair of wings. The serpent stands proudly on a pedestal, without further immediate context, but the motifs in the room are otherwise either Dionysiac or Egyptian.

Megasthenes, who worked under Alexander the Great or Seleucus I, spoke of the marvellous snakes of India in his *Indica*: amongst these are the country's three-foot-long flying snakes (*ophis*, again), similarly with bat-like wings,

---

[55] *LIMC* Typhon *passim*, Gorgo-Gorgones 234–6, 241, 249, 250–3, 258, 260–1, 269, 271, 280, 283–5, 289, 293, 299, 301, 303, 309, 310a, 313–15, 317, 320, 322, 325, 338, 331, 343, 346, 350, Gorgones in Etruria 79, 81, 103–4, 106, 117.

[56] Herodotus 2.75–6 (Egypt, ibises), 3.107–9 (Arabia, frankincense, mating). Aelian *Nature of Animals* 2.38 ascribes the ibises' action to their innate sense of patriotism towards Egypt. Pliny *Natural History* 10.75 notes that the 'Egyptians invoke their ibises against the arrival of serpents'; cf. Solinus 32.32. Lloyd 1976:326–8 and at Asheri et al. 2007:290 suggests that somewhere behind these notions may lie (1) the cobra goddess Wadjet of Buto, who is often given wings in her iconography (as also was another serpent-goddess Meretseger), (2) the flying lizard of South-East Asia (*Draco volans*), or (3) the horned viper, which launches itself at its victims through the air. Mayor 2000:135–6 ambitiously suggests that Herodotus was shown a collection of spinosaur fossils. The Arabian serpents' mating and birthing habits are redeployed by the (initially iv AD) *Physiologus* for its account of the viper: *Physiologus* (first Greek recension) 10; (first Latin recension) 12. For the use of fumigation against snakes and *drakontes*, see also Theocritus *Idylls* 24.88–100 (retrospective); Nicander *Theriaca* 35–56 (a list of twelve useable substances); Virgil *Georgics* 3.414–15; Lucan 9.915–21; Pliny *Natural History* 8.118, 24.54, 28.100; schol. Apollonius *Argonautica* 2.130–1a (pungent substances choke snakes because of the narrowness of their breathing apparatus); Lucian *Philopseudes* 11–13 (for the last of which, see Chapter 8, §8.1 and *passim*). Cf. Jacques 2002:81–4.

that—delightfully—drop a corrosive urine on people below as they fly overhead.[57] Before we leave the realm of cryptozoology, let us also pay tribute to the *iaculus* snake, literally 'the javelin', that Pliny tells us flies (*vibrari, volare*) from tree branches to attack people; however, the point is very much that this snake hurls itself like a weapon shot from a torsion catapult, not that it sports wings. As we have seen, in his engaging excursus on the terrible snakes of Africa, Lucan takes the analogy even further and has a *iaculus* shoot itself directly through the head of one Paulus (Chapter 2, §2.1).[58]

Of particular interest is the phenomenon of pairs of flying *drakontes* that draw chariots through the air in Greek myth, the bulk of the evidence for which is iconographic. We may consider four cases. First, the flying chariot that Demeter lent to Triptolemus was a popular theme in ancient art. In most of the earlier images (in which Triptolemus is the driver) the chariot itself sports wings, this from *c.*490 BC.[59] From *c.*480 BC a pair of serpents sometimes serves as outriders to this winged chariot (Fig. 4.15).[60] From *c.*380 BC we occasionally find the associated serpents now sporting the wings themselves instead of the chariot; they can again serve as outriders, or they can draw the chariot from the front, just like

Fig. 4.15 Triptolemus in the dragon-escorted flying chariot of Demeter. Greek, Attic, terracotta kalpis, attributed to the Niobid Painter, *c.*460–450 BC. Metropolitan Museum, New York, Rogers Fund, 1941, 41.162.98. Public domain.

---

[57] Megasthenes *FGrH* 715 FF21a, 21c.

[58] Pliny *Natural History* 8.85; Lucan *Pharsalia* 9.822–7. Here I must correct a misleading statement at Acker 2012:7–8 (otherwise an excellent piece). Lucan *does not* tell us that *dracones* fly with wings (*cum pinnis*) at *Pharsalia* 9.730. Rather, he is telling us that *dracones* inhale large quantities of air *together with the birds* in it (*pinnae*, 'wings', are used in poetic metonymy). The phenomenon is commonly referred to in ancient texts: cf. e.g. Pliny *Natural History* 8.36–7; and the further references collected at Ogden 2013a:230–1.

[59] *LIMC* Triptolemos 22, etc. For Demeter's chariot more generally, in Triptolemus' hands or her own, see *LIMC* Demeter 333–415 *passim*, Demeter/Ceres 79–83, 126–38, 143–4, 164, 176, Triptolemus 7, 30–157 passim. Discussion at Hayashi 1992; Schwartz 1987, 1997; de Angeli 1998.

[60] *LIMC* Triptolemos 87, etc. Note Sophocles *Triptolemus* F596 *TrGF* (*c.* 468 BC): 'a pair of dragons [*drakonte*] that has taken hold of the axle in their coils' (*c.*468 BC), and Apuleius *Metamorphoses* 6.2, 'the winged chariot of your attendant dragons [*draconum*].'

a pair of horses.[61] And then from c.340–320 BC we find images of a—still flying—wingless chariot with wingless serpent outriders or drawers.[62] The imagery of the serpents, winged or wingless, drawing Triptolemus in his chariot continues into the Roman era, from which the bulk of the surviving examples of it derive. From the first century BC Demeter recovers her serpent chariot for herself, with the serpents initially unwinged.[63] From the first century AD the serpents that draw her chariot sometimes sport wings again.[64]

Second, from c.440 BC we find Athena riding to the Judgement of Paris in a chariot, presumably again a flying one, the bodywork of which consists of a pair of (wingless) drakontes, sweeping over the wheels. In later art she may have ridden a drakōn-drawn chariot in the great battle of the gods against the Giants (always a serpent-intense occasion).[65]

Thirdly, vases from c.400 BC show Medea escaping from Corinth and Jason after the murder of her children in the Chariot of the Sun drawn by a pair of drakontes (Fig. 4.16).[66] Medea was ever a mistress of such creatures.[67] Later traditions find other episodes for Medea's serpent-chariot. Ovid tells that Medea roamed the world in it to find magical herbs with which to rejuvenate Jason's father Aeson; the scent of the collected herbs rejuvenated the dracones as they

---

[61]   LIMC Triptolemos 138 (c.380 BC); cf. 39, 44, 48a, all of the Roman era. An electrum stater coin minted by Cyzicus in 430–400 BC (auction catalogues) carries a crude image of Triptolemus' chariot: it is just possible that already here the wings are to be understood as attached to the serpents rather than to the chariot itself.

[62]   LIMC Triptolemos 145 (340–330 BC); cf. 7, 36–7, 41, all of the Roman era.

[63]   The earliest evidence seems to be LIMC Demeter/Ceres 81, a denarius of 78 BC. Further examples of Demeter's chariot drawn by unwinged serpents: Demeter/Ceres 79 (gemstone, i AD; a poor image, but serpents are seemingly unwinged); 80 (denarius, 48 BC); 82 (lamp, i AD); 83 (lamp, i AD). In other contexts Demeter: (1) sits with an unwinged serpent at her side—LIMC Demeter/Ceres 93 (denarius, 58 BC); (2) sits with a winged serpent on her lap—LIMC Demeter/Ceres 145 (marble urn, first half of i AD), 146 (sarcophagus, c. AD 145), 147 (terracotta fragment, Claudian-Neronian era); and (3) sits before a temple from which two winged serpents emerge—LIMC Demeter/Ceres 137 (marble relief in the Uffizi, late ii AD).

[64]   First-century AD examples include LIMC Demeter/Ceres 138 (sardonyx vase), 164 (silver plate from the first half of the century on which Demeter sits beside her empty serpent chariot), and 176 (sardonyx cameo, Claudian era). Subsequent examples: Demeter/Ceres 126 (sarcophagus, AD 130–50), 127 (sarcophagus, AD 150–80), 128 (sarcophagus, AD 170–80), 131 (sarcophagus, early iii AD), 133 (sarcophagus, AD 220–30), 134 (sarcophagus, AD 230–40).

[65]   Judgement of Paris: LIMC Paridis iudicium 40. In a fragmentary Gigantomachy frieze of c. AD 150 from Aphrodisias (LIMC Gigantes 486) one of the Giants flees a pair of horned serpents, who are thought to have drawn a chariot, and probably Athena's. For Giants and serpents, see Ogden 2013a:82–6.

[66]   LIMC Iason 70 (= Medeia 35), Iason 71–3 (73 = Medeia 37), Medeia 29, 36 (= Fig. 4.17), 38, 41 (where the chariot is actually given a lavish four-team of drakontes). The chariot famously appears at Euripides Medea 1321 (431 BC), but there is no explicit mention of drakontes in the text, though they may have featured in the staging. Even before this the drakōn-chariot's existence may be indirectly attested as early as c.530 BC by the group of closely related images at LIMC Medeia 3–6: see Schmidt 1992 ad loc.; and Ogden 2013a:198–201. At Diodorus 4.51 Medea is associated with another pair of (imaginary) flying serpents: she claims that the goddess Artemis has come to the Iolcians on a flying chariot drawn by snakes, using her drugs to conjure up phantoms of them.

[67]   Cf. Ogden 2013a:198–209.

Fig. 4.16 Medea's dragon-drawn Chariot of the Sun. Greek, red-figure calyx-crater, c.400 BC. Cleveland Museum of Art, Leonard C. Hanna, Jr. Fund 1991.1. Open access.

flew, causing them (aetiologically?) to slough.[68] And a scholium to Aristophanes' *Clouds* explains that Medea sowed the land of Thessaly with the magical herbs upon which its notorious culture of witchcraft was to be based by scattering a casket of them from her chariot as she flew over.[69] On the earlier fourth-century BC vases Medea's *drakontes* remain unwinged. We owe their earliest winged manifestation to a unique later fourth-century BC bell crater in the Hermitage by a Faliscan artist. He combines their wings with prominent beards and crests and positions their rampant necks in such a way as to leave them resembling roosters, perhaps deliberately (albeit unfathomably) so.[70] The wings of Medea's flying *drakontes* are occasionally given explicit mention in Latin poetry.[71]

Also worthy of mention in this connection is the pair of 'crested snakes' (*angues iubati*) that Hera sends against baby Heracles in Plautus' c.200 BC *Amphitruo* (although there is no chariot for them to pull): we are told that they 'fly down' (*devolant*) into Amphitryon's house to make their attack through the *compluvium* (as we infer, because they are said to land in the *impluvium*). Plautus does not specify whether they are actually winged.[72]

---

[68] Ovid *Metamorphoses* 7.179–237, esp. 236–7.   [69] Schol. Aristophanes *Clouds* 749a.
[70] *LIMC* Medeia 39. I am aware of no other extant illustrations of Medea's chariot-serpents as winged prior to the Roman period.
[71] Ovid *Metamorphoses* 7.218 (*volucrum...draconum*) and 234 (*pennis...draconum*; AD 8) and Valerius Flaccus *Argonautica* 5.453 (*aligeris...anguibus*; c. AD 80).
[72] Plautus *Amphitruo* 1091–1124.

These classical winged *drakontes* probably did contribute to the developing notion of the winged *drakōn* amongst the Christians of the Latin West, though they should not be regarded as a sufficient cause of it in themselves. It is just possible that some influential words of Augustine on flying dragons, discussed below, draw in part upon the classical cryptozoological tradition. Images of Demeter's (Tritpolemus') and Medea's winged serpents certainly did flourish as late as the central imperial period; indeed, it is from this period that most of the extant evidence for them derives. From the second and third centuries AD we find fine illustrations of both Demeter's *drakōn*-chariot and Medea's *drakōn*-chariot on relief sarcophagi.[73] The case for some of these images at least having fallen before Christian eyes is a reasonable one given the importance that sarcophagi were to acquire as a locus for early Christian art in turn (as we shall see).[74] Triptolemus is found driving Demeter's chariot with winged serpents on the reverses of coins (ever a durable medium) minted under several Roman emperors, including Hadrian, Antoninus Pius, Septimius Severus, Caracalla, Gordian III, and Philip the Arab, whose reigns fell between AD 117 and AD 249.[75] And no doubt too winged-serpent frescos of the sort found in Pompeii continued to exist and to be viewable in the following centuries.

But the greater importance of the classical material for our question may consist rather in two considerations to which it gives rise. On the one hand it is indicative of a broader propensity across human societies to attach wings to serpents.[76] To this extent it offers another level of explanation for the genesis of the form of the Romanesque dragon. On the other hand, it warns us that dragons need not be endowed with wings to possess the ability to fly, a point we must bear cautiously in mind when considering the earlier Christian texts that speak of flying dragons without actually specifying wings for them.

4.6 The *Drakōn* in Early Christian Art and Thought

Early Christian culture embraced *drakontes* avidly.[77] The Bible had given new meaning to the creature, and it now became an embodiment of Satan, one of his

---

[73] Medea: *LIMC* Medeia, 46, 51, 53, 55, 57, 58, 62, 63; cf. also 66. See Neils 1990 and Schmidt 1992 ad loc. Demeter: *LIMC* Demeter/Ceres 126 (AD 130–50, a superb image in which the serpents sport heavy linked collars or a yoke, to which we must imagine reins to be attached) and 133 (AD 220–30).

[74] Laufner and Klein 1974–5:ii, 93 actually seek to derive some of the dragon imagery in the c. AD 800 *Trier Apocalypse* directly from such representations of Demeter's serpent chariot on ancient sarcophagi. See further below, §4.9.

[75] These coins are not included in *LIMC*: I derive the information from auction catalogues.

[76] Chinese dragons, which are wingless, regularly fly in their rich folktale traditions. Sometimes, though by no means always, they are said to ride on clouds, appropriately enough for the water and rain spirits that they are: see n. 12 above.

[77] See, above all, Merkelbach 1959.

demons, or of evil more generally. The biblical precedents were univocal. Inter alia, the Old Testament provided: the Serpent of Eden; the sea-monsters Leviathan and Rahab; and the promise that the faithful would trample on the lion and the serpent, resumed in Luke's promise that the faithful would trample on snakes. To these the New Testament had added the magnificent seven-headed *drakōn* of Revelation. We shall expound the relevant passages in more detail in Chapter 5 (§5.2.6), where we consider their profound impact on the hagiographical tradition, but of particular interest in this immediate context are Isaiah's prophetic references to flying fiery snakes (viii or vii BC). The more notable of the references speaks of the perilous range of creatures inevitably encountered by those foolish enough to attempt to camel-train through the Negev desert to trade profitlessly with Egypt: lions, lionesses, adders, and flying *saraphs*. The Greek Septuagint's reflex of the final term here was to offer 'the offspring of flying asps', whilst Jerome's Latin Vulgate was to offer 'a flying basilisk'.[78]

As one might have expected, the earliest Christian art adopts classical forms very directly for its *drakontes*. The point is crisply made by an early series of illustrations of the Serpent of Eden from the third and fourth centuries AD. In these a shamed Adam and Eve, clutching greenery to themselves to hide their nakedness, stand on either side of the Tree of Knowledge, around the trunk of which the thoroughly classical Serpent of Eden winds. One could be forgiven for thinking that one was looking at Ladon in his tree with his golden apples, flanked by Heracles and the Hesperid enamoured of him (Fig. 1.2 again), or even at the Dragon of Colchis in his tree, flanked by Jason and Medea (Fig. 4.17). In such images Eve often reaches out a hand to the serpent's head to receive the apple (in an act of narrative compression, since she and Adam are already aware of their nakedness): so it is with the frescos from the catacombs and from Thessaloniki and the sarcophagi from Toulouse (Fig. 4.18) and Córdoba. In making this gesture, Eve strongly recalls the Hesperides and Medea as they reach out to feed their respective serpents, usually from a bowl. Even more remarkable is a late fourth-century Roman ewer from Taprain Law, on which Eve reaches out to the snake's head whilst Adam takes an apple from the opposite side of the tree, just as if he were Heracles stealing an apple whilst the serpent was distracted by a

---

[78] Isaiah 30:6. The Hebrew's term *saraph* (שָׂרָף; plu.: *seraphim*, שְׂרָפִים) literally signifies 'coal', and is used in this context to denote a snake of fiery bite. The Septuagint has ἔκγονα ἀσπίδων πετομένων, Jerome's Vulgate *regulus volans*. The Negev setting leads one to wonder whether a tradition of this sort does not underlie Herodotus' reference, discussed above (§4.3), to the flying snakes that seek to enter Egypt from Arabia through the pass at Buto (2.75–6; Lloyd 1976:326–8 ad loc. and at Asheri et al. 2007:290 ad loc. considers the Isaiah passage worthy of citation, whilst labelling it 'suspect'). Perhaps too the Septuagint-translators had the Herodotean passage in mind when they chose the term *stenochōria* (literally 'narrow place') to express the hardship of the desert in which these creatures are encountered. Isaiah 14:29 warns the Philistines that, though the rod used to strike them is broken, there will be born from it a snake and from that in turn a flying *saraph*; the Septuagint has 'flying snakes' (ὄφεις πετόμενοι), whilst Jerome seemingly misrepresents the original by speaking of 'a basilisk and its bird-swallowing offspring' (*regulus et semen eius absorbens volucrem*).

Fig. 4.17   Medea drugs the Dragon of Colchis from her phiale, whilst Jason filches the golden fleece. Greek, red-figure volute crater, *c.*320–310 BC. Naples Museo Nazionale 82126 (= *LIMC* Iason 42). © 2020. Photo Scala, Florence.

Hesperid offering it a titbit.[79] There is no hint here of the Rabbinic tradition in which the Serpent of Eden had initially sported feet, God depriving him of the use of these in punishment.[80] Thoroughly classical in form too is the *drakōn* of Babylon killed by Daniel in an illustration of the tale from Bel and the Dragon (of the Old Testament Apocrypha) on a late fourth-century AD Roman glass medallion now in the British Museum: the serpent is rampant and crested as it accepts the fatal ball of pitch from Daniel's hand.[81] An honourable mention must go also to the *c.* AD 500 Ashburnham Pentateuch, with its scene of the

[79] The following are some key images. (1–2) Two iii AD frescos from the catacomb of Sts Peter and Marcellinus on the Via Labicana. (3) A similar fresco from a tomb in Thessaloniki's Western Cemetery, *c.* AD 360–70, and now in that city's Museum of Byzantine Culture, illustrated at Spier 2007:215, item 44c. (4) The relief sarcophagus of Junius Bassus, the *praefectus urbi* to the city of Rome who died in AD 359. This was found in 1597 in the remains of Old St Peter's, beneath the current basilica, and remains close to the point of its discovery in what is now Museo Storico del Tesoro della Basilica di San Pietro. (5) A second iv AD sarcophagus believed to have belonged to the child-saint Saint-Clair, Musée Saint-Raymond, Toulouse, Ra 825 (Fig. 4.18); it was discovered in the former priory of Saint-Orens of Auch. (6) A third iv AD sarcophagus found in Córdoba in 1962 and now in that city's archaeological museum. (7) A silver-gilt relief ewer made in Rome or northern Italy in the late iv AD, but found at Traprain Law in Scotland and now in that country's National Museum, illustrated at Spier 2007:253–5, item 75. Discussion at Schade 1968a. For early Christianity's embracing of Heracles, see in particular Simon 1955 and Eppinger 2015.

[80] The tradition was accessible to Greek and Roman Christians: it appears at Josephus *Jewish Antiquities* 1.1.4 and [Basil] *De paradiso* 7 (*PG* 30.67–8); cf. Schmerber 1905; and Kelly 1972:301–3, with further sources and scholarship.

[81] Illustrated at Spier 2007:222 item 48.

Fig. 4.18 Adam and Eve. Lombardian, relief panel from the sarcophagus of Saint-Clair, fourth century AD. Musée Saint-Raymond, Toulouse, Ra 825. © J.-F. Peiré.

animals going in two by two, including, in the foreground, a pair of perky bearded snakes.[82]

4.7 The Demon, Winged or Flying, in Early Christian Art and Thought

We turn now to early Christian thinking about demons.[83] We already find an airborne demon in the *historiola* (little story) of a pagan but Judaeo-Christian-influenced i–ii AD Greek amulet found in Altenburg in Austria. Here a migraine demoness comes out of the sea but is deflected by Artemis before she can enter the 'half-of-the-head'; the demoness' name, Antaura, reveals her identity to be a 'hostile wind'.[84] The physical form of demons is sharpened up for us by Tertullian in an important and influential chapter of his *Apology* of AD 197.

---

[82] Bibliothèque Nationale de France, MS nouv. acq. lat. 2334 folio 10v, illustrated at Spier 2007:156, fig. 116.

[83] On demons in antiquity and early Christianity, see the expansive *RAC* article by many hands, Colpe et al. 1976; amongst recent work see Brakke 2006; Smith 2008; Vos and Otten 2011; Kalleres 2015; Elm and Hartmann 2020.

[84] Kotansky 1994 no. 13, with Barb 1966; cf. Ogden 2009a:266. 'Judaeo-Christian-influenced' because exorcistic in character.

He reaffirms (after Revelation) that demons are constituted by a corrupted stock of angels with Satan as their prince, and catalogues the evils they inflict upon humankind. He declares that, like angels, they are all winged, and that they reside in the air. He proceeds to classify the pagan gods within this group and illustrate the point with reference to a story famously told by Herodotus. The historian had related how Croesus, king of Lydia, had tested various oracles and found Apollo's at Delphi to be the only reliable one. It alone had been able to tell his messenger what the king himself was doing back home in Sardis at the time of the consultation, namely boiling lamb and tortoise together. Tertullian explains that Apollo had been able to declare this truth to the messenger because he was able to cut through the air instantaneously on his wings and observe it. There is no explicit mention of *drakontes* in this connection yet, but they do lurk, for Tertullian goes on to talk about the demons that seem to heal disease, which in fact they are only able to do because it is they themselves that inflict the disease in the first place: clearly, Tertullian has the anguiform healing gods, Asclepius and his fellows, primarily in mind here.[85]

Winged demons (and indeed demons in general) take a surprisingly long time to manifest themselves in the Christian iconographic record. The earliest example of an illustrated demon of any kind seems to be that found on an ivory of c. AD 500 from Murano, in a scene of Jesus' exorcism of a demoniac. The demon emerges from the top of the victim's head in the form of a tiny but (apparently) wingless humanoid figure, his arms outstretched.[86] A clearly winged demon is, however, found in an exorcism scene in the Syriac Rabbula Gospels of AD 586, now in Florence.[87] Another sixth-century winged demon probably appears in one of the fine mosaics of Ravenna's basilica of Sant' Apollinare Nuovo. The sheep Christ has separated from the goats stand before a sufficiently benign-looking winged red angel; the goats stand before a slightly sinister-looking parallel winged angel in blue, the blueness extending to his hands, feet, face, and indeed halo.[88] This is thought to be a fallen angel, a demon: the parallelism he exhibits with the good angel is striking in the light of the way Tertullian had spoken of the two entities as equal and opposite to each other.[89]

---

[85] Tertullian *Apology* 22; cf. Revelation 12.7–9 and Herodotus 1.46–8. Martin 2001 traces the history of the (good) angels' acquisitions of wings; cf. also Grindberg 2013:379–80.

[86] See Artelt 1968:274; and Schiller 1966:i.173 (with illustration at fig. 424); Lunn-Rockliffe 2012:443–5 (with illustration at figs 14.4–5). Thereafter, ivories of the sixth century AD do indeed show such emerging demons as winged according to Artelt 1968:274 (again) and Schade 1968b:466, though I have been unable to confirm this directly.

[87] Rabbula Gospels fol. 8b (the scene illustrating the Gospel canons); cf. also Charcot and Richer 1984:5–6 (with a somewhat crude reproduction); and Lunn-Rockliffe 2012:444–5 (with fig. 14.6, a rather better reproduction).

[88] Cf. Murray and Murray 1996 s.v. 'Devil'.

[89] The first known image of a winged (good) angel comes in a v AD ivory of the baptism of Christ: British Museum 1856, 0623.3. See Martin 2001:17, with illustration at p. 26, fig. 5 (also at Lundberg 1981:81).

In the world of hagiography the Devil is identified with a range of dragon antagonists encountered by the saints, as, importantly, are his subordinate demons too. We shall investigate these themes in some detail in Chapter 6 (esp. §6.5.1),[90] but for now let us single out one aspect of a text to which we will return several times in the course of that chapter. The association between *drakōn* and flying demon is nowhere more apparent than in the late fourth-century AD Greek *Acts of Philip*.[91] St Philip and his colourful team, which includes the cross-dressing Mariamne (a prototype Encratite nun), and a leopard and a goat endowed with human speech, are en route to convert the wicked city of Ophiorhyme, 'Snake Town', i.e. Phrygian Hierapolis, which is in thrall to a great Echidna, or Viper (cf. Chapter 2, §2.3). As they pass by a huge pile of stones, there is an earthquake and a confusion of voices comes forth. The voices identify themselves as belonging to fifty demons, and they seem to say that they find themselves forcibly dislodged from their long resting place in their subterranean cave by the saint's mere approach. Philip uses compulsive, exorcistic language against them, and now a fifty-first voice replies from amongst them, that of the *drakōn* that is their master: he immediately confesses his identity as Satan himself. Philip redoubles his prayers and compels the demons to come forth from the pile of stones, which they do in the form of gigantic serpents, each 60 cubits long, whilst the *drakōn* himself is 100 cubits long, and belches forth fire and venom. The *drakōn* begs Philip to spare them all and promises that they will build a church for him in six days if he does so. The saint agrees and, as he utters another prayer, the fifty serpents are transformed into humanoid shape. They then fly off at once 'like winds', each to fetch a column for the new building. When the church is complete, the *drakōn* now transforms himself into humanoid form, specifically that of an Ethiopian (demons being characteristically considered black already even in pagan culture).[92] He declares that he and the other demons are now taking themselves off into the wilderness. This fascinating tale is full of contradictions and unresolved problems, of which the key one for us lies in the fact that its anonymous author evidently cannot decide whether his demons' *true* or *default* form is serpentine or humanoid. It is not explicitly stated that the humanoid forms are also winged, but their wind-like flying strongly suggests this to be the

[90] Cf. also Tertullian *Ad uxorem* 1.6.3.   [91] *Acts of Philip* 11.2–8 (A).
[92] For the blackness of classical ghosts, see e.g. Lucian *Philopseudes* 16, 30–1; cf. Winkler 1980. For the subsequent assimilation between demons and black-skinned peoples in early Christian culture, see e.g. *Acts of Thomas* 55–7, 64 (demons in the form of a black men and a black boy); Athanasius of Alexandria *Life of Antony* 6 (the Devil in the form of a black boy); Palladius *Lausiac History* 23.5 (a demon in the form of an Ethiopian girl); John Cassian *Conferences* 1.21 (the Devil in the form of a squalid Ethiopian) and *Conversio et passio ii S. Afrae* 7 (a demon in the form of an Egyptian 'blacker than a crow', for which see Chapter 6, §6.5.1). Discussion at Frost 1991; Habermehl 1992:148–60; Boulhol 1994:286–7; Brakke 2001, 2006:157–81; Verkerk 2001; and Bremmer 2017b:139 (with further bibliography).

case. At any rate, it is easy to see how such thinking could lead in due course to the merging of the physical forms of *drakontes* and of winged humanoid demons.

Ps.-Ephraim the Syrian's *The Cave of Treasures* is a Syriac text thought to have originated also in the fourth century AD, though available to us only in a version compiled in sixth century AD or after. Here the Serpent of Eden is given the ability to fly: 'And he [Satan] went and took up his abode in the serpent, and he raised him up, and made him to fly through the air to the skirts of Mount [Eden] whereon was Paradise'.[93] The serpent evidently acquires the power to fly directly from the possessing Satan within.[94]

4.8 The *Drakōn* Takes Wing in its Own Right (*c.* AD 400): The *Questions of Bartholomew*, the *Testament of Solomon*, Jerome, and Augustine

It is time to turn to a series of Christian texts, largely of the turn of the fourth and fifth centuries AD, in which dragons are seemingly given wings more directly in their own right and more fixedly. We shall look at some Greek ones first. If, as is usually thought, the Greek *Questions of Bartholomew* is to be identified with the *Gospel of Bartholomew* mentioned by Jerome, then it will have come into existence by the late fourth century AD, but probably not much before that. In this engaging text Bartholomew has the privilege of posing a series of eschatological questions to the resurrected Jesus. One of his requests is to be shown the great antagonist of humankind. Jesus reluctantly accedes and, to the blast of the archangel Michael's trumpet, 660 angels bring forth the Revelation Dragon from his place of confinement. Now going under the name Beliar, the '*drakōn* of the abyss', he is bound in chains of fire; he is 1,600 cubits in length and 40 in breadth; his face resembles a fiery lightning bolt; his eyes are dark; a malodorous smoke emanates from his nostrils; and his mouth resembles a chill cavern. At the terrible sight of him, Bartholomew and his fellow apostles fall to the ground as if dead. Beliar's description includes one further term: 'His single wing extended for 80 cubits'. Here then, as it seems, the Christian tradition at last gives us an explicitly winged dragon, but as a single-winged creature, it is a truly odd one.[95]

---

[93] [Ephraim the Syrian] *The Cave of Treasures*, British Museum, Additional MS 25875, fols 6b col. 1–7a col. 1; trans. at Budge 1927:63–4.

[94] See Kelly 1972:308–10, with discussion and scholarship.

[95] *Questions of Bartholomew* 4, esp. §§12–14 and §46; the key passage is quoted in Chapter 6, §6.4.4. For the text, see Bonwetsch 1897; for the dating of it, see Jerome *Commentary on Matthew*, prologue, with Quasten 1949–60:i, 127; for general discussion, see Kaestli 1988. The phrase in question reads, somewhat ambiguously, ἦν δὲ καὶ ἡ μία πτέρυξ αὐτοῦ πηχέων ὀγδοήκοντα (§13), and I have in the past been in two minds as to how to interpret it: at Ogden 2013a:394 I read the phrase as I do here, whereas at Ogden 2013b:192, I saw fit to translate it rather, 'and just one of his [sc. two?] wings extended for 80 cubits' (cf. also the translation at James 1924:174). The derived Latin recension of the

The anonymous *Testament of Solomon* is fascinating in content but unfathomable in its textual history. Most would currently date its earliest accessible recension to between the late third century AD and *c.* AD 400, with the caveat that even so one must beware of subsequent interpolations, and the passage of interest to us frankly does not look early. One of the demons (*daimones*) that Solomon summons up before himself is described as 'a winding *drakōn*, with the face and feet of a human and the parts [sc. otherwise] of a *drakōn* and wings [*ptera*] on its back'. Solomon compels it to confess its identity and praxis: 'I am the so-called Wing-Dragon [*Pterodrakōn*]', it declares. Textual difficulties obscure the account of its modus operandi, but it seems to claim that it becomes a wing-form breath (*pneuma pteroeides*) in order to have anal sex with women, albeit only the most beautiful ones. The confession over, the demon proceeds to burn up with a breath (*pneuma* again) projected from its mouth the frankincense wood Solomon had collected for the building of the Temple. Solomon then compels the demon to confess the name of the angel that defeats it: Bazazath. Bazazath is duly summoned, and the demon is thereby put to work on sawing up marble for the Temple. The integration of 'wing' and '*drakōn*' in this demon's very name is striking: it is evidently a strong synthesis of *drakōn* and winged humanoid demon, with its aerial nature indeed being fundamental to its function. It is intriguing that this combination of dragon and flying demon too should be put to work on the construction site of a place of worship, just like the dragons of the *Acts of Philip*. But for all that we have the motifs of fiery *drakōn*, wings, and indeed feet all together here, this creature, with its humanoid head, does not feel quite like an immediate ancestor of the Romanesque dragon.[96]

Meanwhile, what was happening on the Latin side? We find flying dragons in the works of the two greatest Latin fathers, Jerome and Augustine, both writing at the turn of the fourth and the fifth centuries. In his *Commentary on Isaiah* of *c.* AD 395–400 Jerome agonizes over the translation of the term *thennim* (i.e. *tannim*), describing the wild occupants of the desolate Babylon.[97] The Septuagint had rendered it with 'Sirens' and Aquila's (ii AD) Greek translation, as he tells us, with 'Typhons'. In classical art Sirens and Typhons were both winged, it should be noted, with the former sporting the bodies of birds and the heads of women (for the form of the latter, see Chapter 1, §1.6). Jerome preferred, he explains, to

---

text does not throw any light on the matter: *et una ala eius octuaginta* [sic] *cubitos* (p. 501; this recension, based on a single ninth-century AD MS, is edited at Moricca 1921–2). Perhaps the image of Beliar owes something, very broadly, to that of Satan as expressed at Athanasius *Life of Anthony* 24; cf. Boulhol 1994:265; Godding 2000:149–50.

[96] *Testamentum Solomonis* 14, pp. 45–6 McCown; for the text, see McCown 1922 (also at *PG* cxxiii, 1316–58); for translations, see Conybeare 1898; and Duling 1983. For further human-headed *drakontes*, see §4.7.

[97] Isaiah 13:21–2. *Tannim*: תַּנִּים (sing.: *tan*, תַּן). The Hebrew term, which the Septuagint translators partly confused with *tannin/tanninim* (cf. §4.4), in fact signifies 'jackals': Kiessling 1970:173; Heyman 2013:82.

translate the term as 'demons, or monsters of some kind, or indeed as great *dracones*, which are crested and flying'. The fashion in which Jerome seemingly assumes the ready assent of his readership to the notion that *dracones* should be flying creatures is striking. Jerome almost certainly considered them actually to be winged entities too, not only because of the implicit comparison with Sirens and Typhons, but also because he is speaking here primarily about the physical form of his *thennim*, so that the significance in this context of the fact that *dracones* fly ought indeed to be that they are accordingly winged.[98] Following Jerome's lead, Isidore of Seville applies the terms 'Sirens' to the winged snakes of Arabia.[99]

Two related passages of Augustine are also of considerable interest. In his *Literal Meaning of Genesis* (AD 404–20) he makes it his task to unravel the attempts of 'certain philosophers' to classify animals according to the elements. Along with ground-dwelling animals, these philosophers classify birds as 'terrestrial', because they alight on the ground, reserving the term 'aerial' for gods and demons. But, he notes, they classify fish and sea-monsters as 'aquatic' even though they can rest on the earth at the bottom of their waters and in this sense are akin to birds. The philosophers shore-up their separate 'aquatic' classification for fish by noting that (in contrast to ground-animals and birds) they have no feet. But what, protests Augustine, are we then to do with snakes and indeed *dracones*, which can hardly be classed as aquatic?

> Now *dracones*, although they have no feet, are said both to live in caves [i.e. to be highly terrestrial], and to lift themselves into the air [*in aerem sustolli perhibentur*; i.e. to be aerial]. Although they are not easily seen, nonetheless literature, and not just our own, but also that of the pagans, has in no way been silent about this variety of creature.   Augustine *De Genesi ad litteram* 3.9.13[100]

In his *Commentaries on the Psalms* (AD 392–417), Augustine's exegesis of Psalm 148's exhortation to '*dracones* and all abysses' to 'praise the Lord from the earth' includes the following observations:[101]

> *Dracones* live in the region of water. They come forth from caves, and they launch themselves into the air [*feruntur in aera*]; the air is made turbulent [*concitatur*] by them. *Dracones* are massive creatures; there are none greater on the

---

[98] Jerome *Commentary on Isaiah* 13:21–2, PL xxiv, 163: *Sirenae autem* thennim *vocantur, quae nos aut daemones, aut monstra quaedam, aut certe* dracones *magnos interpretabamur, qui cristati sunt et volantes*. His Vulgate does in fact deploy *dracones* to translate the term at this point. For the form of classical Sirens, see *LIMC* Seirenes.

[99] Isidore of Seville *Etymologies* 12.4.29: he also tells that, flying aside, they can run faster than horses, and that they are so venomous that their victims die before they can experience any pain.

[100] For a complete translation of this text, with commentary, see Taylor 1982.

[101] We discuss this curious phrase further ourselves in Chapter 5, §5.2.10.

earth. That is why he begins with the words '*dracones* and all abysses'. There are caves filled with hidden waters, whence springs and rivers come forth. Some come forth to flow over the earth, whilst others go beneath it in secret. All this, all this watery mass, together with the sea and the lower air, is termed 'abyss' or 'abysses', and *dracones* live there and praise God. What? Do we think that *dracones* form choirs and praise God? Away with the idea! But when you think about *dracones*, you give thought to the maker of *dracones*, the creator of *dracones*. And when you wonder at *dracones* and say, 'Great is God who made these things', the *dracones* praise God through the medium of your voices, the *dracones* and all the abysses.   Augustine *Enarrationes in Psalmos* 148.9 on v. 7

If the key phrases here (*in aerem sustolli perhibentur, feruntur in aera*) were taken out of context, one might imagine them to refer only to a serpent's tendency to go rampant, i.e. to lift the forepart of its body up off the ground. But the refutational context of the first text really does require that Augustine is sending his *dracones* into the air like birds. In this text too Augustine makes it explicitly clear that he is drawing, if only in part, upon the classical heritage (as Jerome does for the crestedness of his *dracones*), though it is not clear precisely what part of this heritage he has in mind: the cryptozoology seems the most likely. The second text's association of *dracones* with water sources may similarly be classically derived (cf. Chapter 1, §1.7), but it also, in making them dwellers within the watery abysses, seems to draw them close once again to *kētē*, sea-monsters, as the Judaeo-Christian tradition had a tendency to do.[102]

Augustine does not explicitly state that his flying *dracones* are winged, but the second text's reference to their propensity to make the air turbulent seems to presuppose massive beating wings. Some caution is due: it was well known in both classical and Christian tradition that *drakontes* could pollute the air with their poison breath, inter alia (Chapter 1, §1.7, Chapter 6, §6.1.3). It may be that this is what Augustine is referring to here, though I prefer to think that he is, rather, self-consciously offering a new take on the established notion that *dracones* should compromise the air.

Augustine's words here were influential. First, Cassiodorus, in his reworking of them in his own *Exposition of the Psalms* of c. AD 550, makes it now fully explicit that the *draco* is a flying creature (*volitare narratur*), whilst adding the scientific explanation that the creature lives in watery caves to regulate its body temperature when overheated by the warmth of the day.[103] Second, the great

---

[102] One admires Augustine's skill in marrying this classical notion with: (1) the words of the obscurantist text under exegesis; (2) the notion of the watery *draco* Leviathan; and (3) the established Christian notion that *dracones*, as embodiments or foot-soldiers of Satan, should inhabit the Abyss. Admirable too is his almost sophistic resolution of the paradox that Satanic *dracones* should be said to be praising the Lord.

[103] Cassiodorus *In psalterium expositio* 148.7 (*PL* lxx, 1044).

etymologist Isidore of Seville, writing in the early seventh century AD (he died in AD 636), repeats the notions that the *draco* comes forth from caves, launches itself into the air (*fertur in aerem*), and makes the air turbulent. For Isidore, a strongly influential author in his own right, the cause of this turbulence must surely be wings, not breath, for in the same context he draws attention to the smallness of the creature's mouth and gullet, whilst also adding, again in good classical fashion, that it is crested.[104]

Before finally encountering the wyvern in the ninth century AD, let us briefly note an anomalous but intriguing document supposedly of the century before, a Greek fragment 'on dragons and witches' attributed to the earlier eighth-century AD John Damascene. The author refers dismissively to what is apparently a contemporary scientific hypothesis designed to support the—now widespread?—notion that dragons, presumably even unwinged ones, can fly. The hypothesis claims that they are lifted up into the air (and killed) by thunderclaps (*brontai*).[105]

4.9 Enter the Wyvern: Four Illuminated Manuscripts of the Ninth Century AD: The *Trier Apocalypse*, the *Stuttgart Psalter*, the *St Amand Psalter*, and the *Gospels of Hincmar*

We first begin to find winged dragons in Christian art in Carolingian biblical manuscripts from *c.* AD 800, Apocalypses, Psalters, and Gospels. It is striking that no dragons embellished with wings or feet appear in manuscripts of the *Physiologus*, the great medieval bestiary, until the twelfth century AD, from which point they do, however, come to proliferate in them.[106]

The *Trier Apocalypse* was compiled *c.* AD 800 in Reims, though its seventy-five illustrations are thought to draw in some ways on iconographical schemes

---

[104] Isidore of Seville *Etymologies* 12.4.4. For the narrowness of serpents' gullets supposedly causing them to choke when fumigated against in the classical tradition, see §4.5 above. Isidore's disquisition on snakes throughout 12.4 is grounded in the tradition of classical works such as Nicander *Theriaca*; Pliny *Natural History* 8.32–7, 78–9, 85–7; Lucan *Pharsalia* 9.587–949 (cf. Raschle 2001); Philumenus *On Venomous Creatures and the Antidotes to Them*. At 12.4.29 Isidore also speaks of the (winglessly) flying *iaculus* familiar from Pliny and Lucan (who is quoted) and of the flying snakes of Arabia, which he calls 'Sirens', perhaps under the influence of Jerome (cf. above in this section and Kelly 1972:311).

[105] John Damascene *De draconibus et strygibus*, PG xciv, 1601. However, Litavrin 2003:636–43 contends that the dragon portion of this material was actually written by (the xi AD) Kekaumenos, author of the *Stratēgikon*.

[106] See Kelly 1972:304–5, noting the absence of such creatures from the (ix AD) C-tradition Bern *Physiologus* (*Physiologus Bernensis*, Bern Burgerbibliothek, Codex Bongarsianus 318) and the (x AD) A-tradition Brussels *Physiologus* (Brussels, Bibliothèque Royale 10074). For the *Physiologus* in its original form, see now Schneider 2019, with further scholarship. Examples of other bestiaries subsequently incorporating dragons include the *c.* AD 1120–40 *First Family English Bestiary* (British Library, MS Stowe 1067 fol. 5) and the *c.* AD 1300–10 *Peterborough Bestiary* (fols 204v–205; for a facsimile text, see James 1921; and for a translation, see White 1954, esp. 165–81). Dragons receive an entry also in Brunetto Latini's bestiary-influenced (*c.* AD 1266) *Li livres dou tresor* (1.5.142), regarded as the first modern encyclopaedia.

established as far back as the fifth or sixth centuries AD.[107] Eight times it gives us a
Revelation Dragon with a fully serpentine, coiling body. In most of these images
he has his principal head in the usual place (it may or may not have a slight animalian quality), whilst his other six heads are minuscule and project from the
front of his neck in a column. He also has the ten horns specified by Revelation.
However, they are not distributed across the seven heads, but are all confined to
the principal head where they are arranged closely together in a mohican, to form
a crest of the sort one expects of a classical *drakōn*. Most importantly of all, in five
of the eight images, the dragon sports a pair of fine bird's wings, or rather, it
should be said, wings that match in their form precisely those of the angels and in
particular the fallen angels, the demons, in the manuscript.[108] In none of these
images does the Revelation Dragon sport legs, but a scene in which the dragon is
paired with the Beast is intriguing in this regard: one of the dragon's minuscule
heads, low down on its body, is extending itself and reaching out over the head of
the Beast. In so doing it presents a strongly limb-like effect, and so seems to pave
the way for the generation of a dragon that possesses both wings and legs
(Fig. 4.19).[109] (Laufner and Klein contend that the winged dragons of this Apocalypse
are derived directly from the images of Demeter's winged chariot-drawing serpents
on imperial-period sarcophagi, but their case is a weak one.[110])

---

[107]   Thus Laufner and Klein 1974–5:ii, pp. 43–5; O'Hear and O'Hear 2015:32. Cf. also Palli 1968:523.
[108]   *Trier Apocalypse*, Trier Stadtbibliothek MS 31, fols 37r (Revelation 12:1, 3–5), 38r (Revelation
12:7–9), 39r (Revelation 12:13–16), 41r (Revelation 13:7–8), 42r (Revelation 13:11–15; the dragon is
wingless in this image), 51r (Revelation 16:10 and 12–13), 64r (Revelation 19:19–20:2; wingless again),
65r (Revelation 20:3–4; only the dragon's tail is visible, as Michael drops it into the abyss, but the tight
relationship of this scene with that of 64r invites us to read this version of the dragon too as wingless).
See Laufner and Klein 1974–5 vol. i for a facsimile of the manuscript. Many of the manuscript's images
were copied and elaborated in the fine *Cambrai Apocalypse* of the earlier x AD, Cambrai, Bibliothèque
municipale, MS 386: thus 37r = Cambrai 27r (Laufner and Klein 1974–5:i, Abb. 16); 38r = Cambrai 27
bis r; 41r = Cambrai 28r; 42r = Cambrai 29r; 64 = Cambrai 36r (Laufner and Klein 1974–5:i, Abb. 48);
65r = Cambrai 37r (Laufner and Klein 1974–5:i, Abb. 18).
[109]   *Trier Apocalypse*, fol. 41r. Unfortunately the corresponding illustration in the *Cambrai
Apocalypse*, fol. 28r, omits the figure of the dragon.
[110]   Laufner and Klein 1974–5:ii, p. 93. The case depends upon a comparison of fol. 39r, illustrating
Revelation 12:13–16, with the sarcophagus relief *LIMC* Demeter/Ceres 126 (AD 130–50). The folio
duly shows the dragon vomiting forth its torrent of water at the woman, only for the Earth, embodied
in a female figure projecting from the ground (as typical in classical art), to swallow it up. The winged
dragons aside, they compare the form of the figure of Earth with a prone figure in the sarcophagus
scene somewhat removed from Demeter and her chariot. This comparison is not compelling as it
stands, but in any case depends upon the line-drawn reconstruction of the relief at Robert 1919:iii.3,
460–1, no. 362, which the *LIMC* photograph reveals to be wholly misleading (the fragments of the
relief are unhelpfully divided between the Villa Giustiniani-Massimo and the Vatican's Statue Gallery).
A slightly stronger case could be made on the basis of the complete and broadly similar scene on a
sarcophagus of *c.* AD 220–30 (*LIMC* Demeter/Ceres 133), but again the degree of correspondence
between the Apocalypse's Earth and the prone figure is poor.
    The *Book of Kells*, believed to have been created also *c.* AD 800 in Iona (Scotland) or Kells (Ireland) or
both, is better left out of consideration here. Animal heads (mostly of the same indeterminate sort) and
legs are attached to the ends of the straps of the elaborate, serpentine knot-work throughout the book (a
particularly admired example at fol. 124r), but there is little to indicate that these forms as a whole were
intended to be dragons as opposed to elongated versions of other creatures, whether of pure or composite form. For the book in general, see Fox 1990; Trinity College Dublin offers a full facsimile of the book
on its website.

Fig. 4.19 The Revelation Dragon and the Beast. *Trier Apocalypse*, Trier Stadtbibliothek MS 31, fol. 41r, *c*. AD 800. Redrawn by Mike Adams, Phoenix Mapping.

The *Stuttgart Psalter* was compiled *c.* AD 820–30 in the Abbey of Saint-Germain-des-Prés near Paris.[111] It gives us some still wingless dragons of traditional sort, including a fire-breather, but alongside these it gives us a fine, rampant, vertically meandering, and crested dragon sporting two relatively modest wings fixed high up on its neck.[112] It is noteworthy for our thesis that the same manuscript also contains some fine images of demons. These are black, with distorted faces and clawed hands, and of course they are winged. Their wings too are modest in size and carried similarly high on the back. In short, they are a good match in their configuration for the Psalter's winged dragon.[113] It is accordingly easy to read in these illustrations the implicit argument that dragons should be winged because of their affinity with (humanoid) demons. The *kētē*—we should now be calling them rather *ceti*—of the Jonah scenes in this manuscript also deserve attention. They too appear to have been assimilated to the demons in their own way, for their fore-flippers are distinctly claw-like and as such match the demons' claw-like hands rather well. With their animalian heads and spiky ears too the creatures already look close to the fully developed Romanesque dragon: all that they want for the full effect are wings and pointed tails in place of their fish tails.[114] The *dracones* and the *ceti* of this psalter have little in common with each other despite the fact that they both represent significant steps along the road to the Romanesque dragon. But the one thing that they do have in common is that they have both been attracted in form, in different ways, towards the humanoid demon.

The *Psalter of St Amand* in Valenciennes, also known as the *Valenciennes Psalter*, is imprecisely dated within the ninth century as a whole, with its artwork considered to be of Spanish origin. Its Revelation Dragon remains conservatively serpentine and wingless, though he otherwise has something in common with that of the *Trier Apocalypse*. Again he has one principal head with six minor ones, these now forming a mohican over the main one. The ten horns are distributed across these six with the first and sixth sporting one horn each, those in between sporting two each. But the interest of this manuscript lies rather in the relationship between the representation of this dragon and that of his deputy, the Beast. This has the coiling body and fish-tail of a *cetus*; its principal head is a lion's, in line with Revelation's description; the *cetus*' fore-flippers have again been replaced by animalian claws, a bear's, we may presume; intriguingly, the six extra heads are similarly miniaturized to form a mohican to the main, leonine

---

[111] *Stuttgart Psalter*: Württembergische Landesbibliothek, Stuttgart, Bibl. fol. 23.

[112] *Stuttgart Psalter* fol. 69v. For wingless dragons, see fols 87r (fire-breathing) and 107v (trampled on by Christ).

[113] e.g. *Stuttgart Psalter* fol. 147v, a demon attends the regurgitation of Jonah. See Schiller 1966:i, 143–4 (with the Psalter's demons tempting Christ at fig. 389); and Palmer 1992:23.

[114] Honorable mention should also be made here of the superb clawed *cetus* of the mid-ninth-century AD Chludov psalter: Moscow, Historical Museum, MS D129, fol. 157. A little praying Jonah sits within its belly (or at any rate its coils).

one, but these remain serpentine, like the dragon's own. Given the bridge thereby constructed between these two creatures, one can well understand how the dragon should come in turn to share the Beast's own features of a *cetus*-body and a pair of animalian legs in the fore-flipper position.[115]

A fourth manuscript of importance is the *Gospels of Hincmar*, also known as the *St Thierry Gospels*, dating from the second half of the ninth century AD, and now in the Bibliothèque Municipale in Reims. It sets out the Eusebian canons (of corresponding loci across the Gospels) in six decorated tables on the pediments of which dragons, brown, grey or both, sit or scamper, together with a few other animals. Some take the form of pure serpents, albeit with slightly animalian heads. Most have the stouter fore-body of the *cetus* and that creature's more decisively animalian head, with its spiky ears, whilst their tails end nonetheless in the point of the *draco*. In the *cetus*' fore-flipper position, some have animalian legs, others have wings. Some sport beards and crests. Some blow forth streams of fire. One is ridden by a black demon.[116] Most exhibit the perkiness of young dogs. But it is on folio 19 that the prize awaits: here a fine pair of brown dragons, *cetus*-bodied and *both legged and winged alike*, blow long, hard blasts of fire at the poor bird perched on the apex of their pediment (Fig. 4.20). Here at last is a fully formed Romanesque dragon, in what must be one of its earliest appearances.[117]

The revolution was not instantaneously all-pervasive, and wingless and legless dragons continued to thrive in other manuscripts. We find, for instance, the Revelation Dragon (seyen-headed and coiling) in a still wingless and legless form in the beautifully illustrated Beatus manuscripts, which continue on from the ninth century AD, whilst reproducing the eighth-century commentary on the Apocalypse by Beatus of Liébana (*c.* AD 730–800). However, for a relatively early example of a fully formed Romanesque dragon in another artistic medium, one may look to a panel of Hildesheim Cathedral's bronze Bernward doors, commissioned in AD 1015, a triumph of Ottonian art: as a cringing Adam and Eve are expelled from Eden, a tiny, but perfectly formed, winged, two-legged, *cetus*-bodied, and fire-breathing Serpent of Eden sits at Eve's feet.[118]

---

[115] *Apocalypse of St Amand*, Bibliothèque de Valenciennes, MS 99, fols 23r, 24r (the Revelation Dragon), 25r, 31r (the Beast); cf. also 36r, 37r. The library conveniently offers a complete facsimile of the manuscript online. For the assimilation between the two creatures in this manuscript, see Kelly 1972:305.

[116] Cf. n. 92 above. At Athanasius of Alexandria *Life of Antony* 6 the Devil appears before Antony in the form of a black boy whilst the author designates him by the soubriquet he often applies to him, 'the *drakōn*'. An Armenian monastic apophthegm preserved in a xii AD manuscript reads as follows: 'Abba Avita [?] saw a dragon that had penetrated the desert. A black man was seated upon it. He heard a voice saying, "Darkness has come upon the desert, and gone is the sun of justice." He understood that the desert was bereft of good works' (Arm. ii 430 (79) A Regnault, after the French at Regnault 1977:271; cf. also Brakke 2001:508 n. 31).

[117] *Gospels of Hincmar*, Reims, Bibliothèque Municipale, MS 7, fols 15–20; cf. Palli 1968:521.

[118] Bernward doors, Hildesheim Cathedral, fourth panel down on the left.

Fig. 4.20 Wyvern decorating the canons of Eusebius. Gospels of Hincmar, later ix AD. Bibliothèque Carnegie de Reims, MS 7 fol. 19.2. © Bibliothèque Carnegie de Reims.

4.10 Coda: Two Legs Good, Four Legs Better

Let us return to Paul Acker, with whom we began the chapter. He suggests that *four*-legged dragons did not become the norm prior to *c.* AD 1500, citing the paintings of da Vinci and Raphael as early examples of the phenomenon.[119] I would prefer to pull the significant point of transition back a full century before this. The dragon images extant from these centuries and the surrounding ones are of course far too prolific to be fully encompassable—so how to begin to address the question seriously and systematically? The best way is to drill a fine but deep core out of the data, to serve as a sample and a proxy for the whole of it. An opportunity to do this has recently been given to us by Juliana Dresvina's magnificent survey of the tradition of St Margaret of Antioch in both literature and art. In her fine catalogue of images of Margaret and her dragon produced between the tenth and sixteenth centuries (about seventy examples), all the dragons remain two-legged until *c.* AD 1380–90, when a four-legged creature first emerges in a Keble College manuscript, and from this point on the four-legged variety clearly predominates until the end of the survey-period, whilst the two-legged variety never entirely disappears.[120] With less system, we may further point to some fine

---

[119] Acker 2013:53–4.
[120] Dresvina 2016:278–88; Oxford, Keble College 47. Of course this sampling method need not be fool-proof: it could be, for instance, that the iconography of Margaret's dragon developed to some extent within a micro-tradition of its own, rendering it poorly reflective of broader trends.

examples of pre-1500 four-legged dragons from other contexts too, beginning as early as the *c.* AD 1120 Leviathan of a Ghent manuscript, passing through the fine illuminations of the Boucicault Master, the Master of Sir John Fastolf, Willem Vrelant and Lieven van Lathem, and through Bernat Martorell's painting of *St George and the Dragon*, and concluding with the superb *c.* AD 1475 Languedoc-style gilt alabaster sculpture of St Margaret in the Met (Figs 4.21–4.30).[121] But here I return to a point I made towards the beginning of this chapter: in a world in which the form of the dragon is subject to constant innovation and experimentation at the hands of artists, we must not give undue weight to stray anticipations of configurations that subsequently become established. We may reaffirm the turn of the fourteenth to the fifteenth centuries, *c.* AD 1400, as the birth-point proper of the four-legged dragon.

[121] (1) Leviathan in a *c.* AD 1120 copy of Lambert's *Liber Floridus*, now in the University of Ghent: four sturdy legs support a fine green creature with a squat, scaly body, long, looping serpentine tail (on the end of which the Antichrist sits), wings, and an animalian head decorated with crest, horns, and tusks, from the mouth of which a plume of fire gratifyingly projects: Ghent, Universiteitsbibliotheek, MS 92 fol. 62v. (2) The dragon illustrated in the *Liber de natura bestiarum* in the British Library's Harley MS, dated to AD 1236–*c.*1250; the creature is elongated and linear, boasts two pairs of wings to match its two pairs of legs, and breathes fire: MS Harley 3244, fol. 59r (Fig. 4.21); the same *Liber* also contains magnificent wyverns at fols 39v (Fig. 4.1) and 58v, together with dragons, sea-serpents, and sea-monsters of varying configurations. (3) The dragon of a thirteenth-century Spanish tin-glazed earthenware tile: Metropolitan Museum of Art, 29.113.3 (Fig. 4.22). (4) The squat dragon topping an ivory dagger-hilt from Venice (*c.* AD 1300): Metropolitan Museum of Art, 29.158.658a. (5) The handsome, spotted dragon seizing Agnello Brunelleschi whilst Dante and Virgil attend in a Sienese manuscript of Dante's *Divine Comedy* accompanied by a commentary by Fra Guidone of Pisa (*c.* AD 1328–30): Musée Condé, Chantilly, MS 597 fol. 169v (illustrating *Inferno* canto xxxv). (6) The Revelation Dragon of an Italian painting in the Valencian style, *c.* AD 1405: Metropolitan Museum, New York, Rogers Fund, 1912, 12.192 (Fig. 4.23). (7) The dragon defeated by St George as drawn by the Boucicaut Master in the *Boucicaut Hours* (*c.* AD 1410–15): Musée Jacquemart-André, MS 2 fol. 23v. (8) The dragon trampled by St George in a chestnut-wood sculpture by Hans von Judenburg (*c.* AD 1400): Metropolitan Museum of Art, 64.280. (9) The dragons of the manuscript illustrations in the *Book of Hours* by the Master of Sir John Fastolf (*c.* AD 1430–40): Getty Museum, MS 57 (94.ML.26) fols 27v (St Michael—the dragon's body is rather that of a winged, black demon; Fig. 4.24), 33v (St George; Fig. 4.25). (10) The dragon painted by Bernat Martorell in his *Saint George and the Dragon* (AD 1434–5): Art Institute, Chicago, 1933.786 (Fig. 4.26). (11) The Revelation Dragon drawn by an unknown artist in a copy of Lambert of Saint-Omer's *Liber Floridus* (*c.*1448): Musée Condé, MS 724 fol. 14v. (12) The dragons of manuscript illustrations by Willem Vrelant in the *Arenberg Hours* (early AD 1460s): Getty Museum, MS Ludwig ix 8 (83.ML.104) fols 47 (St George; Fig. 4.27), 57 (St Margaret). (13) The dragons of manuscript illustrations of Sts George, Margaret, and Michael by Lieven van Lathem (AD 1471): Getty Museum, MS 37 (89.ML.35) fols 15v (Michael; Fig. 4.28), 49v (Margaret; Fig. 4.29), 67v (George). (14) The dragon by an unknown artist in a Languedoc-style gilt alabaster sculpture of St Margaret (*c.* AD 1475): Metropolitan Museum of Art, 2000.641 (Fig. 4.30).

Fig. 4.21 An early four-legged dragon (lower right), amongst friends (illumination). Illustrated in the *Liber de natura bestiarum*, AD 1236–*c*.1250. British Library, MS Harley 3244, fols 58v–59r. © British Library Board / Bridgeman Images.

Fig. 4.22 An early four-legged dragon (tile). Spanish, earthenware, tin-glazed tile, xiii AD. Metropolitan Museum, New York, Rogers Fund, 1929, 29.113.3. Public domain.

Fig. 4.23 Saint Michael battles the Revelation Dragon (painting). Italian painting in Valencian style, *c.* AD 1405. Metropolitan Museum, New York, Rogers Fund, 1912, 12.192. Public domain.

Fig. 4.24 Saint Michael battles the Revelation Dragon in the form of a winged demon (illumination). French or English, illustrated manuscript, Master of Sir John Fastolf, *c.* AD 1430–40. The J. Paul Getty Museum, MS 5 (84.ML.723), fol. 27v. Public domain.

Fig. 4.25 Saint George slays the dragon (illumination). French or English, illustrated manuscript, Master of Sir John Fastolf, *c.* AD 1430–40. The J. Paul Getty Museum, MS 5 (84.ML.723), fol. 33v. Public domain.

Fig. 4.26 Saint George slays the dragon (painting). Spanish, painting, Bernat Martorell, AD 1434–5. Art Institute of Chicago, Gift of Mrs Richard E. Danielson and Mrs Chauncey McCormick, 1933.786. Public domain.

Fig. 4.27 Saint George slays the dragon (illumination). Flemish, illustrated manuscript, Willem Vrelant, early AD 1460s. The J. Paul Getty Museum, MS Ludwig IX 8 (83.ML.104), fol. 47. Public domain.

Fig. 4.28 Saint Michael battles dragons (illumination). Flemish, illustrated manuscript, Lieven van Lathem, *c.* AD 1471. The J. Paul Getty Museum, MS 37 (89. ML.35), fol. 15v. Public domain.

Fig. 4.29 Saint Margaret and the Dragon of Antioch (illumination). Flemish, illustrated manuscript, Lieven van Lathem, *c.* AD 1471. The J. Paul Getty Museum, MS 37 (89.ML.35), fol. 49v. Public domain.

Fig. 4.30 Saint Margaret and the Dragon of Antioch (alabaster). French (Toulouse?), alabaster, gilded, *c.* AD 1475. Metropolitan Museum, New York, Gift of Anthony and Lois Blumka, in memory of Ruth Blumka, 2000, 2000.641. Public domain.

PART II
SAINTS

5

Scripture and Shape

5.1 Introduction: The Hagiographical Dragon Fight

The dragon fight is a commonplace episode in the vast hagiographical tradition. It made its first appearance in the *Lives* of the saints in the later second century BC and continued to thrive in them until the early modern age. These dragon episodes cannot be encompassed in their entirety: the number of potentially relevant *Lives* is vast, as, often, is the number of the variants in which they are preserved; many of them remain unpublished or inadequately published; and there is no satisfactory way to search out the relevant episodes systematically, even with the benefit of electronic databases.[1] Nonetheless, this second Part seeks to reconstruct the traditional sequences and motifs of saintly dragon-fight narratives on the basis of a catalogue of some two hundred of them, these drawn from across the full era of hagiography, principally in Greek and Latin.[2] It will be seen that, as a whole, they are remarkably conservative. A second-century AD reader would find little to surprise or challenge him in the narratives of the sixteenth century. A remarkable token of this conservatism consists in the fact that the dragon of hagiographical literature can rarely be seen to have abandoned the strictly anguiform or vermiform shape of classical antiquity, this despite the striking and elaborate evolution of its form in the parallel iconographic

---

[1] An indication of the proportion of the potentially relevant extant saints' *Lives* encompassed in this survey may be provided by the case of St Margaret. Here I have taken into account six versions of her life (see Appendix B); Dresvina's catalogue of all those versions known to her, in Greek, Latin, and the vernacular languages (2016:207–25) extends to forty-one. Admittedly, Margaret was exceptionally popular! On the more positive side, the variations in the details of the dragon story in these different accounts are fractional.

[2] This Part accordingly extends to a considerable degree the database and chronological parameters of the motival analyses of saintly dragon-fights in Rauer 2000 esp. 52–86, 174–93 (an outstanding piece of work); and Ogden 2013a:383–426, 2013b:187–256, and 2019a. Rauer's analysis was based upon a survey of sixty-three Latin narratives; my own earlier analyses on thirty-four Latin and Greek ones. Despite the impossibility of exhaustiveness, the want of serious and extensive catalogues of hagiographical dragon-fights is remarkable and deeply frustrating (a complaint I share with Susi 1995:108 n. 76 and Rauer 2000:52–3). Beyond Rauer one may look to the under-referenced lists at Cahier 1867:i, 314–22; Drake 1916:172–3; and Mackensen 1930:373; and to the brief article of Riches 2003 (written at a considerable distance from the evidence). The title of Mayer 1890 ('Über die Verwandschaft heidnischer und christlicher Drachentödter') is sadly misleading in this regard. There are several dragon-fighting saints in Cahier's list (of about seventy individuals), mainly French ones, for which I have not been able to pin down appropriate literary sources; it appears that he sometimes relies on local oral or iconographic traditions; for the latter note in particular Raison du Cleuziou and Couffon 1966.

traditions, as expounded in the previous chapter. Nonetheless, many individual narratives in the catalogue do exhibit interesting or witty variations in their handling of commonplace motifs.

Given the tricky nature of the source-material exploited in this Part (by classical standards, at any rate), and the need to refer to the same passages repeatedly within the course of the analysis, I have adopted a very particular referencing technique in what follows. The dragon-fight narratives (which are typically about a paragraph in length each, but can on occasion extend over several pages) are identified here, either in the main text or in the footnotes, simply in terms of their saintly hero. If more than one narrative relating to a particular saint falls within the frame of our discussion, then these are differentiated alphabetically: 'Samson ([a])', 'Samson ([b])', etc. The citations may be decoded with reference to Appendix B, where the saints discussed are catalogued, and the relevant texts, their publication details, the specific chapter and verse in question and their dates, precise or approximate, are supplied. Indications of the dates are also generally supplied in the main text and the notes.[3] (I have seldom felt the need to supply the dates for the age in which the saints in question lived, or were supposed to have done so.[4])

5.2 Scriptural Catalysts

The Old Testament and the New are replete with dragons and dragon fights of one kind or another. This fact in itself justifies the prominence of the dragon fight also in hagiography. The saint that fights a dragon not only thereby inscribes himself in a most sacred tradition, he also demonstrates the enduring nature of God's order. But, more specifically, the deeds and gestures of both dragons and saints in the hagiographical stories are to a certain extent bricolaged from biblical narratives and utterances. And beyond this the relevant biblical passages are often cited directly by the hagiographical narrators, or even put into the dragon-fighting saints' own mouths as they present themselves for the fight. The following passages are of particular importance, as we look through the Old Testament, its Apocrypha, and then the New Testament.[5]

[3] Many of these dates indeed remain quite conjectural, as noted by Rauer 2000:58–9. In some of the obscurer cases I have often depended on lapidary reference works of the sort provided by Blatt et al. 1973 and Deckers 1995 in my attempts to pin them down.

[4] Historical and biographical information about the saints in question is most easily accessed, in the first instance, through *Bibliotheca sanctorum* 1961–70, in which most of the individuals in our catalogue are accorded entries; information about their *Vitae* is offered on a patchy basis.

[5] For dragons in the Bible in general, see Beaude 2000. Joines 1974 and Charlesworth 2010:269-351, 425-51 discuss serpent symbolism in the Old Testament. For the use of the terms *drakōn* and *ophis* in the New Testament, see Foerster 1935 and Foerster et al. 1957.

5.2.1 Leviathan

Isaiah's reference to God's aboriginal slaying of the cosmic sea-monster Leviathan becomes a particularly apposite precedent for our saints when considered in its Septuagint rendition:

> On that day God will ply his sword, holy, great, and strong against the dragon-snake [*drakōn ophis*] as he tries to escape, against the twisting dragon-snake, and he will kill the dragon.   LXX, Isaiah 27:1[6]

So it is that Ammon (*c*. AD 395 and *c*. AD 403/4) invokes the precedent of this slaughter before bursting open the Dragon of the Egyptian Desert, and that Margaret reminds God that he 'extinguished the power of the great dragon' as she asks for his help against the dragon that confronts her in her martyr-cell ([b], early ix AD or before). The tradition bearing upon Martha ([a], AD 1187), however, engages with this locus in a rather different way: the Tarasque-dragon she defeats is said to have been the very child of Leviathan, the 'water serpent' (*serpens aquosus*; so too [c], AD 1263–7, [d], 1264).

5.2.2 The Serpent of Eden

At the head of the Bible stands the Serpent of Eden, described as an *ophis* in the Septuagint and a *serpens* in Jerome's Vulgate.[7] In our very first hagiographical dragon fight proper, that of the *Acts of Thomas*, the Dragon of India, compelled to confess its outrages by the apostle Thomas (later ii AD), immediately declares its identity with this serpent: 'I am the one who entered Paradise through the fence and said to Eve everything my father commanded me to say to her.'[8] Thereafter the authors of the dragon fights or the saints featured within them frequently make an alignment between the Eden serpent the dragon in hand.[9] The identification

---

[6] Τῇ ἡμέρᾳ ἐκείνῃ ἐπάξει ὁ θεὸς τὴν μάχαιραν τὴν ἁγίαν καὶ τὴν μεγάλην καὶ τὴν ἰσχυρὰν ἐπὶ τὸν δράκοντα ὄφιν φεύγοντα, ἐπὶ τὸν δράκοντα ὄφιν σκολιὸν καὶ ἀνελεῖ τὸν δράκοντα. For a complete set of references to Leviathan and Rahab in the Hebrew Bible and their reflexes in the Septuagint and Jerome's Vulgate, see Chapter 4, §4.4; for these monsters in their biblical context, see Day 1977 and Batto 1992; for their Near Eastern and Indo-European analogues, see Appendix A; for Leviathan in later Judaism, see Whitney 2006 and Charlesworth 2010:436-7.

[7] Genesis 3:1–20; in Hebrew, *nachash*, שׁחַנָ. Discussions: Cassuto 1961:138–77; Joines 1974:2–3, 16–41, 1975; Morris and Sawyer 1992; Stordalen 2000; Charlesworth 2010:437-9. More generally, see Joines 1974:1–15 and Charlesworth 2010:425–51 for the Hebrew Bible's full lexis of serpent terms.

[8] For the context and the dating of this interesting text, see Chapter 8, §8.1.

[9] Thus: Andrew ([a], late vi AD) and the Dragon of Thessalonica; Caluppan (AD 581–94) and the principal dragon that attacks him in his Cantal cell; Lifard (ix AD) and the Dragon of Meung-sur-Loire; Paulus Aurelianus ([a], AD 884) and the Dragon of the Isle of Battha (Batz); and Vindemialis (xii AD or before) and the Dragon of Vado.

can be peculiarly pointed when the antagonist standing before the dragon is female. When Jesus prepares the apostle Philip ([a], mid- to late iv AD) and his team to take on the Viper-goddess and the serpents of the land of Ophiorhyme, he advises Mariamne to dress as a man rather than as a woman, the form of Eve, so that the serpents will not attempt to exploit her as a means of deceiving others, as they had done with Eve herself. In this we have an aetiology of the masculine dress of the Encratite nuns. And when, in due course, the team encounters the Dragon of the Rocks outside Ophiorhyme, the beast does accordingly claim identity with the Serpent of Eden. Eustratius explicitly compares the deployment by the Devil, a dragon himself, of the Babylonian dragon against Golinduch ([b], vi–vii AD) with his prior deployment of the Serpent of Eden against Eve.[10]

5.2.3 Trampling on Snakes

Three biblical passages of importance evoke the imagery of serpent-trampling. In Genesis God condemns the Serpent of Eden with the following words:

> You will travel on your breast and your belly and eat earth all the days of your life. And I shall establish a hatred between you and the woman and between your seed and hers. Man will be wary of your head, and you will be wary of his heel.   LXX, Genesis 3:15

In the Psalms King David prophesies to the faithful: 'You will step upon the asp and the basilisk, and you will trample on the lion and the *drakōn*.'[11] Luke's Jesus then resumes the promise to his own converts: 'See, I have given you the power to trample on snakes [*opheis*] and scorpions, and upon all the enemy's strength, and he will be able to harm you in no way.'[12] The gesture of the trampling of the neck ('*calcatio colli*') actually has a wider currency in the Bible, and is applied also to vanquished humans. For example, Joshua bids his soldiers trample on the necks

---

[10] We shall not have cause to discuss here the influential portrayal of the Serpent of Eden as a female anguipede by Petrus Comestor/Manducator ('Peter the Eater') in his AD 1170 *Historia scholastica* 1.21; he seemingly attributes the configuration spuriously to Bede (1.21, *PL* cxcii, 1072).

[11] Psalms 91:13: *drakōn* in the Septuagint (ἐπ' ἀσπίδα καὶ βασιλίσκον ἐπιβήσῃ καὶ καταπατήσεις λέοντα καὶ δράκοντα); *draco* in Jerome's Vulgate (in both of which the Psalm is numbered 90). The Hebrew has only a single term corresponding directly to 'asp and basilisk', *pethen* (פֶּתֶן); *drakōn* renders *tannin* (תַּנִּין); cf. Chapter 4, §4.4. In his (iv AD) *Commentary on Job* Didymus the Blind embellishes the list in speaking of the forms in which the Devil can manifest himself: lion, *drakōn*, snake, beast, *kētos* (*PG* xxxix, col. 1129). Christ himself is depicted as trampling on a lion and a dragon in a fine pair of images from Ravenna, a stucco panel from the Orthodox Baptistery (v AD) and the mosaic in the lunette of the *c.* AD 500 Archiepiscopal Chapel: see Quacquarelli 1975:108–9.

[12] Luke 10:19; *serpentes* in the Vulgate.

of the five kings of the Amorites.[13] But its peculiar appropriateness to serpentine enemies, who might be conceptualized as just one big neck, is self-evident.

The imagery was popular with patristic authors,[14] and is already taken up in one of our earliest hagiographical texts, the *Passion of Sts Perpetua and Felicitas* (AD 203). Here Perpetua recounts her famous vision of the ladder to heaven:

> I saw a bronze ladder of marvellous height. Its height reached to heaven. It was narrow, so that no one could climb up it except in single file. Into the sides of the ladder was fixed every kind of iron blade: swords, spears, hooks, knives, and darts. So if anyone were to climb up it in careless fashion or without fixing his gaze upwards, he would be gored and his flesh would cleave to the blades. Under the ladder itself lay a *drakōn* of miraculous size, which came out and attacked people as they tried to climb up and deterred them from attempting to do it. Now Saturus went up first, the one who subsequently gave himself up for us (for we were in the house that he himself had built). But he had not been present at the time we were arrested. When he reached the top of the ladder he turned and said, 'Perpetua, I will help you up. But make sure that that dragon doesn't bite you.' I said, 'It will not harm me, in the name of Jesus Christ.' Hesitantly, as if afraid of me, the creature stuck its head out from underneath the ladder. I trod upon its head as if it were the first step, and mounted up. I saw an enormous garden, and in the middle of it a tall, grey-haired man in the dress of a shepherd, and he was milking his sheep. Many thousands of people in white stood around him. He lifted his head, looked at me and said, 'You did well to come, child.'
>
> *Passion of Sts Perpetua and Felicitas* 4.3–9

Trampling on the dragon is the first, the most challenging, and the most distinctive step in the stairway to heaven.[15] Prudentius (later iv AD) was subsequently to imagine another female martyr, Agnes, already established in heaven, trampling with her heel the fierce dragon that spews its venom over all worldly things and plunges them into hell, and compelling it to lower its fiery crest.[16]

The imagery thrives at the heart of many hagiographical dragon-fight narratives and occasionally informs the actual action of them also. Sometimes the author will make the connection in his own voice, as when Eustratius reminds us, as he narrates Golinduch's ([b], vi–vii AD) encounter with the Dragon of Babylon,

---

[13] Joshua 10:24; cf. Psalms 67:22 and 109:1 (LXX; 68:21 and 110:1 King James). Discussion at Dresvina 2016:173–8.

[14] See Quacquarelli 1975 passim.

[15] For the *Passion of Sts Perpetua and Felicity*, see the detailed edition and commentary of Heffernan 2012, esp. 167–84; see also Amat 1996; White 2008:153–7; Bremmer and Formisano 2012; Gold 2018; and, for the dragon in particular, Godding 2000. Augustine celebrates the episode at *Sermon* 280: 'And so the dragon was trampled by the chaste foot' (*calcatus est ergo draco pede casto*). For the iconographical reflex of Perpetua's trampling, see Dresvina 2016:176–7.

[16] Prudentius *Peristephanon* 14.111–17.

that Christ gave us the power to 'trample on snakes and scorpions'. The narrator of Vindemialis' (xii AD or before) battle against the Dragon of Vado interestingly speaks of the saint trampling on two dragons at once: the Vado Dragon itself, and the Revelation Dragon that is somehow inherent within it.

But often the saints themselves in their stories can be shown to be self-consciously aware of the biblical passages as they act. Examples abound. The Christian brothers associated with Ammon (c. AD 395 and c. AD 403/4), for whom dragon-slaying is almost a sport, cite the promise of Luke's Jesus directly to explain the confidence they have in their activities. Honoratus ([a], before AD 449) cleanses the future Île Saint-Honorat (in the Lérins group off the coast of Cannes) of its host of serpents whilst proclaiming the promises of both the Psalms' David and Luke's Jesus. Margaret of Antioch ([d], x AD) is fortified in her fight against the dragon that manifests itself before her in her martyr cell by recollection of the same Lukan promise. Vigor of Bayeux (AD 1030–45) tells Velosianus that Jesus has given him the power to trample serpents and scorpions (à la Luke) as he proceeds to take on the Dragon of the Cerisy Forest, but then reminds the dragon itself that Jesus had given his followers the capacity to trample on asp, basilisk, lion, and dragon (à la David).[17]

Beyond this, the saints sometimes make explicit the link between their metaphorical 'trampling' of the contingent dragon in hand and the need similarly to 'trample' the Great Dragon, the Devil himself. As Elisabeth ('the Thaumaturge') of Thracian Heraclea ([a], ix–x AD) destroys the Dragon of Constantinople, she directly quotes David's prophecy and finds reassurance in it: 'From that point her hopes were high, one might say, and she developed the firm conviction that, with the support of Christ, she could be victorious over the spiritual dragon just as has she had been over this physical one, and embarked upon her miracle-working boldly.'[18] Theodore Tyron ([g], AD 980–1010) declares that he will trample on the Dragon of Euchaita before killing it with his lance; he then declares that just as God has given him the power to overcome this dragon of the material world,

---

[17] Further examples may be supplied. When Syrus of Genoa (v AD, perhaps with post-ix AD accretions) extracts a pestilential basilisk from its well, its mouth stopped, the gathered crowd heaps praise upon him, recognizing that he is the realization of David's prophecy. Joannicius of Bithynia ([a], AD 846) sings David's psalm as he kills the Dragon of Prusa with his cross. As he goes up against the Dragon of September Island, Machutus (AD 866–72) reminds his comrades that Jesus has given his disciples the power to trample on serpents and scorpions. As Paulus Aurelianus ([a], AD 884) approaches the Dragon of the Isle of Battha (Batz), he bears in mind the Lukan promise. As Maglorius (ix–x AD) goes up against the Dragon of Jersey he prays and reminds God, not entirely accurately, that he had commanded 'women's feet to trample on the serpent's scaly neck' (the words of Genesis are somewhat kaleidoscoped here). Rofillus ([a], xi AD) exhorts Mercurialis to trample—metaphorically—on the Dragon of Forlimpopoli with him. Paris (AD 1533 or before) goes up against the Dragon of Teano in the confidence that Jesus has given his followers the ability to trample on serpents and scorpions.

[18] καὶ τὸν νοητὸν δράκοντα ὡς τὸν αἰσθητὸν τοῦτον.... For Elisabeth, her *Lives*, and her dragon, see White 2008:163–7.

so too he has given him the power to smash the head of the dragon of the immaterial one.

Occasionally the trampling becomes literal, as in other traditions relating to Theodore Tyron, in which he tramples on the carcass of the slain Dragon of Euchaita so that the Euchaitans will have the courage to approach it ([d], *c.* AD 871). Some accounts ([b], late ix AD or before; [c], late ix AD; [f], x AD) offer a particularly delightful treatment of this motif. After praying to God for support against the dragon, Theodore addresses his horse, which understands human speech (at this point at any rate), and instructs it to trample the dragon with its four hooves, which it proceeds to do enthusiastically, before he finishes it off with his sword or lance. He reassures the horse that God protects animals as much as He does humans ([c] only).[19] Thomas Defourkinos (xii AD) quotes the Lukan tag back at God and proceeds to enact the exhortation in a striking way, as he seals his victory over the Dragon of the river Sangarius: with God's help the serpent is drawn down into a ravine, and then buried beneath the ravine's two flanking hills, which collapse in on top of it, creating a plain the saint can then walk over (see Chapter 6, §6.5.4).

A passage of Mark also deserves brief notice here. The risen Jesus tells his followers that they will cast out demons in his name, speak in tongues, and lift up snakes. For all that this gesture would appear to be almost the reverse of that of trampling on snakes, it nonetheless aligns the creatures with demons, an alignment that becomes particularly important in the world of hagiography.[20]

5.2.4 Moses, Aaron, and the Dragon-Staffs

Exodus tells how God (speaking through the burning bush) gives Moses a means to demonstrate to others that He has appeared to him. He commands Moses to throw his staff down on the ground, whereupon it becomes a snake (*ophis*, in the Septuagint). Moses flees from it, but then, at God's bidding, picks it up by the tail, whereupon it turns back into a staff.[21] Subsequently, Moses and his brother Aaron perform the demonstration before Pharaoh (Fig. 5.1):

---

[19] The notion of a horse trampling a dragon reminds us of the iconography of the 'Christian rider', for which see Chapter 9, §9.2.

[20] Mark 16:17–18: ἐν τῷ ὀνόματί μου δαιμόνια ἐκβαλοῦσιν, γλώσσαις λαλήσουσιν καιναῖς, [καὶ ἐν ταῖς χερσὶν] ὄφεις ἀροῦσιν.... This is the biblical text that underpins the practice of snake-handling in Appalachian Pentecostal churches. A sympathetic documentary film may be found in Peter Adair's *Holy Ghost People* (1967). In her 2016 cognitive study of Greek religion Larson briefly contends that, given that fear of snakes is a human universal, snake-handling can be understood to be a means of heightening arousal in ritual contexts (238 n. 159).

[21] Exodus 4:1–5. In Hebrew *nachash* (נָחָשׁ) once again.

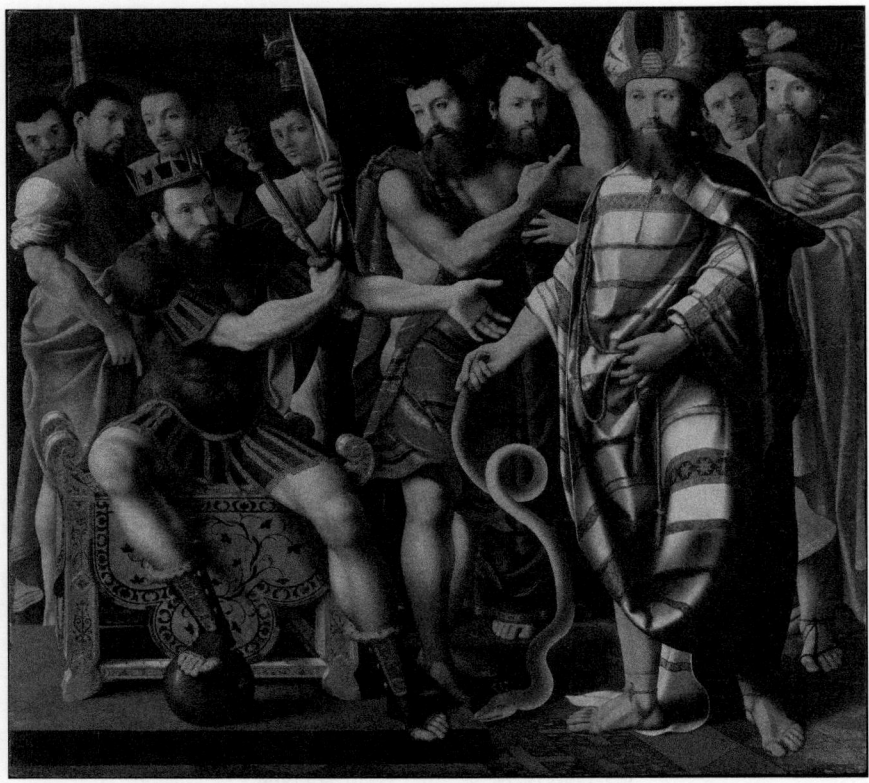

Fig. 5.1 Moses and Aaron before Pharaoh: An Allegory of the Dinteville Family. Flemish or French, painting, AD 1537. Metropolitan Museum, New York, Wentworth Fund, 1950, 50.70. Public domain.

And the Lord spoke to Moses and Aaron, saying: 'If Pharaoh speaks to you, saying, "Give me a sign or a miracle!", then tell your brother Aaron, "Take your staff and throw it on the ground before Pharaoh and before his servants, and it will become a *drakōn*."'[22] Moses and Aaron came before Pharaoh and his servants and they did just as the Lord had bidden them. Aaron threw his staff down before Pharaoh and before his servants, and it became a *drakōn*. Pharaoh summoned the tricksters [*sophistai*] and sorcerers [*pharmakoi*] of Egypt, and the enchanters [*epaoidoi*] of the Egyptians did exactly the same by means of their sorceries. Each of them threw down his staff, and they became *drakontes*. The staff of Aaron gobbled down their staffs. And so Pharaoh's heart hardened, and he failed to heed them, just as the Lord had told them.   LXX, Exodus 7:8–13

[22] In Hebrew *tannin*.

This interesting episode has only a limited *direct* impact on the hagiographical dragon-fight tradition. We may, however, point to the encounter of Philip ([a], mid- to late iv AD) with the Dragon of the Rocks and his cohorts outside Ophiorhyme. Whilst the principal dragon declares his identity with the Serpent of Eden, he declares that his fifty subordinate dragons are, precisely, the staffs of Pharaoh's sorcerers. We may also point to two possible *indirect* impacts on the tradition: first, the saints' frequent deployment of their (inert) staffs against their dragon opponents (see Chapter 6, §6.6.3); and, secondly, the narrative subroutine in which a saint stands before his or her tormentor and the tormentor summons his sorcerers to unloose dragons and serpents against them (see Chapter 7, §7.5).

5.2.5 Jonah's Sea-Monster

Jonah's sea-monster (cf. Chapter 4, §4.4) is invoked as a precedent less often than one might have expected, but then, even if the monster offered a broadly suitable template in its form and in its swallowing of Jonah, there had been no destruction of this ultimately benign creature, which John Chrysostom would even describe as Jonah's 'host', or triumphing over it.[23] However, God's deliverance of Golinduch ([b], vi–vii AD) from the Dragon of Babylon as it tries to devour her is compared by Eustratius to his protection of Jonah in the belly of the sea-monster. And as he makes to slay the Dragon of King Samuel's City, Theodore Tyron ([h], xiv AD) evokes in precedent the fact that God had not allowed Jonah to be burned up whilst he was in the belly of the sea-monster. It is not clear whether the author intends by this to make the sober point that Jonah was not digested, or whether, as is perhaps more likely, he holds that the sea-monster, strongly assimilated to a dragon-proper, was a creature of fire and blew forth this fire from the furnace of its belly.

5.2.6 Fiery Snakes

Neither the Septuagint nor Jerome's Vulgate preserves the fieriness of Isaiah's (viii–vii BC) fiery flying snakes of the Negev Desert (the term is *saraph*, literally 'coal'; cf. Chapter 4, §4.6).[24] In Numbers (v BC?), God sends fiery snakes amongst the Israelites, and in Deuteronomy (vii BC) he leads them through a wilderness infested with them. In both contexts the Hebrew deploys the term *saraph* again and also *nachash* ('snake'). Whilst the Septuagint again fails to acknowledge the fieriness in these two cases (Numbers: 'deadly snakes', *opheis thanatountas*;

---

[23] John Chrysostom *On Psalm 75, PG* lv, 598 (*xenos*).   [24] Isaiah 30:6.

Deuteronomy: 'biting snake', *ophis daknōn*), it is preserved in the Vulgate's renderings (Numbers: 'fiery serpents', *ignitos serpentes*; Deuteronomy: 'the serpent that burns with its breath', *serpens flatu adurens*).[25] The Vulgate surely did much to support the characteristic fieriness of the hagiographical dragon in due course, though it was hardly indispensable in this regard, given the well-established fiery nature of the classical dragon: it is noteworthy that we find a superb fiery dragon already in the *Acts of Philip* ([a], mid- to late iv A D), composed before Jerome set to work (the relevant passage is laid out in Chapter 6, §6.1.4).

5.2.7 The Enemies of the Jews and John the Baptist

The Hebrew Ezekiel (perhaps vi B C) compares Pharaoh to a *tannin*, a sea-monster, in the Nile (cf. Chapter 4, §4.4). The passage would be of little interest to us, were it not that the Septuagint turns him into a *drakōn* and the Vulgate duly into a *draco*.[26] The expansive Hebrew version of Jeremiah we possess is actually thought to post-date the briefer Septuagint version. In a passage found in the Hebrew but not the Greek, the same Hebrew term is deployed as God declares that Nebuchadnezzar has swallowed him down like a *tannin*.[27] The Vulgate then turns Nebuchadnezzar too correspondingly into a *draco*.

As we move into the New Testament, when Matthew's John the Baptist notices a great many Pharisees and Saducees presenting themselves to him for baptism, he rails against them: 'Offspring of vipers [*gennēmata echidnōn*], who warned you to flee before the coming wrath?'[28] This language is then picked up by his Jesus himself, who asks the scribes and Pharisees, 'Snakes and offspring of vipers [*opheis gennēmata echidnōn*], how are you to escape the judgment of Gehenna?'[29] This phraseology is seemingly refracted in the description of the brood associated with the Dragon of the Ophiorhyme Desert destroyed by Philip ([a], mid- to late iv A D), where the creature is said to be attended by 'a host of snakes and a host of the children of snakes' (*plēthos opheōn kai plēthos ekgonōn tōn opheōn*). At a further remove it may inspire other hagiographical episodes in which a saint takes on not merely a single dragon but actually a host of serpents (for which see Chapter 7, §7.1).

No doubt this outburst on John the Baptist's part, together with the Gospels' accounts of his preparatory sojourn in the desert,[30] led to the development of the

---

[25] Numbers 21:6; Deuteronomy 8:15; cf. Joines 1974:7-8, 42-9.

[26] Ezekiel 29:3.   [27] Jeremiah 51:34.

[28] Matthew 3:7: γεννήματα ἐχιδνῶν, τίς ὑπέδειξεν ὑμῖν φυγεῖν ἀπὸ τῆς μελλούσης ὀργῆς; He delivers exactly the same rhetorical question at Luke 3:7, although the explanatory context is less clear there. The words became iconic in the Middle Ages, opening, for example, the *Physiologus*' discussion of the viper: *Physiologus* (first Greek recension) 10; (first Latin recension) 12.

[29] Matthew 23:33: ὄφεις γεννήματα ἐχιδνῶν, πῶς φύγητε ἀπὸ τῆς κρίσεως τῆς γεέννης; Cf. Matthew 12:34, γεννήματα ἐχιδνῶν again.

[30] Matthew 3:1-9; Mark 1:1-8; Luke 3:1-20; John 1:19-28.

post-biblical tradition found in John Chrysostom that 'the *drakontes* and the asps and the horned snakes trembled before John in the desert'.[31] The notion is picked up directly in Sabas' account of Joannicius' attempt to mortify his flesh by throwing himself before the Dragon of Cunduria ([b], before AD 860): 'But this beast felt shame before him, just as of old the asps and the *drakontes* and the horned snakes had bowed down before the Baptist'.[32] At a more general level it may inform the many episodes in which dragons are reduced to passivity or even fawning before their saints (Chapter 6, §6.4.3).

Finally, two examples of the direct exploitation of the Baptist's power over serpents deserve mention. A spectacular example is the use of the thumb bitten from his relic hand to destroy the Dragon of Antioch (John the Baptist [a], x AD). A less spectacular one is the opportunity provided by his feast-day to fumigate against flying dragons ([b], AD 1263–7).

5.2.8 Daniel and the Dragon of Babylon

The apocryphal Old Testament book of Bel and the Dragon (ii BC), surviving in Greek only, had told the spectacular tale of Daniel's destruction of the (first) Dragon of Babylon (Fig. 5.2):[33]

> And there was a great dragon [*drakōn*] and the Babylonians worshipped it. And the king [Cyrus the Great] said to Daniel: 'You will not be able to say that this is not a living god [sc. in contrast to the idol of Bel]. Do obeisance before it!' And Daniel said to Cyrus, 'I will do obeisance before my God, because he is the living God. But king, give me the authorization, and I will kill the dragon without knife or staff.' And the king said, 'I give it you.' And Daniel took pitch and fat and hair and boiled them until they congealed. He then made cakes [*mazai*] and gave them into the mouth of the dragon. Upon eating them the dragon burst open. And Daniel said, 'Behold the object of your worship!'
>
> LXX, Bel and the Dragon (Theodotion version) 23–7

The cakes evidently work by means of at once intensifying the dragon's internal heat and sealing it in. This tale was taken up into the hagiographical tradition in different ways. As with the other biblical dragons, the precedent of the

[31] John Chrysostom Εἰς τὴν ὄρχησιν τῆς Ἡρωδιάδος, καὶ εἰς τὴν ἀποτομὴν τῆς κεφαλῆς Ἰωάννου τοῦ Προδρόμου καὶ Βαπτιστοῦ (*In decollationem sancti Joannis*), PG lix, col. 486: δράκοντες καὶ ἀσπίδες καὶ κεράσται τὸν Ἰωάννην ἐν τῇ ἐρήμῳ ἐτρόμασαν. Cf. the commentary on Psalm 139 spuriously attributed to Chrysostom, PG lx, col. 707: δράκοντες καὶ κεράσται καὶ ἀσπίδες τὸν ἄνδρα ᾐσχύνοντο.

[32] Ἀλλ' οὖν καὶ τούτου τοῦ θηρὸς αἰδεσθέντος, ὡς τὸν Βαπτιστὴν πάλαι ἀσπίδες καὶ δράκοντες ἔπτηξαν καὶ κεράσται.

[33] For discussion of this text, see Goodman 2001:126–8.

Fig. 5.2 Daniel and the Dragon of Babylon. South Netherlandish glass roundel, in the style of Pseudo-Ortkens, *c.* AD 1520. Metropolitan Museum, New York, The Cloisters Collection, 1932, 32.24.49. Public domain.

destruction of the Dragon of Babylon could be invoked in a merely generic way. Thus, as Theodore Tyron ([d], *c.* AD 871) destroys the Dragon of Euchaita, he compares himself to Daniel in his destruction of the Dragon of Babylon with his ball of pitch. Sometimes the invocation could be paired with an invocation of the more canonical and more famous episode of Daniel's plight in the lions' den.[34] So it is that Vindemialis (xii AD or before) aligns himself with Daniel as he goes into battle with the Dragon of Vado: he both compares himself in his approach to the dragon's cave with Daniel entering the lions' den, and compares the dragon itself to the Dragon of Babylon. Magnus of Füssen ([a], *c.* AD 895) goes further. The saint verbally compares his plight before the Dragon of Kempten to that of Daniel in the lions' den, but he then proceeds to kill the dragon in just the same way as Daniel had the Dragon of Babylon, namely with a ball of pitch and resin. Eustratius' *Life* of Golinduch ([b], both vi–vii AD) engages more tightly still with

---

[34] Daniel 6.

this precedent: the dragon this lady saint has to face in Babylon is strongly projected as the successor in office to Daniel's dragon (cf. Chapter 7, §7.7).

5.2.9 Paul in Malta

Luke gives the following episode to Paul in Malta:

Paul gathered together a mass of dry sticks and put them on a pyre. A viper [*echidna*], escaping from the heat, latched onto his hand. When the Maltese saw the creature hanging from his hand, they said to each other, 'By all means this man is a murderer. Although he has been saved from the sea, justice has not allowed him to live.' But he shook the creature off into the fire and suffered no harm. They expected that he was about to become inflamed [*pimprasthai*] or suddenly fall down dead. But as they anticipated this and watched him for a long time, and nothing untoward happened, they changed their opinion and said he was a god.   Acts 28:3–6

Although not explicitly referenced in hagiographical dragon-fight sequences, this scene arguably plays a part in their formulation. On the one hand, the saints occasionally have to go up against vipers (*echidnai*), as well as *drakontes* (see below, §5.3). On the other, as we shall see, the saints sometimes drive their dragons onto pyres, and beyond that burn them up by a variety of methods (Chapter 6, §6.6.2). This technique of disposal mirrors the burning with which serpents and dragons themselves threaten their victims, a point well made already in this passage.[35]

5.2.10 Abysses and the Dragon of Revelation

Let us return to Psalm 148's puzzling exhortation to '*drakontes* and all abysses [*abyssoi*]' to 'praise the Lord from the earth', mentioned in the previous chapter in connection with Augustine's commentary on it (Chapter 4, §4.8).[36] The phrase is knowingly quoted by Eustratius in his *Life of Golinduch* ([b], vi–vii AD) in association with her battle against the Dragon of Babylon.

---

[35] In a brief passing reference at *Golden Legend* 95 Jacobus de Voragine (AD 1263–7) transposes the site of this episode from Malta to Mytilene.

[36] LXX, Psalms 148 l:7: αἰνεῖτε τὸν κύριον ἐκ τῆς γῆς, δράκοντες καὶ πᾶσαι ἄβυσσοι. The Hebrew original deploys the terms *tannin* and *tehom* (תהום), respectively, *tehom* being the embodiment of the primordial sea. The phrase may have a very ancient resonance. Barb 1966, esp. 5 and 10, suggests that the Greek term *abyssos* is ultimately derivative of the Babylonian 'Apsu', the lover of the multiheaded sea-monster or indeed dragon Tiamat (*Enūma eliš* tablets i–iv; see Appendix A). One wonders whether the Hebrew and the Greek phrases alike effectively strive to salute a primeval pair of this sort.

But before Golinduch and the world of hagiography the bond between dragon and abyss enshrined in the phrase presumably had a role in shaping the imagery of the Book of Revelation, which is striking if, again, somewhat baffling. Here a great red *drakōn* with seven heads, seven crowns, and ten horns stands against a woman giving birth (the Church, according to Hippolytus and Augustine), ready to devour her child. The archangel Michael and his fellow angels make war upon the dragon and cast it down to the land, where it pursues the woman. It belches forth a river from its mouth to carry her away, but the earth opens up to swallow the water.[37] Eventually Michael seals the dragon into the abyss (Figs 4.23–4, 4.27):

> And I saw an angel coming down from heaven, with the key of the abyss and a large chain in his hand. He conquered the *drakōn*, the ancient snake [*ophis*], that is the Devil or Satan, and bound him for a thousand years. He cast it into the abyss, and locked it in, making a seal over it, so that it should no longer lead the races of men astray before the completion of the thousand years.
>
> Revelation 20:1–3[38]

As we have seen, the (late iv AD) *Questions of Bartholomew*'s reflex of this dragon, Beliar, is actually identified as 'the *drakōn* of the abyss' (Chapter 4, §4.8).

The Dragon of Revelation is directly invoked as a precedent relatively rarely in hagiographical dragon fights. We may point to the prayer made by Theodore Tyron ([d], *c.* AD 871) before joining battle with the Dragon of Euchaita: he calls upon God's help on the basis that He had bound the Revelation Dragon in the abyss. And, as we have noted, the Dragon of Vado fought by Vindemialis (xii AD or before) is partly identified with the Revelation Dragon: 'for that dragon [of Revelation] had come to inhere in the likeness of this one.' Of this more below (Chapter 6, §6.5.1).

Nonetheless, the model of the Dragon of Revelation lurks behind every episode—and there are a great many of these—in which a saint sends his dragon opponent into the abyss, whether conceived of as a land-based chasm or as watery depths, and every episode—and there are a great many of these too—in which a saint binds his dragon (see Chapter 6, §§6.5.4–7, for these themes). Nor can one avoid thinking of the Dragon of Revelation in those tales in which the archangel Michael returns for an encore of his greatest hit, as when he kills the Dragon of Southern Asia with his fiery sword, hacking it into twelve portions ([a], ix–x AD; cf. [c], xii AD or before) or the Dragon of Mt Garganus in Campania, hacking this one up rather into nine portions ([b], xi AD).[39]

---

[37] Revelation, esp. 12–13; Jerome's Vulgate deploys the terms *draco* and *serpens*. Hippolytus *On Christ and Antichrist* 61; Methodius *Banquet of the Ten Virgins* 8.5–7; Augustine *City of God* 20.8.
[38] For general discussion of the Revelation Dragon, see Koch 2004.
[39] For the archangel Michael in the hagiographical tradition (particularly in Britain and Britany), see Laporte et al. 1965–72; and Rauer 2000:116–24.

5.3 Dragon Terminology

The dragons of our saintly narratives are overwhelmingly defined by the familiar term *drakōn* on the Greek side, as first in the case of Thomas (later ii AD), and most typically on the Latin side by the term derived from it, *draco*. However, as with classical material, Latin often also substitutes *draco* with its indigenous and slightly broader term, *serpens*. Occasionally, as again with the classical material, further terms signifying 'snake' more broadly are employed for what are manifestly dragons, and quite appropriately so when the broods of the lesser reptiles that accompany the great dragons are described (mainly *ophis* in Greek; *anguis*, *coluber*, or *vermis*, 'worm', in Latin; see Chapter 7, §7.1).[40]

When terms beyond these are used, the principal purpose on the authors' part is to celebrate the breadth of their lexis. So it is, for example, when Aldhelm applies the following generous suite of terms to what are evidently the quite standard *dracones* faced by Silvester ([c], [d]), Hilarion ([b], [c]), and Victoria ([b], [c]) in the prose and poetic versions of his *On Virginity* (AD 675–710): *draco*, *serpens*, *coluber*, *boa* ('ox-snake'), *natrix* ('water-snake'), *gypsa* ('?'), *chelidrus* ('water-snake'), *basiliscus* ('basilisk').[41] The only terms in this list sometimes deployed with a degree of meaningful specificity are *boa* and *basiliscus*. Boa-dragons can be said to devour oxen (*boves*; cf. Chapter 6, §6.1.1). The *basiliscus* faced by Pope Leo IV ([a], before c. AD 939; cf. [b], c. AD 939) is described as sporting a cock's crest (of this more anon) and as being able to kill people with its vision as well as with its breath.[42]

An important subcategory of dragon or a creature closely associated with it is the *echidna*, the viper. These are encountered by Jesus himself ([a], ii–vi AD), Philip ([a], mid- to late iv AD), and Joannicius of Bithynia ([a], AD 846). The noun *echidna* is feminine but, beyond this, *echidnas* seem to be characterized in these saintly contexts as distinctively female, setting up a contrast with masculine and male *drakontes*. The key example is the viper-goddess Echidna of Ophiorhyme plunged into the abyss by Philip ([a], mid- to late iv AD), who is described also by

---

[40] *Angues* are faced by Caluppan (AD 581–94), Amand of Mastricht ([a], viii AD), Germanus (xi–xii AD), and Lifard (ix AD); *colubri* are faced by Lifard (again) and by Fronto of Périgueux (xi AD); *vermes* are faced by Petroc ([a], xii AD or before) and Magnus of Füssen ([b], AD 1067–70).

[41] We may compare the extended list of snake-categories Maglorius (xi–x AD) declares God able to control, as he seeks his help against the Dragon of Jersey: *amphisbaena, aspis, basiliscus, chersidrus, dipsas, draco, hemorrois, jaculus, ophites, natrix, praester, seps, serpens*. This list bears a striking resemblance to Lucan's famous catalogue of the dreaded snakes of Libya at *Pharsalia* 9.700–838: *ammodytes, aspis, basiliscus, cenchris, cerastes, chelydrus, chersydrus, dipsas, draco, haemorrhois, jaculus, natrix, Niliaca serpens, parias, prester, scytale, seps*.

[42] But the basilisk encountered by Syrus of Genoa (v AD, perhaps with post-ix accretions) remains just a standard dragon, without any more distinctive features. For the basilisk killing with its vision, see Pliny *Natural History* 29.29 (cf. the ill-expressed 8.32–3, where, however, the basilisk is also said to destroy plants with its breath; so too Solinus 27.50); and Isidore of Seville *Etymologies* 12.4.6–9; cf. Alexander 1963.

that distinctively female term *drakaina*, 'she-dragon', and again as 'the mother of snakes' (cf. Chapter 3, §3.3.1). We shall consider the intriguing phenomenon of the male-female *drakōn-echidna* pair in hagiographical context in Chapter 8 (§8.3.4; cf. Chapter 9, §9.1.5).[43]

What is not can often be as informative as what is. It is a remarkable fact that hardly any dragon featuring in the standard hagiographical dragon fights surveyed here can boast a personal or specialized name.[44] Two exceptions to the rule may be noted. First, Margaret of Antioch's ([a], AD 815–20) dragon, it transpires, glories in the name 'Rouphos', 'Red'. However, this dragon's demonic affinities are emphasized, and it may be that we are to imagine the name as attaching in the first instance to a parallel humanoid manifestation: the case is finely balanced.[45] Second, the dragon encountered by Martha ([a], AD 1187; [b], late xii AD; [c], AD 1263–7; [d], 1264) glories in the name 'Tirascurus' (etc.), i.e. the modern 'Tarasque'.[46] However, this creature is anomalous in almost every way, including its spiny form, as we shall see (§5.5.3). Nonetheless, the case of the Tarasque was perhaps catalyst to the phenomenon of French popular culture (as opposed to hagiography proper) in which saints' dragons did indeed acquire personal names. So it was that the dragon defeated by Clement of Metz ([a], AD 782–6; [b], *c.* AD 1000; [c], *c.* AD 1100; [d], xii AD) in due course became 'Graouilly', focus and star of that city's rogation parades, held in the days leading up to Ascension;[47] that the sundry dragons encountered by Samson of Dol evolved into the 'Guivre';[48] that

---

[43] The Latin translation of *echidna* is *vipera*. However, when the Dragon of Armorica faced by Samson ([c], xii or earlier) is described as a *vipera* (in addition to being described as a *draco*), nothing seems to be at stake beyond stylistic variation.

[44] The Dragon of Revelation has acquired the name Beliar in the (iv AD or earlier) *Questions of Bartholomew* (4.7–17, 18–28, 46, 60), but he appears in the context of a vision rather than that of a fight.

[45] The name is supplied when the humanoid demon Beelzebub subsequently says to Margaret, 'I dispatched my *kinsman Rouphos in the form of a dragon*, so that he might kill you'. On the other hand, it could be that the name Rouphos (i.e. the Latin Rufus) purposefully salutes the Revelation Dragon, which Jerome's Vulgate describes (12.3) as *draco magnus rufus* ('a big red dragon'). For a detailed discussion of the representation of this dragon-demon, see Boulhol 1994:262–9, who rather ties the name to the entity's dragon-manifestation on the basis that it salutes its capacity to belch (ruddy) fire (268–9).

[46] Other variants of the name as expressed in these texts: Tharascus, Tharascurus, Tarasconus, Tirasconus.

[47] For the tradition of the *Lives* of Clement of Metz, see Chazan 2000; for the dragon's role in rogation parades, a once widespread phenomenon, see Wagner 2000; cf. also Mackensen 1930:375–6; Raison du Cleuziou and Couffon 1966:29–31; Gayrard 2001:159–62.

[48] De Cerny 1861:25–6 records a seemingly oral tradition. According to this, Samson of Dol and his entourage go to visit the frugal Suliac in his monastery on Mt Gârot. One of his monks, appalled by the poor quality of the food put before him, but anxious not to give offence by refusing it, secretly tucks a mean bread roll into the bosom of his robe, whereupon he collapses in agony. Suliac, tending to him, opens his robe to reveal a serpent—the Guivre (cf. '*vouivre*')—gnawing at his breast. Suliac subjects it to exorcism, makes a leash for it with his stole, and gives it over to the monk to lead to Mt Gârot's highest point. Once there, Suliac subjects it to exorcism a second time and then casts it down into the sea below. The Guivre is then said—rather contradictorily—to have had its home in a cave beneath the mountain, subsequently shown (at what point can it have utilized this home between its birth in the monk's breast and its expulsion into the sea?). Two years after de Cerny wrote, Dickens published an (unattributed) English summary of her words in his journal *All the Year Round* (1863).

the Dragon of the Fontaine de Vaucluse spring, banished by Veranus of Cavaillon (ix–xi AD), evolved into the Coulobre of the Sorgue, much elaborated in local legend (cf. *coluber*);[49] and that Romanus of Rouen, dragonless in hagiography proper, was gifted with the Gargouille ([a], AD 1394; [b], AD 1609).[50] One may also point here to the legend of the Velue or Peluda that supposedly marauded La Ferté-Bernard in the fourteenth century AD, its spiny, ox-sized body specifically recalling that of the Tarasque.[51]

5.4 The Dragon's Personality

Consonantly with this lack of personal names, few of the hagiographical dragons seem to express anything that could be described as a personality, and we are seldom permitted entry into the beast's head. A notable exception is to be found in the tale of Euflamus (xii AD), where the Dragon of Saint-Efflam (as the location will become) has long defeated King Arthur's attempt to track it down and kill it through its sheer cunning. When Arthur finally goes up against it, it is indignant to be expected to face a challenge from a single man, hardened victor as it is of so many battles against multiple opponents. Beyond this, we may point to two dragons that fall in love with human women: the Dragon of India slain by the

The tale-type is similar to that associated with Brigid (ix AD; see Chapter 6 §6.5.1), in which some of her nuns refuse to eat their pork and conceal their portions in a tree, whereupon the meat is transformed into a pair of serpents.

[49] For Veranus and the Coulobre, see Besson 1994.

[50] The tradition of Romanus (Romain) of Rouen and the dragon known as the Gargouille is one of the most frustrating to attempt to pin down. It goes unmentioned in his *Lives* and evidently thrived primarily in the iconographic register. The earliest literary mention of it is said by those that know to occur in an unidentified vernacular document, an 'enquiry' dated to AD 1394, the key portion of which reads as follows: 'By the grace of God he captured and subdued a great serpent or dragon [*draglon*] which was in the region of Rouen, and was devouring and destroying the people and the animals of the country, to such an extent that no one dared to meet or dwell in that that place.' See Floquet 1833:i, 10–11 (where the text is quoted); Pillion 1903:453; van den Gheyn 1904. The popular tradition that grew up around the dragon served as an aetiology for the Privilege of St Romanus, which endured until 1790. A good account of this is provided by Nicolas Rigault in the (unnumbered) introductory pages of his 1609 edition of one of the *Lives* of Romanus. According to Rigault, this 'false folktale' told that a serpent of exceptional size infested the Seine in the region of Rouen during the reign of King Clotarius, entwining a great many ships in its coils and dragging them down, and snatching and slaughtering men, herds, and flocks. Rouen would have been wiped from the map but for the intervention of its bishop, Romanus. Nobody would accompany him in his quest to deal with the serpent, save for a condemned criminal taken from the gaol. Romanus fitted his stole around its neck in the conventional way and passed it over to the criminal to lead back to the city, where it was burned before the crowd. In memory of the deed Romanus' successor in office, Audoenus (Audoin), secured from the subsequent king Dagobert the privilege that the Bishop of Rouen should be able to liberate a criminal every year during the feast of Ascension (cf. Metz). See also *AASS* Oct. x, pp. 87–8, where some slightly different details, including the term 'Gargouille', are recorded. The Gargouille particularly resembles the Tarasque in the detail of its sinking of ships in the river.

[51] *La Velue* 1813. However, the creature was dispatched not by a saint but by a local hero whose fiancée it had taken. The creature merited inclusion in Borges' 1969 *El Libro de los Seres Imaginarios* (translated as *Book of Imaginary Beings*, 2002).

apostle Thomas (later ii AD) and the Dragon of King Samuel's City slain by Theodore Tyron ([h], xiv AD or before). The Dragon of India, when pressed by the apostle, gives the following justification for his last killing:

> The dragon said, 'There is a beautiful woman in this village opposite. As she passed by me I saw her and fell in love with her. I followed her and kept watch over her. I found this young man kissing her. He also had sex with her and did other shameful things with her. It has been easy for me to reveal this to you, for I know that you are the twin brother of Christ and are always trying to abolish our race. Because I did not wish to upset this woman, I did not kill him there and then, but waited for him to pass by in the evening, and I struck him and killed him then, not least because he had the effrontery to do this on the day of the Lord.'[52]

Perhaps these are lies, but the actions of the Dragon of King Samuel's City speak for themselves: he falls in love with the saint's mother as she comes to fetch water from his spring, captures her, and imprisons her in his cave, but then goes out to capture in addition two boys to keep her company, and even fetches some deer-skins for them all to sit on as they converse.

The case of the Dragon of India—star of the first dragon-fight proper of the hagiographical tradition—highlights a path the developing tradition sadly declined to take. It could easily have imbued its dragons with personalities of all sorts, if it had continued to permit them to speak. But speaking dragons were to be vanishingly rare in it. The one other notable case is that of the Dragon of Rocks encountered by Philip ([a], mid- to late iv AD), which undertakes an extended negotiation with him about the terms of its exorcism, and makes a bargain to build a temple for him.[53]

5.5 The Physical Form of the Dragon

A remarkable feature of the hagiographical dragon-fight tradition is that in general very little attention is given to the physical form of the dragon in its narratives. The dragons are inevitably conceived of as anguiform at the commencement of the tradition in the later second century AD, when they are borrowed into it wholesale from the classical tradition. But the indications are that the dragons

---

[52] For discussion of this episode and others akin to it in the *Acts of Thomas*, see Czachesz 2001.

[53] However, this case is close to being a rule-proving exception, in that the dragon's alternate form, that of an (inevitably speaking) humanoid demon, lies close beneath its skin. Note also the dragon Hilarus of Galatea (vi AD) drags after him after it has threatened his monk Glycerius, with whom the saint proceeds to hold a conversation. But then this creature too is presented as inhabited by a smoky demon, which flies off when it is pulverized: see Chapter 6, §6.5.3.

faced by the saints *for the most part* remained pure anguiforms throughout the full span of the hagiographical era. In some ways this is not surprising: the very fact that the project of the following chapter, a unified motival analysis of the one-and-a-half-millennia-long tradition, is even viable testifies to the extreme and dogged conservatism of that tradition. In other ways it is surprising indeed: our last chapter has shown that in iconography and in the general imagination the form of dragon had undergone a radical evolution by around the mid-point of the life of the hagiographical tradition. That the hagiographical tradition felt the impact of this evolution in only a limited way is testimony not only, again, to its conservatism, but also to its vigorous autarky.

5.5.1 Indications of the Dragon's Anguiform Nature

Given that the saintly dragon is so seldom accorded an explicit physical description, we must infer its (usually) anguiform nature through indirect indications. So it is, for example, with the imagery of the wooden beam: the Dragon of the Egyptian Desert encountered by Ammon (*c.* AD 395 and *c.* AD 403/4) is tracked by a trail it has left in the sand resembling that of a beam; the first of four dragons encountered by Samson of Dol ([b], ix AD) is similarly tracked by means of its beam-like trail (it also leaves the ground around it burned);[54] the Dragon of Montecristo encountered by Mamilianus ([a], vii–viii AD) is described as resembling a massive beam in itself.

More often the clue to the dragon's anguiform nature is given in the description of its coiling or sinuous movement. Venantius Fortunatus describes the gait of the serpent (*draco, serpens, coluber*) expelled by Marcellus of Paris (late vi AD) from the tomb of an adulterous woman in terms that can only fit an anguiform: 'And when the snake returned to the tomb from the wood, coiling about to meet itself by turns, Marcellus uttered a prayer.' The Dragon of Trigg fought by Samson ([a], vii–viii AD; cf. [b], ix AD) coils itself up into a circle and gnaws its own tail at the saint's approach. The Dragon of Thasion banished by Joannicius of Bithynia ([a], AD 846; [b], before AD 860) is said to throw its coils around violently when it senses the presence of the saint outside its cave, or when burned by his prayers. The Dragon of September Island dismissed across the sea by Machutus (AD 866–72) leaves a twisting trail on the shore. The Dragon of Meung-sur-Loire encountered by Lifard (ix AD) attempts to destroy the cross-embellished staff he has planted in the ground before it by biting the top part and coiling around the lower part. The physiology of the snake is also implied when dragons are said to lift their heads to attack (see Chapter 6, §6.4.3).

[54] For Samson and his dragons, see above all Flobert 1997; note also Raison du Cleuziou and Couffon 1966:15–27; Henken 1991:91–3, 157; and Rauer 2000:90–116, 150–9.

The recurring motif of constriction also rather requires that the dragon be conceptualized as of largely anguiform shape.[55] The first of the serpents encountered by Simeon Stylites ([a], shortly after AD 459) winds itself tightly around his leg, up to his knee.[56] The Dragon of Chamaegephyrae destroyed by Donatus of Epirus ([b], AD 1263–7) coils its tail around the legs of the ass the saint is riding as he attempts to bless and purify the spring it has been occupying.[57] A more interesting handling of the motif is found in Gregory of Tours' tale of Caluppan (AD 581–94). Here the saint is assailed by a host of snakes and a pair of *dracones* in his hermit-cave in the Cantal. The snakes attempt to wrap themselves around his neck, whilst one of the *dracones* attempts to wind itself around his legs and feet and constrict them. But, in addition, the other *draco* raises itself off the ground and stares him in the face, seemingly paralysing Caluppan with its hypnotic stare as snakes were popularly supposed to do to their prey. He wishes to make the sign of the cross to protect himself, but finds his limbs frozen. He is only able to unfreeze his hand to make the sign by virtue of an internal prayer. Evidently, the second *draco* is able to inflict a sort of mental constriction by means of the stare.[58] We find a broadly comparable phenomenon in John the Deacon's account of Gregory's ([b], ix AD) monk Theodore, who is afflicted at once by the bubonic plague arising from the miasma of a dragon carcass and by a hallucination that a second dragon is

[55] The motif is actually found in hagiography prior to its first extant dragon fight. Already in the apocryphal *Acts of John* (for which see Bremmer 1996) the apostle John ([a], c. AD 150–80) encounters a snake (*ophis*) acting, anomalously, on behalf of the forces of good. This snake interrupts the work of the wicked Callimachus and his abettor Fortunatus as the former attempts to have sex with the corpse of the Christian woman Drusiana in her tomb. It kills Fortunatus with a single bite and then wraps itself around the legs of Callimachus, pulling him to the ground, whereupon it sits on top of him blowing out a terrible hiss until help arrives in the form of John and his colleagues, with the saint then telling it to depart. The story is delightfully revived in the *Calimachus* [sic], one of the dramas of Hrotsvitha, the learned nun of Gandesheim (John [b], c. AD 1000).

[56] A remarkable vi AD votive silver plaque from the church of Ma'arrat an Numan in Syria and now in the Louvre's Salle de Qabr Hiram depicts a massive serpent winding up around Simeon's pillar to attack him above: Louvre 1952 Bj 2180 (MND 2035).

[57] A further example: a mistaken copyist in the Latin tradition of the Christina legend ([a], ix AD — the London version, after the vi AD Greek original) appears to have had the pair of vipers sent against her by the eparch Julian's snake-wrangler binding her feet tightly (as opposed to licking them).

[58] This episode has some thematic correspondences with one in Felix of Crowland's *Life of Guthlac* (AD 730–40), preserved in both Latin and Anglo-Saxon versions. Here Guthlac retires to a hermit life on the island of Crowland, making his dwelling in a hole in a mound that had been partially excavated by treasure-hunters (one thinks of the barrow in which Beowulf's Firedrake lives; cf. Chapter 11, §11.2). There he is attacked in various ways by the forces of evil, including by a pair of demons that manifest themselves as vipers (inter alia); he dismisses them with the sign of the cross. This rich episode should be compared in turn with that of Bede's *Life of Cuthbert* 17 (AD 721; for text and translation, see Colgrave 1940), in which Cuthbert is similarly assailed by demons when he first makes his hermit-residence on the island of Farne. The Guthlac episode exhibits further affinities (perhaps with particular appropriateness too, if the mound is indeed to be read as a disturbed tomb), with the favourite haunted-house story-type of the pagan and early Christian worlds. In these a figure of moral authority, be it a pagan philosopher or a Christian saint or bishop, is assailed overnight in the house by the occupying ghost in the guise of a series of different animals: see esp. Lucian *Philopseudes* 30–1; and Gregory the Great *Dialogues* 3.4.1–3 (also Plautus *Mostellaria* 446–531; Pliny *Letters* 7.27.5–11; and Constantius *Life of Germanus* 2.10); cf. Ogden 2007:205–24, 2019b:67–73.

currently devouring him. He professes that he is unable to make the sign of the cross against the latter dragon because it is constricting his limbs so tightly.

One of the most significant indications that the dragons are being envisaged (still) as pure anguiforms is a description of them that refers to their length alone, without concern for their other dimensions: it is ever the snake that is, as it were, the creature of a single dimension. Here are some of the figures supplied:

- The Dragon of the Ophiorhyme Desert faced by Philip ([a], mid- to late iv AD): beyond 100 cubits.
- The Dragon of Rocks outside Ophiorhyme encountered by the same saint: around 100 cubits; its fifty cohorts are 60 cubits each.[59]
- The Dragon of Thessalonica destroyed by Andrew ([a] and [b], both late vi AD): 50 cubits.[60]
- The Dragon of the river Narco (near Spoleto) destroyed by Maurus of Syria (viii AD?): 90 feet.
- The Dragon of the Isle of Battha (Batz) confronted by Paulus Aurelianus ([a], AD 884): 120 feet.
- The Dragon of Cerisy Forest encountered by Vigor of Bayeux (AD 1030–45): 40 feet.
- The Dragon of King Samuel's City killed by Theodore Tyron ([h], xiv AD): 12 cubits.

The lengths given here, whilst all impressive by real-world standards, vary much. But there is no reason to think that the Dragon of King Samuel's City, at a mere 12 cubits in length, is supposed to be a modest specimen of the species. The individual authors are merely throwing out numbers that seem impressive to themselves.

In this context, a rare example of a narrative that does indeed supply a width together with a length presents us with a genial puzzle. The dragons destroyed by Artemon ([a], x AD) in the temple of Asclepius in Caesarea are said to have possessed the massive but peculiarly squat dimensions of 80 cubits in length and 20 cubits in breadth. Does the author envisage fully evolved, fat-bodied Romanesque dragons of the sort that had come into existence a century or so before, or is he just throwing out big numbers without thinking their implications through for the overall shape of his creature?[61]

---

[59] Of these 60 cubits, they raise the first 10 into the air with their heads. We are not told the overall length of the Dragon of the Jura Mountains encountered by Donatus of Sisteron (xii AD or earlier), but it lifts 15 cubits of itself into the air to attack him.

[60] For Gregory of Tour's *Acts of Andrew*, see Bremmer 2000.

[61] In a further complication it remains unclear whether these serpents are to be understood as living dragons—the traditional story-pattern would suggest that they are—or merely as graven idols decorating the temple, in which case one would probably have expected relative dimensions more appropriate to Asclepius' serpent avatar. Which Caesarea? Perhaps Ceretapa-Diocaesarea in Phrygia.

A final indirect indication that the shape of a dragon is fundamentally anguiform is their tight association with broods of (more) regular snakes (for which see Chapter 7, §7.1).

5.5.2 Additional Parts: Beards, Crests, Legs, Wings, and Multi-Heads

In the case of the classical dragon, the most frequent exception to the purity of their anguiform shape had been the minor one of an added beard or a crest (Chapter 1, §1.4). These make an occasional impact on the hagiographical tradition too. The Dragon of the Rocks outside Ophiorhyme encountered by Philip ([a], mid- to late iv AD), itself 100 cubits in length, boasts a beard of 20 cubits in length. It probably also has a head like a hill-top surmounted by a crest of iron (unfortunately the text of the *Acts of Philip* is obscure and possibly corrupt at the relevant point). The dragon encountered by Margaret of Antioch ([a], AD 815–20; cf. [b], early ix AD; [c], early ix AD; [f], *c.* AD 1380) in her martyr cell ('Rouphos') has a beard and crest too, both of gold (the key passage is quoted below).[62] Sometimes we find crests without (specification of) beards, as in the case of the dragons that the Ethiopian sorcerers Zaroes and Arphaxat send against the apostle Matthew ([a], late vi AD; [c], xv AD) and the Dragon of Euchaita confronted by Theodore Tyron ([d], *c.* AD 871).

The Basilisk of Genoa faced by Syrus (v AD, with post-ix AD accretions) is said actually to have the crest of a cock upon its head. This surely salutes the conceptualization of the basilisk as a 'cockatrice', and it anticipates the first extant literary account of the subsequently famous mode of its generation. This comes in Theophilus' *c.* AD 1100 *Schedula diversarum artium*: two old cocks are fattened in an underground stone chamber until they have sex with each other and produce an egg. The cocks are then replaced by toads in the chamber, which duly incubate the egg. The creature that is hatched from it resembles a chicken, but after seven days it grows a serpent's tail. This physiology had probably evolved in bestiary illustrations prior to this.[63] At the other end of the tradition the Basilisk-dragon of

[62] In the earliest Latin version of her passion ([b], early ix AD or before) the dragon boasts iron teeth; in the Norse version of her life ([f], c.1380), these become tusks like iron.

[63] Theophilus *Schedula diversarum artium* 3.48. At *De propertatibus rerum* 12.16 (AD 1240) Bartholomeus Anglicus (Bartholomew de Glanville) attributes this information to Bede (c. AD 700), with what warrant it is unclear. Perhaps somewhere in the background to all this lurk (1) the claim made by both Cassian *De incarnatione Christi* 7.5 (v AD) and Theophylact Simocatta *Quaestiones physicae* 14 (vii AD) that the ibis eats so many snakes that basilisks hatch from its eggs and (2) the (originally Greek) tale in the (vii AD) Syriac *Alexander Romance* in which Alexander's world-conquest and death are prophesied when a hen lays an egg on Philip's lap, from which a snake hatches (1.11, pp. 10–11 Budge). See Alexander 1963 esp. 175–9 and, for the history of the basilisk more generally, Breiner 1979; Bondeson 1999:161–92; and Sammer 1999. White 1954:169 reproduces an illustration of a basilisk in the form of a serpent-tailed cock from the xii AD *Peterborough Bestiary*.

the river Élorn in Brittany faced by the warrior saints Neventerius and Derien (AD 1637—a late vernacular text drawing on lost sources) is said to be five fathoms long, to possess the body of a horse and the head of cock, to be covered in hard scales, to be able to devour a sheep with a single bite, and to be able to kill people with its gaze.

As we saw in the Chapter 4 (§4.9), the form of the Romanesque dragon crystallizes in the ninth century AD. From this century onwards we do get just occasional nods in the hagiographical tradition to the dragon's possession of the relevant additional parts.

The description of the gait of the Dragon of the Isle of Battha (Batz) confronted by Paulus Aurelianus ([a], AD 884) suggests that it is an anguiform struggling to evolve, as it were, the ability to walk. It is said to move in an anomalous fashion, arching its spine up rigidly in such a way that it can use its 'flanks' as legs upon which to walk and its scales, proof against all weapons, correspondingly as nails or talons. But the dragon of another ninth-century text, the earliest extant Greek *martyrium* of Margaret of (Pisidian) Antioch ([a], AD 815–20), our 'Rouphos' again, has its legs fully evolved:

> After she had finished her prayer [to be shown the enemy] there was in that place a great earthquake, and the prison was shaken. And suddenly there emerged from the corner a great and most terrifying *drakōn*, with a skin of all colours. Its crest and beard were like gold. Its teeth flashed with lightning, and its eyes were like pearls. A flame of fire and a great deal of smoke issued from its nostrils. Its tongue was like a sword.[64] Snakes coiled around its neck. The corners of its eyes were like silver.[65] ...

The text goes on to specify that, as the dragon cranes its neck over a square stone in the cell (a stone for the binding of prisoners), its 'legs reached the ground, running out from that part of its neck upon which the snakes grew, and the mouth of the dragon gaped open.' The detail lavished on the physical description of the dragon here is rare. When it is said that the creature has a pair of legs growing from its 'neck', a tubular serpentine body is presumably (still) intended by this.[66] In later texts the Dragon of (Syrian) Antioch killed with the thumb of the relic-hand of John the Baptist ([a], x AD) is said to crawl forth from its cave on feet. The dragon of Carhampton (Carrum) fails to deploy its talons when bound by

---

[64] For a dragon whose tongue is literally a sword, see the interesting refraction of the Silvester story at *De promissionibus* 3.43 (at *PL* li, col. 835; v AD): here the Dragon of Rome is no longer a live dragon, but a mechanical device. As the virgins proceeded down the steps of its cavern in the pitch dark, believing they were carrying offerings down to it, they impaled themselves on its sword-tongue, to become the offerings themselves. See Chapter 7, §7.2.

[65] The remainder of this episode is quoted in Chapter 6, §6.4.2.

[66] For representations of Margaret's dragon in art, which are divergent from those of the texts, see Dresvina 2016:178–81, 278–98.

Carantoc (early xii AD),[67] whilst the Dragon of Saint-Efflam dismissed by Euflamus (xii AD) is, however, indeed able to use its talons to tear into King Arthur's shield.

The earliest Latin account of Margaret's passion ([b], early ix AD) is fairly congruent with the Greek version just quoted, but we are actually told that her dragon seemed to have a shining sword in its *hand* (*gladius candens in manu eius videbatur*). Comparison with the Greek version just mentioned suggests this detail originates in a corruption of the contention that the dragon's tongue resembled a sword. But in some ways the error is of little moment: for the author of the Latin version, the notion that the dragon should have hands—and that too hands that could hold and wield things—was an acceptable one.

We turn to wings. When Veranus of Cavaillon (ix–xi AD) banishes the Dragon of the Fontaine de Vaucluse Spring (antecedent of the Coulobre), we are told that it flies (*volare coepit*) to the summit of Mt Debrieso, where it disappears, never to be seen again. No wings are explicitly specified here, but we may probably assume their existence. Subsequently the Dragon of Armorica encountered by Samson ([c], xii AD or before), curiously described as a viper (*vipera*), is explicitly said to be winged and feathered. When Carantoc (early xii AD) binds the neck of the Dragon of Carhampton, we are told that the creature makes no attempt to raise its wings or, again, its talons (*nec exaltavit pennas neque ungulas*). The feast day of John the Baptist ([b], AD 1263–7) offers the opportunity to fumigate against dragons that fly through the air in a state of lustful arousal. The visions of Francisca (before AD 1440) include that of 'a large and terrible black dragon, its mouth open and vomiting forth a great deal of fire, flying through the air on the swiftest course and rushing with the greatest force towards Latium'.

We may also note here the relative scarcity of multi-headed dragons in the hagiographical tradition. This is a little surprising, given their presence in the preceding classical tradition (beginning with the Hydra and Ladon, the Dragon of the Hesperides), and even more so given the notoriously multi-headed nature of the Dragon of Revelation, that great precedent for the hagiographical dragon. Again, the ninth century seems to be the starting point for innovation here, and perhaps the Revelation Dragon does indeed provide the initial impetus. In the description of the dragon encountered by Margaret of Antioch ([a], AD 815–20) just quoted, we note that the creature has minor snake-heads growing from its neck at the same point from which the legs emerge; in the earliest Latin version of the tale ([b], early ix AD or before) these become a single serpent on its neck.[68] We are probably not meant to envisage here a shaggy mane of snake-hair, à la Gorgon, Hydra, or Cerberus. It is more likely that the author has in mind a row of mini-snake heads running down the upper part of the dragon's breast, as we find

---

[67] For Carantoc and the Dragon of Carhampton, see Henken 1991:92.
[68] And then in the Norse version ([f], c. AD 1380) the serpent becomes a single *viper* coiling around the neck.

in the *c.* AD 800 *Trier Apocalypse* manuscript considered in the previous chapter (§4.9, again). Thereafter the Dragon of Trou Baligan on the Cotentin peninsula confined by Germanus of Auxerre ([a], xi–xii AD) boasts seven heads, whilst the Dragon of King Samuel's City killed by Theodore Tyron ([h], xiv AD) must be content with three.

5.5.3 Some Exceptional Individual Dragons: The Loch Ness Monster, the Tarasque, and the Péist of Inis Cathaigh

It is debatable whether the Loch Ness monster should be considered a dragon. Our earliest source for it, Adamnan's *Life of Columba* (*c.* AD 700), describes it only as an 'aquatic beast' (*aquatilis bestia*). Still, his tale of it exhibits some common points with the dragon tales, most obviously the motif in accordance with which Columba is able to drive the beast back from attacking his companion by making the sign of the cross (see Chapter 6, §6.4.2).[69]

The hagiographical dragon with the single most distinctive form is that of the Tirascurus, the modern Tarasque, destroyed at Nerluc, henceforth Tirascon/Tarascon, by Martha of Bethany, sister of Lazarus and, on some readings, Mary Magdalene, as told in the *Life* of her attributed to her servant, Marcilia or Marcella ([a], AD 1187). It is important to note that the *Life* repeatedly describes the creature as a *draco* and specifies that it has a viper-tail (*caudam vipeream*; so too [c], AD 1273–7; [d], AD 1264). We might otherwise have hesitated to classify it as a dragon in form at least, although its story constitutes an absolutely standard dragon-fight narrative. The creature is described in the following terms: it is part land-creature, part fish; it is larger than an ox and longer than a horse; it has the head of a lion; its teeth are as sharp as swords; it has the hair of a horse; its back is as sharp as an axe; its scales are hairy but blade-like; it has six feet and the claws of a bear; it is protected on both sides by shields like those of tortoise. In addition to a distinctive physical form, the Tarasque is also endowed, rather uniquely, with an ancestry. It is said to have come to the Rhône from Galatia in Asia Minor and to have been the child of Leviathan, 'drainer of rivers' and ferocious 'water serpent', and of the Galatian Onachus (or Bonachus), which had enjoyed the ability to shoot its caustic, liquid excrement at its pursuers over a considerable distance, like arrows. Most of these details are recycled in the accounts of Martha's story by Ps.-Hrabanus Maurus ([b], late xii AD), Jacobus de Voragine ([c], AD 1263–7), and Vincent de Beauvais ([d], AD 1264).[70]

---

[69] In the same text Columba deters a massive *cetus* from attacking his ship by blessing it (1.13).

[70] For full discussion of the sources for the Tarasque, its iconography, and the Pentecostal festival in which it came to star, see Dumont 1951; the accounts of [Marcilia], Jacobus, and Vincent are conveniently compared and analysed in parallel at 150–64, with that of [Hrabanus] at 166–9. See also Gutch 1952; Peters 1997.

The monster (*péist*) expelled from the island of Inis Cathaigh by Senán in an Irish text (early xv AD) similarly resembles a dragon only partially in its physical form, but it again resembles one rather more strongly in its story-type. Its dragon-ish elements consist in its body, which is as long as the island of Inis na h-Urclaide, its fiery breath, which emanates from a furnace-bellows-like belly and turns things to embers, and its piercing vision. In other ways it sounds more like a hip-pocamp (for which see Chapter 4, §4.3.5): it has a horse's mane, two thick legs, nails of iron, and the tail of a whale. Its narrative is typical of a saintly island-cleansing (cf. Chapter 6, §6.8.2). With the help of the angel Raphael and the sign of the cross, Senán orders it to depart the island so that he may build his hermit-age on it, and to harm no one anymore; it goes into the sea (which boils around it, owing to its heat) and does not stop swimming until it reaches Dubloch of Sliab Collain, where it does indeed refrain from harming people.[71]

5.6 Conclusion

So much, then, for the scriptural impetuses for the dragon in the hagiographical tradition, and for the creature's form in it. We may turn now to a review of the typical narratives in which the tradition engaged its dragon, and this is where its rather stronger legacy lies.

---

[71] Cf. Riches 2003:196–8.

6

The Etiquette of the Saintly Dragon Fight (i)

Its Principal Narrative Course

I now lay out the principal narrative course, the series of episodes and motifs that structures the vast bulk of hagiographical dragon fights. The order of exposition tracks, so far as practicable, the order the episodes and motifs most usually follow.

6.1 The Initial Problem

The great majority of saintly dragon-fight stories begin with an initial problem of one of three kinds (or indeed a combination of them): the dragon is devastating the local community by marauding; it is denying the community access to a spring or other vital water-source; or it is poisoning the air for all with its toxic breath.

6.1.1 Marauding

It is a well-established commonplace, beginning with the creatures encountered by Ammon and Hilarion at the end of the fourth century AD, that the dragon should be blighting its local community by general marauding. In almost all cases it is specified that the dragon is laying waste to the entire region and devouring men and beasts alike.[1] For all its importance, its productiveness, and durability,

---

[1] Generally marauding dragons are faced by, inter alios: Ammon (c. AD 395 and c. AD 403/4)—the Dragon of the Egyptian Desert; Hilarion ([a], AD 396)—the Dragon of Epidaurus in Dalmatia; Donatus of Epirus ([a], earlier v AD)—the Dragon of Chamaegephyrae; Andrew ([a], [b], both late vi AD)—the Dragon of Thessalonica; Samson of Dol ([a], vii–viii AD; [b], ix AD)—the Dragon of Trigg in Cornwall, the Dragon of Brittany, and the Dragon of the Pental Monastery at St-Samson-sur-Risle (cf. [c] and [d], both xii AD or before; [e], AD 1107–30); Pavacius (ix AD)—the Dragon of le Mans; Joannicius of Bithynia ([a], AD 846; [b], before AD 860)—the Dragon of Prusa; Theodore Tyron ([b], late ix AD or before; [d], AD 871; [c], late ix AD; [f], x AD)—the Dragon of Euchaita; Paulus Aurelianus ([a], AD 884; [b], AD 1637)—the Dragon of the Isle of Battha (Batz); Elisabeth ([a], ix–x AD)—the Dragon of Constantinople; Maglorius (ix–x AD)—the Dragon of Jersey (Angia); Deodatus ([b], x AD)—the Dragon of Blois; Beatus (x AD?)—the Dragon of Vendôme; Fronto of Périgueux ([c], xi AD)—the *coluber* of the river Dronne; George ([a], xi AD; [b], xii AD; [c], AD 1263–7)—the Dragon of Lasia; the archangel Michael ([b], xi AD)—the Dragon of Mt Garganus; Carantoc (early xii AD)—the Dragon of

Fig. 6.1 Saints Peter, Martha, Mary Magdalen, and Leonard. Italian, painting by Corregio, *c.* AD 1515. Metropolitan Museum, New York, John Stewart Kennedy Fund, 1912, 12.211. Public domain.

this motif is subject to very little elaboration in the tradition, though we may note that the Tarasque encountered by Martha ([a], AD 1187; [b], late xii AD; [c], AD 1263–7; [d], AD 1264) expanded the repertoire to include the overturning of ships in the Rhône (Fig. 6.1).

One particular sub-motif here does, however, invite more comment. Amongst the livestock devoured by the dragons oxen are sometimes singled out. So it is, for example, in the case of the Dragon of Metz dismissed by Clement ([a], AD 782–6). We are told that the Dragon of Oña destroyed by Eneco (xvi AD or before) devours humans in a single bite, but takes two to consume oxen. The Dragon of Epidaurus in Dalmatia destroyed by Hilarion ([a], AD 396; cf. [c], AD 675–710) is more specifically designated a *boa* by virtue of the fact that it devours entire oxen (*boves*).[2]

Carhampton; Petroc ([a], xii AD or before)—Dragon of Cornwall; Tudual (xii AD)—the Dragon of Treguier; Armel ([a], xii AD or later)—the Dragon of Rennes; Venerius of Tino (early xv AD)—the Dragon of Luni; Servanus (AD 1510)—the Dragon of Dunning in Strathearn; Eneco (xvi AD or before)—the Dragon of Oña.

[2] In classical tradition, the *boa* snake had been so termed (or so it was thought) for its propensity merely to suck milk from cows' udders, although Solinus knew that in the reign of Claudius one of

No doubt this is why the same term is also applied to the Dragon of Kempten destroyed by Magnus of Füssen ([b], AD 1067–70) and to the Dragon of Teano dismissed by Paris (AD 1533 or before).[3] But the sub-motif was a flexible one, and oxen could be put to other uses too in dragon-slaying tales. We will consider the repeated use of ox-teams to cart away the carcass of a slain dragon below (§6.7).[4]

6.1.2 Springs

Often the dragon seizes control of the spring or the water-source on which the local town depends. It either denies physical access to the spring, or else it poisons it with its venom.

As to denial of access, we find this in the work of the Dragon of Augsburg killed by Narcissus of Gerundum (c. AD 770), the Dragon of Meung-sur-Loire encountered by Lifard (ix AD), the Dragon of Euchaita destroyed by Theodore Tyron ([g], AD 980–1010), and the Dragon of Vaux destroyed by Nicasius (xi AD) and his companions. In a nice twist in the last case, Nicasius proceeds to baptize the local population, duly converted by his killing of the dragon, in the water of their newly liberated spring.

Sometimes the dragon more specifically cuts off the road to the spring in question. We find this in the cases of the Dragons of Prusa faced by Joannicius of Bithynia ([a], AD 846; [b], before AD 860)[5] and by Timothy ([a], x AD; the springs are hot ones in this case), and also in that of the Dragon of le Mans encountered by Pavacius (ix AD). Occasionally we find the motif of the road cut off by a dragon without an actual spring at its destination. The Dragon of Kempten encountered by Magnus of Füssen ([a], c. AD 895) blocks off the Horse-Head Pass. Similarly the Dragon of Forlimpopoli contained by Rofillus and Mercurialis ([a], [b], both xi AD) blocks off a road between that city and the neighbouring city of Forli.[6]

Other water-sources too can be occupied. Syrus of Genoa (v AD, perhaps with post-ix accretions) and John of Reomay (AD 659) confront serpents that have taken up occupancy of a well. Syrus brings his basilisk up alive in a bucket before

---

them had so fattened itself by this method that it had been able to take a child (Pliny *Natural History* 8.37; Solinus 2.33–4; Isidore of Seville *Etymologies* 12.4.28).

    [3] The term applied to the Dragon of Kempten is actually a slight variant: *boas* (sing.).

    [4] Two further uses of the sub-motif. The Dragon of the river Sangarius destroyed by Thomas Defournikos (xii AD) is said to have been as big as an ox, whilst the Tarasque encountered by Martha ([a], AD 1187; [c], AD 1263–7; [d], AD 1264) is said to have been bigger than one; and the disciples of St James ([b], AD 1263–7) encounter the Dragon of Galicia as they search for Queen Lupa's missing oxen.

    [5] For Joannicius and his *Lives*, see Mango 1983; Walter 2003:222–3; Efthymiadis 2011:110–11; and Hinterberger 2014:223–5.

    [6] A further example: the dragon (location unspecified) destroyed by Arsacius of Nicomedia ([a], earlier v AD; [b], AD 1493) inhabits a roadside cave from which it blasts passers-by with its breath and kills them.

dismissing it, whereas John takes the precaution of killing his dragon first, by means of a prayer, and must consequently extract its carcass. In a variant of this motif Parasceve (viii AD) is thrown to 'a dragon and venomous beasts and reptiles' in a—presumably dry—well. Rivers and lakes too can be featured in this way. The Dragon of the river Gorgytes destroyed by Joannicius of Bithynia ([a], AD 846; [b], before AD 860) has come to block off the river's stream with its vast bulk. The Dragon of Rennes destroyed by Armel ([a], xii AD or later) makes its home on a mountain above the river Sicca (Seiche). The Dragon of Lasia killed by George ([a], xi AD; [b], xii AD; [c], AD 1263–7) occupies a lake adjacent to the city, upon which the people depend for their water.[7]

As to the actual poisoning of the spring, the Dragon of Chamaegephyrae destroyed by Donatus of Epirus ([b], AD 1263–7) lives in a spring and poisons it to the extent that anyone drinking from it dies, as Jacobus de Voragine tells us; when Donatus purifies the water with his prayer, the dragon bursts forth from the spring to attack him. And dragons can—on occasion at least—poison waters in other ways too. Jacobus also tells how in death John the Baptist ([b], AD 1263–7) offers his aid against a particularly unpleasant phenomenon. Around the time of his feast day animal bones are burned. This fumigation drives away the dragons that fly through the air in a state of lustful arousal, dropping their ebullient seed into wells and waters, with the potential to cause a year-long plague.[8]

Motifs can sometimes be neatly combined, with the spring in question actually flowing from the cave that appropriately constitutes the dragon's home (for which see §6.3.1). So it is with the Dragon of the Fontaine de Vaucluse spring banished by Veranus of Cavaillon (ix–xi AD). In one of the later *Lives* of Theodore Tyron ([h]; xiv AD) the Dragon of King Samuel's City takes up residence in the cave from which flows the weak spring upon which the city depends, and permits access to it only at the price of regular animal sacrifice. In due course God sends the angel Gabriel to Theodore's aid, and the angel takes the opportunity to break open the spring and turn it into a torrent, which not only liberates him from the cave, in which he has become trapped, but also provides an abundant new water-source for the city.[9]

---

[7] For the George tradition, see Chapter 9, §9.2.

[8] Jacobus is explicitly aware of the ancient roots of this particular piece of natural history. We may also refer to Megasthenes *FGrH/BNJ* 715 FF21a, 21c, where we learn of flying snakes delightfully dropping corrosive urine onto the people below. Cf. also Chapter 1, n. 26.

[9] The Dragon of Teano dismissed by Paris (AD 1533 or before) occupies a cave with an abundant spring; however, little is made of this in the story and the problem the dragon presents to the local community is not denial of access to the vital water-source but rather its fetid breath. Otherwise the dragon can live close by a spring. The Dragon of Prusa destroyed by Timothy ([b], xiv AD) emerges from its adjacent cave to take up residence in a cypress tree beside a spring. The Dragon of the Cerisy Forest encountered by Vigor of Bayeux (AD 1030–45) is said to travel between its cave and the local springs.

A dragon-fight story can also culminate with the saint creating, directly or indirectly, a brand-new spring for the locals. After Mamilianus ([a], vii–viii AD) has killed the Dragon of Montecristo a spring of the coolest water, seemingly a new one, begins to flow out of the cave it has vacated. After Machutus (AD 866–72) has sent the Dragon of September Island off into the sea he strikes his staff into the floor of the dragon's vacated cave to produce a pure spring, à la Poseidon.[10] Although the Dragon of Lasia killed by George ([a], xi AD; [b], xii AD; [c], AD 1263–7) has been occupying the lake upon which the city has hitherto depended for its water, the denouement of the tale curiously consists not in the liberation of this lake, but in George's creation of a new spring for the Lasians within the church they build in his honour. The logic here is perhaps revealed by the case of the Dragon of Huy encountered by Domitianus of Maastricht ([a], [b], both xii AD). This dragon occupies a spring and poisons it, killing the men and beasts that drink from it. After dismissing the dragon, Domitianus encloses the spring within the earth, apparently because it remains irrevocably poisoned, and creates a new one for the people by, again, striking his staff into the earth. The new spring is not merely drinkable, but actually possesses healing powers. In the multiply anomalous tale of Euflamus (xii AD), the saint strikes a rock to bring forth an abundant spring, but this is not to replace any water-source befouled by the Dragon of Saint-Efflam (cf. §6.2.3). Rather, it is to provide a source of refreshment for King Arthur, parched after fighting the beast profitlessly all day long. And when the Dragon of Rennes is destroying people and animals alike by parching them with its flame-vomiting breath, Armel ([b], xiii AD) affords them relief by, again, striking his staff into the ground to create a new spring.

6.1.3 The Dragon's Breath

The most important and most productive category of blight the dragon inflicts on its city or its local area is that of the miasma of its venomous and pestilential breath, which both sickens and kills. Already well established in classical culture, the notion that dragons should give forth terrible breath takes on extra significance as it moves into the world of hagiography.[11] The dragon's miasma—like the dragon itself—is now commonly presented as an actualization of the unbelief in which pagan communities live. At an intellectual level the saint's demonstration of

---

[10] For Poseidon's creation of the spring of Amymone with his trident, see Propertius 2.26.45–50; Apollodorus *Bibliotheca* 2.1.4; Lucian *Dialogues in the Sea* 8; Hyginus *Fabulae* 169, 169a. For his creation of the saltwater 'Sea of Erectheus' with it on the Athenian acropolis, see Herodotus 8.55; Pausanias 1.27.2; Apollodorus *Bibliotheca* 3.14.1.

[11] For the classical: e.g. Ovid *Metamorphoses* 3.49 and 75–6 (the Dragon of Ares' breath, poisonous with its corruption); Silius Italicus *Punica* 6.146–50, 174–80 (the terrible blasts of the Bagrada dragon); Hyginus *Fabulae* 30.3 (the Hydra's fatal breath). Further examples at Ogden 2013a:226–30, cf. also 406–9.

the power of his own faith in disposing of the dread dragon converts the people that witness his deed and leads them to faith in turn; at a cruder and more physical level it brings faith about in them simply by eliminating the source of the gas of unbelief to which they had hitherto been subject (cf. §6.8.1).[12]

An early and striking example of a city miasma is that inflicted by the Dragon of Rome and dealt with by Pope Silvester ([b], c. AD 500; cf. [a], late iv AD; [c] and [d], AD 675–710; [e], AD 1263–7):

There was a most monstrous dragon in the Tarpeian rock, on which the Capitol is located. Once a month, mages, together with profane virgins, used to descend down 365 steps to this dragon, as if to hell, with sacrifices and propitiatory offerings, titbits of which could be given to the dragon, large as it was. This dragon suddenly and unexpectedly came up and, although it did not come out of its hole, nonetheless it corrupted the air around about with its breath. As a result of this came the death of people and, in great measure, mourning for the death of children.[13]

Another striking example of the city-miasma motif is John the Deacon's account of the blight visited upon Metz by the dragon and its brood eventually chased from that city by Clement ([a], AD 782–6; cf. also [b], AD 1000; [c], c. AD 1100):

At the point in time at which the venerable priest came to the aforementioned city, the greatest calamity was destroying the people of the region, for the above-mentioned amphitheatre was filled with such a great multitude of serpents that not only did no one dare to come to this same place, but no one even dared to come near it. Their venomous breaths had given rise to exceptionally cruel deaths, not just of men, but also of horses, oxen, sheep, and other animals. Now, as the most blessed Clement was approaching the walls of the city itself, this same pestilence spread itself out in such a way that there was no means of going to the city and returning safely from it. For if anyone wished to exit the gates,

---

[12] For city and local-area miasmas in addition to those mentioned below in this section, see Narcissus of Gerundum (c. AD 770)—the Dragon of Augsburg; Maurus of Syria (viii AD?)—the Dragon of the river Narco; Gildas ([a], ix AD; cf. [b], xi AD)—the Dragon of Rome; Paulus Aurelianus ([a], AD 884)—the Dragon of the Isle of Battha (Batz); the archangel Michael ([a], ix–x AD; [c], c. AD 1000)—the Dragon of Southern Asia and the Dragon of Mons Tumba, respectively; Pope Leo IV ([a], before c. AD 939; cf. [b], c. AD 939)—the Basilisk of Rome; Vigor of Bayeux (AD 1030–45)—the Dragon of the Cerisy Forest; Nicasius (xi AD)—the Dragon of Vaux; Rofillus ([a], [b], xi AD) and Mercurialis—the Dragon of Forlimpopoli; Germanus of Auxerre ([a], xi–xii AD)—the seven-headed Dragon of Trou Baligan; Donatus of Sisteron (xii AD or earlier)—the Dragon of the Jura Mountains; Tudual (xii AD)—the Dragon of Treguier; Bernacus (xii AD?)—the Dragon of Rome; Honoratus ([b], xii AD?; cf. [a], before AD 449)—the Dragon of the Île Saint-Honorat in the Lérins group off the coast of Cannes; Martha ([b], late xii AD)—the Tarasque; Crescentinus (xiv AD)—the Dragon of Tifernum (Città di Castello); Paris (AD 1533 or before)—the Dragon of Teano.

[13] The direct continuation of this passage is quoted in §6.8.1, where the somewhat parallel [a] version is also given. For the *Acts of Silvester*, see Loenertz 1975; Pohlkamp 1983; Canella 2006.

even under compulsion of the greatest necessity, or indeed to go near them, he would immediately perish in the most wretched way, stricken by the power of the venom. Nor is it surprising if the snake, gliding over its vessels of choice, laid low the bodies of those from whose minds righteousness had as yet least dismissed [lacuna] through the water of the holy baptism. So after the admirable worshipper of the Holy Trinity began to give his mind fully to performing the duty laid upon him of preaching, the countless multitude of the sick soon flocked eagerly to where he was. For they had heard that he was preaching that the true God was the source of succour. They learned from the mouth of the excellent shepherd how they had deservedly been infected by the serpents' venom. When he saw their manifest wretchedness, he made no delay in applying the most healthful medicine. So he pledged that they would have God's mercy all the more quickly if they did not refuse to abandon the detestable worship of idols. And so not only the sick but also the few who remained well promised on the basis of the healthful advice to renounce all effigies once they were delivered, so long as they were not cheated of their promised benefits by the bishop of God on high.[14]

Also worth singling out here is the tale of the Dragon of le Mans encountered by Pavacius (ix AD), given that its toxic breath gives rise to an exclusion zone around the city with a radius of five miles.

The early *Acts of Philip* ([a], mid- to late iv AD) uniquely adds another dimension to the motif of the dragon's breath: that of the infliction of physical and spiritual blindness. When Philip and his team are being tortured in the course of their martyrdom at Ophiorhyme, St John comes to the city and tells the citizens that they are being blinded by the dragon's breath: 'The dragon has blown [*pneō*] into you with its breath and blinded you in three ways, which is to say that it has blinded you in body, soul, and spirit [*pneuma*], and you were stricken by the destroyer.' The imagery of physical blinding is deployed more widely: the second rank of the city's dragon-guards consists of a pair that blind unwelcome visitors by breathing into their eyes. Noteworthy too is Philip's conversion of Stachys, the former head of the city's Echidna (Viper) cult: he achieves this by curing the physical blindness Stachys has accidentally inflicted upon himself by putting the juice from serpent eggs into his own eyes.

Did the sickness caused by the dragon's breath affect unbelievers and sinners alone, or all members of the community regardless? As to the former model, the Dragon of Blerana banished by Senzius (vii–viii AD) is said to inflict its illness on the city's sinners alone. The Dragon of Scythia encountered by Philip in a later account ([b], late vi AD; so too [c], AD 1263–7), the Dragon of Artinas

---

[14] For Clement of Metz and his dragons, see Chazan 2000; Goetz 2000; Michaux 2000; Wagner 2000.

encountered by Julian of le Mans (c. AD 1000), and the first of the five dragons faced by Fronto of Périgueux ([c], xi AD) more directly destroy their own pagan worshippers with their breath as they stand before them.

But the latter model is also found. The Dragon of Trebula dismissed by Victoria ([a], c. AD 500; [b] and [c], AD 675–710) and Dragon of Prusa destroyed by Timothy ([a], x AD) not only kill the local people with their breath, but also their cattle and flocks.[15] However, the Clement narrative (in the passage quoted above) has the animals dying on the one hand, which implies the latter model, but its individual people being healed by conversion, which rather implies the former one. In such cases it may be that the authors have just not thought things through: it might be said that they have failed to resolve the question of whether the dragon's breath constitutes a simple physical blight, or a more abstruse spiritual one. In at least one case we find a dragon blighting the still more innocent plant-world with its breath: when an (actually friendly) dragon takes up residence north of the column of Simeon Stylites ([b], c. AD 830), grass ceases to grow in the area. But here a physical explanation may safely be assumed, given that the dragon in this case is not an embodiment of unbelief or evil of any kind, merely one of God's creatures in distress.

Sometimes the dragon pumps out its toxic breath from the redoubt of its hole in the ground. So it is with the Silvester and the Dragon of Rome, as we have seen. The Basilisk of Genoa encountered by Syrus (v AD, perhaps with post-ix accretions) pumps out is breath from the bottom of a well.

Beyond the confines of their holes dragons can also deploy their breath in a more targeted jet-blast against individual victims. The Dragon of the Egyptian Desert destroyed by Rufinus' Ammon (c. AD 395 and c. AD 403/4) contrives to cause the body of the son of a local shepherd to swell up by the power of its breath alone (for the swelling, see §6.1.5); when Ammon confronts the dragon himself it directs the foulest blasts of its breath against him, albeit to no effect. The Dragon of Heliopolis (Baalbek) destroyed by Eudocia (x AD or before) similarly kills a boy directly with its breath. Individuals can also be targeted by the sucking in of the breath as well as its blowing out: the Dragon of Epidaurus in Dalmatia faced by Hilarion ([a], AD 396) sucks down individual people and animals alike, including entire oxen, as we have seen (§6.1.1).[16] These last two motifs are combined in the case of the dragon (location unspecified) destroyed by Arsacius of Nicomedia ([a], earlier v AD; [b], AD 1493), which targets travellers with the blast of its breath as they pass before its roadside cave.

---

[15] If the point in these cases is that the unbelievers are being further punished by the destruction of their chattels, it is not explicitly stated.

[16] For dragons using a sucking breath to destroy in pagan context, see Pliny *Natural History* 8.36–7; Lucan 9.727–33; and the further material collected at Ogden 2013a:231–2, to which add Nonnus *Dionysiaca* 25.478–80, where the *Dragon* of the river Hermus is said to suck wayfarers into its mouth with its terrible breath, spinning them across the ground as they are drawn in.

Occasionally dragons can produce toxic gases from orifices other than the nose and mouth. In a late version of the tale of the apostle Matthew's encounter with the Ethiopian magicians Zaroes and Arphaxat ([c], xv AD), the fiery-breathed serpents they send against him scatter a sickness-inducing sulphur not only from their noses, but also from their *ears*. More striking still is the rather earlier case of Gregory of Tours' Caluppan (AD 581–94), who is attacked by a pair of *dracones* in his hermit cell in the Cantal:

But one day two snakes of immense size entered the chapel to confront him, initially holding back. One of these, the instigator of all temptation himself, as I think, was stronger than the other. It raised its breast and lifted its face up against the saint's as if it were about to whisper something to him. Caluppan was absolutely terrified and froze, just as if he were cast from bronze. He could not move even a limb, nor could he lift his hand in order to make the sign of the blessed cross against his opponent. When saint and snake had stood there in silence for a considerable time, it occurred to him to pray to the lord in his spirit and to shout out to him with his heart, even if he could not move his lips. As he silently spoke, his limbs, which had been bound by the craft of the foe, gradually began to be loosened. Sensing that he now had his right hand free, he made the sign of the blessed cross before his own face, and then, turning to the snake, he drew the sign of the cross of Christ again, against it... [he prays].[17] As the saint said these and similar things, making the sign of the cross with each assertion, the dragon was confounded by the virtuous power of this sign and in response abased itself and sank to the earth. And while this was happening, that other dragon began to wind itself around the feet and shins of the saint to trap him. When the saintly hermit saw this snake pouring itself around his feet he made a prayer and ordered it to go away, saying: 'Go back, Satan! You could do me no further harm, in the name of my Christ.' But the snake, after retreating as far as the threshold of the little chamber, emitted a loud noise through its lower part and filled the room up with such a stench that it could not be believed to be anything other than the Devil.[18] Thenceforth, however, neither snake nor dragon manifested itself before the saint.

It is difficult to believe that there is not a humorous intent in this case. Such scatology is rare in the tradition of hagiographical dragons, though let us recall the

---

[17] Cf. the episode of John the Deacon's *Life* of Gregory the Great ([c], ix AD), referred to in Chapter 5, §5.5.1 and below, §6.7, in which the monk Theodore, delirious with plague and imagining himself to be constricted by a great dragon, is accordingly unable to free his hands to follow his brother monks' advice to make the sign of the cross.

[18] Whilst it remains unlikely that Gregory appreciated the fact, snakes can actually fart: herpetologists have identified the deployment of 'cloacal popping' as a defensive mechanism in some species and suspect it in others too. See Lillywhite 2014:188.

case of the Galatian Onachus, mother to the Tarasque defeated by Martha ([a], AD 1187; [c], AD 1263–7; [d], AD 1264): as we have noted, she boasted the ability to shoot her excrement at her pursuers. We do find elsewhere the notion that dragons can leave a dreadful smell behind upon departure, albeit without any scatological justification: such is the case with the dragons dismissed by Brigid (ix AD) and Humiliana of Cerci (mid-xiii).[19] However, Humiliana's story at least may yet owe something to Caluppan's. Here the Devil appears to her in her hermit cell in serpent form and she compels him to depart with exorcistic language. The manifestation being incorporeal, he disappears in a puff of smoke, but leaves an unbearable stench behind him. Then a few days later he returns in the form of an all-too corporeal serpent, and remains with her for three days. During this time the serpent winds itself around her feet and presses its head against her cheek, just as the first of Caluppan's dragons had done to him (for the remainder of Humiliana's tale, see Chapter 7, §7.6). (Dragons can be a source of toxic miasmas in another important way too, when their slain carcass begins to rot: see §6.7.)

Compatibly with the dragon's association with unbelief, in later texts it can be asserted that God inflicts a dragon on a community specifically as a punishment for that unbelief. The sending of the dragon as an act of divine punishment is a version of a classical idea: the Lamia had been sent against Argos by Apollo to punish the city for the deaths of his lover and his son (Chapter 3, §3.4.1), whilst the Kētos of Troy had been sent against that city by Poseidon to punish it for the non-payment of a debt and the Ketos of Ethiopia or Joppa had been sent against that land or city by Poseidon again as punishment for its queen's insult to his Nereids (Chapter 4, §4.3.2). So it is that we are told, in the case of the Dragon of Lasia killed by George ([a], xi AD; [b], xii AD; [c], AD 1263–7), that the dragon's arrival in the local lake is in itself a punishment sent by God for the city's paganism (although there is no specific reference to any toxic breath in this case). The locals recognize that God has sent the Dragon of Rennes, destroyed by Armel ([a], xii AD or later), similarly to punish them for their sins. And Carantoc (early xii AD) refuses to kill the Dragon of Carhampton precisely because God has created it to punish sinners. In the Norse Life of Archbishop Nicholas (i.e. the famous St Nicholas of Myra; c. AD 1340) the tale is told of a venal English deacon who is punished by the emergence of a terrible flying dragon (flugdreki) from the sea: it burns up his church and his house with its venom, fire, and brimstone, and so too his ship as he tries to escape with his ill-gotten gains. This dragon seemingly owes much to the dragons of the sagas, which have a habit of raining fire down on ships (see Chapter 11, §11.5.1).[20] The marauding sea-monster 'resembling a dragon

---

[19] For Humiliana, see Petroff 1994:101–7; Schuchmann 2000.   [20] Cf. Acker 2013:56.

rather than a fish' defeated by Paulus Aurelianus ([b], AD 1637) is sent by God to punish the wicked Lord of Faou, who has been persecuting the local Christians.

But this logic does not always apply. With a tighter focus on the mind and motivation of the dragon itself, the earliest *Life* of Silvester ([a], late iv AD) makes the conversion of the local populace the point at which the Dragon of Rome becomes an active problem and starts to emit its pestilential breath. The logic here is that the conversion marks the cessation of its pagan cult and of its main-tenance by the Vestal Virgins with their offerings, with the result that the dragon pumps out the miasma by way of remonstration and as an expression of its displeasure:

> And so, after several days had passed, all the priests of the temples are said to have made a suggestion to august Constantine along the following lines: 'Most holy emperor, ever august, your Roman people is continuously imperilled by the breath of a dragon. For sacred virgins in the temple of Vesta maintained the cus-tom of descending to him every day of the calends and serving cakes of wheat to him. But from the point at which your piety received the Christian law, nothing has been taken in to it, and so, in its displeasure, it plagues the people every day with its breath. Accordingly, we beg you to command that the food that used to be given in tribute to its power be laid out for it, so that the city of Rome can give thanks to your piety for the health of all its citizens.'

Similarly, the ire of the Dragon of Euchaita is raised when Theodore Tyron ([d], *c*. AD 871; cf. [c], late ix AD) attempts to convert the locals. In a later Theodore story ([h], xiv AD or before) the Dragon of King Samuel's City cuts off that city's water supply in retaliation when the distracted King Samuel accidentally forgets to supply it with its animal sacrifice at the point when it falls due.[21]

6.1.4 The Dragon's Smokiness and Fieriness

Closely bound up with the motif of the dragon's toxic breath or miasma is that of its smokiness and, the immediate cause of this, its fieriness. As we have already seen in classical context, the notion that dragons should be fiery is an imaginative extrapolation of the fact that a viper's venom causes a burning sensation. As a dragon's fire is a sort of super-charged venom, so its smoke is a sort of vapor-ized venom.

We do well to start by looking again at the dragons of the marvellous *Acts of Philip* ([a], mid- to late iv AD). We meet the Dragon of the Ophiorhyme Desert

---

[21] See further Chapter 9, §9.1.5.

by night, but, the darkness of the night aside, it carries with itself a dark and smoky mist of its own (*gnophōdēs, gnophos*), the product of its internal fire, the fire that lives in its belly of brazen embers and sparks.[22] The Dragon of the Rocks and his fifty-serpent host subsequently encountered by Philip declare themselves to be the Children of Darkness (*Skotos*) and Blackness (*Melania*). Furthermore, we are told that the Dragon of Rocks himself 'belched forth fire and a great deal of venom in a bursting torrent', and indeed that its whole body resembled fire. Toxic gas and fire are similarly combined in the case of the Dragon of Anjou encountered by Mewan (x–xi AD). This suffocates men with its 'fire-vomited gas and stench' (*ignivomo vapore atque foetore*) and burns up animals with its venomous 'stings' (*venenosis aculeis*)—perhaps, that is, by spitting venom at them. The Dragon of Teano dismissed by Paris (AD 1533 or before) has a breath that is both fetid and fire-vomiting.

In other cases too attention is drawn to the smokiness of the dragon. The second dragon encountered by Simeon Stylites ([a], shortly before AD 459) emits fire and smoke with it. The Dragon of the river Narco destroyed by Maurus of Syria (viii AD?) puffs out a cloud from its nostrils, in conjunction with flames from its eyes. The dragon that confronts Margaret of Antioch ([a], AD 815–20; cf. [c], early ix AD; [f], c. AD 1380) breathes forth a smoky and pestilential breath; this is then seemingly contrasted with the sweetness of the breath that is the Holy Ghost. Margaret prays to God: 'Let the sweetness and goodness of your Holy Ghost/breath [*pneuma*] come to me.'[23] Just as a dragon's miasma can emanate from its cave, so can its smoke. Samson ([b], ix AD) finds smoke emerging from the caves of the Dragon of Trigg and from that of the dragon associated with his Pental Monastery at St-Samson-sur-Risle, fire also, in the latter case (cf. [d] and [e], both xii or before).[24]

Our authors often leave smoke aside to concentrate on the dragon's fieriness alone, and often too specifically on its fire-breathing or fire-vomiting, the most beloved dragon-motif of any modern child. Examples of the simple but undeveloped assertion of this motif abound.[25] In the earliest Latin version of her passion Margaret's dragon lights up her martyr-cell with the fire it emits from its nose and mouth ([b], early ix AD; cf. [c], mid-ix AD; [f], c. AD 1380). In later texts we occasionally find the imagery of the furnace: the Dragon of King Samuel's City killed by Theodore Tyron ([h], xiv AD) is said to deliver furnace-like blasts from its

---

[22] Appropriately, the wicked proconsul that rules the benighted serpent-worshipping city of Ophiorhyme rejoices in the personal name Tyrannognophos, 'Tyrant of Darkness'.

[23] Cf. Boulhol 1994:266.   [24] For the dragons of Samson of Dol, see Rauer 2000:90–116.

[25] For fire-breathing or fire-vomiting, see, e.g., the dragons encountered by: Matthew ([a], late vi AD; [b], AD 1263–7)—the dragons of the Ethiopian sorcerers Zaroes and Arphaxat; Veranus of Cavaillon (ix–xi AD)—the Dragon of the Fontaine de Vaucluse spring; Vigor of Bayeux (AD 1030–45)—the Dragon of Cerisy Forest; the disciples of St James ([a], mid-xii AD or earlier; [b], AD 1263–7)—the Dragon of Galicia; Armel ([a], xii AD or later; [b], xiii AD; [c], AD 1514)—the Dragon of Rennes; Paris (AD 1533 or before)—the Dragon of Teano.

mouth, while the monster expelled from Inis Cathaigh by Senán in an Irish text (early xv AD) is said to turn things to embers with a fiery breath that emanates from a belly resembling furnace-bellows, in a description similar to of that of the Dragon of the Ophiorhyme Desert faced by Philip.

The dragon's fieriness could extend from its mouth and nose to other parts of its body too, most commonly its eyes (cf. Chapter 1, §1.7), as in the cases, once again, of the Dragon of the river Narco destroyed by Maurus of Syria (viii AD?) and of the Dragon of Montecristo killed by Mamilianus ([a], vii–viii AD).[26] In a distinctive example of this phenomenon, the eyes of the dragon that Joannicius of Bithynia ([a], AD 846) encounters in a dark cave resemble glowing coals to such an extent that the saint attempts to build up the fire with some dry leaves. Accordingly, metaphors of bright light can be applied to a dragon's eyes. The dragon that attacks Simeon Stylites as he prays ([a], shortly after AD 459) flashes lightning from its eyes.[27] Whereas the mechanical version of the Dragon of Rome destroyed by the anonymous monk in the (v AD) *De promissionibus* has actual gemstones for eyes,[28] the eyes of the dragon encountered by Margaret of Antioch ([a], AD 815–20; cf. [c], early ix AD) in her martyr-cell are said to resemble pearls.[29] As regards other parts of the body again, the Galatian Onachus, mother to the Tarasque defeated by Martha ([a], AD 1187; [c], AD 1263–7; [d], AD 1264), effectively shoots fire from her rear end: the liquid excrement she shoots at its pursuers has a caustic effect.

Sometimes, as with Philip's Dragon of the Rocks, the entirety of the dragon's body can be fiery. The Dragon of Vaux destroyed by Nicasius (xi AD) is said to 'throw its whole fiery self upon' Quirinus as he approaches it. The full-body fieriness of the dragon has consequences for the land, wherever it travels. Samson of Dol tracks down the first of the four dragons he encounters in his second *Life* ([b], ix AD) by following its burned trail, and as he draws closer he is able to espy it from a distance because of its flaming head; when he subsequently drags along the Dragon of Brittany with his stole, it too leaves a fiery and smoky trail behind it. The Dragon of September Island dismissed over the sea by Machutus (AD 866–72) leaves the twisting trail it had made on the shore smoking. When we are told that the Dragon of Meung-sur-Loire faced by Lifard (ix AD) and the Dragon

---

[26] Further examples of fiery eyes: Theodore Tyron ([b], late ix AD or before; [d], *c.* AD 871; [f], x AD)—the Dragon of Euchaita; Peter of Athos (xiii–xiv AD)—the demon that appears before him in the form of a dragon (sparks).

[27] Rather more curiously, the dragon-demon faced by Margaret ([a], AD 815–20) and the Dragon of Jersey encountered by Maglorius (ix–x AD) are said to have had *teeth* resembling thunderbolts.

[28] *De promissionibus* 3.43, at *PL* li, col. 835.

[29] Our heroine is 'Marina' in Greek but Margarita in Latin. This leads to some irony when, in the earliest Latin version of her passion ([b], early ix AD), the dragon's eyes are again said to shine like pearls (*margaritae*). Mombritius' edition of this passion prints 'Oculi eius velut Margaritae splendebant', curiously construing the line to mean not 'Its eyes shone like pearls' but 'its eyes shone like Margaret's' (!). See Dresvina 2016:22–4.

of the Jura mountains encountered by Donatus of Sisteron (xii AD or earlier) burn up the lands in which they live, it remains unclear whether this is with breath-fire or with body-fire.

6.1.5 Further Effects of the Dragon's Breath and its Bite: Swelling and Lividity

The tale of the Dragon of Vaux destroyed by Nicasius (xi AD) and his companions offers more detail than usual about the actual pernicious effects of the dragon's breath: 'as to those that remained at home sick, after prolonged agonies from the serpent's venom and the tortures beyond compare of fevers and pyrexia, they would fail and die.' It is a nice touch that the diseases the dragon inflicts should be hot and fiery ones. But the most noted effect of the dragon's breath—and indeed of its bite alike—is to produce a swelling and a lividity in its victims. The notion has a good classical precedent in (e.g.) Lucan's description of Nasidius' death at the hands of a *prester* ('hurricane snake'; cf. Chapter 2, §2.1): his body distends to the point where he becomes a single, tumid blob.[30]

Numerous examples can be given of the swelling effect of the dragon's pestilential breath or the foul air it otherwise creates. Thus, the Dragon of the Egyptian Desert destroyed by Ammon (*c.* AD 395 and *c.* AD 403/4) contrives to cause the body of the son of a local shepherd to swell up by the power of its breath alone. Aldhelm interestingly coordinates his account of Silvester and the Dragon of Rome ([d], AD 675–710) with that of the conversion of Constantine. By fitting a tight collar around the dragon's neck the saint brings to an end the plague caused by its pestilential breath, and with it the sin of idolatry in the city. Simultaneously, the emperor is cured of his elephantine swelling of the body (*elefantiosa corporis incommoditas*) upon acceptance of the sacrament of baptism from Silvester. When the rotting bodies of a great dragon and its serpent host are washed down the Tiber in a flood, prior to the papacy of Gregory ([a], AD 594; [b], viii AD; [c], ix AD), they give rise to bubonic plague, the plague, that is to say, that causes groins to swell (*inguinaria*).[31]

As for bites, Joannicius of Bithynia ([a], AD 846) comes to the rescue of one of the workmen that has been building a hermit-cell for him on Mt Alsos. He has been bitten on the temple by an *echidna* (viper), his body has turned black and

---

[30] Lucan *Pharsalia* 9.789–804.
[31] Gregory himself speaks of another bubonic plague, one that fell upon Clermont during the reign of King Sigibert, earlier in the sixth century AD (*Dialogues* 4.31). Here we find plague and serpent brought together in a different syntax: the plague's swellings (*bubones*) were serpent-shaped, and they killed their hosts with their toxicity.

swollen up, and he is at death's door. Joannicius draws the sign of the cross over the wound with his finger whereupon it bursts open and all the foul-smelling venom pours forth.

Serpent-induced swellings are often accompanied by blackness or lividity, as in the case of this Joannicius tale. So too when the Dragon of India destroyed by Thomas (later ii AD) is compelled to reverse its bite upon its last-victim boy by sucking the toxin out of him, the boy's body loses its lividity whilst the dragon itself swells up until it bursts. This interesting episode implies that the body of the victim had been similarly swollen by the bite, with the swelling-inducing toxin going first into the boy before it is taken back into the serpent. Other examples focus on lividity and blackness alone. In the tale of the apostle John ([a], c. AD 150–180), Drusiana restores the wicked Fortunatus to life after he has been bitten by the dragon. Even so, he refuses conversion, whereupon the lividity returns to his body and he dies again. When Eudocia (x AD or before) directs the revivification of the boy 'bound' by the venom of the Dragon of Heliopolis, we learn that 'at once the dead boy rose again, putting off the blackness of the dragon'. The importance of the themes of swelling and lividity will become apparent when we come to look at Lucian and the archaeology of the hagiographical dragon fight (Chapter 8, §8.3.4).

6.1.6 The Dragon's Whipping Tail

A less frequently mentioned weapon in the dragon's armoury is its whipping tail. Thus the second dragon encountered by Simeon Stylites ([a], shortly before AD 459) approaches him beating its tail on the ground as a gesture of aggression. When the dragon encountered by Julian of le Mans (c. AD 1000) bursts forth from the idol of Jupiter at Artinas it destroys its own worshippers not only with its sulphurous breath but also by beating them with its tail. And when, in a similar episode, a dragon bursts forth from the idol of Venus destroyed by Fronto of Périgueux ([c], xi AD), it kills seven of its worshippers with its breath but beats others with its tail.

6.2 The Saint Prepares for the Battle

6.2.1 The Petitioning of the Saint

Whilst saints are perfectly capable of confronting dragons blighting a local community unbidden, they more usually undertake action in gracious response to a specific appeal from it, or from a representative of it, official or otherwise. The motif is seldom elaborated other than by the addition of speeches of appeal.[32]

6.2.2 Prayer and Fasting

The saint will often prepare for his approach to the dragon by praying or fasting, or indeed by enjoining the people of the city blighted by the dragon to undertake one or the other. The motif of the preparatory prayer, occasionally postponed until the point at which the saint is actually facing the dragon, is unsurprisingly all but universal, but is subject to little by way of variation in itself (although the different texts of the actual prayers uttered can sometimes be supplied in direct speech).[33] The motif of fasting in addition is a little less frequent. As with praying,

---

[32] Appeals are addressed to saints in e.g. the following instances: Ammon (c. AD 395 and c. AD 403/4), by the locals—the Dragon of the Egyptian Desert; Victoria ([a], c. AD 500), by Domicianus, the local mayor—the Dragon of Trebula; the apostle Andrew ([a] and [b], both late vi AD), by the mother of a disciple—the Dragon of Thessalonica; Samson of Dol ([a], vii–viii AD), by Count Vediolanus—the Dragon of Trigg; Samson of Dol ([a], vii–viii AD) again, by King Childebert—the Dragon of Brittany; Samson ([c], xii or earlier), by King Budic—the Dragon of Armorica; Senzius (vii–viii AD), by the locals—the Dragon of Blerana; Joannicius of Bithynia ([a], AD 846; [b], before AD 860), by the locals—the Dragon of Prusa; Joannicius of Bithynia ([a], AD 846; [b], before AD 860) again, by Father Daniel and his Christian brothers—the Dragon of Thasion; Michael ([a], ix–x AD), via the local pagan peoples' prayer to God—the Dragon of Southern Asia; Maglorius (ix–x AD), by the locals—the Dragon of Jersey; Mewan (x–xi AD), by a local estate-owning woman—the Dragon of Anjou; Vigor of Bayeux (AD 1030–45), by Volusianus (Velosianus)—the Dragon of the Cerisy Forest; Fronto of Périgueux ([c], xi AD), by the people of Limoges—the Dragon of the river Dronne; Germanus of Auxerre ([a], xi–xii AD), by the locals—the Dragon of Trou Baligan on the Cotentin peninsula; Armel ([a], xii AD or later)—the Dragon of the Rennes; Domitianus of Maastricht ([a], [b], both xii AD), by the locals—the Dragon of Huy; Leo of Cava (xii AD), by the locals—the Dragon of Cava; Martha ([a], AD 1187; [b], late xii AD; [c], AD 1263–7; [d], AD 1264), by the locals of Nerluc/ Tarascon—the Tarasque; Venerius of Tino (early xv AD), by the archbishop of Luni—the Dragon of Luni.

[33] Prayers are uttered by e.g. the apostle Philip ([a], mid- to late iv AD)—the Dragon of the Ophiorhyme Desert; Hilarion ([a], AD 396)—the Dragon of Epidaurus in Dalmatia; Ammon (c. AD 395 and c. AD 403/4)—the Dragon of the Egyptian Desert; Arsacius ([a], earlier v AD)—the Dragon of Nicomedia; Simeon Stylites ([a], shortly after AD 459)—the demon-dragon that manifests itself to him in his Syrian monastery; Victoria ([a], c. AD 500)—the Dragon of Trebula; Athenogenes (vi AD)—the Dragon of the Land of the Goths; Senzius (vii–viii AD)—the Dragon of Blerana; Fronto of Périgueux ([a], viii AD; [b], later x AD)—the Dragon of the river Dronne; Maurus of Syria (viii AD?)— the Dragon of the river Narco; Parasceve (viii AD)—the dragon to which she is thrown at Acireale; Gildas ([a], ix AD)—the Dragon of Rome; Joannicius of Bithynia ([a], AD 846)—the Dragon of Thasion; Joannicius of Bithynia ([b], before AD 860)—the Dragon of Cunduria; Samson ([b], ix AD)—a dragon encountered in the wilderness, and the Dragon of Brittany; Veranus of Cavaillon (ix–xi AD)—the Dragon of the Fontaine de Vaucluse spring and the Dragon of Albingaunum (Albenga, near Genoa); Theodore Tyron ([b], later ix AD or before; [d], c. AD 871; [f], x AD)—the Dragon of Euchaita; Magnus of Füssen ([a], c. AD 895; [b], AD 1067–70)—the Dragon of Kempten; Pope Leo IV ([a], before c. AD 939; [b], c. AD 939)—the Basilisk of the Church of St Lucy in Rome; Eudocia (x AD or before)—the Dragon of Heliopolis; Elisabeth ([b], x AD)—the Dragon of Constantinople; Vigor of Bayeux (AD 1030–45)—the Dragon of the Cerisy Forest; George ([a], xi AD; [b], xii AD; [c], AD 1263–7)—the Dragon of Lasia; Rofillus ([b], xi AD)—the Dragon of Forlimpopoli; Donatus of Sisteron (xii AD or earlier)—the Dragon of the Jura Mountains; Carantoc (early xii AD)— the Dragon of Carhampton; Euflamus (xii AD)—the Dragon of Saint-Efflam; Leo of Cava (xii AD)—the

the fast can be undertaken by the saint himself, or the saint and his Christian brothers, or he can ask the local population as a whole to undertake it with him. The periods of a single night, three, four, and seven days are mentioned.[34] One text that calls for particular attention in this connection is a passage of Jean Gobi's (earlier xiv AD) *Scala coeli*:

> It is told in the *History in Three Parts* that a most wicked *draco* was devouring people and could not be repelled by the power of arms or by the power of men. Upon hearing of this, a certain saint said, 'My dear men, the power of a dragon is no greater than that of a demon, but the power of a demon is repelled by fasting and prayer. So let us mortify our flesh and our bodies by fasting, so that God may take pity on us. When he had done this for ten days, he called all the people together and said, 'So that you may all learn how powerful fasting is, I want you all to spit into my bowl'. Then he took the spittle and made a circle around the dragon. It was unable to escape from the circle and died. Then the saint began to declare in loud voice, 'Just as the power of the corporeal fast killed this dragon, so the power of the spiritual fast repels all a demon's power and temptation.'
>
> Jean Gobi *Scala coeli* 13

Unfortunately, Jean provides no further context here: no place, no time, and no identity for the saint. The reason this text is of particular interest is that it assumes almost a physiological effect for the fasting, not merely a spiritual one: the fasting transforms the quality of the locals' spittle, which then allows it to be used effectively against the dragon. (For more on fasting in association with dragon fights, see §6.2.4, and for more on the use of spittle against dragons, see §6.6.2.)

Dragon of Cava; the monks of Tudual (xii AD)—the Dragon of Treguier; Crescentinus (xiv AD)—the Dragon of Tifernum (Città di Castello); Timothy ([b], xiv AD)—one of the Dragons of Prusa; Venerius of Tino (early xv AD)—the Dragon of Luni.

[34] Syrus of Genoa (v AD, perhaps with post-ix accretions) and the Basilisk of Genoa—a three-day public fast ordained; Silvester ([b], c. AD 500) and the Dragon of Rome—a three-day fast ordained for the church; Samson of Dol ([a], vii–viii) and the Dragon of Brittany—an overnight fast by the saint himself outside the dragon's cave; Senzius (vii–viii AD) and the Dragon of Blerana—a three- or four-day public fast ordained; Fronto of Périgueux ([a], viii AD; [b], later x AD) and the Dragon of the river Dronne—Fronto dismisses the dragon with a prayer, confident in the power of his default fasting; Joannicius of Bithynia ([a], AD 846) and the marauding dragon of a nameless village—a seven-day public fast ordained; Joannicius of Bithynia ([a], AD 846; [b], before AD 860) and the Dragon of Thasion—father Daniel and his Christian brothers asked to perform an overnight vigil (including a fast?); Joannicius of Bithynia ([a], AD 846; [b], before AD 860) and the Dragon of the river Gorgytes—an overnight fast and vigil by saint; Maglorius (ix–x AD) and the Dragon of Jersey (Angia)—a three-day fast by the saint himself; Pope Leo IV ([a], before c. AD 939) and the Basilisk of the Church of St Lucy at Rome—a preparatory fast by the saint; Vigor of Bayeux (AD 1030–45) and the Dragon of the Cerisy Forest—a fast by the saint himself; Rofillus ([a], xi AD) and the Dragon of Forlimpopoli—a fast by the saint himself and his Christian brothers; Venerius of Tino (early xv AD) and the Dragon of Luni—a three-day fast by the saint himself.

6.2.3 Spiritual Armoury

The saint's primary protection against the dragon is his faith. From the ninth century onwards, and especially in that century, this is often conveyed by means of the metaphor of arms. So it is that when Joannicius of Bithynia ([a], AD 846) presents himself before the cave of the marauding Dragon of Prusa, he is barefoot and clothed only in a hair shirt, relying rather on the 'breastplate of his simple faith'. Theodore Tyron ([d], c. AD 871) does carry a lance against the Dragon of Euchaita, but for good measure he also sports a 'helmet of salvation' and a 'shield of faith', alongside a 'golden, life-giving cross'. Pavacius (ix AD) goes up against the Dragon of le Mans armed with a 'cuirass of justice', a 'helmet of salvation', a 'shield of faith', and a 'sword of the Holy Ghost and the Word'.[35]

The celebration of spiritual armour conveys a message that faith is superior to physical arms, that the saint is superior to the soldier (this despite the fact that some distinguished dragon-fighting saints are themselves warriors, such as George and the Theodore just mentioned; see §§6.6.3–4). A similar message is conveyed by the tale of Euflamus (xii AD) and the Dragon of Saint-Efflam, a dragon tale with a more independent spirit than most. The British prince Euflamus is devoted to the monastic life, but forced into a dynastic marriage for the sake of a peace treaty. So he abandons his wife while she sleeps and makes for the coast of Brittany with some like-minded brethren. Here he encounters a dragon returning to a cave and then King Arthur, no less, on the trail of it, the cunning beast having evaded him repeatedly hitherto. Euflamus directs him to the cave, and the king goes into battle with it with a three-knotted club and a shield covered in a lionskin (he sounds somewhat Herculean). They fight the whole day long, but Arthur is unable to inflict a lethal blow, the serpent being protected by the hardness of its skin. However, the dragon is able to pierce Arthur's shield with its talons. They part at nightfall. Arthur now asks Euflamus for a drink, but he has none. Accordingly, the saint prays to God for water, climbs a prominent crag, and strikes the rock, whereupon an abundant spring bursts forth (cf. §6.1.2). Arthur drinks gratefully, asks the saint to bless him and pray for him, and happily departs leaving the dragon's fate in Euflamus' hands. Euflamus prays to God again, asking him to command the dragon to depart. Thereupon the dragon raises its head over a rock, looks about wildly in all directions and emits an anguished bellow, at which even distant places tremble. It vomits blood from

---

[35] Some further examples may be supplied. Samson of Dol ([b], mid-ix AD) approaches the Dragon of the Pental Monastery at St-Samson-sur-Risle similarly sporting a 'shield of faith' and a 'breastplate of hope'. Julian of le Mans (c. AD 1000) encounters the Dragon of Artinas wearing a 'cuirass of faith', a 'helmet of salvation', and a 'sword of the Holy Ghost'. Rofillus ([a], xi AD) takes on the Dragon of Forlimpopoli under the protection of a 'shield of spiritual salvation'; Donatus of Sisteron (xii AD or earlier) is fortified against the Dragon of the Jura Mountains by a 'helmet of faith'; Petroc ([a], xii AD or earlier) goes up against the Dragon of Cornwall armed with a 'shield of faith'; and Servanus (AD 510) kills the Dragon of Dunning armed with a 'cuirass of faith'.

mouth and nose, leaving the rocks reddened as an eternal testimony to the battle (cf. §6.8.2). Finally, it plunges into the sea, never to be seen again.[36] The same message is conveyed by the tale of Martha ([a], AD 1187; [d], AD 1264) and the Tarasque. The lady saint is called in only after military solutions have failed: armed men have been unable to kill the amphibious creature because it quits the forest in which it lives as they hunt it and hides in the river Rhône. It is also said to be able to withstand the attacks of twelve lions or as many bears. And the same message again is conveyed when King Budic and his entire army go down on bended knee to implore Samson ([c], xii or earlier) to save them from the Dragon of Armorica. The contrast between the saint's abilities and those of (normal) soldiery is made even in the case of the warrior saint Theodore Tyron ([f], x AD): we are told that he kills the Dragon of Euchaita with a single blow, whilst a phalanx of ten thousand men would not have had the courage to look upon it.

6.2.4 Angelic Support

When classical heroes had gone into battle against dragons, they were often supported by the goddess Athena: the message is conveyed best in the iconographic tradition where, so often, the goddess is seen to attend the scenes of dragon fights, showing keen interest, whilst not usually intervening herself at the physical level.[37]

The reflex of the supporting Athena in the hagiographical dragon fight is the manifestation of a holy figure, most commonly an angel. Occasionally their intervention takes on a physical dimension, but most manifesting angels content themselves with a hands-off bolstering of their saint's faith in advance of the battle proper. Victoria ([a], c. AD 500) is aided in her exorcistic dismissal of the Dragon of Trebula by the manifestation of her angel-familiar:

> No sooner had she begun to pray and make petition than the angel of the Lord that had appeared to her came to accompany her and began to lead the way, saying to her, 'None of these people can see that I am with you. Be reassured therefore that although I do not show myself to them, I will not abandon you, and I will ensure that your commands to the dragon are fulfilled.'

In her *Lives* Golinduch ([a] and [b], both vi–vii AD) is similarly fortified against the Dragon of Babylon with which she is enclosed in a pit by a manifestation of

---

[36] Arthur joins another British saint too in a dragon episode, that of Carantoc and the Dragon of Carhampton (early xii AD), although in this case there is no attempt to construct a contrast between the martial and the saintly methods of dealing with dragons. Rather, Arthur merely asks Carantoc to demonstrate his power to him by bringing the dragon under control, in exchange for telling him where he can find his marvellous floating altar. This story accordingly inverts the initial relationship between king and saint from the Euflamus story: in the former Arthur asks the saint where he can find the dragon; in the latter the saint asks Arthur where he can find his altar.

[37] See the sources, literary and iconographic, collected at Ogden 2013a:195–6.

her angel-familiar in turn. The angel gives her words of encouragement, but also liberates her from the capacity to feel thirst and hunger by touching her stomach and leaving his sign upon it, so that she is able to endure her lot for three months, deprived of food and drink the while. For, as the narrator of the Greek *Life* ([b]) explains, she herself was rather supposed to be food for the dragon. After the three months her tormentors eventually give up on the dragon and extract her from the pit to face other tortures. She retains her immunity from hunger even after her deliverance, and continues to perform miraculous feats of fasting in her later life (cf. §6.2.2 for fasting in association with dragon fights).[38] The angel that appears in a dream to Theodore Tyron ([d], *c.* AD 871) does so in order to give him specific instructions as to how to deal with the Dragon of Euchaita. The same saint ([h], xiv AD or before) is given physical help by the archangel Gabriel in association with his battle against the Dragon of King Samuel's City, albeit not before or during his battle against dragon itself, but rather after the event, when he, his mother, and two boys are left trapped in the dragon's cave by the bulk of its carcass: Gabriel creates a torrent to blast them free.[39]

Other holy powers can play a similar role. Silvester ([b], *c.* AD 500) is aided in his shutting in of the Dragon of Rome by a manifestation of St Peter, who gives him very particular instructions as to how to proceed against it; in a later version of the same story he is aided rather by the Holy Ghost ([e], AD 1263–7). Margaret of Antioch ([a], AD 815–20) is aided in her fight against the demon-dragon she faces in her martyr-cell by a manifestation of Jesus himself, no less, who materializes to precede her into her dragon's stomach as it swallows her, and so burst it open. And God himself replies in a disembodied voice to the prayers made by George ([a], xi AD; [b], xii AD), before he goes up against the Dragon of Lasia.

6.2.5 Attempted Dissuasion

The holy powers can be strong for the saint, but mortal flesh is weak, and the strength of the saints' faith is further demonstrated by their refusal to

---

[38] For the *Lives* of Golinduch, see Peeters 1944 for the tradition as a whole and Eustratius' Greek version ([b]) in particular; and Garitte 1956 for Stephen of (Syrian) Hierapolis' original Georgian version ([a]), with a helpful rendering of it into Latin. Eustratius' Greek version quickly followed Stephen's original. See also Efthymiadis and Déroche 2011:65.

[39] Some further examples. Hypatius (*c.* AD 450) is lifted by an angel of God beyond the reach of the dragon-headed, camel-bodied demons sent against him by a sorcerer. As Erasmus of Antioch (ix AD or before) is dragged before the statue of Jupiter at Sirmium and compelled to sacrifice to the dragon-demon within, he asks God to send him an angel to strengthen him in his battle (we are left to infer that God does indeed grant the request). Paulus and Juliana of Nicomedia (xiv AD) are protected by an angel in their martyr cell against the host of dragons and other snakes unleashed against them by Aurelian's sorcerers.

countenance the attempts of terrified, well-meaning mortal advisers to dissuade them from going up against their dragons. So it is that the inhabitants of September Island attempt to dissuade Machutus (AD 866–72) from going up against its dragon. The presbyter Tozzo attempts to dissuade Magnus of Füssen ([b], AD 1067–70) and his brethren from tarrying in the region of Kempten, infested as it is with 'worms' which are known to devour local hunters. When a great *boas* appears to attack them, he amusingly scuttles up a tree for his own safety. But it is the military saints above all that are subject to attempts to dissuade. As Theodore Tyron ([a], soon after AD 754; [b], late ix AD; [c], late ix AD; [d], *c.* AD 871; [f], x AD; [g], AD 980–1010) makes his way to his battle with the Dragon of Euchaita, the matronly Eusebia initially tries to discourage him from the attempt, although she does then support him in it when she learns that he is fortified by faith. In the later tale of Theodore's fight against the Dragon of King Samuel's City ([h], xiv AD or before), the part of Eusebia has morphed into that of Theodore's actual mother, whom the dragon has captured, and whom Theodore must now rescue, and so the role of dissuader passes to King Samuel himself, anxious to preserve the life of his best and favourite soldier. But Theodore is adamant, and asks the king rather to look after his estate should he not return, giving the proceeds to widows and orphans and freeing his slaves. When George ([a], xi AD; [b], xii AD; [c], AD 1263–7) encounters princess Sabra, put out in sacrifice for the dragon of Lasia, she repeatedly begs him to flee from the place to preserve his own life, both before and after he articulates the notion of staying to protect her.

6.3 At the Dragon's Lair

6.3.1 The Dragon's Home: Caves, Wells, Tombs, Islands, Groves

One of the most productive motifs of the hagiographical dragon fight is another of those that remains self-evident and readily meaningful to any modern child: the dragon lives in a cave. Caves have a double value. At one level they represent an appropriately inflated version of the elongated hole in the ground in which a common or garden snake might live. At another level they exhibit affinities with both the wilderness and the underworld (as they ever had, in the latter case, since classical times), the two places in which the Christian dragon properly belongs (as we shall see in §§6.5.4–5 and 6.5.7).[40]

---

[40] For the association between classical dragons and caves, see Ogden 2013a esp. 35, 41–2, 46–7, 51, 74–7, 88, 129–30, 132, 144, 161–7, 172, 300, 323, 357, 360, and, for their association with the underworld, 127–9, 247–54.

We find the motif of the dragon's cave-home already in our earliest hagiographical dragon fight proper, that of Thomas (later ii AD) against the Dragon of India: as Thomas happens across the body of the dragon's latest victim, lying in the road, the dragon emerges from its adjacent hole to confront him. Thereafter the motif is found frequently, most commonly as a mere cypher and unelaborated.[41] Doubtless we are to imagine the dragons said to live beneath tumbles of rocks as also living in caves, as in the case of the Dragon of the Rocks and its fifty cohorts encountered by Philip ([a], mid- to late iv AD) and the Dragon of Cunduria encountered by Joannicius of Bithynia ([b], before AD 860).

As we have seen, the spring the dragon controls occasionally emanates from the cave in which it lives. Otherwise, we are seldom invited into the cave to learn anything of its internal topography. The exceptions to this general rule are all unique. The cave in which the Dragon of Rome fought by Silvester ([b], c. AD 500; cf. [a], late iv AD, [c] and [d], AD 675–710, and [e], AD 1263–7) lives is described as being situated at the heart of the city, in the Tarpeian rock; the chamber at the bottom, closable with bronze doors, is approached down a descent of 365 steps, down which virgins had processed in pagan times to offer the dragon sacrifice. Joannicius of Bithynia ([a], AD 846; [b], before AD 860) takes refuge from a storm in a cave, and is initially delighted to find what he takes to be a fire left burning within by a previous occupant. As he attempts to build up the embers into a bigger blaze with the cave's detritus, he realizes that the embers are none other than the glowing fiery eyes of the great dragon that lives there, which now lunges at him. However, Joannicius is protected by God, who holds the serpent back. The saint stealthily withdraws to a different part of the cave, where he waits in safety for the storm to pass. We are left to infer that he quits the cave leaving the dragon unmolested. The furnished cave of the Dragon of King Samuel's City faced by Theodore Tyron ([h], xiv AD) has a central role in his story. Having captured Theodore's mother, the dragon keeps her prisoner in his cave, which is fronted by

---

[41] Cave homes are given to e.g. the dragon tracked by the Christian brothers associated with Ammon (c. AD 395 AD and c. AD 403/4); the Dragon of Nicomedia encountered by Arsacius ([a], earlier v AD); the Dragon of Chamaegephyrae encountered by Donatus of Epirus ([a], earlier v AD); the Dragon of Trebula dismissed by Victoria ([a], c. AD 500); the Dragon of Montecristo killed by Mamilianus ([a], vii–viii AD); the Dragons of Trigg in Cornwall and of Brittany encountered by Samson ([a], vii–viii AD); the host of dragons turned back by baby Jesus ([b], viii–ix AD); the *echidna* killed by Joannicius of Bithynia ([a], AD 846); the Dragon of Euchaita confronted by Theodore Tyron ([d], c. AD 871); the Dragon of Meung-sur-Loire destroyed by Lifard (ix AD); the Dragon of Brittany encountered by Samson ([b], ix AD)—the dragon retreats to the rear of its cave when he prays before it; the Dragon of Vendôme encountered by Beatus (x AD?); the Dragon of Antioch killed with the relic-hand of John the Baptist ([a], x AD); the Dragon of the Cerisy Forest encountered by Vigor of Bayeux (AD 1030–45); the Dragon of Mt Garganus destroyed by Michael ([b], xi AD); the Dragon of Saint-Efflam (to be) encountered by Euflamus (xii AD); the Dragon of Cava destroyed by Leo (xii AD); the Dragon of Treguier destroyed by Tudual (xii AD); the Dragon of Vado dismissed by Vindemialis (xii AD or before); the Dragon of Prusa destroyed by Timothy ([b], xiv AD); the Dragon of Luni dismissed by Venerius of Tino (early xv AD); the Dragon of Teano dismissed by Paris (AD 1533 or before); the Dragon of Caltabellotta in Sicily dismissed by Peregrinus (xvi AD or before).

a lockable door or gate. Within it the woman is made to sit on a stool where she is guarded by a host of snakes, including twelve principal ones, an abominable asp, and an old-man dragon (not to be confused with the dragon proper), the last seated on a golden throne. The dragon proper plans to enhance his cave's soft furnishings when he returns to it with more captives and deerskins for them to sit on (see passage quoted in Chapter 9, §9.1.5). Peregrinus (xvi A D or before) seemingly throws the Dragon of Caltabellotta in Sicily down an abyss-like hole within its own cave (what is envisaged is slightly obscure).

Dragons can also live in other cave-like places. As we have noted (§6.1.2), the Basilisk of Genoa dismissed by Syrus (v A D, perhaps with post-ix accretions) lives down a well, as does the Dragon of Moutiers-Saint-Jean (to be) encountered by John of Reomay (A D 659). Like caves proper, wells exhibit the desirable feature of being elongated (and so suitably serpent-shaped) holes in the ground; and, of course, like the spring-caves occupied by dragons, they constitute a vital water source. We shall have more to say about the significance of wells later on (§6.5.7). Dragons can also be maintained by their human owners in pits, as in the case of the Dragon of Babylon tamed by Golinduch ([a] and [b], both vi–vii A D).[42] And it is at the bottom of a pit that we find a fiery dragon in Barlaam's wonderful parable of the distractions of the material world, in the xi A D romance *Barlaam and Ioasaph*: chased into the pit by an enraged unicorn, the man clings to its sides as he tries to evade the dragon below, symbolic of the ravening belly of hell, but is more interested in the bit of honey dripping down to him from an overhanging tree.[43]

Another sort of hole in the ground in which a dragon could live was the tomb. So it is, for example, that the Dragon of Blerana banished by Senzius (vii–viii A D) lives in a crypt under that city's walls. The imagery of the tomb-home can be particularly rich. Venantius Fortunatus tells of the expulsion by Marcellus of Paris (late vi A D) of a dragon that had taken up residence in the tomb of an adulterous woman, after devouring her corpse there:

> There was a certain matron of high family but low repute, who stained her shining stock with base sin. After the light was taken away and she brought the days of her fleeting life to an end, she was carried out to her tomb with an accompanying (though profitless) procession. What happened after she had been laid in this tomb, and after her funeral rites, I shudder to relate, because it gives rise to a double grief over the dead woman. Anyway, a most enormous serpent began to visit in order to devour her body, and, to speak more plainly, the *draco* itself became the burial place of the woman whose limbs the beast was devouring. The serpentine pallbearer appropriated her luckless obsequies in such a way that her

---

[42] The term used for 'pit' is *lakkos*, the term the Septuagint deploys for Daniel's lion's den (6.16).
[43] [John Damascene] *Barlaam and Ioasaph* 12.112–14 (*bothros*).

corpse was not permitted to lie quiet. Although the ending of her life had permitted her to lie in one place, she was ever being transported around in punishment. What an accursed fate, truly to be dreaded! A woman who had not maintained her integrity towards her husband when in the world did not deserve to retain the integrity of her body in the tomb. For the snake, which had drawn the woman into sin when she lived, continued its cruelty against her corpse. Then the members of her family that remained in the city heard a loud noise, ran together, and saw the huge beast coiling its way out of the tomb and gliding along with its vast bulk and its tail whipping....[44]

After an angel has shown Eucherius ([a], AD 858; cf. [b], after AD 1124) a vision of Charles Martel (grandfather of Charlemagne) being tortured in hell for his seizure of church lands, the saint proceeds to investigate his tomb:

As they opened his tomb, a *draco* was seen suddenly to depart from it, and the whole of the inside of that tomb was found to have been blackened, as if it had been burned out. I have met people involved in this affair who survived into my own lifetime, and they have testified truthfully to me in their own voices about what they heard and saw.

The vignettes established here, particularly that in relation to Eucherius, resemble one recounted by Jacobus de Voragine too, but the context is far different. The pagan Mamertinus has lost an eye and become paralyzed in one hand through the worship of idols. The monk Savinus directs him to seek out Germanus ([b], AD 1263–7), bishop of Auxerre, for a cure. As he makes his way to him he is caught in the rain, and takes shelter in a cell built over the tomb of St Concordian, where he falls asleep. In his sleep he has a vision in which Concordian is invited to a feast with other bishops, but asserts that he cannot come because he must stay and protect a guest from the serpents that are living there. On waking he proceeds with his visit to Germanus and tells him of his experience, begging forgiveness. They return to the tomb together and lift the stone. Within they find a multitude of ten-feet-long serpents. They scatter, with Germanus commanding them to go where they can harm no one any more in the usual exorcistic fashion (see §§6.5.2–3). So in this case the serpents are the embodiment not of the paganism or wickedness of the tomb's actual occupant, Concordian, but of that of his so-called guest, which the buried saint has selflessly taken to himself in order to save him.[45]

---

[44] On this episode cf. le Goff 1980:155–88.
[45] The embodiment of a sinner's sins in a snake is also found in a story Jacob de Voragine tells of St Benedict ([b], AD 1263–7). A boy was sent to Benedict with two jars of wine, but he hid one by the side of the road for himself and delivered only the other. As the boy was leaving the percipient Benedict advised him not to drink directly from the jar he had kept, but tip the contents out carefully

Otherwise the most popular type of home for a dragon was an island, as in the cases of the Dragon of the Isle of Ogia encountered by Amand of Mastricht ([a], viii AD; cf. [b], xii AD) and the Dragon of the Isle of Battha (Batz) off Brittany encountered by Paulus Aurelianus ([a], AD 884).[46] In a doubling of motifs, island dragons can sometimes live in a cave within their island, as in the cases of the Dragon of the Isle of Montecristo killed by Mamilianus ([a], vii–viii AD)[47] and the Dragon of Thasion encountered by Joannicius of Bithynia ([a], AD 846; [b], before AD 860). Sometimes these caves can, more specifically, be sea-caves, as in the cases of the Dragon of September Island dismissed by Machutus (AD 866–72) and the Dragon of Jersey confronted by Maglorius (ix–x AD).

A noteworthy example of an island-based tale is found in the case of the serpent-host of the Isle of Gallinaria (off the Italian coast, near Andora) brought under control by Hilary of Poitiers, as in the following account again by Venantius Fortunatus ([a], late vi AD; cf. [b], AD 1263–7):

It would not be right for us to pass over this distinguished miracle. When he was in the region of the Isle of Gallinaria, he learned from the locals that it was infested with unnumbered and enormous coiling serpents. Because of this, even though they could see the island nearby, they considered it remoter than Africa because of its inaccessibility. When he heard this, the man of God saw that victory was coming to him in a fight against the beasts. He disembarked onto the island invoking God's name and with the succour of the cross before him. Upon seeing him the snakes were turned to flight, because they were unable to tolerate the sight of him. Then he fixed his staff into the ground to serve as a boundary marker by which he designated, by the power of his virtue, the point up to which they were to be permitted to roam. They were no longer allowed to occupy the part he forbade. The island had a sea inlet. Since they ever feared to touch the forbidden part, it was easier for them to cross over the sea than to cross the place at which the saint had spoken: such was the immovable boundary fixed in place by his speech.

Also noteworthy here is the Irish tale of Senán (early xv AD), who expels a fiery monster from the Isle of Inis Cathaigh so that he can build a hermitage on it; the archangel Raphael advises him that God had ensconced the creature there

---

first. As he did so, a snake emerged. Cf., perhaps, Gregory of Tours' slightly obscure tale of Portianus (late vi AD), in which Sigivald compels Portianus to bless a cup of wine, whereupon the cup shatters, pouring its contents to the ground together with a huge and venomous serpent.

[46] Further examples of island-dwelling dragons: Guthlac (AD 730–40)—the demon-vipers on his hermit-island of Crowland; Honoratus ([b], xii AD?; cf. [a], before AD 449)—the Dragon of the Île Saint-Honorat in the Lérins group off the coast of Cannes, which bodily surrounds its island; Siward (xii–xiii AD)—the Dragon of Orkney.

[47] But a later version of his story has it occupying rather the island's mountain-top ([b], xii AD).

(curiously) to keep the place pure of sinners, precisely so that it would constitute a suitable place for his retreat when the time came.

The final category of dragon-home worth mentioning is the grove. Like the cave-home, the grove-home had a good classical pedigree, especially in the context of art, where both Ladon, Dragon of the Hesperides, and the Colchis Dragon hang in their trees with the golden treasures they guard, respectively apples and fleece (see Chapter 1, §§1.2.3–4). And we have seen how, in early Christian iconography, the Serpent of Eden, coiling around the Tree of Knowledge, is the direct descendant of these creatures (Chapter 4, §4.6). Turning to the hagiography, the Dragon of Euchaita killed by Theodore Tyron actually lives in a tree in one of the earlier tellings of its story ([a], AD 754); in another version it lives in a grove on the road outside the city ([e], before AD 890). The Tarasque of Tarascon encountered by Martha ([a], AD 1187; [c], AD 1263–7; [d], AD 1264) likewise inhabits a wood. But caves are never far away. In other versions again of the Theodore Tyron story the Dragon of Euchaita lives in a hole within a dense wood, the latter shaking as it emerges ([b], late ix AD or before; [f], x AD). The Dragon of the Cerisy Forest encountered by Vigor of Bayeux (AD 1030–45) lives in a cave within the forest, whilst the Dragon of Prusa destroyed by Timothy ([b], xiv AD) takes up residence in a cypress tree beside the spring it seeks to monopolize after emerging from its adjacent cave.

6.3.2 The Saint Presents Himself at the Dragon's Lair, or Summons the Dragon

One of the most productive motifs is that of the saint's presentation of himself at the dragon's lair, typically the mouth of its cave, duly prepared for the fight. For all its near-universality, the motif seldom receives much by way of elaboration.[48] Just

[48] Saints presenting themselves before the dragon's lair, ready for battle: Ammon (*c.* AD 395 and *c.* AD 403/4)—the cave of Dragon of the Egyptian Desert (so too in the case of his over-enthusiastic Christian-brother associates); Syrus (v AD, perhaps with post-ix accretions)—the well of the Basilisk of Genoa; Victoria ([a], *c.* AD 500)—the cave of the Dragon of Trebula; Samson ([a], vii–viii AD; cf. [b], ix AD, [d], xii AD or before)—the caves of the Dragon of Trigg and the Dragon of Brittany, and the home (whatever it is—the narrative is vestigial) of the dragon in the region of his Pental Monastery at St-Samson-sur-Risle (to be); Senzius (vii–viii AD)—the crypt of the Dragon of Blerana; Maurus of Syria (viii AD?)—the riverbank of the Dragon of the river Narco; Joannicius of Bithynia ([a], AD 846; [b], before AD 860)—the cave of the Dragon of Prusa and the cave of the Dragon of Thasion; Machutus (AD 866–72)—the cave of the Dragon of September Island; Theodore Tyron ([d], *c.* AD 871)—the cave of the Dragon of Euchaita; Elisabeth ([a], ix–x AD)—the pagan ruins in which the Dragon of Constantinople lives; Maglorius (ix–x AD)—the cave of the Dragon of Jersey; Veranus of Cavaillon (ix–xi AD)—the cave of the Dragon of Albingaunum; Pope Leo IV ([a], before *c.* AD 939)—the cave of the Basilisk of the Church of St Lucy in Rome; Mewan (x–xi AD)—the lair of the Dragon of Anjou; Vigor of Bayeux (AD 1030–45)—the cave of the Dragon of the Cerisy Forest; Fronto of Périgueux ([c], xi AD)—the lair of the Dragon of Limoges and its serpent brood; Nicasius (xi AD)—the spring of the Dragon of Vaux; Rofillus ([a] and [b], xi AD) and Mercurialis—the hole of the Dragon of Forlimpopoli; Martha ([a], AD 1187; [b], late xii AD; [c], AD 1263–7; [d], AD 1264)—the wood of the Tarasque of

occasionally there is an attempt to convey the sense of a journey being made, as, for example, with the employment of a guide or guides to the lair. So it is that Mewan (x–xi AD) is escorted by (unidentified) guides to where the Dragon of Anjou lies and Armel ([a], xii AD or later) is guided by the locals to the lair of the Dragon of Rennes. This motif can be combined with that of the dragon's 'last-victim boy' (for which see Chapter 7, §7.4): such a boy, duly restored to life by the saint, escorts Germanus of Auxerre ([a], xi–xii AD) to where the seven-headed Dragon of Trou Baligan lies.[49] The sense of a journey being made can also be conveyed by the difficulty of the path. Silvester ([a], late iv AD; [b], c. AD 500; [c] and [d], AD 675–710; [e], AD 1263–7) has to progress down the 365 steps of the cave of the Dragon of Rome in order to confront it in its chamber at the bottom. Gildas ([a], ix AD; [b], xi AD) has the mirror-opposite experience: he has to stumble up a mountain above Rome (whatever that is) with his staff to present himself at the cave of his own iteration of the Dragon of Rome.

An anomalous tale deserves mention here. In Sabas' account of Joannicius of Bithynia (before AD 860) the saint approaches the cave of the Dragon of Cunduria with a far different purpose. He is assailed by lustful thoughts, as if by fiery darts, and so he seeks out the dragon in its cave in order to feed himself to it (!) in an attempt to mortify his flesh, rending it himself the while. But the dragon feels shame before him and declines to touch him. At this Joannicius stretches out his hands to God and repels all the demons that have been tormenting him, killing the dragon itself at the same time, and thereafter retaining power over all beasts, seen and unseen.

Just occasionally we find an inversion of the motif of the saint's progress to the dragon's lair, with the saint rather summoning the dragon to wherever he happens to be himself by means of a prayer. So it is with Athenogenes (vi AD) and the Dragon of the Land of the Goths, Eudocia (x AD or before) and the Dragon of Heliopolis, and Carantoc (early xii AD) and the Dragon of Carhampton, when he is challenged by King Arthur to demonstrate his power over the creature.

6.4 The Saint's Mastery of the Dragon

6.4.1 The Dragon Compelled to Self-Harm

The mere approach of the saint can compel dragons to self-harm. The Dragon of India destroyed by Thomas (later ii AD) beats its head and tail on the ground as it

---

Tarascon; Tudual (xii AD)—the cave of the Dragon of Treguier; Venerius of Tino (early xv AD)—the cave of the Dragon of Luni; Paris (AD 1533 or before)—the cave of the Dragon of Teano.

[49] The boy that escorts Samson ([a], vii–viii AD; [b], ix AD; [d], xii AD or before) to the cave of the Dragon of Trigg is seemingly reminiscent of this motif too.

draws close to the saint. The first line of snake-guards of Ophiorhyme, seven in number, bite their own tongues at the approach of Philip ([a], mid- to late iv AD). When the Dragon of Trigg catches sight of Samson of Dol ([a], vii–viii AD; [b], ix AD) before its cave, we are told that 'it shook violently and furiously strove to turn about to gnaw its tail'; another of the dragons Samson ([b]) encounters behaves in a similar way, also biting at the soil and the dust. When the Dragon of Thasion senses the presence Joannicius of Bithynia ([a], AD 846; [b], before AD 860) outside its cave, it begins to throw its coils around violently and to shake the place with its loud hisses. The Dragon of Caltabellotta in Sicily beats the ground (presumably) with its tail in fear at the approach of Peregrinus (xvi AD or before).[50]

6.4.2 The Cross

Prayer aside (§6.1.2) another key tool in gaining mastery over the dragon is the sign of the cross, usually in air-drawn form (the *signum crucis*) but occasionally actual crucifixes are deployed too. The air-drawn cross is a highly productive motif, though one that is seldom elaborated in itself: it can have the effects of merely protecting the saint, of rendering the dragon tame, or of actually destroying it.[51]

A few specific examples of its use may be mentioned. Philip ([a], mid- to late iv AD) makes the sign of the cross in the air with sprinkled holy water to counter the smoky miasma produced by the Dragon of the Ophiorhyme Desert. We have noted (§6.1.3) Caluppan's (AD 581–94) struggle to unfreeze his hands whilst

---

[50] Cf. also the Dragon of Euchaita destroyed by Theodore ([d], AD 871), which beats its tail on the ground before giving up the ghost.

[51] Air-drawn crosses are found in the following cases: Donatus of Epirus ([a], earlier v AD)—the Dragon of Chamaegephyrae; Marcian (mid-v AD)—the dragon that manifests itself in the vestibule of his house; Julian Sabas (mid-v AD)—the Dragon of the Syrian Desert; Columba (*c.* AD 700)—the Loch Ness monster; Guthlac (AD 730–40)—the demon-vipers of the island of Crowland; Clement of Metz ([a], AD 782–6)—the Dragon of Metz and its serpent brood; Amand of Mastricht ([a], viii AD; cf. [b], xii AD)—the Dragon of the Isle of Ogia; Maurus of Syria (viii AD?)—the Dragon of the river Narco; Pavacius (ix AD)—the Dragon of le Mans; Samson ([b], ix AD)—the dragon encountered in the wilderness; Machutus (AD 866–72)—the Dragon of September Island; Theodore Tyron ([b], late ix AD; [d], AD 871; [c], late ix AD; [f], x AD)—the Dragon of Euchaita; Magnus of Füssen ([a], *c.* AD 895)—the Dragon of Kempten; Elisabeth ([a], ix–x AD)—the Dragon of Constantinople; Maglorius (ix–x AD)—the Dragon of Jersey; Veranus of Cavaillon (ix–xi AD)—the Dragon of Albingaunum; Julian of le Mans (*c.* AD 1000)—the Dragon of Artinas; Vigor of Bayeux (AD 1030–45)—the Dragon of the Cerisy Forest; Fronto of Périgueux ([c], xi AD)—the dragon that bursts forth from the idol of Venus at Périgueux and the Dragon of Limoges; George ([a], xi AD; [b], xii AD; [c], AD 1263–7)—the Dragon of Lasia; Agilus (xi–xii AD)—the vision of a venom-spewing dragon at Resbach; Servulus ([a], xii AD or before)—the Dragon of Trieste; Vindemialis (xii AD or before)—the Dragon of Vado; the disciples of St James ([a], mid-xii AD or earlier; [b], AD 1263–7)—the Dragon of Galicia; Girardus of Anjou (*c.* AD 1153)—the Dragon of Brossay; Honoratus ([c], *c.* AD 1300)—the Dragon of the Île Saint-Honorat; Venerius of Tino (early xv AD)—the Dragon of Luni; Senán (early xv AD, Irish text)—the monster of Inis Cathaigh; Severinus of Amiterno (xvi AD or before)—the dragon that manifests itself before him; Paris (AD 1533 or before)—the Dragon of Teano in Campania.

Fig. 6.2 Saint Margaret and the Dragon of Antioch (painting). Italian, painting from the workshop of Agnolo Gaddi, *c.* A D 1390. Metropolitan Museum, New York, Bequest of George Blumenthal, 1941, 41.190.23. Public domain.

subject to the hypnotic stare of one of the pair of dragons that attacks him in his hermitage in the Cantal: eventually he is able to so do by means of an internal prayer, and to proceed to use the sign of the cross against the creature in the usual way. Enclosed in a pit with the Dragon of Babylon, Golinduch ([b], vi–vii A D; cf. [a], vi–vii A D) renders the creature tame as it attempts to devour her by stretching her arms out to express the form of the cross with her body. Strikingly, Margaret (in Greek Marina) of Antioch ([a], A D 815–20; cf. [c], early ix A D; [d], x A D; [e], A D 1263–7) makes the sign of the cross before the dragon that manifests itself in her martyr-cell as it swallows her, with the result that Jesus precedes her into its belly and bursts it open (Figs 4.29, 4.30, 6.2):[52]

It [the *drakōn*] stood in the middle of the gaol roaring and hissing. It ran around Marina in a circle with its sword-tongue unsheathed, and its hissing made a

---

[52] The following passage continues on directly from that quoted in Chapter, 5, §5.5.2, where the dragon's physical form is described.

terrible stench in the gaol. The holy virgin was in great fear. Her limbs gave way, her vision became blurred and she forgot the prayer she had been making. But the lord acted in accordance with it and showed her the enemy and adversary of all men. Now she knelt and began to pray and say, 'Unseen God, by your face the sea and the abyss are dried up. You are the one that sets boundaries to Hades. You are the one that frees the bonds of the earth, so that it may not shake. You are the one that diminishes the power of the good-hating dragon. You are the one that binds Hades and liberates those shut within it. Now look at me and have pity on me. Do not stand by and see me harmed by an evil demon. Let your wish come to pass, Lord, so that I may conquer this creature's flame, the nature of which I did not know.' As she was saying this the dragon, greatly angered, hissed at her. The holy servant of God made a cross on her forehead and over her whole body, and prayed with tears and said, 'Lord, chase this wicked wolf and mad dog and its stench away from me. And let the sweetness and goodness of your Holy Spirit [literally 'breath', *pneuma*] come to me.' And when she had said this the dragon raged against her and overwhelmed her. It raised its neck over the square stone [sc. to which prisoners would have been bound]. Its head was hanging down. Its legs reached the ground, running out from that part of its neck upon which the snakes grew, and the mouth of the dragon gaped open. The dragon drew the holy girl to itself, placed its mouth on her neck, sent its tongue down under her feet, and in this way hoisted her up like a lifting machine and gobbled her down into its belly. With her hands making the sign of the holy Christ, Christ went before her and ruptured the dragon's guts. And so the dragon fell from the square stone, made a loud noise, split in half and died. The holy girl came out of its belly unharmed. Turning back, she said to it, 'Truly you found what you were looking for.' The dragon remained where it was, fallen on the floor. And suddenly from the other corner of the prison a great demon fell upon the knees of the holy Marina....[53]

Joannicius of Bithynia ([a], AD 846) uses the drawn cross in an intriguing way. When Pardus, one of the workmen building a hermit-cell for him on Mt Alsos, is bitten on the temple by an *echidna* (viper), his body turns black and swells up, and he is brought to death's door. As we have seen, the saint draws the sign of the cross over the wound with his finger, whereupon it bursts open and all the foul-smelling venom pours forth (§6.1.5 above; see further Chapter 8, §8.3.4). We have

[53] For Margaret, see Boulhol 1994; Clayton and Magennis 1994; Petroff 1994:97–109; White 2008:157–62; Dresvina 2012, 2016; Bledsoe 2013; Barillari 2017. Boulhol's case that the sequence is strongly influenced by the (late iv AD?) *Questions of Bartholomew* (for which see Chapter 4, §4.8) and its Beliar is persuasive: both Bartholomew and Margaret have asked the lord to show them a vision of the enemy (cf. also Dresvina 2012:196–9). His contention (266–7) that the dragon's swallowing of Margaret is derivative of the classical tradition of the Colchis Dragon's swallowing of Jason is less so: the sole evidence for this episode available to us—which would not have been available to the author of the *Life* of Margaret—is the *c.*480 BC Duris cup (see Chapter 1, §1.2.4 and Fig. 1.4).

an interesting double use of the sign of the cross in the tale the destruction of the Dragon of Vaux by Nicasius (xi AD) and his companions: first Quirinus uses it to tame the dragon and bind its neck; then Nicasius himself uses it to burst the dragon before the assembled crowd.

As to physical crucifixes, Philip ([a], mid- to late iv AD) and his team again, on Jesus' advice, wear the sign to compel the snakes of Ophiorhyme to bow their heads before them. In the earliest Latin *Passion* of Margaret ([b], early ix AD or before), the saint—as it appears—carries a crucifix she has made into the dragon when it swallows her, and this then expands in size inside the dragon, causing it to split in two.[54] Joannicius ([a], AD 846; [b], before AD 860) also uses crucifixes in distinctive ways. He destroys the Dragon of Prusa by making an imprint upon it three times with the crucifix he carries, invoking the Trinity the while; it has the effect of a sword.[55] He kills the Dragon of Cunduria, however, by rather more prosaically bashing it on the head with his cruciform iron staff ([b] only). Magnus of Füssen ([b], AD 1067–70) both makes the sign of the cross in the air and then also deploys a separate crucifix against the Dragon of Kempten. Martha ([a], AD 1187; [b], late xii AD; [c], AD 1263–7; [d], AD 1264) shows her Tarasque-dragon a wooden cross to subdue it (we feel as though we are in the territory of the modern vampire movie here). Tudual (xii AD) carries a flag emblazoned with the cross into his battle against the Dragon of Treguier.

6.4.3 The Dragon's Bowing and Fawning

The dragon often becomes docile before the saint, either by virtue of his mere presence or after a prayer. A precedent for this motif may be found in a post-biblical tradition: John Chrysostom claims that 'the *drakontes* and the asps and the horned snakes trembled before John the Baptist in the desert'.[56] In this regard the dragon is often said to bow down its head: this is indicative of meekness and subjection, of course, and a willingness to submit to the symbolic gesture of trampling (see Chapter 5, §5.2.3), but it is also a gesture significantly antithetical to the serpent's raising of its head from the ground to strike, as found, for example in the Dragon of the Jura Mountains' raising of its head (15 cubits into the air!) to attack Donatus of Sisteron (xii AD or earlier). The point is made when Andrew

---

[54] So, at any rate, I hesitantly interpret the phrase *sed crux Christi quam sibi fecerat beata Margarita crevit in ore draconis et et † in duas partes eum divisit.* That Margaret should have made a physical cross for herself is a slightly awkward notion, but the alternative seems more awkward still: that she should make an air-cross that then mutates into a substantial object before beginning to expand (the textual aporia is not itself of moment here).

[55] So too Athenogenes (vi AD) strikes the Dragon of the Land of the Goths three times with the butt of a spear he uses as a staff, thereby causing it to burst open.

[56] John Chrysostom Εἰς τὴν ὄρχησιν τῆς Ἡρωδιάδος, καὶ εἰς τὴν ἀποτομὴν τῆς κεφαλῆς Ἰωάννου τοῦ Προδρόμου καὶ Βαπτιστοῦ (*In decollationem sancti Joannis*), PG lix, col. 486; cf. Chapter 5, §5.2.7.

([a], late vi AD), in addressing the Dragon of Thessalonica as an avatar of the Devil, commands it, 'Put away the head that you raised in the beginning to the destruction of the human race'. Fronto of Périgueux ([c], xi AD) gives a similar order to the Dragon of Neuilly-Saint-Front (Nogeliacum): 'I command you, deathly dragon, you who have lifted up your head, to subject yourself to me.'

Thus, when Jesus is telling the apostle Philip ([a], mid- to late iv AD) and his team how to take on the terrible snakes of Ophiorhyme, he instructs them to wear the sign of the cross because it will make the snakes bow their heads. When Philip then approaches the city, its first rank of seven snake guardians is dispatched from the shoulders of the human guards to attack him as a stranger to the city's 'abomination', i.e. the worship of the viper-goddess, the Echidna, but instead they just lay their heads on the floor and bite their own tongues. When Venantius Fortunatus' Marcellus of Paris (late vi AD) confronts the dragon that has come to occupy the tomb of an adulterous woman, devouring her body, 'The snake began to beg for forgiveness with its head inclined in supplication and its tail making blandishing gestures'. Machutus (AD 866–72) seemingly compels the Dragon of September Island to incline its head to the earth by holding his staff over its neck. When Quirinus, the companion of Nicasius (xi AD), makes the sign of the cross before the Dragon of Vaux, it lays its head down on the ground.[57] A distinctive subset of taming motifs is found in scenes in which a tyrant has his magicians or wranglers send dragons or snakes against the saint: see Chapter 7, §7.5.

In this respect the dragon is often compared to a tame and harmless animal, most often a sheep or a pet dog. As to sheep, Golinduch ([b], vi–vii AD), the 'lamb of God' herself, renders the Dragon of Babylon as tame as a lamb, to such an extent that it lays its head in her lap, and she fondles its head and lips. After tying his handkerchief around the neck of the Dragon of the Cerisy Forest, Vigor of Bayeux (AD 1030–45) passes it over to his companion Theodemirus (Theudemir) to lead, as if it were a tame sheep. The Tarasque tackled by Martha ([a], AD 1187; [b], late xii AD; [c], AD 1263–7; [d], AD 1264) becomes as tame as a sheep when she throws holy water over it and shows it a wooden crucifix. As to pet dogs, Pavacius (ix AD) has the Dragon of le Mans 'play dead' for him in the road. The Dragon of the Fontaine de Vaucluse spring encountered by Veranus of Cavaillon (ix–xi AD) similarly falls at his feet as if dead. The Dragon of Lasia tamed by George ([c], AD 1263–7) is compared to a tame dog as it follows princess Sabra on a lead made from her girdle (cf., more loosely, [a], xi AD; [b], xii AD). The Dragon of Naples contrives to imitate both animals: it first becomes like the tamest lamb for Gaudiosus (xvi AD or before), before rolling over onto its back for

---

[57] Some further examples: Samson of Dol ([b], mid-ix AD) and the Dragon of Brittany; Germanus of Auxerre ([a], xi–xii AD) and the Dragon of Trou Baligan; Armel ([a], xii AD; [b], xiii AD) and the Dragon of Rennes; Myron of Crete ([b], xiv AD) and the Dragon of Raucia (the dragon also cries a river).

him. Other animals too can be invoked. The Dragon of Metz bows its head to the ground before Clement ([c], *c.* AD 1100) like a goose. The Dragon of Carhampton adds a calf into the repertoire: it initially runs to Carantoc (xii AD) like a calf running to its mother and with eyes downcast (cf. the bowing of the head again); but it then allows itself to be led about like a lamb; finally the saint then leads it into the hall of Cato's (Cadwy's) castle at Dindraithov, where he proposes to feed it as if a pet.[58]

Once fully subjected, dragons can be more constructively employed. So it is that Philip ([a], mid- to late iv AD) has the Dragon of the Rocks outside Ophiorhyme and its fifty attendant serpents build a church for him. Rufinus' hermit Ammon employs a pair of *dracones* to guard his desert cell against the thieves that would steal his bread (*c.* AD 395 and *c.* AD 403/4).

6.4.4 The Binding of the Dragon's Neck with a Stole and the Stopping of its Mouth

From the time of at least the sixth century onwards, one of the most distinctive and productive motifs of the saintly dragon fight is that of the saint binding the neck of the dragon with a garment and leading it along with it, as if on a lead or leash. The biblical genesis of the motif is not entirely clear. The act of binding in itself probably salutes Michael's locking of the Revelation Dragon into the abyss,[59] probably too Jesus' parable as preserved by Mark, 'No one can enter the house of a strong man [sc. Satan] and snatch his possessions without first binding the strong man,'[60] and perhaps also Jesus' words to Peter in bestowing the keys to heaven upon him, as preserved by Matthew, 'whatever you bind on earth will be bound in heaven.'[61]

But for the use of clothing the best we can do is look to the precedents of Paul in Ephesus and to the Daughter of Jairus episode. As to the former, Acts tells how God accomplished so many miracles by Paul's hands, 'that the handkerchiefs [*soudaria*; lit. 'sweatcloths'] and aprons [?—*simikinthia*] that had touched his skin were taken off to the sick, and their diseases left them and the wicked spirits departed from them.'[62] As to the latter, Luke records that, as Jesus makes his way to the house to heal the girl, a woman who has been bleeding continuously for

---

[58] Note also the Dragon of Trou Baligan encountered by Germanus of Auxerre ([a], xi–xii AD): in addition to bowing its head, it begins to behave like a tame animal (species unspecified) at the saint's approach.

[59] Revelation 20:1–3; see Chapter 5, §5.2.10, where the text is quoted.   [60] Mark 3:27.

[61] Matthew 16:19: ὃ ἐὰν δήσῃς ἐπὶ τῆς γῆς ἔσται δεδεμένον ἐν τοῖς οὐρανοῖς; cf. also 18:18, ὅσα ἐὰν δήσητε ἐπὶ τῆς γῆς ἔσται δεδεμένα ἐν οὐρανῷ. I thank my colleague David Horrell for drawing these passages to my attention.

[62] Acts 9:11–12.

twelve years touches the hem of his cloak, and her bleeding stops at once. Jesus
senses that 'power' has gone out from him and asks who has touched him. The
woman confesses, whereupon Jesus bids her go in peace, for she has been healed
by her faith.[63] At any rate this episode would seem to be the principal inspiration
for the role of the hem of Jesus' robe in a striking sequence in the *Questions of
Bartholomew*, which may have served as an intermediary text so far as our motif
is concerned. In the (iv–v AD?) Greek version Bartholomew asks a manifestation
of Jesus to show him a vision of the enemy of humankind, and he reluctantly has
the archangel Michael bring the Revelation Dragon, now rejoicing in the name of
Beliar, forth from his confinement in the abyss:

> He nodded to Michael to blow his trumpet in the height of heaven. There was an
> earthquake, and out came Beliar under the control of 660 angels, and he was
> bound in chains of fire. He was 1,600 cubits in length and 40 in breadth. His face
> resembled a lightning bolt of fire. His eyes were dark. A malodorous smoke
> emanated from his nostrils. His mouth was like a chill cavern. His single wing
> extended for 80 cubits.[64] As soon as they saw him the apostles fell down on the
> earth on their faces and became as dead.... Frightened, Bartholomew said,
> 'Lord Jesus, give me the hem of your cloak, so that I may be bold as I approach
> him'. Jesus said to him, 'You cannot take the hem of my cloak, for this cloak of
> mine is not the one I wore before my crucifixion'.
>
> *Questions of Bartholomew* 4.12–14, 18–19[65]

The Greek version's 'hem [*kraspedon*] of your cloak' becomes 'the jerkin [*torax*]
from your shoulders' in the (vi–vii AD) so-called 'Latin 2' version of the text.[66]
For all Jesus' refusal, the seed of the idea that the robe of a holy person could be
efficacious against a dragon was seemingly sown.

In the relevant hagiographical narratives, which are largely on the Latin side,
the garments said to be deployed in this way are the following: the *orarium*
('handkerchief', 'napkin');[67] the *zona* ('belt', 'girdle');[68] the *stola* ('stole', 'upper

---

[63] Luke 8:40–9 (40: τοῦ κρασπέδου τοῦ ἱματίου).

[64] Cf. Chapter 4, §4.8, for discussion of this tricky phrase.

[65] For the Greek text, see Bonwetsch 1897; and for the Latin 2 text, see Moricca 1921–2; for discussion, see Kroll 1932; Kaestli 1988.

[66] Κύριε Ἰησοῦ, δός μοι κράσπεδον ἀπὸ τῶν ἱματίων σου. *Domine, da mihi toracem* [= *thoracem*] *desuper umeros tuos*.

[67] Marcellus of Paris and the dragon occupying the tomb of the sinful woman (late vi AD); Vigor of Bayeux (AD 1030–45) and the Dragon of the Cerisy Forest; Samson of Dol ([c], xii AD or before) and the Dragon of Armorica.

[68] Samson of Dol and the Dragon of Trigg ([a], vii–viii AD; cf. [d], xii AD); Samson and the Dragon of the Pental Monastery at St-Samson-sur-Risle ([b], ix AD); Martha ([b], late xii AD) and the Tarasque; George ([c], AD 1263–7) and the Dragon of Lasia—the girdle is princess Sabra's (cf. [a], xi AD, a Georgian word translated as 'girdle', and [b], xii AD, the Greek equivalent, *zōnē*); Honoratus and the Dragon of the Île Saint-Honorat ([c], AD 1300).

garment');[69] the *palliolum* ('little cloak');[70] the *sudarium* ('handkerchief'; cf. the Acts passage);[71] and the *cingulum* ('girdle', 'ladies' belt').[72] Of these items, it is the *stola* that appears most frequently. Sometimes the term would appear to be used to define an appropriately scarf-like ecclesiastical garment that we might properly translate with the modern English term 'stole', but this is not always the case, and it may often be intended to denote nothing more specific than an upper garment of a general nature. The garment Mewan (x–xi AD) deploys to bind the neck of the Dragon of Anjou is defined by the otherwise unknown word *monopalium*, evidently a supposed derivative of *pallium*, 'cloak', 'upper garment', perhaps translatable as 'single cloak'. But the term is principally designed to serve as an aetiology for the name of the monastery, the Monopalium, that Mewan founds in the aftermath of the fight.

In many cases, not least those involving 'handkerchiefs', it is difficult to see how the garment can be large enough to fit around the serpent's neck, let alone offer sufficient further length to make a lead from it. Occasionally there is a consciousness on the part of the author about these issues. Thus, when Carantoc (early xii AD) binds the neck of the Dragon of Carhampton with his stole, the narrator rather exceptionally explains that the serpent's neck was as broad as that of a 7-year-old bull, so that the stole could just about be passed round it. Other texts offer more practical solutions. We are told that when Paulus Aurelianus ([a], AD 884) has bound the neck of the Dragon of the Isle of Battha (Batz) with his stole, he then inserts his crook into the binding so as to be able to draw the creature along; Mewan (x–xi AD) does the same. George ([b], xii AD) has the princess of Lasia (later Sabra) give him her girdle (*zōnē*) and also his own horse's bridle (*schoinion*); he attaches the two together so as to have a mechanism by which the princess can then comfortably lead the dragon along.

Sometimes the point seems to be made that the clothing deployed is of exceptional delicacy, with the result that the miracle of the binding is accordingly all the more impressive. George ([b], xii AD), as we have seen, uses the girl Sabra's girdle for the Dragon of Lasia, and Martha ([a], AD 1187; [b], late xii AD; [c], AD 1263–7; [d], AD 1264) similarly uses her own girdle too against the Tarasque. Perhaps these garments acquire miraculous power also through their association with virgin girls. Paris (AD 1533 or before) deploys against the Dragon of Teano a

[69] Clement of Metz ([a], AD 782–6; [b], c. AD 1000; [c], c. AD 1100) and the Dragon of Metz; Paulus Aurelianus ([a], AD 884; cf. [b], AD 1637) and the Dragon of the Isle of Battha (Batz); Pavacius (ix AD) and the Dragon of le Mans; Nicasius (xi AD) and the Dragon of Vaux; Rofillus ([a] and [b], xi AD) and the Dragon of Forlimpopoli; Germanus of Auxerre ([a], xi–xii AD) and the Dragon of Trou Baligan; Armel ([a], xii AD or later; [b], xiii AD) and the Dragon of Rennes; Vindemialis (xii AD or before) and the Dragon of Vado; Carantoc (early xii AD) and the Dragon of Carhampton; Tudual (xii AD) and the Dragon of Treguier; cf. also Neventerius and Derien (AD 1637) and the basilisk-dragon of the river Élorn in Brittany ('*escharpe*').

[70] Samson of Dol ([b], ix AD) and the Dragon of Brittany.

[71] Petroc ([a], xii AD or before) and the Dragon of Cornwall.

[72] Martha ([a], AD 1187; [c], AD 1263–7; [d], AD 1264) and the Tarasque.

garment described, obscurely, as a *re(s)ticulum*, which ought to imply some sort of net: perhaps the intention is to suggest that the item was flimsy and lace-like.

Finally, some variations of this motif. Veranus of Cavaillon (ix–xi AD) ties a mundane chain around the neck of the Dragon of the Fontaine de Vaucluse spring, before drawing it along in the usual way. More interestingly, Rofillus ([a] and [b], xi AD) and Mercurialis, taking on the Dragon of Forlimpopoli as a pair, both tie their stoles around the dragon's neck before dragging it off between them. The case of Thomas Defourkinos (xii AD) is particularly striking. He commands the dragon to follow him, whereupon it clamps its teeth onto the end of his stole and permits the saint to drag itself along in that fashion—to its death (see §6.5.4).

A partly convergent motif with this one is that of the stopping of the dragon's mouth—an obviously desirable objective given the threat of the dragon's pestilential breath. When the Basilisk of Genoa is afflicting the population of that city with its pestilential breath Syrus (v AD, perhaps with post-ix accretions) approaches the well in which it lives. He orders the serpent to hold in its breath and close its mouth, and to get into the bucket that he sends down for it. When he draws it up the gathered crowd can see that the terrible serpent's mouth has been stopped by the saint. Senzius (vii–viii AD) binds shut the mouth of the Dragon of Blerana before driving it out of its crypt with his stick. Silvester's stopping of the evil breath of his iteration of the Dragon of Rome becomes ever more pointed as his story develops. At first ([b], late v AD) he chains and locks the doors to the dragon's chamber at the bottom of its great descent, in a fashion directly reminiscent of the archangel Michael's locking of the Revelation Dragon into the abyss. In Aldhelm's subsequent versions of the tale ([c] and [d], AD 675–710), the saint rather more vividly fixes a tight, fume-proof collar around the dragon's neck. Finally, in Jacobus de Voragine's version, Silvester binds up the dragon's actual mouth with a rope and seals it with a signet ring bearing the motif of the cross ([e], AD 1263–7), the deployment of the seal again recalling Michael's treatment of the Revelation Dragon directly.

6.5 The Dragon Is Subject to Exorcistic Banishment

The most usual fate of the dragon in a saintly dragon fight is not death but banishment to a wilderness or abyss, where it will never be seen again, and where it can do no harm to man or beast. Such exorcistic banishment is wholly appropriate to (immortal, unkillable) demons, and much can be made of the assimilation of dragons to demons and indeed, as is often found, their full identification with them.[73] In Chapter 4, §§4.7–8, we contended that this assimilation was the prime cause of the dragon's acquisition of wings in its broader tradition.

[73] For the importance of exorcism to the early church—perhaps, in Brown's phrase, its 'most highly rated activity'—see Brown 1981:108; Young 2016:28.

6.5.1 Dragons, Demons, and the Devil

As explained in Chapter 5, §5.2, there is a general sense in which all hagiographical dragons are re-embodiments of the great dragons of the Bible, including Leviathan-Rahab, the Serpent of Eden, and the Revelation Dragon—all in turn manifestations of the Devil. The flipside of this association is that the Devil, even in contexts in which he is ostensibly devoid of active serpentine characteristics, can be referred to under the soubriquet of 'the *Drakōn*'.[74] Accordingly, hagiographical dragon fights often explicitly celebrate the dragon's identity as the Devil or as one of his demons, or its assimilation to or affinity with one or the other of these.

Dragons as the Devil. In a number of cases the dragon is simply identified as a manifestation of the greatest demon of them all, the Devil himself, and we find this already in the case of the Dragon of India destroyed by Thomas (later ii A D). We are told of Clement of Metz ([a], A D 782–6) that, 'putting his trust in the Lord of Heaven and Earth, he courageously entered the vaults of the amphitheatre to fight the ancient serpent, that is, the Devil'. Vigor of Bayeux (A D 1030–45) addresses the Dragon of the Cerisy Forest directly as 'Satan'. Sometimes we are given something less than a full identification. As Nicasius (xi A D) prepares to destroy the Dragon of Vaux before the assembled crowd of pagans, he merely compares the serpent lying before them to 'the Devil, the ancient serpent'. After the apostle Matthew has dismissed the serpents sent against him by the Ethiopian magicians Zaroes and Arphaxat ([c], xv A D), he preaches to those that wish to liberate themselves from 'the dragon-Devil'.[75]

Entities hovering between dragon and humanoid demon. A number of our antagonists are indicated to shift their form between that of dragon and that of humanoid demon, or otherwise are presented as some sort of indistinct or unresolved amalgamation of the two. Let us begin with cases where the transition between forms is at least partially explicit. As we saw in Chapter 4, §4.7, in the *Acts of Philip* ([a], mid- to late iv A D), the serpent host of the Dragon of the Rocks is identified with demons to such an extent that the anonymous author is unable to decide whether their base form is anguiform or humanoid. On Philip's mere approach they cry out to him in terror in a hubbub of voices that reminds us of Legion of Gerasa.[76] Whilst they emerge from the rocks in serpent form, they adopt humanoid form in order to build a church for him, and before his final departure to banishment the presiding Dragon finally reveals himself as a demon 'in the form of a rather black Ethiopian'. When Margaret of Antioch ([a], A D

---

[74] E.g. in Athanasius' (mid-iv A D) account of the Devil's temptation of St Anthony: *Life of Anthony* 6.

[75] Cf. also the two Syriac tales discussed in Chapter 7, §7.6, in which the Devil manifest in the form of a serpent is defeated by Mary ([a], iv B C; [b], originally vi–vii A D).

[76] Mark 5:1–20; cf. Luke 8:26–39.

815–20; cf. [b], early ix; [c], early ix AD; [d], x AD; [e], AD 1263–7) asks God to show her enemy (*echthron*) to her in her martyr-cell, a terrible golden-bearded dragon manifests itself. After she has defeated it by bursting it open, a humanoid demon then manifests himself, whom she disposes of by pulling out half of his beard, knocking his right eye out with it, and then striking him on the forehead with a bronze hammer. The demon calls himself Beelzebub, and asserts that he had just sent his kinsman (in [b], specifically brother) Rouphos to kill her 'in the form of a dragon'. Margaret then addresses the humanoid Beelzebub in turn as a dragon (*drakōn*) as she attacks him. This would seem to imply that the kindred bearded pair were both equally capable of manifesting themselves in serpentine and humanoid forms.[77] Another female saint, Brigid (ix AD), confronts an entity in her nunnery that is seemingly stranded between the forms of dragon and humanoid demon. It is initially described as 'an unclean spirit, twisting about its flaming eyes, gnashing its teeth, streaming fire from its maw, standing on black and twisted legs and hurling insults'. When she comes to command it to flee, however, it is described more simply as a *draco*, and as leaving a putrid smell behind it, as we have noted (§6.1.3).[78]

Demons manifesting themselves as dragons and dragon visions. The antagonist can more simply be presented as of humanoid demon form by default but currently manifesting itself in the form of a dragon, as in the case of the Dragon of Mt Garganus in Campania (*recte* Apulia) destroyed by the archangel Michael ([b], xi AD) in an Old Irish text. John Parvus (or Colobus, xii AD or before) experiences a vision of a dragon—explicitly said in this case to be a demon—coiled around him, eating his flesh, and vomiting it back into his face. The anchorite Peter of Athos (xiii–xiv AD) is beset by a demon that appears before him in the form of a terrible dragon at the head of an army of snakes. When Severinus of Amiterno (xvi AD or before) and his companion are confronted by a dragon, the saint dismisses it with the sign of the cross, telling his companion that it is really a *diabolus*.[79]

An interesting sub-group of the demon-manifesting-as-dragon motif is found in the case of possessing demons emerging in the form of a dragon as they are expelled from their host. Thus, when Palladius' Paulus Simplex (AD 419–20) is called upon to expel a demon from a demoniac in the Egyptian Desert, the demon emerges in the form of a dragon no less than 70 cubits long before being swept away into the Red Sea. Pagan idols can be possessed too. When Erasmus of

---

[77] In the Latin tradition the dragon-demon is known as Rufus or Rufo.

[78] We are also told of the Lenten evening on which two of her nuns refused to eat the pork she had given them, no other food being available. They hid their portions in a tree. The following morning Brigid sent them back to the tree to look at their portions, whereupon they discovered that they had been transformed into a pair of terrifying snakes. Brigid then transformed the snakes again into (still anguiform) loaves, which could be used for Easter.

[79] Note also the four demons sent against Hypatius (*c.* AD 450) in the form of camels with dragon-heads.

Antioch (ix AD or before) is made to sacrifice before the great bronze statue of Jupiter at Sirmium, the demon (*diabolus*) within emerges in the form of a great dragon; we shall consider below further tales in which dragons emerge from pagan idols (Chapter 7, §7.3).

A range of dragon-visions should probably be classified here even if there is no explicit reference to a demon in association with them, as in the case of Caesarius of Arles (vi AD). Whilst reading a profane text given to him by the grammarian Pomerius, Caesarius falls asleep with it under his arm and in his sleep sees the arm in question and its shoulder entwined and gnawed at by a dragon. Upon waking he conceives a contempt for worldly wisdom. Agilus of Resbach (xi–xii AD) experiences a vision of a dragon spewing venom at him in a church one morning, but is able to dismiss it with the sign of the cross. So too a dragon vision has the effect of confining an errant monk within Benedict's ([a], AD 593; [b], AD 1263–7) monastery. The feckless individual attempts to abandon his monastery, despite Benedict's pleas, but on emerging from it finds his path blocked by a dragon that shows itself intent on devouring him. He returns to the monastery, never to leave it again. Dominic (xiii AD) has a vision of a monstrous dragon devouring some of his brethren. This, it transpires, foretells their absconding from him; he is unable to persuade them to stay, but he subsequently succeeds in bringing them back by prayer.

Dragons in company with demons. In some instances dragons and demons are shown as close associates, without it being stipulated that they are cut from precisely the same cloth. Already in the *Acts of Thomas* (later ii AD) the Dragon of India is aligned with a demon that appears later in the narrative by virtue of the fact that both of them distinctively fall in love with a woman. In the latter case a woman is approached by a shape-shifting demon in the form of young man desperate to sleep with her as she leaves the baths. She rejects him, but when she wakes the following morning, she finds that he has appeared in her bed and violated her. He then continues to attack her in this way for five years (the wording suggests that these are real-world as opposed to in-dream assaults). Thomas duly sends the demon on its way, comparing it to a snake (*ophis*) in the meantime; it professes the genuineness of its love for the woman as it departs. The fact that the Dragon of India can speak *tout court*, rather anomalously for a dragon, also assimilates it to the demonic, as, furthermore, do the claims it makes for itself in its speech (cf. Chapter 5, §5.4).[80] In the Confession section of the (iv AD) *Acts of*

---

[80] The young-man demon: *Acts of Thomas* 42–50; the same demon reappears to possess another pair of women at 62–81 (esp. 75), where Thomas now dismisses it with the help of a wild ass he has endowed with human speech. Discussion at Czachesz 2001. Bath houses were notorious as haunts of demons: see above all Dunbabin 1989:35–46; also Hopfner 1921–4:i.45 §195 (ὑλαῖοι δαίμονες); Bonner 1932. For a particularly rich account of a bathhouse demon, see Gregory of Nyssa *Life of Gregory the Thaumaturge* 92–4 Maraval (= *PG* xlvi 952a–953a), a tale with much in common with the ancient world's favourite Haunted House story-type, for which see Chapter 5, §5.5.1.

Cyprian and Justina Cyprian tells of his initiation into pagan magic. Like the sorcerer of Lucian's 'Sorcerer's Apprentice' tale, he had received instruction in an innermost sanctuary in Egypt, at Memphis in this case.[81] There he had been exposed to a number of visions, including '*drakontes* in company with demons and the wickedness that proceeded from them, to the destruction of those on the Earth'. In speaking of how Justina had subsequently undeceived him, he tells that she taught him that demons are merely smoke and without power, and that with her he saw the dragon that had blown out so much (sc. venom?) unable to display the strength even of a gnat; in the familiar biblical image, he declares that 'the dragon was trampled by Justina as if a mere worm'.[82] Dragons and demons are drawn tightly together also in the second *Conversion and Passion of St Afra*, wherein Narcissus of Gerundum (*c.* AD 770) redeems the soul of Afra at Augsburg from a demon who manifests himself in the form of an Egyptian, 'blacker than a crow, naked, his body covered with the scars of elephantiasis', by promising to render another soul to him in place of hers on the following day. But he tricks the demon into taking, instead of a human soul, that of a dragon that has come to occupy and befoul a local spring. The demon duly remonstrates: 'O that lying bishop! And, what is more, he has bound me with an oath to kill my friend, and if I do not kill him I will be forced to go into the abyss.' The affinity between the professional colleagues here comes out all the more strongly in the light of Philip's Dragon of the Rocks, who, as we saw, manifests himself both in the form of a dragon and in the form of an Ethiopian. It is interesting to note the theological anomaly in the Narcissus tale that the dragon should be credited with a soul—but theology should not be allowed to get in the way of a good story. Sabas' Joannicius of Bithynia ([b], before AD 860) seemingly kills the Dragon of Cunduria and the lustful demons that have been tormenting him simultaneously in a single act of prayer.

Dragons as creatures possessed by demons. One of the more interesting methods of combining dragons and demons is found in the conceit that, like people, dragons can be substantial host-creatures possessed or inhabited by insubstantial demons. When Lifard (ix AD) has burst in half the Dragon of Meung-sur-Loire, the aerial demons whose 'shrine' the dragon had constituted are expelled from its carcass and remonstrate with the saint for rendering them homeless. The dreadful noise they make draws the locals to the scene, and they glorify God upon finding the dragon destroyed, with many of them joining him in the monastic life. Magnus of Füssen ([b], AD 1067–70) intriguingly commands that the demon (*diabolus*) that is lying hidden within the Dragon of Kempten (Campidona,

---

[81] Lucian *Philopseudes* 33–6; cf. also [Thessalus of Tralles] *De virtutibus herbarum* 1–28 Friedrich.

[82] *Acts of Cyprian and Justina*, Confession, 3.5 (ἐκεῖ εἶδον δρακόντων κοινωνίαν μετὰ δαιμόνων καὶ ἐξ αὐτῶν προηγμένην κακίαν εἰς ὄλεθρον τῶν ἐπιγείων), 8.2–5 (τοὺς δαίμονας ὅτι καπνοί εἰσι καὶ οὐδεμίαν δύναμιν ἔχουσιν...τὸν τοσαῦτα φυσῶντα δράκοντα μήτε κώνωπος ἰσχὺν ἐπιδεικνύμενον...δράκων ὡς σκώληξ πρὸς τῆς Ἰουστίνης κατεπατήθη). The first resort for this fascinating text is now Bailey 2017, a superb McGill University thesis.

Cambodunum) should itself kill its host creature (although he then proceeds to knock the creature on the head with his own staff and burst it open thereby). He subsequently observes, once the dragon's attendant worms have fled in the aftermath, that the place has been cleansed of both worms and also of demons. As we have seen, Vindemialis (xii AD or before) partly identifies the Dragon of Vado with the Revelation Dragon, itself a manifestation of the Devil: 'for that dragon [of Revelation] had come to inhere in the likeness of this one' (Chapter 5, §5.2.10). The notion expressed here seems to hover between the idea that, on the one hand, the Vado dragon is possessed by the spirit of the Revelation Dragon, on the model of other host-dragons, and the idea that, on the other hand, it is in some way an instantiation of the Revelation Dragon, an earthly manifestation of its form. The notion of the dragon as a creature possessed by a demon is both established and then undermined by a later telling of the tale of Myron of Crete ([b], xiv AD) and the Dragon of Raucia:

A terrible dragon, with an unclean demon living within it, appeared out of some ancient ruins[83] and was harming many. Seeing the saint going past, it began to cry a river of tears and to incline its head down. First, the saint drove out the demon that had made its lair inside the dragon, and all saw it being driven away like a puff of smoke in the wind.[84] Then he said to the dragon: 'You are to depart beyond these borders. Let no one ever see you, and do not harm anybody.' Immediately it crawled off to another place, and disappeared.

Once the demon is exorcised from the dragon, it ought to be harmless, but it is rather then subject to a sort of second exorcism itself, as if also a demon in its own right. The dragon's emergence from ancient ruins here also invites comment. The Dragon of Constantinople destroyed by Elisabeth ([a], ix–x AD) similarly emerges from the ruins of the Hebdomon, the city's old pagan heart. Evidently there is a notion that these dragons represent entities that had formerly passed themselves off as pagan gods, now emerging, in the age of Christianity, from the homes to which they had long been accustomed (cf. again Chapter 7, §7.3).

6.5.2 Exorcistic Imagery

Accordingly, demons or the Devil could be assimilated to dragons particularly at the point at which they were expelled in exorcism. The point is crisply made by an

[83] So it is that I construe ἐκ συμπτωμάτων ἀρχαίων. The Latin translation given in *AASS* interprets the phrase to mean rather 'from some ancient events' (*ex antiquis…eventis*). The vignette may be inspired by the vignette in Jerome's Vulgate of the ruins of the desolate Babylon occupied by *dracones* (Isaiah 13:19–21); cf. Chapter 4, §4.8.

[84] Cf. Lucian's exorcist, discussed below, who expels demons as smoky black forms.

exorcistic prayer prescribed in the (viii AD) *Gellone Sacramentary*. The exorcist is to address three adjurations to the demon: 'And so I adjure you, ancient serpent [*serpens*]; I adjure you, not by means of my own weakness, but by means of the strength of the Holy Ghost; and so I adjure you, dragon [*draco*] most evil.'[85]

It is no surprise, then, that the circumstances of the dragon's expulsion in the hagiographical tradition often strongly resemble those of the exorcism of demons in general. Early Christian and classical (but nonetheless Judaeo-Christian-influenced) descriptions of the exorcisms of demoniacs tend to follow a strong pattern: (1) the demon is ordered out of the person in which it hides, typically in the name of a great power; (2) the demon confesses its identity and its crimes (the game is won once it has admitted its presence); (3) the demon gives a visible token of its departure.[86] Thus, Mark tells how Jesus ordered the 'Legion' demons out of the demoniac of Gerasa; at his demand they supplied their name; and they demonstrated their departure by entering a herd of pigs and driving them into a lake.[87] Josephus tells how the Jewish exorcist Eleazar used the name of Solomon (together with a magic ring) to draw a demon out of a demoniac by the nose before Vespasian; the demon gave proof of its departure by knocking over a cup of water on the way out.[88] Lucian tells how 'a Syrian from Palaestine' would order demons out of the possessed; the demons would confess their origin and they would be seen to depart as a black and smoky shape.[89] A fine hagiographical example is provided by the (v AD?) *Passion of St Trypho*. This tells how Gordiana, the cherished daughter of the emperor Gordian III, falls to the possession of a demon which ever cries out the name of Trypho the goose-herd with dread. Troops eventually track him down in an obscure Phrygian village and bring him to Rome. Upon arrival he calls the demon out in the name of Christ, and it emerges in the form of a black (NB) dog with fiery eyes. Trypho compels it to confess its identity—the son of Satan—and after a protracted interview sends it off to the place of fiery punishment.[90]

In the world of the hagiographical dragon fight, the saint will order his dragon in the name of God to depart its current place (= 1). Since the saintly dragon is

---

[85] *Gellone Sacramentary* §2405; for the text see Dumas 1981; cf. Young 2016:46. Pace Czachesz 2001:45–6, for all that the ventriloquist demon exorcised by Paul from the slave-girl at Acts 16:16–18 is described as 'python spirit' (πνεῦμα πύθωνα), I doubt that it was actively conceptualized as a dragon. The term *pythōn*, a generic one for such ventriloquist demons, need not have had any etymological connection with the Delphic dragon, nor need it have been perceived to do so. See Hesychius s.vv. ἐγγαστρίμυθος, πύθων (4314–15: δαιμόνιον μαντικόν), *Suda* s.vv. ἐγγαστρίμυθος, πύθωνος, schol. Plato *Sophist* 252c; discussion at Ogden 2001:112–14.
[86] The schema is laid out more fully at Ogden 2009:166–71. Discussion at Oesterreich 1930; Thraede 1967; Brenk 1986:2107–16; Twelftree 1986, 1993, 2007a, 2007b; Edwards 1989; Levack 2013; Young 2016 esp. 27–60; Bremmer 2017b:202–8; cf. also Lunn-Rockliffe 2012.
[87] Mark 5:1–20.   [88] Josephus *Jewish Antiquities* 8.42–9.
[89] Lucian *Philopseudes* 16.
[90] *Passio S. Tryphonis* 1–2 (*BHG* no. 1856); for the text, see Franchi de' Cavalieri 1908:45–74 (at pp. 45–54); for the tradition of Trypho's life, see now Macchioro 2019. Cf. the fiery-eyed dog-demon of Ephesus defeated by Apollonius of Tyana at Philostratus *Life of Apollonius* 4.10.

rarely endowed with the power of speech, we seldom get the confession sequence, but we do get a fine one in the case of the earliest dragon-fight proper, that of the battle of Thomas (later ii A D) against the Dragon of India: he compels it to admit that it is the Devil in serpent form and also to produce a litany of its previous crimes (= 2). And the final departure of the dragon from its current place, typically for the wilderness, is manifest and graphic (= 3).

A minor variant of the ordering-to-depart motif in some ways brings us closer to the traditional demoniac model. The dragon ordered to depart normally lives in plain sight, but in a few cases we do actually have a hiding dragon forced from its place of concealment. Thus, in the complex episode of the Dragon of the Rocks encountered by Philip ([a], mid- to late iv A D) outside Ophiorhyme, the fifty-one serpent-demons are compelled to blurt out admission of their presence by Philip's mere approach. In due course the saint compels them to bring themselves out into the open by, in good exorcistic style, invoking the name of God:

> Praying in this way, he cried out and said, 'I adjure you in the glorious name of the Father, in the name of His only-born son, in the name of the highest God, show yourselves, demons, show your number, and show what form you are'.

In this case the serpents do half the saint's job for him in volunteering their own presence. In other cases the saint's mere approach, or little more than that, is sufficient to bring dragons out into the open. Sabas' Joannicius of Bithynia ([b], before A D 860) encounters the Dragon of Cunduria when he is walking over a mountain psalming and a great pile of rocks quakes and collapses. Again, a massive dragon shoots out from them—presumably forced forth by the psalming, although Sabas does not make this explicit. When Erasmus of Antioch (ix A D or before) is compelled to sacrifice before the great bronze statue of Jupiter at Sirmium, the dragon-demon (*diabolus*) that lives within emerges even before Erasmus has done anything: it is compelled to reveal itself simply upon looking into the saint's face. We may compare here too the Dragon of Raucia that begins to cry a river simply because Myron of Crete ([b], xiv A D) walks past it: once again, the simple presence of the saint can have an exorcistic effect, even despite the man himself.

6.5.3 Exorcistic Banishment to the Wilderness

The dragon's exorcistic banishment to the wilderness is a highly productive motif. For example, the Dragon of the Rocks and his fifty fellow demon-dragons encountered by Philip ([a], mid- to late iv A D) finally bid adieu: 'We are off, Philip, to a place we will no longer be seen by you….' In a later account Philip ([b], late vi A D) similarly banishes the Dragon of Scythia to the wilderness, where it can harm no one. So too Victoria ([a], *c.* AD 500; [b] and [c], AD 675–710) orders the Dragon of Trebula to depart into the wilderness, a place where neither man nor animal live. Veranus of Cavaillon (ix–xi AD) banishes the Dragon of the Fontaine de Vaucluse spring to a mountain-top.[91]

A milder version of the banishment motif has the dragon banished not *to* some remote wilderness, but merely *from* a more local portion of territory. Hilary of Poitiers (late vi AD) confines the serpents of Gallinaria to one portion of that island, demarcating the boundary with his crozier. Clement of Metz ([a], AD 782–6) renders the soil of the amphitheatre of Metz, in which the city's dragon and its serpent brood have hitherto lived, toxic to serpents. Similarly, after Patrick's ([c], AD 1263–7) banishment of the snakes from Ireland the island's earth remains toxic to all snakes—though in point of fact the tradition that Irish earth should be toxic to snakes went back even further than the historical St Patrick (see Chapter 7, §7.1).

Carantoc's (early xii AD) dismissal of the Dragon of Carhampton is rather anomalous. After he has led it into the hall of Cato's castle at Dindraithov and proposed to feed it as if it were a pet (cf. §6.4.3), he is prevented from doing so by the courtiers that rather wish to kill it. But Carantoc refuses to let them do so on the basis that God has sent it into the world with the purpose of destroying sinners, and also to allow himself to demonstrate God's power. He then takes it outside the castle gates, releases it, and, seemingly with a rather gentler command than is usual in these situations, asks it not to harm anyone and not to return. This narrative perhaps wins the prize for the most sympathetic and indulgent hagiographical treatment of a dragon (at any rate in the context of a dragon-fight proper): it too is one of God's creatures and part of God's plan.

Many of the themes noted in this and the two foregoing sub-sections (§§6.5.1–3) are brought together nicely in a tale attached to Hilarus of Galatea (vi AD). When one of his brethren, the sweetly named Glycerius, feels temptation to eat a ripe grape in a vineyard, he confesses it to Hilarus. Hilarus suspects the work of a demon and tells the monk to follow his desire, for God will not forsake him. As he reaches out to pick the grape, it is transformed into a monstrous serpent. Glycerius rushes back and reports again to Hilarus. Hilarus runs to the scene, finds the serpent standing on its tail, and recognizes it for the demon it is. He grabs the serpent (by the tail?) and drags it after him, whereupon the demon

---

[91] Some further examples: in the Syriac tradition, Mary ([a], iv AD; [b], originally vi–vii AD) and the Devil in dragon-form detached from a young girl, with the help of baby Jesus (these interesting texts are discussed in more detail in Chapter 7, §7.6); the apostle Matthew ([a], late vi AD; [b], AD 1263–7; [c], xv AD) and the serpents sent against him by the Ethiopian magicians Zaroes and Arphaxat; Marcellus of Paris (late vi AD) and the dragon of the adulterous woman's tomb (to the desert or the sea); Myron ([a], x AD; [b], xiv AD) and the Dragon of Raucia; Julian of le Mans (*c.* AD 1000) and the Dragon of Artinas; Fronto of Périgueux ([c], xi AD) and both the Dragon of Périgueux and the Dragon of Limoges; Germanus of Auxerre ([b], AD 1263–7) and the serpents of St Concordian's tomb.

cries out from the serpent's mouth, protesting that it is being burned by the hottest fire. He compels the demon to confess that it had cast the temptation to taste the grape into Glycerius; it also asserts that, had it been able to make the monk actually taste the grape, it would have been able to detach him from Hilarus. Hilarus prays, whereupon the serpent cries out and is reduced to a pile of dust, from which emerges some smoke blacker than pitch—the demon, of course. As all look on, the smoke flees off to the wilderness. Here we perhaps detect an affinity between the black smoky form of a disembodied demon and the black smoke a dragon is inclined to emit (§6.1.4).

6.5.4 The Dragon Sent to the Abyss (i): The Underworld

Just as the archangel Michael sent the Revelation Dragon into the abyss (Chapter 5, §5.2.10), so the more earthly saints are often destined to do the same with their dragons. The term 'abyss' (*abyssos*) may be understood in pagan and Christian writing alike to signify either a deep hole in the land, leading down to an underworld, or the vast depths of the sea. Saints dismiss their dragons into abysses in both senses of the term. Let us consider first the underworld sense. After Thomas (later ii A D) has killed his dragon by bursting it open, the ground opens up to swallow the carcass down into the abyss, presumably by divine command. In the course of his final martyrdom Philip ([a], mid- to late iv A D) calls a great curse down on the citizens of Ophiorhyme and the Echidna, their viper-goddess, with the result that Hades opens up and swallows them all down, some seven thousand men, together with their wives and children. He has gone too far. Christ manifests himself and restores the inhabitants to the light, all except the wicked proconsul that has presided over them and the Echidna herself. In praying to God to help her cope with the dragon manifest before her, Margaret of Antioch ([a], A D 815–20, translated at pp. 193–4; cf. [b], early ix A D or before) appeals most appropriately to his control of the abyss and the boundaries of Hades.

A particularly striking case of a dragon being plunged into the earth is provided by the tale of Thomas Defourkinos (xii A D). This rich narrative, to which we will continue to refer on a number of occasions, is worth quoting in full. The Devil renews his attack on this Thomas in his hermitage by the river Sangarius, assembling all the snakes over which he presides to do so:

> Many consider the tale practically incredible. For the father could undertake no activity of any kind without the manifestation of some sort of snake. Whichever way he turned, there was a snake. If ever he picked up a pot for any reason, he found a snake lurking inside it. This didn't happen once or twice, but continually. Nor was he harassed by the snakes for a period of just one year or two, but for a full eleven years, during which time he could get no rest. For whenever he

decided to lie down on his usual bed, snakes would lie down on it together with him, on both sides. However, with care and forethought, he managed to keep himself safe from them. Then, one day, when he was conducting the service of the bloodless sacrifice and was coming to the end of the ceremony, a terrible *drakōn* crawled out from somewhere and arranged itself around the apse of his oratory. At that point the brother that was helping the father in the role of deacon was coming in with the offering of the wine. The creature broke away from the apse and came to rest by the entrance doorway. It was as big as an ox and made a bizarre sight. When the priest had come to the customary part of the rite, he realized that the man ministering the wine was taking his time. Deciding to look over in his direction, he saw the creature blocking the doorway, and the deacon standing there atremble. He filled himself with the Holy Spirit. 'Come in, and don't dally!', he said to the brother, and then proceeded with the making of the offering, not allowing himself to be distracted any further. Emboldened by the father's encouragement, the brother mounted over the creature as if winged, and entered in accordance with Thomas' invitation. The ceremony complete, and before changing out of his stole, the priest approached the creature without trembling and said to it: 'If God's providence has a purpose for you, follow me!' The creature held onto the end of his garment with its teeth and was drawn and dragged along. When the father had come to a ravine, flanked by a hill on each side, he separated himself from the creature by the distance of an arrow's flight. He stood in prayer and, after everything else, finished with these words: 'Lord, who told those who have faith in you to trample over snakes and scorpions, grant that I, as small as I am, should be over this creature at this ravine, in accordance with what you said.' When he had said this, the creature was drawn down from above into the chasm, and the hills on either side fell in with it, with the result that the ravine was filled in and the place became a plain. The old man thanked God and returned to his cell, whereupon another extraordinary miracle was revealed. When the snakes that had been living beneath the cell and torturing the saint over so many years looked upon his glorious face, they were unable to bear it, just as if it were burning fire. They sped off at once to the place where the dragon had been entombed. By the providence of God all the countless snakes perished there. Birds, equal in number to the snakes, flew in from somewhere, as if on a mission, made a meal of the dead snakes, and went off again. From that point the father was released from his ordeals.

The notion of the sending down of the dragon into an abyss can sometimes be refracted more indirectly. Samson of Dol ([a], vii–viii AD) drags the Dragon of Trigg to the edge of a precipice and casts it down from a great height; similarly Armel ([a], xii AD or later) drags the Dragon of Rennes to the summit of a mountain to cast it down into the river Sicca (Seiche) below. This saint similarly sends the Dragon of Brittany off beyond the river Sigona (Seine) to dwell beneath a rock, presumably deep in the earth. We shall consider below the possibility that Lucian's tale in his *Philopseudes* (*c.* AD 170s), in which Eucrates deploys a magic ring to open up the earth and thereby plunge a massive, serpentine manifestation of Hecate down into the abyss, already refracts the imagery of the Christian dragon fight.

6.5.5 The Dragon Sent to the Abyss (ii): The Sea

Alternatively, many of the banished dragons are sent into the sea. Examples of this motif abound.[92] The 70-cubit dragon that Palladius' Paulus Simplex (AD 419–20) produces from a demoniac in the Egyptian desert is at once swept away into the Red Sea. Syrus (v AD, perhaps with post-ix accretions) orders the Basilisk of Genoa he has extracted from a well to throw itself into the sea. When Venantius Fortunatus' Marcellus of Paris (late vi AD) confronts the dragon that has occupied the tomb of an adulterous woman, he dismisses it either to the desert or to the sea. Senzius (vii–viii AD) drives the Dragon of Blerana across the river Minione and then on to the sea, where he is said to have bound it (remotely, by prayer, presumably) 'in the depth of the abyss'. Patrick ([b], AD 1200–10) famously drives Ireland's great brood of snakes over a precipice on Croagh Patrick (an intimation of an underworld abyss here too) and down into the sea. In a slight variation of this motif Samson ([c], xii AD or before) binds the winged Dragon of Armorica to a rock in the middle of the sea. In another variation, when the archangel Michael ([a], ix–x AD) has destroyed the Dragon of Southern Asia with his fiery sword, the locals drag its carcass to the sea in portions and dump it in, to avoid the ensuing stench.

An intriguing early example of a saint consigning a dragon to the watery abyss, albeit in an iconographic and symbolic context rather than a narrative one, is found in Eusebius' *Life of Constantine* (AD 340). Eusebius tells us that the emperor hung an encaustic painting in the vestibule of his palace (probably the one in Constantinople) in which he was shown, a cross above his head, trampling (NB) upon and spearing a *drakōn* in the company of his sons, with the *drakōn* being

---

[92] In addition to those given in this paragraph: Samson of Dol ([a], vii–viii) and the Dragon of the Pental Monastery encountered at St-Samson-sur-Risle; Mamilianus ([a], vii–viii AD) and the Dragon of Montecristo; Samson of Dol ([b], ix AD) and the Dragon of Trigg; Machutus (AD 866–72) and the Dragon of September Island; Paulus Aurelianus ([a], AD 884; [b], AD 1637) and the Dragon of the Isle of Battha (Batz); Veranus of Cavaillon (ix–xi AD) and the Dragon of Albingaunum; Vigor of Bayeux (AD 1030–45) and the Dragon of the Cerisy Forest; Fronto of Périgueux ([c], xi AD) and the Dragon of the river Dronne; Gildas ([b], xi AD) and the Dragon of Rome (the language used suggests that the abyss envisaged is a watery one); Euflamus (xii AD) and the Dragon of Saint-Efflam; Tudual (xii AD) and the Dragon of Treguier; Vindemialis (xii AD or before) and the Dragon of Vado; Venerius of Tino (early xv AD) and the Dragon of Luni; Paris (AD 1533 or before) and the Dragon of Teano; Neventerius and Derien (AD 1637) and the Basilisk-Dragon of the river Élorn in Brittany.

carried down into the 'abyss of the sea'. Versions of the image survive on medallions. In his explication of it Eusebius identifies the dragon both with the Dragon of Revelation, the besieger of the Church, and with Leviathan, by means of a quote from Isaiah.[93]

6.5.6   Across or down the River; over the Sea

Rivers often play a key role in the banishment or disposal of the dragon. When the dragon is banished to the wilderness, the local river often constitutes the boundary that demarcates it—an unnervingly close one, one might think. In a relatively early and simplistic tale,ˑ Martin of Tours ([a], c. AD 400; cf. [b], AD 1263–7) and his companions find a serpent crossing a river from the opposite bank to attack them; he simply commands it to turn back. His companions admire the miracle, whereas Martin merely sighs and laments that serpents heed his word, but people do not. Samson of Dol ([a], vii–viii AD; cf. [b], ix AD) sends the Dragon of Brittany off beyond the river Sigona (Seine) to dwell beneath a rock, as we have seen. Clement ([a], AD 782–6; cf. [b], AD 1000; [c], c. AD 1100) sends the Dragon of Metz and its great serpent brood off to live beyond the river Salia (Seille).

When the dragon is rather sent into the abyss of the sea, a river is the usual conduit for this. So, for example, Maurus of Syria (viii AD?) is able, after some difficulty (cf. §6.7), to send the carcass of the Dragon of the river Narco away down that river and into the Tiber, of which it is a tributary, and thence into the sea. Fronto of Périgueux ([c], xi AD) sends the Dragon of the river Dronne down that river and into the sea; and Paris (AD 1533 or before) throws the Dragon of Teano into the river Saon to be carried away to the sea, never again to harm anyone, or to be seen.[94] More anomalously, Senzius (vii–viii AD) drives the Dragon of Blerana across the river Minione and from there on to the sea (i.e. by land, not down the river itself).

---

[93] Eusebius *Life of Constantine* 3.3; Isaiah 27:1. Constantine II adapted the image, whilst also assimilating it to the 'Holy Rider' type (for which see Chapter 9, §9.2), for a series of gold coins he issued to celebrate his AD 353 victory over Magnentius: on these Constantine II sits on a rearing horse whilst spearing a coiling dragon below; the legend is *debellator hostium*. Discussion at Grabar 1936:43–5; Mango 1959:22–4; Merkelbach 1959:243–5; Cameron and Hall 1999:255–6; and Kuehn 2011:103–4 (with citations for the coins).

[94] A further example: Veranus of Cavaillon (ix–xi AD) sends the Dragon of Albingaunum to the sea by means of the local river (unnamed—presumably the Centa). Sometimes we are told merely that the saint throws the dragon, dead or alive, into the river; we may assume that in these cases too the dragon is to be carried to the sea. So it is when Mewan (x–xi AD) throws the Dragon of Anjou into the river Loire; when Donatus of Sisteron (xii AD or earlier) compels the Dragon of the Jura Mountains into the river Durance, never to be seen again; and when Armel ([a], xii AD or later; [b], xiii AD) casts the carcass of the Dragon of Rennes into the river below from a precipice (once again, an intimation also of the underworld-abyss here).

In a further variant of this sort of motif, the dragon is dispatched to go and live in a land beyond not a river but a lake or a sea. When Joannicius of Bithynia ([a], AD 846; [b], before AD 860) burns the Dragon of the islet of Thasion with the rays of the morning sun, or with his prayers, it throws itself into the surrounding Lake Apolloniatis, but once in the water crosses to the shore opposite and disappears into the mountains beyond.[95] Vigor of Bayeux (AD 1030–45) is said to have sent one of the total of three dragons he encounters 'across the strait of the sea'. Petroc ([a], xii AD or before) drags the Dragon of Cornwall to the sea so as to dispatch it to 'the wildernesses beyond the sea'. In an Irish text Senán (early xv AD) expels the fiery monster of Inis Cathaigh into the sea, whereupon it makes landfall at Dubloch of Sliab Collain; nonetheless, it adheres to his stricture not to harm anyone any more.

6.5.7 Circularity of Banishment

There is often, oddly, and almost self-defeatingly, a sense of a banished dragon being returned to its home, or somewhere that could well have served as such. This is already a pagan trope. When Zeus finally overwhelms the great dragon Typhon, he confines him within the bowels of the Earth by burying him under Mt Etna: but Typhon is himself a creature of the Earth, and had previously lived deep within it with his consort, the Echidna.[96]

As we have seen, the 'abyss' is a favourite destination for the banished dragon in the hagiographical dragon fight, and this might well be thought of as the proper place of belonging for the dragons. Let us bear it in mind that long before the archangel Michael had cast Satan, in the form of the Dragon of Revelation, down into the abyss and locked him in there,[97] Psalm 148 had been making (puzzling) appeal to a yoking of '*drakontes* and all abysses'.[98] When Silvester ([b], late v AD) salutes Michael's great deed by locking the Dragon of Rome in at the bottom of its own cavern, down a descent of 365 steps, the dragon does not move at all, even if its pestilential breath is cut off. This case rather makes the point that the dragon's standard cave home, a great hole in the ground, is already a kind of abyss. The point is well made by a later text, too. Peregrinus (xvi AD or before), having cap-

---

[95] The original tale, as told in these accounts by Peter the Monk and Sabas (for which see Mango 1983), locates the tale on the tiny islet of Thasion (the modern Kiz) in Lake Apolloniatis (the modern Ulubat), named for the city of Apollonia ('by the Rhydacus') on its shore. Modern tradition transfers the tale's location to the island of Thasos, adjacent, more or less, to the Apollonia on the Thracian coast.

[96] See especially Hesiod *Theogony* 295–318, 820–80; Pindar *Pythians* 1.15–28; Strabo C750–1; Apollodorus *Bibliotheca* 1.6.3; Nonnus *Dionysiaca* 1–2 passim; cf. Ogden 2013a esp. 69–80, 148–50, 152–3, 161–5, 218–20, 247–8, 292, 2013b:19–38.

[97] Revelation 20.

[98] LXX Psalms 148:7; we have discussed this curious phrase at Chapter 4, §4.8, and Chapter 5, §5.2.10.

tured the Dragon of Caltabellotta in Sicily by thrusting his staff into its mouth, drags the dragon to its own cave on top of the local mountain. He then seemingly (what is envisaged is slightly obscure) throws the dragon down a hole within this cave, whence it never emerges again. Once again the oddly circular identification between the dragon's lair and the abyss itself is pointed up.

We have seen that a variant of the cave-home chosen by dragons is the well, as in the cases of the Basilisk of Genoa dismissed by Syrus (v AD, perhaps with post-ix accretions), the Dragon of Moutiers-Saint-Jean (to be) encountered by John of Reomay (AD 659), and the dragon and its venomous cohorts to which Parasceve of Sicily (viii AD) is thrown. In this light it is remarkable that it is the fate of other dragons precisely to be sealed into wells by their saints. Thus Rofillus ([a] and [b], xi AD) and Mercurialis throw the Dragon of Forlimpopoli down a well and seal it by placing a monument on top of it. So too Germanus of Auxerre ([a], xi–xii AD) plunges the Dragon of Trou Baligan into a cistern and has the entrance to it stopped up. In this way again we see a curious merging between the dragon's home and its place of banishment.

Similarly, other dragons live beneath piles or tumbles of rocks, from which they emerge at the approach of a saint. This is most strikingly the case with the Dragon of the Rocks and his fifty fellow demon-dragons encountered by Philip ([a], mid- to late iv AD) outside Ophiorhyme. So too Joannicius of Bithynia ([b], before AD 860) encounters the Dragon of Cunduria when he is walking over a mountain psalming and a great pile of rocks quakes and collapses, with the massive dragon emerging from them.[99] But then when Samson of Dol ([a], vii–viii) banishes the Dragon of Brittany beyond the Sigona (Seine) river in exorcistic fashion, he compels it to dwell—precisely—beneath a certain rock.

The *Historia apostolica*'s account of the apostle Matthew ([a], late vi AD) and the serpents of the Ethiopian magicians Zaroes and Arphaxat has Matthew invoking the Holy Ghost (as the name of power) in the following fashion: ' "I adjure you, Spirit, that you compel [sc. the serpents] to *return to their place* in all tameness, in such a way that they come into contact with no one, that they harm no one, not man, not four-footed beast, not bird." At this word the serpents lifted their heads and began to go. The gates opened, they departed in public view, with all looking on, and never more appeared.'

6.6 The Dragon Is Killed

Dragons—evidently not regarded as immortal or fully demonic in these cases—can also be killed by the saints, and a wonderful variety of methods and weapons

---

[99] Similarly, when Theodore Tyron ([d], c. AD 871; [c], late ix AD) calls the Dragon of Euchaita forth from its cave, the earth shakes. The Dragon of Luni dismissed by Venerius of Tino (early xv AD) shatters the rock under which it lies hidden in its deep cavern out of frustration as it is sent away.

is recorded.[100] But the carcass left behind can then present the community with a further problem.

6.6.1 The Saint Commands the Dragon to Die or Actively to Commit Suicide; the Dragon's Belching of Venom and its Bursting Open

It is a commonplace that the saint is able to take full command of the dragon and turn it into his obedient slave, as we have seen (§6.4). So it is that he can also command it to die or actively to kill itself. A plain example of the former is offered by the case of Gildas ([a], ix AD), who simply orders his iteration of the Dragon of Rome to die in its cave.

A pair of related productive motifs bears upon the (usually hands-off) infliction of death upon the dragon. In the first of these the dying dragon vomits forth its venom. Andrew ([a] and [b], both late vi AD) simply commands the Dragon of Thessalonica to die. According to Gregory of Tours' account of this ([a]):

Then the saint of God said to it, 'Killer, put away the head that you raised in the beginning to the destruction of the human race, submit to the servants of God and die'. At once the serpent let out a deep roar, coiled around a large oak which was nearby and, winding itself around it and vomiting out a stream of venom, died.

Similarly, when Fronto of Périgueux ([c], xi AD) merely orders the Dragon of Neuilly-Saint-Front (Nogeliacum) to submit itself to him, the beast at once vomits forth its venom, with a bellow, and dies. When Maglorius (ix–x AD) commands Dragon of Jersey to die it belches forth its venom, before falling down the side of a rocky mountain, to be shattered into pieces below.[101] In a variant of this motif, the Dragon of Saint-Efflam subdued by Euflamus (xii AD) vomits blood from mouth and nose in defeat, although it does live on to be banished to the sea. There is a specific reason for the tweaking of the motif in this case: the blood left behind is an aetiology for the local 'Red Rock', the Roch-Ru, still to be seen.

In the second of these productive motifs the dragon is made to burst open. This evokes Daniel's bursting open of the Dragon of Babylon, of course (see Chapter 5, §5.2.8), but also the well-established classical tradition of the Marsi, the snake-bursting people of Marruvium.[102] Many examples can be

---

[100] The heavily demonic Dragon of the Rocks encountered by Philip ([a], mid- to late iv AD) presents an anomalous case in this regard, pleading, as it does, for exorcistic banishment as an alternative to annihilation.

[101] A further example: Samson ([b], mid-ix AD) and the dragon he encounters in the wilderness.

[102] For the Marsi's snake-bursting, see Lucilius Book 20 F7 Charpin (575–6 Marx); Virgil Eclogues 8.70–1; Horace Epodes 17.29; Ovid Amores 2.1.23–8, Metamorphoses 7.203, De medicamine faciei femineae 39; [Quintilian] Declamationes maiores 10.15; discussion at Letta 1972 esp. 139–45; Piccalugia 1976; Tupet 1976:187–98; Dench 1995:159–66; Phillips 1995; Ogden 2013a:213–14.

given.[103] Already in the *Gospel of Thomas* Jesus ([a], ii AD) bursts open the viper that has just bitten Jacob. And then in the *Acts of Thomas* Thomas (later ii AD) himself compels his remonstrating Dragon of India to restore its last-victim boy to life by sucking out the bile with which it had envenomed him and taking it back into itself. But this then causes the dragon to inflate (*ephusato, phusētheis*) and burst. The most striking example of the bursting of a dragon comes in the case of Margaret of Antioch ([a], AD 815–20 or before, translated at pp. 193–4; [b], early ix AD; [c], early ix AD; [d], x AD; [e], AD 1263–7; [f], *c.* AD 1380). She achieves this by making the sign of the cross as it swallows her down; in bursting forth alive from the belly of the dragon she makes herself into the patron saint of childbirth. The Dragon of Meung-sur-Loire encountered by Lifard (ix AD) bursts itself in half as it strains to destroy the cross-embellished staff the saint has planted in the ground before it. Eudocia (x AD or before) prays that the Dragon of Heliopolis should burst itself and die. The dragon is not present, but the prayer acts as a summons: no sooner has she finished praying than the dragon arrives on the scene, inflates itself, and indeed bursts open (the passage is quoted in Chapter 8, §8.3.2). Dragons can also be burst open with slightly more hands-on techniques. Thus, Athenogenes (vi AD) causes the Dragon of the Land of the Goths to burst open by rapping it on the head three times with his spear-butt. According to one account Magnus of Füssen ([b], AD 1067–70) bursts open the Dragon of Kempten in a similar way, by striking it with his staff. According to another ([a], *c.* AD 895) he bursts it open rather by feeding it a ball of pitch, precisely after the method Daniel had used in Babylon. And Timothy ([a], x AD) bursts open his iteration of the Dragon of Prusa by hurling at it a woven bag or a cloth in which he has been carrying some holy loaves.[104]

The two motifs outlined here can be combined. Thus, the Dragon of the Egyptian Desert belches out its venom as Ammon (*c.* AD 395 and *c.* AD 403/4) bursts it open. We find an appeal to both imageries when Joannicius of Bithynia

[103] In addition to those mentioned in this paragraph: Ammon (*c.* AD 395 and *c.* AD 403/4) bursts open the Dragon of the Egyptian Desert by the power of his prayers; Simeon Stylites ([a], shortly before AD 459) bursts open, seemingly lengthways, the first of the two dragons that assail him; Parasceve (viii AD) bursts open by the power of prayer alone 'the dragon and venomous beasts and reptiles' to which she is thrown; Fronto of Périgueux ([c], xi AD) bursts in half the dragon he encounters on the road to Metz; Nicasius (xi AD) and his companions burst open the Dragon of Vaux with the sign of the cross before an audience of unbelieving locals; the disciples of St James ([a], mid-xii AD or earlier; [b], AD 1263–7) burst open the fiery Dragon of Galicia in the middle by making the sign of the cross; Servulus ([b], AD 1493) bursts open the Dragon of Trieste by blowing upon it.

[104] Dragons can be reduced to pieces in other ways too: the archangel Michael reduces dragons in Southern Asia ([a], ix–x AD) and on Mons Tumba, the future St Michael's Mount ([c], *c.* AD 1000), into twelve pieces each with his fiery sword, and the dragon of Mt Garganus to nine pieces in a similar way ([b], xi AD). Maglorius (ix–x AD) compels the Dragon of Jersey to throw itself down a steep mountainside so as to shatter in smithereens at the bottom.

([a], AD 846) heals the workman Pardus, bitten by an *echidna* (viper): his swollen wound bursts open and all the foul-smelling venom within pours forth.

Occasionally the dragon can be commanded to commit suicide in a more active way. Jerome's Hilarion ([a], AD 396) commands the Dragon of Epidaurus in Dalmatia to mount a pyre. Sozomen's Arsacius of Nicomedia ([a], earlier V AD) compels his dragon to kill itself by dashing its head against the ground.

6.6.2 Reciprocal Weapons against the Dragon: Breath, Spittle, and Fire

Our saints exploit a series of weapons designed to be equal and opposite to the terrible weapons of which the dragon itself disposes.[105] As we have seen, the dragon's principal weapon is the emission of its pestilential and fiery breath. The saints can in turn use their own breath against the dragon by blowing upon it. Compatibly, the blowing-upon method was, separately, an established technique for dismissing demons: so it is that we find St Justina blowing upon and thereby dismissing two of the three demons sent to seduce her by the wicked mage Cyprian in the (mid-iv AD) *Acts of Cyprian and Justina* (cf. Chapter 8, §8.3.3).[106] Accordingly, Theodoret's Marcian (mid-v AD) burns up the dragon that attacks him as he prays in the vestibule of his house merely by breathing on it. Simeon Stylites ([a], shortly before AD 459) blows upon the second of a pair of dragons that attacks him and it simply disappears. When Servulus of Trieste ([b], AD 1493; cf. [a], xii AD or before) blows upon that city's dragon, and the blowing in itself has the effect of bursting the serpent in half.

The human weapon that corresponds to serpent venom most directly is spittle. The deployment of saintly spittle seems to represent a perfect synthesis of pagan and Christian notions. On the classical side, Aristotle had briefly noted in the *History of Animals* that human spittle was deleterious to most venomous creatures.[107] Pliny had gone into greater detail: snakes flee as if scalded when spat on, especially by people under fast; if they actually swallow the saliva, they die; one bursts them open by spitting into their mouths.[108] On the Christian side Jesus had healed the deaf and the blind by the application of his spittle to their ears and eyes, respectively.[109] Turning to the hagiographical tradition, Sozomen's Donatus of Epirus ([a]) destroys the Dragon of Chamaegephyrae by spitting into its mouth (earlier V AD; so too [b], AD 1263–7). We have quoted above Jean Gobi's marvellous (earlier xiv AD) tale of an anonymous saint who destroys a dragon by having

---

[105] Cf. Ogden 2013a:215–46 and esp. 404–11.
[106] *Acts of Cyprian and Justina*, Conversion, 5 and 8 Bailey.
[107] Aristotle *History of Animals* 607a.
[108] Pliny *Natural History* 7.14–15 (reworked by Aulus Gellius 16.1), 28.7, 28.30–1.
[109] E.g. Mark 7:33, 8:23; John 9:6; cf. Dresvina 2016:178.

the people of the community against which it marauds fast for ten days and then collect their spittle in a bowl (§6.2.2). He pours the spittle out in a circle around the dragon, which the serpent is then unable to cross, and so dies.[110] This sheds retrospective light on the traditions relating to St Elisabeth of (Thracian) Heraclea (a.k.a. 'the Thaumaturge'). Her *Life* ([a], ix–x AD) tells us that she destroyed the Dragon of Constantinople by spitting on its head. A summary reference to this killing in the *Synaxarion of Constantinople* ([b], x AD) offers what, in context, looks like a non sequitur: 'She killed a very large and terrible snake [*ophis*] with a prayer, she abstained from bread for extended periods, and she tasted not even the tiniest bit of olive oil.' The relevance of the abstinence from food is apparently that it armed Elisabeth's spittle in the appropriate way. The motif of fasting has such a strong resonance in Christian terms generally that it is quite surprising to note that, in this particular context, its most direct antecedent is pagan (Pliny).

More specifically, the spittle of female saints can be effective against serpent-induced illness. When Philip ([a], mid- to late iv AD) seeks to cure Stachys' blindness, a blindness both physical and spiritual, caused by the liquid from snake eggs, he does so by applying the saliva of his companion, the holy virgin Mariamne, to his eyes. Monegundis (late vi AD) heals a young boy who has drunk something toxic and now has a nest of serpents writhing inside his stomach. She moistens a vine-leaf with her saliva, makes the sign of a cross on it, and sticks it on his belly. The pain is eased and he is soon able to pass the snakes from his system.

Similarly to spittle, holy water could also be deployed against the dragon. Philip ([a], mid- to late iv AD) and his team counter the smoky miasma produced by the Dragon of the Desert and its serpent host, met with on the road to Ophiorhyme, by sprinkling cups of it into the air in the pattern of the cross. Martha ([a], AD 1187; [c], AD 1263–7; [d], AD 1264) throws it over the Tarasque-dragon to reduce it to docility. And when, in his Norse *Life*, Bishop Gudmund's (mid-xiv AD) ship is obstructed by a massive seaborne dragon (*ormr*) with twelve coils, en route between Nidaross and Bergen, he prays and sprinkles holy water on it. The ship then rides over the dragon and it bursts into twelve corresponding pieces, which are washed ashore.[111]

Against the dragon's fire-breathing and fieriness in general, the saint can deploy various kinds of fire in turn. We may identify four broad categories of use, but the distinctions between them can be fine. The saint can: use external fire;[112] turn the

---

[110] Jean Gobi *Scala coeli* 13.

[111] See, for the episode, Evans 2005:245–6; and, for Gudmund's *Lives* more generally, Skórzewska 2011.

[112] External fire and caustic substances had been deployed against dragons in the classical tradition too. Heracles and Iolaus famously used fire against the Hydra (Diodorus 4.11.5–6; Apollodorus *Bibliotheca* 2.5.2, etc.) and a Ps.-Aristotelian text preserves a marvellous story in which a Thessalian witch destroys a 'Sacred Snake' by charming it across a circle of parching herbs, thereby burning it up (*Mirabilium auscultationes* 845b, iii BC–ii AD); see Ogden 2013a:218–26, with further examples.

dragon's own fire against it; produce fire from his or her own body; and subject the dragon to the perception or hallucination of burning.

As to the use of external fire, let us turn first once again to the Dragon of the Ophiorhyme Desert and its snake host encountered by Philip ([a], mid- to late iv AD) and his team; these are destroyed, together with their eggs in their lairs, by the lightning brought down from heaven in response to the saint's prayers: Zeus' elemental battle against Typhon perhaps still lurks in the background here. Gregory the Great's Florentius of Valcastoria (AD 594) likewise destroys the snakes infesting a deacon's cell by calling down a thunderbolt from God.[113] In a conceit of broadly the same type, the Dragon of Thasion encountered by Joannicius of Bithynia ([a], AD 846) is burned by the rays of the morning sun and so throws itself into Lake Apolloniatis, before disappearing into the mountains of the mainland opposite. Hilarion ([a], AD 396; [b] and [c], AD 675–710) more directly destroys the Dragon of Epidaurus in Dalmatia by commanding it to mount a pyre he has prepared for it, burning the creature alive whilst the local people look on. In the same vein, Eneco (xvi AD or before) has a large pyre built on a mountain-top before commanding the Dragon of Oña to throw itself into its flames. We are told, vestigially, that Eumenius (x AD) burned up a dragon 'with torches'.

As to turning the dragon's own fire against it, Magnus of Füssen ([a], c. AD 895) feeds the Dragon of Kempten a ball of pitch, so that it overheats internally, after the method Daniel had used against the Dragon of Babylon. Pope Leo IV ([b], c. AD 939) would seem similarly to be exploiting the creature's internal fire when he deploys the sign of the cross against a dragon said to be particularly fiery and thereby reduces it to ashes.

As to the saint's production of fire from himself, when Philip ([a], mid- to late iv AD) arrives at Ophiorhyme itself, the city's second rank of guardian dragons, the pair on sentry-duty at the gate, die on sight of the 'light of the monad' in his eyes. Similarly, after Thomas Defourkinos (xii AD) has destroyed the dragon that has attacked him in his oratory near the river Sangarius, the dragon's bereft attendant brood of snakes can no longer bear the sight of the saint's glorious face, which burns them like fire, and they flee off (see §6.5.4). Theodoret's Marcian (mid-v AD) burns up the dragon that attacks him as he prays in the vestibule of his house merely breathing on it, as we have just noted: it disintegrates like a burning reed. With the help of Mary ([b], vi–vii AD) a girl defends herself against the attack of a demon in dragon form by draping baby Jesus' swaddling clothes over her head,

---

[113] The motif of the destruction of a dragon by directing lightning at it is found more recently in Bram Stoker's *The Lair of the White Worm* (1911), the lightning being directed inadvertently into the Worm's well-lair down a wire running from a kite (the Worm, which manifests itself in humanoid form as Lady Arabella, is avowedly modelled on the great worms of English folklore, the Lambton Worm, which inhabits a well, and the Laidly Worm of Spindleston Heugh, a princess transformed).

whereupon flames and embers leap forth from it and attack the dragon's own head and eyes.

As to the inducing of the perception of burning in the dragon, when Hilarus of Galatea (vi AD) drags the dragon that has threatened his monk Glycerius after him, it cries out that it is being burned by the hottest fire. When Eudocia (x AD or before) needs to summon the Dragon of Heliopolis, after it has surreptitiously killed a boy, she prays and it rushes to the scene 'pursued by fire', which we are probably to understand as hallucinatory (cf. Chapter 8, §8.3.2).

We may note one final kind of reciprocity. The swelling up of the dragon that precedes its bursting open by saints (§6.6.1) can be seen as reciprocal to the swelling (usually combined with lividity) that the dragon inflicts on men by breath and bite alike (§6.1.5). The reciprocity of these actions is almost made explicit in the early *Acts of Thomas* (later ii AD), where the Dragon of India is made to suck the lividity—and no doubt too the swelling—out of its last victim, whereupon, in taking the toxin back into itself, it swells up and bursts.

6.6.3 Staffs

The saint's principal physical weapon against the dragon is his staff, which is sometimes specified to be a crook, and is sometimes to be read more specifically as a crozier. The use of the staff can be totemic or symbolic, and can prevent a dragon from passing. Hilary of Poitiers ([a], late vi AD; [b], AD 1263–7) uses his staff to demarcate the line on the Ligurian Isle of Gallinaria that the snake brood that infests it will henceforth be forbidden to cross. Similarly, Lifard (ix AD) encourages his fearful pupil Urbitius to protect them from the Dragon of Meung-sur-Loire, which is on its way to attack them, by taking his cross-embellished staff and planting it in the ground in its path. The serpent bites the upper part of it and coils its body around the lower part of the shaft in an attempt to destroy it, but it can achieve nothing, and bursts itself in half as it strains against it. When Rofillus ([b], xi AD) and Mercurialis have enclosed the Dragon of Forlimpopoli in a well, they plant their croziers in the ground over it; the croziers put roots down into the well's waters and grow into great trees. The significance of Maurus of Syria's (viii AD?) staff is more indirect. He fixes it into the ground after arriving before the lair of the Dragon of the river Narco, whereupon it miraculously puts forth leaves and flowers. Inspired by this sign, he begins to build break stones to build himself a hermitage there. His fight with the dragon will follow.

At other times the staff can function simply and directly as a lethal weapon. Mamilianus ([a], vii–viii AD) kills his dragon by knocking it on the head with his staff, as do Arsacius ([b], AD 1493) with the Dragon of Nicomedia and Magnus of Füssen ([b], AD 1067–70) with the Dragon of Kempten; in the last case the blow has the effect of bursting the dragon open. Maglorius (ix–x AD) drives his staff through the throat of the Dragon of Jersey, as does Servanus (AD 1510) with the Dragon of Dunning.[114]

The staff can also be used, less lethally, in taming the dragon. Machutus (AD 866–72) seemingly subdues the Dragon of September Island by holding his staff over its neck, after which it bows its head to the earth in the familiar, productive gesture; he then strikes the same staff into the floor of the dragon's former cave to produce a pure spring. When Paris (AD 1533 or before) knocks the dragon of Teano on the head with his staff, described more specifically as his walking stick, his purpose is merely to send the dragon to sleep, extinguishing all its fire and venom in the meantime.

More particularly, the staff can be used in the leading-and-parading process to which the tamed dragon is subject, usually in association with the binding of the neck with one of the saint's garments. We saw above (§6.4.4) that Paulus Aurelianus ([a], AD 884) and Mewan (x–xi AD) insert the crooks of their staffs into the binding garment they have put around their dragons' necks, so as to be able to draw them along. Two garment-less variations of this motif deserve attention here. First, Senzius (vii–viii AD) drives the Dragon of Blerana along with his staff like an ass, as if it were a cattle-prod or a whip. Second, Peregrinus (xvi AD or before) pretends to be one of the attendants presenting the Dragon of Caltabellotta with his daily meal of a boy-sacrifice, but as the dragon draws near to gobble the boy down, he thrusts his staff into its maw instead and is able to use it to drag the dragon it off to the top of the local mountain. It is not clear exactly what is envisaged here: does the staff just somehow magically inhere in the mouth? Does he use the crooked end of the staff like a fish-hook?[115]

6.6.4 Other Physical Weapons, Conventional and Unconventional

The so-called 'military saints' use the conventional weapons of lance and sword against their dragons. Theodore Tyron ([a], soon after AD 754; [b], late ix or before; [d], c. AD 871; [e], before AD 890; [g], AD 980–1010; [f], x AD) kills the Dragon of Euchaita by launching his lance (*lonchē*) through its head or its liver. In other versions of this story ([e], before AD 890; [c], late ix AD) he deploys rather a sword, as he does in the killing of the Dragon of King Samuel's City ([h], xiv). George ([a], xi AD; [b], xii AD; [c], AD 1263–7) similarly kills the Dragon of Lasia with his sword.[116]

---

[114] Also, Leo (xii AD) kills the Dragon of Cava with a big stick.

[115] But sometimes a staff is just a staff: more mundanely, Gildas ([a], ix AD) uses his staff merely to help him hike up a mountain so that he can confront the Dragon of Rome in its high cave.

[116] Further examples: Crescentinus (xiv AD) kills the Dragon of Tifernum with his lance; the archangel Michael ([a], ix–x AD), a quasi-military saint, kills the Dragon of Southern Asia with his fiery (NB) sword.

On occasion non-military saints too can use weapons of a broadly conventional sort. Athenogenes (vi AD) strikes the Dragon of the Land of the Goths on the head three times with the spiked butt (*styrax*) of the spear that serves him as his staff; even so, the effect of this is symbolic rather than physical: the dragon bursts open as opposed to dying of a headwound. In a more directly physical fashion Joannicius of Bithynia ([a], AD 846) kills the Dragon of the river Gorgytes by striking it on the head with an iron axe he has brought from his own hermit cave. As an alternative to the usual story of Donatus of Epirus ([b], AD 1263–7) killing the Dragon of Chamaegephyrae by spitting in its mouth, Jacobus de Voragine notes the tradition that he had rather killed it with a whip.[117] Maurus of Syria (viii AD?) kills and beheads the Dragon of the river Narco with the iron tool with which he is in the process of building his hermitage.

The use of some more unconventional physical weapons may also be noted. Narcissus of Gerundum (*c.* AD 770) weaponizes a demon-associate of the Dragon of Augsburg by tricking him into undertaking to kill the beast on his behalf. Timothy deploys some unusual weapons against his iteration of the Dragon of Prusa. In the earlier account of his tale ([a], x AD) we are told that he kills the dragon by throwing at it a bag in which he has been carrying some holy loaves, thereby causing it to burst open directly. In the later account ([b], xiv AD) the bag contains rather some prayers he is delivering on behalf of his brother monks to a pious lady newly arrived in the region. Transferring the prayers to the sleeve of his cloak, he screws the bag up and slings it at the creature, before passing on his way. As he returns by the same road, the prayers now duly delivered, he finds the dragon lying dead.

Unusually, Mamilianus of Palermo ([b], xii AD or before) is said to have throttled the Dragon of Montecristo—presumably with his bare hands, therefore.

6.7 The Stench of the Dragon's Carcass and its Disposal

Dragons continue to pollute the air even in death: the putrefaction of their carcasses, perhaps combined with the remnants of their venom, is the cause. Consequently, slain dragons can constitute almost as great a threat as living ones, and the disposal of their carcass presents the local community with a challenge. This theme was well established in classical tradition: Delphi had acquired its byname of Pytho from the rotting (*pythesthai*) of the huge carcass of the dragon slain there by Apollo (variously identified as Delphyne and Python);[118] and the

---

[117] When Victoria ([a], *c.* AD 500) dispatches the Dragon of Trebula to the wilderness, it is said to flee *as if* being beaten with whips.

[118] *Homeric Hymn* (3) *to Apollo* 300–6, 352–73; Ovid *Metamorphoses* 1.59–60; Plutarch *Moralia* 294f; Pausanias 10.6.5–6; Macrobius 1.17.50–1. Discussion at Ogden 2013a:229–30.

rotting carcass of the Bagrada Dragon beside its river created such a stench that it had forced Regulus' army to move camp.[119]

In hagiographical tradition, the threat the dragon's rotting carcass constitutes is well conveyed by Gregory of Tours' *History of the Franks*. This tells how in AD 589 Rome's Tiber River flooded, carrying down with it a multitude of snakes together with a huge log-like *draco*. The creatures were destroyed in the salt sea, but then washed back up onto shore again, whereupon their carcasses gave rise to a bubonic plague that killed Pope Pelagius, resulting in Gregory the Great's ([a], AD 594; so too [b], viii AD) ascent to office. The story is taken further in John the Deacon's *Life* of Gregory ([c], ix AD). Here we are told how a monk in Gregory's monastery, Theodore, fell victim to the disease and became delirious, believing that he was being devoured by a great *draco* that already had his head in its mouth (cf. Chapter 5, §5.5.1). When Ammon (*c.* AD 395 and *c.* AD 403/4) destroys the dragon of the Egyptian Desert, the locals have to cover its carcass with sand; as we have seen, this dragon is actually said to have belched out its venom as it was burst open by the saint. When John of Reomay (AD 659) has killed a serpent inside the well in which it lives, and extracted it, it has to be 'cast away far from the place'.

Sometimes God can help with the problem of the venomous, festering carcasses. When Gregory the Great's Florentius of Valcastoria (AD 594) has destroyed the host of snakes infesting a deacon's cell with a thunderbolt, he is faced with the problem of how to dispose of all the rotting corpses. In response to his plea, God sends a flock of birds, equivalent in number to the snakes: each one carries away a carcass to dispose of. Similarly, after the massive brood of snakes that had been torturing Thomas Defourkinos (xii AD) for eleven years die at the site of their presiding dragon's entombment, a flock of birds, again equal to the snakes in number, appears 'as if on a mission' and gobbles up the carcasses before disappearing off again (see §6.5.4 for the full tale). After Honoratus ([c], *c.* AD 1300) has destroyed the host of serpents infesting the future Île Saint-Honorat with the sign of the cross, he is faced with the problem of clearing the island of their foul carcasses. He climbs the palm tree at the island's highest point and prays, whereupon God sends a tsunami to sweep them all away. But God does not wait to be asked by Nicasius (xi AD) how to solve the problem of the carcass of the Dragon of Vaux: 'The sign of the cross was made and the dragon was burst open at the invocation of Christ's name, in such a way that no trace of its wickedness or its carcass remained in that place.'

A common solution is the hacking up of the body and the carting away of it to a place of safety by means of ox-teams. After Donatus of Epirus ([a], earlier v AD) has killed the Dragon of Chamaegephyrae, its carcass must be hauled off to a

---

[119] Valerius Maximus 1.8 ext. 19.

nearby plain by eight yoke-pair of oxen, so that it can be burned before it befouls the air. When the carcass of the Dragon of Montecristo destroyed by Mamilianus ([a], vii–viii AD) is lifted and thrown into the sea, it is remarked, curiously, that not even four yoke-pair of oxen could have shifted it 'whilst it was alive'; the implication is perhaps that that was how many yoke-pair it took to remove the carcass from harm's way. The archangel Michael destroys dragons in Southern Asia ([a], ix–x AD) and on St Michael's Mount (Mons Tumba; [c], c. AD 1000) with his fiery sword, hacking each of them into twelve portions. The respective groups of locals must then drag away each of the portions using twelve teams of oxen and dump it in the sea to avoid the ensuing stench. When, according to an Old Irish text, St Michael hacks the Dragon of Mount Garganus into nine parts ([b], xi AD), we are told that each of the separate parts had the weight of ten oxen—a striking and interesting detail, and one that perhaps originates in a claim that it had taken teams of ten oxen to drag each portion off. (See §6.1.1 above for the other uses to which oxen are put.)

One of the most elaborate treatments of this theme comes in the tale of Maurus of Syria's (viii AD?) disposal of the enormous, decapitated carcass of the Dragon of the river Narco. He heaves it into the river, but it is too vast for the waters to carry away, so he rolls a stone (presumably a massive boulder) onto the top of the body. Over the space of three days this squeezes a huge quantity of blood out of it, at which point it is at last carried away successfully from the Narco into the Tiber.

6.8 Lasting Results

6.8.1 The Conversion of the Local People

The typical result of the saint's banishment or killing of a local dragon is the conversion of the people. The conversion operates on two levels, as we have already noted (§6.1.3). Most obviously, at an intellectual level, the saint's victory over the dragon demonstrates the power of his faith, and thereby wins converts. At a more physical or indeed a symbolic level, the dragon (together with its miasma) is an embodiment of unbelief, and so the saint's removal of it ipso facto lifts the condition of unbelief away from its erstwhile victims.

The extent to which dragon-fights are proofs of the faith of those that undertake them is made clear at a relatively early stage in Rufinus' tale of the group of Christian brothers associated with Ammon the hermit (c. AD 395 and c. AD 403/4). They are delighted to find the trail of a huge draco in the Egyptian Desert and rush after it, with the boast to their non-Christian companions that they have killed many such dragons and snakes before by the power of their own faith. For them, as we have noted, dragon-slaying appears to have become almost a sport (cf. Chapter 5, §5.2.3).

The conversion (or sometimes re-conversion) of an unbelieving local population is a productive theme of dragon-mastery.[120] After Philip ([a], mid- to late iv AD) has overcome the Dragon of the Rocks outside Ophiorhyme and compelled its fifty-serpent host to build a church in the place they had formerly lived, no fewer than three thousand men are attracted to the spot, together with their wives and children, and begin to glorify Christ. The second account of Silvester's victory over the Dragon of Rome is framed by the issue of conversion ([b], c. AD 500; cf. [c] and [d], AD 675–710; [e], AD 1263–7):[121]

St Silvester was having an argument with some pagans in defence of the truth, and it came to a point at which the pagans said to him, 'Silvester, go down to the dragon and in the name of your God make it desist from killing the human race even for just one year, so that we may believe that your Christ possesses the virtue of divinity'. St Silvester said to them, 'My Christ, full of the virtue of divinity, will deign to demonstrate his virtue in this place. But in your lack of faith you will ever be looking for bogus objections to his divinity that can be of no benefit to your cause'... [Silvester locks the dragon and its breath in]. The whole city was liberated from the breath of the dragon from that day and thenceforth. But when one year had passed, and then a second, all the servants of the dragon, agreeing amongst themselves that it had been truly overcome and shut in, prostrated themselves before St Silvester, put their faith in Christ, and were baptized.

When the town of Trebula is afflicted by the blasts of the local dragon's breath, Victoria ([a], c. AD 500; cf. [b] and [c], AD 675–710) tells the mayor Domicianus that the dragon will flee if the people abandon their idols and worship Christ instead. Domicianus responds rather that if she expels the dragon, he will ensure that all the citizens become Christians. Veranus (ix–xi AD) goes up against the Dragon of Albingaunum, to which the locals give annual sacrifices of virgin boys and virgin girls; on the one hand they claim that the dragon confers fertility and safety upon them, but on the other they promise Veranus to convert if he can chase it away for them. George kills the Dragon of Lasia on condition that the local pagans it has been harassing convert, and proceeds to baptize variously 45,000 ([a], xi AD), 240,000 ([b], xii AD), or 20,000 ([c], AD 1263–7) of them.

---

[120] In addition to the examples listed in the main text that follows, the local population or the crowd of onlookers is converted after a saint's manifest victory over a dragon in the following cases: Philip ([b], vi AD) and the Dragon of Scythia; Athenogenes (vi AD) and the Dragon of the Land of the Goths; Senzius (vii–viii AD) and the Dragon of Blerana; Columba (c. AD 700) and the Loch Ness monster; Clement of Metz ([a], AD 782–6; [b], c. AD 1000) and the Dragon of Metz; Samson of Dol ([b], ix AD) and the Dragon of Trigg; Eudocia (x AD or before) and the Dragon of Heliopolis; Julian of le Mans (c. AD 1000) and the Dragon of Artinas; Fronto ([c], xi AD) and the Dragon of Périgueux; Nicasius (xi AD) and the Dragon of Vaux; Crescentinus (xiv AD) and the Dragon of Tifernum.

[121] The following continues directly from the passage quoted in §6.1.3 above.

When the local population petitions Germanus of Auxerre ([a], xi–xii AD) to rid them of the seven-headed Dragon of Trou Baligan on the Cotentin peninsula, he responds that they would have their wish if only they had faith in Christ. His banishment of the dragon to a cistern then occasions their conversion and baptism.

Sometimes such conversions can be effected at a more individual level too. The thieves that would steal the hermit Ammon's (c. AD 395 and c. AD 403/4) bread in the Egyptian Desert are converted when they observe his command over the pair of dragons he employs as guards for his desert cell. Mamertinus is converted after Germanus of Auxerre ([b], AD 1263–7) has expelled the serpents that embody his paganism from the tomb of St Concordian.

In light of this, the modesty of Theodoret's Julian Sabas (mid-v AD) is rather curious. He kills a dragon he meets whilst walking in the desert alone, as is divined by his disciple James, who comes across the carcass. Only with difficulty does James force the admission from the modest Julian that it was indeed he that had killed the dragon, and the old man forbids him from telling anyone else of it until after his death.

6.8.2 Memorialization: The Building of a Church, Monastery, or Hermitage

Occasionally, less often than one might imagine, our authors write with a consciousness that the glorious story they are telling can in itself constitute a monument to the saint's achievement. Jerome, for example, notes that the tale of the burning of the Dragon of Epidaurus in Dalmatia by Hilarion ([a], AD 396) is told by mothers to their children, so that it will be handed down to posterity.[122] But the hagiographical tradition is not much given to self-reflection, and it prefers to concentrate on celebrating the more tangible monuments that can proceed from a victory over a dragon.

Accordingly, we hear much of the building of churches or monasteries and of the establishment of more modest hermitages for the saints themselves either at the place at which the dragon has been defeated or even within its former home. In practice a great many saintly dragon tales have the look of being, first and foremost, retrospective aetiologies of a venerated building or site. An incunabular version of the motif is found already in the tale of the destruction of the Dragon of India by Thomas (later ii AD). After the earth has opened to swallow its carcass, Thomas commands that workmen should fill in the hole and build houses over it for visitors, presumably, that is to say, for pilgrims.

---

[122] For Jerome's *Life of Hilarion* in general, see Leclerc et al. 2007.

Let us begin with churches. After Philip ([a], mid- to late iv AD) has gained mastery over the Dragon of the Rocks and his fifty-serpent host, the dragon makes a surprising offer as it begs him for banishment instead of annihilation:

'...Just as we served our just lord Solomon in Jerusalem (and it was by virtue of our service that he built God's temple), so let us complete a dwelling in this place for you in six days, and it will be called the Church of the Living God. And I will make seven eternal springs flow forth in the name of the crucified one. Only do not annihilate us'...And at once the dragon and the fifty snakes revealed their true form and flew off right away, like winds, and cried out, 'Let us bring the building at once!' Before three hours had passed they had brought fifty tall columns through the air and they said, 'Arrange these columns as you wish, Philip, and on the sixth day you will see the building, the seven springs and the consecration of the church'. After six days the building had been completed, and rivers gushed forth. In a few days more three thousand men, together with many women and small children, were attracted to the spot, and they glorified Christ.

Clement of Metz ([a], AD 782–6) builds a chapel as well as a hermitage for himself in the vaults of the Metz amphitheatre from which he has expelled the city's dragon and its serpent host. Fronto of Périgueux ([c], xi AD) is a serial founder of churches: he founds one at the spot in which he has killed a dragon at Neuilly-Saint-Front (Nogeliacum), another at the spot from which he has banished a dragon at Limoges, and a third at the spot beside the river Dronne from which he has banished yet another one. Selbius builds a church for George ([a], xi AD; [b], xii AD; [c], AD 1263–7) after his defeat of the Dragon of Lasia. Donatus of Sisteron (xii AD or earlier) makes his bed in the place where the Dragon of the Jura Mountains, banished to the river Durance, had made its nest, before going on to build a chapel named for St Martin on the summit of the hill above.[123]

Let us move on now to monasteries (although the narratives do not always trouble to make a strong distinction between churches and monasteries). This is the aftermath of the banishment of the Dragon of Trebula by Victoria ([a], c. AD 500; cf. [b] and [c], AD 675–710):

Then the dragon, with the speediest of courses, departed in flight, in such a fashion that you would think it was being thrashed with whips. But neither its smell nor any trace of it could be detected any more. Then they praised St Victoria, saying, 'She is a goddess'. But she entered the dragon's cave and, calling the people

---

[123] A further, late, example: the warrior saints Neventerius and Derien (AD 1637—in a vernacular text preserving older material) secure the agreement of the local baron that he will build a church for them if they dispose of the Basilisk-dragon that has been terrorizing the region of the river Élorn in Brittany; they compel the creature to throw itself into the sea.

together, said, 'Hear me, and build here a place of prayer and give me virgin girls to help me'. Girls were found of nine years of age and above, whom their parents brought to her at their request, with the result that within a short time more than sixty were in conversation with her. She instructed them in hymns and psalms and canticles, working constantly with them....

Samson of Dol ([a], vii–viii A D; cf. [b], ix A D, [d], xii or before) has his monks build monasteries at the sites of the former caves of the Dragon of Trigg and the Dragon of Brittany, after killing the former and banishing the latter. After liberating the island of Jersey of its Dragon, Maglorius (ix–x A D) takes a seventh part of it to maintain himself and his monks. Mewan (x–xi A D) builds a monastery on the estate he has liberated of the Dragon of Anjou, and further memorializes his deed by giving the monastery the name Monopalium, supposedly after the garment he has used to bind the dragon's neck in the conventional way. When Vigor of Bayeux (A D 1030–45) has sent the Dragon of the Cerisy Forest into the sea, the forest's owner Volusianus makes the land over to him for the purposes of building his monastery. Sometimes the building of a church or monastery can be, as it were, contractual: the people of Mons Tumba, the future St Michael's Mount, promise God they will build him a church and a monastery if he delivers them from their dragon, and he accordingly sends them the archangel Michael ([c], c. A D 1000) to do the job.[124]

The circumstances in which saints construct more modest hermitages or cells for themselves can be similar to those of churches or monasteries, as in the cases of Clement and Donatus just noted. Veranus of Cavaillon (ix–xi A D) too builds a hermitage for himself at the site of the Fontaine de Vaucluse spring, after delivering it from the possession of a dragon. Like Victoria's convent, such hermitages often occupy the very cave vacated by the dragon (and cf. again Clement's amphitheatre-crypt). Joannicius of Bithynia ([a], A D 846) takes over a cave for his hermitage after killing its previous occupant, an evil *echidna* (viper). Beatus (x A D?) destroys the Dragon of Vendôme before taking up residence in its cave too; the necessary improvements include the ejection of the serpent's dung.[125] Peregrinus (xvi A D or before) makes his hermitage in the cave of the Dragon of Caltabellotta in Sicily, after he has thrust the dragon itself down a hole within the cave.[126]

Small islands too can be made into hermitages. After driving the Dragon of the Isle of Battha (Batz) into the sea, Paulus Aurelianus ([a], A D 884) makes his home

---

[124] Further examples of monastery-building: John of Reomay (A D 659) founds a monastery by the well in which he has destroyed the Dragon of Moutiers-Saint-Jean (to be) that was occupying it; after dismissing the Dragon of Cornwall Petroc ([a], xii A D or before) founds a monastery for eighty brethren. Pavacius' (ix A D) taming of the Dragon of le Mans is memorialized in association with ecclesiastical architecture in a more modest way, in a painting in the city's episcopal palace.

[125] For the legend, cult, and *Lives* of Beatus, see Moretus 1907.

[126] Further examples of hermit-cell building: Deodatus ([a], x A D; [b], x A D) and the Dragon of Blois; Crescentinus (xiv A D) and the Dragon of Tifernum.

on it for the remainder of his life. Mamilianus of Palermo ([b], xii AD or before) builds a little hut for himself on the hilltop of the Isle of Montecristo, after killing the dragon that had previously lived there. In an Irish text Senán (early xv AD) expels a fiery monster from Inis Cathaigh with the very purpose of building a hermitage on the island: as we have noted (§6.3.1), the archangel Raphael advises him that God has been using the monster specifically to keep sinners away from the island, so that it would be able to provide a suitably pure place for his retreat.

Sometimes the establishment of the hermitage (etc.) can be the first act in the story, with the saint then being subsequently attacked in it by dragons or broods of snakes, or himself using it as a base from which to attack them. Thus, when Gregory of Tours' Caluppan (AD 581–94) makes his hermitage in a cave on a high crag in the Cantal, he is attacked by a host of serpents under the leadership of a pair of dragons of immense size, which Caluppan is eventually able to dismiss from his cell by prayer. It is not clear whether Caluppan gets to the cave first, where he is arbitrarily attacked by the serpents, or whether he is in effect taking up residence in the cave in which they already live. Florentius of Valcastoria (AD 593) comes to the aid of a deacon whose established cell has been beset by a plague of snakes, calling down a thunderbolt upon them. Maurus of Syria (viii AD?) starts to build a hermitage before the lair of the Dragon of the river Narco. When the dragon duly presents itself, the saint is economically able to dispose of it with the axe with which he has been cutting stones. A viper (*echidna*) attacks the workman Pardus as he is building a chapel at the behest of Joannicius of Bithynia ([a], AD 846).[127] Prior to engaging with the local dragon, Magnus of Füssen ([b], AD 1067–70) commands his follower Theodore to build a home for himself and a chapel in the worm-infested region of Kempten.[128] The Dragon of Treguier first imposes itself on Tudual's (xii AD) attention when it interferes with the workmen attempting to build a monastery on its patch. Thomas Defourkinos (xii AD) is harassed by a plague of snakes in his cell for a full eleven years, until matters come to a head in his confrontation with their presiding dragon (see §6.5.4).

Victories over dragons can also be memorialized by permanent changes to the local landscape.[129] The creation of new water-sources is the most common motif in this regard (cf. §6.1.2). Seven new rivers flow forth after Philip's ([a], mid- to late iv AD) defeat of the Dragon of the Rocks outside Ophiorhyme, in conjunction with the construction of a church by the dragon and his fifty serpent cohorts.

---

[127] The passage is quoted in Chapter 8, §8.3.4.

[128] In an earlier tale Magnus of Füssen ([a], *c.* AD 895), more unusually, renders an area suitable for more general home-building by destroying the Dragon of the Horse-Head Pass in the Julian Alps.

[129] For the propensity of classical dragons (and sea-monsters) to leave their marks on their landscapes, see Ogden 2013a:161–5. To the examples collected there should be added Ovid *Metamorphoses* 7.358 and 11.55–60: as the decapitated head of Orpheus washes up on the shore of Lesbos, a *draco* makes to take a bite out of it, but is petrified by Apollo before it can do so; it survives in the form of a landmark rock at Pitane on the mainland opposite.

The spring that Euflamus (xii AD) creates to refresh King Arthur after his abortive battle with the dragon is still shown at Toul-Efflam. After slaying the dragon of Lasia, George ([a], xi AD; [b], xii AD; [c], AD 1263–7) brings forth a spring by the altar of the church subsequently founded at the site.

The landscape can be marked in other ways too. When the archangel Michael ([c], c. AD 1000) destroys the Dragon of Mons Tumba, St Michael's Mount to be, he does so in the form of a giant bird, and leaves behind his talon marks in the stone, where he had stood to do the deed. Venerius of Tino (early xv AD) affords a similar example. In dismissing the Dragon of Luni, he must descend into its cave to encounter it: his feet leave impressions on the hard rock as if he is walking through snow. In addition to the spring Euflamus (xii AD) created at Toul-Efflam, the Roch-Ru or Red Rock can still be seen at Saint-Efflam, where he caused the dragon he defeated to vomit forth its blood.[130] Keyne (xiv AD or before) turns the plague of snakes she encounters at the future Keynsham in Somerset to stone: these stones, as her *Life* says, can still be found today in the streets and fields and look as if they have been carved by a sculptor. This is thought to be a reference to fossilized ammonites.

Otherwise, the site of the fight can change its name to remember the saint's achievement. So it is, beyond 'Euflamus' and 'Saint-Efflam', and 'Keyne' and 'Keynsham', that the place at which John of Reomay (AD 659) kills a dragon in a well becomes Moutiers-Saint-Jean; that Mons Tumba becomes St Michael's Mount after Michael's ([c], c. AD 1000) killing of its dragon; that the mountain on which the Dragon of Rennes had lived is renamed for St Armel ([a], xii AD or later) after he has destroyed it. However, it is the dragon's name, not the saint's, that is in remembered in the name of Tarascon (Tirasconus), where Martha ([a], AD 1187; [b], late xii AD; [c], AD 1263–7; [d], AD 1264) destroyed the Tarasque (Tirascurus). Similarly, after Servanus (AD 1510) killed the Dragon of Dunning, the valley in which he had done so was named 'The Valley of the Dragon' in memory of the deed.

Rather differently, the victory of Victor of Marseilles over the local marauding dragon was memorialized in the display of the creature's skin in the Benedictine monastery named for him, the Abbaye Saint Victor. It was seen there and recorded by Hans von Waltheym ('*trache*') in the course of his pilgrimage in AD 1474.[131]

Let us conclude by noting the prodigious memorialization that resulted from the overcoming of a single dragon in Provence: Honoratus ([c], c. AD 1300) gave

---

[130] Cf. the classical tradition of the battle between Zeus and Typhon. At Apollodorus *Bibliotheca* 1.6.3 Typhon hurls a mountain at Zeus, who blasts it back at him with his thunderbolt, and blood gushes forth from it (Typhon's, or the mountain's own?), whence it acquires the name Haemus (cf. *haima*, 'blood').

[131] This is the earliest literary reference to Victor's dragon fight, though it is attested first iconographically on a shield of the city of Marseilles of AD 1243, for which see Bedos 1980:306–9; cf. Coulet 1995:120, 122.

his name to the Île Saint-Honorat, from which he expelled it, whilst the dragon itself conferred its own designation upon Draguignan on the mainland, where he finally killed it, at the same time leaving its parched bones behind there to be admired in perpetuity. When credit for the triumph was subsequently transferred to another saint, Armentarius (AD 1540), the local town already named for him, Saint-Hermentaire, retrospectively came to celebrate his triumph over the creature in turn (see Chapter 7, §7.1, for more on this nexus of traditions).[132]

6.9 Conclusion

Such, then, is the principal narrative course of the saintly dragon fight. By way of conclusion, let us imagine an ideal total narrative that encompasses versions of all of the episodes and motifs laid out above.

A dragon takes up residence in a cave, a well, a tomb, a grove, or an island. From this lair it sallies forth to make depredations on the local flocks of sheep and herds of cattle, and also on its human neighbours. The creature is possessed of a caustic venom, which it breathes forth as fire or in the form of a smoky, pestilential miasma, and this, an actualization of their unbelief, sickens and kills the local people. It also poisons with its venom a spring upon which they depend. Its venomous bite induces swelling and lividity.

The locals petition a saint to put an end to the menace. He prepares for his encounter with the beast by fasting and praying, or by asking the locals to undertake this themselves. He dons arms of a spiritual nature, most typically a breastplate of faith. He is encouraged in his endeavour by an angel, whilst his human companions, less secure in their faith, attempt without success to dissuade him from the deed.

The saint presents himself at the dragon's lair. His very approach can induce the dragon to harm itself. He subjects it to himself by praying again and by making the sign of the cross or indeed brandishing a crucifix. The dragon bows its head before the saint and behaves towards him like a fawning animal. He is thereby able to leash its neck with a garment of a slight nature, most typically a stole, and thereby parade it harmlessly before the astonished locals. The binding of the neck in this way seals off the dragon's pestilential breath.

The dragon is often demon-like, and occasionally an alternative humanoid-demon aspect is made manifest. Dragons of such a sort cannot normally be killed, only subjected to the exorcistic banishment appropriate to demons. It is banished either to the wilderness, often a place specifically beyond a river boundary, or to

---

[132] Cf. Gayrard 2001.

the abyss. The abyss can be conceived of either as the underworld, in which the dragon is confined, or as the sea, into which it is plunged directly, or into which it is sent by means of a river. This dismissal of the dragon can be seen as a sending of it home to the place whence it originally came.

But sometimes the dragon can indeed be killed. In these cases the saint can merely command it to die or to kill itself; it belches forth its (liquid) venom in the process, or bursts open. But weapons can also be used. Sometimes these can be weapons that mirror the dragon's own armoury: the saint's own breath, his own spittle, or fire, deployed in various ways. Sometimes they can be objects the efficacy of which lies only or principally in their holiness, such as a bag for holy loaves, or the saint's staff or crozier. But weapons of the cruder physical sort are not disdained: swords, lances, axes, and whips are all deployed.

The dead dragon's carcass continues to constitute a public hazard as it rots and releases its venom into the atmosphere. Different means, divinely aided and miraculous or merely banal, can be deployed in its safe disposal. Often it is hacked into sections, which are wheeled away on ox-carts.

There are lasting results from the battle. The local people are converted by this token of the power of faith, or confirmed in their faith if they have lapsed, or simply released from the actuality of their unbelief by the killing of the dragon. There are more physical monuments too: sometimes the battle leaves its mark on the landscape; more often the landscape is modified by the construction of a hermitage, a church, or a monastery, on occasion actually in the dragon's former lair.

In the course of our review we have noted the reflexes of the six core dragon-fight motifs the hagiographical tradition shares with the classical and Germanic traditions, namely: the dragon's marauding (§6.1.1); its fire (§§6.1.4, 6.6.2); its pestilential breath (§§6.1.3, 6.8.1; cf. §6.7); its cave-home (§§6.3, 6.5.4, 6.5.7); its control of a water source (§6.1.2); and its generation from a corpse (§6.3.1—albeit the key discussion of the relevant hagiographical material here is deferred to Chapter 11, §11.3).

Beyond the spine of this principal narrative course the hagiographical tradition deploys a number of further recurring themes or subroutines of a distinctive nature. It is to these that we turn in the next chapter.

7

The Etiquette of the Saintly Dragon Fight (ii)

Some Important Narrative Subroutines

We now turn to a number of motifs and episode-types which, whilst being subordinate to the principal narrative course described in the previous chapter, or indirectly associated with it, are nonetheless frequently found and are often highly elaborated. We also consider some matters of what might be termed 'meta-narrative' interest, namely the impact of the attribution of multiple dragon-fights to a single saint (e.g. Silvester and Fronto) and, more intriguingly, the impact of the attribution of fights against what is effectively the same dragon to different saints, the case of the Dragon of Rome constituting the *ne plus ultra* example of this phenomenon.

7.1 The Great Dragon and its Serpent Brood

A motif that recurs strongly in the hagiographical tradition, without becoming dominant, is that of a single great dragon presiding over a pullulating host of lesser dragons or snakes.[1] The motif was probably present already in pagan tradition. Hyginus' *Astronomica* (ii AD) cites Polyzelus of Rhodes, who lived at some point prior to the first century BC:

> Their [the Rhodians'] island was overrun by a multitude of serpents, and so the citizens named it Ophiussa ['Snake-land']. In the midst of that multitude was a dragon [*draco*] of vast size, which had killed very many of the people, and accordingly the island had begun to become a wasteland, bereft of men. [The Thessalian] Phorbas, the son of Triopas by Hiscilla, the daughter of Myrmidon, is said to have been carried to the island by a storm and to have killed all the wild creatures and that dragon. He is said to have been translated to the stars

---

[1] For massive 'social aggregations' of actual snakes, the purpose of which is temperature regulation during winter, a phenomenon particularly associated with northern latitudes, see Lillywhite 2014:108: his striking image (fig. 4.7) of red-sided garter snakes so massing in Manitoba disquiets even your ophidiophile author. For a modern take on the terror of a burgeoning brood of serpents, see Mikhail Bulgakov's 1925 novella *The Fatal Eggs*.

[i.e. transformed into the constellation of Ophiuchus] because he was very much loved by Apollo, so that he could be seen killing the dragon and so be remembered and praised.

[Hyginus] *Astronomica* 2.4 =
Polyzelus of Rhodes *FGrH/BNJ* 521 F7[2]

In hagiography the motif is found already in the *Acts* and the *Martyrium* of Philip ([a], mid- to late iv AD), and no less than three times there. We have had occasion to refer to each group several times already. First, Philip is sent on a mission against the *drakaina*-goddess known as the Echidna, the viper-goddess, object of worship of the Ophianoi ('People of the Snake') and their city of Ophiorhyme ('Snake-town'). She is described as 'the Mother of Snakes' and it emerges that she presides over not only the human citizens of this benighted place, but also a profusion of snakes, which the citizens handle. Indeed, at one point she is said to preside over a wilderness not merely of *drakontes* but actually of *drakainai*: she is the brood-mother of brood-mothers. Second, when Philip and his team are then on the desert road to Ophiorhyme: 'a very great and dark *drakōn* attacked the servants of God from out of the darkness itself…. His body extended beyond a hundred cubits. There attended upon him a host of snakes and a host of the offspring of snakes.' This dragon is projected as male, a king presiding over a snake host, but the notion of pullulating snakes still lurks in the reference to 'the offspring of snakes', as it does in the following observation that the lightning directed by Philip's prayers 'penetrated the openings of the lairs and pulverized the eggs of the snakes'. Third, when Philip and his team pass by a great pile of rocks on the approach to the city they bring forth from it fifty serpents of sixty cubits each presided over by a huge *drakōn* of a hundred cubits in length (see Chapter 6, §§6.1.4, 6.5.1, 6.8.2).

There are numerous further examples of the phenomenon. Fronto of Périgueux ([a], viii AD; [b], later x AD) and his brethren encounter a dragon accompanied by a serpent host at the site of the future Neuilly-Saint-Front on the river Dronne in Soissons. Whilst his companions are terrified, Fronto, confident in the power of his fasting, expels them, never to be seen again, with a mere prayer. Clement of Metz ([a], AD 782–6; [b], *c.* AD 1000) confronts a massive pestilential serpent brood gathered in that city's amphitheatre, where a single large dragon presides over them. Clement dismisses the dragon across the river Seille and tells it to take its host with it: 'I command that you should do no harm to man or beast and that you should at once cross this river together with the whole of your venomous entourage and go into those parts where mankind cannot live.' When Joannicius

---

[2] The story is also told at Diodorus 5.58, where we are given overweening snakes (ὄφεις ὑπερμεγέθεις), albeit without the singling-out of a presiding dragon. Aelian *Nature of Animals* 9.21 tells how Helen cleansed the island of Pharos of its snakes by planting a snake-repellent herb on it.

of Bithynia ([b], before AD 860) expels from the islet of Thasion the dragon and
its serpent host that are blighting the lives of Father Daniel and his Christian
brothers there, the dragon plunges into the sea to escape to the mainland opposite, and its host of snakes throw themselves into the water with it. When Magnus
of Füssen ([a], *c.* AD 895; [b], AD 1067–70) visits the site at which Narcissus of
Gerundum had killed his dragon in the Julian Alps, he destroys the Dragon of
Kempten that lives there in the midst of a great brood of 'worms'; the dragon
dead, the remaining worms flee off, never to be seen again. Thomas Defourkinos
(xii AD) is harassed in his hermit cell and oratory beside the river Sangarius for
eleven years by a plague of snakes before finally being permitted a confrontation
with their presiding dragon (see Chapter 6, §6.5.4). After he has buried this in the
earth, the countless snakes that have been nesting under his cell rush to the spot
at which the dragon has been entombed, and promptly die there.[3]

Gregory of Tours' *History of the Franks* gives us a vision of just such a brood and
its presiding dragon frozen in death. As we have seen, he tells how in AD 589 Rome's
river Tiber flooded, carrying down with it a multitude of snakes together with a
single huge *draco* like a log. The creatures were destroyed in the salt sea, but then
washed back up onto shore again, whereupon their carcasses gave rise to a bubonic
plague that killed Pope Pelagius, resulting in the succession of Gregory the Great
([a], AD 594; cf. [b], viii AD; cf. Chapter 6, §6.7).

An interesting treatment of the theme of the brood and its dominant dragon is
offered by the earlier *Life* of the Cornish saint Petroc ([a], xii AD or before). Petroc
arrives in the west of Britain and comes to a place that had been ruled over by the
cruel tyrant Teudur. In his savagery he had had various serpents and all sorts of
deleterious worms gathered together into a marsh, and he had been punishing
criminals by throwing them into it. When this king died and his more humane
son had taken over, he had abandoned the practice. And so the serpents, starving
now that they were deprived of their criminal suppers, began to devour each
other instead until only one was left, a dragon of, inevitably, enormous size. This
had then turned to marauding against beasts and men.

Some texts appear to move towards the concept of a brood-pair responsible for
such a serpent plague. Caluppan (AD 581–94) is harassed by a host of snakes in
his hermit-cave in the Cantal, until one day he is confronted by a pair of massive
ones, to at least one of which the term *draco* is applied. One of the pair tries to
hypnotize the saint into submission, whilst the other winds itself around his feet.

---

[3] Some further examples still. The Dragon of Euchaita slain by Theodore Tyron ([a], soon after AD
754) is said to inhabit a region full of 'beasts and reptiles crawling on the ground'. Parasceve of Sicily
(viii AD) is confined to a well occupied by 'a dragon and venomous beasts and reptiles'. At Limoges
Fronto of Périgueux ([c], xi AD) encounters an enormous dragon ensconced with a multitude of serpents; he banishes dragon and serpents alike to the wilderness. Donatus of Sisteron (xii AD or earlier)
comes across a mass of snakes in a barren spot at the foot of the Jura Mountains, in the midst of which
lies an enormous dragon. Peter of Athos (xiii–xiv AD) is attacked by a demon that appears before him
masquerading as a terrible dragon at the head of an army of snakes.

Caluppan's victory over them of course liberates the cave of all the snakes. We may think that we have in this pair the mummy and the daddy of the lesser snakes, though the narrator, Gregory of Tours, gives us no further clue that this might be so. In the late and anomalous but very rich account of Theodore Tyron's ([h], xiv AD) battle against the Dragon of King Samuel's City, the dragon proper maintains a complicated arrangement back home in his cave. Here he has a host of lesser snakes, which guard his human captives for him, and these are presided over more directly by an 'old-man dragon', who sits on a golden throne, and an 'abominable asp', which is arguably characterized as female. We shall return to the passage in question for a more detailed discussion below (Chapter 9, §9.1.5, where the text is also quoted), but here we may note the possibility of a male-female pair presiding directly over the lesser serpents in the cave.

Sometimes we are just given the brood itself without specification of a king or queen. So it is with Venantius Fortunatus' tale of the snake infestation on the Isle of Gallinaria contained by Hilary of Poitiers (late vi AD). So it is too with Gregory the Great's tale of Florentius of Valcastoria (AD 594): when Gregory visits a remote deacon he finds his cell infested with snakes and destroys them by calling down a thunderbolt from God. We find the phenomenon again in one of the West's most famous saintly dragon-stories, which tends to go unrecognized as such precisely because the traditions give no attention to any presiding master: the tale of St Patrick cleansing the land of Ireland of its snakes, first attested directly by Gerald of Wales ([a], AD 1187).[4] But, let us note, this tradition does exhibit two tell-tale motifs of a standard dragon saga: in Jocelin of Furness' slightly later but fuller account ([b], AD 1200–10), we learn that Patrick is aided by an angel in his work, and that he causes the snakes to plunge into the sea from a high rock (cf. also [c], AD 1263–7). When Keyne (xiv AD or before) crosses the Severn from Wales to the future Keynsham in Somerset and asks the local king to give her a place in which she can pursue a life of solitude, he laughs and gives her a place rendered unhabitable to man and beast by its multitude of serpents. She prays, and at once the brood is killed and turned to stones.[5]

---

[4] But the tale is indirectly attested (without Patrick's name) already at Bede *Ecclesiatical History of the English People* 1.1 (AD 731). The tradition in itself that Ireland is inherently snake-free is far older, indeed classical, being found already at Solinus 22.3 (iii AD); Solinus tells the same also of Crete, Thanet, Ibiza, Gauloe: 11.12, 22.8, 23.11, 29.5. For discussion of Patrick and 'Irish earth', see Krappe 1941a, 1947.

[5] Some further examples. In the Gospel of Ps.-Matthew, baby Jesus ([b], viii–ix AD) himself, no less, turns back a host of *dracones* that emerges from a cave to attack the holy family: they depart worshipping him. George of Suelli in Sardinia (xii AD) comes to the rescue of one Judex, who is subject to a curse partly reminiscent of that experienced by King Phineus in Greek myth, whose food was ever snatched from before him by the Harpies (Apollonius *Argonautica* 2.179–434; Valerius Flaccus *Argonautica* 4.425–528; Apollodorus *Bibliotheca* 1.9.21; Hyginus *Fabulae* 19, etc.). Every time Judex sits down to a meal he is overwhelmed by a plague of snakes (these take the prime focus), together with plagues of beetles, hornets, toads, and frogs. When, by way of solution, George is invited to lunch and presents himself at the table, snakes and frogs duly leap forth, but the saint kills them all with a simple benediction.

Whilst one might understand that the great serpent broods proceed from their presiding dragons in the context of their narratives, in the context of narrative history the direction of genesis can on occasion be the reverse. The case is made by the developing tradition of the Provençal dragon briefly noted at the end of Chapter 6, §6.8.2. In Hilary of Arles' sermon on the life of his distinguished predecessor Honoratus of Arles ([a], before AD 449), we are told that Honoratus cleansed the future Île Saint-Honorat, in the Lérins group off the coast of Cannes, of its venomous animals and 'host of serpents' (*turba serpentium*) to make his monastery there. As his legend matured, the host produced in its place a dragon proper, which by the twelfth century AD ([b]) was surrounding the island and deterring sailors from it with its pestilential breath. A *Life* of *c.* AD 1300 ([c]) then tells that when Honoratus destroys the host of snakes with the sign of the cross, a single pestilential dragon escapes to the mainland and flees to the region subsequently to be known as Draguignan. There it takes up residence in a cave in a valley. In due course it is driven forth by heavy rains and rising water levels, and so inflicts itself upon the region of the town subsequently to become known as Saint-Hermentaire, laying the lush fields to waste and penning the townspeople up behind their walls. It ambushes a group of ten pilgrims from Arquinand as they make their way to Honoratus' monastery and constricts and devours one of their number in front of the rest of them. The survivors find their way to Honoratus and make appeal to him. He ties the creature with his belt (*zona*) and leaves it bound to the crag of the cave in which it had made its home, where its dry bones can still be seen.[6] By AD 1540 the starring role in this tale had been transferred, for readily intelligible reasons, to the namesake of Saint-Hermentaire himself, Armentarius, the fifth-century bishop of Antibes—as we read, in expansive detail, in the *Discours de la vie de Saint Hermentaire* of the local historian Jean de Nostredame, brother of Michel, the famous Nostradamus.

Whilst, according to one account, the brood of venomous reptiles that infested Tarascon disappeared, as we might have expected, upon Martha's destruction of the presiding Tarasque ([b], late xii AD), Gervase of Tilbury gives us a rather different aftermath. In his *Otia imperialia* of AD 1209–14 he reports a contemporary folk tradition associated with the spot in the Rhône in which the Tarasque had once had its lair, this being a deep hollow of the river beneath the precipice on which Tarascon was built.[7] The place is now, he tells us, frequented by *draci*. Despite their name, and their evident association with the Tarasque, these creatures are not dragons in any obvious way and seemingly have more in common with the medieval Greek *drakos* (for which see Chapter 9, §9.1). These entities lure people into the river, where they (usually) devour them, sometimes by taking on human form, sometimes by taking on the form of tempting golden objects

---

[6] Gayrard 2001:52–3 ('*vaincu*') seems to misread *vinxit* as *vicit*.
[7] Gervase of Tilbury *Otia imperiala* 3.85 (pp. 39–40 Liebrecht); discussion at Dumont 1951:164–6.

floating on the surface. Gervase recounts a pair of recent occurrences. In one of these, a few years before, a voice was heard to issue forth continuously for three days from the hollow in the river that had been home to the Tarasque: 'The hour is past, but the man comes not!' At the same time, a *dracus* in human form was seen to be running back and forth along the river bank. On the afternoon of the third day the *dracus* itself was now screaming out this same utterance with yet greater anguish, when a young man arrived at the river bank, running apace, only to be swallowed down whole.[8] At that the cry was silenced. In the second tale, a nursing mother of Gervase's acquaintance was lured into the river by a *dracus* masquerading merely as a wooden goblet. This woman wasn't killed, but kept in servitude in the *dracus'* expansive palace at the bottom of the river, where she was made to nurse its son for seven years (*draci* particularly seeking out nursing mothers for this purpose), but then released. One day the *dracus* had given her an eel sandwich for her meal, and she had accidentally brushed some of the fish's fat into one of her eyes. This gave her the ability to see clearly under water, but after her release she found that it also gave her the ability to recognize the *dracus* whilst disguised in human form. This she did one day in the marketplace of Beaucaire (the town opposite Tarascon on the western bank of the Rhône). To ensure that it should not happen again, the *dracus* poked her eye out.[9]

7.2 Virgins Sacrificed to the Dragon

One of the ancillary motifs of the hagiographical tradition has the dragon actually being worshipped by its locals. Thus we are told that the Dragon of Vado dismissed by Vindemialis (xii AD or before) receives daily sacrifices from its locals in the pagan style (cf. Chapter 6, §§6.1.3 and 6.8.1, for the tendency for the dragon to serve an embodiment of the community's paganism or unbelief). More particularly, it can be specified that the local dragon is worshipped and placated by means of offerings carried to it by virgins. In due course this motif morphs, quite understandably, into the simpler, more lurid, and more pleasing one of human sacrifice.

The notion of the dragon being fed by virgin girls is found early in the traditions bearing upon the Dragon of Rome, in association with Silvester and others. The ultimate inspiration here lies in the actual pagan cult of Juno Sospita, which had been based not in Rome itself, but outside it at Lanuvium (Fig. 7.1). Here, in a fertility rite, blindfolded virgins had carried honey-cakes down many steps into a

---

[8] *Totus imbibitur: imbibo* suggests that it is the river that does the swallowing; *totus* rather the *dracus.*

[9] See the commentary at Banks and Binns 2002:718–21, where the first of these tales is compared with the folklore of the Scottish Water-Kelpie.

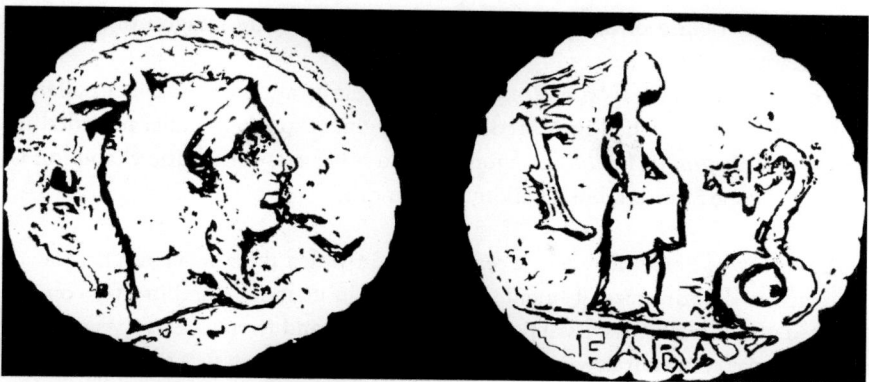

Fig. 7.1 A veiled virgin (right) feeds the sacred snake of Juno Sospita (left) with honey-cakes. Coin of L. Roscius Fabatus, 64 BC: Sydenham 1952: 152 no. 915 and pl. 25. Redrawn by Eriko Ogden.

steep cavern, and presented them to the dragon that lived below. Woe-betide the girl that was not truly a virgin, for the serpent would refuse to accept her honey-cakes.[10] In the earliest Silvester tradition ([a], late iv AD) the dragon and its many-stepped hole are transferred to the heart of the Roman forum, where, supposedly, it had been maintained in the same fashion by the rather more distinguished Vestal Virgins. But, now that Christianity had come to predominate, the girls had ceased to provide their service, and the dragon had begun to pump out its toxic breath in anger (cf. Chapter 6, §6.1.3). We find similar themes alive and well at the other end of the hagiographical tradition. When Paris (AD 1533 or before) arrives at the city of Teano in Campania, he finds the citizens worshipping a local dragon. The dragon lives in the cave of a large spring near the city gate and has been infecting the air with its stinking and fire-vomiting breath, causing the people to fall sick; we may imagine that it has also been infecting the spring, or at any rate has been threatening to monopolize it. In fear the people have consequently built a temple to the dragon above the spring and have come to serve it fine meats every day; they compete with each other in presenting the dragon with the tastiest offerings. Paris encounters Tranquillina, the virgin daughter of the distinguished Simpronius, standing before the dragon's cave with her girl attendants. She is there to present the dragon with the choicest morsels as its daily placatory offering. Paris substitutes himself for the girl in order to accost the dragon, in a motif that partly reflects Heracles' taking of the place of Hesione before the *Kētos* of Troy (see Chapter 4, §4.3.2), and

---

[10] Propertius 4.8.2–14; Aelian *Nature of Animals* 11.16. Discussion at Douglas 1913; Pailler 1997; Ogden 2013a:205–6, 2013b:221–7.

Menestratus' taking of the place of Cleostratus before the Dragon of Thespiae (see Chapter 3, §3.4.1).

We return to the Dragon of Rome for an early indication that sacrifices offered by virgins have morphed into sacrifices of virgins, though the tale, recorded in the (v AD) *De promissionibus*, is anomalous in other respects.[11] The champion is no longer Pope Silvester, but an anonymous monk:

In the city of Rome there was a certain cave in which there was a mechanical dragon of amazing size. It brandished a sword in its mouth, and its eyes consisted of red gemstones. Its appearance was fearful and terrible. Every year virgins, decked out with flowers, were dedicated to it, and given to it in sacrifice in that fashion. Unawares, they would carry offerings down to it. But when they reached that step of the staircase where the dragon hung, by the craft of the Devil, the impact of the sword would kill them and shed their innocent blood. The dragon was destroyed in the following fashion by a certain monk who was well known to the imperial courtier Stilicho on account of his good offices. He felt his way carefully down the staircase step by step with his hand and his staff, examining the steps carefully. He perceived that Devil's trap as soon as he touched it and so evaded it in his descent. He hacked the dragon up and dashed it into pieces. He also demonstrated that gods cannot be made by human hand.

Intriguingly, the tale in itself seems to enact the transition from virgin-offering-sacrifice to virgin-sacrificed.

In later texts we find human sacrifices being made to dragons-proper, which will of course devour them, as in the case of the boy Athenogenes (vi AD) comes across in the Land of the Goths:[12]

Towards the end of that journey, he came to a village near a mountain and a profoundly deep lake, and a boy tied up in it.[13] For between the mountain and the lake there lived a very great dragon [*drakōn*] that used to maraud dreadfully against all those that dwelled nearby and to snatch four-footed animals and children. For this reason, the people that lived there, in the grip of a great fear and as directed by the oracle of some demon or other, had at that time chosen a boy by lot, and were keeping him tied up at that time,[14] so that they could appease the beast through the death of the boy. When the blessed Athenogenes saw this, he

---

[11] *De promissionibus* 3.43, at *PL* li, 835.

[12] For the dating of Athenogenes' *Passion*, see Maraval 1990:11–12; Bremmer 2017a:34–7.

[13] 'It': the village or the lake? Both are possible grammatically. Maraval 1990:33 keeps his translation ambivalent. Bremmer 2017a:35 prefers the lake, but this raises a number of questions. Why hasn't the boy drowned? Is he on a jetty, an islet, a boat? I prefer the village, and I take it that Athenogenes in effect interrupts the villagers as they are in the course of preparing the sacrifice: note the subsequent imperfect, ἐδέσμευον, 'they were keeping him tied up'.

[14] The second 'at that time' may be a scribal error for 'in that place'.

was amazed. The boy told him why he had been tied up and that he was about to be devoured by the dragon. Athenogenes made the sign of the cross over the boy and freed him from his bonds. Standing him by his side, he invited him to pray with him and to invoke the name of the lord Jesus Christ. Extending his hands, together with the boy and his entourage, he said: 'God, lord of the ages and of all creation, since you called me to come across this place and find the boy about to be horribly devoured by the dragon, hear the prayer of me, your servant, and even more so that of this boy who cries out to you with pure heart. Come to the aid of your suppliants and demonstrate here too the power of your goodness. Bring the dragon here and render it powerless, breaking it apart, so that all the onlookers and the local inhabitants may learn your ineffable power and glorify your great and miraculous name for ages to come. And I, your servant, with good cheer will continue the journey I will make in your name.' As he prayed the dragon was dragged before them and revealed as a terrible and fearful sight. St Athenogenes, looking up to heaven and sighing, struck the dragon thrice on the head with the butt of the spear-shaft that he was in the habit of carrying in his hand to serve as a staff. And immediately the beast was broken apart and destroyed. After accomplishing this amazing miracle, the blessed man restored the boy to his parents, safe and sound, and instructed all the locals in the praising of Christ the Lord and the acceptance of his godhead. The man currently established as bishop there, upon learning this, and moved also by a vision, raised Athenogenes, beloved of god, to the rank of chief priest, bestowing upon him the honour of the bishopric.

In his *Life of Golinduch* ([b], vi–vii AD) Eustratius considers it a possibility that the Babylonians had been worshipping the dragon to which they attempted to feed Golinduch in its pit; the other possibility he considers is that they maintained it merely to punish Christians with.[15] The Dragon of Albingaunum (Albenga) chased off by Veranus (ix–xi AD) is given annual sacrifices of virgin boys and virgin girls (in addition to animals) by the locals, who claim that the beast confers fertility and safety upon them. The Dragon of Antioch destroyed by the relic thumb of John the Baptist ([a], x AD) similarly receives the annual sacrifice of a virgin girl. The story of its demise, as told by Theodore Daphnopates, is worth quoting for the vividness of its visualization of the rite and its setting:

In the territory of Antioch there lurked in a cave a certain dragon[*draco*], whom, on the advice of the gods, they used to honour with an annual sacrifice. That

---

[15] In the Georgian version of Golinduch's *Life* by Stephen of (Syrian) Hierapolis ([a], vi–vii AD), the model for Eustratius', it is told more simply that the Babylonians worshipped a dragon as they had in the time of Daniel (it is not specified whether it is the same one), and that they had the custom of feeding criminals to it.

sacrifice, however, was a virgin girl, who had just recently come to puberty. She was kept as a sacrifice for the dragon on account of the purity of her virginity. The people of Antioch would flood to the actual site of the dragon's cave and pack the theatre around it. When they had led the girl around, they would offer her to the dragon to be devoured. The dragon would crawl forth out of its cave and—a dreaded and incredible manifest marvel—would creep and crawl on its feet, its body curving because of the nature of its breath within. With gaping mouth and distended breast it would receive the sacrifice, and tear it apart with its teeth. However, it was their custom to use the lot, and one day this fell upon a certain Christian man, requiring that he give his daughter to be sacrificed to the dragon. Understandably stricken in this situation, he prayed from the heart to the greatest Forerunner of Christ. He devised the following sort of plan, so that his daughter could be saved from death. He concealed a great sum of gold on his person and sought permission to adore the holy hand [sc. the relic hand of John the Baptist] from its keeper, who acceded to the request. As he proceeded, he poured out all the gold he had secretly brought, ostensibly to give in worship, onto the ground, and then went right up to the hand to adore it. The sacristan looked at the gold with covetous eyes and ran to gather it up. But the man that had sought the permission to perform the adoration curved his body and bent himself over the reliquary. Spurred on by divine desire, whilst kissing the thumb of the venerable right hand and applying his lips to it, he snapped it off with a bite of his teeth and hid it, then withdrew from the temple as quickly as possible. Now when the day of the sacrifice had come, and all the citizens that lived around had gathered into the theatre, the father stepped forward to lead his girl to sacrifice. When he was near the dragon, and saw it making a huge gape with its mouth, terrifying all that heard with its dreadful hiss, and eager for the sacrifice, he threw that sacred and venerable thumb into middle of its gullet, and by the throwing of it he immediately brought death upon the dragon.

The inhabitants of Lasia offer human sacrifices (in addition to animals) to the local dragon, killed by George ([a], xi AD; [b], xii AD; [c], AD 1263–7), as a means of mitigating its marauding, with the lot eventually falling on the emperor's own daughter (the first two of these passages are quoted in Chapter 9, §9.2). It is not specified in this case that the people offered up should be virgins, although they are the children of the city's families, and much is indirectly made of the focal princess Sabra's virginity, given that her father speaks of her as a bride as he presents her to the dragon. The Dragon of Caltabellotta disposed of by Peregrinus (xvi AD or before) is given a boy to eat every day to prevent it desolating the entire region. Peregrinus rescues its latest victim by substituting himself for the attendant presenting the boy to the dragon (cf. the case of Paris of Teano, above).[16]

---

[16] Another late example: in the case of the marauding Basilisk-Dragon of the river Élorn in Brittany defeated by the warrior saints Neventerius and Derien (AD 1637), the locals had been compelled to

Some of these themes are refracted in the account of the Dragon of King Samuel's city encountered by Theodore Tyron ([h], xiv AD or before, quoted and discussed in Chapter 9, §9.1.5): here again we have regular (animal) sacrifices to the dragon, and the dragon's interest in a beautiful girl, albeit of a rather strange kind.

7.3 Statue, Sacrifice, and Dragon

Another variety of dragon-worship sequence is also popular in the tradition. This is the sequence in which a saint is dragged before a pagan idol and compelled to worship it; the idol is inhabited by a dragon, which is duly forced from cover and must now be dealt with.

Let us begin by returning to Philip's ([a], mid- to late iv AD) adventures in the land of the Ophianoi and their city of Ophiorhyme. Here the people worship the Echidna, 'the viper', and offer her wine, after taking which she may sleep— evidently this is a form of propitiation. It is implied that her sanctuary contains an idol of her, together with the goddess herself. There is no direct confrontation between Philip and the idol—unless, that is, we are to imagine that the goddess, whom Philip plunges into the abyss, is one and the same with her idol, which is not impossible. However, we do then get an explicit encounter between saint and idol in the *Apostolic History*'s later biography of Philip ([b], late vi AD; cf. [c], AD 1263–7). Here the setting is transferred to Scythia. Philip is brought before a statue of Mars and compelled to make sacrifice to it. In the course of this a huge dragon emerges from underneath the idol's base: presumably it is forced out by the mere presence of the apostle (cf. Chapter 6, §§6.5.1–2). It at once kills the son of the priest and the two presiding tribunes, whilst bringing the remainder of the onlookers to death's door with its pestilential breath. Philip tells the people that the cure for their sickness is to smash down the statue and replace it with a cross, before banishing the dragon and reviving the dead. All are converted.

In a similar sequence the Roman emperor drags Erasmus of Antioch (ix AD or before) before the 12-cubit high bronze statue of Jupiter in his temple at Sirmium and commands him to make sacrifice. The saint asks God to send an angel to his aid. As soon as the demon within the statue looks into the martyr's face, it collapses into dust and a huge dragon emerges from it and kills almost a third of the assembled people. Those remaining alive beg Erasmus to deliver them from the serpent, whereupon Erasmus tells them they will be safe if they have faith in the God that he does. He then commands the serpent to harm no more people. Similar too is one of the tales of Fronto of Périgueux ([c], xi AD). Here the saint forces himself into a temple of Venus. As he invokes Christ, the great statue

sacrifice a person (of some sort) to it every Saturday, the family from which the victim was to come being selected by lot.

collapses into dust and an enormous dragon bursts forth from it, killing seven worshippers with its pestilential breath and beating others with its tail. Fronto banishes it to the wilderness. We find a slight variation of this motif in the tale of Julian of le Mans (c. AD 1000): a dragon bursts forth of its own accord from an overturned idol of Jupiter at Artinas to destroy its own worshippers with its breath and whipping tail alike; Julian similarly banishes it to the wilderness.[17]

Like the story-type of the last-victim boy to which we shall turn shortly (§7.4), the story-type of the saint dragged before the dragon-possessed idol was so compelling and influential that it also manifested itself in disaggregated forms. John of Euboea's tale of Parasceve of Sicily (viii AD) appears to constitute a disaggregated version of the story-type associated with Philip ([b]), Erasmus, and Fronto, whilst also exhibiting the influence of Golinduch's story-type. Parasceve approaches the idols (gods unspecified) of her own accord, followed by a crowd of pagans, who think she is going to make sacrifice to them. But instead she stands before them and declares, 'My lord Jesus Christ commands that these idols shall fall to the ground'. Immediately they collapse into dust and the crowd cries out, 'Great is the God of the Christians'. But those that are 'unclean of idols' now demand of their leader that he 'kill this mage'. She is given as food to a 'dragon and venomous beasts and reptiles' in a deep well, where she bursts them open by the power of prayer.[18] Fronto ([c], xi AD) himself also features in a second tale that looks like a disaggregated version of his first: he first destroys the temple, idols and all, of an unnamed pagan deity, perhaps a goddess again, beside the river Dronne with a thunderbolt, building a church in its place; but he then crosses the river (walking over it) to banish a marauding serpent, a *coluber*, that is making mischief on the other side of the river.[19]

So far we have seen saints shattering statues of Mars, Jupiter, and Venus. But what about the god that was most strongly associated with dragons and serpents in the classical world, Asclepius? He does indeed feature in tales of this story-type too, but the serpents of the two tales of interest seem to be those that would have formed part of his ancient pagan statue. Thus, Artemon ([a], x AD; [b], xii AD) is dragged into a temple of Asclepius in Caesarea and compelled to worship its idol. Instead, he turns it into dust, à la Erasmus: 'Entering the temple of Asclepius he turned the idol itself to dust and he turned the dragons to dust too, even though they were huge, a terrible sight to behold. For they say that they were 20 cubits in

---

[17] Similarly again, a dragon emerges from the statue before which Modestinus (AD 1613) is compelled to worship in Campania; it kills many, but disappears at the saint's command.

[18] For some observations on the text of John of Euboea's *Encomium of St Parasceve*, see Vinogradov 2013.

[19] Perhaps the pressure of the story-type lurks behind the following note on Crescentinus (xiv AD) too: 'he realized that the city [of Tifernum—Città di Castello] was deceived by the tricks of that ancient serpent, the Devil, and for that reason was worshipping empty and silent idols. This was the cause of the pestilence produced by their dragon (God himself permitting it).'

breath and 80 in length.'[20] The dimensions of the serpents are odd, but context and phraseology seem to imply that they are stone idols like the statue of Asclepius itself, rather than living dragons produced from the collapse of the statue. This is clearer in the case of Callinicus (xi AD or before) at Apollonia:

> Understanding this, Baudus commanded his servants to tonsure their hair and lose their beards. When they had done this, Callinicus tied his head- and beard-hair together and threw it at an idol of Asclepius, with the words, 'Most wicked of demons....' Two hours after he had said this the statue moved. After this, it fell down with an enormous crash, and was broken into three parts. In one place lay Asclepius' hands, with his dragon and his rod, in another his lower body and feet, and in a third his head and torso.[21]

The two-hour delay is a nice touch. One has to wonder whether this Asclepius sub-type was actually the origin-point of the broader story-type, with the attacking live dragon evolving out of the stone dragon destroyed as part of his statue.

For the early Christians Asclepius was certainly the god to beat: no pagan god was more popular across the later classical world.[22] In the early fourth century AD Lactantius was referring to him, in the context of his transference to Rome in the form of a giant serpent, as the 'arch-demon' (deploying the Greek word *daimoniarchēs*), whilst later in the same century the *Acts of Cyprian and Justina* could imagine him actually to be the father of the other pagan gods (perhaps via an identification with Zeus).[23] He was, furthermore, uncomfortably similar to Jesus in a number of ways, his devotion to healing aside: unlike most pagan deities, he was uniquely beneficent, an avuncular, caring presence;[24] and he had died and risen from the dead, twice in fact.[25] One can well understand why in AD 331 Constantine ordered the temple of Asclepius at Cilician Aegae to be destroyed because the demon that appeared by night to those sleeping in it was drawing people away from their true Saviour and into deceit.[26] Here it is relevant that although we have surprisingly few examples of pagan sanctuaries being converted directly into Christian basilicas before the seventh century AD, some historians and archaeologists have contended that Asclepieia were in particular singled out

---

[20] καὶ εἰσελθὼν ἐν τῷ ναῷ τοῦ Ἀσκληπιοῦ αὐτό τε τὸ ξόανον συνέτριψεν καὶ τοὺς δράκοντας συνέτριψεν ὑπερμεγέθεις ὄντας, φρικτὸν θέαμα τοῖς ὁρῶσιν. Φασὶν γὰρ αὐτοὺς πήχεις εἴκοσι τὸ πλάτος ἔχειν, ἐκτείνεσθαι δὲ ἐπ' ὀγδοήκοντα.

[21] Cf. the Margaret of Antioch tradition ([a], AD 815–20, etc.) in which Margaret destroys Beelzebub, kinsman of the dragon-demon Rouphos she has just encountered, with his own beard.

[22] Riethmüller 2005 catalogues over 900 still-detectable temples and shrines for the god.

[23] *Acts of Cyprian and Justina*, Martyrdom 5.3, with the note of Bailey 2017 ad loc.

[24] See e.g. *EMI* generally, and the literary sources collected at Ogden 2013a:316–17.

[25] See Justin Martyr *Apology* 21.1–2 and the sources collected at Ogden 2013a:342–3, 418–20.

[26] Eusebius of Caesarea *Life of Constantine* 3.56; Sozomen *Ecclesiastical History* 2.5; Zonaras *Epitome historiarum* 12c–d.

for such conversion in the late antique period.[27] The case is not uncontentious, but there is at least one emphatically clear example of such a conversion, that of the great Asclepieion of Athens, no less. We know that the site was still a pagan sanctuary in AD 450 and perhaps even as late as AD 485, but by AD 500 its walls had been levelled, its votive stelae had been defaced, and a church had been built over the site not only of the temple itself, but also over its sacred spring and over the all-important stoa where the god's patients had incubated. An inscription tells us that the church was dedicated to none other than St Andrew, the patron saint of healing.[28]

There are perhaps intimations of the pagan worship of Asclepius in other saintly dragon-slaying stories. When Philip ([a], mid- to late iv AD) and his team arrive at Ophiorhyme (Phrygian Hierapolis), the city of the Echidna, the viper goddess, they are confronted by a first rank of guards that carry venomous serpents on their shoulders, in a configuration that perhaps recalls one of the traditional iconographic poses of the goddess Hygieia (Salus), daughter of Asclepius, with her serpent avatar (cf. Chapter 1, §1.3.1).[29] The team subsequently establish themselves in a disued clinic and begin offering healing services there.[30] They attract the custom of one Stachys, who had contrived to blind himself forty years before by applying a liquid from snake-eggs to his eyes, in an attempt to test its curative power, but instead leaving them chronically inflamed (*en phlegmonēi*— the fire motif again). The message would seem to be that Asclepius, he of the snakes, is not the great healer the pagans imagine him to be, but the very opposite of that (cf. Chapter 6, §6.6.2).

Later hagiography continues to arrange battles between dragons and healing saints, though such sequences can no longer be animated by the urgency of the campaign against Asclepius. After Domitianus of Maastricht's ([a] and [b], both xii AD) battle against the Dragon of Huy, he replaces the spring the dragon has poisoned indefinitely with a fresh one, striking his staff into the ground, and this fresh one offers healing properties. The ejection of serpents that have invaded the body becomes a speciality. Monegundis (late vi AD) expels a nest of snakes writhing in a young boy's poisoned stomach by sticking a vine leaf inscribed with the sign of the cross to his belly with her saliva. In one of the miracles from beyond

---

[27] In support of the notion: Delehaye 1909:143–5; Travlos 1939–41. Against it: Frantz, 1965:194–5; Speiser 1976:310, 312; and (on balance) Gregory 1986:237–9 (with 233 for the relative lack of sanctuary conversions prior to the vii AD).

[28] The shrine's last pagan use is documented by Marinus *Vita Procli* 29 Boissonade (for this text and its context, see now Männlein-Robert 2019). The archaeology: Travlos 1939–41:51–7; Gregory 1986:287. The inscription: Bayet 1878:71 no. 13; Creaghan and Raubitschek 1947:29 no. xi.

[29] *LIMC* Hygieia, Salus passim.

[30] For the recent—brilliant—discovery of the iv–v AD church dedicated to Philip at Hierapolis (adjacently to his well-known octagonal martyr-shrine there), which incorporates his original i AD tomb and retains the detritus of healing practices, see D'Andria 2011–12 and 2016–17 (both with superb illustrations and reconstructions); cf. also de Stefano 2013.

the grave ascribed to the healing saints Cosmas and Damian (AD 1263–7), they come to the rescue of a peasant. He has fallen asleep whilst harvesting and a serpent has slipped into his open mouth and taken up residence in his belly, giving him severe cramps. He runs to their church whereupon he falls asleep again, and the serpent emerges from his belly by the same route. Similarly, Petroc ([a], xiii–xiv AD) cures a woman who has taken in a tiny serpent whilst drinking water. He gives her a medicine composed of earth and water to drink, whereupon she vomits forth a rather larger serpent, three feet in length, but dead.[31]

Noteworthy here too is one the more curious subcategories of saintly dragon tales. In this story-type a dragon, the erstwhile creature of Asclepius, actually makes appeal to a saint for healing for itself. Such a dragon takes up residence to the north of Simeon Stylites' 40-cubit column in the life of the saint attributed to Antonius ([b], c. AD 830). But the dragon does no more harm than stopping the grass from growing in that area (either, presumably, because of its noxious breath or because of its general fieriness). One day the dragon crawls up to the door of the monastery adjacent to the saint's column and lays its right eye on the threshold, lying there for three days without doing any harm to those entering the building. It transpires that the dragon is blinded in its left eye by a piece of wood. Simeon commands that earth and water be poured over the creature, and immediately a piece of wood a cubit long springs forth from the blinded eye. The dragon continues to lie there harmlessly for some time, coiled up. Eventually it bestirs itself and prays for two hours before the monastery door, before returning to its lair. A similar tale is told of Petroc ([a], xiii–xiv AD): a great dragon presents itself outside his cell with a piece of wood stuck in its right eye. Petroc washes it out with a medicine made from water and earth from his beaten floor, and the serpent returns to its nest. One immediately thinks of a pagan precedent here, the tale of Androcles and the lion; but it is the Bible again that more immediately lends this story its shape, with the parable of the 'beam in the eye'.[32]

7.4 The Revival of the Last-Victim Boy

A striking motif that enjoyed particular success throughout the hagiographical tradition is that of the saint's restoration to life, either from the point of death or from death itself, of the dragon's last victim, almost always a boy or young man, in coordination with his defeat of the serpent. The motif of course represents a

---

[31] Note again here the marvellous (vi–vii AD) tale of the healing of Callimachus in the church of Sts Cyrus and John at Menuthis, after the boy had swallowed a *drakaina*'s egg: Sophronius *Narratio miraculorum sanctorum Cyri et Joannis* 34.10 (cf. Chapter 3, §3.3).

[32] Androcles (Androclus) and the Lion: Aulus Gellius 5.14. The beam in the eye: Matthew 7:5.

celebration of the resurrection of Jesus and indeed of the resurrection that ultimately awaits all.[33]

Let us begin with a pair of early, Thomasine texts. First, in the *Acts of Thomas*, in the course of his mission to India, the apostle Thomas (later ii AD) and his followers discover an attractive young man lying dead. The apostle knows at once that this is the work of the Devil in *drakōn* form. No sooner has he come to this conclusion than the dragon emerges from his adjacent hole and, surprisingly, speaks to him. Even more surprisingly, he professes that he has killed the boy because he had witnessed him having sex with a local woman with which he, the dragon, had fallen in love, and that too on the sabbath day. Nonetheless, the saint compels the dragon to restore the boy to life by sucking his venom back out of him. The boy's body loses its lividity and recovers its former whiteness.[34] Restored to life, he immediately leaps to his feet and throws himself down before the apostle. Meanwhile the dragon's body is inflated and burst open by the venom he has taken back. Here the revival of the boy and the destruction of the dragon are fully, indeed almost hydraulically, integrated.[35] Second, in one of the scenes of the *Infancy Gospel of Thomas*, which also seems to have roots in the second century AD, the boys Jesus ([a]) and Jacob are gathering firewood when a viper (*echidna*) bites the latter's hand. He is at the point of death when Jesus restores him to life by blowing upon the wound, whereupon the creature itself is ipso facto destroyed (cf. Chapter 6, §6.6.2, Chapter 8, §8.2, where the text is quoted).[36]

Many further examples can be given. Ammon's (*c.* AD 395 and *c.* AD 403/4) destruction of the Dragon of the Egyptian Desert is initiated when petitioning locals bring him the dragon's last victim as part of their plea. The boy, the son of a shepherd, is not quite dead yet: rather, the sight of the dragon has turned him mad, whilst its breath has rendered his body so swollen that he has to be carried (cf. Chapter 6, §§6.1.5 and 6.6.2 on swelling). Ammon cures him by anointing him with oil. Andrew ([a] and [b], both late vi AD) first destroys the Dragon of Thessalonica with a simple suicide-command, before then happening across the body of the boy who had been its last victim. He invites a woman amongst his associates to raise him from the dead. The Dragon of Heliopolis destroyed by

---

[33] For Christ's resurrection, see Matthew 28; Mark 16; Luke 24; John 20–1; Acts 1. For the common resurrection, see Matthew 11:23–33; Mark 12:18–27; Luke 14:14, 20:27–40; John 5:25–9, 6:39–59, 11:24–5; Acts 4:2, 17:32, 26:3–8, 24:15, 24:21; Romans 8:11; 1 Corinthians 4:14, 5:1–2, 6:14, 15:12–13; Philippians 3:12; 1 Thessalonians 4:13–16; 2 Timothy 2:11, 2:18; Hebrews 6:2.

[34] ἐλευκαίνετο: in contrast to the lividity's blackness; cf. the tale of Eudocia (x AD), as quoted at p. 267.

[35] For commentary on this episode, see Klijn 2003:90–8 (on §§30–3). We are to take the dragon's disapproval of fornication on the sabbath with a pinch of salt, of course, but it is noteworthy that in Ezra's visionary tour of hell in the *Vision of Ezra*, a mid-vi AD Latin translation of a probably late ii AD Alexandrian Greek original, he finds those that had sex on the sabbath being attacked by dragons and dogs and burned by fire (§9). For the Ezra text, see Bogaert 1984; for datings and discussion, Bremmer 2018 esp. 179–80.

[36] *Gospel of Thomas* 16.1–2 (A), p. 147 Tischendorf. Another, more indirect, early testimony to the motif may be found in the tale of Fortunatus in the *Acts of John* ([a]), discussed below.

Eudocia (x AD or before) kills a boy, the only son of a widow, with its breath as he sleeps in a garden at midday. Eudocia leads the neophyte Diodorus to the scene, where they find the dead boy 'bound' by the venom. Under her guidance, Diodorus prays, 'and at once the dead boy rose again, putting off the blackness of the dragon'. She proceeds to pray that the dragon should kill itself (cf. Chapter 8, §8.3.4, where the passage is quoted more fully). Two tales of Fronto of Périgueux ([c], xi AD) are of interest here, one of which we shall consider below. As to the other, when he is accompanying Clement of Metz on the road to Metz, they find a boy either killed or at any rate severely wounded (*valde laesum*) by a dragon; Fronto bursts the dragon open with a prayer, and the boy is ipso facto restored to health. This direct coordination of the killing of the dragon and the revivification of the last victim recalls the Thomasine tales. Finally, Germanus of Auxerre ([a], xi–xii AD) restores to life the last-victim boy killed by the Dragon of Trou Baligan on the Cotentin Peninsula.

This story-type too was incredibly powerful, with the result that its influence can be detected even in narratives where it is not itself formally told. Thus, when Philip ([b], vi AD; [c], AD 1263–7) is brought before the statue of Mars in Scythia and compelled to sacrifice to it, the dragon that emerges from beneath it kills three people, the first mentioned being the son of the temple's priest. After banishing the dragon, Philip, we are told, resuscitates all, but the particular emphasis the narrative at this point places upon the son of the priest, evidently a boy, clearly expresses the influence of the story-type. Notably, we often find dragon-fight episodes collocated with ostensibly unrelated boy-revivification episodes. So it is that Samson ([a], vii–viii AD; cf. [b], ix AD) is accompanied on his quest against the Dragon of Trigg by a boy he has just revived after he had broken his neck falling from a horse two hours before. Immediately after Maurus (viii AD?) has killed the Dragon of the river Narco, he is approached, on the basis of that achievement, by a widow whose (only?) son has died in circumstances unexplained to us. Maurus delegates the boy's revivification to his associate Felix. As Petroc ([a], xii AD or before) is dragging the duly subdued Dragon of Cornwall to the sea, so as to be able to dispatch it to the wildernesses beyond, he encounters a funeral cortege for the king's son consisting of three hundred men. They all collapse in terror at the sight of the beast, but Petroc prays and restores all to strength, whilst bringing the boy himself back to life.

In a pair of disaggregated narratives of this type, one featuring Martha and a second one featuring Fronto, the revived boy is specifically said to have died by drowning. It is initially curious that, when Martha ([a], AD 1187; [c], AD 1263–7; [d], AD 1264) accosts the Tarasque she has been summoned to kill, she finds it in the course of devouring a man it has just jugulated and yet makes no attempt to restore him to life. But then, a few sentences later, we are treated to the story of her revivification of a youth (*iuvenis*) who had drowned and been dead for two days (he had been attempting to swim across the Rhône to hear the saint preach).

Fronto of Périgueux ([c], xi AD) walks over the river Dronne (his feet remaining dry)[37] in order to banish the marauding *coluber*-dragon that has been ravaging beyond it and then immediately restores to life a boy that has been dead for three days after drowning in the river Garonne. This narrative is of especial interest for the fact that the dragon-fight episode actually lies at the heart of a doubly disaggregated complex. For, as we saw above, it is immediately preceded by an episode in which the saint pulverizes a pagan temple and its idols by calling down thunderbolts upon them, so that we would appear to have also a disaggregated version of the story-type in accordance with which a saint fights a dragon that emerges from a statue he has pulverized.[38]

Given the banal ability of saints to revive a dragon's recent victims, and the desirability that they should be seen to do it, dynamic tales in which saints rush to the rescue of a victim in the course of a dragon-attack are few and far between (episodes in which the saint intervenes in a human sacrifice aside). One notable exception here is offered by the nice, simple tale of Girardus of Anjou (*c.* AD 1153). A peasant attacked unexpectedly by a *draco* as he walks in the forest at Brossay cries out. Girardus hears the cry from his chapel and runs to the scene, where he is able to repel the serpent with the sign of the cross.

The peculiar importance of the story-type considered here, in which the revival of the last-victim boy is coordinated with the victory over the dragon, in both its aggregated and disaggregated forms, will become apparent when we come to consider the archaeology of the saintly dragon-fight narratives more generally in the next chapter.

7.5 Dragons Sent Back against their Magician Masters

Another distinctive subroutine of the saintly dragon-tale is a story-type in accordance with which magicians, usually acting at the behest of a wicked tyrant, send dragons against the saint, only to have the saint turn them back against them.[39] A partial precedent for the story-type obtains in Exodus, where the wicked

---

[37] Cf. Matthew 14:25, etc.

[38] Two further tales may be cited as exhibiting, in different ways, the impress of the story-type. First, in the very early *Acts of John* ([a], *c.* AD 150–80), a serpent bites and kills the wretched steward Fortunatus instantaneously as he abets Callimachus in having sex with the corpse of the Christian woman Drusiana. Drusiana, restored to life by John, in turn revives Fortunatus. However, the steward continues to refuse conversion despite his exemplary experience, whereupon the lividity caused by the serpent's venom returns to his body, and he dies again, for good this time. Second, Peregrinus (xvi AD or before) rescues the latest boy given in sacrifice to the Dragon of Caltabellotta in Sicily by its attendants just before he is eaten. Cf. further on Christina below (§7.5).

[39] For the general profile of magicians in middle Byzantine hagiography, see de Abrahamse 1982; she does not, however, discuss the topos considered here.

Pharaoh has his sorcerers turn their staffs into serpents before Moses and Aaron (see Chapter 5, §5.2.4, where the text is quoted).[40]

In Callinicus' *Life* of Hypatius (*c.* AD 450) a sorcerer (so he appears to be, though he is not explicitly so described) of servile appearance and matted hair sends four demons against Hypatius in the form of camels with the necks and heads of dragons. But an angel of God appears and lifts him up beyond their reach. He then shows Hypatius a vision of the sorcerer sitting on his bed and tells him that he is the sender, whereupon Hypatius instructs the demons to attack the one that sent them instead, and the sorcerer begins to gnaw at his own tongue and fingers. In the course of the extended martyrdom of Christina of Tyre ([a], ix AD, after a lost vi AD original; cf. [b], AD 1263–7), the eparch Julian has a sorcerer described both as an 'enchanter of serpents' (*incantator serpentium*) and as a 'serpent-wrangler' (*serpentarius*) send six snakes against her. A pair of 'serpents' (tout court) lick her feet, a pair of asps hang from her breasts like babies, and a pair of vipers coil round her neck and lick away her sweat. She prays to God and sends them back upon the enchanter, killing him. But, after this, with God's help and an appeal to the precedent of Lazarus, she restores him to life again—and here too we feel the impress of the last-victim boy motif.[41] The *Apostolic History* tells how during his mission to Ethiopia the apostle Matthew ([a], late vi AD; cf. [b], AD 1263–7; [c], xv AD) encounters the mages (*magi*) Zaroes and Arphaxat. They accost him with a *draco* each. The creatures are crested, blow fire from their mouths and lethal sulphurous gases from their noses. But they at once fall asleep tamely at the apostle's feet. Matthew tells the sorcerers that, had he not just prayed, he would have turned the snakes back upon them. As it is, he merely sends them off, permanently tamed and never to be seen again. The claim is evidently a knowing one on the author's part, for we can see that that was precisely the traditional denouement of this story-type. In a similar narrative, Paulus and Juliana of Nicomedia (xiv AD) are imprisoned by Aurelian. In the course of the many torments to which he subjects them, he summons all his enchanters of reptiles (*epaoidoi tōn herpetōn*). These bring along all the vipers, asps, horned-snakes, and *drakontes* they possess and shut them in with the martyrs. The creatures merely gather at their feet and stare raptly into their faces as they psalm and hymn, without harming them in any way (cf. Chapter 6, §6.4.3, for the fawning motif). After three days of this Aurelian's messengers peep into the cell to see whether they have been destroyed yet, and find an angel standing before the serpents, forbidding them to approach Paulus and Juliana and stopping up their mouths. Aurelian then orders the enchanters to gather up their serpents and bring the martyrs before his tribunal. They approach the cell door and from without attempt to engage their creatures with their magical language, but they pay them no heed.

---

[40] Exodus 7:8–13.   [41] For Christina, see Paschini 1925.

When they then open the door, the creatures charge out en masse and kill all the faithless in the offing, before fleeing off to the wilderness.

A refraction of the motif of the magician pair is found also in Jacobus de Voragine's account of Silvester and the Dragon of Rome ([e], AD 1263–7). Silvester has made his way down the steep steps into the cavern with two assistant priests and has successfully bound up the dragon's maw to prevent it from spewing forth its noxious breath. But as they remount the steps back to the surface they come across the near-dead bodies of a pair of magicians who have followed them down to see whether they were going to go all the way down to the dragon itself. They have been overcome by the dragon's fumes (which the priests have of course been protected against by their faith). The priests carry them out. They are revived and, together with a limitless crowd, undergo conversion.

7.6 Female Dragon-Fighting Saints

Whilst one might be tempted to think of dragon-fighting as a characteristically male activity, both the hagiographical world and indeed the classical world before it were familiar with female dragon-fighters. In the classical world we think first of Medea and the Hesperides: these virgin women are fundamentally dragon-tenders or -wranglers, but both ultimately deploy drugs against their respective charges, whether to send them, unsleeping as they are, to sleep, or to kill them, on behalf of the men with whom they have become infatuated (see Chapter 1, §§1.2.3–4). For a more active martial engagement on the part of a mortal woman (albeit again alongside a male hero), let us take note of the oldest surviving image of Heracles' fight against the *Kētos* of Troy, a Corinthian black-figure column-crater of *c*.560 BC: as Heracles shoots arrows at the creature, Hesione stands actually in advance of him and pelts it with rocks.[42] In the divine sphere we may also look to Athena, who directly battles against serpents as a warrior in the context of the Gigantomachy at least.[43]

Initially, female saints fight their dragons in the context of visions—their own or others'—only. So it is that the distinguished early female saint Perpetua (AD 203), in her famous vision of the ladder to heaven, treads on the head of the dragon that lurks beneath the lowest rung by way of making the first step of her ascent (the text is quoted in Chapter 5, §5.2.3). In doing this she is of course following precisely the biblical exhortations to trample on serpents. As we have also seen (Chapter 5, §5.2.3, again), in the fourth century Prudentius was to have a vision of the heavenly Agnes similarly trampling a dragon that was an embodiment

---

[42] *LIMC* Hesione 3.   [43] See the copious evidence collected at Ogden 2013a:195–8.

of all things earthly.[44] In the *Acts of Xanthippe and Polyxena* Polyxena (mid-iii AD) experiences a dream in which a hideous dragon appears before her and summons her to itself. She refuses to approach, but it charges and swallows her feet-first. Then a beautiful youth, 'the brother of Paul' (presumably, in context, Jesus) addresses her from the light of the sun, tells the dragon has no power, takes her hand in his own, which has the odour of sweet balsam (the antithesis of the fetid smell of the dragon), and draws her out of the creature, whereupon it disappears. When she awakens from her dream she tells her older sister Xanthippe of it, who presses her to accept baptism, and to ask to be delivered from the snare of the dragon in the course of the rite.[45]

In a Syriac tale a woman falls into the toils of a seemingly more tangible dragon, to be delivered from it, at arm's length, by no less than Mary. In the initial version ([a], iv AD) a noblewoman contrives to tempt Satan by swimming naked in a river whilst she is supposed to be washing clothes in it. He leaps out in the form of a serpent and coils himself around her body. The woman then runs to Mary and asks to kiss baby Jesus, whereupon the Devil is repelled by the sweet odour of his body (again, the antithesis of the dragon's foul stench), abandons his grip on her and departs never to be seen again. A more elaborate version of the tale was told in another Syriac text of the sixth or seventh century AD; it is now lost, but reflected in the *Arabic Infancy Gospel* (Mary [b]).[46] Here a girl is possessed by Satan, who manifests himself to her in the form of a dragon that threatens to devour her whilst in the meantime sucking out her blood and leaving her corpse-like. A healed leper-woman advises the girl's mother to approach Mary on her daughter's behalf. Mary gives her some of the water in which she has bathed Jesus, to pour over her daughter, and one of the cloths in which she has swaddled him for her daughter to show to the dragon. When the dragon next manifests itself the girl drapes the cloth over her head and eyes, whereupon flames and embers leap forth from it and attack the dragon's own head and eyes. The dragon disappears for good, remonstrating against Jesus' interference.

Women saints would never combat dragons in a martial mode, of course, although they are pressed to do so in a metaphorical way as early as Methodius' c. AD 300 *Banquet of the Ten Virgins*. Here Methodius urges virgins to don the

---

[44] Prudentius *Peristephanon* 14.111–17.

[45] Dragon-visions were also experienced at the other end of the hagiographical tradition by Francisca of Rome (before AD 1440), these being recorded contemporaneously by her confessor Giovanni Mattiotti. Her visions include one of a black, fire-vomiting dragon hurtling through the air towards Latium, and a most elaborate one of a great, fiery, stench-emitting, ever-open-mouthed dragon chained down in hell and bound to Satan himself (cf. the work of the archangel Michael). Attendant demons feed the newly arrived sinners' souls to this latter dragon, but, after spending some time in its belly, they return from it and are passed on to judgement before Satan and thence to further tortures, as appropriate. Only the souls of the excommunicated fail to return from the dragon's belly, but rather pass down its tail to arrive at a place of pitch, sulphur, boiling oil, and molten iron.

[46] On this text, see Elliot 1993:100–7, which does not, however, reproduce the passage of interest here.

helmet, breastplate, and greaves of salvation in order to fight the Dragon of Revelation, broadly along the lines of the (weaponless) female figure thought to embody the Church in that book.[47] But when we come to the turn of the sixth century AD, at least, we start to find female saints taking on seemingly tangible dragons in the standard fashion of the male saints, and dealing with them, inevitably, by hands-off prayers or exorcistic means.

So it is that Victoria ([a], c. AD 500; [b] and [c], AD 675–710) banishes the Dragon of Trebula to the wilderness in exorcistic fashion. Christina of Tyre ([a], ix AD, after lost vi AD original; [b], AD 1263–7) simply dismisses the six snakes that have been sent against her (and which have fawned upon her) verbally, telling them to harm no one in the future. Golinduch ([b], vi–vii AD), the 'lamb of God', renders the Dragon of Babylon as tame as a lamb in turn by stretching her arms out to express the form of the cross with her body. Parasceve (viii AD) bursts open 'the dragon and venomous beasts and reptiles' to which she is thrown merely by the power of prayer. Margaret of Antioch ([a], AD 815–20 or before; [b], early ix or before; [d], x AD; [e], AD 1263–7) bursts open the dragon in her martyr cell, the form in which the demon Rouphos is manifest before her, simply by making the sign of the cross (or brandishing a crucifix) as it swallows her. The influence of the Polyxena narrative, or something akin to it, is palpable. It is by prayer alone that Eudocia (x AD) bursts open the dragon of Heliopolis (Baalbek) and that Keyne (xiv AD or before) turns to stone the plague of serpents that besets her place of hermitage at the future Keynsham.[48]

In due course female saints develop a slightly greater degree of physicality in their engagement with their dragons. Elisabeth of Heraclea ([a], ix–x AD; [b], x AD) destroys the Dragon of Constantinople by praying and making the sign of the cross, but also by spitting on its head. Martha ([a], AD 1187; [b], late xii AD; [c], AD 1263–7; [d], AD 1264) renders the Tarasque-dragon tame by throwing holy water over it, showing it a wooden cross, and then tying it with her girdle. After having initially harassed Humiliana of Cerchi (mid-xiii AD) in her hermit cell in the form of an incorporeal serpent (for which see Chapter 6, §6.1.3), the Devil appears to her again a few days later, now in the form of an all-too corporeal serpent, and remains with her for three days, winding itself around her feet and pressing its head against her cheek. Terrified that, as she sleeps, the serpent may 'secretly enter her naked body from the direction of her feet and penetrate her to a certain degree' (ne subintraret a pedibus serpens et attingeret aliquatenus corpus nudum), she binds her legs together with her clothing and her belt.

---

[47] Methodius Banquet of the Ten Virgins 8.12 (in an inset poem the Dragon of Revelation is compared to the Chimaera).
[48] It is perhaps better not to classify Juliana of Nicomedia here, as she is only shown acting against the snakes with which she is imprisoned in conjunction with Paulus (xiv AD). The pair render the creatures tame and harmless by psalming.

Ultimately, she commands the serpent to coil itself up, carries it to her window, and sends it off from there.

7.7 Back by Popular Demand: Serial Dragon-Fighters and Repeat-Offender Dragons

A few saints are presented as dragon specialists, insofar as they take on multiple dragons. When saints do this within the same texts, it is noteworthy that they are shown to deal with the dragons in different ways, with some typically being killed and others being subject to exorcistic banishment. *Variatio* may be the main motivation here, but even so this variation seemingly entails contrasting conceptions of what a dragon actually is: mortal creature vs. immortal demon. Otherwise, the same saint can encounter ostensibly different dragons in discrete texts. In the latter case it can be a philosophical question as to whether he is indeed encountering distinct dragons or repackaged versions of the same one.

The phenomenon appears early with the apostle Philip ([a], mid- to late iv AD), who is given an extended and multifaceted adventure in the land of the Snake-people, the Ophianoi, where he must confront, inter multa alia: the Dragon of the Desert with its serpent brood, which he destroys by calling down lightning on them; the Dragon of the Rocks with its fifty serpent colleagues, which he subjects to exorcistic banishment; the first line of defence of the Ophianoi's city of Ophiorhyme (Phrygian Hierapolis), the seven shoulder-riding snakes, whom he compels to tameness; the city's second line of defence, the pair of dragons that flank its gateway, which he compels to die by means of the light of the monad in his eyes; and, last but not least, the Echidna (Viper), the mother of snakes that presides over the Ophianoi and their city, which he plunges into the underworld abyss. Then in later texts Philip ([b], late vi AD; [c], AD 1263–7) encounters a dragon in a far different place, Scythia, the dragon emerging from the statue of Mars before which he is compelled to make sacrifice.

In his first *Life* Samson of Dol ([a], vii–viii AD) progresses from the killing of the Dragon of Trigg in Cornwall to the exorcistic banishment of the Dragon of Brittany and on again to the killing of a third dragon in the region of his Pental Monastery at St-Samson-sur-Risle. As to the second of these, King Childebert of Brittany petitions him to deal with the latter on the basis of his fame for having dealt with the former one. In a slightly later *Life* ([b], ix AD) these three dragons have now expanded to four. Here the narrator writes with a proper sense of narrative build in introducing the third dragon as 'fiercer than the previous ones'.

Peter the Monk's Joannicius of Bithynia ([a], AD 846; [b], before AD 860) similarly boasts four encounters: first, he kills the marauding Dragon of Prusa; second, he banishes the Dragon of the Islet of Thasion to the shore of Lake

Apolloniatis opposite; third, he kills the Dragon of the river Gorgytes, together with its companion *echidna* and, finally, he takes shelter for the night in a cave that turns out to be occupied by a fourth dragon, but leaves it unharmed on his departure.

Fronto of Périgueux ([c], xi AD) enjoys no fewer than five encounters with dragons in a single *Life*.[49] First, in defiance of local resistance, he destroys the statue of Venus at Périgueux. A dragon bursts forth from it, killing seven with its breath and beating other worshippers with its tail. Fronto sends it to the desert with the sign of cross, and the people are converted. Second, at Neuilly-Saint-Front on the river Dronne in Soissons, he kills a dragon that raises its head against him and builds a church there.[50] Third, whilst he is accompanying Clement of Metz to that city, the pair of them find a boy killed by a dragon on the road; they revive him and burst the dragon in two.[51] Fourth, he expels a dragon and its multitude of snakes from a site near Limoges and builds a church in the spot. Fifthly, and finally, he commands a massive marauding *coluber*-dragon to plunge itself into the sea, which it duly does, by means of a river.

The archangel Michael, veteran of the Revelation Dragon, is given three extraordinarily similar dragon-slayings in three different locations across three different texts. He is said to have killed the Dragon of Southern Asia ([a], ix–x AD) and the Dragon of Mons Tumba, the future St Michael's Mount ([c], c. AD 1000) in identical ways: he kills each of them with his fiery sword, hacking it into twelve portions; the locals must then drag away each portion using twelve teams of oxen and dump it in the sea to avoid the ensuing stench. Between these accounts Michael ([b], xi AD) is also said to have killed the Dragon of Mt Garganus in Campania in a fashion only slightly different, hacking it up into nine parts this time, each one of which is said to have weighed ten oxen as it was taken off to be burned. What are we to conclude? The same story, the same dragon re-appropriated to the glory of each new location? Or is it rather that Michael has a much more determinate modus operandi than the other serial dragon-fighters?[52]

---

[49] For discussion of the tradition of Fronto's *Lives* and of their dating, see Coens 1930, 1957; Herrick 2010; Otero Pereira 2014.

[50] This is the sole dragon he had been permitted to encounter in his earlier *Lives* ([a], viii AD; [b], later x AD).

[51] The association between Fronto and Clement of Metz, the great dragon-slayer in his own right, here raises a further point of interest, namely that dragon-slayers can share prosopographical links. Another example is provided by Maglorius (ix–x AD), battler against the Dragon of Jersey and cousin to the great Samson.

[52] Two examples of saints that have distinctively different encounters with serpents in different texts. In an earlier text Simeon Stylites ([a], shortly before AD 459) blows upon a hostile dragon to make it disappear, before enduring a manifestation of the Devil in the form of a dragon coiling around his feet and biting one of them. In a later text ([b], c. AD 830) he finds himself healing a friendly and petitioning dragon, which has a beam lodged in its eye. In an earlier text Germanus of Auxerre ([a], xi–xii AD) seals the seven-headed Dragon of Trou Baligan on the Cotentin Peninsula into a cistern. In a later one he dismisses the nest of 10-foot snakes, embodiments of Mamertinus' sin or unbelief, from the tomb of St Concordian ([b], AD 1263–7).

Let us move on now to a more interesting prospect: that of the returning dragon that must be fought repeatedly by different saints, or otherwise the successor dragon that resumes the role and the location of the former one. The *ne plus ultra* example here is the Dragon of Rome, which has a truly rich and multifaceted history. As we have seen, it has its origins in an actual pagan serpent cult based at Lanuvium, the serpent there being tended by local virgin girls (§7.2). Silvester ([a], late iv AD; [b], *c.* AD 500; [c] and [d], AD 675–710; [e], AD 1263–7), who was Pope AD 314–35, heroically locks in the dragon, now tended by the Vestal Virgins, at the bottom of its steep cavern in Rome's Tarpeian rock, to prevent it killing the people of the city with its deadly breath, and completes their conversion to boot. Despite this achievement, we learn from the (v AD) *De promissionibus* that the dragon is causing trouble again in the age of Stilicho (i.e. *c.* AD 400), although it has now morphed into a mechanical device, kept at the bottom of a steep cavern in Rome (surely the same one), which effects the sacrifice of its virgin attendants by impaling them on its sword-like tongue; an anonymous monk is now called upon to smash it up.[53] The dragon is back again in something more akin to its Silvestran form in the age of the British saint Gildas, whose historical floruit fell in the earlier seventh century AD. We learn from his *Lives* ([a], ix AD; [b], xi AD) that it is once again killing the people of Rome with its pestilential breath. Although there is no explicit reference back to Silvester here, the later of these *Lives* further salutes Silvester's iteration of dragon in explicitly locating the dragon's cave actually within the Tarpeian rock again. Gildas makes his way up the mountain (descent has now morphed into ascent), staff in hand, and addresses himself to the cave, commanding the dragon to die in the name of Christ, which it duly does, and thereby raising the pestilence. And this same dragon or something very much like it appears again in the reign of Pope Leo IV ([a], before *c.* AD 939), who occupied the papacy between AD 790 and 855: 'In the first year of his pontificate, there was born in some foul, hidden caves near the church of the blessed martyr Lucy [i.e. St Lucy at Selci in Rome], a serpent of a dreadful sort, termed basilisk in Greek, *regulus* in Latin'; Leo sends it off. Finally, the *Life* of Bernacus (Brynach, xii AD?) also credits this British saint, whose historical floruit fell in the fifth century AD, with killing a dragon at Rome.

We have a nice conundrum in the case of two different recensions of essentially the same *Life* of Vigor of Bayeux (AD 1030–45): in one recension this banisher of the Dragon of the Cerisy Forest is vestigially credited with the banishment of two further dragons. In the other recension, more intriguingly, it is said rather that his two further banishments were *of the same dragon*, which he evidently had to keep following around and moving on from place to place.

---

[53] *De promissionibus* 3.43, at *PL* col. 51, 835.

In the cases of some successor dragons we detect a relatively high degree (by the standards of hagiography) of what might be termed literary self-awareness on the narrator's part. Let us consider two examples. Eustratius' *Life of Golinduch* introduces the Dragon of Babylon, into whose pit the locals cast Golinduch ([b], vi–vii AD), in the following fashion: 'They [the Babylonians] had or still have a dragon (like the ancient one, which Daniel killed with the cake), which they keep shut in a pit....' Eustratius seems to be self-consciously composing his own tribute to the Daniel story. He is also explicitly aware, we may note, of Golinduch's place in a wider network of Christian tales: he compares her to other women that had encountered dragons, Eve (this comparison is of course to Golinduch's advantage) and Thecla, trampler of the dragon beneath her heavenly ladder; he also compares her to Jonah, who psalmed in the belly of the sea-monster, just as Golinduch psalms and glorifies God in her confinement with the dragon. Magnus of Füssen's dragon fight ([a], *c.* AD 895; [b], AD 1067–70) begins when the saint conceives the wish, by way of pilgrim, fan or tourist, to visit the site at which his hero Narcissus of Gerundum had killed the Dragon of the Julian Alps by tricking its demon associate. Upon arrival, he finds that the place is occupied not only by another dragon, the Dragon of Kempten, but also by a host of worms. One feels that the real fan of Narcissus here is not so much Magnus as the creator of his tale, keen to revisit a beloved dragon story.

In a rather different way, the first of the dragons encountered by Samson in his second *Life* ([b], ix AD) is a clear literary tribute to that encountered by the associates of Ammon in Rufinus' *History of the Monks of Egypt* (*c.* AD 395 and *c.* AD 403/4). Both of these dragons are discovered by the distinctive motif of their beam-like trails, and the Samson narrative explicitly salutes the Ammon one by bestowing the name of Ammon on Samson's companion in the episode. However, whereas the associates of Ammon abandon their dragon-hunt in Rufinus' tale, Samson and the new Ammon complete theirs.

What is remarkable about the repeat-offender dragons and the successor dragons is that these hero dragons (sic!) prove to be rather more popular and consequently rather more enduring than the saints that line up against them. That a dragon should continue as an active peril for subsequent saints to address, or be substituted with a replacement, makes a mockery of the efforts—and the faith—of the predecessor saints. One is put in mind of Dracula's wonderful inability to stay dead (perhaps one should rather say 'out of play'), despite his glorious annihilation at the end of every Hammer Horror movie in the franchise.

7.8 Conclusion

We have surveyed here a number of recurring motifs and story-patterns that sit aslant the principal narrative course of the saintly dragon-fight narrative, and then some recurring characters, human and serpentine. As to the latter, the (effective) recurrence of the same dragon in the *Lives* of diverse saints is a truly remarkable phenomenon, in which the medium of the good story triumphs over the message conveyed. As to the former, the following recurring motifs have been noted: the serpent brood, the plague of snakes over which the great dragon presides; the sacrifice of a virgin to the dragon; the emergence of the dragon as a saint is compelled to make sacrifice before a pagan idol; the revival of the dragon's last victim, most typically a boy; the saint's sending back of the dragons against their magician masters; and the female dragon-fighting saint. Amongst these the motif of the sacrifice of a virgin to the dragon retains a strikingly current resonance. But two of these motifs at least—that of the brood and that of the last-victim boy—are particularly ancient and go back to the very beginning of the hagiographical tradition, as we shall see in the following chapter.

8

Close to the Point of Origin

Lucian's Chaldaean Snake-Blaster

8.1 Introduction and Text

The pagan Lucian's *Philopseudes* or *Lover of Lies* will have been composed at some point between the AD 160s and the AD 180s.[1] This text incorporates what is evidently a satirical parody of a saintly dragon-fight narrative. In so doing it entails that the tradition of such narratives was well established already before the point of its composition. This is a position for which I have argued more than once before.[2] The argument was a bold one, given that, as it seemed, the earliest surviving hagiographical dragon fight proper, namely Thomas' battle against the Dragon of India in the *Acts of Thomas*, was not to be dated until half a century later, *c.* AD 220–40. But the *Acts of Thomas* has recently been radically and persuasively backdated to the later second century AD—to, that is to say, the same zone as the *Philopseudes* itself.[3] All of a sudden, the hypothesis seems rather less bold than it did.

If the hagiographical dragon-fight tradition is to be well-established by the time that Lucian wrote, then it must have been thriving already for some

---

[1] As with most of Lucian's works, the *Philopseudes* cannot be dated accurately: it most probably derives from the AD 170s, but it may also derive from one of the decades on either side of this. See Ogden 2007:2–3.

[2] See esp. Ogden 2013a:411–15; cf. also 2007:65–104, 2013b:199–202. The discussion I now present is based on the more extensive catalogue of hagiographical dragon fights reviewed in the foregoing chapters (and catalogued in Appendix B), and in consequence it is able to draw more nuanced and more far-reaching conclusions than my previous discussions have done.

[3] For the *Acts of Thomas* in general, see Bremmer 2001a (with Adamik 2001 for the serpent episode in particular); Klijn 2003. The question of the date of the *Acts* is bound up with the question of its provenance. It has long been held that the Syriac version is the original, and that the Greek version is derivative of it; for statements of this traditional view, see Bremmer 2001b:74–9 (with the further citations in n. 1), 2001c:152–9; Klijn 2003:1, 15; and, for Syriac hagiography more generally, see Brock 2011. However, in a Vorstudie anticipating a major study, Lanzillotta now argues powerfully that the Greek version is the original and the Syriac version the derivative, and he demonstrates that it belongs in the milieu, chronological and other, of the other four great early sets of apocryphal *Acts*, namely those of Peter, John, Paul, and Andrew, i.e. in the later second century AD (Lanzillotta 2015, esp. 127 for the date; subsequently to this, Bremmer 2017b:167–70). But if the hypothesis of Greek priority moves the *Acts of Thomas* closer to Lucian chronologically, it takes it further away from him in a certain cultural sense. We can no longer assume that it was first composed in Syrian Edessa (cf. Lanzillotta 2015:106), a mere 25 miles from Lucian's birthplace of Samosata. The hypothesis of Greek priority also prompts us to ask whether Thomas' dragon owes anything to the rich classical lore of Indian serpents mentioned briefly in Chapter 1, §1.1.

time—some decades?—even before that point. But then the *Acts of Thomas* rather suggests this in itself: its dragon fight is far from incunabular in feel. Rather, it is an expansive and elaborate narrative that one can well imagine draws on its own mature traditions. Of course, these traditions may have been largely oral. Perhaps, cautiously and scrupulously, we should designate them 'proto-hagiographic'.

An element of boldness remains, however, for we will now contend that Lucian's tale more particularly demonstrates the second-century AD currency of a range of hagiographical dragon-fight motifs that in some cases are not otherwise attested until many centuries later. In so doing the tale testifies both to the depth and fulness of that tradition at this early stage and also to its subsequent durability and to the degree of its conservatism. (It is, we should note, almost inconceivable that the authors of saintly dragon-fight narratives were themselves reading Lucian, and completely inconceivable that they were de-satirizing his text and drawing inspiration from it.) Lucian's tale reads as follows:

Said Ion, 'I'll tell you an amazing story. It took place when I was a lad, just about 14 years old. Someone came with news for my father that Midas the vine-dresser, a generally strong and hard-working slave, had been bitten by a viper [*echidna*] at around noon, and was lying there with his leg already going rotten. For, as he had been tying up the vine tendrils and winding them around the props, the creature had crept up on him and bitten him on his big toe. Then it had slipped off again and shot down its hole, whilst he was left to wail, dying from the pain. This was the news, and then we saw Midas himself being carried in on a stretcher by his fellow slaves, his whole body swollen and livid. He looked clammy, and he was only just still breathing. My father was upset, but a friend who happened to be present said, "Don't worry. For I'll go after a Babylonian fellow, one of the Chaldaeans, as they say, right away, and he will cure your man." To make a long story short, the Babylonian came and set Midas back on his feet by driving the venom out of his body with an incantation. Also, he tied a rock he had chipped off a virgin's tombstone to his foot. You may think this a rather ordinary achievement. Even so, Midas himself picked up the stretcher on which he had been brought and went off straight back to the farm. That was power of the incantation and the piece of tombstone. And the Babylonian did other things too that were truly marvellous.

'He went out to the farm at dawn, recited seven sacred names from an old book and purified the place with a sulphur-torch, encircling it three times. He called out all the reptiles within its boundaries. There came as if drawn to the incantation many snakes, asps, vipers, horned snakes, darting snakes, common toads, and puff-adders [*phusaloi*]. Only one ancient dragon [*palaios drakōn*] was left behind, unable to crawl out by reason of old age [*hupo gerōs*] or too deaf to hear the command. The mage said there was one missing, and chose out the youngest snake and sent it with a message, and shortly that snake too arrived. When they were fully assembled, the Babylonian blew upon [*en-ephusēse*] them all. At once they were all burned up by the blast [*phusēmati*], and we looked on in amazement.'

'Tell me, Ion,' I [Tychiades] said, 'did the young snake that took the message lead the snake of, as you say, advanced age [*gegērakota*] back by the hand, or did the old snake have a stick with which to support himself?'

Lucian *Philopseudes* 11–13[4]

8.2 Gospel Allusions

Lucian establishes the Christian frame of reference for this parodic story in the distinctive vignette of the healed Midas leaping to his feet and carrying his own stretcher home. The motif is unknown in the prior classical (pagan) tradition, but memorably features in descriptions of Jesus' healing miracles in all four of the Gospels, as, for example, in Matthew: "'Get up, pick up your bed, and go off home.' And he got up and went home.'[5]

We are strongly reminded too of an episode in the apocryphal *Infancy Gospel of Thomas*, thought to have its roots in the second century AD:[6]

Jacob went off into the wood to bind faggots, to cook bread. Jesus went off with him. As they were collecting the firewood an abominable viper [*echidna*] bit Jacob on his hand. As he was laid out flat and dying the boy Jesus ran to Jacob and blew upon [*kat-ephusēsen*] the bite, and at once the bite was healed. And the beast was killed and Jacob was saved.

Infancy Gospel of Thomas 16.1–2 (A), p. 147 Tischendorf (= Jesus [a])

This brief text, again featuring an *echidna*, a bite that brings a young man to the point of death, a magical blowing, a miraculous healing and a snake-destruction, serves to convey the unity underlying Lucian's seemingly broken-backed, two-episode tale, both in the direct coordination of the act of healing with the act of snake-destruction, and in the kaleidoscopic application of the motif of the blowing to the former instead of the latter (cf. Table 8.1 below).

---

[4] For a commentary, see Ebner et al. 2001:50–2, 118–20.

[5] Matthew 9:6–7; so too Mark 2:9 and 11–12; Luke 5:24–5; and John 5:8–9. Betz 1961:158 considers that Lucian is alluding to the New Testament here without parodying it, whereas des Guerrois 1920:317 considered that parody of the New Testament was indeed Lucian's intent: 'an unworthy parody of the evangelist.' My own view, as will be clear, is that the principal target of Lucian's parody is the hagiographical dragon-slaying tale: if nothing else, the New Testament imagery helps to signpost this.

[6] For the date of the text, see Quasten 1949–60:i, 123–5. The text or part of its tradition at any rate is referred to at Irenaeus *Against the Heretics* 1.13.1 (c. AD 174–89). For general discussion, see Quispel 1957; Gero 1971; Fallon and Cameron 1988; Valantasis 1997; Uro 2003; Gathercole 2012.

Table 8.1 Motival correspondences between Lucian's tale of the Chaldaean and the tale of Eudocia

Motif	Lucian *Philopseudes* 11–13	*Life of St Eudocia* §15
Serpent attacks boy…	*Echidna* attacks Midas	*Drakōn* attacks Zeno
at midday…	✓	✓
in a cultured landscape.	Farm	Garden
Serpent(s) blow(s) forth breath.	Presence of puff adders (*phusaloi*)	*Drakōn* kills with pestilential breath; eventually inflates itself to death
Boy is brought to the point of death.	✓	✓ (Indeed dies)
Boy's flesh becomes livid.	✓	✓
The wonder-worker travels to the scene of the attack.	✓	✓
The boy is healed by the wonder-worker…	Chaldaean	Eudocia (with Diodorus)
who puts him back on his feet.	✓	✓
A second wonder is announced.	By the narrator, Ion	By Eudocia
Wonder-worker summons serpent(s) verbally for destruction…	The Chaldaean summons the *drakōn* (and other serpents) with a spell	Eudocia summons the *drakōn* with a prayer
deploying breath against it/them…	The Chaldaean blows on the serpents	Eudocia compels the *drakōn* to over-inflate and burst
and deploying fire against it/them.	Fiery breath	Pursuing fire

8.3 Engagement with the Hagiographical Tradition

Let us now lay out the hagiographical narratives, or groups thereof, that appear to engage retrospectively with this text—which is to say, rather, that they attest, often long after the event, the pre-existence of the saintly dragon-fight motifs that Lucian himself is engaging with.

8.3.1 The Serpent Brood Presided Over by a *Drakōn*; the Old-Man *Drakōn*

As we have seen (Chapter 7, §7.1), the productive theme of a great *drakōn* presiding over a brood of lesser serpents is attested already at a relatively early stage of the hagiographical tradition, as, notably, in the case of Philip ([a], mid- to late iv AD). But of particular interest here is a late but rich account of the Theodore Tyron story ([h], xiv AD), which is laid out more fully in Chapter 9 (§9.1.5). When Theodore penetrates the cave of the Dragon of King Samuel's City in search of his kidnapped mother, the principal Dragon himself is absent, but he finds his mother within sitting on a stool and guarded by twelve large snakes, a hissing asp, and a host of smaller snakes, whilst an old-man dragon (*gerōn drakōn*) sits on a golden throne and evidently presides over them. This text is of value for giving us, on the one hand, a *drakōn* so strongly characterized as the ruler of a brood and, on the other, a *drakōn* so distinctively characterized, like Lucian's, as an old man.[7] In immediate context the old-man dragon has the appearance of being an awkward doublet of the principal one. However, some striking comparanda from a Norse text, *Konráðs saga Keisarasonar* (also xiv AD), considered in Chapter 11, §11.2.4, may militate against such a supposition.

Lucian takes the identification of an ancient dragon with an old man to a logical conclusion for humorous purposes, and so characterizes it as harmlessly decrepit. But the Theodore tale gives a glimpse of the horror of an aged *drakōn* in the more serious register. And indeed it can be shown that both of the specific tokens of the *drakōn*'s decrepitude that Lucian gives us, that of it being deaf and that of it, absurdly, using a walking stick, make light of phenomena that are sinister and terrible in established dragon-lore.

As to the first, Psalms (in the Septuagint version) speaks of the threat posed by asps (vipers) that are deaf or that have the ability to deafen themselves: 'Their heart resembles that of the snake [*ophis*], as it were of the asp [*aspis*] that is deaf and plugs its ears, so that it will not hear the voice of charmers, the voice of the sorcerer, and the one using sorcery ill-advisedly.'[8] In his fifth-century retelling of Genesis in hexameter verse Avitus of Vienne speaks of the efforts of the magical Italian race of the Marsi—the standard topos of Latin poetry—to control snakes: 'Sometimes the charmer dies, if a deaf snake scorns his clever mutterings.' Avitus is probably remoulding his classical source-material in the light of the Psalms passage.[9] Isidore of Seville (*c.* AD 600) knows of yet more sinister asps: when the enchanter calls and attempts to draw the asp forth from its cave, it presses one ear against the ground and sticks its tail in the other one so as not to hear the compulsive words.[10]

---

[7] In a considerably earlier text the Dragon of Euchaita destroyed by Theodore Tyron ([a], AD 754) had also been specified to be of great age.

[8] LXX, Psalms 57:5–6. The Hebrew (58:4–5) deploys the terms *nachash* and *pethen* (cf. Chapter 5, §§5.2.2–3). The familiar King James version reads: 'Their poison is like the poison of a serpent: they are like the deaf adder that stoppeth her ear; which will not hearken to the voice of charmers, charming never so wisely'; the quotation is one of Bertie Wooster's favourites.

[9] Avitus of Vienne *De spiritalis historiae gestis* 2.303–13. Wood 2001:267–9 esp. 268 n. 32 believes Avitus found his deaf snakes in a classical source here, a view to which I have myself previously been sympathetic: Ogden 2013a: 243–4. For Avitus' work in general, see Shanzer and Wood 2002. For the Marsi, see Chapter 6, §6.6.1.

[10] Isidore of Seville *Etymologies* 12.4.12.

As to the second token, that of the walking stick, the case is made well by one of the superb inset tales of the *Metamorphoses* (AD 150s–80s) of Lucian's contemporary Apuleius. Here the narrator Lucius has contrived to turn himself into an ass after meddling in the workshop of a Thessalian witch. In the course of his many adventures in this shape he has become the possession of a band of runaway slaves. As the slaves recuperate on a wooded hillside, they espy an old goatherd. They ask him whether he has any milk or cheese to sell them. He tells them he does not, before expressing surprise that they should be interested in such things in their current circumstances: do they not know the nature of the place in which they are relaxing? Without elaborating further, he hurries off with his animals, leaving the slaves terrified. In due course another old man appears on the adjacent road. He is of enormous size, but stooped with age, leaning on a stick, and dragging his feet. He is crying profusely. He grasps the knees of each of the young men in supplication and begs them to help him rescue his little grandson, who has fallen down a hole beneath some bushes as he was trying to grab a singing swallow from them. One of the younger and stronger slaves goes off with the old man towards the bushes he indicates in the distance. In due course, when the party of slaves is ready to move on, they call out to their companion, but there is no reply. Eventually they send another of their number to fetch him back, and he returns pallid and shaking. He had found a massive dragon (*draco*) in the course of devouring the missing slave, pinning him down on his back as it did so, and now almost finished with its meal. Of the old man there had been no sign. The slaves realize that it was this that had been the subject of the first old man's warning, and flee from the place as fast as they can, beating ass-Lucius with their clubs to urge him on as they go.[11]

It is one of the charms of this story that Apuleius does not quite join up all the dots for us, but of course we are to infer that the second old man and the dragon are one and the same.[12] The dragon has transformed into humanoid form in

---

[11] Apuleius *Metamorphoses* 8.19–21; see Scobie 1977 for a folkloric perspective on this tale. The sharing of the walking-stick motif between Lucian and Apuleius raises, once again, the question of the authorship of the lost Greek original upon which Apuleius based the *Metamorphoses*, given that an influential school of thought holds that it too was by Lucian, e.g. Perry 1967:211–82; Anderson 1976:34–67; and Bowie 1994:444. It is quite possible that 'Lucius of Patras', the autobiographical narrator of the lost Greek *Metamorphoses*, a substantial summary of which, the *Onos*, is transmitted with Lucian's own oeuvre (*Onos* 55; Photius *Bibliotheca* cod. 128), is an alter ego of Lucian himself, just as another of Lucian's characters with a name reminiscent of his own, Lycinus, is often so held to be (the latter appearing in *Dance, Dipsads, Hesiod, Eunuch, Hermotimus, In Defence of Portraits, Lapiths, Lexiphanes, Portraits, Ship*). For the relationship between the text of Apuleius' *Metamorphoses* and that of the *Onos*, see van Thiel 1971–2; Frangoulidis 2008:13–45. However, the gothic tone of our dragon tale (which in any case does not appear in the summary *Onos*) gives it the feel of being an Apuleian insertion, as, apparently, are the splendid gory witch tales of Apuleius' first three books, with the exception, of course, of that of Pamphile, the witch integral to the focal transformation episode, who is the equivalent of the *Onos*' wife of Hipparchus (Apuleius *Metamorphoses* 3.15–25). Bremmer 1998:167–71 dates the lost Greek *Metamorphoses* to *c.* AD 170 and Apuleius' version to *c.* AD 180.

[12] As Scobie 1977:340–3 realizes.

order to lure away a tasty young man to a place of privacy where it can return to its base form and devour him. In retrospect, there were clues: the dragon's original and true form peeped through his humanoid disguise, in the old man's great size and age (presumably *drakontes* never stop growing, and so the older the *drakōn*, the bigger and the more terrible it is); in the crookedness of his back, which replicated the serpent's sinuous form; and in the dragging of his feet, which replicated the serpent's slithering gait.

We almost certainly have another example of a dragon that can manifest itself in the form of a humanoid old man in a hagiographical text. In the (xii–xiii AD) Latin *Life of Waldevus* (i.e. Waltheof) we are initially told of the deeds of the saint's father, Siward, the Danish Earl of Northumbria. First, he defeats a marauding dragon on one of the islands of the Orkneys and drives it off. This is a desultory episode and its function is really to set up the more interesting one that follows. When Siward then sails on to Northumbria he hears of another such dragon and is eager to rout it in a similar way. But he cannot find it. Instead he finds a steep hill with an old man sitting on the top of it, and asks him for information about the creature. The mysterious old man already knows Siward's name and why he has come, but tells him that his efforts are in vain and that he will not be able to find the dragon. Instead, he tells him to return to his companions and gives him a prophecy of the good fortune he will find in London, giving him a raven banner as a token. Siward reluctantly returns to his companions and proceeds to London. We cannot doubt that the mysterious old man, sitting atop his hill,[13] with his arcane knowledge, and so sure that Siward will never find the dragon, is anything other than the (friendly) dragon himself in transformation. The tale is reduced to arbitrariness without such an assumption.[14]

8.3.2 The Last-Victim Boy

The most striking and over-arching motif with which Lucian's tale engages is that of the boy that is the last victim of the dragon being revived by the saint (or an agent thereof) in some sort of co-ordination with his triumph over the dragon itself (see Chapter 7, §7.4). If not a boy, the last victim Midas at any rate retains the vigour of youth. An oddity of Lucian's tale in relation to the hagiographical tradition is that the serpent that attacks the boy is not the great dragon itself, but rather a member of the serpent brood over which the dragon evidently presides—an oddity mitigated, however, by consideration of the Joannicius material

---

[13] For another mountain-top dwelling dragon, cf. the Dragon of the Island of Montecristo killed by Mamilianus ([b], xii AD).

[14] For discussion, see Rauer 2000:125–33, who, however, prefers to see in the old man a refraction of Odin, adopting an advisory role as he sometimes does (128–31).

discussed below (§8.3.4) and the Theodore material discussed later on (Chapter 9, §9.1.5). In terms of the co-ordination between the two actions, the revivification of the boy and the destruction of the dragon, the motif appears in three variants:

- The saint deals with the dragon in a single action with the revivification of the boy, as in the case of Jesus ([a]) and the *echidna* in the *Infancy Gospel of Thomas*, as laid out above, and as in the case of Thomas himself and the Dragon of India, in his *Acts* (later ii AD), where the saint makes the dragon suck its own venom back out of boy, killing itself in the process.
- The dragon is dealt with (killed or dismissed) first, and the last-victim boy then restored to life in a separate feat in the aftermath: so it is with the tales of Ammon (*c.* AD 395 and *c.* AD 403/4), Andrew ([a] and [b], both late vi AD), and Fronto of Périgueux ([c], xi AD).
- The last-victim boy is restored to life first, and the dragon dealt with in a separate feat in the aftermath. So it is with Eudocia (x AD or before) and the Dragon of Heliopolis.

It is the third variant here to which Lucian's narrative most closely conforms, with the boy being restored to life before any attention is given to the dragon, and indeed its alignment with the Eudocia narrative extends further, as we can see when we consider the latter more fully (the motival correspondences are laid out in Table 8.1):

At that point the holy martyr [Eudocia] was in the house of Diodorus, preaching the word of God, when a massive dragon [*drakōn*] arrived in a garden near his house. A young man was sitting there at midday; he was the only son of a widow. The dragon killed him by blowing on him [*prosphusēmati*]. His mother was terribly grief-stricken, and wailed loudly over her son. Eudocia, the lamb of God, realizing what had happened, said to Diodorus, 'come and see another revelation of God's goodness and compassion.' He readily went off with her. She found the young man bound by the creature's venom, and said to Diodorus, 'Here is an opportunity for you to demonstrate the perfection of your faith in the Lord. Lift up the eyes of your heart and pray, and raise the dead body'.... After he had made these prayers, Diodorus said to the dead boy, 'In the name of Jesus Christ, who was crucified by Pontius Pilate, rise up, Zeno!' And at once the corpse rose again, putting off the dragon's blackness. When this had taken place, all glorified the God of heaven and earth and put their faith in him. When the crowds were minded to withdraw, Eudocia, the blessed lamb and servant of Christ, said to them, 'Wait a moment, brethren, for our saviour Jesus Christ is to be glorified further'. As they listened, she raised a great cry, and spoke as follows: 'Lord God...heed my humble prayer and command the enemy, the dragon that preys upon your servants, to come, harried by your vengeance, and to burst itself open and die...'. After she had made this prayer, lo! the terrible dragon came, harried by fire, burst itself open completely, and, after its over-inflation, breathed its last [*diaphusēsas exepneusen*].[15]

Just as Midas is bitten around noon, so too Zeno is bitten at midday. Both are attacked in a place where man attempts to impose order on nature: a farm in the first case, a garden in the second. In both cases attention is drawn to the lividity of the stricken boy. As we enter the second episode, in both cases again the wonder-worker, travelling to the scene of the crime, forces the dragon to present itself to himself or herself with a verbal summoning, a spell or a prayer. Whereas Lucian's Chaldaean destroys his dragon with fiery breath, Eudocia's is brought to the place of its destruction by divinely sent fire, perhaps to be considered hallucinatory. The theme of destructive breath lurks on both sides of the equation in both stories: Lucian's serpent brood contains puff-adders; Eudocia's dragon kills with its pestilential breath; Lucian's Chaldaean kills the dragon and its brood by blowing on it; Eudocia kills her dragon seemingly by compelling it to over-inflate itself.

8.3.3 Blowing on the Drakōn and Burning It

The Chaldaean destroys his *drakōn* by blowing on it and causing it to burst into flames. This finds a direct parallel in Theodoret's Marcian (mid-v AD), who burns up the dragon that attacks him as he prays in the vestibule of his house, again merely breathing on it; it disintegrates like a burning reed. More generally, we find the separate motifs of killing-the-dragon-by-blowing (Chapter 6, §6.6.2) and of killing-the-dragon-by-burning used widely and productively in the hagiographical tradition (Chapter 6, §6.6.2).

8.3.4 The Echidna, the Wounded Workman, and the Healing Digit

A narrative with a peculiar degree of alignment with the first part of Lucian's is to be found in one of the many serpent episodes Peter the Monk gives to Joannicius of Bithynia ([a], AD 846):

Joannicius moved out of his cave and mounted Mt Alsos, as it is called, on which the all-holy man, dweller in the heavenly city, was building the most miraculous

---

[15] The last phrases, from 'completely', seem to be slightly corrupt. LSJ note only a transitive use for *diaphusaō* in the sense of 'inflate', but I suspect that (as the text stands, at any rate) it is intended intransitively here: the dragon bursts itself by over-inflating. The alternative is to read *diaphusēsas* as signifying that the dragon blows out in all directions as it dies—which, given the lethal nature of its breath (*hinc illae lacrimae*), hardly seems appropriate.

church in the name of the soldier-martyr Eustathius. He was making haste with the construction of a chamber to receive and give shelter to Eustathius' most sacred remains. Having surveyed the place and drawn up plans for the building, he instructed the builders to proceed with all due care, and retreated into the nearby wilderness. As the work was nearing completion and evening was coming on, the builders all turned to sleep. And lo, at the prompting of the Devil, a wicked viper [echidna] came out, struck one of the workmen, whose name was Pardus, on the temple and sped off again. Feeling the pain and roused from his sleep, the man cried out with a great shout. Now all the builders were roused from their sleep, and they asked him why he was shouting out so loudly. He told them that he had an unbearable pain in his head, but that he had absolutely no idea what had happened. As the toxin spread across his head and his whole body, it caused it to turn black and to swell up enormously, and he was brought to the very point of death. St Joannicius knew from God what had happened in the place and departed from where he was. He got back to the builders at dawn, at the third hour. As soon as the men saw the saint, they threw themselves at his feet and besought him to have pity on the victim. He took Pardus up and stood apart from the other builders, about a stone's throw distant. He stood in prayer and lifted his arms towards heaven in the shape of a cross. When he had finished the prayer, he touched the place in which Pardus had been bitten with his holy finger and drew the shape of the glorious cross into it. And at once that dreadful swelling burst open and all the stinking venom poured forth. Cured, Pardus glorified God, who had healed him instantaneously through the agency of his servant Joannicius, and applied himself to his work just as before. This Pardus is still alive today, proclaiming the kingdom of heaven and telling of the saint's healing of him to all. He tells the tale with such clarity that all who hear him glorify God and give praise to his servant Joannicius.

The motival correspondences with Lucian's tale of Midas largely speak for themselves. It will be sufficient to tabulate them (Table 8.2; for convenience, I also compare the *Infancy Gospel*).

The only correspondences here that may require more particular comment are rows 9 and 10. As to the former, the use of the term 'stone' is very different in the two narratives. In the Lucian narrative it is a healing tool, whereas in the Peter narrative it merely appears in the context of a metaphor, albeit at the very same point in the expositional sequence. Even so, the correspondence seems too tight to be coincidental, and Peter's metaphor surely represents a dim refraction of (or a conscious tribute to?) an original Christian motif more closely resembling the paganized parody of it found in Lucian. The original Christian motif may have had the saint deploying a stone from the tomb of a holy virgin or, for reasons we shall see, of a patriarch. As to row 10, the common motif of the digit does seem to

Table 8.2 Motival correspondences between Lucian's tale of the Chaldaean and Peter the Monk's tale of Joannicius

Motif/theme	Lucian	Peter the Monk	*Infancy Gospel*
1. The victim: the workman at his work.[16]	Midas, the vine-dresser	Pardus, the builder	Jacob, at work in firewood-collection
2. Specification of time of attack.	Midday	Evening	—
3. Viper (*echidna*) creeps out, strikes workman, and shoots off again.	✓	✓	✓ (Shooting off not specified)
4. Attacked body-part specified.	Toe	Temple	Hand
5. The workman's body becomes black and swollen.	✓	✓	—
6. He is brought to the point of death.	✓	✓	✓
7. Miracle-worker brought in from local area.	The Chaldaean (Babylonian)	St Joannicius	Jesus (already present)
8. Verbal technique of healing.	Incantation	Prayer	—
9. Reference to a stone.	The Chaldaean heals with a stone chipped from a virgin's tombstone	Joannicius stands apart 'by a stone's throw'	—
10. Application and digit.	The Chaldaean applies the healing stone to the victim's *toe*	Joannicius applies his *finger* to the victim's temple	(Affected part is hand)
11. The venom is driven out of the wound.	✓	✓	—
12. Instantaneous recovery...	✓	✓	✓
13. ̇ expressed in the workman's immediate return to normal and vigorous activity.	Midas carries his own stretcher home	Pardus returns to his building work	—
14. Praise for the miracle-worker's achievement.	(extra-narrative)	(intra-narrative)	—

[16] The theme of workmen disturbed in their work by a serpent is also to be found in the (early iii AD) alpha recension of the *Alexander Romance*: (A) 1.32 ≈ (Arm.) §§86–7 Wolohojan. As we saw in Chapter 1, §1.3.2, the builders of the first dwellings of the city of Alexandria have their work repeatedly interrupted by the visitations of a *drakōn*. Alexander, from afar, orders it to be killed, but then has a hero-shrine built for it, and it becomes, as Agathos Daimon (Good Demon), the patron deity of the new city.

lurk: in Lucian the healer applies the medicine to the digit (toe) of the victim; in Peter the healer applies his own digit (finger) to the victim's wound.[17]

Peter's *echidna* story in his *Life of Joannicius* is not *directly* coordinated with a tale of dragon-destruction on the part of Joannicius, as Lucian's is, but his *Life* does include a number of other dragon-fight stories, as we have seen (Chapter 7, §7.7), and no less than three of these may also, in their various ways, reflect the influence of a prototype shared with Lucian's broader tale. In the first of these he destroys the Dragon of Prusa, a conventional marauder, by stamping the sign of the cross into it three times with his signet ring. The number three here may salute the Trinity, but we are also reminded that Lucian's Chaldaean had also exploited the number three in carrying his sulphur-torch around the snake-infested farm three times. The technique Joannicius uses to kill the dragon, a physical impression of the cross, is broadly the same as the technique he uses to expel the *echidna*'s venom from Pardus. This at any rate serves to create a vague link between Peter's *echidna* story and a dragon-destruction story, even if they are not syntagmatically integrated.

In the second story Joannicius answers the petition of Brother Daniel and his fellow monks on the Islet of Thasion in Lake Apolloniatis: they are plagued by a most dreadful *drakōn* and the unnumbered host of snakes over which it presides. Joannicius maintains a prayer vigil overnight before the dragon's cave. As the sun rises at dawn the dragon shoots out of its cave 'as if driven by fire' and throws itself into the lake, swimming to shore and disappearing into the land beyond. Peter does not specify what becomes of the rest of the brood, though Sabas' parallel Joannicius narrative ([b], before AD 860) specifies that the other snakes all went into the lake together with the dragon. Even though the dragon and his cohorts are not destroyed here, the tale brings us reasonably close to Lucian's second episode in its themes: again we have a serpent-brood, again the dragon is dealt with by means of fire, and again the dragon shares a common fate with its brood.

In Peter's third story Joannicius takes it upon himself to deal with the Dragon of the river Gorgytes. The beast is so huge that when it unfolds itself across the river's stream it blocks its flow. After due preparation by fast and prayer Joannicius presents himself at the dragon's cave and kills it by bringing an iron axe down on its head. Peter finishes his tale with an additional note taken over from one Eustratius to the effect that 'Joannicius, the servant of God, also killed, by means of prayer, a wicked viper [*echidna*] that had been living in that cave over many years.' This is a fascinating detail: it strongly suggests that this *echidna* was the

---

[17] Worthy of note again here too is the wonderful story preserved by Theodore Daphnopates of the virgin girl about to be sacrificed to the Dragon of Antioch: her Christian father secretly bites the *thumb* from the relic hand of John the Baptist ([a], x AD) whilst pretending to kiss it and throws it into the dragon's mouth, destroying the creature instantaneously (Chapter 7, §7.2).

consort of the Dragon of the river Gorgytes, just as the great Echidna of myth, the great brood mother, was the consort of the great dragon Typhon, deep under the earth.[18] This prompts us to turn also to the later Theodore narrative ([h], xiv AD) laid out below (Chapter 9, §9.1.5) and in particular to its singling out of the abominable asp for attention. Evidently this asp has a privileged status, seemingly serving, at least, as the chief of the serpent-guards. But the way in which it is twice paired with the old-man dragon in the exposition, together with its repeated representation by a feminine noun (with coordinated adjective and pronoun),[19] tends to project the creature as the consort of the old-man dragon.

This raises the intriguing possibility that Lucian's viper (*echidna*), the initial cause of all the trouble, or at any rate its Christian prototype, might also have had a special status within the serpent community of the farm in question, and indeed that it might, similarly, actually have been the consort of the old *drakōn*. Was this *echidna* even, perhaps, the brood-mother of all the snakes, like the Echidna of Ophiorhyme, the *drakaina* plunged into the abyss by Philip ([a], mid- to late iv AD; cf. Chapter 6, §6.5.4)?

8.3.5 The Chip from the Virgin's Tombstone

Lucian's Chaldaean's use of a chip from a virgin's tombstone to drive the venom from Midas' wound initially seems quite an exotic gesture. One must assume that, in its pagan context, the ghost of the dead virgin girl is being called upon, by means of the physical material associated with her corpse, to accomplish the deed. For the pagans, the ghosts of those dead before marriage, the *agamoi*, especially female ones, were particularly restless, vigorous, and susceptible to magical exploitation, as is clear from the world of the curse tablets.[20]

But we can in fact contextualize this gesture much more closely in both classical and Christian registers. Aristotle tells that in Libya there is a little snake (*opheidion*) that lives in the silphium, and that its bite is cured by a stone taken from the tomb of an ancient king: one puts the stone in wine and drinks.[21] In the *Acts of Thomas* (later ii AD) again, after King Misdaeus has martyred the apostle, his son falls to possession by a difficult demon, and so he conceives the plan to

---

[18] Hesiod *Theogony* 295–308. For another great dragon of pagan tradition with a distinctive female-serpent consort, we may turn again to Nonnus' account of the marauding Dragon (*drakōn*) of the river Hermus: after the Giant Damasen has killed it with a tree, it is revived by its wife, a 'female snake' (θῆλυς ὄφις) with the jaws of (NB) an *echidna* (ἐχιδνήεντι γενείῳ), by means of a magic flower (*Dionysiaca* 25.451–552; cf. Chapter 3, §3.2).

[19] ἀσπίδα μιαρὰ [sic]...ἡ μιαρὰ ἀσπὶς...αὐτῆς.

[20] For the vigorous ghosts produced by dead virgin girls see Johnston 1999:161–99. For curse tablets more generally, see Tomlin 1988; Gager 1992; Ogden 1999.

[21] Aristotle *History of Animals* 607a: γίνεται δὲ καὶ ἐν τῷ σιλφίῳ τι ὀφείδιον, οὗ καὶ λέγεται ἄκος εἶναι λίθος τις, ὃν λαμβάνουσιν ἀπὸ τάφου βασιλέως τῶν ἀρχαίων καὶ ἐν οἴνῳ ἀποβάψαντες πίνουσιν.

open up Thomas' tomb, take a bone from it, and attach it to the boy as an amulet, in the confidence that he will be cured thereby. But when he comes to the tomb he finds the bones have been stolen: one of Thomas' brethren has taken them off to the west. Still, Misdaeus takes some of the dust (*konis*) in which the bones had been lying and attaches that to his son instead, proclaiming his faith in Christ the while. The boy is cured, and Misdaeus joins the brethren.[22] Also of interest is a fifth-century AD (?) Christian narrative pseudonymously attributed to Epiphanius. This survives in two recensions of its own, but it is reflected, in on the whole better, though not perfect, condition, in the seventh-century AD *Chronicon Paschale*. All three accounts are confusing, because of the omission of vital details, but, when they are overlapped, the nature of the original tale becomes apparent. It is accordingly told that when Alexander the Great was founding Alexandria, he went off to visit the tomb of the prophet Jeremiah, who had been an averter of snakes in life, and learned his mysteries. He then transferred his remains to Alexandria and arranged them in a circle around the city, with all due honour. In this way Alexander was able to protect his city from the race of venomous asps.[23] We are, as it seems, to imagine Alexander sprinkling the dust of Jeremiah's body around the circuit of the city, much as, in the city's earlier foundation legend, he had marked out the course of the city walls for his architects and builders by sprinkling a circle of grain (which, by way of good omen, was promptly eaten by birds).[24] It is noteworthy that Lucian's Chaldaean makes use of an isolating circle-barrier—this one created by a sulphur-fumigation—in handling his snakes, just as Alexander does.

On this basis, we can easily imagine that the early Christian tradition Lucian is already parodying involved the use of a stone either from the tomb of a suitable patriarch, or of a holy man, perhaps even a holy girl, whose virgin status may have had its own, rather different, power in Christian context.

8.3.6 The Abyss: A Displaced Motif?

One of the distinctive features of the *Philopseudes* is Lucian's propensity for displacing motifs from one of the story-types he is parodying and merging them

[22] *Acts of Thomas* 170.

[23] [Epiphanius] *De prophetarum et obitu* (first recension) p. 9 Schermann and (second recension) p. 62 Schermann; *Chronicon Paschale* p. 293 Dindorf. For the two Epiphanian recensions, see Schermann 1907; Schwemer 1995. The relevant portions of all three constituent texts are now reprinted at Barbantani 2014:228–32, which should also be consulted for helpful further discussion, together with Ogden 2013a:293–5, 2013c; and Djurslev and Ogden 2018. An alternative tradition, preserved at John Moschus *Pratum spirituale* 77 (c. AD 600), has it that Alexander rather buried Jeremiah's bones at Alexandria's Tetrapylum (four-column colonnade). These stories belong in the Alexandrian Agathos Daimon tradition, for which see Chapter 1, §1.3.2.

[24] Strabo C792; Valerius Maximus 1.4 ext. 1; Curtius 4.8.6; Plutarch *Alexander* 26.5–6; Arrian *Anabasis* 3.2.1–2; Stephanus of Byzantium s.v. Ἀλεξάνδρειαι; Amyntianus (?) *Fragmentum Sabbaiticum, FGrH* 151, §11; *Alexander Romance* (A) 1.32.4; *Itinerarium Alexandri* 49; Ammianus Marcellinus 22.16.7; Eustathius *Commentary on Dionysius Periegetes* 254.

into another one. The clearest example of the technique is found in his handling of the tales of the Sorcerer's Apprentice and of the Haunted House. Analogues of the Sorcerer's Apprentice story lead us suppose that at its heart the great Egyptian sorcerer, Pancrates, should be seen to be in possession of an all-important grimoire or spell-book. But no mention is made of this in the course of the Sorcerer's Apprentice tale itself. However, the motif does indeed pop up elsewhere, in the Haunted House tale, where the Pythagorean philosopher Arignotus, the former pupil of Pancrates, reads through Egyptian spell-books as he waits for the terrible ghost to appear: we cannot doubt that he had got these from Pancrates.[25]

In light of this, it is worth taking note of the fact that a further tale in the *Philopseudes*, that of the terrible manifestation of the goddess Hecate, culminates in the earth opening up to swallow a serpentine monster into the underworld (the passage is quoted in Chapter 3, §3.3.4), in a pattern of action that does not seem far removed from the hagiographical motif of the earth opening up to swallow the defeated dragon into the abyss. From the examples of hagiographical dragons being swallowed down into a (land-based) abyss considered above (Chapter 6, §6.5.4), the single most pertinent one here is perhaps that of the Echidna of Ophiorhyme. In the course of his final martyrdom Philip ([a], mid- to late iv AD) utters a great curse with the result that Hades opens up and swallows down the Echidna, the city's viper-goddess, together with a host of its citizens. As we have also seen above (Chapter 3, §3.3.1), we are probably to imagine the Echidna here to be an anguipede, which draws her form particularly close to that of Lucian's Hecate. We may also look to the Dragon of India, the carcass of which is swallowed down into the abyss when the ground opens up after it has been killed by Thomas (later ii AD).

8.4 Pagan Flavours

In paganizing his Christian story Lucian evidently had to eliminate its hero-saint and replace him with a pagan miracle worker.[26] Why did he choose to substitute the saint specifically with a Chaldaean, a Babylonian?[27] Their more general magical associations aside,[28] Chaldaeans can be shown to have had two roles in

[25] Lucian *Philopseudes* 29–31 (the Haunted House tale), 33–7 (the Sorcerer's Apprentice tale). See Chapter 5 n. 58 for the Haunted House tradition in antiquity, and Ogden 2007: 237–41 for Lucian's displacement of motifs between stories in this text.

[26] Compare Lucian's *Alexander* or *The False Prophet*, in which, if we read between the lines, we can see that Lucian has largely substituted Epicureans for the Christians that must have been the actual leaders of the historical campaign against Alexander of Abonouteichos: Ogden 2009b. For a review of Lucian's explicit references to Christians, see Betz 1961:5–13.

[27] Daniel's destruction of the (first) Dragon of Babylon, it should hardly need saying, is not relevant here: Lucian must be using a Chaldaean for reasons that make sense in *pagan* tradition, not in *Christian* tradition, for which he presumably cares little.

[28] E.g. Strabo C762; Pliny *Natural History* 30.5; Lucian *Menippus* 6; Diogenes Laertius 8.3; SHA *Marcus Aurelius* 19.

pagan lore that made them particularly suitable for such a task as this. First, they probably had an established association with revivification (as well as with necromantic reanimation): in his lost novel *Babyloniaca* Iamblichus of Emesa, whose floruit coincided precisely with Lucian's own, has a Chaldaean restoring a dead girl to life as he happens upon her funeral.[29] Second, strange as it may seem, men described as 'Chaldaeans', who doubtless had no association with Babylon whatsoever, may have been held to hang around the farms of the Roman world. Already in *c.*160 BC Cato had been prescribing his ideal farm steward (*vilicus*): 'He should not wish to have consulted any haruspex, augur, diviner, or Chaldaean.'[30] And then we meet an intriguing pair of Chaldaeans in Eunapius' quasi-*Life* of the (earlier iv AD) miracle-worker Sosipatra of Ephesus, a female version of the 'divine man' (*theios anēr*) figure.[31] When Sosipatra is a child of 5, two old men with full wallets and dressed in clothes made of animal skins arrive at her parents' country estate and prevail upon the estate's steward to put them in charge of the vines. The result is an exceptional grape harvest, so exceptional indeed that Sosipatra's father, visiting the estate, suspects divine intervention and invites the two men to join him for dinner, where they meet the charming little girl. They then make a surprising offer: if her father leaves the girl on the estate with them for five years, staying away from it himself in the meantime, they will confer a divine mind upon her, a gift that will render her famous, whilst in the meantime the estate as a whole will flourish of its own accord. The father agrees and the men proceed to initiate the girl into their mysteries. Five years later her father returns and can barely recognize his daughter, now grown tall and beautiful and resembling a goddess; she immediately shows him that she possesses the gift of remote sight by revealing to him the details of the journey he has just made. Only at this point, with the father pressing them much, do the old men reveal, reluctantly, that they are Chaldaeans. Their work done, it is now time for them the leave and they do so discretely whilst he is sleeping. Before departing, they hand over to Sosipatra in a sealed chest her initiation garments, some mystic symbols, and some (presumably sacred) books, and tell her that they are travelling to the Western Ocean. In the light of Lucian's first episode incorporating a vine-dresser and a Chaldaean, it leaps to the attention that Eunapius as it were kaleidoscopes these motifs by giving us vine-dressing Chaldaeans. A case could be made, indeed, that Eunapius' tale kaleidoscopes other motifs too from the episode: the grown Sosipatra, again using remote sight and also, seemingly, remote healing powers, rescues her relative Philometor from danger when he has hurt his *legs* in a carriage accident and is being *stretchered* out of it.[32]

---

[29] Iamblichus *Babyloniaca*, as summarized at Photius *Bibliotheca* cod. 94, §74b.

[30] Cato *De agricultura* 5: *haruspicem, augurem, hariolum, Chaldaeum nequem consuluisse velit.*

[31] Eunapius *Lives of the Philosophers and Sophists* 6.5–11; her *Life* is concatenated with those of her husband Eustathius and her son Antoninus; for a good discussion, exposing the considerable interest of this biography, see Addey 2018.

[32] Cf. Ogden 2018a:9–11.

8.5 Conclusion

It is remarkable enough that we should possess any pagan parody of early hagiography, let alone such a sophisticated one; it is more remarkable still that this parody should coincide chronologically with the first attestation of the saintly dragon-fight tradition it is parodying; but it is most remarkable by far that this parody should directly witness, at such an early stage, a number of themes and motifs not otherwise attested in the hagiographical tradition itself until many centuries later. Lucian's tale demonstrates that the elaborate world of the holy man's dragon fight must have become fully established in all its glory already by the middle of the second century AD. Even more than the expansive analysis of themes and motifs laid out in Chapters 6 and 7, this helps us to appreciate the extraordinary and deep-rooted conservatism of the dragon-fight tradition over the millennium and a half of its existence.

9

Theodore and George

Two Military Dragon-Slaying Saints in Context

The hagiographical tradition bequeaths us a pair of distinguished warrior saints, Theodore Tyron and George, who, in contrast to the vast majority of their saintly peers, fight their dragons in a duly martial fashion, and it is to these we turn in this chapter. However, their physical fight is typically brief, desultory, and anticlimactic, an adjunct or coda to a more spiritual battle that has already been won.

9.1 A Later Theodore Narrative in Secular Context

Hitherto we have been considering our hagiographical narratives rather as if self-contained or hermetically sealed within their own vigorous and prolific tradition, occasional glances at classical motifs aside. But secular dragon traditions did also thrive in the Greek and Roman world outside and around the world of hagiography and these made a detectable impact on one of the later Theodore Tyron narratives.[1] Remarkably, the narrative in question is the one referred to already in Chapter 8 (§8.3.1), the *Miracle and Story of the Saint and Glorious Great-Martyr Theodore Tiron, Concerning his Mother being Taken Captive by the Dragon* ([h], xiv AD)—remarkably, because in that chapter we were able to trace some of this same narrative's motifs back to the very earliest form of hagiographical dragon-fight, a millennium before. The tale is a truly striking one for the complexity and the reach of its affinities (Fig. 9.1).

We shall proceed now by laying out two precious examples of secular dragon-fight narratives from the Byzantine world, a relatively short one from the epic poem *Digenis Akritis*, and then a rich and expansive one from the verse romance *Callimachus and Chrysorrhoe*. We shall give some consideration to these texts in their own right, particularly in the latter case, before proceeding to demonstrate the impact of their motifs and sequences on the Theodore tale. In all three narratives the dragon is arguably partly attracted in form and modus operandi to the medieval and folkloric *drakos*, a more *humanoid* variety of monster, a kind of demon or ogre.[2]

---

[1] So far as dragon-slaying is concerned, no purpose is served by attempting to disentangle the concatenated (or rather bifurcated) traditions of Theodore Tyron (Tiron, Teron) of Euchaita and Theodore Stratelates. For the concatenation, see Delehaye 1909:12–43; Walter 1999 esp. 185–9, 2003a:44–66; White 2013 esp. 72; Haldon 2016:1–17.

[2] For the *drakos*, see Lawson 1910:280–1; Dawkins 1953:23; Megas 1970:liii–lv, 253; Scobie 1977 (with further references).

Fig. 9.1 Saint Theodore slays a many-headed dragon. Byzantine, agate intaglio, AD 1300 or later. Metropolitan Museum, New York, Gift of Nanette B. Kelekian, in memory of Charles Dikran and Beatrice Kelekian, 1999, 1999.325.227. Public domain.

9.1.1 *Digenis Akritis*

Digenis Akritis is a once popular Byzantine epic poem, which has been described as a piece of 'secular hagiography'.[3] The earliest manuscript of it, the Grottaferrata, derives from *c.* AD 1300, but it reflects a world largely of the ninth and tenth centuries AD, and this period, in consequence, is likely to have been the age of its principal composition. The protagonist himself, Digenis Akritis, is a trouble-making Byzantine frontiersman. Here, he has carried off the daughter of a general, Doukas:

At noon I turned to sleep.[4] The noble girl sprinkled me with rose water whilst the nightingales and other birds sang. The girl felt thirsty and went off to the spring. As she was pleasantly dipping her feet, a *drakōn* transformed itself into a handsome boy and accosted her with the intention of leading her into sin. But she recognized it for what it was and said, '*Drakōn*, give up your plan. I am not deceived. The man that loves me has been keeping vigil and has only just gone to sleep.' (To herself she said, 'This is a *drakōn*. I have never yet seen such a sight.') 'If he wakes and discovers you, he will punish you.' But the *drakōn* leaped up shamelessly and tried to rape her. The girl screamed at once and called to me, 'Wake up, my lord, and save your dearest girl!' The sound of her voice went right to my heart and I quickly sat up and saw the troublemaker, for I had advisedly slept in a place directly opposite the spring. No sooner had I drawn my

---

[3] For an edition of the two basic versions, with a helpful introduction, see Jeffreys 1998. For further discussion, see Trapp 1972; Huxley 1974; Beaton 1981, 1989 esp. 27–48 (with the quote at 41–2); Kuehn 2011:118–35.

[4] Noon is ever the 'dangerous hour', the hour at which demons and other unwelcome supernatural phenomena are wont to manifest themselves: see Blum and Blum 1970 esp. 331–2. Cf. also Table 8.2 above, p. 270.

sword than I found myself at the spring, for my feet carried me as swiftly as wings. As I got there it turned itself into a huge, terrifying vision, fearful for men: it had three massive heads, all shooting forth flame. From each of its heads it sent forth a lightning-like flame. It made the sound of thunder as it moved, with the result that the earth and all the trees seemed to shake. It inflated its body whilst drawing its heads together, but it drew in its hinder part and sharpened its tail. Alternately coiling and uncoiling, it launched its whole body against me. But I set what I saw at nought. I raised my sword up high, with all my strength, and brought it down upon the heads of the most terrible beast and took them all off at once. It fell to the ground and unravelled itself, twitching its tail up and down in its death throes. I wiped off my sword and put it back into my scabbard. I called my boys over from where they were, some distance away, and ordered them to remove the *drakōn* immediately.

Digenis Akritis (Grottaferrata version) 6.42–80

The unrestrained narrative, appropriate in style to a vernacular epic, has a number of motifs in common with hagiographical dragon-fight narratives: the dragon's association with a spring, its fire-breathing, the carting of its carcass out of harm's way (cf. Chapter 6, §§6.1.2, 6.1.4, 6.7). The dragon's human impulses here (desire for a human woman) and humanoid manifestation can also be paralleled from ancient hagiographical narratives. Indeed, in the earliest extant hagiographical dragon fight-proper, that of the *Acts of Thomas* (later ii AD), we have a *drakōn* falling in love with a human woman, or at any rate claiming to have done so. Similarly, we have seen a number of cases in which ancient hagiographical dragons can manifest themselves in humanoid form, beginning with the Dragon of the Rocks and his associates in the *Acts of Philip* (mid- to late iv AD). Even so, Jeffreys is probably right that the significance of the term *drakōn* here partly leans towards that of the modern Greek term *drakos*.[5]

9.1.2 *Callimachus and Chrysorrhoe* (i): Introduction

We have two witnesses to what was evidently the open and perhaps partly oral tradition of the Byzantine-romance poem *Callimachus and Chrysorrhoe*: an anonymous full telling of it, at 2,607 lines, preserved in an early sixteenth-century AD manuscript in Leiden,[6] and an early fourteenth-century summary by Manuel Philes of a telling of it that had recently been written by Andronikos (Komnenos

---

[5] Jeffreys 1998 ad loc.
[6] For the text, see Pichard 1956, with French translation; for an English translation, see Betts 1995:33–93; for further discussion, see Beaton 1989:101–2, 107–9, 115–17, 144–9, 185–7, 190–4; Aerts 2003:384–7.

Branas Doukas Angelos) Palaiologos, the cousin of the Byzantine emperor.[7] So we know that the tradition had come together by this point.[8] But the manuscript version is unlikely to represent (or simply to represent) Andronikos' version, because Philes' summary of the latter shows that it treated some episodes slightly differently to the manuscript,[9] featured some minor episodes not found in the manuscript,[10] and presented the whole as a cloying religious allegory hard to reconcile with the manuscript's secularity and eroticism.[11]

Even without the evidence of the summary, the anonymous poem, our focus henceforth, tells us of its own accord that it swam in a sea of variant versions. It resembles the *Odyssey* in that it preserves within itself narrative sign-posts that at first sight lead to dead ends, the ghosts of alternative story-paths not taken. As with the *Odyssey*, the reason for this must lie in the pressure of the rich competing traditions (and perhaps too largely oral ones) behind the version of the poem with which we are actually presented. And, also as with the *Odyssey*, the effect is an enchanting one, conferring a degree of animation upon the narrative thread that we are actually given, and conferring upon it too something of the mysterious effect of a hall of mirrors.[12]

Coincidentally, the poem also salutes the *Odyssey* in its themes and broad structure. In its relatively fast-moving first half the hero travels to a strange and mysterious place to encounter a man-eating monster (cf. the Cyclops) and a shape-conjuring witch (cf. Circe), whilst also having time to enjoy enchanted gardens (cf. those of Alcinous) and a dalliance (cf. Calypso). The second half of the poem slows to relate a minutely observed domestic drama, in which the hero disguises himself as a beggarly man in order to penetrate a palace with the aid of one of its old retainers (cf. Eumaeus), and by this means re-establishes contact with the queen, his lost wife (cf. Penelope); the tale closes with a striking female execution (cf. Odysseus' maids).

There is no real indication as to when or where in the world the poem's action takes place. The love-rival king is said to enjoy visiting 'the monuments of the Greeks' (l. 857), but it is not clear whether his interest is an internal one or an external one, and it may in any case be that the phrase is deployed merely in a generic way to signify 'ancient monuments' tout court. Camels, bathhouses, and eunuchs may strike the modern western reader as distinctively middle eastern, but all were at home in Byzantine society.

---

[7] Manuel Philes *Epigram on a Book of Romance by the Emperor's Cousin*; discussion at Knös 1962, with the text of the epigram reproduced at pp.280–4; cf. also Pichard 1956:xvi–xxiii; Beaton 1989:101–2, 190–2; Betts 1995:33; and Aerts 2003:386. Manuel neither supplies a title for the poem he is summarizing nor names any of the characters in it.

[8] For further precision, see Pichard 1956:xxiii–xxviii.

[9] Notably the episode of the recognition-token ring (ll. 74–7).

[10] E.g. before they arrive at the Dragon's castle, the three brothers capture some cities and the hero kills a lion (ll. 45–9).

[11] *Epigram* lines 84–115.

[12] These points are articulated slightly differently at Betts 1995:34.

9.1.3 *Callimachus and Chrysorrhoe* (ii): Summary

The course of the poem runs as follows. A king decides to bestow his kingdom upon whichever of his three sons, of whom Callimachus is the youngest, makes the greatest achievement.[13] All three go out into the world together with the army he has given them. Eventually they come across a great mountain, which takes them three months to climb. On the summit, higher than the birds, they find a plateau on which there sits a magnificent castle built from gold and precious stones, and guarded by dragons and serpents:[14]

> Before the shut gates stood living snakes, great snakes, frightening supernatural beasts, keen, unsleeping guards of the great castle, terrifying dragons, gate-keeping creatures. If one had seen them, one would have died simply through fear alone.   *Callimachus and Chrysorrhoe* 189–93[15]

Only Callimachus is brave enough to approach the castle, which he does by borrowing a magic ring from his eldest brother, and this allows him, upon taking it into his mouth, to grow wings and fly over the heads of the guardian monsters and the castle wall.

Callimachus wanders through the castle's fabulous rooms, gardens, and baths and at last comes to its master's special room. Here he finds a beautiful girl, Chrysorrhoe, naked (as we will subsequently learn)[16] and suspended by her hair from the ceiling. He falls in love with her:

> [448] *He reveals, with lamentation, how the girl was hanging.*
>
> For in the middle of it [the Dragon's decorated ceiling]—but it is so painful to tell!—a girl was hanging by her hair, all alone. It rocks my senses, it rocks my mind! By her hair! Ah! An insane thing dreamed up by Fortune! The girl was hanging by her hair.... I silence myself—there, I silence myself, and I proceed to record this with a deadened heart. A girl full of charm was hanging by her hair. As soon as that third son gazed directly at her there on her own, the third son, Callimachus, that beautiful and desirable man, that man of daring, capable, and

---

[13] We need not doubt that the greatest prowess is that shown by Callimachus, but he never returns to his homeland to claim his prize, preferring to tarry rather in the Dragon's luxurious and automatic castle; nor indeed are we told the resolution of this competition: did the original kingdom then go to one of Callimachus' other brothers?

[14] For the motif of the castle as a distinctive post-Frankish (i.e. post-Fourth Crusade) motif in the Greek romance tradition, see Betts 1995:xxiv.

[15] Cf. Ulrich von Zatzikhoven *Lanzelet* l. 5048 (*c.* AD 1195–1200), where the castle in which the wicked Valerin has imprisoned Guinevere (as Chrysorrhoe is imprisoned here) is said to be surrounded by a forest of serpents, a 'worm-garden' (*würmegarte*).

[16] The author oddly delays telling us that Chrysorrhoe had been naked from the first as she hung. And indeed, both she and the supposedly chivalrous Callimachus themselves are curiously slow to address the matter of her modesty even after her rescue: they exchange a good deal of conversation

determined heart, at once he was rooted to the spot as if made of stone.[17] All he could do was gaze at her; he stood there just gazing; she too, he declared, was one of the illustrations. To such an extent does beauty have the power to grab souls, to snatch tongues and voices, and to stop hearts. Gazing at all the charms and the outstanding beauty of the woman, the virgin girl, he stood there gazing at her directly, his heart stolen. He stood there gazing, without being able to speak, for two reasons: he was dumbfounded by her beauty, and he felt sympathy for her pain. He just let forth a groan from his afflicted soul.

Callimachus and Chrysorrhoe 448–69

She urges him to hide before the castle's master, the great man-eating Dragon, returns. Upon his return, the Dragon whips Chrysorrhoe with a willow twig before briefly allowing her to rest her feet on a golden stool whilst she eats the morsel of bread and drinks the single gulp of water he permits her. He then gorges himself on a personal banquet. He falls asleep after his meal, whereupon Callimachus emerges from hiding to kill him and chop him in two with his own sword, burning the carcass:

'…This is the abode of a Dragon [*drakōn*], the house of a man-eater. Do you not hear the thunder, do you not see the lightning-bolts? He is coming! Why are you just standing there now? He is coming! Flee now, hide yourself! He is an ogre [*drakos*] in his strength, this child of a man-eater! If you hide and conceal yourself, just perhaps, you will save your life. Do you see the silver basin lying over there? If you get yourself underneath and shelter under it, just perhaps, you will escape the Dragon's irresistible strength. Flee, get down, hide, keep quiet! He is coming now.' He took the girl's advice and obeyed her words, as she hung there by the hair. He hid immediately, concealing himself under the basin.

---

before the matter is raised, and even then Callimachus busies himself with disposing of the Dragon's body before finding her something to wear (she is released at l. 581; she draws attention to her nakedness and asks for clothes at ll. 629–31; Callimachus finally gives her a dress at l. 643). A much later digression (ll. 1550–63) contains another oddity, in that it now tells us that the dress with which Callimachus had clothed Chrysorrhoe had the magical ability to heal any wounds and bruises it covered, even seemingly fatal ones. It is curious that this interesting and important detail should be withheld for so long after the episode of Chrysorrhoe's release and recovery, but it is also barely compatible with that former episode, for we are told in it, to good effect, sympathetic and erotic alike, of Callimachus' soothing of Chrysorrhoe's wounds in the all-important bath they go on to share (ll. 775–8). Perhaps the release-and-recovery episode as we have it results from the imperfect merging of two variants: in the one Chrysorrhoe is initially naked, given a non-magical dress by Callimachus with appropriate promptitude and then healed by him in the bath; in the other a non-naked Chrysorrhoe is, at a slower pace, re-clothed and healed by Callimachus with the magic dress discovered in due course amongst the Dragon's belongings.

[17] The author delays the introduction of Callimachus' name until this line (l.457), a full fifth of the way through the poem of which he has been the focus from the start. But the name is introduced at a significant point, as the hero first catches sight of Chrysorrhoe and falls in love with her. It is as if his love for her creates his identity.

[501] *The Dragon's arrival in that chamber.*

The Dragon came; he arrived with inhuman thoughts. Who could describe, with calm mind and iron heart, the dragon's inhuman frenzy? Who could write of his iron mind, his implacable heart, who could put the Dragon's guts of stone into words? He took up a willow branch that was lying there and subjected the hanging girl to a prolonged whipping with it, right down to her feet, from her head to the tips of her toes. Eros sat enthroned there, in painted form, the inflamer of people's insides, the enslaver of hard hearts, but he was unable to kindle the Dragon's heart, he was unable to soften his hard mind.[18] The Dragon's hardness escaped the fire of love. For the Dragon had no fear of Eros' flame or bow. After that terrible punishment, the Dragon, in his inhuman fashion, brought an all-gold stool to place under that woman's golden feet. With difficulty, the girl was just about able to set her feet on the stool. However, her hair was not released from the ceiling even during this time.

[521] *Observe the food given to the beautiful girl by the Dragon.*

He brought a morsel of bread and gave it to her, hardly anything to speak of, and water, just a single gulp, no more than that, in a cup made of precious stone, true emerald. In truth, he was preserving her only for further punishment. She drank the water, in a state of agony from her sufferings—from her sufferings, from her tortures, and from hanging by her hair. At once the Dragon removed the stool from under her feet, and once again the girl was hanging by her hair.

[530] *Observe the Dragon's words, his order, his command, and all the instantaneous service he received. Learn this, and wonder upon hearing it.*

A small bed—a precious one, you would say—lay in that Dragon's amazing chamber, or rather the girl's torture-chamber and prison. You would not be far off the mark to call the chamber an instrument of torture. The small bed lay there, low, raised just a little from the floor, made from precious stones. The Dragon sat alone on the bed and gave an order, and all at once the table came of its own accord with precious foods for the insatiable Dragon's mouth. He devoured a great deal, and struggled to sate himself. For he had no compassion for the hanging girl. Once he was satisfied, the Dragon reclined and went to sleep.

[545] *Learn about the Dragon's sleep and his killing—a deep and fatal sleep, as you will learn from the story.*

---

[18] Eros apparently forms the centrepiece of the hall's decorated ceiling. His presence puts us in mind of the Cupid and Pysche episode of Apuleius' *Metamorphoses* (esp. 5.1-23): here too we have a marvellous palace, similarly bedecked with jewels and gold, and in a remote and inaccessible place; a beautiful ingenue, Psyche, detained in it; animated furniture, no, but a retinue of invisible serving-girls; and the palace's master, and the girl's admirer, is mendaciously claimed by her wicked sisters to be a great serpent (*serpens, coluber*).

When the girl saw that the Dragon was asleep, very drunk, sated, and content, and that he was snoring as he slept, completely extended—for the sleep was induced by the food and the large quantity of drink—so when Chrysorrhoe then saw the Dragon in a deep sleep, completely insensible...

[553] *Chrysorrhoe's words to the man in hiding.*

...she said to the man in hiding, 'Man, are you alive in a state of terror, or are you dead? Do not be afraid, but rather show more courage! Come out now! Do not be frightened, if, by chance, you have recovered from the sight of all my tortures and your fear of the beast. Come out quickly, kill the beast at once!'

At her voice he came out, fearfully. The girl said to him, 'Don't be timid in any way! See, this is your opportunity: kill the beast whilst he sleeps. In the first place, save your own skin and your own life! You carry a sword: draw it, and strike the man-eater! You be the slayer of the slayer of so many men, and bring darkness to the eyes of the one that has cast a pall of darkness over my heart!'

He got up, groaned, drew his sword and, with a fine action, with a fine act of bravery, struck the sleeping Dragon with as much strength as he was able to. However, the Dragon was not roused by the blow. The girl groaned and said to Callimachus, 'Cast aside your sword, which is worth little more than a piece of wood, lest we soon be killed. Take the key from his pillow. Do you see the Dragon's wall-cupboard there? Open the wall-cupboard: you will find the Dragon's sword within. It has a fine spinel-stone handle. If you have the strength to wield it, if you do not tremble from fear, if you can stand your ground and strike the beast with it, you will chop him in two.'

He took the key from the pillow and opened the Dragon's wall-cupboard. He took the Dragon's sword from within and struck him with it, rending him in two at once. And so he freed the hanging girl, delivered her tortured body from pain, and liberated her fine, lovely, well-formed, beautiful body from its confinement and its bitter sufferings.   *Callimachus and Chrysorrhoe* 489–584

He liberates Chrysorrhoe and (eventually) clothes her, and for a brief time they live a blessed life of love and luxury together in the splendid castle, making the most of its breath-taking baths and gardens, with Callimachus soothing Chrysorrhoe's wounds in the former.[19] In the course of this Chrysorrhoe tells Callimachus how the Dragon had fallen in love with her and compelled her parents to surrender her to him. This he had done by withholding the water upon which their kingdom

---

[19] The author's discretion and tendency to euphemistic periphrasis renders it unclear at precisely what point we are to imagine that the union is actually consummated: probably after Callimachus has soothed Chrysorrhoe's wounds in the bath, when he is said to 'pick the sweet flower of pleasure' (l. 781), but the modern English imagery of defloration may mislead here.

depended, which flowed down from his mountain. They, perforce, had consented to the union, but she herself had not. Hence the continuing programme of torture that Callimachus had witnessed:

'Because I was the fair and noble daughter of a wealthy, splendid, and respected ruling family, this Dragon fell in love with my beauty—where is my beauty now?—and wanted to marry me. He compelled my parents, the king and queen, to make this bitter alliance and unnatural marriage. They made the arrangement for fear of the beast. For he prevented the water from the river that flows from the summit of the mountain from coming down to my father's kingdom, lands, and castles. For my inhuman fortune had contrived this: that across the whole of my parents' empire there should not be any other water, just this river alone, and that it should be under the control of this insane Dragon. They spoke with him, then made the arrangement, but I would not obey. The terrible beast... [lacuna].... Rather, he reverted to his dragon-type and all at once he sucked down all the animals of my parents' land like a cup of water. And still he wanted to marry me and again he sought my hand. They did not want to give me, and raised their lament. This made him angry and inflamed his dragon nature. Again he threatened me and tried to compel me to marry him. But whatever he did, I refused the marriage. Not even in a dream would I want to live with a dragon. So then, all at once, he sucked everybody down: the small, the large, the men, the women, the old people, and the children too, just everybody; he left no one behind. They went from his tongue to his gullet to his belly. And then my parents and masters, the rulers themselves—oh disaster, grief, oh outrage! How was it that I was left behind, how is it that I live, that I am still here now?—he ate them, he gobbled them down and that was the end of them. He left me behind, utterly bereft of hope. The one kindness he did them is that he gobbled them down on their own and killed them on their own, separately from the common people and the aristocrats. Oh outrage! How was it that the foul belly of the all-consuming Dragon did not split or burst open at that time? So what happened after their death? What happened after all this? He seized me and wanted to have me against my will. But I refused to obey him in any way, and was subjected to such great suffering. After all those tortures and all that pain, I triumphed over the Dragon's pitiless heart: I have kept myself an undefiled virgin to this very day.' *Callimachus and Chrysorrhoe* 648–93

Some time later an unnamed king ascends the mountain and catches sight of Chrysorrhoe at a window of the castle, and also of Callimachus. He determines to dispose of the protector and take her for himself. His army refuses to attack the castle, for fear of the monsters, but an old witch approaches him and offers her services. She lures Callimachus out of the castle by putting herself into the clutches of a phantom dragon she has magicked up and by screaming for help.[20] Callimachus runs out to her rescue and kills the dragon:

[1281] *Yes, evil fate, yes, crazed fortune, accomplish your desire quickly, do not delay!*

He ran and leaped towards the cry, and he heard a whistle. A terrible dragon emerged from the wood. The old woman had manufactured it by a trick with her magic. It held the old woman in its mouth and was on the point of devouring her. With an evil look the dragon watched him approach in all his courage and with his sword drawn so that he could wield it. It put the old woman down and rushed at him at once. Callimachus in turn rushed at the dragon. He hit it with his sword and immediately struck its head off. But it was just a magical contrivance, a device, and an illusion.   *Callimachus and Chrysorrhoe 1281–92*

The old woman now pretends to thank him by throwing a golden apple to him. But it is a magic apple that kills anyone who clutches it to their breast (whilst rousing back to life any dead person to whose nose it is applied). On catching the apple, Callimachus automatically brings it to his breast, and falls dead. The king seizes the distraught Chrysorrhoe, who has run out after Callimachus, and takes her off to his kingdom to be his queen.[21]

Meanwhile, Callimachus' brothers learn from dreams that he is in peril and come to find his body, together with the apple. An inscription on the apple explains its revivifying properties, of which they immediately make use. Callimachus, restored to life, now wanders the world alone to find Chrysorrhoe. He eventually comes to a land where all the people, young and old, are compelled by their new young queen to wear clothes of mourning, as she grieves for her lost love. She is misunderstood by the locals to have been the daughter of a dragon and, accordingly, repeatedly designated a *drakaina* by them.[22] Callimachus realizes that the queen must be Chrysorrhoe. He infiltrates her palace grounds by disguising himself as a poor man and prevailing upon the gardener to take him on as his labourer. He indicates his presence to Chrysorrhoe by leaving a ring she has given him on a tree for her to find. Chrysorrhoe has a pavilion built in the garden in which, now reunited with Callimachus, she holds secret trysts with him. But their secret is in due course revealed to the king by a maid and the court

---

[20] Frustratingly, there is a seemingly large lacuna at the heart of this episode (between ll. 1261 and 1262), and it may be that we have lost a detailed account of the method by which the witch was able to conjure up the phantom dragon, no doubt with the help of her familiar demons. A pity indeed. Perhaps a page was destroyed at some point in the manuscript tradition precisely because it contained such material.

[21] This episode bears a broad similarity with the central episode of another Byzantine romance, *Libistros and Rhodamne* (S1600-1731; xiv AD). Here Libistros is living a life of bliss with his wife Rhodamne in their Silver Castle when a disappointed suitor of the girl, Berderichos, king of Egypt, employs a witch of his country (somewhat reminiscent of the Old Woman of Bessa at Heliodorus *Aethiopica* 6.12–15) to paralyse Libistros so that he can carry her off home. For the text, see Kriaras 1955:85–130; for a translation, see Betts 1995:95–185.

[22] *Callimachus and Chrysorrhoe* 1515, 1539–40, 1587. Cf. Chapter 3, §3.3.

eunuchs. The pair are put on trial, but Chrysorrhoe, speaking in her own defence, persuades the king to see the justice of their case and have pity on them. He releases them to return to their life of bliss in the Dragon's castle. The witch, meanwhile, is burned at the stake, and the poem comes to an end.[23]

9.1.4 *Callimachus and Chrysorrhoe* (iii): The Poem's Dragons

What can we say of the form and nature of the great man-eating Dragon (*drakōn*) himself? Frustratingly, there is no attempt to supply a physical description of the narrative's most interesting character, and it is not entirely clear how the author envisages him, or whether indeed he has a stable conception of him. There are a number of indications that he is a dragon of traditional form, i.e. a large fiery serpent:[24]

- He is described repeatedly as a 'beast' (*thērion*).[25]
- The nature of his associates. The creatures that guard his castle are themselves also described as dragons (*drakontes*),[26] as great snakes (*opheis*),[27] and as beasts (*thēria*).[28] These are no doubt serpents of a traditional guardian sort. Such is indicated by their unsleeping nature, which resembles that of the great guardian serpents of Greek myth, Ladon and the Colchis Dragon (Chapter 1, §§1.2.3–4).[29] They also recall the two sets of traditional snakes and dragons that guard the gate to the city of Ophiorhyme in the *Acts of Philip*[30] and more generally, of course, the serpent brood over which the great dragon often presides in a hagiographical context (Chapter 7, §7.1). Furthermore, Callimachus' eldest brother conjectures, on sight of these snakes, that they are presided over by a 'man-eating *drakōn*-king',[31] whilst the love-rival king's attendants eventually raise the hypotheses that the castle's interior is inhabited either by normal human beings or by dragons and

---

[23] One of the frustrations of the romance is that the witch is not allowed to answer the rival king's excellent question to her before she is burned: why indeed did she give her magic apple a double power, to confer life as well as to kill (ll. 2578–87)? Perhaps because she wasn't all bad and didn't see why Callimachus should not be allowed to live again once Chrysorrhoe had been taken from him. Indeed, the Dragon aside, no character in the romance is wholly bad: even the rival king does the right thing by Callimachus and Chrysorrhoe in the end, whilst his eunuchs and his maid, for all that the author designates them as wicked, act merely out of loyalty to the king and on the basis of what (given what they know) they believe to be right.

[24] For a rather less committed discussion of this issue, see Betts 1995:35, who does, however, compare *Digenis Akritis*' *drakōn*.

[25] *Callimachus and Chrysorrhoe* 557, 560, 576, 654, 664.

[26] *Callimachus and Chrysorrhoe* 192, 904.

[27] *Callimachus and Chrysorrhoe* 189, 204, 218, 904, 961, 1034, 1053, 1185.

[28] *Callimachus and Chrysorrhoe* 963, 998, 1001; cf. 913.

[29] *Callimachus and Chrysorrhoe* 191, 905, 1148.

[30] Philip ([a], mid- to late iv A D).   [31] *Callimachus and Chrysorrhoe* 221.

beasts 'just like' the (serpentine) gate-wardens.[32] These hypotheses are surely designed to reflect precisely the castle's situations before and after Callimachus' slaying of the great Dragon, and thereby they tell us that the great Dragon did indeed resemble in form the lesser snakes that guarded him.

• Similarly, there is no reason to doubt the traditional anguiform nature of the poem's second significant *drakōn*, the phantom one magicked up by the witch. This is imagined by Callimachus to be a creature of 'marauding savagery' (*lēistrikēn ōmotētan*) and to be able to hold the witch in its mouth.[33]

• The Dragon's approach is heralded by thunder and lightning. This recalls Digenis Akritis' dragon in both respects, whilst the lightning more specifically recalls the fire breathed out by or flashed from the eyes of a traditional *drakōn* (see Chapter 1, §1.7, Chapter 6, §6.1.4).[34] It is possible that both of these associations also carry a demonic resonance, for when the author subsequently pours out a torrent of abuse about the witch, 'the vessel of demons', he describes her as, inter alia, 'a companion of lightning and a mother of thunder'.[35]

• When the Dragon relaxes in sleep after gorging himself on his food and drink, he is said to be 'completely extended' or 'completely unfurled', literally 'completely unfolded into a single layer' (*exaplōmenon holōs*).[36] This gesture, which seems to be particularly at home with a creature of serpentine form, is associated with other dragons in other contexts: it is associated with Theodore Tyron's old-man *drakōn* ([h], xiv AD or earlier) as it departs from the throne on which it has been sitting, and it is associated with Digenis Akritis' dragon as it stretches itself out in death (in the latter case the very same verb is used—*hēplōthē*; see Table 9.1 below).[37]

• The manner of the final dispatch of the Dragon, the chopping of him in two, is suggestive of an elongated serpentine body, and in particular makes appeal to the hagiographical motif of the hacking up of the body of a slain dragon into portions so that each part can be removed from harm's way more easily (see Chapter 6, §6.7).[38]

• The Dragon's marauding depredations upon the animals and people of the land alike are typical of the classical and hagiographical anguiform dragon (see Chapter 1, §1.7, Chapter 6, §6.1.1), and the reference to the people

---

[32] *Callimachus and Chrysorrhoe* 913–14.   [33] *Callimachus and Chrysorrhoe* 1264, 1286.
[34] *Callimachus and Chrysorrhoe* 490.   [35] *Callimachus and Chrysorrhoe* 1305.
[36] *Callimachus and Chrysorrhoe* 549.
[37] The normally unsleeping Colchis dragon similarly stretches itself out to sleep at Apollonius *Argonautica* 4.166; cf. p. 16. However, given that a normal snake would curl itself up to sleep, the unfurling gesture properly fits the *Digenis Akritis* dragon's death rather better. In the case of the *Callimachus and Chrysorrhoe* Dragon the gesture salutes at once both his anguiform shape and his partly human modus operandi and mentality humans lying flat out to sleep. We should note that in this same text precisely the same phrase (*exaplōmenon holōs*) is subsequently applied, in a somewhat awkward calque, to the fully human Callimachus himself when the witch kills him with her golden apple (l. 1313). At this point we must, perforce, render it along the lines of 'laid out completely flat'.
[38] *Callimachus and Chrysorrhoe* 575, 580.

Table 9.1 Theodore Tyron, Callimachus, and Digenis Akritis

Motif	Miracle and story of... Theodore Tyron... (xiv AD or before)	Callimachus and Chrysorrhoe (early xiv AD)	Digenis Akritis (ix–x AD)
Initial city presided over by benign king.	Nameless city presided over by King Samuel	Nameless city presided over by Callimachus' father, the king	—
King thereof, promoter of the hero's prowess.	Theodore is King Samuel's great champion; the king celebrates his victory over the Saracens (to the neglect of the Dragon)	The king tells his three sons to go out into the world to achieve feats of greatness, to determine the succession	—
Dragon-proper controls waters.	Weak spring on which King Samuel's city depends flows from Dragon-proper's cave	River upon which Chrysorrhoe's city depends flows down from the Dragon-proper's mountain	Dragon possesses or lives in spring
Dragon-proper falls in love with beautiful local young woman.	Dragon-proper falls in love with Theodore's young mother	Dragon-proper falls in love with Chrysorrhoe	Dragon is seized with desire for general Doukas' daughter
Dragon-proper uses his control of the water to force the woman into his physical power.	Theodore's mother approaches the Dragon-proper's spring out of pity for her horses, where he snatches her	Dragon-proper attempts to compel Chrysorrhoe's parents to give her to him by withholding water from their city	The dragon attempts first to seduce and then to rape Doukas' daughter as, feeling thirsty, she takes water from his spring and dips her feet in it
Woman is kept over protracted period.	In comfortable circumstances: the Dragon-proper fetches a skin for her to sit on and human company for her	In circumstances of torture: she is hung naked by her hair from a ceiling and subjected to cyclical whipping	—
A host of snakes of different types guards the Dragon-proper's home and its prisoner within.	Theodore's mother guarded within Dragon-proper's cave by; (1) an old-man dragon; (2) an abominable asp; (3) twelve snakes in a circle; (4) other lesser reptiles	Dragon-proper's castle, where Chrysorrhoe is held, is guarded without by 'beasts': (1) dragons; (2) other snakes	—
Interior of Dragon-proper's home is decorated with luxurious furniture.	Golden throne	Extended descriptions of the Dragon-proper's golden and bejewelled luxuries, including tables and bowls	—

Continued

Table 9.1 *Continued*

Motif	Miracle and story of... Theodore Tyron... (xiv AD or before)	Callimachus and Chrysorrhoe (early xiv AD)	Digenis Akritis (ix–x AD)
Humanoid behaviours by dragons.	Old-man dragon sits on golden throne; possibility that he manifests himself in human form; use of gate by Dragon-proper	Dragon-proper makes direct use of human luxuries, specifically stool, cup, table, bed, and pillow; also possesses luxurious bowls, swords, baths, and gardens; uses whip to torture Chrysorrhoe	Dragon manifests himself in the form of a beautiful young man
Dragon-proper is three-headed.	Dragon-proper has three heads	—	Dragon has three heads
Dragon-proper is fiery.	Furnace-like blasts from mouth	Dragon-proper's arrival preceded by lightning	Dragon shoots forth lightning-like flame from each head
Dragon-proper moves with sound of thunder.	—	Dragon-proper's arrival preceded by thunder	Dragon moves with sound of thunder
Hero penetrates Dragon-proper's home in his absence and waits for his return in order to attack him in it.	Having slaughtered the lesser-serpent guards, Theodore waits for Dragon-proper to return to his cave	Having flown over the lesser-serpent guards, Callimachus conceals himself in the castle to ambush the Dragon-proper on Chrysorrhoe's advice	—
Attempts to dissuade hero, and to encourage him.	King Samuel attempts to dissuade Theodore from going up against the Dragon-proper	Chrysorrhoe tells Callimachus to hide before the Dragon-proper returns, before then encouraging him to attack him as he sleeps	—
Hero kills Dragon-proper with sword.	Theodore kills Dragon-proper with sword (and so too the lesser serpents)	Callimachus kills Dragon-proper with his own sword	Digenis kills dragon by striking it on all three heads with a sword
Hero disposes of Dragon-proper's carcass.	Theodore prays to God, who has Gabriel wash the dragon's carcass away with a newly formed torrent	Callimachus hacks up carcass with the sword and carries it away	Digenis orders his boys to remove the carcass
A dragon unfurls itself (a motif with transferable significance).	The old-man dragon unfurls itself to return from human form to serpent form (?): καὶ ὁ γέρων ἐτανύθη, ὥστε μηκέτι τὸν ἄνθρωπον αὐτὸν θεωρῆσαι.	Dragon-proper unfurls itself to stretch out in drunken sleep—ἐξαπλωμένον ὅλος.	Dragon unfurls itself on the ground in death—πρὸς γῆν ἡπλώθη.

disappearing down his 'gullet' (*laimos*) in particular seems well suited to a serpent.[39] Chrysorrhoe is admittedly speaking metaphorically when she talks of Callimachus having 'entered the jaws (*stomata*) of the Dragon' in penetrating his castle, but the metaphor surely makes significant appeal to the notion of a voracious serpent, rather than to a monster of more humanoid shape.[40]

- The Dragon's destructive control of a water-source, in this case a river is typical of a hagiographical dragon (see Chapter 6, §6.1.2; cf. Chapter 1, §1.7).[41]
- Chrysorrhoe's surprise that the Dragon's belly did not split or burst open after he had devoured every living thing in her parents' kingdom makes appeal to the propensity of classical and especially Christian serpents and dragons to be burst open (Chapter 6, §6.6.1). An appeal to the bursting open of the Margaret of Antioch's dragon upon devouring her ([a]–[f]) might be thought to lie particularly close at hand.[42]

There are contradictory indications of the Dragon's size. The thunder that precedes his arrival suggests that he is huge, as does his ability to suck down all the animals and all the people of a kingdom at single sittings. But after killing him Callimachus is said to carry him out of the chamber on his shoulders;[43] however, he has of course been chopped in half (at least) by this point.

Does the Dragon have wings? None are mentioned, but they would certainly have facilitated his travel to and from his inaccessible, pathless castle—and we recall that Callimachus himself flies into it, using his magic ring.[44]

As is manifest from all the luxuries and accoutrements of his castle, the Dragon lives an emphatically human lifestyle. Is he thereby a *drakos* in part? On one occasion the term *drakos* is actually applied to him: 'he is a *drakos* in his strength.'[45] The creature has only just been introduced for the first time three lines earlier as a *drakōn*, and so it makes little sense now to say of him, in effect, 'he is a *drakōn* in his strength.'[46] Rather, *drakos* should carry a differentiated meaning here. Admittedly, given that the expression is ostensibly metaphorical, our author ought not to be signing up to the creature's full identity with a *drakos*: strictly speaking, if the *drakōn* metaphorically has the strength of a *drakos*, he ought not actually to be one in fact.

What of other potential humanoid attributes? Does the Dragon have hands? Callimachus' actual reference to the Dragon's hands is purely metaphorical (and

[39] *Callimachus and Chrysorrhoe* 666–7 (*laimos*), 674–7.
[40] *Callimachus and Chrysorrhoe* 588; cf. 738.
[41] *Callimachus and Chrysorrhoe* 655–63.   [42] *Callimachus and Chrysorrhoe* 686–7.
[43] *Callimachus and Chrysorrhoe* 639.   [44] *Callimachus and Chrysorrhoe* 271–9.
[45] *Callimachus and Chrysorrhoe* 492. However, Pichard 1956 ad loc. considered the use of the term merely to be an insignificant variation of *drakōn*. We may also note that dragons are twice associated closely with demons elsewhere in the poem (1035–6, 1040).
[46] At least, such an argument would be a compelling one in the case of a less pervasively repetitive author than the present one. And indeed the phrase could just about be construed to mean 'he is every bit as strong as you would expect him to be, given that he is *drakōn*'.

in a rather less complicated way than with *drakos*): he speaks of Chrysorrhoe being delivered (sc. by fortune) 'into the hands' of the inhuman Dragon.[47] Whilst the Dragon lives in a palace suitable for humans and full of human paraphernalia as we have just noted, e.g. his bed and pillow,[48] he does not necessarily need hands to manipulate it, given that the accoutrements are enchanted or animated. This is already implied with the description of the seemingly self-running bathhouse furnace,[49] and becomes explicit with the introduction of the table that delivers food to the Dragon of its own accord.[50] It should be made clear that these objects are inherently enchanted, and are not subject to telekinesis on the Dragon's part. This is why Callimachus, eventual inheritor of the castle, can open its great gates with a word alone.[51] However, before the introduction of the table, and the marvellous revelation it brings with it, we have been told that the Dragon whips Chrysorrhoe with a willow branch, sets a golden stool under her feet, gives her a cup to drink from and removes the stool again.[52] If these things are accomplished without enchantment, does he need hands to do them? None are mentioned, but it is just possible to imagine that he holds these three objects in his mouth.

Can the Dragon speak? Seemingly so. He gives an order to his animated table, he snores in his drunken sleep, and Chrysorrhoe's account of his (failed) wooing of her probably entails a spoken suit. This is a human enough trait, but one not completely alien to hagiographical dragons, as is already the case with the Dragon of India encountered by Thomas (later ii AD), and the Dragon of the Rocks encountered by Philip ([a], mid- to late iv AD).

And the Dragon does have something of a personality. Despite everything, he is not wholly unchivalrous: he takes genocide in his stride, but cannot contemplate rape. The goal of all the horrors he perpetrates is to secure Chrysorrhoe's consent to their union. Since he is unable to achieve this, she remains a virgin when he is killed.[53] He is also careful to respect social hierarchies, making a point of gobbling down the royal family separately from the common people, albeit possibly with a hint of irony.[54]

9.1.5 Theodore Tyron Compared

We may now compare with *Callimachus and Chrysorrhoe* the late Theodore Tyron narrative, the remarkable *Miracle and Story of the Saint and Glorious*

---

[47] *Callimachus and Chrysorrhoe* 626.
[48] *Callimachus and Chrysorrhoe* 571.
[49] *Callimachus and Chrysorrhoe* 349–54.
[50] *Callimachus and Chrysorrhoe* 540.
[51] *Callimachus and Chrysorrhoe* 1280.
[52] *Callimachus and Chrysorrhoe* 507–9, 517–18, 522–5, 528.
[53] *Callimachus and Chrysorrhoe* 693.
[54] *Callimachus and Chrysorrhoe* 683–5; cf. Pichard 1956 ad loc.

Great-Martyr Theodore Tyron, Concerning his Mother being Taken Captive by the Dragon ([h], xiv A D or before).[55] This tells how the city of King Samuel depends upon a weak spring emanating from a cave in which a Dragon has made his home.[56] He now has to ransom access to the spring, by sacrificing to the Dragon twelve bulls, twenty-five rams, and an unspecified number of other animals on each occasion. But one day he is distracted by a victory of Theodore, his favourite soldier, over the Saracens, and neglects the offering, with the result that the dragon revokes access to the spring, and his people are deprived of water. In despair, and out of pity for the horses in particular, Theodore's mother—a dim refraction of the matronly Eusebia figure in the earlier Theodore tradition—takes upon herself the courage of a man and approaches the spring with her own horse and a water jar. The spring is located in a region 'terrible and fearful, with holes and clefts and entrances and exits for unnumbered reptiles'. The Dragon notices that she is 'a girl [*korē*] lovely in her youthfulness, shapely to look at and completely beautiful'. This is an odd way to describe the mother of an established soldier: it is as if she has morphed into the role of the virgin ingenue played by George's princess Sabra. The Dragon accordingly conceives a desire to snatch her, though he sets about it in a curiously passive way. On her third visit to the spring she hears the dragon hissing at the door of his cave and faints, whereupon he carries her inside, securing the door behind. Her servants realize what has happened when they find the horse and the water jar abandoned, and alert Theodore. The next morning, he arms himself and heads off to the cave to fight the Dragon, despite the king's attempts to stop him for his own sake. When he sees that he cannot shake Theodore's resolve, he relents and prays to God to protect him in his endeavour. The king follows Theodore to the cave and sits down outside waiting for him to return from it; when, after three days, Theodore has not reappeared, he returns to his palace and asks his priests to pray for him. Meanwhile:

Theodore penetrated to the inner cave and to the lair of the Dragon,[57] and he found there his mother in the form of a girl sitting on a stool and twelve snakes in a circle around her and an abominable asp lay before her. An old-man dragon [*gerōn drakōn*][58] was sitting on a golden throne and other reptiles too, great and small, were guarding the girl. Theodore was terrified at the sight of them. Seeing his mother's beauty again, he wanted to embrace her.

[55] The earliest MS to preserve this text, Θαῦμα καὶ διήγησις τοῦ ἁγίου καὶ ἐνδόξου μεγαλομάρτυρος τοῦ Θεοδώρου Τήρωνος περὶ τῆς μητρὸς αὐτοῦ τῆς αἰχμαλωτισθείσης ὑπὸ τοῦ δράκοντος, is *Codex Vindobonensis historicus graecus* 126, of xiv A D; cf. *AASS* Nov. iv p. 51.
[56] I capitalize 'Dragon' in this exegesis partly to help differentiate the principal and presiding dragon, the 'Dragon-proper', from his minion, the old-man dragon.
[57] Apparently the Dragon has left the door unlocked at this point: there is no need for it, given that his prisoner is guarded within by the serpent host.
[58] Not to be confused with the presiding Dragon, who is distinguished on his return to his cave by the description 'the great Dragon'.

The oddness continues: one perceives the impact here of an erotic narrative in which rescuer and rescued are destined to become lovers. The narrative proceeds:

> As he moved towards her, the snakes roused themselves against him and swelled themselves up over him. The abominable asp hissed and *took her lips to the floor*, whilst the old man unravelled himself, *with the result that he no longer looked like a man*.[59] Each of the small snakes was keen to gobble him down, as one would expect of their wicked nature. Seeing the multitude of reptiles, Theodore, the servant of God, took fear and prayed, saying, 'Lord God.... Give power to my right hand and strengthen my heart, so that I may not hesitate but put to flight these venomous, terrible, and abominable dragons [*drakontes*], to the glory of your holy name, Lord.' He drew his sword and slew the twelve snakes and destroyed the asp and killed the dragon and all his host.

Theodore proceeds to embrace his mother, whereupon the 'great' Dragon, the Dragon-proper, returns. Only at this point, with the narrative being partly focalized through Theodore, are we treated to a physical description of him: he is (a rather modest) 12 cubits in length, but he does boast three heads. He brings with him two little boys and three deerskins so that they can sit with the girl-woman and be company for her. On seeing the devastation of his community, he becomes angry and blows upon them all with furnace-like blasts from his mouth. Theodore prays again, invoking, inter alia, God's preservation of Jonah in the belly of the sea-monster and of Daniel in the lions' den, and proceeds to kill the Dragon with his sword. But in death the Dragon winds himself up and blocks the door so that they cannot escape, nor can anyone else get in. They are trapped for seven days, but eventually God heeds their prayer and sends the angel Gabriel to liberate them from the cave. He does this by breaking the weak spring open into a now torrential flow of water (which presumably washes away both the Dragon's

---

[59] *Καὶ ἡ μιαρὰ ἀσπὶς ἐσύριζεν καὶ ἐδάφιζεν τὰ χείλη αὐτῆς. Καὶ ὁ γέρων ἐτανύθη, ὥστε μηκέτι τὸν ἄνθρωπον αὐτὸν θεωρῆσαι.* I confess myself uncertain as to how to construe the italicized parts of this (corrupt or merely vernacular?) sentence. I am reasonably certain that the asp 'took her lips to the floor', but am puzzled by the metonymy of 'lips' and unclear what the significance of the action might be: perhaps she is threatening Theodore from below, whilst the lesser snakes threaten him from above? I am puzzled to a far greater extent by the phrase I have provisionally translated 'with the result that he no longer looked like a man', which is aggravating, because so much depends on it. The translation that classical syntax at any rate ought to dictate here is rather 'with the result that the man [i.e. Theodore] could no longer see him [i.e. the old-man dragon]'. But in that case it is hard to understand why the dragon's unravelling should prevent Theodore being able to see him, particularly as he then proceeds to slay him effortlessly with his sword, without any intervening episode of revelation. The translation I have opted for, which, at the cost of no little awkwardness, construes the phrase as meaning literally '(with the result that) he [the Dragon] <was> no longer the man for looking at', at least has the virtue of some intelligibility. We no longer need to worry how Theodore is able to see him to kill him. He has certainly been presented in a strongly anthropomorphic way hitherto, as an 'old man' and as sitting on a throne. Does he actually morph between humanoid and serpentine forms?

carcass and the door) and shows Theodore how to sail out of the cave with his mother and the boys. They return to the city, and to the joy of King Samuel.

The Theodore narrative and the *Callimachus* narrative share a central vignette in which the hero penetrates the Dragon-proper's own home, guarded by lesser serpents, in order to rescue a beautiful woman the Dragon has desired and captured, and to kill the Dragon himself with a sword. And here in the Theodore narrative too the Dragon-proper seems to exhibit humanoid affinities, not in form, but by virtue of falling in love with a human woman, understanding human social needs, and inhabiting a home with luxurious furniture (the golden throne) and a door or gate. But there are many further motival correspondences beyond these, which are most efficiently conveyed in the format of a table (Table 9.1). The importance of all these corresponding motifs lies not merely in their number but also in the *systemic* overlap between the *sequences* of them. Both narratives offer a more restricted, though still healthy, series of correspondences with the briefer *Digenis* narrative in turn, despite the intervening cultural rift of the Fourth Crusade and its aftermath. Not the least intriguing point of correspondence in this case is the one motif the Theodore narrative does not share with the *Callimachus* narrative, the distinctive motif of the dragon sporting three heads.

No claim is made here that the author of the Theodore narrative was working directly with the *Callimachus* and *Digenis* narratives (indeed he may have worked before the composition of the former). Rather these two narratives are to be taken as examples of the slightly different sort of traditional dragon fight that was thriving in Byzantine secular literature alongside that of the hagiographical tradition… and just occasionally impacting upon it.

9.2 George: Text and Image

In looking at Lucian in Chapter 8 we have seen how deep-rooted and ancient many of the motifs of the hagiographical dragon fight are, even those that seem to emerge in the tradition at a relatively late stage. As we turn to the best-known dragon-fighting saint of them all, St George, we learn a similar lesson.[60] From the iconographical perspective at least, George's slaying of the dragon goes back not merely to the beginning of the Christian era, but actually to the very beginning of classical antiquity.

---

[60] For the George tradition in general, see Delehaye 1909:45–76; Fontenrose 1959:515–21; Fischer 1975–; Didi-Huberman et al. 1994; Castellana 2000; Hansen 2002:119–30; Walter 2003a:109–44; Woods 2009. For a fine collection of (principally xix A D) icons depicting George with his dragon, see Haustein-Bartsch 2016:90–137.

St George is first depicted a dragon as early as the seventh century AD. The two earliest images of St George in his role as dragon-slayer, in both of which he is paired with another saint, are the following:

1. A vii AD wall-painting from a church in Mavrucan (Güzelöz) in Cappadocia, Marvucan no. 3. George and our own Theodore, both on horseback, spear a pair of serpents twining, caduceus-like, around a central tree (in this regard they are slightly reminiscent of the Serpent of Eden).[61]
2. A terracotta plaque from Vinica, North Macedonia (the former FYROM), now in the Skopje museum and probably dateable to before AD 733 (when Vinica came under Byzantine control) by the fact that its inscription is in Latin. Sts George and Christopher, the latter gratifyingly in cynocephalus (dog-headed) aspect, stand (horseless) and spear human-headed serpents on the ground below them.[62]

Such imagery need only be symbolic (it belongs, broadly, to the Holy Rider tradition, of which more anon), and need not entail the existence also at this date of a fully developed associated narrative.

The earliest narrative of St George's battle against the dragon to survive is probably *in effect* that of the Greek *Miracula Sancti Georgii* preserved in a twelfth-century manuscript, the *Codex Romanus Angelicus* (George [b]).[63] According to the *Miracula*, God resolves to punish Selbius, the wicked king of the pagan city of Lasia, by bringing forth a marauding dragon in the lake upon which the city depends for its water. The dragon is partly controlled by the annual sacrifice to it of young people, chosen by lot, but the lot eventually falls on Selbius' own daughter, princess Sabra (as she is named in later versions). En route home from the wars the soldier George finds her pinned out for the dragon and enquires about the circumstances. Inter alia, he questions her about her people's gods, and she tells him that they worship Heracles, Scamander, Apollo, and the great goddess Artemis, to which George replies that she must believe rather in his God, and

---

[61] See Walter 2003a:125, with illustration at fig. 27, and Pancaroğlu, 2004:154. For an interesting early illustration of a standing Theodore spearing his serpent on the ground before him, see the vii–viii AD lead seal of Bishop Peter of (Theodore's own) Euchaita; Walter 1999:173, with fig. 2; and Haustein-Bartsch 2016:26, fig. 2; cf. Haldon 2016:3–5, 12, 30 for the earlier stages of Theodore's tradition.

[62] See Walter 2003a:52–3, with fig. 24; and Kuehn 2011:106–7, with fig. 104. On some late imperial coins Valentinian III and Honorius are depicted trampling human-headed serpents whilst piercing them with their *labarum*, a spear topped with a cross and a chi-rho (in the latter case the serpent sports the face of Attila the Hun); see Dresvina 2016:174.

[63] *Miracula Sancti Georgii, Codex Romanus Angelicus* 46, §12; text at Aufhauser 1911:52–69. At Ogden 2013a:402–3 and 2013b: 249–52 (no. 160) I was wrong to state, *without qualification*, that the codex preserves the earliest attested version of George's dragon-slaying story. For the early stages of the tradition of St George and his dragon generally, see Walter 1995 and 2003a:109–44.

take courage. Despite her urgings that he should run for his life, he stays and fights the dragon, tames it, and puts a leash on it made from the maiden's girdle. He leads the girl and the dragon alike back to her city, and, upon receiving the citizens' en masse promise to convert, slays it before them with his sword. There is no marriage between the princess and this continent hero.[64]

The shorter Georgian version of this tale found already in an eleventh-century manuscript in Jerusalem (George [a]) appears to be an edited-down version of an already-existing text, probably a Greek one again, similar to that of the *Miracula*.[65] This can be seen if we align translations of the two texts (Table 9.2).

Walter takes the chronological priority of the Georgian account, together with George's contemporary popularity in Georgia and Cappadocia, to indicate that the tale actually had a Georgian origin.[66] Even if that were true, the Georgian tale would have to be strongly grounded in the Graeco-Roman hagiographical tradition nonetheless, as is indicated by its deep saturation with the motifs reviewed in Chapters 6 and 7 above:

- The idolatry of a local people embodied in a dragon (cf. Chapter 6, §§6.1.3 and 6.8.1).
- The dragon's monopolization of a vital water-source (cf. Chapter 6, §6.1.2).
- The failure of armies (or at any rate 'measures') against the dragon (cf. Chapter 6, §6.2.3).
- The dragon's random marauding (cf. Chapter 6, §6.1.1).
- The containment of the dragon's marauding by means of human (virgin?) sacrifice to it (cf. Chapter 7, §7.2).
- The attempted dissuasion of the saint from going up against the dragon (cf. Chapter 6, §6.2.5).
- The saint's prayer for divine aid (cf. Chapter 6, §6.2.2).
- The manifestation of that divine aid (in the form of a disembodied voice) (cf. Chapter 6, §6.2.4).
- The deployment of the sign of the cross (cf. Chapter 6, §6.4.2).
- The taming of the dragon (cf. Chapter 6, §6.4.3).
- The binding of the dragon with an item of clothing, and the leading of it as if on a leash (cf. Chapter 6, §6.4.4).
- The conversion of the local people (cf. Chapter 6, §6.8.1).
- The killing of the dragon (cf. Chapter 6, §6.6).
- The creation of a spring (cf. Chapter 6, §6.1.2).

---

[64] The tale is well illustrated in the xii-xiii AD fresco from the church at Ikvi, Georgia: Princess Sabra leads the dragon with her belt, whilst, in a narrative compression, George spears the creature from horseback. See Walter 1989a:357, drawing 3.

[65] Patriarchal Library, Jerusalem, cod. 2. For Georgian hagiography, see Martin-Hisard 2011.

[66] Walter 2003a:121, 140–2; so too White 2008:152.

Table 9.2 St George and the Dragon: The Georgian version ([a]) and the *Miracula Sancti Georgii* version ([b]) aligned

Georgian version: Patriarchal Library, Jerusalem, cod. 2 (xi AD)[67]	Greek version: *Miracula Sancti Georgii*, Codex Romanus Angelicus 46, §12 (xii AD)
	Miracle of George the great martyr in connection with the dragon [drakōn]. *Lord, bless it!* Turning, amongst miracles, to that of George, the great martyr and miracle-worker, let us give glory to God, who exalted him and displayed the nature of his grace through the all-glorious martyr George. Has anyone through the ages ever yet heard of or seen a miracle of the sort performed by the all-blessed George?
In the city of Lasia reigned a godless emperor, the idolater Selinus. As a punishment for his unbelief, God sent to a nearby lake like a terrifying dragon which devoured the inhabitants of the city.	In these times there was a city named Lasia and it was ruled by a king named Selbius. He was a wicked idolater, lawless, impious, and without pity or compassion for the believers in Christ. The Lord gave his people requital for their deeds. Near the city there was a lake with plentiful water. In that water was born a wicked dragon and every day it would come out and eat them.
On many occasions, the emperor took measures against the dragon but in vain, so huge and awful was it.	Often the king would assemble all his armies and go out and do battle against the beast, but it would churn the waters up into turmoil so that they could not even get anywhere near the place. Since it was eating them, they were wickedly oppressed.
The time came when the inhabitants of the city met together to reproach the emperor for his ineffectiveness and to insist that he take some steps. Then the emperor proposed that a list should be drawn up of the inhabitants, such that each would sacrifice a child, and he promised that he would offer his only daughter when the time came.	The people of the city came together and cried out to the king, 'See, king, our city is a fine and beautiful one to live in, but we are being destroyed in wicked fashion.' The king said, 'A lot is to be given to each of you and you must all register a name on it. I have an only daughter, a young girl, and I will put her name on my lot, just as you will name your own children on yours. And by this means let us not be wiped out of our own city.'

[67] This translation is provided at Walter 2003a:141. It is derived from the intervening Russian translation at Privalova 1977:73.

And so it was decided. When the emperor's turn came, he dressed his daughter in the imperial purple, and, having decked her as for a wedding, with tears and weeping he brought her along.

The emperor offered the people gold and silver and his empire in compensation if he could keep his only daughter; but the people were inexorable. They all met to look at the emperor's daughter.

However, the Lord wished to perform a miracle in the name of St George, who was alive at the time. He was returning home from Diocletian's army to his estate in Cappadocia…

when he stopped by the lake to water his horse. Then he saw the girl weeping on the bank.

The speech pleased all, and they all began to provide their own children, day by day, until the king's lot came up. The king clothed his daughter in purple and linen and decked her out in gold, precious stones, and pearls. Embracing her longingly, he kissed her, and, lamenting tearfully over her, as if she were already dead, said, 'Off you go, my sweetest child, light of my eyes. Upon whom, my sweetest child, shall I look hereafter to take even the tiniest cheer? When shall I arrange your marriage? When shall I see your bridal chamber? When shall I light the wedding torches for you? When shall I sing the wedding song for you? When shall I see the fruit of your belly? Alas, my sweetest child, go off to the place where you must die alone and without me.'

Then the king said to the people, 'Take gold, silver and my kingdom, and let my daughter go.' But no one would concede this to him because of the decree that the king himself had issued. So the king gnashed his teeth bitterly and sent the girl to the lake. The whole of the city, the great and the small alike, flocked together to watch her.

God, who loves mankind and knows pity, and who does not want sinners to die but rather to turn to him and live, wanted to bring about a sign by means of George, the all-glorious great martyr. This was the age of St George. He had the rank of count. It happened that his army had been lost, and he was travelling back to his fatherland, the land of Cappadocia.

By God's design the saint arrived in that place and took his horse into the lake so that it could drink. He saw the girl sitting there, wetting her knees with tears, glancing about this way and that and wailing. St George said to her, 'Lady, why are you sitting crying in this place?'

Continued

Table 9.2 *Continued*

Georgian version: Patriarchal Library, Jerusalem, cod. 2 (xi AD)	Greek version: *Miracula Sancti Georgii*, Codex Romanus Angelicus 46, §12 (xii AD)
The girl told the handsome youth that he should flee to escape death; she told him of her plight.	The girl said to him, 'I see, my lord, that you are handsome and brave, and I feel pity for your handsomeness and your youth. Why have you come here to die in a dreadful way? Get back on your horse and escape quickly!' The saint said to her, 'Lady, who are you and who are the people standing yonder and watching you with great lamentation?' The girl said, 'It is a long story, and I cannot tell it to you. But escape before you are killed in a dreadful fashion!' The saint said to her, 'Tell me the truth, lady. For, by Lord God, I will die alongside you, because I surely will not leave you in the lurch.' Then the girl groaned bitterly and said, 'My lord, our city was a fine and beautiful one to live in, but then a wicked dragon was born in the lake water. Every day it would come out of the water and eat the people of the city. I am the king's only daughter. My father issued a decree and everyone gave up their children for the dragon to eat. And then the decree rebounded upon my father, and he sent me off for the beast to eat. See now, I have told you everything. Get away from here in haste!' Hearing this, the saint said to the girl, 'Fear not henceforth, but take courage!'
George asked her what god was worshipped in her city. She replied: Hercules, Apollo, Scamander, and the great goddess Artemis.	He asked her, 'What is the religion of your father and his people?' The girl said, 'They worship Heracles, Scamander, Apollo, and the great goddess Artemis.' **The saint said to the girl, 'But you must believe in my God. Fear not henceforth, but take courage.'**
George reassured her, and, lifting his eyes to God, asked him to perform a miracle and help him to vanquish the dragon, so that all might see that God was with George. And a voice replied: 'Do what you wish; I am with you.'	The blessed one raised his voice to God and said, 'O God, you who are enthroned over the Cherubim and Seraphim and who watch over the abyss, the one enduring, true God. You know that the hearts of men are foolish. You showed the dreadful signs to your servant Moses. Show your pity through me too, and engineer with me a sign for the good. Make the terrible beast fall at my feet, so that people will know that you are always with me.' Then there came a voice from heaven, which said, 'Your prayer has been heard by the ears of the Lord. Do what you wish.'

At that moment the dragon appeared.

George hastened towards it, made the sign of the cross and asked the Lord to change the wild beast into an animal which would be docile with him. As George said this, the dragon fell at his feet.

The saint tied it with the girl's girdle, handed it to her and told her to go to the city nearby.

The people, seeing this, were terrified and prepared to flee. George calmed them and required them to become Christian. After that, all acknowledged their faith in Christ.

Then George took out his sword and killed the dragon.

Then the people assembled and prostrated themselves at the saint's feet and gave thanks to the Lord. Then St George sent for **Bishop Alexander** who baptized the emperor, his court, and all the people in the course of the following days, in all 45,000 persons. And there was great joy in the city.

The emperor had a shrine built in honour of the saint, and St George went into the shrine and performed a miracle. By the altar, he caused a lifegiving spring to flow which even now performs miracles.

At once the girl cried out, 'Alas, my lord, get away, because the terrible beast is coming.'

The saint ran to meet the dragon and made the sign of the cross, with the words, 'Lord my God, make the beast a call to faith for the faithless people.' When he had said this, by the help of the same God and the prayer of the saint the dragon fell at his feet.

The saint said to the girl, 'Take off your belt and my horse's bridle and bring them to me here.' The girl took her belt off and gave the items to the saint. By God's design he tied them onto the dragon and handed it over to the girl with the words, 'Let us take it to the city.' Taking the dragon, they went to the city.

When the people saw the unexpected miracle they took fear, and were on the point of fleeing for fear of the dragon, but St George shouted to them, 'Do not be afraid, but stay, see the glory of God, and believe in our Lord Jesus Christ, the true God, and I will kill the dragon.' The king and the entire city cried out, 'We believe in the Father, the Son, and the Holy Ghost, and in the consubstantial and indivisible Trinity.'

Upon hearing this, the saint unsheathed his sword, killed the dragon, and handed the girl over to her father.

Most of the people gathered round and kissed the saint's feet, glorifying God. St George summoned **the archbishop of Alexandria**, baptized the king, his nobles, and the whole people, some 240,000, over a period of fifteen days. There was great joy in that place.

Then the city of Lasia raised up a most sacred temple in the name of St George. As the temple was being built, the saint stood in a certain place and prayed, and a sacred spring burst forth. Then they believed in the Lord. St George authored many miracles and signs through the grace he had been given.

However, that the Georgian version is an edited-down version of a fuller narrative already akin to that of the *Miracula* is indicated by the fact that, when George asks the princess what gods her people worship, she replies, 'Heracles, Apollo, Scamander, and the great goddess Artemis', but elicits no further response from him, in something of a narrative cul-de-sac. One badly expects a response from George here along the lines found in the Greek version: 'The saint said to the girl, "But you must believe in my God. Fear not henceforth, but take courage"' (as indicated in bold font in the table). Furthermore, the Georgian version's 'Bishop Alexander', which has no particular significance, has the look of being a corruption of the Greek's 'archbishop of Alexandria', which is significant indeed, Alexandria being one of the three great episcopal sees (alongside Rome and Antioch) in the third century AD, the broader historical context in which George's *Life* is situated. Whether that original fuller narrative already akin to that of the *Miracula* was in Georgian again (with the *Miracula* representing something like a full translation of it) or in Greek (i.e. the actual text of the *Miracula* or something very closely akin to it) is less clear, though I would favour the latter. The fame of George's dragon-slaying became secure in the Latin West when Jacobus de Voragine subsequently included it in his AD 1263–7 *Golden Legend* ([c]).[68]

St George snaps us right back to classical antiquity, though not necessarily in the way that has conventionally been imagined. It is commonly claimed that this *drakōn* story is a reworking of the ancient myth of Perseus, Andromeda, and their *kētos*.[69] But it is actually closer in its details to the myth of Heracles, Hesione, and their *kētos*, in which again there is no love-bond between the male and female principals (for both of these myths see, Chapter 4, §4.3.2). It may be significant that Heracles' name is cited in the *Miracula*, whilst the Lasians' worship of the river Scamander locates their city in the region of Troy, home to Hesione. But perhaps we are wrong to search for classical antecedents in a very specific way. The Eurybatus and Menestratus tales (cited in Chapter 3, §3.4.1) may suggest that this sort of story-type was widespread in antiquity (and perhaps female-victim versions of such actual *drakōn* tales existed alongside the male-victim ones).[70]

It is rather in the realm of iconography that St George forges his most emphatic direct link back to classical antiquity. The traditional and canonical image of St George, thriving still in modern media, has him riding a rearing horse, from

---

[68] Jacobus de Voragine *Golden Legend* 58. The *c.* AD 1400 *South English Legendary* (University of Minnesota MS Z.822. N.81) includes a delightful, rhyming Middle English account of the tale derived from Jacobus' version (fols 215v–216v): 'a wonder fowle dragone...both uggely and grete and so lothely to se'; for text and commentary, see Whatley et al. 2004:89–102. Alas, George acquired his dragon narrative too late for its inclusion in the late ix AD Old High German *Georgslied*, for which see Haubrichs 1979; here George has to content himself with getting the better of a hell-hound (*hellehunt*).

[69] See Hartland 1894–6:iii, 38–47; Fontenrose 1959:515–21; Fischer 1975–; Hansen 2002:119–30; Walter 2003a:121–2; Lestón Mayo 2014:38–9.

[70] More broadly, the St George story belongs to one of the best-established international folktales in the Aarne-Thompson-Uther catalogue: ATU 300.

which he spears a typically supine or backwards-turning dragon on the ground below him. We think, for example, of Raphael's *c.* AD 1504–6 treatment of the subject in the National Gallery of Art in Washington DC (Fig. 9.2; cf. Figs 4.25–7). The earliest surviving examples of George in this image-type *proper* hail from Cappadocia. The earliest of all may be the principal fresco from the Yilanli kilise rock-cut church at Yeşilköy (Ihlara), which may go back to the mid-ninth century AD. Here George spears the dragon below his horse, whilst a mirroring Theodore does exactly the same.[71] The earliest example of St George killing his dragon in

Fig. 9.2 Raphael *St George and the Dragon, c.*1506. National Gallery of Art, Washington DC. Andrew W. Mellon Collection. Open access.

[71] Thierry 1963:91. Yilanli Kilise means 'Snake Church'. The same church offers another similar scene, in a x AD (?) fresco over its vestibule door, for which see Pancaroğlu, 2004:155 with fig. 4 and Kuehn 2011:107–8 with fig. 106 (but I suspect these scholars misread the partly preserved image: George and Theodore will surely have been fighting a pair of intertwined serpents—cf. the Mavrucan image, discussed above—rather than a single two-headed one). In yet another of the church's frescoes, a three-headed serpent devours a trio of sinners. See Walter 1989a:352 and 2003a:127–9, who points to a total of six further such images of St George and his dragon of this type deriving from the tenth and eleventh centuries AD in Cappadocian churches: Pürenli seki kilisesi (x AD?); St Barbara at Soğanle; Yusuf koç kilisesi at Avcilar; Sakh kilise (Göreme 2a); Church of the Rock at the necropolis of

this configuration without a mirroring Theodore may be that found in the church of St Barbara at Soğanle (Soğanli) and dated to AD 1006–21.[72] (The earliest two surviving images of George spearing the dragon *tout court* derive, as we have seen above, from the seventh and eighth centuries AD: they may, just possibly, already be construed to represent variations on this configuration.)

In the first instance this horseback image-type may be taken back to the magical 'Holy Rider' intaglio-amulets of late antique Egypt, usually made of haematite: on these an unnamed rider, haloed and with the butt of his spear sur-mounted by a cross, spears a supine serpent beneath his horse, whilst the accom-panying inscription usually reads, 'The one God conquers all evils'.[73] Yet the image-type goes back further still from here to the pagan scenes of Bellerophon spearing the Chimaera from the back of his flying horse Pegasus (Figs 1.13, 9.3). This scene was popular in late antique Roman mosaics, where, significantly, it could sit alongside explicitly Christian imagery, as in the case of the fourth-century AD mosaic from Hinton St Mary, England, in which the Bellerophon scene is the subject of one of its two major roundels, a portrait of Christ with the chi-rho symbol the other.[74] But versions of it can be found already in the middle of the Greek archaic period.[75] An Apulian lekane of *c*.330 BC deserves particular atten-tion, given that its Chimaera is of an anomalous type and much more anguiform than usual: the goat element is gone, and the creature consists simply of the front half of a cat-like lioness merging into the (large) back end of a coiling serpent, to make the feline equivalent of an anguipede.[76]

Göreme; Yilanli kilise (Göreme 26). Cf. also Palli 1968:521. For other early versions of this type, see the xi–xii AD bas-relief of a mirroring George and Theodore from the monastery of St Michael in Kiev (illustrated at White 2013:129 fig. 8) and the xii–xiii AD fresco from the church at Ikvi, Georgia (cited above, n. 62).

[72] De Jerphanion 1925–42 Planches iii, pl. 189.2; cf. Walter1989a:352.

[73] I give three examples. (1) A British Museum intaglio, G 1986, 5–1, 14 = Michel 2001 no. 450 (V AD; the nonsense inscription is post-antique). (2) An amulet formerly in the Beirut Avyaz collection, Bonner 1950 no. 324. (3) An amulet formerly in Strasbourg, Vikan 1991–2. See Walter 1989b, 1989–90, 2003a:3 3–8; Fauth 1999; Pancaroğlu 2004:152–3 (with further references); Kuehn 2011:102–5; and Dresvina 2012:196. These 'Holy Rider' intaglio-amulets developed in part from a Graeco-Jewish amulet-type in which a rider, sometimes explicitly identified as 'Solomon', similarly spears a supine female demon—Lilith or Obyzouth—below him on the obverse, with the Greek inscription 'Seal of God' on the reverse. See the fine example from the Benaki museum reproduced at Walter 2003a fig. 17. The amulets salute the tradition found in the iii–iv AD *Testament of Solomon* (discussed at Chapter 4, §4.8), according to which the archangel Michael gave Solomon a signet ring with which he could exercise power over demons, among them the female demon Obyzouth, strangler of newborns; cf., more generally, Josephus *Jewish Antiquities*, 8.2.5. The Holy-Rider amulets' substitution of the Solomon amulets' demon with a dragon once again speaks of the affinity between these two entities.

[74] Illustrated at Spier 2007:119, fig. 86. Cf. also the iv AD Bellerophon mosaic at Lullingstone villa in Kent.

[75] See *LIMC* Chimaira, Chimaira in Etruria, Pegasos. Note especially *LIMC* Pegasos 152, a *c*.660 BC plate from Thasos.

[76] *LIMC* Pegasos 155.

Fig. 9.3 Bellerophon slays the Chimaera from the back of Pegasus (ring). South Italian, gold box bezel ring, attributed to the Santa Eufemia Master, *c.*340–320 BC. The J. Paul Getty Museum, 88.AM.104. Public domain.

9.3 Conclusion

We have contextualized traditions associated with the two principal military dragon-slaying saints, Theodore Tyron and George, in very different ways. In Chapter 8 we took much of the saintly dragon-fight tradition, including some elements that manifest themselves in it at a very late stage, all the way back to the later second century AD. In this chapter we have now been able to take what today survives as the tradition's principal living relic, the iconography of St George, back further still, even to the very beginning of classical antiquity. We have also seen that one of the key texts in the Chapter 8 exercise, the (xiv AD) tale of Theodore and the Dragon of King Samuel's City, despite its deep roots in the saintly tradition, additionally exhibits the clear imprint of a popular and secular dragon-slaying tradition that remained largely external to hagiography.

PART III
VIKINGS

10

Worms (Still) and Wyverns

The Form of the Germanic Dragon

We turn, in these final two chapters, to the last major component in the modern western conception of the dragon, the story-types and motifs of the dragon in medieval Germanic culture. The present chapter considers the question of form once again. The next returns to the question of narrative etiquette. In both of these contexts the partial impact of Christian-Latin culture (and through it classical culture) is apparent. The vast majority of texts considered in these chapters are Norse, and the vast majority of these in turn derive from the thirteenth century A D.[1] Texts written in other languages (Anglo-Saxon, Middle High German, Latin, Danish, and English) are clearly badged as such. As with Chapters 5–9, a substantial number of texts is cited repeatedly as we work through the analysis of recurring motifs. Editions and translations are supplied in a checklist in Appendix C.[2]

10.1 'Worms' and 'Dragons': *Ormr* and *Dreki*

Old Norse deployed two words of basic interest to us: *ormr* (cf. Anglo-Saxon *wyrm*, Middle High German *wurm*) and *dreki* (cf. Anglo-Saxon *draca*, Middle High German *drache/trache*, all derivative of Latin *draco*).[3] The scholarly

---

[1] For general discussion of the Germanic, especially the Norse, dragon see Mackensen 1930; Lecouteux 1979; Lionarons 1998, 2000; Evans 2000, 2005; Rauer 2000; Jakobsson 2010; Larrington 2010; Acker 2012, 2013; Rebschloe 2014:149–360 (a substantial treatment, albeit sometimes written at some distance from the evidence); Barreiro 2019. Tolkien's famous dictum that 'in northern literature there are only two [dragons] that are significant...the dragon of the Volsungs, Fafnir, and Beowulf's bane' (1936:252–3) is surely ironic, whilst, as we shall see, the contention of Finlay 2000:15 n. 36 (commenting on *Bjarnar saga Hítdælakappa*) that 'References to dragons are common in the *fornaldarsögur* [the legendary sagas set in the age before the colonisation of Iceland]...but [sc. they] are rarely said to fly' could not be more wrong. Helpful orientation in all matters and texts Norse (dragons aside) is provided by Pulsiano's encyclopedia, *Medieval Scandinavia* (1993), which puts the *Oxford Classical Dictionary* to shame.

[2] I shall typically cite Norse works by means of English translations of their titles in the main text, for reasons of readability and accessibility, but by their Norse form in the accompanying notes.

[3] The *e* of *dreki* entails that the word was imported into Norse prior to (or during) the period of the i-mutation (i-umlaut), which took place *c.* A D 500–900; cf. Evans 2005:227. It is a pity that no passage of the Septuagint or the New Testament featuring the word *drakōn* is reflected in the surviving portions of Wulfila's (later iv A D) Gothic Bible. Although much of the New Testament is represented, Revelation, alas, is not; Acts, which would have given us Paul's Maltese viper, is also missing. *Ophis*

consensus, from which I do not demur, is that the former term *originally* defined a ground-based, pure vermiform creature of a traditional type, wingless and legless, whilst the latter *originally* defined a flying dragon, winged and legged, introduced into the Germanic world from Christian Latin culture.[4] It may be that the introduction of the latter overwrote a pre-Christian winged dragon genuinely indigenous to Germanic culture, but if so it is difficult to demonstrate that now. In a Germanic context more broadly we may assume—what we emphatically could not do in a classical context—that if a dragon can fly it is ipso facto in possession of wings: no texts or images compromise this simple inference. But, importantly and interestingly, the opposite is not true: a dragon in possession of wings does not necessarily fly, at any rate in the context in which it is immediately featured. We shall consider a possible reason for this in due course.

Sometimes in our texts the two terms are treated as effectively interchangeable. In the *Skaldskaparmal* section of the *Prose Edda* (c. AD 1220) Snorri Sturluson provides a list of things termed *ormr*, and the first of these is *dreki* itself.[5] Fafnir is described both as an *ormr* and *dreki* in the *Saga of the Volsungs* (c. AD 1200–70),[6] as are the third dragon of *Thidrek's Saga* (c. AD 1230–50)[7] and the Dragon of Tartary released from a cellar by Knut (Sigrgardr in disguise) in the *Saga of Sigrgardr the Valiant* (xv AD; see further §10.3.11 below, where the latter text is quoted).[8]

But other writers remain careful to distinguish their usages of the terms. The *Saga of Ketil Trout* (xiii AD) is strongly conscious of the difference between an *ormr* and a *dreki*. It is careful to specify that the dragon encountered by Ketil has coils and a tail like an *ormr* (worm), but wings like a *dreki*. Accordingly, the text offers a useful, as it were, programmatic, distinction between the two words and concepts.[9] We may also cite here a pair of texts in which ground-based wingless dragons and flying winged ones co-exist and are duly differentiated in the same way by this terminology. In the chivalric *Konrad's Saga* (xiv AD) the first dragon Konrad encounters, the Dragon of Pezcina (or Persina), is afforded quite a tight description. As he comes across it, it is attempting to carry a lion off to its lair, and is described as squeezing its claws into the lion's shoulders, whilst coiling its tail

---

('snake'), applied to the Serpent of Eden (2 Corinthians 11:3) becomes *vaúrms* ('worm'; cf. also Matthew 7:10, Luke 10:19) and John the Baptist's 'offspring of vipers' (Matthew 3:7, Luke 3:7) becomes *kuni nadrê* ('kin of adders'; nom. sing. is *nadrs*). For the text of the Gothic Bible (with Greek and Vulgate versions conveniently reproduced facing-page) see Massman 1857.

[4] The case was first formulated by Müllenhoff 1849 and has been endorsed in more recent times by Wild 1962:10–12; Lionarons 1998:14; Rauer 2000:85–6; Evans 2005:217, 225–30; Acker 2012 passim, and 2013 passim. For the (often subtle) Christian lens through which Norse literature looks upon its pagan myth, see Clunies Ross 2000.

[5] *Prose Edda* Skáldskaparmál §57. Also listed here are a number of individuals discussed elsewhere in this chapter: the Midgard Worm (as Jormundgandr), Nidhögg, Fafnir, and Grim Aegir.

[6] *Völsunga saga* §18—within the space of three lines, indeed.

[7] *Þiðrekssaga* §§416–22. Lionarons 1998:100 maintains that those dragons that are *consistently* designated *ormr* in this saga remain wingless.

[8] *Sigrgarðs saga frœkna* §13.114–16.   [9] *Ketils saga hœngs* §1, p. 153 Jónsson.

around the middle of the lion's body, and attempting to hoist it into the air that way. The description is only really compatible with a wyvern, and the creature is designated directly as a *dreki* and indirectly as a *flugdeki* ('flying dragon').[10] However, in Konrad's (magnificent) second dragon episode, at the dragon castle at the edge of the world, we are given no reason to believe that any of the myriad serpents Konrad encounters there, including the presiding one, with its crown and crest of dread, is anything other than a pure vermiform, and indeed Konrad avoids some of them by vaulting over them with his spear, which further suggests that they are confined to the ground. These are designated throughout with the term *ormr*.[11] In *Ector's Saga* (xiv–xv A D), when Ingifer turns himself into a dragon to lie on his gold, there is no indication that he is anything other than a pure vermiform. But when Arthur's knight Sir Trancival encounters another dragon later in the same text, this one again fighting a lion, it is made clear that this dragon has both wings and claws, as it tries to lift the lion up into the air. This text too is seemingly scrupulous in its terminology: the first of these creatures is defined as an *ormr* and the second as a *dreki*.[12]

The distinction between the vermiform dragon and the winged dragon is reflected at a grand level in the configurations of Norse mythology's two great eschatological dragons. The Midgard Worm (Midgards*ormr*—the 'Mid-Yard-' or 'Middle-Earth-worm', also known as Jormungandr) salutes its 'worm' configuration in its name, and there is never any indication that it is winged. In the *Prose Edda* again Snorri Sturluson tells that the Worm was the son of Loki. Odin cast it into the ocean that surrounds all the lands, where it grew to an enormous size and coiled around the lands, biting its tail. Utgarda-Loki (Loki of the 'Out-Yard' or 'Outer Regions') disguised the serpent as a simple cat and tricked Thor into attempting to lift it off the ground in a trial of strength. Thor could do no more than raise one of the cat's paws. Upon discovering the trick, the angry Thor went out onto the ocean to fish for the serpent with the giant Hymir. He baited his hook with an ox-head, and this was taken by the serpent, which resisted so hard on the line that Thor's feet were forced through the bottom of the boat, and he then had to brace his feet against the sea-bed beneath as the fight continued, with the serpent spitting venom over him. Thor was eventually able to draw the serpent to him and reached for his hammer to strike it, but Hymir, terrified by the beast, cut the line at the last minute with the bait knife, whereupon Thor punched him and threw him overboard. Thor flung his hammer down into the water after the serpent and, according to some, as Snorri says, struck its head off with it. But

---

[10] *Konráðs saga Keisarasonar* §6 (*flugdreki*), §8 (*dreki*).

[11] *Konráðs saga Keisarasonar* §10. At *Göngu-Hrólfs saga* §33 (xiv A D) the shape-shifter Grim Aegir is said to be able to turn himself into a variety of different animals, amongst which *flugdreki* and *ormr* are deployed to designate distinct creatures ('now a flying dragon, now a worm'); boar and bull are also specified.

[12] *Ectors saga* §§8 and 10.

Snorri himself knows different: the serpent continued to live on in the ocean that surrounds the world. He goes on to protest that at Ragnarök (the 'Twilight of the Gods') this still-living Midgard Worm will writhe in fury and attack the land, spewing venom again into air and sea. Thor will again fight the serpent, and kill it again, but he will also die himself from the venom it spits over him. The fact that the Midgard Worm is ocean-based might in itself lead us to presume that it is wingless, but that would be fallacious: as we shall see, the Dragon (*dreki*) of Tartary encountered by Knut (Sigrgardr) can also swim.[13]

By contrast Nidhögg, the other great eschatological dragon of Norse mythology, is said to be winged in the *Poetic Edda* (*c.* AD 1270), which also applies the term *dreki* to him: he comes forth from below, flying from Nidafjöll, the dark mountains of the underworld, carrying the bodies of men on his wings.[14] Not least because of the application of the term *dreki* to him here, Christian influence has been suspected.[15] Snorri Sturluson's *Prose Edda* (*c.* AD 1220) twice associates Nidhögg with the term *ormr*, but neither of these cases can be considered diagnostic. First, in the *Gylfaginning* section we are told that he gnaws from below at the root of the great universal ash tree Yggdrasill that stands over the boiling spring of Hvergelmir in Niflheim (the murky hell); he lives in the spring together with a vast number of serpents (*ormar*, pl.), so many that even he cannot count them; and here he tears apart the curses of the most wicked of the dead.[16] His association with *ormar* here does not entail that he is himself an *ormr*: the motif seemingly recalls that of the great dragon presiding over the (mere) snake brood, familiar from hagiographical culture (see Chapter 7, §7.1) and Norse culture (see Chapter 11, §11.4.2) alike.[17] And second, as we have already seen, in the *Skaldskaparmal* section Snorri lists Nidhögg as an entity that may be termed an *ormr*—but at the same time, and in parallel, he declares that a *dreki* may also be so termed.[18] However, in the *Poetic Edda* (*c.* AD 1270) we are given a slightly

---

[13] Snorri Sturluson *Prose Edda* Gylfaginning §§34, 46–8, 51, 53 (*c.* AD 1220). The *Poetic Edda* Hymiskviða §§17–26 (*c.* AD 1270) tells a simpler version of the killing of the Midgard Worm, with Hymir's intervention omitted: Thor pulls the serpent on board and strikes its head with his hammer. The Midgard Worm is thought to lie ultimately behind the Orkney tradition of Assipattle and the Mester Stoor Worm, for which see Marwick 1974:139–44; Simpson 1980:137–41. Knut's flying dragon: *Sigrgarðs saga frækna* §13.114–16 (§§88–90 Loth).

Thor is, however, given a *dreki* opponent in an odd context. In the Christianizing, classicizing, and euhemerizing melange that constitutes the Prologue to the *Prose Edda* (3), Snorri tells that King Priam of Troy had a son named Tror (cf. Tros), the Norse Thor. In the course of his wanderings he overcame one of the greatest dragons (*dreki*), alongside sundry berserkers and giants.

[14] *Poetic Edda* Völuspá §§38–9, 66 (with the term *dreki*).

[15] Acker 2013:55; cf. also Lionarons 1998:11, 115 n. 36.

[16] Snorri Sturluson, *Prose Edda* Gylfaginning §§15–16, 52. The hawk Vedrfölnir sits atop Yggdrasill, and the squirrel Ratatöskr runs up and down the trunk carrying envious words between him and Nidhögg. The gnawing of the root and the messaging of Ratatöskr are referred to also at *Poetic Edda* Grímnismál §§32, 35. For Nidhögg's partial identification with Odin via the soubriquet Svafnir, see Lionarons 1998:54.

[17] Cf. in particular (the xiii AD) *Yngvars saga viðförla* §5, ii.436 Jónsson, where the great *dreki* Jakulus lives on a hill of *ormar*.

[18] Snorri Sturluson, *Prose Edda* Skáldskaparmál §57.

different portfolio of facts about Nidhögg, in addition to the flight from Nidafjöll just mentioned. Murderers, adulterers, and oathbreakers are dispatched after death to the Hall of Nastrand, the wattle of which consists of live woven serpents, whose heads face inwards and constantly blow forth venom, which also drops down from the smoke-vent, so that the hall runs with rivers of it. Here Nidhögg sucks their blood, whilst they are torn by a wolf.[19]

10.2 Ground-Based Dragons

A number of Germanic dragons remain resolutely vermiform, however designated. In the chivalric *Saga of Tristram and Isönd* (AD 1226) the Dragon of Wexford, repeatedly defined as a *dreki* and never as an *ormr*, evidently conforms to this pattern: 'he saw the *dreki*, which came slithering, bore its head high, thrust out its eyes and its tongue, and blew forth venom and fire in all directions.'[20] Three of the dragons of Saxo Grammaticus' Latin *Gesta Danorum* ('Deeds of the Danes', early xiii AD) appear to be of a fully traditonal worm style. First, the dragon (*serpens, belua*) encountered by Frothi (Frode): repeated emphasis is laid upon its coils and spirals as it sits on its pile of treasure, and it is also given a flickering, three-forked tongue.[21] (For all its vermiform configuration this dragon—which Frothi kills after learning of a single vulnerable spot in its belly— perhaps constitutes Tolkien's most immediate model for Smaug in *The Hobbit*, although the name of its antagonist, evidently the prototype of 'Frodo', is deferred to *The Lord of the Rings*.[22]) Second, the massive dragon or 'snake' (*draco, anguis, belua*) fought by Fridleif seems to be wingless. It emerges from the sea, possesses a great many coils, and carves out a trench in the ground as it slithers.[23] Third, the pair of overweening vipers destroyed by Ragnar Lodbrok (*anguis, serpens, belua, vipereum genus*), absolutely dragons in their preternatural appetites, their fiery, pestilential breath, and their story-type (the princess' hand is offered to the warrior that can kill them...) clearly remain simple, coiling snakes in form.[24] The indications seem to be also that the dragon (*dreki*) encountered by Yngvar in Scythia in *Yngvar's Saga* (xiii AD) is a pure worm in form: it crawls along its path to the river and spins around (a motion suggestive of coils) on top of its pile of gold when it realizes that some of it has been stolen.[25]

---

[19] *Poetic Edda* Völuspá §§38–9, 66; cf. Davidson 1943:86.
[20] *Tristrams saga ok Ísöndar* §§35–6.   [21] Saxo Grammaticus *Gesta Danorum* 2.1.1–4.
[22] Tolkien 1937 esp. chh. 12–13. For appreciations of Tolkien's Smaug against the context of Norse literature see Evans 1998 and Jakobsson 2009; however, neither notices the point made here.
[23] Saxo Grammaticus *Gesta Danorum* 6.150. The reference to the serpent's 'groin' (*inguen*) seems from context to signify no more than its 'underbelly': it does not entail that it has legs.
[24] Saxo Grammaticus *Gesta Danorum* 9.252–3.   [25] *Yngvars saga víðförla* §6, ii.442 Jónsson.

It may be that a group of Middle High German texts, close in date, give us dragons of lindworm configuration (i.e. legged but unwinged). Gottfried von Strassburg's Middle High German *Tristan* (AD 1210) offers an expansive narrative of Tristan's battle against the Dragon of Wexford. The dragon, defined principally as a *trache* and a *serpant*, never leaves the ground, and there is no mention of wings. It is, however, specified to have claws, and these are indeed put to use in the fight, where they kill Tristan's horse.[26] The case is similar with the dragon (*wurm*) of *Ortnit* (*c.* AD 1217–25) and the related *Wolfdietrich B* (*c.* AD 1225–50). *Ortnit* describes its dragon as beaked, its mouth being the size of a door, and as possessing a prehensile tail; again there is no reference to wings. We would suppose it to be wholly vermiform were it not for a single reference to the bloody footprints (*wurmes staphen... bluotic*) it leaves outside its cave after killing Ortnit. *Wolfdietrich B* seemingly takes the ball offered here and runs with it. The dragon described in this text has a horny skin, a flank of 12 ells and, again, a prehensile tail, and it is explicitly specified to possess feet—no less than twenty-four of them![27] At least three of the four dragons slain by Gawein in Heinrich von dem Türlin's *Diu Crône* (*c.* AD 1220s) are credited with claws, but there is no mention of wings. To these creatures the terms *wurm* and *drache* (also *dracke, trache, tracke*) are applied interchangeably. The first pair, the sorcerer Gansguoter's dragons, are additionally described actually as *lintracken*; a horn is specified for one and red scales over a green hide for the other, though they are seemingly identical twins.[28]

10.3 Flying Dragons

But the bulk of the dragons we encounter in Germanic texts are described as winged or flying, and many of them are further specified to be legged (and

---

[26] Gottfried von Strassburg *Tristan* ll. 8901–9096 (for the principal episode; Book 12 in Hatto's 1960 translation). *Trache*: 8945, 8965, 8969, 8973, 8988, 9014, 9060, etc. *Serpant*: 8907, 8984, etc. The work is derivative of French forebears, chiefly Thomas of Britain's (xii AD) Anglo-Norman *Tristan*, which is largely lost. As Gottfried embarks on his tale of the dragon, he notes that it is from the *geste* that he has learned that the dragon had its lair in the valley of Anferginan. Cf. Blaisdell 1964; Acker 2012:11, 2013:56–7. The dragon episode in the slightly earlier MHG *Tristrant* of Eilhart von Oberge is jejune (ll. 1645–85; *c.* AD 1190). For discussion of dragons in Germanic Arthurian literature more generally, see Rebschloe 2014:251–308.

[27] *Ortnit* §§571, 585; *Wolfdietrich B* §§ 673–4. The dragon episodes of these poems soon inspired a slew of imitations in the MHG Dietrich literature, which cannot be encompassed here: inter alia, *Eckenlied* (*c.* AD 1230); *Rosengarten zu Worms C* and *D* (*c.* AD 1250–1300); *Virginal* (*c.* AD 1250–1300); *Das Buch von Bern/Dietrichs Flucht* and the related *Rabenschlacht* (*c.* AD 1275–1300); (*Der jüngere*) *Sigenot* (before AD 1300); and the probably somewhat later *Wunderer*. In *Sigenot* the giant Sigenot casts Dietrich into a snake-pit, where he is protected by a jewel given to him by the dwarf Baldung until rescued by Hildebrand. Cf. Heinzle 1978, 1999; Rebschloe 2014:214–47.

[28] *Diu Crône* ll. 12776–808, 13384–513 (Gansguoter's pair at the Castle of the Bridle; *lintracken* at 12788), 15032–223 (the Dragon of Aufrat). It may be that the fourth dragon, that of the Mountain, is a pure vermiform (ll. 26608–764): no claws are mentioned, it protects its spring by coiling around it; and it is slain in Fafnir-fashion, as it glides over a ditch.

clawed) too. A recurrent scenario here is that of its human antagonist attempting to fight it from the ground as it flies overhead.

10.3.1 Anglo-Saxon Flying Dragons

Dragon-heads, as it is supposed, are found embellishing the shield, the helmet, and buckles from the vi–vii AD Sutton Hoo burials. It is claimed that a 27 cm-long gilt-bronze appliqué figure from the shield (which may actually have been made in Sweden) represents a serpentine dragon with three sets of wings in a row furled closely to its body and a tail that culminates in a pair of big-toed feet, but I remain dubious about this entire interpretation, and am inclined rather to see the creature more simply as an ornate bird.[29] The (viii AD?) *Finnsburg fragment* does, however, speak of a flying dragon and that too a fiery one. Here the sight from a hall of a torch-bearing army approaching is denied to be the dawn in the east, the hall's gables burning, or a flying dragon: 'nor does a dragon fly here' (*ne her draca ne fleogeð*).[30] We find similar creatures in the *Anglo-Saxon Chronicle* for the year AD 793 (presumably the prodigies were initially gathered in soon after Lindisfarne's disaster):

> AD 793. At this time cruel prodigies came over the Northumbrians' land and frightened the folk terribly. There were violent storms and flashes of lightning, and fiery dragons were seen flying in the air [*wæron geseowene fyrene dracan on þam lyfte fleogende*]. A great hunger soon followed these tokens, and shortly after this, in this same year, on the sixth day before the Ides of January, in terrible fashion the plundering of heathen men destroyed God's church in Lindisfarne through rapine and murder. *Anglo-Saxon Chronicle*, AD 793[31]

10.3.2 The Dragons of *Thidrek's Saga* and *Erex's Saga*

Thidrek's Saga (*c.* AD 1230–50) is a Norse saga based on lost German material.[32] Thidrek is better known as Dietrich of Bern (i.e. Verona), a distant refraction of

---

[29] See Bruce-Mitford 1975–83:ii.13, 37–8, 63–7, 103–6, figs. 6, 8, 29–30, 50, and 79, pll. 1 and 3 (the supposed winged dragon on the shield); ii.85, fig. 67 (the shield); ii.152–63 and figs 115–19 and, dubiously, 126 (the helmet); iii.758–87 and fig. 545 (buckles). There is much serpent imagery to be found now also amongst the (martial) objects of the 'Staffordshire Hoard' discovered in 2009. For a survey of the serpent in Anglo-Saxon art, see Ball 2017:185–235.

[30] *Finnsburg fragment* l.3. For the text, see Dobbie 1942:3–4; Fry 1974.

[31] MS D, Cotton Tiberius B.iv, and MS E, Bodleian MS Laud 636. MS D was left unfinished when rudely interrupted in AD 1066, which gives us a firm terminus ante for the text (MS E is later); for the text, see Irvine 2004:42. Cf. Wild 1962:24; Lionarons 1998:14–15; Rauer 2000:49–50; Symons 2015:76.

[32] For the dragons of this saga, see Lionarons 1993.

Theodoric the Goth, who ruled Rome between AD 493 and 526. The saga is a
peculiarly rich source of flying dragons, containing three major episodes of interest: we shall consider the first two here and the third later (§10.4.4). In the first
episode Thidrek and Fasold rescue Sistram from a flying dragon that has snatched
him up as he slept. The episode seems to have a comic edge, and would not have
been out of place in a modern spoof like *Monty Python and the Holy Grail*:[33]

> When they left the forest [of Rimslo], they saw something profoundly strange
> and surprising. They saw a massive flying dragon [*flugdreki*]. It was both long and
> thick. It had thick legs and claws both sharp and long. Its head was massive and
> awful. It flew nearly on the earth itself, and it was as if the earth had been scored
> with the sharpest iron, wherever its claws touched it. In its mouth it held a man,
> and it had swallowed him feet first all the way up to his hands. His head and his
> shoulders were sticking out of its mouth. His hands hung below the jaws, but the
> man lived yet. When he espied the two men riding there, he called to them.
> 'Good brave men', he said, 'ride this way and help me. This massive devil seized
> me as a I slept on my shield. If I had rather been awake and on my mettle, then
> this great creature would not have been able to harm me. When the partners
> heard that, Thidrek and Fasold, they leaped down from their horses, brandished
> their swords, and both hacked at the dragon [*dreki*] at once. Thidrek's sword bit
> into it a little, but Fasold's not at all. Although this dragon was big and strong, it
> was more than the creature could do to lift the man together with his weapons,
> and it could not get up aloft to fly and protect itself, in the way it would have
> done if unimpeded. The man who was in the dragon's mouth said to Fasold,
> 'I see that your sword cannot bite into the creature, so hard is it. Take this sword
> here from the dragon's jaws. There is greater hope that it might bite most suc-
> cessfully at whatever comes under its edge, if a man of the braver sort has it.'
> With great valour Fasold leaped up, thrust his hand into the dragon's mouth,
> and took the sword. At once he hacked at the creature. The sword bit it no worse
> than the sharpest hair-knife does a beard. The same man said to Fasold, 'Be care-
> ful as you hack. My legs are lying a very long way down the dragon's neck, so
> please take care, because I do not want to get a wound from my very own sword.
> Do be careful, given that the sword is so very sharp.' He now spoke to them both:
> 'Hack as hard as possible, good brave men, because this wicked dragon is now
> squeezing me so hard with his jaws that blood is shooting from my mouth, and

---

[33] Differing views as to whether the humour is intentional at Kalinke 1981:195 and Lionarons
1998:100–3. The dragon's seizing of Sistram whilst he sleeps is ostensibly calqued on the MHG tradition of the (flightless) Dragon of Garda's fatal seizure of Ortnit as he is bound in a three-day sleep
after having closed his eyes beneath an enchanted linden tree: *Ortnit* (c.1217–25) §§568–75,
Wolfdietrich B (c. AD 1225–50) §§515–30. Despite the grimmer outcome, there is ostensibly humour
in these texts too, as Ortnit's dog, horse, and tame elephant desperately try to rouse him as the dragon
approaches, with the first running back and forth between the dragon and his master, and the last
rolling him around.

I cannot yet tell the outcome of your attack.' And now they hacked hard, until the dragon was dead.   *Thidrek's Saga* §105

In a second episode Ostasia, daughter of King Runi of Austriki in Russia and queen to King Hertnid of Vilkinaland, and a witch to boot, magically summons an army of beasts to make war on the invading army of King Isung of Bertangaland. The army consists of lions and bears, amongst other beasts, but is dominated by a squadron of flying dragons (*flugdrekar, drekar*) explicitly endowed with both wings and claws. She also transforms herself into a flying dragon to preside over the army. As with Sistram's dragon, particular attention is given to the dragons' claws here, with the largest dragon actually picking up the eldest of Isung's sons in its claws and squeezing him in them until his breastplate and torso shatter (Thetlief meets a partly similar fate).[34]

The first of the *Thidrek's Saga* episodes (and so too the third, as will be seen) is seemingly the inspiration for a rather flatter episode in *Erex's Saga* (xiii AD, although the episode in question may be a later interpolation; the saga as a whole is based on Chrétien de Troyes'—dragonless—*Érec et Énide*). Here Erex and his lady Ovid are riding through the forest when they find a winged and legged dragon (*flugdreki, dreki*) similarly flying low and trying to get off the ground with a knight called Plato in its mouth. He hacks at the dragon's shoulder from horseback, presumably with his sword, whereupon the dragon falls on its knees and releases Plato. Erex then dismounts and kills the dragon with a spear through the mouth, but as it collapses it falls on his horse and kills it.[35]

10.3.3 The Dragon of Adalsyssla

Burnt Njal's Saga (AD 1270–90) lapidarily informs us that in the course of his adventures Thorkell Hakr (Foulmouth) killed a flying dragon (*flugdreki*) in Adalsyssla.[36]

10.3.4 The Dragon of the Southern Seas

In the *Saga of Björn, Champion of the Men of Hitardal* (xiii AD) a winged dragon attacks Canute's ship, making much use of its claws:

In the summer after that Björn travelled west to England. He acquired a good reputation there. He remained there two winters with the mighty Canute. That is

---

[34] *Þiðrekssaga* §§349–55.   [35] *Erex saga Artuskappa* §10, pp. 48–51 Blaisdell.
[36] *Brennu-Njals saga* §119 Sveinsson.

when the following took place. When Björn followed the king and sailed with his troops for southern seas, a flying dragon [*flugdreki*] flew over the king's troops, made an attack on them and wanted to claw a man up. However, Björn was standing near and sheltered him with his shield. But the dragon nearly clawed all the way through the shield. Then with one hand Björn grabbed hold of the dragon's tail, and with the other he delivered a chop to it behind its wings. It was riven asunder and fell down dead.

Saga of Björn, Champion of the Men of Hitardal §5

10.3.5 The Dragon of the Rhine

In the *Saga of Silent Sigurd* (xiv AD) the Dragon (*dreki*) of the Rhine makes thundering noises from the high mountain in which it lives, the mountain glowing at night with its flames, and flies over the army of Halfdan and Vilhjalmr, spewing venom over it and killing sixty of their men. It swallows one of them down and flies off with two others in its claws. Sigurd the Silent subsequently finds the dragon attempting to fly off with a lion in these same claws, and initiates his attack against it by wounding it under the wing (explicitly specified) with his spear.[37]

10.3.6 The Dragon of England

A relatively unique dragon-slaying story in the Norse tradition that pays particular attention to the physiology of the dragon, its wings and its claws, is that of Unus and the Dragon of England, as recounted in the *Saga of King Flores and his Sons* (xiv AD). For this reason, and because, to the best of my knowledge, the saga is not available in English, I reproduce it in full. Unus (Felix) begins by telling how, as a boy, he was rescued from the sea after a shipwreck:

Then some people came to me on a longship and brought me to England and to a king called Grando. He had a daughter and a handsome son. They gave me to the king. I gave myself the name Unus but I didn't want to say more, because I didn't know their tongue. The king found me a home in his city. My foster mother was called Silvia. That's where I grew up, until I was 15 years old. The king had me instructed in chivalry, until it came to the point where no one could surpass me in the saddle. I got on well with the princess, and for that reason the prince bore a grudge against me, as well as for the fact that I garnered more

---

[37] *Sigurðar saga þögla* §§13, 16.

praise than he did. But he didn't allow himself to show it. One day we were riding in the forest, and there was a page with us. The prince asked me how long we
should live such a soft life without deeds of great glory. I asked him what oppor-
tunities were available to us. He said that he knew of a flying dragon [*flugdreki*]
in a forest in a lake, and that the gold underneath it exceeded even what the king
owned. I told him I would follow his advice. Then we took a ship and rowed to
the island. It was such a long way that little of the day was left. There were lofty
cliffs around the island. High on these cliffs there was a cave, and a precipice
projected out over it. In this cave lay the dragon [*dreki*], and it was dangerous to
approach. There was a narrow path to the cave along the cliffs. One had to leap
down from the path into the cave, but the leap was so far down that one could
not get up to the path again unless one was drawn up on a rope. The others
attended to the rope, and I went along the path. Then I jumped down into the
cave. I had no weapons other than a single spear. But when I had steadied myself,
the prince drew the rope back up. Then they took the boat and rowed off, abandoning me there. It seemed that I was not in a good spot, because to throw
myself down into the water meant death, but I could not get back up to the path.
When I came down, the dragon was asleep, and I supposed that things would
not improve for me when it woke up. I could kill it, but even so I could not get
out of the cave. Then it occurred to me to climb up as high as I could over the
cave-entrance. I was in a difficult position. Then the dragon woke up and realized that there had been an intrusion into its home. So it stuck its head out of the
cave entrance and peered all around. I jumped down between its wings and
embraced its neck in my arms. The dragon now flew forth from its cave and up
over the water, and then back over the forest. Then I took my spear and thrust it
in under the dragon's left wing until it stopped in its heart. It reacted violently,
and thrashed the forest with its wings, with the result that the oaks were shattered. Then I fell down, and the dragon fell on top of me. Its spasms were violent
and it thrashed me with its wings, until I lay in a daze. I did not recover my
senses until the dragon was dead. I was covered in blood, and I stumbled my
way out of the forest. I had one of the dragon's claws with me. I found a little
cottage, and I stayed there until I was healed. It was a long way from the king's
hall. I travelled incognito until I could get to the princess. She was delighted to
see me. I told her how her brother had abandoned me, and asked her to give me
some protection. She said she would do all in her power to help me. Then she let
me prepare a ship in secret and chose out some of her trusted men for me.
Altogether there were twenty-four of us. She was unsparing with gold and silver
for us. Before we parted, I gave her the dragon's claw. It could serve as a large
drinking up. But I kept hold of the bone that had lain inside it. Then we swore
oaths and made a pledge together, that she should marry no man before I sent
her the bone, and that I should marry no woman before she sent me the claw.
After that we parted, in great sorrow. I sailed off. I put in at the forest in which

I knew the prince was wont to ride. I went into it and looked out for him. I found him accompanied by two others. I thanked him for abandoning me. Our encounter came to an end when I killed them all. Then I sailed away from England.   *Saga of King Flores and his Sons* §20

10.3.7 Valr and his Sons and Gull-Thorir as Dragons

Both the *Saga of Gold-Thorir* (xiv AD) and the *Saga of Halfdan Son of Eystein* (xiv AD) speak of the (permanent) transformation of the Viking Valr and his sons into flying dragons (*drekar, flugdrekar*, in both texts) as they sit on their gold in the cave into which they have retreated near Dumbshaf. We know specifically that they are winged too, by virtue of the fact that they keep their swords under their wings, their former arms, evidently.[38] Their gold is taken by Gull-Thorir ('Gold-Thorir'), and at the end of his (at any rate human) life he becomes a dragon himself and lies down on his treasure-chests in turn: henceforth he is to be seen flying across the adjacent fjord and into his mountain.[39]

10.3.8 Harek as a Flying Dragon

It is into a flying dragon (*flugdreki*) that Harek, Valr's uncle, temporarily transforms himself in the the *Saga of Bosi and Herraud* (before AD 1350), when wounded and angered by Smidur. Consonantly with this, he proceeds to engage in a sky-fight with a monstrous bird, a *skergripr*.[40] In the *Saga of Halfdan Son of Eystein* (xiv AD) Harek again transforms into a flying dragon (*flugdreki*), although the focus in this narrative is not on his wings but on his legs and their claws. Grubs contrives to cut off one of his dragon feet, but Harek then grabs him with the other one and tears open his groin in doing so—a nice confirmation that he possesses two legs in the standard wyvern format.[41]

10.3.9 The Dragon of Wexford (à la Norse)

In the *Saga of Tristram and Isodd* (*c.* AD 1400), there is no doubt about the Dragon of Wexford's fully wyvern configuration (in contrast to its earlier configuration in Gottfried von Strassburg's *Tristan*, for which see §10.2 above): it flies out of its

---

[38] *Gull-Þóris saga* §§3–4; *Hálfdanar saga Eysteinssonar* §26.   [39] *Gull-Þóris saga* §20.
[40] *Bósa saga ok Herrauðs* §14, iii.319 Jónsson.   [41] *Hálfdanar saga Eysteinssonar* §20.

cave, whereupon Tristan spears it, and it falls dead upon his horse, which is killed in turn when the dragon's claws tear through its ribs.[42]

10.3.10 The Dragon of *Valdimar's Saga*

In *Valdimar's Saga* (xv AD) the battle between the army of the giant king Arkistratus and Aper's host of trolls is interrupted when Arkistratus' wife, the troll-queen Lupa, flies from his castle in the form of a dragon (*flugdreki*) and spews venom down on them from above. But the dragon meets its match in the sky when challenged by a massive vulture that flies up from the sea and emits twelve or more arrows from its mouth at every breath. The two creatures then engage in a battle to the death in the sky as the two armies pause their fighting to watch. As the creatures wound each other they fill the valleys below with blood. The vulture eventually prevails and is revealed to be the giantess Nigra in transformation.[43]

10.3.11 The Dragon of Tartary

In the *Saga of Sigrgardr the Valiant* (xv AD) Knut (Sigrgardr) kills the witch Hlegerdr in her bower on a lake-island, and then investigates the cellar below:

Down beneath the bower he found a cellar. There lay a dragon [*ormr*]. At once it blew venom but it did not harm Knut because of the old woman's sorcery. The dragon flew out of the opening. There was gold and treasure there in abundance. He filled up his ox-horn. He took as much of the gold as was pleasing to him. Then he went out. He came now to his boat and made to row to the shore. But as he passed onto the water the dragon came up out of it with mouth agape, attacked the boat and hoisted a limb [*lit.* shoulder *or* flipper] onto the prow. He wielded his club and dashed it against the dragon's nose. But it drew the boat underwater with itself. Knut leaped onto the back of the dragon [*dreki*] and embraced its neck. And they travelled until they were close to shore. He took something from the old woman's bag and sprinkled it over the dragon. It was so drained of strength that it sunk into the water. Knut made for the shore.

Saga of Sigrgardr the Valiant §13.114–16 (§§88–90 Loth)[44]

---

[42] *Tristrams saga ok Ísoddar* §10 = §§35–6 Gísli Brynjólfsson = pp. 121–8 Vilhjálmsson.
[43] *Valdimars saga* §3; cf. §1.
[44] It should be noted, however, that the translation offered by Hall et al. 2012–13 for this particular passage differs in an important respect from my own, construing the dragon's attack with its 'shoulder'

This is an oddity indeed: a dragon described as both *ormr* and a *dreki*, and equally at home in both the sky and the sea. How we are to imagine the limb it hoists over the ship we can only speculate. The easiest solution is to suppose that it is a wing, deployed for the purposes of flying and swimming alike, as it is with puffins. (There is no indication of wings in the cases of other aquatic dragons, the Midgard Worm or that encountered by Fridlief, for both of which see above, §§10.1, 10.2.)

10.4   Dragons Stranded between the Worm- and the Winged-Dragon Configuration

A number of Germanic texts seem to exhibit a schizophrenic conception of the dragon, with winged dragons on occasion at least seeming not to make use of their wings properly, as if the starring role in a story-type designed for and long inhabited by a pure vermiform dragon has been superficially re-cast with a dragon of the more modern (?) and exciting winged variety.

10.4.1 *Beowulf*'s Firedrake

The phenomenon begins already with the Anglo-Saxon *Beowulf*'s Firedrake, bane of the Geats.[45] The date of the epic has long been controversial, with guesses ranging from the seventh to the tenth centuries AD. In recent times the linguistic criteria for the dating have been addressed with a new rigour, principally by Fulk, who concludes that its composition falls within the gratifyingly early span of *c.* AD 685 to *c.* AD 725 (which makes the author broadly contemporary with

---

or 'flipper' (*bægslit*) rather as an attack with its 'wide jaws'. But cf. Cleasby and Vigfusson 1874 s.v. *bæxl*; Zoëga 1910 s.v. *bæxl*; and Acker 2013:57.

[45] *Beowulf* ll. 2200–3182. For general discussions of the *Beowulf* dragon, see Klaeber 1911–12; Lawrence 1918; Neckel 1920; Tolkien 1936; Sisam 1958; Chadwick 1959; Bonjour 1962; Wild 1962; Mitchell 1963; Carlson 1967; Brown 1980; Brynteson 1982; Tally 1983; Tripp 1983; Evans 1984, 1985, 2005; Schichler 1986; Sorrell 1994; Orchard 1995, 2003; Shilton 1997; Lionarons 1998:23–48; Rauer 2000; Ball 2017:102–15. For the (at least partially) Christian perspective of the *Beowulf* poem, see Klaeber 1911–12; Goldsmith 1963; Dronke 1969; Anderson 1997:142–3; Irving 1997; Lionarons 1998:40–7; and above all Rauer 2000:14–15 and passim. For a most useful doxographically focused handbook on the poem, see Bjork and Niles 1996. The Nowell codex, sole source of *Beowulf*, also contains other works with an interest in dragons: the (*c.* AD 1000?) Anglo-Saxon version of the *The Wonders of the East* (*De rebus in oriente mirabilibus*) tells of a land beyond the Brixontes that boasts dragons of 150 feet in length (§16), whilst the entirety of the third book of the (vii–viii AD) Latin *Liber monstrorum* is devoted to the monstrous serpents of the classical tradition, including the Hydra, the Bagrada Dragon, and the serpents of India; cf. Sisam 1953:65–96. Texts and translations of both these works are provided by Orchard 1995 and Fulk 2010. Momma 2016 discusses the deployment of the term *wyrm* across the codex as a whole; her observation (211) that 'dragons are not a staple of hagiography' alarms.

Aldhelm).[46] The creature is designated both by the term *wyrm*[47] and the term *draca*, as well as by several interesting compounds of the latter.[48] Its ability to fly is repeatedly adverted in its epithets,[49] and this indeed is how it propels itself when off to burn the buildings of men in its rage. But its wings as such are never specifically mentioned, and that too despite the fact that several physical details are supplied in the course of the expansive narrative: thus, it is 50 feet in length, it coils and breathes fire.[50] More strikingly still, there is no indication that the serpent ever leaves the ground in the course of its climactic battle with Beowulf, though it ought to have been to its considerable advantage to do so. We get the impression that the dragon of this battle had long been a pure vermiform in its tradition, and that its substitution with a flying and presumably winged dragon has been somewhat cosmetic.[51]

10.4.2 Pfetan

It is rare to find a named dragon in the Germanic tradition other than one that has evolved out of a correspondingly named human. An exception is 'the great worm Pfetan' (*der grôze wurm Pfetân*), the cave-dwelling dragon slain by the titular hero in Wirnt von Grafenberg's Middle High German verse romance *Wigalois* (c. AD 1205–10).[52] Wirnt accords the creature an elaborate physical description. It has

---

[46] Fulk 1992 esp. 368–81, 390–1. Fulk's conclusion has been supported by further linguistic and metrical studies, including those of Niedorf 2014 (an edited collection, with more from Fulk himself) and 2017. The older consensus (broadly sceptical but inclined towards a dating at the later end of the spectrum) is represented by the pieces collected in Chase 1981 and by Bjork and Obermeier 1997. North 2006 is speculative and controversial.

[47] The creature is designated by the term *wyrm* eighteen times in all: l. 2287, etc.; a full list at Rauer 2000:32 n. 26. For the full semantic field of *wyrm* in Anglo-Saxon literature, see Ball 2017:21–3 and passim.

[48] *Draca*: ll. 2212, 2290, 2402, 2549, 3131. *Niðdraca* ('enemy dragon'): 2273. *Lîgdraca* ('fire dragon'): 2333, 3040. *Fyrdraca* ('fire dragon', 'firedrake'): 2689. *Eorðdraca* ('earth dragon'): 2712, 2825. See Wild 1962:14–15; Lecouteux 1979:18; and esp. Lionarons 1998:28–9 and Rauer 2000:32–3. Note also that Grendel's mere is infested with 'sea-dragons' (*sæ-dracan*), amongst other 'worm-kin' (*wyrm-cynn*, 1425–6), on which see Honegger 2017.

[49] Thus: *lyftfloga* ('air-flier', l.2315), *guðfloga* ('battle-flier', 2528), *wîdfloga* ('wide-flier', 2536), *uht-floga* ('dawn-flier', 2760). Cf. again the (viii AD?) *Finnsburg fragment* l.3: *ne her draca ne fleogeð* ('nor does a dragon fly here').

[50] A point well noted by Shilton 1997:68.

[51] In his flyting with Unferth Beowulf claims to have slain, by night, nine sea-monsters in the course of a swimming competition across the Gulf of Bothnia, ll. 529–81. The term is *nicor* (575; cf. 422, 845, 1411, 1427); for discussion of the use of this term both here and in other Anglo-Saxon texts, see Ball 2017:81–102. A more recent reflex of the word is found in the title of the 'Lyminster Knucker', for which see Simpson 1973:31–9, 1978:90–1, 1980:130–3.

[52] The principal episode is at *Wigalois* ll. 4707–5140; the cave at 4774–5; the name Pfetan at 4856 (quoted) and 5013. General discussion at Thomas 1977:1–70 (the episode in question falls at pp. 156–61 in his curiously unarticulated translation); cf. also Rebschloe 2014:283–91. It is noteworthy that this dragon episode does not appear in either of the two texts regarded as Wirnt's principal models, Renaut de Bâgé/Beaujeu's *Le Bel inconnu* (c. AD 1190–1200), in which the champion's name is revealed to be Giglain, and Ulrich von Zatzikhoven's *Lanzelet* (c. AD 1195–1200). However, both of

(in roughly head-to-tail order): a large, black, shaggy head, which is carried low to the ground; a fathom-long pointed 'beak' with boar-tusk teeth; red eyes; a cockerel's comb (inspired by the basilisk?); mule-ears; a throat knotted like the horn of a mountain goat; a body round like a candle; horny scales; a green belly; yellow flanks; a pale yellow, sharp-ridged spine of the sort crocodiles use to bisect ships above; a long, prehensile tail in which it is able to grasp a clutch of four knights, winding it three times around them. It also has ugly feet (number unspecified), resembling a griffin's but hairy like a bear's, and a pair of beautiful wings made up of peacock-like feathers.[53] In Wirnt's original order of exposition the feet and then the wings are specified last, as they are here. The latter at least give the feel of being a somewhat awkward attachment, even in the context of the preceding farrago, and perhaps the former do too. Everything else, certainly, speaks of an elongated, snake-like form: the fathom-long toothed 'beak' (perhaps this too is imagined along the lines of a crocodile's mouth?), the neck capable of knotting, the candle-body, and the tail capable of such generous constriction. The few actions ascribed to the creature are compatible with and even favour a pure vermiform. It travels slowly, fearing nothing.[54] When Wirnt first approaches it, he hears it bringing the great trees of a forest crashing down as it *slips* along (*sleif*).[55] Wigalois drives his lance through the dragon's heart before it notices him, whereupon it drops the four knights it is carrying, turns after him and squeezes him instead (similarly in its tail, we must infer), shattering his chain mail and forcing blood from his nose and ears in its death throes. At the same time, somehow or other, it also tears his horse to pieces.[56] So here, it would appear, we have a dragon of ancient worm form that has yet to discover the use of the feet and wings with which it has been decorated.

10.4.3 Fafnir

In the *Saga of the Volsungs* (*c.* AD 1200–70) Sigurd is said to plunge his sword up into (*dreki* and *ormr*) Fafnir's left shoulder from the ditch in which he is hiding below him, as he travels along the path from his cave to the river to drink. This ought to imply that Fafnir is possessed of legs or wings or both. But neither feature is really compatible with the remainder of the narrrative, in which Fafnir

---

these texts contain an episode in which a fair princess has been transformed into a serpent and can only return to human form by kissing the champion. Giglain so kisses the fiery, carbuncle-eyed *wivre/guivre* Esmerée (*Le Bel inconnu* ll. 3101–373), whilst Lanzelet so kisses the bearded (!) *wurm* Clidra/Elidia (*Lanzelet* ll. 7817–8040). The references to flight in the latter case (ll. 7877, 7935) would seem to be metaphorical expressions of speed, given that she is said, as a worm, to slither on her belly (l. 8022).

[53] *Wigalois* ll. 5028–76.   [54] *Wigalois* ll. 4986–7.   [55] *Wigalois* ll. 5004–8.

[56] *Wigalois* ll. 5088–140. However, as we have seen, at Þiðrekssaga §§349–55 Queen Ostasia's largest dragon shatters King Isung's son's torso, breastplate and all, in its claw (§10.3.2 above; Chapter 11 §11.7.4).

surely crawls along his path in the manner of a pure snake (as expounded at greater length below: Chapter 11, §11.8). Again we may suspect that we have a dragon stranded between paradigms: he can be given wings and other embelishments in direct description, surely enough, but the force of tradition behind his story keeps him cleaving closely to the ground.[57]

10.4.4 The Dragon of Bergara: The Third Dragon of *Thidrek's Saga*

The third dragon of *Thidrek's Saga* (*ormr* and *dreki* alike, *c.* AD 1230–50) is introduced as a full-service winged and clawed creature. It lives in a mountain cave in a forest in King Hertnid's Bergara. In an excess of bravado, King Hertnid goes up against it alone. It seizes him in its claws and takes him off to its cave, where it casts him down dead before its three young to eat. Thidrek subsequently hears the sounds of the dragon fighting a lion in the forest and tracks the warring pair down by following the great trail that the dragon has left in the forest floor. This detail surely belongs with a worm-style dragon rather than a winged and stoutlegged one.[58] (The remainder of this tale is expounded in Chapter 11, §11.7.1.) Even in a text so emphatically devoted to winged, flying dragons as *Thidrek's Saga* is, it seems that the influence of worm-dragon story-types cannot be completely shaken off.

10.4.5 The Jakulus of Scythia

In the *Saga of Yngvar the Far-Traveller* (xiii AD) the hill of golden treasure investigated by Valdimar in (as it seems) Scythia is covered in sleeping serpents (*ormar*). When he accidentally wakes one of these, it rouses all the others until what is evidently the presiding entity is also roused, the Jakulus (or a dragon called Jakulus), which is a flying *dreki* that proceeds to wreak destruction from the air. It may be that in this case a winged dragon presides over a wingless snake brood.

---

[57] *Völsunga saga* §18. Lionarons 1998:64 takes 'shoulder' to imply 'legs'. Acker 2013:54–5, 57 rightly holds that wings could equally well be implied. For the Sigurd-Siegfried legend, see (in addition to the general discussions of the dragon in Norse literature cited above) Ploss 1966; Lecouteux 1995; Lionarons 1998:49–92; Jensen 2017:207–10; Neubauer 2019. For Wagner's reflex of the Siegfried story, see McCreless 1982; Tally 1983; Donington 1990; Millington 2011. For a once very popular retelling of the Sigurd-Siegfried story in English, see William Morris' *The Story of Sigurd the Volsung and the Fall of the Niblungs* (1876, Book 2). For the improbable theory that Sigurd-Siegfried is a dim refraction of the historical Arminius, who famously destroyed Varus' three legions at Kalkriese in the Teutoburg forest in AD 9, see Vigfusson 1886; Höfler 1961, 1978; Beck 1985; Lionarons 1998:16–17. Cf. Chapter 11 nn. 11 and 118 for similar speculations.

[58] *Þiðrekssaga* §§ 416–22. The story-type is repeated at *Blómsstrvalla saga* §25 (xv AD), as discussed below, although there is no suggestion here that the dragon concerned is of the worm-type.

The term Jakulus, a direct borrowing from the Latin *iaculus* ('javelin', more particularly 'javelin-snake') is both appropriate and inappropriate for the creature in question. As we know, not least from the striking passage of Lucan (cf. Chapter 2, §2.1), the *iaculus* is indeed a flying snake that can launch itself through the air and drive itself, javelin-like, through a man's head, emerging from the other side before disappearing; however, in resembling a javelin in its physical form, and being able to achieve feats of that kind, it is of course emphatically wingless.[59]

10.4.6 The Dragon of Colchis

The *Saga of the Trojans* (xiii AD) is a free adaptation of Dares Phrygius' Latin *History of the Sack of Troy*. The dragon (*dreki*) of Colchis slain by Jason here (it does not feature at all in the Dares text) does not fly in its featured episode, but it is explicitly said to possess wings, for Jason stabs it under one of them. Medea has drugged it to sleep first, as in classical tradition, but it is nonetheless roused again as Jason kills it. It is also, quite uniquely, said to possess many eyes. The source of this unique motif is clear, for in this narrative the dragon is co-guardian of the fleece alongside King Medius' servant, the hundred-eyed Argus (Medius stepping into the role of Aeetes).[60]

10.5 Norse Iconography and Ships

Let us briefly consider the development of flying dragons in the Norse realm now from the iconographic perspective. Already from *c.* AD 1050 onwards dragons can acquire wings and forelegs on Swedish runestones, in a departure from the formerly pure-serpent style found, for example, in the Fafnir image of the well-known Rasmund stone of *c.* AD 1010–40.[61] The Norman Bayeux Tapestry of the 1070s (regarded fundamentally as a product still of Norse culture) gives us a pair of winged dragons each with two feet beneath the figures of the lady Aelfgyva and William.[62] From the twelfth century onwards we find winged and two-legged dragons in the relief carvings of Norwegian stave churches. Such, for example, is the Fafnir found on the door-jamb from the (lost) Hylestad stave-church, perhaps

---

[59] *Yngvars saga viðförla* §5, ii.436 Jónsson. Lucan *Pharsalia* 9.822–7; cf. also Solinus 27.30. Discussion at Acker 2012:4–7.

[60] *Trójumanna saga* §§9–10.

[61] Düwel 1988:133–6; Acker 2013:58–61, with a winged example reproduced at his fig. 3.3. The earliest examples of dragons on runestones derive from the viii AD: we have examples from Lindkoeping and Uppsala.

[62] Wilson 1985:178 (part 18); cf. Acker 2013:65.

the best-known image of Fafnir to survive: he sports a foreleg and the vestige of a now broken wing (Fig. 10.1).[63]

The Vikings' dragon-prowed ships are not the modern myth their horned helmets are supposed to be.[64] On the literary side, the sagas abound with references to dragon-headed longships.[65] More specifically, gilded-headed dragonships are mentioned in Oddr Snorrason's (originally xii AD) *Saga of Olaf, Son of Tryggvi* [66] before featuring prominently and repeatedly throughout Snorri Sturluson's *c.* AD 1230 history of the kings of Norway, *Heimskringla*. Most notable here is Snorri's description of Raud's ship, the most beautiful one in Norway, as possessing both a dragon-head prow and a dragon-tailed stern, both gilded, with its sails giving the impression of wings when unfurled.[67] A number of items may be mentioned on the iconographic side:

- The spiral prow of the Oseberg Ship now in Oslo's Viking Ship Museum of *c.* AD 800 or before ends in a small serpent head; the neck of the prow is also, separately, decorated with relief carvings of intertwining serpents.[68]
- A 30 cm gilded brooch from the early Viking age, now in the National Museum, Copenhagen, seems to evoke a dragon-headed vessel in its shape.[69]
- A manuscript of the Latin *Cicero's Aratus* (often misleadingly referred to as an 'Anglo-Saxon manuscript') made in Wiltshire in *c.* AD 1050–75 illustrates the constellation of (Jason's ship) Argo with a superbly detailed and colourful picture of a ship with a dragon-head prow and a dragon-tail stern (Fig. 10.2). The head is rendered in a light-yellow colour that speaks of gilding.[70]

[63] Lindholm and Roggenkamp 1968 pll. 64, 48, and 103l; cf. Acker 2013:63–5, with his fig. 3.5. Neubauer 2019 contends that the image earned its place in a Christian church by virtue of the fact that it could evoke a martial Christian saint's slaying of his dragon—but the timing might be a little tight for knowledge of George's story in the west. Let us note also an interesting xii AD pillar base from Nes in Telemark in which a crudely carved Sigurd emerges from a pit to stab a lindworm-style Fafnir (i.e. two legs but no wings) from below: see Düwel 1988:139 and 154 fig. 7. For the Sigurd-Siegfried legend in Germanic art more generally, see Kermode 1907; Ellis 1942a; Lindholm and Roggenkamp 1968; Wilson 1970; Blindheim 1972; Margeson 1980; Düwel 1988; Byock 1990b; Hohler 1999; Bailey 2000; Acker 2013; Symons 2015:88–91.

[64] However, in the far distant past...the magnificent pair of horned helmets from Veksø, of Bronze Age date, now in the National Museum of Denmark (illustration at Nielsen 2016:115).

[65] Two random examples: *Göngu-Hrólfs saga* §8 (xiv AD) *Egils saga* §10 (xiii AD).

[66] Oddr Snorrason *Óláfs saga Tryggvasonar* §67.

[67] Snorri Sturluson *Heimskringla Óláfs saga Tryggvasonar* §87. For other references to dragon-prowed ships in the *Heimskringla*, many of them again specified to be gilded, see Óláfs saga Tryggvasonar §§20, 85, 95, 111; Óláfs saga helga §§154, 157, 160 (St Olaf); Haralds saga hárfagra §§19, 35, 61–3; Sigurðar saga jórsalafara §27; Saga Inga Haraldssonar ok brœðra hans §§31–2. Cf. Brøgger and Shetelig 1951:113, 116.

[68] It is less clear that the animal-head fittings also found with the ship could have served as prowheads (for other vessels, presumably), nor is it clear that they represent dragons, but the case for both is made by Brøgger and Shetelig 1951:214–18; they also contend (162–3) that the (later ix AD) Gokstad ship must have once sported a dragon-head.

[69] Illustration at Nielsen 2016:225.

[70] British Libary MS Cotton Tiberius B.v, Part 1, fol. 40v. Note also the depiction of Noah's ark with dragon heads on stern and prow alike in the *Old English Hexateuch*, British Libary MS Cotton Claudius B.iv, fol. 15r (xi AD).

Fig. 10.1 Sigurd slays Fafnir. Carving from the Hylestad stave church, xii A D.
© Werner Forman Archive/Heritage Images.

- Dragon-headed ships are found in good numbers with the Vikings in their Norman reflex in the (1070s A D) Bayeux Tapestry. Again their yellow colour suggests gilding.[71]
- A dragon-headed ship is represented in an iron mounting on the Norman south-west door of St Helen's church in Stillingfleet, Yorkshire.[72]

[71] Wilson 1985 pll. 5–6, 26, 33, 37, 40–3.   [72] Illustrated at Brøgger and Shetelig 1951:217.

Fig. 10.2 Viking ship. Illustration from a Latin MS of *Cicero's Aratus, c.* AD 1050–7. British Library, MS Cotton Tiberius B. V. Part 1, f40v. © British Library Board / Bridgeman Images.

- The 'Bryggen shipstick', a juniper stick of *c.*25 cm in length excavated at Bergen and now in the city's Maritime Museum is dated archaeologically to between AD 1248 and 1332 (Fig. 10.3). Its complex graffiti includes a superb drawing of a dragon-headed ship with an elaborate stern (tail?) curving back over the vessel.[73]
- Several of the graffiti images carved on Norwegian stave churches (xii AD onwards) collected by Blindheim seem to depict or refract dragon-headed vessels.[74] Perhaps something of the culture of the dragon-head prows is preserved also in the superb wooden dragon-head gables of these churches, developed principally in the late eleventh century AD.[75]

Given this culture, it is unsurprising that Norse literature should have celebrated the theme of dragons attacking ships at sea, as in the cases of: the Midgard Worm,

[73] See Christensen 1995; le Bon 2001. The stick also contains a runic inscription, *hér ferr hafdjarfr*, 'Here fares the sea-bold one'.

[74] Note especially Blindheim 1985:33 and pl. xxxiv (Hopperstad, a clear example); 44 and pl. lviii (Rødven, seemingly an image of a creature tout court in the first instance, but nonetheless strongly evocative of a ship with a dragon-head prow); 46 and pl. lxiv (Torpo).

[75] For the stave churches themselves, see Lindholm and Roggenkamp 1968.

Fig. 10.3 The Bryggen ship-stick. Bergen Maritime Museum, between AD 1248 and 1332. © Werner Forman Archive/Maritime Museum, Bergen/Heritage Images.

which battles with Thor as he fishes for it from a boat in Snorri's *Prose Edda* (*c.* AD 1220; cf. §10.1 above);[76] the Dragon of the Southern Seas, which attacks Canute's ship in the *Saga of Björn, Champion of the Men of Hitardal* (xiii AD; cf. §10.3.4 above);[77] the Jakukus, which rains down fire on two of Yngvar's ships in *Yngvar's Saga* (xiii AD; cf. §10.4.5 and Chapter 11, §11.5.1);[78] and the dragon into which Harek transforms himself to rain down venom on Smidur's ship in the *Saga of Bosi and Herraud* (before AD 1350; cf. Chapter 11, §11.1).[79] Of particular interest are a pair of dragons that emerge *from the sea* to make their attacks on humans: in Saxo Grammaticus' Latin (xiii AD) *Gesta Danorum* Fridlief is attempting to dig up a treasure buried on an unnamed island when a dragon rises up out of the waves of the sea to attack him (cf. Chapter 11, §11.2);[80] and the Dragon of Tartary similarly emerges from the sea to attack Knut's (Sigrgardr's) ship in the (xv AD) *Saga of Sigrgardr the Valiant* (cf. §10.3.11, above).

10.6 Conclusion

The ancient and traditional Germanic dragon was probably ever a simple worm in form, doubtless a fiery one, as the classical dragon had been, and as indeed the Indo-European dragon had been. The exciting new format of the winged dragon

---

[76] Snorri Sturluson *Prose Edda* Gylfaginning §§34, 46–48, 51, 53; cf. *Poetic Edda* Hymiskviða §§17–26 (*c.* AD 1270). This leads us to a slight oddity of the Germanic tradition, as we approach it from the perspective of the classical and hagiographical traditions, namely the partial assimilation of dragons to fish. In *Ketils saga hœngs* (§1; xiii AD), upon seeing the great flying dragon emerge from the hill to the north, Ketil, who is similarly engaged in fishing at the time, remarks to himself that he has never seen such a fish before. In *Ragnars saga loðbrókar* (§§2–4; xiii AD) Ragnar twice uses the concept of fish in kennings for Thora's dragon: 'earth-fish' and 'heath-salmon'. Admittedly, both Ketil's and Ragnar's analogies are intended to be partly disjunctive.

[77] *Bjarnar saga Hítdaelakappa* §5.   [78] *Yngvars saga viðförla* §5, ii.436 Jónsson.

[79] *Bósa saga ok Herrauðs* §14, iii.319 Jónsson.

[80] Saxo Grammaticus *Gesta Danorum* 6.150.

of Christian-Latin culture was embraced avidly and was often substituted into established dragon-fight tales. But on occasion the substitution remained superficial and cosmetic, with the new winged creatures remaining strangely flightless in their featured fights. Just as the winged dragon gives the appearance, in this way, of being a new and only semi-digested arrival in the *c.* AD 685 to *c.* AD 725 Anglo-Saxon text of *Beowulf*, so too it often gives a similar appearance in the Norse literature of the thirteenth century AD, half a millennium later. Does this pattern reflect the later arrival of Christianity on Scandinavian shores—or was it, rather, that medieval Germanic narrative tradition simply never could come to digest the winged dragon fully?

11

To the River and Back

The Etiquette of the Germanic Dragon Fight

As this chapter's subtitle indicates, our project here is to review the persistently recurring motifs of the Germanic dragon fight just as we did for the hagiographical dragon fight in Chapters 6 and 7. And, again as in the case of the hagiographical chapters, we shall begin with those motifs that can be sequenced into what might be considered a principal narrative course before turning (in §11.11) to a pair of more independent motifs.

11.1 Genesis (i): Shape-Shifters

Where do dragons come from? The classical and hagiographical traditions generally remain incurious about this, but it is a matter of intense interest in the Germanic one. It has four broad explanations to offer: (i) a human voluntarily shape-shifts into a dragon; (ii) a human is caused to change into a dragon by lying on treasure; (iii) a human corpse is transmuted into a dragon in its tomb; and (iv) a mysterious tiny snake or worm grows into a huge dragon, often with the help of human nurture. These four modes of explanation are often concatenated. A recurring phenomenon in Germanic literature is the human or humanoid that can, by one means or another, turn himself into a dragon—or vice versa.[1] As an example of the latter we have already met the Dragon of Northumbria that appears to Siward in the form of an old man on top of a mountain in the Latin *Vita S. Waldevi* (xii–xiii AD; Chapter 8, §8.3.1).[2]

Three magical and seemingly serial shape-shifters are of particular interest. First, Queen Ostasia of *Thidrek's Saga* (c. AD 1230–50), whom we have already encountered briefly (Chapter 10, §10.3.2). She is beautiful, wise, and wicked, an experienced witch, instructed in the craft of magic in childhood by her step-mother. She uses this craft of the old times, as it is described, to summon up her beast army against the forces of King Isung of Bertangaland, this beast army being dominated by its squadron of flying dragons, and indeed to transform herself into another flying dragon to command them all. Eventually, the author notes, King

---

[1] For general discussion of the phenomenon, see Evans 2005:248–61.
[2] *Vita S. Waldevi* pp. 104–7 Michel.

Isung and all his sons lie dead owing to Ostasia's magic. After the successful battle, her husband King Hertnid returns to his castle to find Ostasia ill, and three days later she dies. As a result of this Hertnid understands where the helpful army of beasts and dragons has come from. It is less clear to us how he is able to make this connection. Is it that, in taking on the role of a dragon in the battle, Ostasia has exhausted herself to the point of death? Is it that she has been exhausted less by her physical efforts as a dragon, than by the exercise of magic in itself: has this drained her life-force? Or is it, more simply, that the dragon into which she transforms herself is to be regarded as identical with the largest dragon, the one that attacks King Isung and his eldest son, being wounded by the latter in foot and flank in the process? Does she, then, simply die from her (identifying) wounds?[3]

Second, Grim Aegir of *Walking-Hrolf's Saga* (xiv AD). Fighting in battle on behalf of King Eirik against Hrolf and his men, he transforms himself into a winged dragon several times. When he finds himself unable to raise a field of dead warriors to make a new army for Eirik, because the corpses have been given magical protection by the dwarf Mondul, his eyes blaze with fire and he emits a stinking smoke from his mouth and his nostrils. He dives down into the earth, as if into water, to ambush Hrolf's warriors as he re-emerges from it. He now spews out venom and fire, taking off into the air to rain venom down on Hrolf and others. As Hrolf is finally killing him with the help of Mondul, he warns Mondul not to hack off his limbs, for anything hacked from him will immediately turn into a venomous serpent. Also, they must avoid looking at his face as he dies, or they will themselves be killed by it; they cover it with a shield before driving a sword through him, and his body crumbles into dust.[4] We encounter a similar character in the *Saga of Baering the Fair* (xiv AD). Here Baering defeats one Skadevalldr, who turns into a dragon, breathes fire, and spews venom.[5]

Third, in *Valdimar's Saga* (xv AD) the troll-queen Lupa, wife of the giant-king Arkistratus, possesses a dragon-skin which she dons to transform herself into a fiery flying dragon (*flugdreki*). It is in this form that she snatches up Valdimar's sister, princess Marmoria, and subsequently intervenes, to her own demise, in the battle between her husband and Aper.[6]

It is noteworthy that transformation into a dragon sometimes follows directly upon the receipt of a wound in human form. In the *Saga of Bosi and Herraud* (before AD 1350) Harek is enraged when Smidur is able to knock his teeth out with a sword charmed by the witch Busla and so transforms himself into a flying

---

[3] *Þiðrekssaga* §§349–55. One thinks here of the classical claim at Zenobius *Epitome* 404, with scholium (at *CPG* i, 83), that Thessalian witches have to sacrifice a child or an eye when they perform their trick of drawing down the moon, and also of the 1973 Ray Harryhausen movie *The Golden Voyage of Sinbad*, in which the wicked magician-prince Koura (Tom Baker) loses a decade or so of his life each time he practices one of his spells, and is consequently anxious to secure access to a fountain of youth.
[4] *Göngu-Hrólfs saga* §§2, 31, 33.   [5] *Bærings saga fagra* §22, pp. 118–19 Cederschiöld.
[6] *Valdimars saga* §§1 (*hun attj eirn dreka ham*) and 3.

dragon and spews venom down over Smidur's ship, killing many of his men, before diving down and swallowing Smidur himself.[7] In the *Saga of Halfdan Son of Eystein* (xiv AD) we meet Harek again. Here he transforms himself into a dragon after Skuli cuts off one of his ears and cheeks. He then grabs Skuli in his tail, rendering him unconscious. As we have seen (Chapter 10, §10.3.8), another warrior, Grubs, then cuts off Harek's dragon's foot, but he tears open his groin with the claws of his other foot. Finally, he is killed by Halfdan, who delivers a blow to his neck.[8] In the *Saga of Sörli the Strong* (xv AD) Tofi similarly shapeshifts into a dragon when Sorli pokes him in the eye and tears the flesh off his cheeks, so that his beard hangs down over his chest.[9]

11.2 Genesis (ii): Lying on Treasure

> The dragon is to be in its barrow, old and wise, proud of its treasures.
>
> Anglo-Saxon gnomic proverb,
> [*Cotton*] *Maxims* ii, 26a–27b (x AD?)[10]

Of greater interest are those men that make a one-off shift into dragons as they retreat into a remote cave with their ill-gotten golden treasure in order to lie on it jealously forever. The most famous case is of course that of Fafnir. He is found first (though not named) in a passing reference in the Anglo-Saxon *Beowulf* (*c.* AD 685 to *c.* AD 725):

> Great fame sprang up for Sigemund after the day of his death. For the doughty warrior had laid low the worm [*wyrm*], the guardian of the hoard. Under the grey stone the prince's son attempted an audacious deed. He did not have Fitela with him. Nonetheless, it fell to him that his sword transfixed the portentous worm, so that the noble iron stood in the wall. The dragon [*draca*] died in the killing. By valour the dread warrior enabled himself to acquire the treasure-hoard, as he wished. Wael's son [cf. 'Völsung'] loaded up his sea-going boat and bore the adornments in the bosom of his ship. The hot worm melted.[11]
>
> *Beowulf* 884–97

In subsequent versions of this tale the role of Sigemund here is taken by his son, Sigurd-Siegfried. Prime amongst these, moving back into Norse territory, is that

---

[7] *Bósa saga ok Herrauðs* §14, iii.319 Jónsson.   [8] *Hálfdanar saga Eysteinssonar* §20.
[9] *Sörla saga sterka* pp. 381–3 Jónsson.
[10] *Draca sceal on hlaewe/ frod, fraetwum wlanc*. For the text, see Dobbie 1942:55–7. Discussion at Beekman Taylor 1997:230–1; Evans 2005:261–3; and Barreiro 2019:59 (the latter seemingly confused).
[11] See Talbot 1983 for the intriguing but frankly challenging contention that this tale constitutes a dim refraction of the historical episode in which the Batavian chieftain Civilis burned the Roman camp at Vetera, the subsequent Xanten, in AD 69, as told at Tacitus *Histories* 4.60; Xanten is Sigemund's home in the *Nibelungenlied*. Cf. Chapter 10 n. 57 and n. 118 in this chapter for similar speculations.

supplied by the *Saga of the Volsungs* (*c.* AD 1200–70). Here the greedy Fafnir kills his father Hreidmar and deprives his brother Regin of his share of the gold they had all forcibly extorted from the Aesir-gods, Odin, Loki, and Hoenir, in compensation for their killing of a third brother, Otr, the man-otter. He takes it off into the wilderness of Gnita-Heath and is there transformed into a great worm-dragon that then lies upon the gold in his cave, forever guarding it. Regin persuades his foster-son Sigurd to go off to the heath and kill Fafnir, misleadingly telling him that he is no bigger than a water-snake. As a smith, he reforges Sigurd's broken sword Gram for him, rendering it so strong and sharp that it will slice through an anvil. Regin advises Sigurd on method: he is to dig a ditch in the track along which Fafnir comes down from his cave to the nearby river to drink. He is to sit in this and then thrust his sword up into Fafnir's heart as he crawls overhead. As he is digging the ditch a local old man advises him rather to dig several, so as to catch all the serpent's blood, and he does so:

> So Sigurd made the trench after the fashion in which he had been instructed. And when the dragon [*ormr*] crawled to the water there was a great earthquake, with the result that the land shook all around. He snorted out venom, blowing it over the path before him. But Sigurd wasn't frightened by this, nor was he afraid of the noise. When the dragon crawled over the trench Sigurd stuck his sword into him under his shoulder in such a way that it only stopped at the hilt. Then Sigurd leaped up out of the trench and pulled the sword to him. He had his arms all covered in blood up as far as the shoulders. When the great dragon perceived his death-wound he beat his head and tail on the ground, with the result that he smashed apart everything before him.   *Saga of the Volsungs* §17

The dying Fafnir now prophesies to Sigurd. He tries to discourage him from taking his hoard of gold, warning him that it brings death to all that possess it (it has already been the death of its original owner, the dwarf-pike Andvari, from whom the gods had taken it, before then of Hreidmar and now of Fafnir himself). Regin rejoins Sigurd and drinks some of Fafnir's blood, in the knowledge that it will bestow the gift of prophecy upon him. He asks Sigurd to roast Fafnir's heart for him. As he does so he tests its juices by dipping his finger in them and licking it. In this way he too acquires the gift of prophecy, by means of the ability to understand the language of birds. The song of the nuthatches tells him at once that Regin is planning to betray him, and so he strikes his head off with Gram. Riding to Fafnir's lair, he finds its massive iron doors open and proceeds to take the hoard, in defiance of the dragon's warning (or otherwise believing that in getting the better of Regin he had already subverted the prophecy).[12]

---

[12] *Völsunga saga* §§13–20. Snorri Sturluson's version of this story at *Prose Edda* Skáldskaparmál §§46–7 (*c.* AD 1220) proceeds broadly along the same lines. The *Poetic Edda* (*c.* AD 1270) repeats many of the *Prose Edda*'s details in turn. However, from its Reginsmal we learn that Regin is himself a dwarf,

The motif is a productive one and further clear examples of it may be supplied. The *Saga of the Jomsvikings* (*c.* AD 1200) conveys the brief report that 'Bui turned into a worm [*ormr*] and lay on his gold' at Hjörungavagr.[13] The *Saga of Gold-Thorir* (xiv AD) and the *Saga of Halfdan Son of Eystein* (xiv AD) tell how the Viking Valr and his sons similarly retreat into a cave behind a waterfall with much gold, lie down upon it, and are transformed into dragons. An intriguing oddity of this episode, made clear in both texts, is that even in their transformed shape they retain their swords under their wings and their helmets on their heads.[14] The *Saga of Gold-Thorir* finishes its account of Gull-Thorir's life with the tradition that he had lain down on his treasure (formerly Valr's) and become a dragon in turn.[15] In *Ector's Saga* (xiv–xv AD) Ingifer, expelled from his city, takes with him two chests of gold, retreats to a cave, turns himself into a serpent, and lies on the gold there; after lying on the gold for thirty years, he is slain by Fenacius.[16] Also worthy of brief mention here is the *Saga of Viktor and Blavus* (xiv AD), in which Viktor and Blavus are said to have defeated the pair of berserkers and shape-shifters called Falur and Soti, who spew out venom in battle. Whilst these shift into dragons (or into the dragonish behaviour of venom-sprewing—cf. Grim Aegir and Skadevalldr) only on a temporary basis, they do leave behind them a hoard of gold and silver, to which Viktor and Blavus proceed to help themselves.[17]

These narratives are not very forthcoming about the mechanism of transformation. In *Thidrek's Saga* (*c.* AD 1230–50) Regin (here in the role of Fafnir: see n. 12 above) is said, rather vaguely, to have become a dragon as a result of his devotion to sorcery—probably, therefore, though not necessarily, by his own design.[18] As to Fafnir himself, the *Poetic Edda* (*c.* AD 1270) tells that his transformation was effected by his donning of Hreidmar's Helm of Dread; Snorri Sturluson's *Prose Edda* (*c.* AD 1220) may already imply the same. The *Saga of the Volsungs* (*c.* AD 1200–70), however, remains discreetly silent on the matter.[19] These explanations, such as they are, have the feeling of being (semi-)rationalizations. One feels that if the phenomenon of transformation-into-dragon-on-treasure as a whole has a profound justification, it must lie elsewhere: we will consider a possibility in the following section.

Germanic mythology gives us several further examples of dragons lying jealously on their piles of gold or treasure, usually in their caves or cave-like retreats,

whereas from its Fafnismal we learn that both Regin and Fafnir are giants; cf. also Gripisspa. In the (German-derived) *Þiðrekssaga* §§163–7 (*c.* AD 1230–50) Sigurd is portrayed as particularly doltish, whilst the role of the dragon is transferred from Fafnir to Regin and the role of the dragon's brother is transferred from Regin to Mimir.

[13] *Jómsvíkinga saga* §38; discussion at Sävborg 2014.

[14] *Gull-Þóris saga* §§3–4; *Hálfdanar saga Eysteinssonar* §26.   [15] *Gull-Þóris saga* §20.

[16] *Ectors saga* §8 (pp. 110–14) Loth; for an English resumé (*c.*50 per cent) see Fellows-Jensen in Loth.

[17] *Viktors saga ok Blávus* 14v–16v (pp. 77–83) Chappel = §§9–11 (pp. 26–31) Loth.

[18] *Þiðrekssaga* §§163–7.

[19] *Poetic Edda* Reginsmal and Fafnismal; Snorri Sturluson *Prose Edda* Skáldskaparmál §§46–7.

without indicating that they had a humanoid origin. The earliest example here may not, however, be what it seems. The Anglo-Saxon *Beowulf*'s (*c.* AD 685 to *c.* AD 725) great Firedrake sits on its pile of treasure in an ancient tomb, and peaceably so until a runaway serf steals a single jewelled cup from it, whereupon it flies out to unleash its terror and its fire on the local communities. Although there is indeed no explicit claim of a human origin in the case of this beast, hints of such may nonetheless lurk, as we shall see.[20] Subsequent examples of dragons lying jealously on their treasure are more straightforward. The tale of the Scythian dragon encountered by Yngvar in the *Saga of Yngvar the Far-Traveller* (xiii AD) has a similar set-up to the standard Fafnir tale: again we have a dragon (*dreki*) lying on its gold in its cave, and again we have a path between the cave and the local river frequented by the dragon. But in this case the plan is simply to delay the dragon returning to its cave whilst the gold is stolen rather than to kill it. Yngvar and his men sprinkle the path with salt and deposit on it the foot of a giant they happen to have with them. As the serpent returns from the river (as it must be, although the action is confusingly expounded), it is delayed as it licks up the salt, accordingly returning to the river to drink three times, and as it devours the foot. In the meantime Yngvar and his men can remove some of the serpent's gold. An interesting detail here is that the gold appears to be in the form of a single near-molten mass, being as hot as if it had just been brought from the forge, and Yngvar and his men must hack what they can away from it with their axes. We must infer that this is all the result of the dragon's heat, which has presumably congealed what was originally a pile of separate treasure-pieces.[21] Also in *Yngvar's Saga*, in the course of their voyages Yngvar and his men discover a hill that shines in the distance like a half moon. Valdimar goes off to investigate it: it turns out to be a mound of golden treasure, and it is, accordingly, covered in serpents (*ormar*). Since they are all asleep, Valdimar reaches into the pile to hook out a gold ring for himself on the end of his spear. But in so doing he wakes up a baby snake, which in turn rouses all the others, and disaster ensues (cf. Chapter 10, §10.4.5, and below, §10.5.1).[22]

In Saxo Grammaticus' Latin *Gesta Danorum* (early xiii AD) Frothi casts around for a source of money with which to pay his troops. He encounters a countryman who tells him of a nearby island in the hills of which lives a coiling, venom-spewing dragon that sits on a pile of treasure.[23] In this same text Fridleif, Frothi's son, is directed to a treasure guarded by another dragon. The treasure is buried in the ground on an unnamed island, and as Fridlief attempts to dig it up he is attacked by a dragon that rises up out of the waves of the sea to attack him, as we have seen (Chapter 10, §10.5).[24]

---

[20] *Beowulf* ll. 2200–2390.   [21] *Yngvars saga viðförla* §6, ii.442 Jónsson.
[22] *Yngvars saga viðförla* §5, ii.436 Jónsson.   [23] Saxo Grammaticus *Gesta Danorum* 2.1.1–4.
[24] Saxo Grammaticus *Gesta Danorum* 6.150.

In the *Saga of Sigurd the Silent* (xiv AD), after killing the Dragon of the Rhine, Sigurd makes his way to its cave, with the trusty lion companion he has rescued from the creature; he finds a pile of gold (and bones) within, with two baby dragons sitting on top of it.[25] The *Saga of Konrad* (xiv AD) is closely congruent: after killing the Dragon of Pezcina in the course of rescuing a lion from it, Konrad makes his way to its cave and kills the pair of baby dragons he finds there before bringing away some of the gold on which they had been sitting.[26] In the *Saga of King Flores and his Sons* (xiv AD) the Dragon of England lies on its pile of gold in its cave high in a sea-cliff.[27] In the *Saga of William of Sjodr* (xiv–xv AD), after killing the Dragon of the Lutuvald Forest, Vilhjalmr tracks down its treasure-hoard and helps himself to it.[28] Then in the *Saga of Sigrgardr the Valiant* (xv AD) Knut, as we have seen (Chapter 10, §10.3.11) discovers an underground hole in Tartary. A dragon lies within on a pile of much gold and treasure. It blows out venom at him, but Knut remains unharmed because protected by a witch's magic. The dragon escapes past him and Knut proceeds to help himself to the treasure.[29]

Finally, we find a rather different take on the motif in the *Saga of Ragnar Lodbrok* (xiii AD). When King Herrudr of the Geats has given his daughter Thora a tiny heather snake to keep as a pet, because of its beauty, she appropriately—but ominously—keeps it in a little ashen box on a bed of gold. Intriguingly, as it grows and comes to occupy ever more space, the pile of gold beneath it also magically grows too. When it becomes too large and difficult to cope with, Herrudr offers Thora's hand to whoever can destroy the snake, and also offers the gold too as her dowry.[30] See further §§11.4.1 and 11.6 below.

A notable submotif here is that in which the dragon is roused to anger and revenge when only a part, even a tiny part, of its treasure is stolen by a human. In *Beowulf* a serf steals a single jewelled cup. In the *Saga of Yngvar* Valdimar steals a single ring. In the same text we see Yngvar and his men similarly steal only a portion of the Scythian dragon's gold by virtue of the fact that they must, with difficulty, hack it off from the molten mass (cf. §11.5.2).[31]

11.3 Genesis (iii): Spine-Snakes and Corpse-Dragons

The motif of the dragon sitting protectively and possessively on its treasure partially coincides with a further motif of some interest, though rather occluded, that of

---

[25] *Sigurðar saga þögla* §§17.   [26] *Konráðs saga Keisarasonar* §8.
[27] *Flóres saga konungs ok sona hans* §20.   [28] *Vilhjálms saga sjóðs* §13.
[29] *Sigrgarðs saga frækna* §13.114–16 (§§88–90 Loth).
[30] *Ragnars saga loðbrókar* §§2–4. So too *Bósa saga ok Herrauðs* §15 (before AD 1350).
[31] Treasure-guarding dragons survive in English folklore too. Not the least example is the Dragon of Cadbury and Dolbury, which, according to a tradition first attested in the seventeenth century, flies across the Exe Valley every night between the two respective hill-forts, where it keeps its treasure; see Brown 1964:147–8; Simpson 1978:87, 1980:30.

the corpse-dragon. An intriguing classical notion that seems to have passed into the Germanic world—or that at any rate was somehow replicated in it—held that in certain circumstances a serpent could be generated from a corpse. Ovid's Pythagoras observes that, 'There are people that hold that when a spine has rotted, enclosed in the tomb, the human marrow is transformed into a snake', whilst Pliny similarly notes that, 'Many have told us that a snake is produced from the marrow of a man's spine'. Plutarch tells that when a mysterious serpent manifested itself and coiled around the head of the body of the Spartan king Cleomenes III as it hung in Alexandria, wise men explained that this was not the omen it appeared to be: the snake had simply been produced from a coagulation of the juices of his (presumably spinal) marrow, just as the corpses of oxen generate bees, of horses wasps, and of asses beetles. Aelian alone specifies that the spine-snake transformation was confined to the corpses of the wicked.[32] In a variation of this theme, Philostratus' vinedresser tells that a Peparethian friend had once dug up a corpse of twelve cubits in length with a *drakōn* dwelling in its skull.[33] Just as it was believed that individual snakes could be generated from individual human corpses, so it was held that races of snakes could be generated from corpses of terrible monsters of a part humanoid and part serpentine nature. Acusilaus (early fifth-century AD, probably) had told that the race of snakes in general had been generated from the blood of the great dragon Typhon.[34] Similarly, Apollonius of Rhodes and then after him Lucan, famously, had told how the terrible snakes of Libya were generated from the blood that dripped from the Gorgon's severed head as Perseus flew over the land with it.[35]

The idea of the spine-snake passed into early Christian tradition. The pagan Celsus had evidently taken over the notion from Plutarch or a closely parallel source, both of them associating it with ox-bees, horse-wasps, and ass-beetles. In writing against Celsus, the Christian Origen (iii AD) readily accepts the premise nonetheless.[36] And similarly Isidore of Seville (early vii AD) takes over the claim

---

[32] Ovid *Metamorphoses* 15.389–90; Pliny *Natural History* 10.188; Plutarch *Cleomenes* 39; Aelian *Nature of Animals* 1.51. See Ogden 2013a:347–54 for more examples of this sort of phenomenon, and further contextualization. By contrast with Aelian, Stobaeus 1.49.44.321 Hense-Wachsmuth (v AD) credits Hermes Trismegistus with the notion that righteous men are transformed into the outstanding animals of their category after death: if they become a bird, they become an eagle, if a quadruped, a lion, if a sea-creature a dolphin, and if a reptile, a *drakōn*. Cf. Beaulieu 2016:120. Küster 1913:62–5 holds that the notion of the spine-snake derives from corpse maggots.

[33] Philostratus *Heroicus* 8.5–10; cf. Garstad 2011:685–6.

[34] Acusilaus *FGrH* 2 F14 = F14 Fowler; cf. Aeschylus *Suppliants* 264–7. In later texts the great dragon Typhon is replaced in this role, somewhat illogically, by his non-serpentine brothers the Titans, presumably under the influence of Orphic thought: [Hesiod] F367 M-W; Nicander *Theriaca* 8–21; Timothy of Gaza p. 9 Haupt; cf. Jacques 2002:77–8.

[35] Apollonius of Rhodes *Argonautica* 4.1513–17, *Foundation of Alexandria* (Apollonius F4 Powell = schol. Nicander *Theriaca* 12a); Lucan *Pharsalia* 9.696–726. Cf. Chapter 2, §2.1, with further references.

[36] Origen *Contra Celsum* 4.57.

that Ovid had put in Pythagoras' mouth.[37] The idea of the spine-snake surely shapes a narrative found in an early hagiographical text, the early third-century AD *Acts of John*. In this tale the corpse of the newly dead Christian woman Drusiana is protected from the wicked Callimachus' attempts to have sex with it by a snake that emerges 'from somewhere': the serpent kills Callimachus' abettor Fortunatus and pins down Callimachus himself until John and his associates can arrive on the scene to save the day.[38] At somewhat more of a remove, perhaps, it may also inform the rich hagiographical stories bearing upon tomb serpents, discussed in Chapter 6, §6.3.1. We think in particular of Venantius Fortunatus' (late vi AD) tale in which Marcellus of Paris had to dismiss the dragon that had come to visit the tomb of a wicked matron, where it devoured her body, becoming her tomb in turn; and of the tale of Eucherius (AD 858) in which the tomb of the wicked Charles Martel was found, upon its opening, to be occupied not by his corpse but by a fiery dragon.

In Norse tradition an assimilation between the powerful and often dangerous revenant (*draugr*) in his barrow, vigilant still, and the dragon in his cave seems to be enshrined in the curious motif of emergent flames. Flames can be seen to emerge from a revenant's barrow, where they appear to constitute an emanation from the treasure or the shining arms within;[39] and equally they can be seen to emerge from dragons' lairs, where they appear to emanate either simply from the dragon itself or both from the dragon and from the hoarded treasure within alike.

As to the former, in the *Saga of Gold-Thorir* (xiv AD) Gull-Thorir is drawn to the berserker Agnar's barrow, where his ghost or revenant lives with his pile of treasure, by a bluish flame that emerges from it.[40] The *Saga of Hervör and Heidrek* (*c.* AD 1250) preserves the Eddic poem *Hervararkvida*, which records a dialogue between Hervör and the revenant of her father Angantyr at his barrow, as she

---

[37] Isidore of Seville *Etymologies* 12.4.48.   [38] *Acts of John* 71.

[39] On this phenomenon, see Ellis 1942a:475–6; Chadwick 1946:106; de Vries 1956:i.232; Lionarons 1998:58–9; Evans 2005:257–61 (noting the assonance between the plural forms *draugar* and *drekar*). Such revenants could also be known by the term *haugbúar*, 'howe-dwellers'. For *draugr* in general, see Ellis 1943 esp. 90–6, 156–64, 191–4; Chadwick 1946; Hume 1980; Glauser 1993; Jakobsson 2011; Pedersen 2019:116–22.

[40] *Gull-Þóris saga* §3. A compelling analogue for this phenomenon is to be found in the folklore of xix AD Transylvania, as documented by Emily Gerard (1885:134): 'In the night of St. George's Day (so say the legends) all these [sc. ancient Roman] treasures begin to burn, or, to speak in mystic language, to "bloom" in the bosom of the earth, and the light they give forth, described as a bluish flame resembling the colour of lighted spirits of wine, serves to guide favoured mortals to their place of concealment.' The notion was duly appropriated in 1897 by Bram Stoker for *Dracula* (ch. 1, Jonathan Harker's Journal, 5 May; ch. 2, Jonathan Harker's Journal, 7 May; cf. his preparatory notes for the novel, as reproduced at Eighteen-Bisang and Miller 2013:120–1). On his final approach to Dracula's Transylvanian castle, on St George's Eve, Jonathan Harker espies some strange blue flames emerging from the ground. Dracula subsequently explains to him that on that night of the year alone 'a blue flame is seen over any place where treasure has been concealed.' The land around his castle is particularly rich in buried treasure, after having been fought over for centuries by different peoples, but it remains undiscovered because the local peasants are fearful to emerge from their houses on the night in question, this being the night of the year when 'all evil spirits are supposed to have unchecked sway.'

seeks his permission to take his sword Tyrfingr; when he opens up the barrow for her, it is surrounded with fire.[41]

As to the latter, in the *Saga of William of Sjodr* (xiv–xv AD) Vilhjalmr is guided to the treasure-hoard of the Dragon of the Lutuvald Forest by the flames it has left behind it.[42] The *Saga of Sigurd the Silent* (xiv AD) Halfdan and Vilhjalmr espy from afar flames emerging from the Dragon of the Rhine's mountain cave by night.[43] In just the same way in *Konrad's Saga* (xiv AD) Konrad espies flames from the mountain where the Dragon of Pezcina has its home.[44] In both cases, as we have noted, within are found pairs of baby dragons sitting on piles of treasure. The *Saga of Gold-Thorir* (xiv AD) makes it clear that in cases like this both the dragons and the treasure alike can be responsible for the flames. After penetrating their initially dark cave behind a waterfall, Gull-Thorir discovers the dragons into which Valr and his sons have mutated in an inner chamber, which glows with a light that emanates from *both the gold and the dragons alike*. For Thorir's men, watching from outside the cave, a growing glow behind the waterfall heralds the emergence of the dragons from within.

The identification between revenant and dragon in this respect is particularly strong in *Grettir's Saga* (c. AD 1320). Here Grettir's attention is drawn to the tomb of Kar the Old by the fact that he sees flames emerging from it, and it is this that he takes to be a sign that treasure lies within. As he penetrates the barrow to steal the treasure, Kar returns to life and attacks him. Grettir eventually chops his head off and sets it between his buttocks. After the fight he utters a verse in which he refers to the tomb as 'Fafnir's den'.[45]

It could be argued that we already find a merged context for this motif in *Beowulf* (c. AD 685 to c. AD 725): when the king and his companion Wiglaf first approach the Firedrake's treasure-laden tomb-home, they find steam and fire issuing forth from its arches.[46] The text is worth considering in more detail. It tells how a wealthy pagan, the last of his race, has been buried in an elaborate barrow on a headland. Inside the giant-built barrow is a secret stone vault of pillars and arches that contains the entire wealth of the lost people. The Firedrake has come to occupy the tomb and to cherish the treasure as its own. A runaway serf happens upon the tomb and steals a jewelled cup whilst the dragon sleeps. Unable to track down the missing vessel or the thief when it wakes the following day, the dragon awaits nightfall and then exacts a terrible revenge on the local Geats, spewing fire and burning their dwellings, including Beowulf's own great hall, to

---

[41] *Hervarar saga ok Heiðreks* §5.   [42] *Vilhjálms saga sjóðs* §13.
[43] *Sigurðar saga þögla* §13.   [44] *Konráðs saga Keisarasonar* §8.
[45] *Grettis saga* §18. Other sequences too may be compared with this one. In *Göngu-Hrólfs saga* §16 (xiv AD) Hrolf means to penetrate Hreggvid's tomb to retrieve his arms, but finds the revenant king already standing on top of his barrow to welcome him; he gives him not one but two sets of arms, and reveals that he can transform into a swallow. At *Landnámabók* (*Book of Settlements*) §3.1 (c. AD 1100) it may be implied that the reason that Skeggi is unable to possess himself of Bodvar Bjarki's sword Laufi, when he breaks into the tomb the latter shares with King Hrolf (*kraki*) and Hjalti, is that his revenant offers resistance.
[46] *Beowulf* ll. 2545–9.

the ground. And so the scene is set for Beowulf's climactic duel with the creature. Whilst the text does admittedly make it clear that the dragon comes from elsewhere to inhabit the tomb, this nonetheless feels like a rationalization of the simpler notion that the dragon had evolved directly out of the occupying corpse—and this would also explain perfectly (insofar as any explanation is needed) why the dragon should have such a strong sense of ownership of the treasure in the tomb.[47]

One suspects, similarly, that the motif of the dragon evolving out of the corpse lurks behind and structures the tales of Fafnir, Valr, and Ingifer considered in the previous section: as we have observed, hints at the involvement of sorcery in Fafnir's transformation have the look of being secondary, of being, as it were, 'rationalizing' explanations with which the ancient motif of the corpse-dragon has been overlaid. Perhaps it was once known that Fafnir, Valr, and Ingifer died in their cave retreats as they refused to abandon their piles of treasure, and that their dragon-selves came after.

We may note two interesting variations on this theme. First, the *Saga of Arrow-Odd* (xiii AD) seems to tell us that snakes can also be generated from the corpses of horses too. Odd meets his end when he and his men find the old, bleached skull of a giant horse, which he guesses to be the skull of Faxi. He prods it with his spear, but as he does so a snake shoots out from underneath the skull and delivers him a fatal bite above the ankle, whereupon his entire leg swells up as high as the thigh.[48] Second in *Walking-Hrolf's Saga* (xiv AD) the sorcerer-dwarf Mondul warns Hrolf that he must kill the venom-spewing sorcerer Grim Aegir with a single blow, for, as we have seen, any limbs that he hacks off his body will immediately turn into venomous snakes.[49]

The theme of the generation of a dragon from a corpse is alive and well in a modern Germanic society: our own. A folktale recorded as recently as 1968 at Norton Fitzwarren in Somerset tells of a local dragon that was spontaneously generated from a pile of dead bodies after an ancient battle.[50]

11.4 Genesis (iv): The Small Snake

11.4.1 A Tiny Snake Grows into a Troublesome Dragon

Absolute indications of a dragon's size are rare in the Germanic tradition. A striking exception comes in the case of the *Saga of the Volsungs*, where the precipice

---

[47] *Beowulf* ll. 2200–3182. This theory is an old and familiar one, though not an uncontroversial one, amongst Beowulf scholars: see Ettmüller 1850:177; Lawrence 1918; Chadwick 1959; Smithers 1961; Davidson 1950:181, 1964:161; Goldsmith 1970:94, 129; Jones 1972:19 n. 1; Tripp 1983 (who, however, depends on radical alterations to the text); Braeger 1986; Jensen 1993; Orchard 1995:169 n. 4; Lionarons 1998:27, 119 n. 29; Shilton 1997:71–3; Rauer 2000:39–40. Different approaches at Beekman Taylor 1997; Barreiro 2019:72–3.
[48] *Örvar-Odds saga* §31.   [49] *Göngu-Hrólfs saga* §33.
[50] Palmer 1976:77–8; cf. Simpson 1978:84–5 and 1980:38, 50–1.

from which Fafnir dips his head down to drink from his local river is said to be thirty fathoms above it, which would suggest that 180 feet constitutes a relatively small proportion of his length.[51] However, our immediate interest here follows not the large dragons but rather the—initially—small ones.

A productive motif is found in the theme of the tiny harmless snake that grows into the huge and terrible dragon,[52] the locus classicus for which is a tale attached to the historical but heavily mythologized Ragnar Lodbrok ('Hairy Breeches'), to which we have briefly referred above. In his Latin *Gesta Danorum* (early xiii AD) Saxo Grammaticus tells how Herrudr, King of the Swedes, found baby vipers whilst hunting in the woods and gave them to his daughter Thora to rear (no further explanation is supplied as to why he should have taken this strange decision). She feeds them an entire ox carcass each day (!) with the result that they grow to an unusual size and come to burn up the local district with their pestilential breath (we recall the ox-devouring dragons of the hagiographical tradition: Chapter 6, §6.1.1). The king now offers Thora's hand to whoever can deal with the menace, and it is Ragnar that steps forward.[53] The *Saga of Ragnar Lodbrok* (xiii AD) handles the motif in a more satisfactory way. Here Herrudr gives his daughter just a single tiny snake, a heather snake, because of its exceptional beauty, and she begins by keeping it in a little ashen box. As the snake grows it first becomes too big for the box, and eventually has to be taken outside where it can touch its own tail as it coils around her bower, at which point it becomes difficult to handle and (now) requires a whole ox for its meal.[54] In the *Saga of Bosi and Herraud* (before AD 1350) Herrudr is said to have found the tiny golden snake in a vulture's egg (there is perhaps a vague intimation of a basilisk's origin here).[55]

However, Saxo also applies the Ragnar-Thora story-type to the tale of Alf and Alfhild, and in this case the king's thinking in giving his daughter a pair of snakes is made clear. Here Siward, king of the Goths, gives his beautiful but modest daughter Alfhild a viper and a snake to rear so that, when they are grown, they will be able to protect her chastity (in addition, he rules that any man caught attempting to enter her bower should be impaled on a stake). The notion that the snakes should be protecting the girl's chastity makes sense of the motif in the Ragnar tradition in accordance with which the (single) overgrown snake is said to coil all the way around Thora's maiden bower.

---

[51] *Völsunga saga* §18.

[52] The basic notion is just about classical: Ctesias *FGrH* 688 F45r (= Aelian *Nature of Animals* 5.3) speaks of the terrible Indian *skōlēx*, which is born the size of a woodworm and grows to seven cubits in length.

[53] Saxo Grammaticus *Gesta Danorum* 9.252–3. For the episode, see Larrington 2010; and for the Ragnar tradition more generally, see McTurk 1991. The young dragons infiltrated into the kingdom of Garda are similarly initially maintained on an ox a day at *Ortnit* (c. AD 1217–25) §§315–16.

[54] *Ragnars saga loðbrókar* §§2–4; so too Saxo Grammaticus *Gesta Danorum* 7.190–1 (early xiii AD), *Ragnarssona þáttr* §1 (xiii AD), and *Bósa saga ok Herrauðs* §15 (before AD 1350).

[55] *Bósa saga ok Herrauðs* §15; for the generation of the basilisk, see Chapter 5, §5.5.2.

In the Middle High German *Ortnit* (*c.* AD 1217–25) and the related *Wolfdietrich B* (*c.* AD 1225–50) the propensity of dragons to grow from tiny to vast is weaponized. Machorel, the heathen king of Tyre, takes revenge on the Lombard king Ortnit, who has stolen his daughter, Liebgart, by having agents— variously a huntsman or the giant couple Helle and Runze—infiltrate a pair of dragon eggs into a cave adjacent to his capital of Garda. When the baby dragons grow to maturity and begin to maraud, Ortnit feels duty-bound to go up against them and thereby meets his end.[56]

The folktale analogues, Nordic and others, for the tiny harmless worm that grows into a terrible dragon are rich.[57] Particularly worthy of note is the wonderful Middle Persian tale of the Worm of Haftvad. Haftvad's daughter finds the worm in a windfall apple and, recognizing it to be a luck-bringing creature, keeps it in her spindle case. The worm transforms her poor father into a rich and ever-fortunate tyrant, but gradually grows to the size of an elephant, and has to be accommodated in a vast pit (cf. the tradition that Thora's little snake, as it grew, commensurately inflated the bed of gold on which it lay). Ardeshir eventually gains access to the pit and destroys the dragon by pouring molten brass or lead down its throat. Having broken Haftvad's luck thereby, he is able to defeat him.[58] Worthy of note too are some British folktales. The Mordiford Dragon is first discovered in the woods by a little girl, Maud, at the size of a cucumber. She secretly keeps it and feeds it on milk, but as it grows it comes to devour chickens, sheep, cows, and human beings.[59] The Lambton Worm is initially caught on a fishing line by the Lambton heir in tiny form (the evil catch is explained by the fact that the heir is profanely fishing on a Sunday). He casts it down a well, where it gradually grows to vast size.[60]

11.4.2 Principal Dragon and Brood

Small snakes have a wider role to play in Norse traditions. As in the hagiography, we sometimes encounter a threat in the form of a principal dragon with its attendant brood of lesser serpents. A superb example of this motif is found in a curious episode of Snorri Sturluson's *Heimskringla* (*c.* AD 1230). Here King Harald asks a wizard to shapeshift and go spy on Iceland. He makes the journey across the sea

---

[56] *Ortnit* §§484–575; *Wolfdietrich B* §§473–530.

[57] See Krappe 1941b; Davidson and Fisher 1998:ii, 152–3.

[58] *Deeds of Ardeshir* §§6–8 Ântiâ/§§7–9 Grenet (soon after AD 706; the French translation of Grenet 2003 is to be preferred to the English one of Ântiâ et al. 1900) and Firdausi *Shahnameh* C.1381–1391 (*c.* AD 1000; translation at Warner and Warner 1912:vi, 232–45; and Davis 2006:544–53). Krappe 1941b considers that the tale-type actually originated in the Near East and was brought home to Scandinavia by Byzantium's Viking mercenaries.

[59] For text, see Devlin 1848; cf. Simpson 1980:37–9, 58–62, 85–7.

[60] For text, see Simpson 1980:124–9; cf. 36–7, 111–12, 116–17.

in the form of a whale. But as he attempts to come ashore at Vapnafjord a huge dragon rushes down the valley towards him, accompanied by a train of snakes, frogs, and toads, all of which blow venom at him.[61] In *Yngvar's Saga* (xiii AD) Valdimar discovers that a hill that shines in the distance like the moon is, on closer inspection, a pile of golden treasure covered with sleeping snakes: when he accidentally disturbs a tiny one by trying to hook a ring out of the pile for himself, word quickly gets passed up the chain of command until response is made by a huge and terrible Jakulus, which rains down fire on the ships—presumably the master of the brood.[62] We find a presiding dragon, or perhaps two, in the case of the squadron of dragons assembled by the witch-queen Ostasia as part of the great beast army she summons up against the forces of Isung in *Thidrek's Saga* (*c.* AD 1230–50). Ostasia transforms herself into a dragon to command them, but attention is also given to the largest of the dragons, the one that destroys both King Isung and his eldest son, whilst sustaining a wound from the latter. As we have already noted, it is not entirely clear, but this largest dragon is probably identical with the dragon into which Ostasia has transformed herself.[63] In the German *Horn Siegfried Lay* (early xvi AD), after killing a principal dragon (unnamed, but in the role that traditionally belongs to Fafnir), Siegfried finds an enclosed valley writhing with many more dragons and snakes, and proceeds to burn them up.[64]

The Middle High German *Wolfdietrich B* (*c.* AD 1225–50) gives us a small but colourful brood in the environs of Garda. The parent dragon (male, it transpires) leaves the all-but dead Wolfdietrich in its cave for its clutch of young to play with whilst it goes for a snooze outside. They play a game of catch with him as if he is a ball. Their home is a charnel house indeed: amidst the detritus on the cave floor Wolfdietrich discovers Ortnit's helmet, his head still inside (he proceeds to kiss it); and when, after butchering the brood, he makes for the parent outside, he stumbles as he negotiates the intervening pile of corpses, which almost allows the dragon to get the better of him.[65] In *Thidrek's Saga* the Dragon of Bergara seizes King Hertnid when he comes to attack it and carries his carcass off to its mountain cave for its three young to eat there, rooting his armour out of the cave afterwards, like a bird of prey cleaning its nest. It subsequently brings them a lion for a second meal and Thidrek for a third, the last to its own demise.[66] In closely similar tales in *Konrad's Saga* (xiv AD) and the *Saga of the Flower Plains* (xv AD) the parallel dragons' young are reduced to two in number.[67] We could also be said to

---

[61] Snorri Sturluson *Heimskringla* Óláfs saga Tryggvasonar §37.
[62] *Yngvars saga viðförla* §5, ii.436 Jónsson.   [63] *Þiðrekssaga* §§349–55.
[64] *Lied vom hürnen Seyfrid* §§1–11.
[65] *Wolfdietrich B* §§690, 698–707 (f. §528 and *Ortnit* §§574–5).   [66] *Þiðrekssaga* §§416–22.
[67] *Konráðs saga Keisarasonar* §8; *Blómsstrvalla saga* §25. Some further examples may be given. At *Sigurðar saga þögla* §17 (xiv AD), when Sigurd the Silent investigates the cave of the Dragon of the Rhine he has just destroyed, he finds two large baby dragons sitting on the pile of gold within. Similarly, at *Vilhjálms saga sjóðs* §13 (xiv–xv), after killing the Dragon of the Lutuvald Forest, Vilhjalmr discovers a brood of three baby dragons in its nest-cum-treasure-hoard.

encounter a dragon together with a mini-brood in a cave when, in both the *Saga of Gold-Thorir* (xiv AD) and the *Saga of Halfdan Son of Eystein* (xiv AD), as we have seen, the Viking Valr and his sons retreat into a cave behind a waterfall and are transformed into dragons together as they sit on their gold within.[68]

The most remarkable example of a presiding dragon and its brood is to be found in *Konrad's Saga* (xiv AD). Its story deserves to be relayed at length. Princess Matthildr of Constantinople dispatches Konrad with detailed instructions on a mission to the edge of the world, far beyond the five islands of Ethiopia, to fetch a precious green gemstone. After a number of animal adventures, he arrives at his destination, a mysterious castle built from gold, silver, tin, glass, and precious stones. The castle is infested with serpents, but they are all in a trance-like sleep, because he has advisedly timed his arrival to coincide with Whit Sunday. As he enters the outer gate, he must vault over a massive serpent blocking the path with his spear, and do the same again to get over the further pair of serpents that guard the inner gate. The path from the inner gate to the central hall is also lined with serpents, and as he progresses down it he sees serpents occupying the tops of the castle's towers above and hanging from its windows. The hall itself is piled high with gold and bejewelled treasures, and crammed with yet more serpents. At the end of it the great dais is occupied by the largest serpent of them all, which extends from one side of the hall to the other. On its head it sports both a classical crest, specifically a 'crest of dread' (resembling Fafnir's helm of dread...) and, appropriately, a crown. Before the dais two small serpents, one white as snow, the other red as blood, play a game of catch with the green gemstone, catching it in their snouts and never letting it touch the floor. These are the only two serpents not in the state of a trance-like sleep. Konrad intercepts the green gem with his sword before the white serpent can catch it, and puts in his pouch. The serpent glowers at him before winding its way into the ground. Konrad now prises another precious stone out of a table. When he has done so the white serpent returns with a white gemstone, and resumes the game of catch with this. This time Konrad catches the gem before the red serpent can do so. That serpent too glowers at him before winding its way into the ground. When Konrad has prised a second gem from the table, the red serpent returns with a red gemstone and resumes the game of catch with this one. He takes this one too, and they both now glower at him and wind into the earth together. As they do so they create a sort of earthquake, so that everything in the hall, including the sleeping serpents, is upheaved. Konrad grabs some more treasure, including a magical goblet, and makes his way back across the unstable floor, supporting himself with his spear. He hears crashing and hissing behind him, but, following Matthildr's advice, he does not look behind him until he has made his way back to the outer gate, vaulting

---

[68] *Gull-Þóris saga* §§3–4; *Hálfdanar saga Eysteinssonar* §26.

over the serpents on the path again. When he does then look at the scene behind, he sees that all the gold is gone, and all that is left are blackened ruins beneath clouds of dust and steam.[69] This tale is strangely reminiscent, in some regards, of two other fourteenth-century AD tales we have already considered, and already found, despite their very different contexts, to resemble each other in some important respects. The castle built of precious metals and jewels, filled with yet more precious objects, surrounded by serpents and presided over by a dragon lord, is strongly reminiscent of the dragon's castle in the *Callimachus and Chrysorrhoe* romance. But the hierarchical arrangement we find within the hall, where we find a principal dragon presiding over all, and then, as it seems, beneath him a special pair of serpents, and then beneath them a serpent host, is reminiscent of the late narrative of St Theodore ([h]), where within the cave of the Dragon of King Samuel's City are found—in the absence of the Dragon-proper himself—a presiding pair consisting of an old-man dragon and an abominable asp, and beneath them twelve mid-ranking serpents, and beneath them again a serpent host.[70]

The motif continues in more recent Germanic folktales from (amongst other places) the Tyrol. For example, in a folktale from Steeg recorded by Zingerle in 1859, the town is beset by a proliferation of snakes. A foreign sorcerer undertakes to rid them of their curse by building a pyre and charming all the snakes into it by reading out spells. He succeeds, but the final snake to arrive is a white one, wearing a crown, and before it too throws itself on the pyre, it pierces the sorcerer through, leaving him dead.[71] In a closely similar tale recorded in Friedlach in 1911 by Pehr, with Fridelo as its hero, it is made clear that the final white snake is larger than the others and specifically their queen.[72]

11.5 The Dragon's Weaponry

11.5.1 Venom and Fire (and Marauding)

Germanic texts for the most part tend to focus either on a dragon's fieriness or on its venomousness. Even so, one feels the two phenomena are more closely identified with each other than they are in classical or in Graeco-Latin hagiographical texts. Whilst the dragon's venom can be conceptualized as a pestilential gas, it more often seems to be conceptualized, even when 'blown out', rather as a sort of

---

[69] *Konráðs saga Keisarasonar* §§9–10. At §11 we encounter the belated and stray speculation that the serpents must have taken the castle over from an original group of human occupants.

[70] This comparison admittedly constitutes an argument against apparent dittography (between the roles of the Dragon-proper and the old-man dragon) in the Theodore narrative.

[71] Zingerle 1859: 181–2 no. 302; trans. at Ogden 2013b:277, source C9.

[72] Pehr 1913:37 no. 18; trans. at Ogden 2013b:277, source C10. Cf. Brednich 1975–; Schmidt 1975–.

burning, napalm-like substance the dragon spews forth, particularly at its attackers. We may cite four cases in which the identification seems to be tight. In *Iven's Saga* (xiii AD) the dragon *singes* the lion it is fighting with the *venom* it blows out at it.[73] The dragon encountered by Frothi in Saxo Grammaticus' Latin *Gesta Danorum* (early xiii AD) is said to *spew venom*, whilst its *slaver burns* up anything it falls upon; Frothi must protect himself against it by covering his shield and body with bulls' hides, leaving no limb exposed. In the same text the marauding pair of vipers reared by Princess Thora is said to *burn up* the local district with their *pestilential breath*.[74] In the *Saga of Gold-Thorir* (xiv AD) the dragons into which Valr and his sons have mutated *spurt fire and venom together* from their mouths.[75] When Tofi shapeshifts into a dragon in the *Saga of Sörli the Strong* (xv AD) he proceeds to blow *venom* over his opponent Sorli, with the result that he is surrounded by black, asphyxiating *smoke*; however, he is able to hack the dragon to pieces before falling unconscious.[76] More ambivalent is *Walking-Hrolf's Saga* (xiv AD), in which the shape-shifter Grim Aegir *alternately* spews fire and venom at Hrolf as they grapple on the battlefield.[77] In this case venom and fire are at once partly assimilated and partly differentiated.

As to cases in which emphasis is laid more upon the dragon's fieriness, we note again that the flying dragons of the *Anglo-Saxon Chronicle* for AD 793 are already said to be fiery, and also, indeed, to be associated with thunderbolts. Beowulf's dragon (c. AD 685 to c. AD 725) is famously a 'Firedrake' (*ligdraca* and *fyrdraca*). It spews down fire on the Geats, burning up their dwellings, including Beowulf's own great hall, in anger at the theft of his jewelled cup. When Beowulf and his companion Wiglaf first approach its tomb-home, they find flames issuing from the tomb's arches (cf. §11.3). In the course of his final duel against Beowulf the dragon then encloses him in a ring of fire.[78] Similarly, the proto-Fafnir of *Beowulf* would also appear to have been fiery. As we have seen, Sigemund killed it by pinning it to the wall of its cave with his sword, but after this, we are told, in lapidary fashion, 'the hot worm melted': presumably this was the effect of the dragon's internal fire, which built up in intensity when no longer being breathed out.[79] By contrast, the poem is relatively sober in its handling of venom: Beowulf is eventually killed, slowly, by the venom of the Firedrake he duels with, this after it has bitten a chunk out of his neck and presumably envenomed him in the process.[80]

Let us look next at three Middle High German texts. The fieriness of the dragon of Wexford faced by Gottfried von Strassburg's Tristan in his *Tristan* (AD 1210) is repeatedly adverted to in a detailed narrative. This marauder is said to belch forth

---

[73] *Ívens saga* §10.   [74] Saxo Grammaticus *Gesta Danorum* 2.1 (Frothi), 9.252–3 (vipers).
[75] *Gull-Þóris saga* §4.   [76] *Sörla saga sterka* pp. 381–3 Jónsson.
[77] *Göngu-Hrólfs saga* §33; cf. 2 and 31.
[78] *Beowulf* ll. 2200–3182; *ligdraca*: 2333, 3040; *fyrdraca*: 2689.
[79] *Beowulf* ll. 884–97.   [80] *Beowulf* ll. 2688–820. See Rauer 2000:74–7.

smoke, flames, steam, and wind; when wounded by Tristan it burns up thickets in its rage, and turns his shield to cinders.[81] In Heinrich von dem Türlin's *Diu Crône* (*c.* AD 1220s) the Dragon of Aufrat kills Gawein's horse and burns his armour off him with its fire; when he plunges a sword into its mouth, it melts it to the hilt.[82] The principal Dragon of Garda and the local serpent (*sarpant*) of *Wolfdietrich B* (*c.* AD 1225–50) are similarly characterized by their fieriness: the former's breath turns Wolfdietrich's sword red hot, the latter's his armour, so that he must jump into an adjacent lake to cool off.[83] In the Norse version of the Tristan tale, the *Saga of Tristram and Isönd* (AD 1226), Tristan kills the dragon by driving his lance through its mouth, its heart, and out through the side of its body, whereupon a stream of fire flows out of the carcass, killing his horse.[84]

There are many examples of such fieriness from the Norse realm. The Scythian dragon encountered by Yngvar in *Yngvar's Saga* (xiii AD) is so hot in itself that it has melted the pile of treasure on which it lies into a single mass of near-molten gold.[85] The flying dragon encountered by Ketil in the *Saga of Ketil Trout* (xiii AD) has fire flaming from its mouth and eyes.[86] In *Iven's Saga* (xiii AD) the dragon's mouth is compared to a furnace.[87] In the *Saga of William of Sjodr* (xiv–xv AD) Vilhjalmr is alerted to the presence of a dragon in the Lutuvald forest by the sight of the fire it has kindled from afar, and which will eventually lead him to its hoard of treasure (cf. §11.3, again). In the course of his fight with it, the dragon blows more fire at him through its nose and mouth.[88]

As to the emphasis rather on venomousness, a number of texts give us dragons spewing venom before them as they go. So it is that in the *Saga of the Volsungs* (*c.* AD 1200–70) Fafnir blows out venom over the path before him as he travels from his cave to his river for a drink.[89] Snorri Sturluson's *Prose Edda* (*c.* AD 1220) tells how the Midgard Worm spits venom over Thor in the course of their great battle at sea. At Ragnarök the serpent will again spew venom into air and sea, Thor will again fight the serpent, and kill it again, but this time he will indeed die himself from the venom. And then in Snorri's *Heimskringla* (*c.* AD 1230) a dragon and its attendant host of snakes, frogs, and toads together blow venom over a wizard sent by King Harald to spy on Iceland in the form of a whale.[90] In Saxo Grammaticus' Latin *Gesta Danorum* (early xiii AD) Fridleif, Frothi's son, must protect himself from the venom of the island dragon whose treasure he is stealing by covering himself in a bull's hide, as his father had. And in the same text again

---

[81] Gottfried von Strassburg *Tristan* ll. 8901–11370.   [82] *Diu Crône* ll. 15032–223.

[83] *Wolfdietrich B* §§524, 673–5, 722–30.

[84] *Tristrams saga ok Ísöndar* §§35–6. Cf. also *Tristrams saga ok Ísoddar* §10 = §§35–6 Gísli Brynjólfsson = pp. 121–8 Vilhjálmsson (*c.* AD 1400).

[85] *Yngvars saga víðförla* §6, ii.442 Jónsson.   [86] *Ketils saga hœngs* §1, p. 153 Jónsson.

[87] *Ívens saga* §10.   [88] *Vilhjálms saga sjóðs* §13.

[89] *Völsunga saga* §17; the suggestion of Lionarons 1998:64 that Fafnir here is venomous but *not* fiery seems unsafe.

[90] Snorri Sturluson *Prose Edda* Gylfaginning §§48 (Midgard Worm), 52 (Nastrand); *Heimskringla* Óláfs saga Tryggvasonar §37.

the two vipers reared by Princess Thora, which emit venom in the form of a toxic gas, to the distress of the local area, also spit venom (and vomit) over Ragnar Lodbrok, as well as blasting their pestilential breath at him when he comes to attack them.[91] In the *Saga of the Trojans* (xiii AD) the multi-eyed Dragon of Colchis, roused from the magical sleep Medea has cast upon it as Jason stabs it, spews venom over him.[92] In *Walking-Hrolf's Saga* (xiv AD) again the shape-shifter Grim Aegir takes off into the air to rain venom down on Hrolf, but Hrolf's ally, the dwarf Mondul, catches it in a bag before it can touch him, and then throws the bag in the face of Grim's ally Sorli Long-Nose, killing him at once. Grim proceeds to kill a further nine men with his venom before reverting to human form.[93]

But a dragon's venom can destroy bigger targets too. In *Yngvar's Saga* (xiii AD) the Jakulus dragon accidentally roused by Valdimar flies over Yngvar's fleet and attacks one of his ships, the one captained by a pair of priests, by raining down venom on it. The author is clear both that the crew are killed and that the boat itself is destroyed. It is interesting, accordingly, that the he should have specified venom rather than fire in this context.[94] Similarly, in the *Saga of Bosi and Herraud* (before AD 1350) Harek, transformed into a flying dragon, pours down venom on Smidur's ship.[95] In the *Saga of Sigurd the Silent* (xiv AD) the Dragon of the Rhine spews venom over the army of Halfdan and Vilhjalmr as it flies over, killing sixty soldiers (it will subsequently spew venom over Sigurd the Silent too, as he lops off its legs and tail from the ground).[96] In *Valdimar's Saga* (xv AD) a flying dragon spews venom over two battling armies below (one of giants and trolls).[97]

In this connection we find dim refractions of more particularly hagiographical motifs. As we have seen, the hacking up of the dragon's body into chunks and the disposal of the chunks by ox-teams, to forestall the pestilence to which it will give rise, is a prime motif in the hagiography (Chapter 6, §6.7). In the Anglo-Saxon *Beowulf* (c. AD 685 to c. AD 725) Beowulf's companion Wiglaf heaves the Firedrake's carcass over the cliff into the sea before proceeding to bury Beowulf in a magnificent tumulus: a threatened pestilence is implied.[98] When, in the *Saga of Tristram and Isönd* (AD 1226), Tristan hacks the carcass of the Dragon of Wexford in half, after already having slain it, this is presumably as a preliminary to its disposal.[99] The wicked Steward of Gottfried von Strassburg's Middle High German *Tristan* (AD 1210) has the head of the Dragon of Wexford, which he claims to have decapitated, brought to court on a wagon pulled by a team of four

---

[91] Saxo Grammaticus *Gesta Danorum* 6.150 (Fridleif), 9.252–3 (Ragnar). With the last compare *Ragnarssona þáttr* 1 (xiii AD).
[92] *Trójumanna saga* §§9–10.   [93] *Göngu-Hrólfs saga* §§31, 33.
[94] *Yngvars saga viðförla* §5, ii.436 Jónsson.   [95] *Bósa saga ok Herrauðs* §14, iii.319 Jónsson.
[96] *Sigurðar saga þögla* §13.   [97] *Valdimars saga* §3.
[98] *Beowulf* ll. 3131–3; a different explanation at Porck and Stolk 2017:19–20.
[99] *Tristrams saga ok Ísöndar* §§35–6.

horses.[100] In *Ector's Saga* (xiv–xv AD) we find another more distinctively hagiographical motif when Ingifer, turning himself into a dragon and retreating to a cave for thirty years to sit on his gold, becomes a problem for the local city because of his poisoning of the waters of its river (cf. Chapter 6, §6.1.2); he is also said to spew venom in the usual way, as indeed is another dragon mentioned in this text, which is slain by Sir Trancival.[101]

However, a dragon's venom need not always be deleterious in the Germanic tradition: in the proper magical context it can also confer beneficial qualities on men, as we shall see when we come to consider the uses of the dragon's blood (§11.10).

11.5.2 Sound?

It is not entirely clear how the Scythian dragon encountered by Yngvar in *Yngvar's Saga* (xiii AD) contrives to kill those of his men who disobey his orders and expose themselves to it. We are told that the dragon, angry at the theft of some of his gold, rears up, spins round on the gold that is left, and makes a sound like a man whistling. The men live to report to Yngvar what they have seen, but then drop down dead. Have they been killed by the seemingly innocuous sound the dragon has made, with delayed effect? Or has the dragon cursed them in some way?[102]

11.6 The Hand of the Princess

A king will often offer the hand of his daughter to the champion that can unburden his land of its dragon. Let us consider first some Middle High German texts. In Wirnt von Grafenberg's *Wigalois* (c. AD 1205–10), the primary task the spirit of King Lar sets for the knight Wigalois, as he aspires to the hand of his daughter Larie, is the killing of the marauding dragon Pfetan.[103] In Gottfried von Strassburg's *Tristan* (AD 1210) the terrible fiery Dragon of Wexford is burning up

---

[100] Gottfried von Strassburg *Tristan* ll. 9219–20. Cf. the (x AD) 'Nine Herbs Charm' recipe-poem preserved in the Anglo-Saxon medical compilation *Lacnunga* (for the text of the poem, see Dobbie 1942:119–21). It prescribes for the preparation of a salve to prevent against infection, and this is to be applied to the accompaniment of a sung charm, a paradigmatic magical mini-narrative or 'historiola': 'A snake [*wyrm*] came a-crawling; it bit a man in two. Then Woden took up twelve glory-twigs, and struck the viper [*næddre*] in such a way that it flew asunder into nine pieces'. Cf. Symons 2015:86–8; Ball 2017:66–71.

[101] *Ectors saga* §§8, 10.

[102] *Yngvars saga viðförla* §6, ii.442 Jónsson. Cf. the Tyrolean folktales cited above (§11.4.2), in which the terrible snake-queen arrives either to a whistling or to a ringing sound.

[103] *Wigalois* ll. 4783–4.

the country and people of that region. Gurmun, the king of Ireland, offers the hand of his daughter Isolde to the hero that slays it. Thousands of hopefuls die as a result. In the course of an extended battle (expansively narrated) the dragon eats half of Tristan's horse, but he eventually tracks it down, kills it, and cuts out its tongue. He stumbles away from the immediate scene only to be overcome by a mixture of exhaustion, the dragon's heat, and the noxious fumes exuded by the tongue he has with him. Whilst he is out of action, the king's craven steward comes across the dragon's body, arranges for its head to be chopped off and brought to court, and then runs to the king, purporting to be its slayer and accordingly demanding Isolde's hand. In due course, however, there is a protracted show-down at court in which the steward produces the head as evidence for his story, but is confuted by Tristan's production of the tongue. And so Tristan wins Isolde.[104] This distinctive story-type returns in *Ortnit* (*c.* AD 1217–25) and the related *Wolfdietrich B* (*c.* AD 1225–50). Here the doomed Ortnit makes Liebgart, his widow-to-be, promise to marry (and thereby transmit his kingdom to) only the man that will have avenged him by slaying the (or rather *a*) Dragon of Garda: as proof of the slaying, she should accept only a tongue, not a head. It is Wolfdietrich that duly succeeds in the task of slaying the father dragon and his baby dragons together. The wicked Count Wildung of Viterbo attempts to seize both Liebgart and the kingdom by bringing the heads he has taken from the carcasses into the court, but he is confuted when Wolfdietrich produces the tongues. In the ensuing fracas the count is himself beheaded in turn.[105]

In Saxo Grammaticus' Latin *Gesta Danorum* (xiii AD), when the pair of vipers King Herrudr has foolishly given his daughter Thora to rear become unmanageable, he resolves to offer her hand in marriage to whoever can destroy them. Many young men present themselves for the challenge and are killed before Ragnar Lodbrok steps forward, successfully completes it and wins the girl's

---

[104] Gottfried von Strassburg *Tristan* ll. 8901–11370. So too in the Norse versions of the tale at *Tristrams saga ok Ísöndar* §§35–6 (AD 1226) and *Tristrams saga ok Ísoddar* §10 = §§35–6 Gísli Brynjólfsson = pp. 121–8 Vilhjálmsson (*c.* AD 1400), where the principals are Tristan and Ísodd and, in the second of these, the steward becomes a courtier named Kaei. A Norse version of this tale also seems to underlie the Jersey folktale of lé Dragon d'la Hougue Bie (cf. *haugr* and *býr*, 'barrow' and 'settlement'): the Lord of Hambie overcomes the dragon but collapses from his wounds, whereupon his wicked squire cuts his throat and claims to have killed the dragon himself; cf. Bois 2010:i.42–54. The same story-type is found (with the Huntsman in the Tristan role and many ancillary details of interest, including animal helpers) in the complex Grimm Brothers' folktale 'The Two Brothers': Grimm no. 60 = ATU 303 (section C); discussion at Ranke 1934.

[105] *Ortnit* §§544–9; *Wolfdietrich B* §§708, 752–84. Both texts are somewhat confused about the number of dragons in play. Both have two eggs or baby dragons initially infiltrated into the kingdom of Garda, and these are transformed into a pair of marauding adults in due course. But when it comes time for Ortnit and then Wolfdietrich to fight the creatures, the focus switches to a single adult dragon tending a small brood (nice proof that the original two had been a mating pair). Only towards the end of *Wolfdietrich B* is it remembered that the second adult dragon is hitherto unaccounted for, and it is belatedly retrieved for a cursory episode in which she—explicitly the mother of the brood (*die würminne diu ir aller muoter was*)—snatches up Liebgart before being bisected by Wolfdietrich (§§787–92).

hand.[106] The *Saga of Ragnar Lodbrok* (xiii AD) specifies, appropriately for a good folktale, that Thora was the most beautiful of all women, and so given the nickname Borgarhjört, 'Hart of the Village'.[107] As we have seen, Saxo similarly has King Siward of the Goths offer his daughter Alfhild to anyone that can slay the viper and the snake he has given her to help her protect her chastity. And this function of the serpents confers an added significance upon the king's decision that the warrior that destroys the snake should also become her husband: there is a sense in which in destroying the serpent he is ipso facto getting physical access to the girl. However, as it turns out, Alf, the vanquisher of the serpents, is initially denied his bride when Alfhild's mother then poisons her mind against him and she puts on men's clothing and takes up the life of a wandering shield-maiden.[108]

In *Ector's Saga* (xiv–xv AD) King Castor offers the hand of his beautiful daughter Mabil to the warrior that can destroy the dragon Ingifer has turned himself into. It is Fenacius that succeeds in the task and wins the girl.[109]

11.7 The Slayer's Weaponry

11.7.1 The Special Sword

The most typical tool in the killing of the Germanic dragon is the suitably martial and heroic sword. Perhaps there is a sense in this of fighting fire with fire. It has recently been shown that 'biting' swords are conceptually identified with serpents in Viking culture, not least in their decoration and in the kennings used for them in skaldic poetry.[110] But it is often the case that not just any old sword will do when one is dealing with a dragon: it has, rather, to be a named one or an otherwise special one. (Named swords, it should be made clear, are a broader feature of Germanic tradition; they are not specifically reserved for dragon-slaying.)

In the Anglo-Saxon *Beowulf* (c. AD 685 to c. AD 725) Beowulf brings his great named sword Naegling down on the Firedrake's head, but it shatters without effect. However, his companion Wiglaf too has a special sword, a golden one, and he is able to drive it into its belly below, whereupon Beowulf slits the belly open

---

[106] Saxo Grammaticus *Gesta Danorum* 9.252–3.

[107] *Ragnars saga loðbrókar* §§2–4; so too *Ragnarssona þáttr* §1 (xiii AD) and *Bósa saga ok Herrauðs* §15 (before AD 1350).

[108] Saxo Grammaticus *Gesta Danorum* 7.190–1.   [109] *Ectors saga* §8.

[110] Brunning 2015, esp. 56–8 (with table 2.1) for the kennings, including 'battle snake', 'shield snake', 'wound snake', and 'corpse snake'. As to the sagas (55–6), Egil has a sword called Naður, 'Adder' (*Egils saga* §53, xiii AD), whilst the hilt of Sköfnungr, the sword Skeggi gives to Cormac, is inhabited by an *yrmlingr*, a 'wormling' (*Kormáks saga* §9, xiii AD). Note too that a sword-hilt discovered by Beowulf in Grendel's mere is decorated with a *wyrm*: *Beowulf* l. 1698; cf. Symons 2015.

with his dagger, killing it.[111] In *Beowulf* too we are first told of the killing of (proto-)Fafnir. Details are sparse in the brief summary of the episode supplied, but we learn that Sigemund kills the dragon by pinning it to the wall of his own cave with his iron sword.[112] The Norse sources make more of this sword. In the *Saga of the Volsungs* (c. AD 1200–70) Regin reforges Sigurd's broken sword Gram for him so as to make a suitable weapon with which to kill Fafnir: it becomes so sharp that Sigurd can slice through Regin's anvil with it.[113] In the *Story of Norna-Gest* (xiv AD) Regin gives Sigurd another named sword that he had forged from scratch with which to kill Fafnir, Ridil.[114]

In the Middle High German *Wolfdietrich B* (c. 1225–50) the champion shatters his ordinary sword on the head of one of the dragons of Garda. Carried by the dragon to its lair for its young to devour, he finds amid the detritus of its cave, not only King Ortnit's helmet, the remains of its head still within, but also his special sword Rose (Rôse), which had been given to him by his father, the wilderness dwarf Alberich. Snatched up by the dragon whilst bound in an enchanted sleep, Ortnit had not himself had the chance to deploy it. The sword has a gemstone pommel with a relic of St Pancratius sealed within. Wolfdietrich tests Rose by striking it against a rock, and proceeds to slaughter the baby dragons, guided by its inherent gleam, and then the father dragon alike with it.[115] Encountering the mother dragon at a later stage, as he shows Leibgart the site of her husband's demise, he is able to cut her in half with the same Rose.[116]

In *Thidrek's Saga* (c. AD 1230–50) the conventional swords of Thidrek and Fasold prove useless against the Dragon of the Rimslo Forest that has snatched up Sistram and is trying to launch itself from the ground with the armed man in its mouth. They can make no impact upon it as they slash at it as it passes just over-head. Sistram has to hand his own more special sword down to the pair from the dragon's mouth, so that they can more successfully hack into its belly with it.[117] *Thidrek's Saga* also gives us an episode closely aligned with that of Wolfdietrich in the Garda Dragon's cave, even down to the level of personnel, with Wolfdietrich here being reduced to Thidrek, i.e. Dietrich (tout court) of Bern, and Hertnid sporting a name derived from an original 'Hartnit', as does Ortnit. Thidrek similarly shatters his work-a-day sword on the back of the Dragon of Bergara and at this point regrets leaving his own special sword, Ekkisax, at home. Consequently

---

[111] *Beowulf* ll. 2200–3182.   [112] *Beowulf* ll. 884–97.   [113] *Völsunga saga* §15.

[114] *Norna-Gests þáttr* §§5–6. Prior to this Sigurd has already cut through Regin's anvil with Gram, as in *Völsunga saga*, though here it is a sword Regin has forged from scratch, and its cutting power is further conveyed by the claim that it could cut through even a tuft of wool tossed into the flowing Rhine.

[115] *Wolfdietrich B* §§694–708. For Alberich's gift of the sword, see *Ortnit* (c. AD 1217–25) §116. Cf., loosely, Heinrich von dem Türlin's *Diu Crône* ll.15032–223 (c. AD 1220s): when the Dragon of Aufrat backs Gawein into its own cave, he is able to salvage not one but two swords from the detritus, and thereby continue his fight against it.

[116] *Wolfdietrich B* §§791–2.   [117] *Þiðrekssaga* §105.

defenceless, he is brought to its cave to make a meal for its young. Groping around in the darkness, he finds King Hertnid's sword, which the dragon had failed to root out of its cave with the rest of his arms. He strikes it against the stone wall of the cave to make sparks and a fire, and uses the light so created to kill the baby dragons as they sleep. As to the parent dragon, he climbs onto its back and drives the sword down into its spine until it is cut in two.[118] A very similar tale is told also in the *Saga of the Flower Plains* (xv AD). Here a flying dragon seizes the Red Knight, his brother Aki and a third armed warrior in its claws and carries them off to its cave situated in a golden and bejewelled forest. The dragon drops Aki en route, but upon arrival at its cave devours the third warrior with its two young. They fall asleep after the meal, whereupon the Red Knight, released from the dragon's grip, rummages in the detritus of its cave to equip himself with armour and an outstanding sword, driving the latter into the dragon under its wing. He then kills the two young, making off with gold and silver from the cave, and helping himself to a horse with a golden saddle from the forest outside.[119]

In the *Saga of Sigurd the Silent* (xiv AD) Sigurd the Silent does battle against the Dragon of the Rhine with the enchanted sword given to him by Count Lafranz. The sword cannot be blunted, even by magical means, and one edge is permanently poisoned. Attached to the handle in a little bag is a red healing stone. The sword has a long and distinguished pedigree, with which we are regaled. It was initially made by dwarfs for the king of Sicily (cf. Ortnit's Alberich) and had passed through several hands before coming to the count. After dealing the creature an initial wound with his spear as it flies over, he then leaps up to lop off its legs and eventually, whilst dodging the showers of venom, its tail, the latter wound finally bringing the creature down to the ground, whereupon he decapitates it.[120]

In the *Saga of Pole-Ladder Hrolf and the Rhymes of Bjarki* (c. AD 1400) Bodvar drives his sword (not necessarily a special one) through the shoulder and into the heart of the under-described but surely dragon-like beast that is harassing King Hrolf's Danish court (see §11.10 below on this dragon's blood). The sword initially sticks in his scabbard for suspense. When Bodvar then puts the dead beast back on its feet so that his companion Hott can be seen to slay it by the king and his court, who watch from afar, Hott hacks at it with the special named sword he has borrowed from the king himself, Gullinhjalti, 'Hilt of Gold'. To celebrate

---

[118] *Þiðrekssaga* §§416–22. Scholarship is surprisingly dismissive of this episode's tight alignment with *Wolfdietrich B*: see Thomas 1986:xii, xxiii (with xx for the—surely remote—possibility that the figure of Ortnit refracts the historical Odoacer).

[119] *Blómstrvalla saga* §25. The broader motif of the monster snatching the champion back to its lair, where he discovers the special sword he needs to defeat it amid its detritus, is already to be found in *Beowulf* (c. AD 685 to c. AD 725): Grendel's mother seizes Beowulf in her mere and drags him to her cavern below; the named sword he has brought for the purpose, Hrunting, proves useless against her, but he is able to decapitate her with the giant-made sword (*eotenisc...giganta geweorc*) he comes across in the cavern itself (ll. 1557–69; cf. 1489–90).

[120] *Sigurðar saga þögla* §16.

Hott's great feat, even though he suspects that the beast has really been killed by Bodvar, Hrolf renames Hott 'Hjalti', after the sword used.[121]

Special swords can be useful against those that shape-shift into the form of dragons too. In the *Saga of Bosi and Herraud* (before AD 1350) Harek, who can transform himself into a dragon, is invulnerable in human form except to weapons charmed by a witch, and so it is that Smidur is able to bash out all his teeth with a special short sword that has been enchanted by the witch Busla.[122] In the *Saga of Viktor and Blavus* (xiv AD) Blavus deploys a special sword, the gift of Dimus, against the shape-shifting, venom-spewing berserkers Falur and Soti.[123] In *Walking-Hrolf's Saga* (xiv AD) the only sword that can penetrate the venom-spewing sorcerer Grim Aegir is the enchanted sword that had formerly belonged to King Hreggvid, this sword having the ability to cut through stone as if it were flesh. It has healing stones set in its pommel, reminiscent of the sword with which Sigurd the Silent kills the Dragon of the Rhine. The sorcerer-dwarf Mondul deals the key disabling blow to Grim when he enhances the sword's power further by smearing it with his own spittle, before dragging it across his calves and cutting his tendons. It then falls to Hrolf to deal the final death-blow with the same weapon.[124] In the *Saga of Gold-Thorir* (xiv AD) Gull-Thorir and his men stab the dragons into which the Viking Valr and his sons have mutated seemingly with their own (the Vikings') swords, found in their cave beside them (this despite the fact that the ghost or revenant of Agnar has just given Gull-Thorir a special one from his tomb).[125]

11.7.2 Spears and Lances

Spears or lances come into their own when the dragon is a flying one; when the champion is fighting the dragon as a chivalric knight from horseback; or when an appropriate trick is called for.

Flying dragons first. In the great battle of *Thidrek's Saga* (*c.* AD 1230–50) between, on the one hand, Queen Ostasia's army of flying dragons and other beasts and, on the other, the forces of King Isung of Bertangaland, the only

---

[121] *Hrólfs saga kraka og Bjarkarímur* §§35–6, pp. 68–71 Jónsson.

[122] *Bósa saga ok Herrauðs* §14, iii.319 Jónsson.

[123] *Viktors saga ok Blávus* 14v–16v (pp. 77–83) Chappel = §§9–11 (pp. 26–31) Loth.

[124] *Göngu-Hrólfs saga* §§1, 3, 31, 33.

[125] *Gull-Þóris saga* §§3–4. Further examples may be given in which no special qualities are explicitly claimed for the swords used. After darts prove useless against the dragon encountered by Frothi in Saxo Grammaticus' Latin *Gesta Danorum* 2.1.1–4 (early xiii AD), he kills it by plunging his iron sword into its belly; his son Fridleif uses his sword in a similar way against island dragon he encounters at 6.150. At *Ívens saga* §10 (xiii AD) St Iven hacks apart the dragon he encounters, first in half and then into many small pieces, with, so far as can be told, an ordinary sword. At *Konráðs saga keisarasonar* §§6–7 (xiv AD) Konrad hacks off with his sword first the tail and then the claws of the flying Dragon of Pezcina.

weapons we hear mention of are spears, one of which is launched by King Isung itself at the principal dragon, to no effect. The dragon dodges it before swooping down on the king, taking him up in its mouth and claws and devouring him. It is then attacked in turn by his eldest son, who drives his spear through its foot and into its body, before it snatches him up in its claws and squeezes him to death. Similarly, Thetlief (Detlef) throws a spear through the neck of one of the worst of the other dragons as it flies over, but the dragon takes him and his horse to death with itself, falling upon him and grabbing him in its claws in its last moments.[126] As we have just seen, in the *Saga of Sigurd the Silent* (xiv AD) Sigurd the Silent must deal the initial blow to his flying dragon with a spear beneath the wing, before he can get to work on it with his special sword.[127] In the *Saga of Gold-Thorir* (xiv AD) Björn, taking a vantage point on a precipice, spears the largest of the dragons into which Valr and his sons have been transformed—presumably Valr himself—as it flies out of its cave behind a waterfall below.[128]

Second, the knight. In Wirnt von Grafenberg's Middle High German *Wigalois* (c. AD 1205–10) Wigalois is able to drive his lance through the dragon Pfetan's heart before the creature is even aware of his presence. This is a special weapon indeed. It had been made in 'inner India' and then given by an angel to the spirit of King Lar, who has passed it on to Wigalois in turn.[129] In Gottfried von Strassburg's *Tristan* (AD 1210), Middle High German also, Tristan deals the key wound to the Dragon of Wexford similarly with his lance. Indeed, he does so by driving his lance home with such force that his horse dies from the shock, the dragon proceeding to eat half of it. But it is significant that he finishes the creature off with a sword to the heart.[130] In the *Saga of Tristram and Isönd* (AD 1226) Tristan this time kills the dragon of Wexford outright with his lance, driving it through the dragon's mouth and heart and out of the side of its body. But he does then use his sword to hack the tongue out of the dragon's mouth and to cut its carcass in half.[131]

Third, the trick. In Saxo Grammaticus' Latin *Gesta Danorum* (xiii AD) Ragnar Lodbrok attacks the problematic pair of vipers reared by Princess Thora with a spear strapped to his hand, and he is able to drive this successfully through both.[132] In the *Saga of Ragnar Lodbrok* (xiii AD) Ragnar attacks the single serpent

---

[126] *Þiðrekssaga* §§349–55.   [127] *Sigurðar saga þögla* §16.

[128] *Gull-Þóris saga* §4. Some further examples. In an episode of *Erex saga Artuskappa* (§10, pp. 48–51 Blaisdell; xiii AD or later) derivative of *Þiðrekssaga*'s Sistram and Thetlief episodes, Erex first hacks with his sword at the flying dragon that has snatched up Plato, but has to finish the job by driving his spear through its mouth. In *Tristrams saga ok Ísoddar* (§10 = §§35–6 Gísli Brynjólfsson = pp. 121–8 Vilhjálmsson; c. AD 1400), Tristan plainly and simply kills the Dragon of Wexford with a spear alone, launching it into the creature as it flies over him. In *Ectors saga* (§8; xiv–xv AD) Fenacius kills the dragon Ingifer has become by first spearing it through the mouth, but then, presumably with a sword again, chopping its head in half.

[129] *Wigalois* ll. 4747–73, 5088–99.

[130] Gottfried von Strassburg *Tristan* ll. 8901–9096.   [131] *Tristrams saga ok Ísöndar* §§35–6.

[132] Saxo Grammaticus *Gesta Danorum* 9.252–3.

of this version with a spear from which he has removed the nail that pins the head to the haft, so that he can leave the head lodged in the serpent's spine whilst withdrawing the haft. His purpose is to kill the serpent anonymously at first (for reasons that are not entirely clear), and subsequently to reveal himself as the killer by producing the haft that matches the head. Despite the lack of clarity here, we recognize the motif familiar from the Tristan story of the dragon-slayer revealed by a missing-piece token.[133] In the *Story of Ragnar's Sons* (xiii AD) Ragnar again kills the serpent with a spear, but then cuts off its head afterwards, presumably with a sword.[134]

11.7.3   Other Weapons

In the account of the Sigurd story provided by (the German-derived) *Thidrek's Saga* (c. AD 1230–50) Sigurd is portrayed as more doltish and thuggish than usual, and accordingly his weapons are appropriately cruder. Dragon-Regin attacks him whilst he is burning charcoal in the forest, and so Sigurd withdraws a great beam from his fire and strikes him dead with it, before proceeding to chop off his head with an axe. It is noteworthy that although Regin's role has morphed here from that of the smith he is in the standard version of Sigurd's story into that of the dragon, his fate of decapitation remains the same.[135] In the *Saga of Ketil Trout* (xiii AD) Ketil cuts down a fiery flying dragon with his axes, chopping it in half.[136] In the version of the Ragnar story-type Saxo Grammaticus applies to Alf in his Latin *Gesta Danorum* (early xiii AD), Alf kills the viper that is protecting Alfhild by using a pair of tongs to plunge a piece of molten iron into its mouth as it gapes to attack him. More conventionally, he destroys the second protecting snake by plunging a spear into its mouth.[137]

11.7.4   Protective Clothing

In Germanic texts conventional armour is seldom sufficient protection against a dragon. We note its failure when, in *Thidrek's Saga* (c. AD 1230–50), the largest of Queen Ostasia's dragons picks up the eldest of Isung's sons in its claws and squeezes him in them until his breastplate and torso alike shatter.[138] In the Middle High German *Ortnit* (c. AD 1217–25), Ortnit's strong armour retains its integrity

---

[133] *Ragnars saga Loðbrókar* §§2–4; cf. also the use of the dragon's claw and the bone from inside it as tokens at *Flóres saga konungs ok sona hans* §20 (xiv AD), and the simpler use of the dragon's two claws as tokens at *Konráðs saga keisarasonar* §8 (xiv AD).

[134] *Ragnarssona þáttr* §1.   [135] *Þiðrekssaga* §166.

[136] *Ketils saga hœngs* §1, p. 153 Jónsson.

[137] Saxo Grammaticus *Gesta Danorum* 7.190–1.   [138] *Þiðrekssaga* §353.

but is still of little use to him: the parent dragon carries him alive to its cave, where its young suck his flesh and blood out through the links in his chainmail.[139]

Our texts are more interested in the tricky use of soft clothing for protecting against the dragon's venom. As we have seen, in Saxo Grammaticus' Latin *Gesta Danorum* (early xiii AD) both Frothi and Fridlief dress themselves in bull's hides to protect themselves against the venom of the dragons they encounter.[140] Magic is often afoot. In the Middle High German *Wolfdietrich B* (*c.* AD 1225–50) Wolfdietrich is protected both against the principal dragons (*würmer*) of Garda and also against a lion-fighting fiery serpent (*sarpant*) of the place by the shirt Else-Sigminne has given him, which consists of seventy-two layers of palmate silk into which she has sown a (second) relic of St Pancratius. This remains effective whilst his outer mail-shirt glows red with the heat blown at him by the serpent.[141] In Heinrich von dem Türlin's *Diu Crône* (also Middle High German, *c.* AD 1220s) Gawein is similarly preserved when the Dragon of Aufrat burns his armour off, with his underclothes being protected by a belt into which he has inserted a magic jewel taken from Fimbeus.[142] In the *Story of Ragnar's Sons* (xiii AD) Ragnar is initially protected by a silk jacket Aslaug has made for him when thrown into a snake-pit by Ella (Ælla), king of Northumbria; when the Northumbrians strip him of it, the snakes are at last able to kill him.[143] In the *Saga of Viktor and Blavus* (xiv AD) Kador gives Viktor the skin of a mysterious animal, an *osalabra*, to protect him from the venom spewed by the shape-shifting berserkers Falur and Soti, and Blavus an enchanted shirt that is similarly proof against the venom (Viktor also wears some sort of glass visor before his eyes). In the course of the battle Falur does indeed spew venom over Viktor; this disintegrates his armour and it falls away like a decayed husk; the skin, however, continues to protect him.[144] In *Walking-Hrolf's Saga* (xiv AD) Hrolf is protected from the shape-shifter Grim's venom by a special cloak his ally the dwarf Mondul has given him, the blade-proof and venom-proof cloak made by Vefreyja.[145] In the *Saga of Gold-Thorir* (xiv AD) Gull-Thorir penetrates the cave of the dragons derived from Valr and his sons wearing a tunic given to him by the ghost or revenant of Agnar that will protect him from their fire.[146] More prosaically, when Harald Hardrada encounters a venomous serpent in a dungeon in *Morkinskinna* or *Mouldy Vellum* (*c.* AD 1220), he soaks up its venom in his cloak as he attacks it.[147]

The most distinctive protective clothing adopted when going into battle with serpents is that deployed by Ragnar Lodbrok against the two overweening vipers of the Swedish princess Thora in Saxo Grammaticus' Latin *Gesta Danorum* (xiii AD).

---

[139] *Ortnit* §§574–5.   [140] Saxo Grammaticus *Gesta Danorum* 2.1, 6.150.
[141] *Wolfdietrich B* §§687–8, 722–9.   [142] *Diu Crône* ll. 15032–223.
[143] *Ragnarssona þáttr* §3.
[144] *Viktors saga ok Blávus* 14v–16v (pp. 77–83) Chappel = §§9–11 (pp. 26–31) Loth.
[145] *Göngu-Hrólfs saga* §§4, 31, 33.   [146] *Gull-Þóris saga* §§3–4.
[147] *Morkinskinna* §13 Unger.

He dons woollen and shaggy clothing, and then throws himself into water, allowing the soaked garments to harden into ice in the frost. Perhaps there is a notion (though this is not explicitly articulated) that the ice should also protect him from the serpent's burning breath by virtue of its coldness. As King Herrudr congratulates him after their successful slaying, he laughs at his 'hairy breeches', and this is the origin of Ragnar's famous nickname.[148] In the *Saga of Ragnar Lodbrok* (xiii AD) Ragnar less interestingly hardens his hairy clothes by boiling them in pitch and then rolling in sand. In this version of the story he faces a single serpent. When he wounds it a jet of it corrosive blood strikes him between the shoulder-blades, but he remains unharmed (cf. §11.10).[149] In the version of this story-type that Saxo applies rather to Alf, Alf imbues his clothes not with ice or with pitch but actually with blood—he wears bloodstained hides—specifically in order to incite the snakes against himself. This is apparently so that he can kill both of them by thrusting weapons into their mouths as they gape to attack him.[150]

Other varieties of protective magic can also be deployed. In Wirnt von Grafenberg's Middle High German *Wigalois* (*c.* AD 1205–10) the spirit of King Lar fortifies Wigalois for his battle against the carrion-breathed dragon Pfetan by giving him a sweet blossom from his paradisical plot—presumably, therefore, an enchanted one; the knight duly takes a sniff from it before riding to the attack.[151] In *Konrad's Saga* (xiv AD) Konrad carries a magical green gemstone given to him by Princess Matthildr to protect him from the mass of serpents in the mysterious golden castle at the edge of the world (cf. again Wolfdietrich's shirt). The white gemstone he then seizes from the pair of serpents playing catch with it in the castle is itself subsequently revealed similarly to protect its bearer from snakes, toads, and other poisonous animals.[152] In *Ector's Saga* (xiv–xv AD) Fenacius is protected against the venom of the dragon Ingifer by a lotion he has received from a dwarf for the price of a gold ring.[153] In the *Saga of Sigrgardr the Valiant* (xv AD) Knut remains unharmed by the venom the Dragon of Tartary blows at him after being rendered immune to it by the magic of an old witch.[154]

11.8 The Path from Cave-Lair to River

The common classical and hagiographical motif of the dragon seizing control of or blighting a water-source vital to humans is all but absent from the Germanic

---

[148] Saxo Grammaticus *Gesta Danorum* 9.252–3. Saxo does make it clear that, despite the specifics of the nickname, Ragnar clothes his entire body in padded (and soakable) clothing: we should not think that the serpents are able to strike him only below waist, with all that that would imply for the modesty of their size.

[149] *Ragnars saga loðbrókar* §§2–4; so too *Ragnarssona þáttr* §1 (xiii AD).

[150] Saxo Grammaticus *Gesta Danorum* 7.190–1.   [151] *Wigalois* ll. 4736–46, 4991–3, 5063–5.

[152] *Konráðs saga keisarasonar* §§9–10.   [153] *Ectors saga* §8.

[154] *Sigrgarðs saga frækna* §13.114–16 (§§88–90 Loth).

tradition. Two exceptions may be noted. In Heinrich von dem Türlin's Middle High German *Diu Crône* (c. AD 1220s) the unsleeping Dragon of the Mountain slain by Gawein has the mission of protecting a spring that confers proof against enchantment upon its drinkers; it does so by enveloping it so completely in its coils that it cannot be seen.[155] In *Ector's Saga* (xiv–xv AD) Ingifer, upon being transformed into a dragon, poisons a local river.[156] However, Norse tradition develops a distinctive and productive motif of its own embracing dragon and river: this motif has the dragon frequenting a path between its cave-lair and a local river, which it visits to drink from, with the path becoming a locus of action. So it is with the dragon destroyed by Frothi in Saxo Grammaticus' *Gesta Danorum* (early xiii AD). It is returning to its cave after drinking water when Frothi attacks it.[157] So it is too with Fafnir in three of his principal accounts (all xiii AD): Sigurd kills him by digging a trench across his path and stabbing him from below as he passes over it on his way to drink.[158] In *Yngvar's Saga* (xiii AD) Yngvar and his men sprinkle the path of the Scythian dragon with salt and deposit on it the foot of a giant they happen to have with them, so as to delay the serpent in its return to the cave as they remove the gold from it.[159] We find a Christianized take on the motif in the brief *Story of Curious Thorstein* (later xiv AD). Thorstein is sent on a quest to an island of golden trees presided over by a dragon (*ormr*). He waits for the dragon to crawl to its water before cutting off two golden branches. However, the dragon discovers the theft before he can get away and stands rampant before him, challenging him. But Thorstein prays to St Olaf, whereupon the dragon settles down peaceably into its coils.[160] This traditional scenario evidently envisages the dragon being confined to its path and so it would seem to have been designed for a worm-style dragon.

An inversion of the scenario is found in a later version of the Tristan story, the *Saga of Tristram and Isodd* (c. AD 1400). Here the Dragon of Wexford's water-source is actually located within its own cave (a sometime classical and hagiographical conceit)[161] up on Mt Sukstia, and so the emphasis is laid not upon the dragon's need to frequent a river from its cave, but rather on its need to frequent its cave from its general marauding. Accordingly, Tristan waits until the dragon enters the cave before positioning himself below it to attack it as it re-emerges.

---

[155] *Diu Crône* ll. 26608–764.   [156] *Ectors saga* §§8, 10.

[157] Saxo Grammaticus *Gesta Danorum* 2.1.1–4.

[158] *Völsunga saga* §§13–20 (AD 1200–70); Snorri Sturluson *Prose Edda* Skáldskaparmál §§46–7 (c. AD 1220); *Poetic Edda* Reginsmal and Fafnismal (c. AD 1270).

[159] *Yngvars saga viðförla* §6, ii.442 Jónsson.

[160] *Þorsteins þáttr forvitna*; cf. Evans 2005:248.

[161] Similarly, the spring of Dirce is located within the cave of the Dragon of Ares destroyed by Cadmus (Ovid *Metamorphoses* 3.28–98), whilst the spring upon which King Samuel's City depends issues from the cave of the dragon destroyed by Theodore Tyron (Θαῦμα καὶ διήγησις τοῦ ἁγίου καὶ ἐνδόξου μεγαλομάρτυρος τοῦ Θεοδώρου Τήρωνος = Appendix B, Theodore Tyron [h]; xiv AD or before).

One reason for the inversion of the scenario here—or at any rate a compatibility with the inversion of it—is that the author is giving us an actively flying dragon this time: Tristan thrusts his spear up into it as it is about to fly from the rock.[162]

The motif persists in a Danish folktale recorded in the early nineteenth century AD. In this King Gram Guldkølve sends his most courageous courtier Henrik against a venomous dragon (*lindorm*) that has been attacking the people and animals of Vendsyssel. He finds the dragon's hole, and waits for it to emerge to drink the local water, as it does three hours after it has eaten. He positions himself by the water, but downwind of the dragon, and begins his attack by firing an arrow at the creature.[163]

11.9 The Vulnerable Spot

The notion that a dragon should possess a single vulnerable spot is a familiar one to fans of Tolkien's Smaug. The motif is indeed found already in the tale that was surely Tolkien's most immediate model for the Smaug episode, that of the dragon encountered by Frothi in Saxo Grammaticus' *Gesta Danorum* (early xiii AD). This creature has a scaly hide that cannot be penetrated, with only a single, soft, vulnerable spot at the bottom of its belly. The darts Frothi casts against the creature prove useless until he is able to plunge his iron sword into this vulnerable part.[164]

The same motif lurks in other texts. In the Anglo-Saxon *Beowulf* (c. AD 685 to c. AD 725), after Beowulf himself has failed to make any impact on the Firedrake by smashing his sword over its head, Wiglaf has more success by seemingly striking it in its belly.[165] In the *Saga of the Volsungs* (c. AD 1200–70), it is again to be inferred that Fafnir's belly, or some point thereof, constitutes a uniquely vulnerable spot. That is why Regin and Odin (in the guise of an old man) advise Sigurd to dig a pit across the path Fafnir takes from his cave to the river, and to plunge his sword up into his heart from beneath.[166] In Saxo's *Gesta* again the island dragon fought by Fridleif, Frothi's son, similarly has a scaly back impervious to all the hero's darts, and all he can do is attack its underside. The fashion in which he does this constitutes an interesting variation on the method by which Sigurd usually kills Fafnir. The dragon, having emerged from the sea, carves out great ditches as it writhes across the shore in attacking him. Fridlief then stations himself in one of these ditches so that he can stab the dragon in the groin from below with his sword as it now travels transversely across them.[167]

---

[162] *Tristrams saga ok Ísoddar* §10 = §§35–6 Gísli Brynjólfsson = pp. 121–8 Vilhjálmsson.
[163] The tale is recorded at Thiele 1843:i, 125–7; for a translation, see Rauer 2000:170–3 (Text 10).
[164] Saxo Grammaticus *Gesta Danorum* 2.1.1–4.   [165] *Beowulf* l. 2699: *nioðor hwéne slóh*.
[166] *Völsunga saga* §1.
[167] Saxo Grammaticus *Gesta Danorum* 6.150. Sigurd's method of killing Fafnir is recalled also in Heinrich von dem Türlin's Middle High German account of Gawein's slaying of the Dragon of the

In other sagas it is suggested that a winged dragon's most vulnerable spot is just underneath its wing. This is the spot in which Jason stabs the Dragon of Colchis in the *Saga of the Trojans* (xiii AD); this is the part of Dragon of the Rhine at which Sigurd the Silent aims his spear in the *Saga of Silent Sigurd* (xiv AD)—the blow weakens the dragon, but does not kill it outright, and he must continue to work on it with his sword;[168] this is the spot in which Gull-Thorir stabs the dragons into which Valr and his sons have been transformed in the *Saga of Gold-Thorir* (xiv AD);[169] this is the spot in which Unus stabs the flying Dragon of England as he is riding on it in the *Saga of King Flores and his Sons* (xiv AD)—he stabs it beneath its left wing specifically, and thereby penetrates its heart;[170] and this is the part of the dragon into which the Red Knight drives his sword in the *Saga of the Flower Plains* (xv AD), after the beast has carried him off.[171]

The motif of the dragon's uniquely vulnerable spot persists in the (xix AD) Vendsyssel folktale to which we have just referred (§11.8). Henrik opens his attack by firing an arrow at the creature, but this just bounces off it and enrages it. It makes for him, regarding him as a 'light snack'. Henrik jams the dragon's mouth open with a barbed iron crook he has had a blacksmith make for him, though the handle breaks off in Henrik's hands. The dragon dashes him to the ground with its tail and scratches him with its claws. Eventually he is able to stab the dragon in its belly, under which he is pinned, at the point at which its scales are weakest. The people of Vendsyssel retrieve him from under the dragon's carcass and take him back to the king, to whom he entrusts his family before dying. His descendants sport a dragon on their coat of arms.

11.10 The Dragon's Blood (and Venom Again)

On occasion the dragon's blood can be as deleterious to man as one might have expected it to be on first principles. When Gawein kills the Dragon of Aufrat by driving his sword into it in Heinrich von dem Türlin's Middle High German *Diu Crône* (c. AD 1220s), its blood, acting together with its venom, burns the sword away like a straw.[172] When, in the *Saga of Ragnar Lodbrok* (xiii AD), Ragnar's special protective clothing deflects the jet of blood from Thora's wounded serpent that strikes him between the shoulder blades (cf. §11.7.4), we can only assume

---

Mountain, *Diu Crône* ll. 26608–764 (c. AD 1220s): he stabs it from below as it passes over a pre-existing ditch.

[168] *Sigurðar saga þögla* §§16.   [169] *Gull-Þóris saga* §4.
[170] *Flóres saga konungs ok sona hans* §20.   [171] *Blómstrvalla saga* §25.
[172] *Diu Crône* ll. 15032–223. One is reminded of the scene in the movie *Alien* (dir. Ridley Scott, 1979), in which a modicum of blood squirts forth from the 'facehugger' (which will ultimately produce the dragonish 'xenomorph') when it receives a superficial leg-wound: acid-like, it burns down through floor after floor of the metal spaceship and threatens to pierce its hull.

that that blood is viciously corrosive.[173] And in the *Saga of Gold-Thorir* (xiv AD), when Björn spears the largest of the dragons into which Valr and his sons have been transformed, presumably Valr himself, as it flies overhead, the blood that gushes forth from the wound strikes him in the face and kills him instantaneously; at the same time Hyrningr is wounded when some falls on his foot.[174]

However, and paradoxically, the dragon's blood is more often presented as conferring a range of beneficial properties on humans. The Middle High German epic *Nibelungenlied* (*c.* AD 1200), which originated in Austria, refers to Siegfried's slaying of Fafnir only in passing. It tells that when he had slain the dragon (*lintrache*) he bathed in its hot blood, which made his skin grow horny, so that no weapon could penetrate it. However, as he was bathing, a leaf fell from a linden tree above and came to rest between his shoulder blades, with the result that he could still be wounded at that spot—such was his 'Achilles' heel'. The wicked Hagen tricks Siegfried's wife Krimhild into revealing the spot to him, so that he can treacherously slay him.[175] The (early xvi AD) German *Horn Siegfried Lay* offers an interesting development of this motif. As we have seen (§11.4.2), after killing a principal dragon in the role of Fafnir, Siegfried finds an enclosed valley writhing with many more dragons and snakes. He casts trees down in amongst them and sets them all ablaze with fire from his charcoal burner. A molten horn substance oozes forth from the flames, and so he coats his entire body with it—but again, cannot reach the single key spot in the centre of his back.[176] The motif of a single spot of vulnerability is one pleasingly shared with the great dragons themselves, as we have just seen (§11.9).

In the *Saga of the Volsungs* (*c.* AD 1200–70) the dragon's blood has a different virtue. As we have seen (§11.2), once Sigurd has killed Fafnir at Regin's behest, Regin drinks some of Fafnir's blood, so as to acquire the gift of prophecy. But Sigurd too acquires the gift of prophecy whilst roasting Fafnir's heart for Regin and testing its juices. More specifically, he acquires the ability to understand the language of birds and hears the nuthatches singing that Regin is planning to betray him, and so he takes pre-emptive action by striking off his head.[177] Snorri Sturluson has a slightly different version of the tale in the *Prose Edda* (*c.* AD 1220).

---

[173] *Ragnars saga loðbrókar* §§2–4; so too *Ragnarssona þáttr* §1 (xiii AD). This represents an inversion of the motif from the Sigurd-Fafnir story, discussed next, in which the spot between Sigurd's shoulder blades is the one part of his body that the *protective* blood of Fafnir *fails* to reach.

[174] *Gull-Þóris saga* §4. We may compare the effect of Grendel's blood at *Beowulf* ll. 1572–90, 1606–17, 1666–8.

[175] *Nibelungenlied* §§100 and 906. Lionarons 1998:71–92 addresses the short shrift given to dragon-slaying in this epic.

[176] *Lied vom hürnen Seyfrid* §§1–11; some discussion at Rebschloe 2014:201–5. In *Göngu-Hrólfs saga* §17 (xiv AD) Soti's skin is similarly hardened in a magical bath made for him by his foster-mother, a witch.

[177] *Völsunga saga* §20.

Here Sigurd tastes the prophecy-conferring juices of the hot heart when he accidentally touches it whilst it is cooking and sucks his fingers by reflex.[178]

In *Thidrek's Saga* (c. AD 1230–50) the dragon's blood offers both of these functions, protection and prophecy. Here, having killed Regin (in the dragon-role that usually belongs to Fafnir), Sigurd stews up his carcass to make a meal for himself, scalds his fingers in the soup, and sucks them. Acquiring the prophetic language of birds thereby, he learns from them that Mimir (in the dragon's-brother role that usually belongs to Regin) is plotting to kill him and so returns to him and kills him first. He fortifies himself for the task by smearing the dragon's blood (or just possibly its sweat: the manuscript reading is insecure) over himself to acquire an impenetrable horny skin. However, once again he is unable to reach a patch in the centre of his back and has to leave it vulnerable.[179]

The Norse reflex of Beowulf's battle with the dragon is found in the *Saga of Pole-Ladder Hrolf and the Rhymes of Bjarki* (c. AD 1400), where the roles of Beowulf and Wiglaf are taken on by Bodvar Bjarki and Hott, respectively. In this version of the story we are never told directly that the monster in question, which attacks King Hrolf's Danish court, is a dragon, though it is winged, legged, and marauding and is referred to vaguely by Hott as 'the worst kind of troll'—this last in contradiction of Bodvar's suggestion that it may be a mere animal, and so seeming to signify in the first instance that it is rather some sort of supernatural creature. Having killed the monster, Bodvar forces his cowardly companion Hott to drink two mouthfuls of its blood and also to eat a piece of its heart, in order to endow him with courage (the mighty Bodvar has rescued the gibbering Hott from the bone pile in King Hrolf's feasting hall, where he is pelted with bones by the king's arrogant and bullying champions, and has even taken to building himself a wall from the thrown bones to protect himself). Bodvar decides to help the magic along, however, as we have seen, by setting up a great feat for Hott to perform in public view so as to establish his new reputation. He mounts the slain beast back onto its feet and has the king and his court, removed to a great distance, spectate as Hott approaches it and kills it all over again, hewing at it and pushing it over with King Hrolf's special sword (§11.7.1).[180]

Similarly, whereas a dragon's venom is normally a terrible thing in the Germanic tales, as we have seen in some detail (§11.5.1), on occasion snake venom at any rate can, upon ingestion in the correct magical context, bestow a range of beneficial powers upon men akin to those conferred by dragon's blood. Two episodes of Saxo Grammaticus' *Gesta Danorum* (early xiii AD) deserve

---

[178] Snorri Sturluson *Prose Edda*, Skáldskaparmál §§46–7.   [179] Þiðrekssaga §§163–7.
[180] *Hrólfs saga kraka og Bjarkarímur* §§35–6, pp. 68–71 Jónsson. Similarly, the Norse reflex of Beowulf's battles with Grendel and his mother is to be found in the Sandhaugar episode of *Grettis saga*, §§64–7, and in a broader series of 'two-troll' stories. For all these analogues, see Andersson 1997:123–34.

attention. In the first, Balder's strength is sustained by food prepared by three wood-maidens, who drain the venomous slaver of three snakes into it. In the second, Roller's mother Kraka makes him a dish into which again she has drained the venomous slaver of three snakes, two black and one white, by hanging them from ropes over the food as she prepares it. However, it is Erik that contrives to eat the food instead of Roller, and so it is rather he that gains the benefit of wisdom, eloquence, and the ability to understand the languages of animals.[181]

11.11   Two Narrative Subroutines

In our analysis of the structure and motifs of the traditional hagiographical dragon fight we noted some recurring episodes of interest that tended to stand outside the principal narrative course or to operate more as bolt-ons to it (Chapters 6 and 7). Two episode-types with a similar relationship to the traditional Germanic dragon fight may be noted here.

11.11.1   Dragon and Lion

In Chrétien de Troyes' c. AD 1180 French *Yvain ou le Chevalier au Lion* Yvain is wandering in a wood when he comes across a battle between a fiery and venomous dragon (*serpant*) and a lion. After a little hesitation, he decides to intervene on behalf of the lion, the dragon being a treacherous creature and the lion a noble one. He has to cut off a piece of the lion's tail in order to get at the dragon's head. He reasonably expects the liberated lion to turn on him, but it rather stretches out its paws in obeisance and becomes his loyal companion in the hunt. We learn nothing more of this dragon's form or nature, but must suppose it to be unwinged.[182] This episode was to have a *grande fortune* in Germanic literature, on both the Middle High German and the Norse sides. Chrétien's narrative is closely replicated in Hartmann von Aue's Middle High German adaptation of *Yvain*, *Iwein* (c.1203), where the dragon is again described as fiery and malodorous, but the detail of the lion's tail is omitted.[183] And similarly it is closely replicated in the

---

[181]   Saxo Grammaticus *Gesta Danorum* 3.68–9 and 5.110; cf. Davidson and Fisher 1979–80:ii, 55 n. 1. Cf. Ctesias *FGrH* 688 F45l (= Aelian *Nature of Animals* 4.36), where the Indian purple snake is similarly hung up and its venom drained into a bronze vessel below. This coagulates to produce a toxin with different effects depending upon whether the snake is alive or dead as it is drained; at *FGrH* 688 F45r (= Aelian *Nature of Animals* 5.3) Ctesias similarly tells how the Indian *skōlēx*, once caught and killed, is hung up for thirty days whilst five pints of a napalm-like oil are drained from its body.

[182]   Chrétien de Troyes *Yvain* ll. 3335–409. Discussion at Acker 2012:15–16.

[183]   Hartmann von Aue *Iwein* ll. 3822–74.

Norse adaptation, *Iven's Saga* (xiii AD), in which the grateful lion behaves with rather less dignity, rolling over onto its back like a pussy cat.[184] Thereafter:

- No less than three sequences in the Middle High German *Wolfdietrich B* (*c.* AD 1225–50) are impacted upon. Let us consider them in reverse order. First, and most conservatively, Wolfdietrich intervenes in a battle he happens upon between a lion and a fiery serpent (*sarpant*) near Garda. The serpent turns his armour red hot, but he is eventually able to carry the lion away safely from it, entrusting it to Liebgart to nurse back to health. In due course the lion will intervene on his behalf in his dispute with Wildung of Viterbo over the credit for killing the first Dragon of Garda.[185] Second, before this, Wolfdieterich comes across this same Dragon of Garda in the forest in battle with a lion. He intervenes in the fight on the lion's behalf because he has a red lion for his blazon and because the lion looks to him appealingly. The dragon carries both off to its lair, where the lion will be devoured by the dragon and its young but Wolfdietrich will eventually get the better of it.[186] Third, before this in turn, Ortnit comes across this same dragon in the forest in battle with an elephant. Intervening in the battle on the elephant's behalf because he has a red elephant for his blazon, he chases the dragon off and acquires a loyal friend in the creature, which subsequently attempts to rouse him when the dragon returns to attack Ortnit as he sleeps under the enchanted linden, and then gives up its own life in defence of him.[187]
- *Thidrek's Saga* (*c.* AD 1230–50) gives us an episode strongly akin to the middle one of *Wolfdietrich B*. As we have seen (Chapter 10, §10.4.4), Thidrek finds a dragon doing battle with a lion in the forest and resolves to help the latter, the symbol of his blazon. The dragon carries both of them off to its lair, where the lion is devoured at once by the dragon and its brood, but Thidrek is reserved for a second meal, giving him the opportunity to plot their killing.[188]
- In the *Saga of Sigurd the Silent* (xiv AD) Sigurd the Silent comes across the Dragon of the Rhine attempting to fly off with a lion it has caught, which in turn is attempting to cling on to the treetops with its claws. Sigurd is moved to intervene on the lion's behalf because his shield blazon is a lion and draws near. The lion looks to him appealingly and pulls more tightly on the trees to

---

[184] *Ívens saga* §10. Although we may often suspect the influence of non-Germanic sources on the dragon episodes of the Norse chivalric sagas (*riddarasögur*) in particular, this is the only case in which a relationship can be directly documented. *Erex's Saga* is directly based on Chrétien's *Érec et Énide* and *Trójumanna saga* is directly based on Dares Phrygius' *De excidio Troiae historia*, but both originals remain dragonless.
[185] *Wolfdietrich B* §§722–30, 746, 783–4.   [186] *Wolfdietrich B* §§668–84.
[187] *Wolfdietrich B* §§511–25.   [188] *Þiðrekssaga* §§ 416–22.

draw the dragon down and more closely within Sigurd's reach; he proceeds to kill it with a combination of spear and sword, and the grateful lion becomes his pet and companion (cf. Chapter 10, §10.3.5).[189]

- In *Konrad's Saga* (xiv AD) Konrad similarly intervenes to save from a dragon the lion that he boasts on his blazon (although the connection is not made explicitly in this case). The lion attempts to cling onto the earth as the dragon tries to lift it. Once liberated, the lion sheds tears and again rolls over and becomes his trusty companion (cf. §§11.4.2, 11.7.1, and Chapter 10, §10.1).[190]

- In *Ector's Saga* (xiv–xv AD) Sir Trancival similarly rescues a lion from a flying dragon that is trying to carry it away in its claws, and this lion likewise becomes his friend and companion for life (cf. Chapter 10, §10.1).[191]

- In the *Saga of William of Sjodr* (also xiv–xv AD) Vilhjalmr similarly delivers a lion from a dragon attempting to carry it off from the forest of Lutuvald; this lion clings onto the trees so hard that it is actually uprooting them. He is able to cut off the dragon's head from the vantage-point of a mountainside, but he must then cut the lion free from the dead dragon's claws. Once again, the lion becomes his inseparable companion (cf. §11.2).[192]

These last four texts seem to shed some light on the archaeology of the earlier *Thidrek's Saga*. The motif of the uprooted trees is here too, for when, in the course of the battle, Thidrek shatters his sword on the dragon, he uproots a tree to provide himself with an alternative weapon. This looks like a refraction or elaboration of the motif of the lion's uprooting of trees and so suggests that these last four texts, for all their later dates, may preserve a motif that thrived already prior to *Thidrek's Saga*.

11.11.2 Snake Pits

The motif of the hero cast into a snake pit—itself closely allied to the motif of the serpent brood, for which see §11.4.2 above—is a productive one in Germanic literature, and it attaches in particular to individuals with other dragon- or serpent-affinities. In the *Prose Edda* (c. AD 1220) Snorri Sturluson tells that after Gunnar (Gunther) had buried Fafnir's gold, together with Högni (Hagen), they were captured by King Atli (Attila). He had Högni's heart cut out of him alive, but Gunnar cast into a snake pit, his arms bound. However, he was secretly given a harp, which he was able to play with his feet, and this charmed the serpents to sleep, all except for a single adder, which burrowed through his breastbone and tunnelled

---

[189] *Sigurðar saga þögla* §§16.   [190] *Konráðs saga keisarasonar* §8; cf. §6 for the blazon.
[191] *Ectors saga* §10.   [192] *Vilhjálms saga sjóðs* §13.

Fig. 11.1 Gunnar in the snake pit. Carving from the Hylestad stave church, xii A D.
© Werner Forman Archive/ Universitetets Oldsaksamling, Oslo/ Heritage Images.

into his liver until he died (Fig. 11.1).[193] The *Saga of the Volsungs* has the same
tale, with the only significant variation being that the adder tunnelled rather into
Gunnar's heart.[194] The selection of an adder for the snake in this role prompts us
to wonder whether appeal is being made the notorious deaf adder of the Psalms,
the one that can remain immune to the voice of charmers (cf. Chapter 8, §8.3.1).[195]

The principal sources for Ragnar Lodbrok, he of Thora's little snakes, similarly
tell of his confinement in a snake-pit. Saxo Grammaticus' Latin *Gesta Danorum*
(early xiii A D) relates how, after the usurping king Harald attempts to introduce
Christianity to Denmark in Ragnar's absence, Ragnar returns, ousts him, and
restores the old religion. God then punishes him by allowing him to be captured
by the Northumbrian king Ella, who casts him into a snake-pit, where adders
devour his liver and heart (that snake-variety and those two organs again).
Whilst this is going on, he sings all his achievements.[196] The same tale is found in

[193] Snorri Sturluson *Prose Edda* Skáldskaparmál §41.
[194] *Völsunga saga* §39. For a useful review of all the Old Norse sources for the death of Gunnar, see
Guðmundsdóttir 2012; cf. also Jensen 2017:2010–11.
[195] Psalms 57:5–6.   [196] Saxo Grammaticus *Gesta Danorum* 9.262.

the *Saga of Ragnar Lodbrok* (xiii AD) and the *Story of Ragnar's Sons* (xiii AD), with the further detail that the snakes refuse to touch Ragnar whilst he remains clothed but, once he is stripped, they hang off every part of him (cf. §11.7.4).[197]

The *Morkinskinna* or *Mouldy Vellum* (*c.* AD 1220) gives us a similar set-up, albeit with a single and rather larger serpent. Harald Hardrada is captured and thrust down into a bell-shaped dungeon with two of his companions. The dungeon is the home of a large and venomous serpent (*eitrormr*) and bestrewn with the fragments of the bodies of the men that have constituted its previous meals. Fortunately, the serpent is asleep as they arrive. After debating what to do whilst sitting on a headless corpse, and making a prayer to St Olaf, they attack it. Harald manages to plunge the small knife he still has with him through its mouth and into its heart, using his cloak to absorb its venom as it thrashes about.[198]

11.12 Conclusion

We have reconstructed an idealized principal narrative course for the medieval Germanic dragon fight that runs as follows. The dragon is created when a man is confined in a remote dark hole with his treasure. In some cases a jealous man retreats to a cave with his treasure to cherish and protect it and he is transformed into a dragon—or transforms himself into a dragon—as he lies on his gold and jewels, this in line with the abilities of shapeshifters, for whom the dragon can constitute a transformation of choice. In other cases a dragon is spontaneously generated from the corpse of a man sealed into his tomb (often a barrow) with his precious grave-goods. In either case, the attempt of another to take the treasure, or some of it, results in conflict. In a rather different scenario, the dragon originates as a mysterious tiny worm that is found and fostered until it grows to enormous and uncontrollable size. The marauding dragon's chief weapon is its fire and venom, which tend to be identified with each other to a rather greater extent than they are in the classical and hagiographical traditions. The king of the blighted land offers his daughter's hand to the champion that can defeat the dragon. The champion arms himself with special protective clothing manufactured by magic or at any rate by an imaginative trick. He then attacks the dragon most typically by ambushing it as it crawls between its cave and its water-source. He strikes it in a uniquely vulnerable spot, whether this is its underbelly or a pit beneath its leg or wing. The weapon deployed is either a special, named sword or a spear or lance.

---

[197] *Ragnars saga loðbrókar* §15; *Ragnarssona þáttr* §3. The latter text makes Ragnar's killing the cause of the invasion of England by his sons at the head of their Great Heathen Army. Lionarons 1998:50, noting that the youngest of the sons was known as Sigurðr ormr-í-auga, 'Sigurd Worm-in-the Eye', makes the intriguing suggestion that the winning but mysterious epithet of the eldest of them, Ivar the Boneless (*beinlausi*), may refer similarly to a serpentine nature.
[198] *Morkinskinna* §13 Unger.

The champion benefits from the magical properties of the blood of the slain dragon, which confers the gift of courage, strength, invulnerability, wisdom, or prophecy.

We have also investigated a pair of recurring narrative subroutines. In the first of these the champion intervenes on a lion's behalf upon coming across it engaged in a fight with a dragon, and after killing the dragon has a lifelong loyal pet in the lion. In the second the champion is cast into a snake pit, with varying outcomes.

In the course of our review of the Germanic dragon-fight tradition in this chapter and the last we have noted the reflex of the six core dragon-fight motifs it shares with the classical and hagiographical traditions, namely: the dragon's marauding (esp. §11.5.1); its fire (§11.5.1, Chapter 10, §10.4.1); its pestilential breath (§§11.4.1, 11.5.1, Chapter 10, §§10.2, 10.3.10); its cave-home (passim, esp. §§11.2, 11.4.2, 11.7.1, 11.8, Chapter 10, §§10.3.6, 10.3.7, 10.3.9, 10.4.3, 10.4.4); its generation from a corpse (§11.3); and, with a little variation, its control of a water-source (§11.8).

Conclusion

The Introduction established this volume's teleological project in posing the question as to whence the dragon familiar in the modern West derives, both in terms of its form and in terms of its typical narratives and associations. The issue of form has been chiefly addressed in Chapters 1, 3, 4, 5, and 10, where it is contended that the classical dragon's fundamentally pure serpentine form evolved into the wyvern shape through the long process of its merging, on the one hand, with the wide-bodied and animalian-headed sea-monster and, on the other, with the winged but otherwise generally humanoid demon. This process reached its completion by the ninth century AD. It was some five centuries after this that the four-legged variety of dragon became properly established.

The issue of the dragon's typical narratives and associated motifs has been chiefly addressed in Chapters 1, 6, 7, 8, 9, and 11. Already in the Graeco-Roman tradition dragon narratives evince the six core motifs that are to be shared by all three of the culture-groups under consideration here, namely: the dragon's marauding nature, its fieriness, its pestilential breath, its cave-home, its control of a water-source, and, a less prominent one, its generation from a human corpse.

These motifs persist into the era of Graeco-Latin hagiography where they are consolidated and joined by others, including the appeal of the locals to the saint, the saint's presentation of himself at the dragon's lair, his use of prayer and the sign of the cross, his taming and binding of the dragon, his dismissal of it to the wilderness or abyss, his conversion or reconversion of the locals as they look on, and his foundation of a religious institution at the site of the battle or in the dragon's vacated lair. The extraordinarily conservative nature of the hagiographical tradition means that its dragons, whilst seldom accorded much by way of physical description, tend to remain purely anguiform or vermiform, even as, beyond the bounds of this specific genre, the Christian dragon evolves into the wyvern.

The dragon-fight culture of Germanic tradition similarly evinces the six core narrative motifs. These may constitute, to some unfathomable extent, a shared Indo-European inheritance as opposed to a more recent borrowing from Latin hagiography. The tradition also shares with broader classical culture a motif that by-passes the hagiography, namely the offer by the king of a blighted land of his princess-daughter's hand in marriage to the champion that can defeat the troublesome monster in question (but then saints may not, of course, marry, once they have embarked upon their holy life). To these motifs the Germanic tradition added a different set of its own: the antagonist's transformation into a dragon whilst lying on his treasure, either dead or alive; the alternative origin of the dragon in a mysterious tiny worm; the champion's special weapon and magical protective clothing; his ambush of the dragon between cave and river; his exploitation of the dragon's sole vulnerable spot; and his subsequent exploitation of the magical qualities of the dragon's blood, which confers gifts such as invulnerability or prophecy.

Germanic tradition gives us more full-blown, physical, martial fights against dragons than the hagiographical one does. Whilst hagiography bequeaths us a pair of distinguished warrior saints, Theodore and George, who fight their dragons in a duly martial fashion, their physical fights are brief, desultory, and anticlimactic, an adjunct or coda to a more spiritual battle that has already been won. By contrast with hagiography too, medieval Germanic literature is more interested in celebrating the dragon's wyvern form, and specifically its winged nature, explicitly in the course of its story-telling. But, and now rather in common again with hagiography, the depth and conservatism of its story-telling traditions similarly exercise a retardant effect upon its dragon-fight construction, which has the curious result of often leaving explicitly winged dragons marooned on the ground, where they remain relatively easy prey for their human slayers.

I concluded my earlier book *Drakōn* by contrasting intra-narrative and extra-narrative perspectives on the dragon. Dracontophiles, I noted, may lament the death of the dragon in his story, but console themselves with the reflection that he is, after all, a creature of story, and that he lives again whenever his story is retold—and, as a good story, it does not want for the retelling.[1] I conclude now by contrasting intra-narrative and extra-narrative perspectives on the dragon in a different way. In his story, the dragon is a figure of destruction; outside it, he is a figure of integration. The shared recognizability, enjoyability, and indeed comfort of his story expresses a fundamental bond between the peoples and cultures of Europe across time and space, from archaic Greece, through imperial Rome, early medieval France and late medieval Iceland, to the Britain of today.

Hafi hverr þökk, er hlýðir ok sér gerir skemmtan af, en hinir ógleði,
er angrast við ok ekki verðr at gamni. Amen.

---

[1] Ogden 2013a:426. 'Dracontophile' is not my coinage: if not by others, it is deployed by Wendy Perriam in her 1989 novel, *Devils, for a Change.*

The Myths of Typhon and of Other Indo-European and Near Eastern World-Foundational Dragons Compared

The Greek Typhon narratives evince a story-type with a deep history in Indo-European mythology, and in the mythologies of the Near Eastern cultures the Greeks were in contact with in both prehistoric and historical times.[1] The reconstructed story-type may be summarized as follows. On the one side stands a great serpent, with an ambition to seize control of the world. It is often fiery, and it is often multiheaded. It is often the child either of the earth or of an evil god. It often lives in a cave or a hole in the earth, but it is also often associated with the chaotic sea or with flood waters. Against the serpent stands the storm god, who does battle against the serpent with his fiery thunderbolts (answering the dragon's fire), which are often identified with other weapon-types, such as clubs or hammers. Both protagonists can also direct winds against each other. The dragon can have an army of allies, seldom clearly defined; the storm-god is sometimes aided by a human, whose help he secures by allowing him to sleep with an allied goddess. The dragon can succeed in stealing body-parts form the storm god, and these are recovered either by his human helper or an allied deity deploying a seductive technique (music, sex, food, beer). In the end, the storm god succeeds either in binding the serpent beneath the earth, or in hacking it up into pieces.[2]

The sources in question are laid out in Table A.1, where they are, listed in chronological order of attestation, with the examples in Indo-European languages indicated as such (I-E). Table A.2 then lays out in detail the available constituent motifs for each example of the story-type.

[1] See the discussions in Fontenrose 1959; Walcot 1966; West 1966:379–81, 1997:300–4, 2007:255–9; Day 1977; Delcor 1977; Burkert 1987; Diény 1987:149–56 (a Chinese reflex?); Forsyth 1987; Batto 1992; Penglase 1994; Duchemin 1995:89–103; Watkins 1995; Katz 1998; Haider 2005; López-Ruiz 2006 esp. 79–94, 2010 esp. 88–94, 109–13; Bremmer 2008:1–18, 317–320; Lane Fox 2008:255–73; Rodríguez Pérez 2008:23–68; Kuehn 2011:87–92, 118–19; Yasumura 2013:117–31; Ayali-Darshan 2015; Noegel 2015; Scully 2015:50–68; Bachvarova 2016:250–65; Stephenson 2016:48–53; and my own earlier discussions at Ogden 2013a:10–15, 75–8 and esp. 2013b:257–62 (appendix A), 2017:117–34.

[2] We may note the frequent persistence still in the hagiographical tradition of the motifs bearing upon the dragon's fate: that to be (re-)confined beneath the earth, and that to be chopped up into pieces (see Chapter 6, §§6.5.4, 6.7).

Table A.1 Indo-European and Near Eastern world-foundational dragon myths: sources

Culture	Date	Source	Text	Translation
Sumerian: Ninurta against Azag	Late third millennium BC	*Lugal*-e, esp. 282–337	van Dijk 1983	Jacobsen 1987:233–72; van Dijk 1983 (French)
Egyptian: Ra against Apophis	c.2000 BC	*P. Bremner-Rhind* xxvi–xxviii	Budge 1910: pll. i–xix.	*ANET*³ 6–7 (J. A. Wilson)
Babylonian: Marduk against Tiamat	Early second millennium BC	*Enūma eliš* tablets i–iv	Lambert and Parker 1966; Talon 2005	*ANET*³ 60–72 (E. A. Speiser—obsolete; Dalley 2000:228–77 (reprinted at López-Ruiz 2018:14–16); Foster 2005; Talon 2005 (French)
Indian: Indra against Vritra (I-E)	c.1500–1000 BC	*Rigveda* 1.32; cf. also 1.52, 1.80, 2.11–12, 3.32, 4.18, 5.32, 6.17, 8.96, 10.113	van Nooten and Holland 1994	Arya and Joshi 2001; West 2004 (1. 32 only); Brereton and Jamison 2014
Canaanite-Ugaritic: Baal-Sapon (Adad) against Yam/Litan	c. xiv BC	Baal and Yam—*KTU* 1.1–2 (= *CTA* 1–2); Baal, Yam, and Litan—*KTU* 1.3 (= *CTA* 3) iii 35–52 and 1.5 (= *CTA* 5) i 2•–3	Smith 1994	*ANET*³ 129–42 (H. L. Ginsberg—obsolete; Caquot et al. 1974 (French); Coogan 1978; Gibson 1978; Meier at López-Ruiz 2018:177–91
Hurrian-Hittite: Teshub against Hedammu	c.1250 BC, reflecting Hurrian material up to two millennia older	*CTH* 348	Siegelova 1971:38–71	Hoffner 1998:51–5; Siegelova 1971:38–71, esp. 44–5, 54–61; *TUAT* iii.856–8 (German); Bachvarova at López-Ruiz 2018:158–67
Hittite: Tarhunna against Illuyanka (I-E)	c.1250 BC	*CTH* 321	Beckman 1982:12–18	*ANET*³ 125–6 (A. Götze—obsolete); Beckman 1982:18–20; Hoffner 1998:11–14; Bachvarova at López-Ruiz 2018:150–3

			Edition	Translation
Iranian: Atar and Thraētaona against Aži Dahāka (I-E)	c. x–v BC	Atar against Aži Dahāka—Avesta, Yašts 19.46–50; Thraētaona against Aži Dahāka—esp. Avesta, Yašts 5.28–35, 9.13–15, 14.40, 15.18–25, 9.7–8; Avesta, Vidēvdat/Vendidād 1.17, Dēnkard 7.1.26, Bundahish 29.8–9	Avesta: Geldner 1886–96; Dēnkard: Sanjana 1874–1928; Bundahish: Justi 1868	Avesta: Darmesteter and Mills 1880–7; Dēnkard: Sanjana 1874–28; Bundahish: Justi 1868
Jewish: God against Leviathan/Rahab	c. x–iv BC	Job 3:8, 7:12, 9:5–13, 26:5–14, 40:15–41.34; Psalms 74:13–14, 89:9–10, 104:26; Isaiah 27:1, 51:9–10	Kittel et al. 1997	NEB, etc.
Greek: Zeus against Typhon (I-E)	c.700 BC–vi AD	Hesiod Theogony 820–80; Pindar Pythians 1.15–28; Strabo C750–1; Apollodorus Bibliotheca 1.6.1–3; Oppian Halieutica 3.15–25; Nonnus Dionysiaca 1–2	(sundry)	Ogden 2013b:19–35 (DSS nos 5–9)
Norse: Thor against the Midgard Worm (I-E)	c. AD 1220	Snorri Sturluson Prose Edda, Gylfaginning §§34, 46–8, 51, 53; Poetic Edda, Hymiskvitha §§17–26	Prose Edda: F. Jónsson 1931; G. Jónsson 1935; Faulkes 1998; Poetic Edda: Dronke 1969–2010	Prose Edda: Brodeur 1916; Byock and Poole 2005; Poetic Edda: Belows 1936; Dronke 1969–2010; Larrington 1996

Table A.2 Indo-European and Near Eastern world-foundational dragon myths: motifs

	Sumerian (late third millennium BC)	Egyptian (c.2000 BC)	Babylonian (early second millennium BC)	Indian (c.1500–1000 BC; I-E)	Canaanite (c. xiv BC)	Hurrian (c. 1250 BC)	Hittite (c. 1250 BC; I-E)	Iranian (c. x–v BC; I-E)	Jewish (c. x–iv BC)	Greek (c. 700 BC–vi AD; I-E)	Norse (c.1220 AD; I-E)
The dragon	Azag	Apophis	Tiamat	Vritra, 'Blockage'	Yam/Litan	Hedammu	Illuyanka, 'Serpent'	Aži Dahāka (cf. *ophis*)	Leviathan/Rahab	Typhon	Midgard Worm
The dragon's form	Serpent? Hardwood tree? Has snake-like sky-weapon (cf. Ninurta's previous victories over seven-headed serpent, etc.)	Serpent	Female, multiheaded, serpentine	Serpent, but with shoulders?	Seven-headed serpent	Sea-serpent	Serpent	Three-mouthed, six-eyed serpent	Twisting sea-serpent	Complex compound dragon	Great serpent (capable of disguising self as cat)
Genesis of dragon	Child of Heaven and Earth			First-born of the serpents		Child of the underworld god Kumarbi and Sertapsuruhi, daughter of the Sea God		Created by Spenta Mainyu, Evil Principle		Child of Earth and Tartarus (Ap.)	Son of Loki
Dragon and water				Vritra pens up the world's waters, released by Indra	Yam, Litan's associate, is the Principle of the Sea	Hedammu lives in the watery deep; child of Sertapsuruhi, daughter of the Sea God		Aži Dahāka offers sacrifices to the Waters	Leviathan presides over chaotic ocean, pacified by God	Typhon becomes the Orontes (Str.); comes from the Ocean abyss (?) (Opp.)	Midgard Worm lives in the waters that surround the earth, and itself surrounds the lands

Dragon and Earth	Child of Heaven and Earth	Lives in cave in mountains of the West				Child of the underworld god Kumarbi	Illuyanka lives in hole		Typhon inhabits and uses series of caves; striking 'incest' scene (Non.); child of Earth and Tartarus (Ap.)	
Dragon's purpose	To seize throne of storm god							Competition for kingly splendour	To seize throne of storm god	
The storm god	Ninurta (and his father Enlil brings rainstorm)	(Ra, Sun god)	Marduk	Indra	Baal-Sapon (Adad)	Teshub	Tarhunna	(Angra Mainya, Good Principle; Thraetaona)	Zeus	Thor
Weapons of storm god	Battle-mace Sharur, also conceptualized as a lion-headed bird	Spear, arrows, sword, flame, magic spells	Winds, arrow	Thunderbolts fashioned by Tvastar; dragon also uses lightning and rain (?)	Throwing-clubs (i.e. thunderbolts) named 'Expeller' and 'Chaser', made for him by the smith-god Kothar; compared to eagles			(Atar, Principle of Fire)	Thunderbolts (repeatedly), harpe (dual-blade sickle); Typhon steals the thunderbolts	Thor's hammer, Mjölnir
Use of fire or venom by dragon (equivalent to thunderbolt)	Landscape set alight		Marduk holds herb to counter Tiamat's venom					Fire-breathing	Fire all-pervasive; landscape set alight	Worm spits venom

Continued

Table A.2 *Continued*

	Sumerian (late third millennium BC)	Egyptian (c.2000 BC)	Babylonian (early second millennium BC)	Indian (c.1500–1000 BC; I-E)	Canaanite (c. xiv BC)	Hurrian (c. 1250 BC)	Hittite (c. 1250 BC; I-E)	Iranian (c. x–v BC; I-E)	Jewish (c. x–iv BC)	Greek (c.700 BC–vi AD; I-E)	Norse (c.1220 AD; I-E)
Use of winds on both sides			By Marduk, to inflate Tiamat like a bladder before popping her					Aži Dahāka offers sacrifices to Vayu ('Storm-Wind')		By Typhon, before and after death (Hes.)	
Dragon's allies	Army of stones		Further anguiform monsters						Partisans of Rahab	Anguipede Delphyne(?) (consort?)	
Storm god's divine allies						Sauska, sister of Teshub	Inara (brings Hupasiya)			Hermes, Aegipan	
Storm god's human allies							Hupasiya			Cadmus (cf. Athena and Giants: brings Heracles, Ap.)	
Mortal's liaison with goddess							Hupasiya sleeps with Inara			Cadmus offered Athena, Leto, Charis, Aphrodite by Typhon; given Harmonia by Zeus/Ares	

Dragon removes and stores storm god's body parts					Eyes			Sinews (Ap, Non.)—sinews akin to thunderbolts?	
Seduction of the dragon				Sauska, with music, beer, love potion, sex ('love runs after her like puppies')	Inara, with feast, beer, wine, etc.			Cadmus, with flute (and promise of lyre, made from Zeus' sinews) (Non.); Pan with fish dinner (Opp.)	
Binding and deep burial of dragon	Ra binds Apophis beneath the Earth				Bound	Bound beneath Mt Demavend		Bound beneath Etna	
Dragon's body hacked up	Hacked up	Hacked up					Rahab hacked in pieces		Thor strikes off serpent's head (?)
Key locations			Mt Sapuna = Kasios		Kiskilussa			Kasios (Jebel Aqra), Cilicia (Kilikia), Corycian cave, Sicily (Sikelia), Arimoi	

APPENDIX B

Hagiographical Dragon Fights: The Sources

Saint	Date of text	Citation	Text/edition	Language	Translation
anonymous monk	v AD	*De promissionibus et praedictionibus Dei* 3.43, col. 835 PL	*PL* li, coll. 733–858	Latin	*DW* p. 240; *DSS* no. 140
anonymous saint	earlier xiv AD	Jean Gobi *Scala coeli* §13	Polo de Beaulieu 1991	Latin	*DW* p. 181
Agilus of Resbach	xi–xii AD	*Vita S. Agili* 6.31, p. 585 AASS	AASS Aug. vi pp. 574–87; *BHL* no. 148	Latin	—
Amand of Mastricht [a]	viii AD	[Baudemond] *Vita S. Amandi episcopi Traiectensi* 1, p. 849 AASS	AASS Feb. vi, pp. 848–54; *BHL* no. 332	Latin	—
Amand [b]	xii AD	Philip of Harveng *Vita S. Amandi* pp. 859–60 AASS	AASS Feb. vi pp. 857–73; *BHL* no. 334	Latin	—
Ammon	c. AD 395 (Greek original); c. AD 403/4 (Rufinus' Latin trans.)	*Historia monachorum in Aegypto*; Rufinus of Aquileia *Historia monachorum in Aegypto* 8	Festugière 1971 (Greek original); *PL* xxi, 387–460 (Rufinus' Latin trans.)	Greek and Latin	*DSS* no. 145 (based on Rufinus)
Andrew, apostle [a]	late vi AD	Gregory of Tours *Life of Andrew* 19	Prieur 1989; *BHL* no. 430	Latin	*DW* p. 215; *DSS* no. 149
Andrew [b]	late vi AD	Ps.-Abdias *Historia apostolica* at pp. 483–4 Fabricius	Fabricius 1719:i, 402–742.	Latin	—
Armel (Ermel, Armagilius) [a]	xii AD or later	*Vita S. Armagili ex veteri breviario Leonensi* 4, pp. 170–3 Ropartz	Ropartz 1864:163–74; *BHL* no. 678	Latin	

Continued

Continued

Saint	Date of text	Citation	Text/edition	Language	Translation
Armel [b]	xiii AD	*Breviary of St Malo* p. 299 AASS	AASS Aug. iii 298–9; *BHL* no. 679	Latin	—
Armel [c]	AD 1514	*Breviary of Rennes* p. 457 Duine	Duine 1904–5	Latin	—
Armentarius (Hermentaire) of Antibes	AD 1540	Jean de Nostredame *Discours de la vie de Saint Hermentaire* pp. 39–41 Gayrard	Gayrard 2001:33–48 (orthography modernized)	French	—
Arsacius (Arsace, Ursacius) of Nicomedia [a]	earlier v AD	Sozomen *Ecclesiastical History* 4.16	Bidez and Hansen 1960	Greek	Hartranft 1890
Arsacius [b]	AD 1493	Petrus de Natalibus *Catalogus sanctorum et gestorum eorum* 7.67	Petrus de Natalibus 1493; *BHL* no. 715b	Latin	—
Artemon of Laodicea [a]	x AD	*Synaxarium ecclesiae Constantinopolitanae* Synaxarium mensis Aprilis Day 12 §2	Delehaye 1902	Greek	—
Artemon [b]	xii AD	*Analecta Hymnica Graeca* canones Aprilis 13.18	Halkin and Festugière 1984; *BHG* no. 2047	Greek	—
Athenogenes	vi AD	*Passio Athenogenis* 5–7	Maraval 1990; *BHG* 197b	Greek	*DW* pp. 240–1; Maraval 1990 (French)
Beatus (Beat, Bienheuré, Bié) of Vendôme	x AD (?)	*Vita S. Beati* p. 366 AASS	AASS Mai. ii, 363–6; *BHL* no. 1064	Latin	—
Benedict of Nursia (of Montecassino) [a]	AD 593	Gregory the Great *Dialogues* 2.25	de Vogüé and Antin 1979	Latin	Zimmerman 1959
Benedict [b]	AD 1263–7	Jacobus de Voragine *Golden Legend* 49	Graesse 1850	Latin	Ryan 1993
Bernacus (Bernachius, Brenach, Brynach) of Nevern	xii AD	*Vita S. Bernaci* p. 6 Rees	Rees 1853:5–12; *BHL* no. 1186.	Latin	—

Name	Date	Source	Language	Edition	Reference
Brigid of Kildare	ix AD	[Chilienus/Coelan of Inis-cealtra] (probably by Donatus of Fiesole) *Vita iii S. Brigidae* pp. 143, 153 *AASS*	Latin	*AASS* Feb. i pp. 141–55; *BHL* no. 1458	—
Caesarius of Arles	vi AD	Cyprian of Toulon et al. *Vita S. Caesarii Arelatensis* 1.9, p. 460 *MGH*	Latin	*MGH Scriptores rerum Merovingicarum* iii pp. 433–501; Morin 1937–42:ii; *BHL* no. 1508	Klingshirn 1994:1–70
Callinicus	xi AD or before	*Passio SS. Thyrsi, Leucii, Callinici* p. 823 *AASS*	Latin	*AASS* Jan. ii pp. 817–24; *BHL* no. 8279	*DW* p. 245
Caluppan	AD 581–94	Gregory of Tours *Liber vitae patrium* 11.1	Latin	*MGH Scriptores rerum Merovingicarum* i.2, 259–60; *BHL* no. 1535	*DW* p. 173; *DSS* no. 150
Carantoc (Carantocus, Caradocus, Cernathus Carannog)	early xii AD	*Vita S. Carantoci* §4, p. 99 Rees, pp. 144–6 Wade-Evans	Latin	Rees 1853:97–101; Wade-Evans 1944:142–7; *BHL* no. 1563	Rees 1853:396–401; Wade-Evans 1944:142–7
Christina of Tyre/Tyro/Bolsena [a]	vi AD (lost Greek original); ix AD (surviving Latin versions thereof)	*Passio S. Christinae* pp. 185–6 Cross and Tuplin (London version) and pp. 200–1 (Turin version)	Latin (after Greek)	Cross and Tuplin 1980; *BHL* no. 1749	—
Christina [b]	AD 1263–7	Jacobus de Voragine *Golden Legend* 98	Latin	Graesse 1850	Ryan 1993
Clement of Metz [a]	AD 782–6	Paul the Deacon *Gesta episcoporum Mettensium* coll. 711–13 *PL*	Latin	*PL* xcv, 709–22; *MGH Scriptores* x, 534–44	*DW* pp. 170–1; *DSS* no. 156
Clement [b]	c. AD 1000	*Vita I S. Clementis* 4–7, pp. 8–10 Sauerland	Latin	Sauerland 1896; *BHL* no. 1859	—
Clement [c]	c. AD 1100	*Vita II S. Clementis* 12–21, pp. 497–502 *Catalogus*	Latin	*Catalogus codicum hagiographicorum Bibliothecae regiae Bruxellensis* 1886–9:i.2 pp. 486–502; *BHL* no. 1859	—

Continued

Continued

Saint	Date of text	Citation	Text/edition	Language	Translation
Clement [d]	xii AD	*Vita III S. Clementis*	Paris BN lat. 16735 foll. 112r–114v; Chazan 2000:29–30 (excerpts only)	Latin	—
Columba (Cholmcille)	c. AD 700	Adamnan *Life of St Columba* 2.28	Anderson and Anderson 1961; *BHL* no. 1886	Latin	Anderson and Anderson 1961
Constantine the Great	AD 340	Eusebius *Vita Constantini* 3.3	Winkelmann 1975	Greek	Cameron and Hall 1999
Cosmas and Damian	AD 1263–7	Jacobus de Voragine *Golden Legend* 143	Graesse 1850	Latin	Ryan 1993
Crescenti(a)nus of Umbria	xiv AD	*Acta S. Crescentini Martyris* 1–2, p. 59 AASS	AASS Jun. i, pp. 59–60; *BHL* no. 1983	Latin	—
Deodatus (Dié) of Blois [a]	x AD	*Vita S. Deodati*, AASS Apr. iii, 273	AASS Apr. iii, 273–4; *BHL* no. 2130	Latin	—
Deodatus [b]	x AD	*Vita S. Deodati*, AASS Apr. iii, p. 274	AASS Apr. iii, pp. 274–6; *BHL* no. 2128	Latin	—
Dominic of Osma (Dominican founder)	xiii AD	Bartholomaeus Tridentius *Vita S. Dominici* p. 560 AASS	AASS Aug. i pp. 559–61; *BHL* no. 2214	Latin	—
Domitianus of Maastricht [a]	xii AD	*Vita S. Domitiani* 4, p. 147 AASS	AASS May ii pp. 146–7; *BHL* nos 2254–5	Latin	—
Domitianus [b]	xii AD	*Vita S. Domitiani* 8–9, p. 149 AASS	AASS May ii pp. 147–52; *BHL* no. 2253	Latin	—
Donatus of Epirus [a]	earlier v AD	Sozomen *Ecclesiastical History* 7.26	Bidez and Hansen 1960	Greek	DSS no. 146
Donatus of Epirus [b]	AD 1263–7	Jacobus de Voragine *Golden Legend* 115	Graesse 1850	Latin	Ryan 1993
Donatus of Sisteron (Jura)	xii AD or earlier	*Vita S. Donati* 3–4, pp. 309–10 *Catalogus*	*Catalogus* 1889–93:i, 309–15; *BHL* no. 2310	Latin	—

Name	Date	Source	Edition	Language	Reference
Elisabeth of Thracian Heraclea (the Thaumaturge) [a]	ix–x AD	*Vita S. Elisabeth* p. 259 Halkin	Halkin 1973; *BHG* (Sup.) no. 2121	Greek	Karras 1996
Elisabeth [b]	x AD	*Synaxarium ecclesiae Constantinopolitanae, Synaxarium mensis Aprilis* Day 24 §1	Delehaye 1902	Greek	—
Eneco (Íñigo) of Oña	xvi AD or before	*Acta S. Eneconis*, pp. 116–17 AASS	*AASS* Jun. i, pp. 111–26; *BHL* no. 2545	Latin	—
Erasmus of Antioch	ix AD or before	*Passio S. Erasmi* (reconstructed from several sources) 215–16	*AASS* Jun. i, pp. 213–17	Latin	—
Eucherius of Orleans [a]	AD 858	*Epistola Synodi Carisiacensis ad Hludowicum regem Germaniae directa*	*MGH Leges, Capitularia regum Francorum* ii, pp. 432–3	Latin	*DW* p. 188
Eucherius [b]	after AD 1124	*Miracula S. Prudentii* p. 351 AASS	*AASS* Oct. iii, 349–78; *BHL* no. 6979	Latin	—
Eudocia of Heliopolis	x AD or before	*Vita S. Eudociae* §15, p. 885 AASS	*AASS* Mar. i, pp. 875–85; *BHG* no. 604	Greek	*DW* pp. 267–8
Euflamus (Efflam) of Brittany	xii AD	*Vita S. Euflami confessoris* pp. 284–8 de la Borderie	de la Borderie 1891:282–96; *AASS*, November iii, pp. 134–8; *BHL* no. 2664	Latin	—
Eumenius of Gortyn	x AD	*Synaxarium ecclesiae Constantinopolitanae, Synaxarium mensis Septembris* Day 18 §3	Delehaye 1902	Greek	—
Florentius of Valcastoria	AD 593	Gregory the Great *Dialogues* 3.15.11–12	de Vogüé and Antin 1979	Latin	*DSS* no. 153; Zimmerman 1959
Francisca (Francesca, Frances) of Rome	before AD 1440	Giovanni Mattiotti *Acta S. Franciscae* pp. 106, 163–5	*AASS* Mar. ii, pp. 92–176; *BHL* no. 3094	Latin	Miguet 1900

Continued

Continued

Saint	Date of text	Citation	Text/edition	Language	Translation
Fronto of Périgueux [a]	viii AD	*Vita S. Frontonis* 9, pp. 351–2 Coens	Coens 1930:343–60; *BHL* no. 3181t	Latin	—
Fronto [b]	later x AD	[Gauzbert] *Vita S. Frontonis* 10, p. 357 Coens	Coens 1957:351–65; *BHL* no. 3182d	Latin	—
Fronto [c]	xi AD	[Sebald of Périgueux] *Vita S. Frontonis, episcopi Petragoricensis* pp. 409, 411, 412 AASS	*Vita S. Frontonis, episcopi Petragoricensis*, AASS Oct. xi pp. 407–14; *BHL* no. 3185	Latin	—
Gaudiosus of Salerno	xvi AD or before	*Vita S. Gaudiosi* p. 908 AASS	AASS Oct. xi pp. 906–9; *BHL* no. 3281	Latin	—
George [a]	xi AD	MS, Patriarchal Library, Jerusalem, cod. 2	—	Georgian	Walter 2003:140–2 (English trans., after the intermediary Russian of Privalova 1977:73)
George [b]	xii AD	*Miracula Sancti Georgii (Codex Romanus Angelicus* 46), §12	Aufhauser 1911:52–69	Greek	DW pp. 298–301; DSS no. 160
George [c]	AD 1263–7	Jacobus de Voragine *Golden Legend* 58	Graesse 1850	Latin	DSS no. 161; Ryan 1993
George of Suelli in Sardinia	xii AD	*Vita S. Georgii episcopi Suellensis* p. 218 AASS	AASS Apr. iii, pp. 217–18; *BHL* no. 3410	Latin	—
Germanus (Germain) of Auxerre [a]	xi–xii AD	*Vita S. Germani* 4.12–13, p. 265 AASS	AASS May i, 261–9; *BHL* no. 3452	Latin	—
Germanus [b]	AD 1263–7	Jacobus de Voragine *Golden Legend* 129 (Life of Mamertinus)	Graesse 1850	Latin	Ryan 1993
Gildas of Rhuys [a]	ix AD	*Vita i S. Gildae* p. 95 MGH	*MGH Auctores Antiquissimi* xiii.1, 91–106; *BHL* no. 3541	Latin	DSS no. 141

Gildas [b]	xi AD	Vita ii S. Gildae p. 184 Catalogus	Catalogus 1889–93: ii, 182–91	Latin	—
Girardus of Anjou	c. AD 1153	Vita S. Girardi p. 495 AASS	AASS Nov. ii Pars i, pp. 493–501; BHL no. 3548	Latin	—
Golinduch [a]	vi–vii AD	Stephen of Hierapolis The Endurance and the Trial of the Blessed Gulanducht in Persia 9	Kekelidze 1955:197–250	Georgian	Garitte 1956:426–40 (Latin)
Golinduch [b]	vi–vii AD	Eustratius Vita S. Golinduch 12–14	Papadopoulos-Kerameus 1897–98: iv, 149–74; v, 395–6; BHG no. 700–1	Greek (after Syriac)	—
Gregory the Great [a]	AD 594	Gregory of Tours History of the Franks 10.1 (cf. 4.31)	Krusch and Levison 1951	Latin	Thorpe 1974
Gregory [b]	viii AD	Vita S. Gregorii Magni p. 132 AASS	AASS Mar. ii, pp. 130–7; BHL no. 3640	Latin	—
Gregory [c]	ix AD	John the Deacon Life of St Gregory 1.5.36–8, p. 144 AASS	AASS Mar. ii pp. 137–210; BHL no. 3641	Latin	—
Gudmund	mid-xiv	Arngrímr Brandsson Guðmundar saga §62, p. 129 Vigfusson and Sigurdsson	Vigfusson and Sigurdsson 1858–78:ii.1–220	Old Norse	—
Guthlac	AD 730–40	Felix of Crowland Life of Guthlac 4–8	Colgrave 1956; BHL no. 3723	Latin and Anglo-Saxon	Colgrave 1956
Hermas	AD 130–50	Shepherd of Hermas vision 4 (4.1–3)	Whittaker 1967	Greek	Ehrman 2003:161–474
Hilarion [a]	before AD 396	Jerome Life of St Hilarion 39	Bastiaensen 1975; BHL no. 3879	Latin	DSS no. 143
Hilarion [b]	AD 675–710	Aldhelm De virginitate (poetic version) p. 387 Ehwald, ll. 808–11	R. Ehwald, ed. MGH Auctores Antiquissimi xv, 350–471	Latin	Lapidge and Rosier 1985

Continued

Continued

Saint	Date of text	Citation	Text/edition	Language	Translation
Hilarion [c]	AD 675–710	Aldhelm *De virginitate* (prose version) pp. 266–7 Ehwald	R. Ehwald, ed. *MGH Auctores Antiquissimi* xv, 226–323	Latin	Lapidge and Herren 2009
Hilarus of Galatea	vi AD	*Vita Hilari*, §9, p. 475 AASS	AASS May iii, pp. 473–5; *BHL* no. 3913	Latin	–
Hilary of Poitiers [a]	late vi AD	Venantius Fortunatus *Vita S. Hilarii [Pictavensis]* 35–8	*MGH Auctores Antiquissimi* iv.2, pp. 1–7; *BHL* no. 3885	Latin	*DW* p. 189; *DSS* no. 152
Hilary of Poitiers [b]	AD 1263–7	Jacobus of Voragine *Golden Legend* 17	Graesse 1850	Latin	Ryan 1993
Honoratus of Arles [a]	before AD 449	Hilary of Arles *Sermo de vita sancti Honorati episcopi Arelatensis* 3.15, col. 1257 *PL*	*PL* l [= 50], 1249–72; AASS Jan. ii, pp. 17–24	Latin	–
Honoratus [b]	xii AD?	*Vita S. Iacobi, Episcopi Tarentasiensis* pp. 26–7 AASS	AASS Jan. ii pp. 26–8; *PL* clxiii, 1411–14; *BHL* no. 4112	Latin	–
Honoratus [c]	c. AD 1300	*Vita S. Honorati* 1.22–3, 2.26	Marchant and Petit 1511	Latin	Gayrard 2001:52–3 (part only)
Humiliana (Umiliana, Aemiliana) of Cerchi	mid-xiii AD	Vito of Cortona *Vita S. Humilianae* 2.20–1, pp. 391–2 AASS	AASS Mai. iv pp. 385–400; *BHL* no. 4041	Latin	–
Hypatius	c. AD 450	Callinicus *Vita sancti Hypatii* 28.19–23	Bartelink 1971; *BHG* no. 760	Greek	–
James, apostle, the disciples thereof [a]	mid-xii AD or earlier	*Liber S. Iacobi* p. 293 Whitehill	Whitehill 1944:i, 289–99; *BHL* no. 4072	Latin	–
James, apostle, the disciples thereof [b]	AD 1263–7	Jacobus de Voragine *Golden Legend* 99	Graesse 1850	Latin	Ryan 1993

Jesus [a]	ii–vi AD	Infancy Gospel of Thomas 16.1–2 (A), p. 147 Tischendorf	Tischendorf 1876 pp. 140–63	Greek	DW p. 262; Elliot 1993:68–83
Jesus [b]	viii–ix AD	Gospel of Ps.-Matthew 18, p. 81 Tischendorf	Tischendorf 1876 pp. 51–112	Latin	Elliot 1993:84–99
Joannicius of Bithynia [a]	AD 846	Peter the Monk Life of Joannicius pp. 400–1, 405–6, 407–8, 412 AASS	AASS Nov. ii pars I pp. 384–436; BHG no. 936	Greek	DW pp. 268–9
Joannicius [b]	before AD 860	Sabas Life of Joannicius pp. 343–4, 354–5, 360–1 AASS	AASS Nov. ii Pars i pp. 343–84; BHG no. 935	Greek	—
John, apostle [a]	c. AD 150–80	Acts of John 71–86	Lipsius and Bonnet 1891–1903:ii.1, 151–216; Junod and Kaestli 1983 BHG nos 899–915	Greek	Elliot 1993:303–46
John, apostle [b]	c. AD 1000	Hrotsvitha Comoediae sex, iii. Callimachus	Goullet 1999; Berschin 2001; PL cxxxvii, coll. 1001–14	Latin	St John 1923; Wilson 1998; Goullet 1999 (French), Bonfante 2013
John the Baptist [a]	x AD	Theodore Daphnopates Oratio in translationem manus S. Praecursoris Antiochia Constantinopolin 12–13, pp. 617–18 Migne	PG cxi, 611–20	Latin (after Greek)	DW pp. 241–2
John the Baptist [b]	AD 1263–7	Jacobus de Voragine Golden Legend 86	Graesse 1850	Latin	Ryan 1993
John Parvus/Colobus	xii AD or before	Narratiuncula rhythmica, appendix, AASS Oct. viii p. 48	AASS Oct. viii pp. 47–9; BHL no. 4383	Latin	—
John of Reomay (Reomaus, Réome)	AD 659	Jonas Vita S. Johannis Monachi et Abbatis Reomaensis pp. 507–8 MGH	MGH Scriptorum rerum Merovingicarum iii pp. 506–17; BHL no. 4434	Latin	—

Continued

Continued

Saint	Date of text	Citation	Text/edition	Language	Translation
Julian of le Mans	c. AD 1000	Létald de Micy, *Vita S. Iuliani* p. 765 *AASS*	*AASS* Jan. ii pp. 762–7; *BHL* no. 4544	Latin	–
Julian Sabas	mid-V AD	Theodoret *History of the Monks of Syria* 2.6	Canivet and Leroy-Molinghen 1979; *BHG* no. 969	Greek	Price 1985
Keyne (Keane, Cain, Ceinwen, etc.)	xiv AD or before	*Vita S. Keynae* p. 277 *AASS*	*AASS* Oct. iv pp. 276–7; *BHL* no. 4653	Latin	–
Leo IV, Pope [a]	before c. AD 939	*Vita S. Leonis* p. 110 Duchesne	Duchesne 1892:ii,106–39	Latin	–
Leo IV, Pope [b]	c. AD 939	Flodoard of Rheims *De Christi triumphis apud Italiam* pp. 816–17 *PL*	*PL* cxxxv, 595–886	Latin	–
Leo of Cava	xii AD	*Vita S. Leonis* p. 461 *AASS*	*AASS* Jul. iii, 460–1; *BHL* no. 4840	Latin	–
Lifard/Liphardus of Meung-sur-Loire	ix AD	*Vita SS. Lifardi et Urbitii* 5–8, pp. 300–1 *AASS*	*AASS* June i, 300–2; *BHL* no.4931	Latin	–
Machutus (Malo, Maclou, Machutes, Maclovius) of Alet	AD 866–72	Bili, *Vita S. Machutis* pp. 38–40 Yerkes	Yerkes 1984; *BHL* no. 5116	Latin	–
Maglorius (Magloire) of Dol	ix–x AD	*Miracula S. Maglorii* pp. 308–10 *Catalogus*	*Catalogus* 1889–93:iii, 308–12; *BHL* nos 5139–43	Latin	–
Magnus (Magnoaldus) of Füssen [a]	c. AD 895	*Vita S. Magni Faucensis vetus* pp. 144–8 Walz (= *AASS* Sept. ii, 749)	Walz 1989; *AASS* Sept. ii, pp. 735–58; *BHL* no. 5162	Latin	–
Magnus [b]	AD 1067–70	Otloh of Saint-Emmeram, *Vita S. Magni confessoris* §16, pp. 205–7 Coens	Coens 1963; *BHL* no. 5163	Latin	–

Name	Source	Date	Edition	Language	Translation
Mamilianus of Palermo [a]	Vita Senzii, AASS Mai. vi, pp. 71–2	vii–viii AD	Vita Senzii, AASS May vi, pp. 71–3; BHL no. 7581	Latin	—
Mamilianus [b]	Vita S. Mamiliani (summary at p. 49 AASS)	xii AD or before	Vita S. Mamiliani (summary only); BHL no. 5204d	Latin	—
Marcellus of Paris	Venantius Fortunatus Life of Bishop Marcellus of Paris 10, pp. 53–4 MGH	late vi AD	MGH Auctores Antiquissimi iv.2, 49–54; BHL no. 5248	Latin	DW pp. 187–8 DSS no. 151
Marcian	Theodoret History of the Monks of Syria 3.7	mid-v AD	Canivet and Leroy-Molinghen 1979	Greek	Price 1985
Margaret of Pisidian Antioch (a.k.a. Marina) [a]	Martyrium of St Marina pp. 24–7, 29 Usener	AD 815–20 (based on an earlier text)	Usener 1886; BHG no. 1165	Greek	DW pp. 161, 193–4; DSS no. 158
Margaret [b]	Passio S. Margaritae virginis et martyris 12–14, p. 192 Mombritius; pp. 204–7 Clayton and Magennis	early ix or before	Mombritius 1910:ii, 190–6; Clayton and Magennis 1994:194–218; BHL no. 5303	Latin	Clayton and Magennis 1994:194–218
Margaret [c]	Old English Life of St Margaret (Cotton Tiberius A iii) 11–14	mid-ix AD or before	Clayton and Magennis 1994:112–39	Anglo-Saxon	Clayton and Magennis 1994:112–39
Margaret [d]	Passion of St Margaret ('The Rebdorf passio') AASS Jul. v pp. 37–8	x AD	AASS Jul. v pp. 33–9; BHL no. 5308	Latin	—
Margaret [e]	Jacobus de Voragine Golden Legend 93	AD 1263–7	Graesse 1850	Latin	Ryan 1993
Margaret [f]	Margretar saga 5; i, p. 478 Unger	c. AD 1380	Unger 1877:i, pp. 474–81	Norse	Pálsson and Edwards 1985

Continued

Continued

Saint	Date of text	Citation	Text/edition	Language	Translation
Martha [a]	AD 1187	[Marcilia] *Vita S. Marthae* pp. 235–6 Mombritius	Mombritius 1910:ii.231–40; Dumont 1951:150–4; *BHL* nos 5545–6	Latin	–
Martha [b]	late xii AD	[Harbanus Maurus] *Vita beatae Mariae Magdalenae et sororis eius Marthae* 40–1, coll. 1497–8 *PL*	*PL* cxii, 1431–1508; Dumont 1951:166–7; *BHL* no. 5508	Latin	Mycoff 1989
Martha [c]	AD 1263–7	Jacobus de Voragine *Golden Legend* 105	Graesse 1850; Dumont 1951:150–4	Latin	Ryan 1993
Martha [d]	AD 1264	Vincent de Beauvais *Speculum historiale* 10.99	de Beauvais 1473; Dumont 1951:150–4	Latin	–
Martin of Tours [a]	c. AD 400	Sulpicius Severus *Dialogues* 3.9, coll. 217 *PL*	*PL* xx, coll. 183–222	Latin	–
Martin [b]	AD 1263–7	Jacobus de Voragine *Golden Legend* 166	Graesse 1850	Latin	Ryan 1993
Mary, Virgin [a]	iv AD	*History of the Blessed Virgin Mary* i pp. 44–5, ii pp. 51–2 Budge	Budge 1899:i	Syriac	Budge 1899:ii
Mary [b]	vi–vii AD (for the Syriac archetype)	*Arabic Infancy Gospel* 33–4	Provera 1973	Arabic (after Syriac)	Roberts et al. 1886
Matthew, apostle [a]	late vi AD	Ps.-Abdias *Historia apostolica* at ii 638, 642–4 Fabricius	Fabricius 1719; *BHL* no. 5690	Latin	–
Matthew [b]	AD 1263–7	Jacobus de Voragine *Golden Legend* 140	Graesse 1850	Latin	Ryan 1993
Matthew [c]	xv AD	*Acta S. Matthaei* pp. 221–2 AASS	AASS Sep. vi pp. 220–5	Latin	–
Maurus of Syria	viii AD (?)	*Vita beati Mauri Syri et Felicis eius filii apud Vallem Narci prope Naris ripam* 5–8, pp. 132–5 Susi	Susi 1995:130–6; *BHL* no. 5791m	Latin	–

Name	Date	Work	Edition	Language	Reference
Mewan (Mevennus, Maianus, Men, Méen) of Brittany	x–xi AD	*Vita S. Mevenni* 16–17, pp. 153–4 Plaine	Plaine 1884; *BHL* no. 5944	Latin	—
Michael, archangel [a]	ix–x AD	*Homiliary of St Père* pp. 33–4 Cross	Cross 1986; Rauer 2000:158–61	Latin	Rauer 2000:158–61
Michael [b]	xi AD	Leabhar Breac Homily no. xvi ('On the Archangel Michael') pp. 213–19 Atkinson	Atkinson 1887:ii, 213–19	Old Irish	Atkinson 1887:ii, 453–4
Michael [c]	c. AD 1000	*Apparitio S. Michaelis in Monte Tumba*	Poncelet 1910:369; *AASS* Sept. viii, pp. 76–8; *BHL* no. 5951	Latin	—
Modestinus	AD 1613	Filippo Ferrari *Catalogus sanctorum Italiae in Menses duodecim distributus* p. 98 (Feb. 14)	Ferrari 1613; cf. *AASS* Feb. ii, p. 900	Latin	—
Monegundis	late vi AD	Gregory of Tours *Liber vitae patrium* 19.3 p. 289 *MGH*	*MGH Scriptores rerum Merovingicarum* i.2, 211–94	Latin	James 1991
Myron of Crete [a]	x AD	*Synaxarium ecclesiae Constantinopolitanae*, August, Day 8, §3	Delehaye 1902	Greek	—
Myron [b]	xiv AD	Epitome *Vita S. Myronis* p. 345 *AASS*	*AASS*, Aug. ii pp. 344–5; *BHG* no. 1312	Greek	*DW* p. 205
Narcissus of Gerundum (Girona)	c. AD 770	*Conversio et passio ii S. Afrae* 7, p. 60 *MGH*	Krusch ed., *MGH Scriptores rerum Merovingicarum*, iii, 55–64; *BHL* no. 109	Latin	*DSS* no. 155
Neventerius and Derien	AD 1637	Albert le Grande *Vie de S. Riok* 2–5	Thomas and Abgrall 1901:40–2	French	—

Continued

Saint	Date of text	Citation	Text/edition	Language	Translation
Nicasius, Quirinus, and Scuviculus/Scubiculus	earlier xi AD	*Passio SS. Nicasii episcopi, Quirini presbyteri, Scuviculi diaconi cc.2–5*, pp. 629–30 de Smedt	de Smedt et al. 1982; *BHL* no. 6082	Latin	—
Nicholas of Myra	c. AD 1340	*Niklaus saga erkibiskups* pp. 57–9 Unger	Unger 1877:ii.21–158	Old Norse	
Parasceve of Sicily	viii AD	John of Euboea, *Passio S. Parascevae* 8–9	Halkin 1966; *BHG* no. 1420p	Greek	—
Paris of Teano	AD 1533 or before	*Vita S. Paris* p. 75 AASS	AASS Aug. ii pp. 74–8; *BHL* no. 6466		
Patrick [a]	AD 1187	Gerald of Wales *Topographia Hibernica* 1.28	Brewer, Dimock, and Warner 1861–9:v	Latin	*DSS* no. 159
Patrick [b]	AD 1200–10	Jocelin of Furness *Vita S. Patricii* §148, p. 574 AASS	AASS Mar. ii, pp. 540–80; *BHL* no. 6513	Latin	*DSS* no. 159
Patrick [c]	AD 1263–7	Jacobus de Voragine *Golden Legend* 50	Graesse 1850	Latin	*DSS* no. 159; Ryan 1993
Paulus Aurelianus of Léon (Pol de Léon) [a]	AD 884	Wrmonoc *Vita S. Pauli Aureliani* 18.52–6, pp. 245–8 Plaine	Plaine 1882; *BHL* no. 6585	Latin	—
Paulus Aurelianus [b]	1637 AD	Albert le Grand *Vie de S. Jaoua* 6–11	Thomas and Abgrall 1901:52–6	French	—
Paulus Simplex (Haplos)	AD 419–20	Palladius *Historia Lausiaca* (recension G) 22.9–13	Bartelink 1974	Greek	Clarke 1918
Paulus and Juliana of Nicomedia	xiv AD	*Martyrium of Paulus and Juliana* 13–15, pp. 8–9 Trautmann and Klostermann	Trautmann and Klostermann 1934; *BHG* no. 964	Greek	—
Pavacius of le Mans	ix AD	*Vita S. Pavacii* cc.5–7, p. 541 AASS	AASS Jul. v, 540–3; *BHL* no. 6602	Latin	—
Peregrinus	xvi AD or before	*Vita S. Peregrini*, pp. 1153–4 AASS	AASS Jan. ii pp. 1153–4; *BHL* no. 6626	Latin	—

Name	Date	Work	Edition	Language	Bibliography
Perpetua	AD 203	*Passion of Sts Perpetua and Felicitas* 4.3–9	Heffernan 2012; *BHL* no. 6633; cf. *BHG* no. 1482	Latin	*DSS* no. 129; *DW* p. 143; Heffernan 2012; Gold 2018:165–74
Peter of Athos	xiii–xiv AD	Gregorius Palamas *Orationes asceticae* Oration 2.23	Chrestou 1992:157–260	Greek	—
Petroc (Pedrog) [a]	xii AD or before	*Vita S. Petroci antiquior* §10, pp. 493–4 Grosjean	Grosjean 1956b; *BHL* no. 6639	Latin	—
Petroc [b]	xiv AD or earlier	*Vita S. Petroci* pp. 157–8 Grosjean; p. 383 AASS	Grosjean 1956a; *Acta Sanctorum* Jun. i, 391–4; *BHL* no. 6640	Latin	—
Philip, apostle [a]	mid- to late iv AD	*Acts of Philip* 8, 11, 13–15, *Martyrion of Philip* 2, 7, 12–20, 24–8, 32, 39, 42	Amsler et al. 1999; *BHG* nos. 1516–26	Greek	*DW* pp. 207, 227; *DSS* no. 134; Bovon and Matthews 2012; Amsler et al. 1996 (French)
Philip [b]	late vi AD	Ps.-Abdias *Historia Apostolica* at ii 738–40 Fabricius	Fabricius 1719; *BHL* no. 6814	Latin	*DSS* no. 135
Philip [c]	AD 1263–7	Jacobus de Voragine *Golden Legend* 65	Graesse 1850	Latin	Ryan 1993
Polyxena	mid-iii AD (?)	*Acts of Xanthippe and Polyxena* 22	James 1893–7:ii.58–85	Greek	Craigie 1880
Portianus	late vi AD	Gregory of Tours *Liber vitae partum* 5.2 p. 228 MGH	*MGH Scriptores rerum Merovingicarum* i.2, 211–94	Latin	James 1991
Rofillus (Rufillus, Rophilus, Rophius) of Forlimpopoli [a]	xi AD	*Vita Rophili seu Rufilli episcopi* 2.11–14, pp. 381–2 AASS	AASS Jul. iv 379–82; *BHL* no. 7283	Latin	—
Rofillus [b]	xi AD	*Vita S. Mercurialis* p. 756 AASS	AASS Apr. iii, pp. 752–7; *BHL* no. 5932 [misprinted as 5032]	Latin	—
Romanus (Romain) of Rouen [a]	AD 1394	'Inquiry' cited at Floquet 1833:i, 10–11	Floquet 1833:i	French	—

Continued

Saint	Date of text	Citation	Text/edition	Language	Translation
Romanus [b]	AD 1609	Rigault 1609, Introduction	Rigault 1609	Latin	–
Samson of Dol [a]	vii–viii AD	*Vita i S. Samsonis* 1.48–51, 58–60, pp. 218–20, 230–2 Flobert	Flobert 1997; *BHL* nos 7478–9	Latin	Taylor 1925; *DSS* no. 154 (part)
Samson [b]	mid-ix AD	*Vita ii S. Samsonis* pp. 109–11, 128–30, 144–5 Plaine	Plaine 1887; *BHL* nos 7480–4	Latin	Rauer 2000:151–9 (part)
Samson [c]	xii AD or before	*Vita S. Teliavi* pp. 440–1 Loth	Loth 1893–4; cf. Loth 1894–5; *BHL* no. 7997	Latin	–
Samson [d]	xii AD or before	*Book of Llan Dâv*, *Vita S. Samsonis* pp. 20–1 Evans and Rhys	Evans and Rhys 1893:6–24	Latin	–
Samson [e]	AD 1107–30	Baudri (Balderic) of Bourgeuil *Vita S. Samsonis* fols 47v–50r, 77r–80r, 99v–101v	Paris, Bibliothèque nationale, lat. 5350 fols 1–105 (unedited MS); *BHL* 7486	Latin	–
Senán	early xv AD	*The Book of Lismore* ll. 2194–227, pp. 66–7 Stokes (text), pp. 213–14 (trans.)	Stokes 1890	Irish	Stokes 1890
Senzius	vii–viii AD	*Vita Senzii*, *AASS* May vi, pp. 72–3	*Vita Senzii*, *AASS* May vi, pp. 71–3; *BHL* no. 7581	Latin	–
Servanus (Serf, Serbán)	AD 1510	*Aberdeen Breviary* p. 58 AASS	*AASS* Jul. i, pp. 57–8; *BHL* no. 7610	Latin	–
Servulus of Trieste [a]	xii AD of before	*Passio beatissimi Christi martyris Servuli Tergestinae civitatis ac diocesis lectio* ii	Kandler 1847, part iv (*Atti dei santi martiri Tergestini*: unpaginated); *BHL* no. 7642	Latin	–
Servulus [b]	AD 1493	Petrus de Natalibus *Catalogus sanctorum et gestorum eorum* Book v §36	Petrus de Natalibus 1493; cf. *BHL* no. 7642	Latin	–

Subject	Date	Work	Edition	Language	Reference
Severinus, Bishop of Amiterno	xvi AD or before	Vita S. Severini AASS Jan. i p. 1105	AASS Jan. i p. 1103–7; BHL no. 7664	Latin	—
Silvester [a]	late iv AD	Acts of Silvester (A) 1	Pohlkamp 1983; BHL nos 7725–42	Latin	DW p. 175 DSS no. 136
Silvester [b]	c. AD 500	Acts of Silvester (B) 1	Duchesne 1897; BHL no. 7743	Latin	DW pp. 160, 225; DSS no. 136
Silvester [c]	AD 675–710	Aldhelm De virginitate (poetic version) p. 376 Ehwald, ll. 545–56	R. Ehwald, ed. MGH Auctores Antiquissimi xv, 350–471	Latin	Lapidge and Rosier 1985
Silvester [d]	AD 675–710	Aldhelm De virginitate (prose version), pp. 257–8 Ehwald	R. Ehwald, ed. MGH Auctores Antiquissimi xv, 226–323	Latin	Lapidge and Herren 2009
Silvester [e]	AD 1263–7	Jacobus de Voragine Golden Legend 12	Graesse 1850	Latin	Ryan 1993
Simeon Stylites [a]	shortly after AD 459	Life of Simeon Stylites pp. 529–30, 548–50	Bedjan 1894:507–644; BHO no. 1121	Syriac	Lent 1915
Simeon Stylites [b]	c. AD 830	Antonius Vita S. Simeonis Stylitae, PL 73, col. 330 (= AASS Jan. i p. 271)	Antonius Vita S. Simeonis Stylitae, PL 73, coll. 325–33 (= AASS Jan. i pp. 269–74); BHL no. 7957	Latin	Waddell 1934:22–3
Siward	xii–xiii AD	William of Ramsey (?), Vita S. Waldevi pp. 104–7 Michel	Michel 1836–40:i, 104–20; BHL 8778	Latin	Rauer 2000:163–5 (part only)
Syrus of Genoa	v AD, perhaps with post-xi AD accretions	Vita Syri Genuensis episcopi et confessoris pp. 549–50 Mombritius	Mombritius 1910:ii, pp. 549–51; BHL no. 7973	Latin	—
Theodore Tyron/Tiron/Teron/Stratelates/of Euchaita/of Heraclea [a]	soon after AD 754 (Walter 1999:167–8, 2003a:47); x–xi AD (Delehaye 1909:33; Haldon 2016:39–41)	Βίος πρὸ τοῦ μαρτυρίου καὶ ἡ ἐκ παιδὸς ἀναγωγή τε καὶ αὔξησις καὶ θαύματα ἐξαίσια τοῦ ἁγίου καὶ πανενδόξου μεγαλομάρτυρος Θεοδώρου §§4–5, pp. 187–90 Delehaye	Delehaye 1909:183–201 (App. v); AASS Nov. iv, pp. 49–55; BHG no. 1764	Greek	Haldon 2016:92–111

Continued

Continued

Saint	Date of text	Citation	Text/edition	Language	Translation
Theodore [b]	late ix AD or before	Μαρτύριον τοῦ ἁγίου μεγαλομάρτυρος Θεοδώρου τοῦ στρατηλάτου §§3–6, pp. 153–6 Delehaye	Delehaye 1909:151–67 (App. iii); *BHG* no. 1751	Greek	—
Theodore [c]	late ix AD or before	Augarus/Abgar *Acts of Theodore* §§3–6	van Hooff 1883; *BHG* no. 1750	Greek	—
Theodore [d]	c. AD 871	Bonitus *Life of Theodore* pp. 31–3 AASS	AASS Feb. ii pp. 30–8; *BHL* no. 8086	Latin	—
Theodore [e]	text originally vi–vii AD, but dragon episode a later interpolation, before AD 890 (Delehaye 1909:19, 25–6; Haldon 2016:20, 28–30, 40)	*Martyrium of St Theodore Tiron* p. 127 Delehaye	Delehaye 1909:127–35 (App. i); Hengstenberg 1912; *BHG* no. 1762d	Greek	Haldon 2016:83–9
Theodore [f]	later x AD	Μαρτύριον τοῦ ἁγίου μεγαλομάρτυρος Θεοδώρου τοῦ Τήρωνος §3, pp. 137–8 Delehaye	Delehaye 1909:136–50 (App. ii); *BHG* no. 1763	Greek	—
Theodore [g]	c. AD 980–1010	Nikephoros Ouranos *Vita Theodori* 6–10	Halkin 1962 = Halkin 1974 no. 9; *BHG* no. 1762m	Greek	—
Theodore [h]	xiv AD or before	Θαῦμα καὶ διήγησις τοῦ ἁγίου καὶ ἐνδόξου μεγαλομάρτυρος τοῦ Θεοδώρου Τήρωνος περὶ τῆς μητρὸς αὐτοῦ τῆς αἰχμαλωτισθείσης ὑπὸ τοῦ δράκοντος	AASS Nov. iv pp. 46–8; *BHG* no. 1766	Greek	*DW* pp. 293–4
Thomas, apostle	later ii AD	*Acts of Thomas* 30–3	Lipsius and Bonnet 1891–1903:ii.2, 99–291; Klijn 1962; *BHG* no. 1800	Greek	*DW* p. 156; *DSS* no. 131; Schneemelcher 1991–2:ii, 99–291; Elliot 1993:439–511; cf. Klijn 2003 (trans. of parallel Syriac version)

Name	Date	Source	Reference	Language	Additional
Thomas Defourkinos	xii AD	*Synaxarium ecclesiae Constantinopolitanae*, Synaxarium mensis Decembris, Day 10, §2, Recension M, coll. 295–8 Delehaye	Delehaye 1902	Greek	*DW* pp. 209–10
Timothy of Prusa [a]	x AD	*Synaxarium ecclesiae Constantinopolitanae*, Synaxarium mensis Junii, Day 10, §1, coll. 741–2 Delehaye	Delehaye 1902	Greek	—
Timothy [b]	xiv AD	*Synaxarium Chiffletianum seu Divionense*, extract at AASS Jun. ii p. 274	AASS Jun. ii pp. 273–5	Greek	—
Tudual (Tutgual, Tugual, Tutwal, Tual) of Treguier	xii AD	*Vita iii S. Tuguali* 7, p. 27 de la Borderie	de la Borderie 1887: 21–45; *BHL* no. 8353	Latin	—
Venerius of Tino (Tyro)	early xv AD	*Vita S. Venerii, Eremitae in Tyro Majore* p. 116 AASS	AASS Sept. iv, pp. 115–20; *BHL* no. 8535	Latin	—
Veranus (Veran, Voran, Vrain) of Cavaillon	ix–xi AD	*Vita S. Verani* 15–16, pp. 467, 468–9 AASS	AASS Oct. viii, 467–70; *BHL* no. 8536	Latin	—
Victor of Marseilles	AD 1474	Hans von Waltheym *Pilgerfahrt* p. 45 Welti	Welti 1925	German	—
Victoria [a]	c. AD 500	*Passio S. Victoriae* 5–7, pp. 158–9 Delehaye	Delehaye et al. 1883; *BHL* no. 8591	Latin	*DW* pp. 181, 227–8; *DSS* no. 147
Victoria [b]	AD 675–710	Aldhelm *De virginitate* (poetic version), pp. 450–1 Ehwald, ll. 2385–415	R. Ehwald, ed. *MGH Auctores Antiquissimi* xv, 350–471	Latin	Lapidge and Rosier 1985
Victoria [c]	AD 675–710	Aldhelm *De virginitate* (prose version), pp. 308–9 Ehwald	R. Ehwald, ed. *MGH Auctores Antiquissimi* xv, 226–323	Latin	Lapidge and Herren 2009
Vigor of Bayeux	AD 1030–45	*Vita S. Vigoris* pp. 300–1 AASS	*Vita S. Vigoris*, AASS November i, pp. 297–305; *BHL* nos 8608–11	Latin	—
Vindemialis	xii AD or before	*Vita S. Florentii et S. Vindemialis* p. 272 AASS	AASS Mai. i, 271–2; *BHL* no. 3053	Latin	—

Germanic Dragon Fights

Texts and Translations

Works in languages other than Norse are so indicated. Norse works are given first under their Norse title, with English translation(s) following, with the exception of the *Poetic Edda* and Snorri's *Prose Edda*. Saga classifications: FS—*fornaldarsaga*/legendary saga; IS—*Íslendingasaga*/saga of the Icelanders; KS—*konungasaga*/saga of kings; RS—*riddarasaga*/chivalric saga, romance; SS—*skáldasaga*/bardic saga.

Text	Date	Editions	Translations
Anglo-Saxon Chronicle, MS D, Cotton Tiberius B.iv, and MS E, Bodleian MS Laud 636 [Anglo-Saxon]	before AD 1066	Classen and Harmer 1926; Irvine 2004	*DW* p. 315; Swanton 1996 (based on MSS A and E)
Baerings saga [fagra] (*The Saga of Baering [the Fair]*) [RS]	xiv AD	Cederschiöld 1884	—
Beowulf [Anglo-Saxon]	AD 685–725? (otherwise, viii–x AD)	Klaeber et al. 2008; Fulk 2010:85–296	*DW* p. 334; Porter 1991; Fulk 2010:85–296
Bjarnar saga Hítdaelakappa (*The Saga of Bjorn, Champion of the Men of Hítardal*) [IS, SS]	xiii AD	Nordal and Jónsson 1938:111–211	*DW* pp. 317–18; Bachman 1985; Finlay 2000
Blómstrvalla saga (*The Saga of the Flower Plains*) [RS]	xv AD	Möbius 1855	—
Bósa saga ok Herrauðs/Herrauðs saga ok Bósa (*The Saga of Bosi and Herraud*) [FS]	before AD 1350	Jónsson 1954a:iii, 283–322	Pálsson and Edwards 1985
Brennu-Njáls saga (*Burnt Njal's Saga*) [IS]	AD 1270–90	Sveinsson 1954	Cook 2001

Continued

Text	Date	Editions	Translations
Ectors saga (*Ector's Saga*) [RS]	xvi–xv AD	Loth 1962–5:i, 79–186	Dodsworth in Loth ad loc. (c.50% précis)
Egils saga (*Egil's Saga*) [IS]	xiii AD	Jónsson 1986:i	Scudder at Hreinsson 1997:i–ii
Erex saga Artuskappa (*The Saga of Erex, Arthur's Champion*) [RS, after Chrétien de Troyes' French *Érec et Énide*]	xiii AD (with later interpolations?)	Blaisdell 1965	Blaisdell 1965; Blaisdell and Kalinke 1977
Finnsburg fragment [Anglo-Saxon]	viii AD?	Fry 1974	Hall 1940
Flóres saga konungs ok sona hans (*The Saga of King Flores and his Sons*) [RS]	xiv AD	Lagerholm 1927:121–77	DW pp. 318–20; Kreutzer 1998 (German)
Göngu-Hrólfs saga (*Walking-Hrolf's Saga*) [FS]	xiv AD	Jónsson 1954a:iii, 161–280	Pálsson 1980
Gottfried von Strassburg, *Tristan* [Middle High German, after Thomas of Britain's (lost) Anglo-Norman *Tristan*]	AD 1210	Krohn 1980	Hatto 1960
Grettis saga Ásmundarsonar (*Grettir's Saga; The Saga of Grettir Son of Asmundar*) [IS]	c. AD 1320	Boer 1900; Jónsson 1936	Byock 2009
Gull-þóris saga (*Saga of Gold-Thorir*); a.k.a. *Þorskfirðinga saga* (*The Thorskafjördur Saga*) [IS]	xiv AD	Kålund 1898; Vilmundarson and Vilhjálmsson 1991:173–227	Cardew 2000
Hálfdanar saga Eysteinssonar (*The Saga of Halfdan Son of Eystein*) [FS]	xiv AD	Schröder 1917	germanicmythology.com (Hardman)
Hartmann von Aue *Iwein* [Middle High German]	c. AD 1203	Edwards 2007	Edwards 2007
Heinrich von dem Türlin *Diu Crône* [Middle High German]	c. AD 1220s	Scholl 1852	Thomas 1989
Hervarar saga ok Heiðreks (*The Saga of Hervör and Heidrek*) [FS]	c. AD 1250	Helgason 1924; Turville-Petre 1956	Kershaw 1921:79–150

Hrólfs saga kraka og Bjarkarímur (Hrolf's Saga; The Saga of Pole-Ladder Hrolf and the Rhymes of Bjarki) [FS]	c. AD 1400	Jónsson 1904; Jónsson 1954a:i, 1–105	Jones 1961; Byock 1998; Tunstall 2003
Ívens saga (Iven's Saga) [RS, after Chrétien de Troyes' French Yvain]	xiii AD	Blaisdell 1979:3–147	Blaisdell 1979:150–233
Jómsvíkinga saga (Saga of the Jomsvikings) [KS]	c. AD 1200	Blake 1962	Blake 1962
Ketils saga hœngs (The Saga of Ketil Trout) [FS]	xiii AD	Jónsson 1954a:ii, 151–81	germanicmythology.com (Chappell)
Konráðs saga keisarasonar (Konrad's Saga; Saga of Konrad, Son of the Emperor) [RS]	xiv AD	Cederschiöld 1884:43–84; Zitzelsberger 1988	Zitzelsberger 1980
Kormáks saga (Kormak's Saga) [SS]	xiii AD	Sveinsson 1939:201–302	Hollander 1949
Lied vom hürnen Seyfrid (Horn Siegfried Lay) [German]	early xvi AD	King 1958	Lecouteux 1995 (French)
Morkinskinna (The Mouldy Vellum: sagas of the kings of Norway) [KS]	c. AD 1220	Jónsson 1932a	Andersson and Gade 2000; Acker 2007, 2012:12–13 (snake episode only)
Nibelungenlied (The Song of the Nibelungs) [Middle High German]	c. AD 1200	Reichert 2005	Hatto 1965
Norna-Gests þáttr (The Story of Norna-Gest) [FS]	xiv AD	Nordal 1944–5	Kershaw 1921:14–37
Oddr Snorrason Óláfs saga Tryggvasonar (The Saga of Olaf, Son of Tryggvi) [KS]	originally xii AD	Jónsson 1932b	Andersson 2003
Ortnit [Middle High German]	c. AD 1217–25	Amelung and Jänicke 1871:3–77	Thomas 1986:1–42
Örvar-Odds saga (The Saga of Arrow-Odd) [FS]	xiii AD	Boer 1898; Jónsson 1954a:ii, 199–363	Pálssson and Edwards 1985:25–137
Poetic Edda (Norse: Sæmundar Edda)	c.1270	Dronke 1969–2011	Belows 1936; Larrington 1996; Dronke 1969–2011

Continued

Continued

Text	Date	Editions	Translations
Ragnars saga loðbrókar (*The Saga of Ragnar Lodbrok/Hairy-breeches*) [FS]	xiii AD	Olsen 1906–8	van Dyke 2003
Ragnarssona þáttr (*The Story of Ragnar's Sons*) [FS]	xiii AD	Jónsson 1954a:i, 289–303	germanicmythology.com (Tunstall)
Saxo Grammaticus *Gesta Danorum* (*Deeds of the Danes*) [Latin]	early xiii AD	Olrik and Raeder 1931; Friis-Jensen and Fisher 2015	Elton 1894; Davidson and Fisher 1979–80; Friis-Jensen and Fisher 2015
Sigrgarðs saga frækna (*The Saga of Sigrgarðr the Valiant*) [RS]	xv AD	Loth 1962–5; Hall et al. 2012–13	*DW* p. 321; Hall et al. 2012–13
Sigurðar saga þögla (*Saga of Sigurd the Silent*) [RS]	xiv AD	Loth 1962–1965:ii, 93–259	Dodsworth in Loth ad loc. (c.50% précis)
Snorri Sturluson *Heimskringla* (*Orb of the World; History of the Kings of Norway*) [KS]	c. AD 1230	Aðalbjarnarson 1941–5	Laing 1844
Snorri Sturluson *Prose Edda* (Norse: *Snorra Edda*)	c. AD 1220	F. Jónsson 1931; G. Jónsson 1935; Faulkes 1988	Brodeur 1916; Byock and Poole 2005
Sörla saga sterka (*Saga of Sörli the Strong*) [FS]	xv AD	Jónsson 1954a:iii, 367–410	germanicmythology.com (Hardman)
Þiðrekssaga/Þiðrekssaga af Bern (*Thidrek's Saga, The Saga of Thidrek of Bern*) [FS, RS, after a lost German original]	c. AD 1230–50	Bertelsen 1905–11; Jónsson 1954b	*DW* pp. 316–17; Haymes 1988
Þorsteins þáttr forvitna (*The Story of Curious Thorstein*)	later xiv AD	Jónsson 1986:xii.179–81	—
Tristrams saga ok Ísoddar (*The Saga of Tristram and Isodd*) [RS]	c. AD 1400	Vilhjálmsson 1949–54:vi, 85–145	Hill 1977
Tristrams saga ok Ísöndar (*Saga of Tristram and Isönd*) [RS, after a lost Anglo-Norman original]	AD 1226	Jorgensen 1999	Jorgensen 1999
Trójumanna saga (*Saga of the Trojans*) [RS, after Dares Phrygius' Latin *De excidio Troiae historia*]	xiii AD	Louis-Jensen 1981	Eldevik 1987 (*non vidi*)

Work	Date	Edition(s)	Translation(s)/notes
Ulrich von Zatzikhoven *Lanzelet*	c. AD 1195–1200	Hahn and Norman 1965	Kerth et al. 2004
Valdimars saga (*Valdimar's Saga*) [RS]	XV AD	Loth 1962–5:i, 51–78	Fellows-Jensen in Loth ad loc. (c.50% précis)
Viktors saga ok Blávus (*Saga of Viktor and Blavus*) [RS]	XIV AD	Loth 1962–5:i, 1–50; Chappel 1972	Chappel 1972; Dodsworth in Loth ad loc. (c.50% précis)
Vilhjálms saga sjóðs (*Saga of William of Sjodr*) [RS]	XIV–XV AD	Loth 1962–1965:iv, 1–136.	Fellows-Jensen in Loth ad loc. (c.50% précis)
Vita S. Waldevi (*Life of St Waltheof*) [Latin]	xii–xiii AD	Michel 1836–40:i, 104–20	Rauer 2000:163–5 (dragon episode only)
Völsunga saga (*Saga of the Volsungs*) [FS]	c. AD 1200–70	Olsen 1906–8; Finch 1965; Thorsson 1990	DW p. 335; Finch 1965; Byock 1990a
Wirnt von Grafenberg *Wigalois* [Middle High German]	c. AD 1205–10	Kapteyn 1926	Thomas 1977
Wolfdietrich B [Middle High German]	c. AD 1225–50	Amelung and Jänicke 1871:167–301	Thomas 1986:43–97
Yngvars saga viðförla (*Yngvar's Saga; The Saga of Yngvar the Far-Traveller*) [FS, KS]	xiii AD	Jónsson 1954a:ii, 423–59	Pálsson and Edwards 1989

References

Abeghian, M. 1899. *Der Armenische Volksglaube*. Leipzig. English trans. (R. Bedrosian): M. Abeghyan [sic] *Armenian Folk Beliefs*. Long Branch, NJ, 2012.

Acker, P. 2007. 'The dragon episode in *Morkinskinna*'. *American Notes and Queries* 20.3, 65–8.

Acker, P. 2012. 'Death by dragons'. *Viking and Medieval Scandinavia* 8, 1–21.

Acker, P. 2013. 'Dragons in the eddas and in early Nordic art', in P. Acker and C. Larrington, eds, *Revisiting the Poetic Edda: Essays on Old Norse Heroic Legend*. London. 53–75.

Acta Sanctorum. 1643–1940. Editio novissima. 68 vols. Antwerp and Brussels.

Adamik, T. 2001. 'The serpent in the *Acts of Thomas*', in Bremmer 2001a, 115–24.

Addey, C. 2018. 'Sosipatra: prophetess, philosopher and theurgist. Reflections on divination and epistemology in late antiquity', in R. J. Evans, ed., *Prophets and Profits: Ancient Divination and its Reception*. London. 144–61.

Aðalbjarnarson, B., ed. 1941–5. *Snorri Sturluson: Heimskringla*. 3 vols. Reykjavik.

Aerts, W. J. 2003. 'The "Entführung aus dem Serail"-motif in the Byzantine (vernacular) romances', in S. Panayotakis, M. Zimmerman, and W. Keulen, eds, *The Ancient Novel and Beyond*. Leiden. 381–92.

Aguirre Castro, M. 2002. 'Scylla: hideous monster or femme fatale? A case of contradiction between literary and artistic evidence'. *Cuadernos de Filologia Clásica: Estudios griegos e indoeuropeos* 12, 319–28.

Alexander, R. McN. 1963. 'The evolution of the basilisk'. *Greece and Rome* 10, 170–81.

Amat, J. 1996. *Passion de Perpétue et Félicité suivi des Actes: introduction, texte critique, traduction, commentaire et index*. Paris.

Amelung, A., and O. Jänicke, eds, 1871. *Deutsches Heldenbuch*. iii.1. Berlin.

Amsler, F. 1996. 'The apostle Philip, the viper, the leopard, and the kid: the masked actors of a religious conflict in Hierapolis in Phrygia (*Acts of Philip* vii–xv and *Martyrdom*)', in *Society of Biblical Literature 1996 Seminar Papers*. SBL Seminar Papers 35. Atlanta. 432–7.

Amsler, F. 1999. *Acta Philippi*. 2 vols [Vol. 1: *Textus*; Vol. 2: *Commentarius*]. Corpus Christianorum, Series Apocryphorum nos 11–12. Turnhout.

Amsler, F., F. Bovon, and B. Bouvier 1996. *Actes de l'apôtre Philippe*. Turnhout.

Anderson, A. O., and M. O. Anderson, eds and trans. 1961. *Adamnan, Life of Columba*. London.

Anderson, G. 1976. *Studies in Lucian's Comic Fiction*. Leiden.

Andersson, T. M. 1997. 'Sources and analogues', in Bjork and Niles 1997, 125–48.

Andersson, T. M., trans. 2003. *The Saga of Olaf Tryggvason by Oddr Snorrason*. Ithaca.

Andersson, T. M., and K. E. Gade, trans. 2000. *Morkinskinna: The Earliest Icelandic Chronicle of the Norwegian Kings (1030–1157)*. Ithaca.

Andreae, B. 1989. *Laokoon und die Gründung Roms*. Mainz am Rhein.

Andreae, B., and B. Conticello. 1987. *Skylla und Charybdis: Zur Skylla-Gruppe von Sperlonga*. AbhMainz 14. Mainz am Rhein.

Artelt, W. 1968. 'Besessene, Besessenheit'. *LCI* i, 273–7.

Asheri, D., A. B. Lloyd, and A. Corcella. 2007. *A Commentary on Herodotus Books i–iv*. Oxford.

Atkinson, R., ed. 1887. *The Passions and the Homilies from Leabhar Breac: Text, Translation, and Glossary*. Royal Irish Academy: Todd Lecture Series 2. 2 vols. Dublin.

Arvanitaki, A. 2012. Ὁ Δίας ἐναντίον ἑνός δράκοντα: μια διαφορετική απεικόνιση του μύθου της αναμέτρησης του Δία με τον Τυφώνα στην Κόρινθο;, in E. Kephalidou and D. Tsiaphaki, eds, Κεραμέως παῖδες: Ἀντίδωρο στον Καθηγητή Μιχάλη Τιβέριο από τους μαθητές του. Thessaloniki. 171–8.

Arya, R. P., and K. L. Joshi, eds. 2001. *Rgveda Samhita: Sanskrit Text, English Translation, Notes and Index of Verses*. 4 vols. Delhi.

Aufhauser, J. B. 1911. *Das Drachenwunder des heiligen Georg in der griechischen und latein-ischen Überlieferung*. Byzantisches Archiv 5. Leipzig.

Aufstieg und Niedergang der römischen Welt. 1972–. Multiple volumes and parts. Berlin.

Ayali-Darshan, N. 2015. 'The other version of the story of the storm-god's combat with the sea in the light of Egyptian, Ugaritic, and Hurro-Hittite texts'. *Journal of Ancient Near Eastern Religions* 15, 20–51.

Bachman, W. B., Jr., trans. 1985. *Four Old Icelandic Sagas and Other Tales*. Lanham, MD.

Bachvarova, M. R. 2016. *From Hittite to Homer: The Anatolian Background of Ancient Greek Epic*. Oxford.

Bailey, R. 2017. 'The *Acts* of Saint Cyprian of Antioch: Critical Editions, Translations, and Commentary'. Diss., McGill. Montreal.

Bailey, R. N. 2000. 'Scandinavian myth on Viking-period stone sculpture in England', in G. Barnes and M. Clunies Ross, eds, *Old Norse Myths, Literature and Society: Proceedings of the 11th International Saga Conference*. Sydney. 15–23.

Ball, C. 2017. '"A Creeping Thing": The Motif of the Serpent in Anglo-Saxon England'. Diss. Leicester.

Banks, S. E., and J. W. Binns, eds, and trans. 2002. *Gervase of Tilbury: Otia Imperialia, Recreation for an Emperor*. Oxford.

Barb, A. A. 1966. 'Antaura the mermaid and the Devil's grandmother'. *Journal of the Warburg and Courtauld Institutes* 29, 1–23.

Barbantani, S. 2014. 'Mother of snakes and kings: Apollonius Rhodius' *Foundation of Alexandria*' *Histos* 8, 209–45.

Barillari, S. 2017. 'L'arcivescovo e il dragone: riflessioni sulla fortuna iconografica e testuale di un episodio della *Vita di santa Margherita*', in G. Ameri, ed., *Arte e letteratura a Genova fra XIII e XV secolo. Temi e intersezioni*. Genoa. 42–61.

Barreiro, S. 2019. 'The hoard makes the dragon: Fáfnir as a shapeshifter', in S. Barreiro and L. Russo, eds, *Shapeshifters in Medieval North Atlantic Literature*. Amsterdam. 53–82.

Barrenechea, F. 2018. *Comedy and Religion in Classical Athens: Narratives of Religious Experiences in Aristophanes' Wealth*. Cambridge.

Bartelink, G. J. M. 1971. *Callinicos: Vie d'Hypatios*. Sources chrétiennes 177. Paris.

Bartelink, G. J. M. 1974. *Palladio: la storia Lausiaca*. Verona.

Basset, E. L. 1955. 'Regulus and the serpent in the *Punica*'. *CP* 50, 1–20.

Bastiaensen, A. A. R., ed. 1975. *Vita di Martino—Vita di Ilarione—In memoria di Paola*. Milan.

Bastiaensen, A. A. R., A. Hilhorst, et al., eds, 1987. *Atti e passioni dei martiri*. Milan.

Bates, R. 2002. *Chinese Dragons: Images of Asia*. New York.

Bates, R. 2007. *All about Chinese Dragons*. Beijing.

Batto, B. F. 1992. *Slaying the Dragon: Mythmaking in the Biblical Tradition*. Louisville.

Bayet, C. 1878. *De titulis Atticae Christianis antiquissimis*. Paris.

Beaton, R. 1981. 'Was *Digenes Akrites* an oral poem?' *Byzantine and Modern Greek Studies* 7, 7–27.

Beaton, R. 1989. *The Medieval Greek Romance*. Cambridge.

Beaude, P.-M. 2000. 'Les dragons dans la Bible', in Privat 2000, 135–43.

Beaulieu, M.-C. 2016. *The Sea in the Greek Imagination*. Philadelphia.

Beck, H. 1985. 'Zu Otto Höflers Siegfried-Arminius Untersuchung'. *Beiträge zur Geschichte der deutschen Sprache und Literatur* 107, 91–107.

Beck, H., and P. C. Bol, eds, 1983. *Spätantike und fruhes Christentum*. Frankfurt am Main.

Beckman, G. 1982. 'The Anatolian myth of Illuyanka'. *Journal of the Ancient Near Eastern Society* 14, 11–25.

Bedjan, P. 1894. *Acta martyrum et sanctorum*. iv. Paris and Leipzig.

Bedos, B. 1980. *Corpus des sceaux français du Moyen Age*. Vol. 1: *Les sceaux des villes*. Paris.

Beekman Taylor, P. 1997. 'The Dragon's treasure in *Beowulf*. *Neuphilologische Mitteilungen* 3, 229–40.

Bellows, H. A., trans. 1936. *The Poetic Edda*. 2 vols. Princeton.

Beneventano della Corte, F. 2017. 'Φάσμα. Una categoria del sovrannaturale nella cultura della Grecia antica'. Diss. Siena.

Bernard, F. 2014. *Writing and Reading Byzantine Secular Poetry, 1025–1081*. Oxford.

Berschin, W. 2001. *Hrotsvit: Opera omnia*. Leizpig.

Bertelsen, H., ed. 1905–11. *Thidriks Saga af Bern*. 2 vols. Copenhagen.

Bertini, F., ed. 1995. *Letaldo di Micy: Within Piscator*. Florence.

Besnier, M. 1902. *L'île Tibérine dans l'antiquité*. Paris.

Besson, L. 1994. *Véran de Cavaillon, le saint, la source et le dragon*. Les Cahiers de L'Académie 2. Beaumes-de-Venise. [*non vidi*]

Betts, G. 1995. *Three Medieval Greek Romances*. New York.

Betz, H. D. 1961. *Lukian von Samosata und das Neue Testament*. Religionsgeschichtliche und paränetische Parallelen Texte und Untersuchungen der altchristlichen Literatur 76. Berlin.

Bibliotheca hagiographica Latina. 1898–1901. 2 vols. Brussels.

Bibliotheca sanctorum. 1961–70. 13 vols. Rome.

Bidez, J., and G. C. Hansen, eds, 1960. *Sozomenus: Kirchengeschichte*. Die griechischen Schriftsteller 50. Berlin.

Bile, M. 2000. 'Etymologies', in Privat 2000, 121–33.

Bjork, R. E., and J. D. Niles, eds, 1996. *A Beowulf Handbook*. Lincoln, NE.

Bjork, R. E., and A. Obermeier. 1997. 'Date, provenance, author, places', in Bjork and Niles 1997, 13–34.

Björklund, H. 2017a. 'Metamorphosis, mixanthropy and the child-killing demon in the Hellenistic and Byzantine periods'. *Acta Classica* 60, 22–49.

Björklund, H. 2017b. 'Protecting against Child-Killing Demons: Uterus Amulets in the Late Antique and Byzantine Magical World'. Diss. Helsinki.

Blaisdell, F. W., Jr. 1964. 'The composition of the interpolated chapter in the *Erex saga*'. *Scandinavian Studies* 36, 118–26.

Blaisdell, F. W., Jr., ed. 1965. *Erex saga Artuskappa*. Copenhagen.

Blaisdell, F. W., Jr., ed. 1979. *Ívens saga*. Copenhagen.

Blaisdell, F. W., Jr., and M. E. Kalinke, eds, 1977. *Erex Saga and Ivens Saga: The Old Norse Versions of Chretien de Troyes's Erec and Yvain*. Lincoln, NE.

Blake, N. F., ed., and trans. 1962. *Jómsvíkinga saga: The Saga of the Jomsvikings*. London.

Blatt, F., et al., eds, 1973. *Index scriptorum novus mediae latinitatis ab anno DCCC usque ad annum MCC*. Copenhagen.

Bledsoe, J. C. 2013. 'Practical hagiography: James of Voragine's *Sermones* and *Vita* on St Margaret of Antioch'. *Medieval Sermon Studies* 57, 29–48.

Blindheim, M. 1972. *Sigurds saga i middelalderens billedkunst*. Exhibition Catalogue. Oslo.

Blindheim, M. 1985. *Graffiti in Norwegian Stave Churches c.1150–c.1350*. Oslo.

Blum, R., and E. Blum. 1970. *The Dangerous Hour: The Lore and Culture of Crisis and Mystery in Rural Greece*. London.

Blust, R. 2000. 'The origin of dragons'. *Anthropos* 95, 519–36.

Boardman, J. 1986. 'The ketos in India', in L. Kahil et al., eds, *Iconographie classique et identités régionales*. BCH Suppl. xiv. Paris. 447–53.

Boardman, J. 1987. 'Very like a whale—classical sea monsters', in A. E. Farkas, eds, *Monsters and Demons in the Ancient and Medieval Worlds*. Mainz. 73–84.

Boardman, J. 1990. 'vii. Herakles in other undefined encounters'. *LIMC* v.1, 118–21.

Boardman, J. 1992. 'Lamia'. *LIMC* vi.1, 189.

Boardman, J. 2003. 'Three monsters at Tillya Tepe' *Ancient Civilizations from Scythia to Siberia* 9, 133–46.

Boardman, J. 2007. 'Central Asia: west and east', in J. Cribb and G. Herrmann, eds, *After Alexander: Central Asia before Islam*. Oxford. 9–25.

Boardman, J. 2015. *The Greeks in Asia*. London.

Boedeker, D. 1983. 'Hecate: a transfunctional goddess in the Theogony?' *TAPA* 113, 79–93.

Boer, R. C., ed. 1898. *Örvar-Odds saga*. Leiden.

Boer, R. C., ed. 1900. *Grettis saga Ásmundarsonar*. Halle.

Bogaert, P.-M. 1984. 'Une vision longue inédite de la "Visio Beati Esdrae" dans la légendier de Teano (Barberini lat. 2318)'. *Revue Bénédictine* 94, 50–70.

Bois, G. J. C. 2010. *Jersey Folklore and Superstitions*. 2 vols. Milton Keynes.

Bondeson, J. 1999. *The Feejee Mermaid and Other Essays in Natural and Unnatural History*. Ithaca.

Bonfante, L. 2003. *The Plays of Hrotswitha of Gandersheim*. Wauconda, IL.

Bonjour, A. 1962. 'Monsters crouching and critics rampant: on the *Beowulf* dragon debated', in *Twelve Beowulf Papers, 1940-60*. Neuchatel. 97–114.

Bonner, C. A. 1932. 'Demons of the bath', in F. L. C. Griffith hon., *Studies Presented to F. L. C. Griffith*. London. 10–20.

Bonner, C. A. 1950. *Studies in Magical Amulets, Chiefly Graeco-Egyptian*. Ann Arbor.

Bonwetsch, G. N. 1897. 'Die apokryphen *Fragen des Bartholomäus*' *Nachrichten von der königlichen Gesellschaft der Wissenschaften, Philol.-hist. Kl.* [no serial no.], 9–29.

Boosen, M. 1986. *Etruskische Meermischwesen.Untersuchungen zu Typologie unde Bedeutung*. Rome.

Borges, J. L. 1969. *The Book of Imaginary Beings*. 3rd ed. New York.

Bortolani, L. M. 2016. *Magical Hymns from Roman Egypt: A Study of Greek and Egyptian Traditions of Divinity*. Cambridge.

Boulhol, P. 1994. 'Hagiographie antique et démonologie: notes sur quelques Passions grecques (*BHG* 962z, 964 et 1165–66)'. *Analecta Bollandiana* 112, 255–303.

Bovey, A. 2002. *Monsters and Grotesques in Medieval Manuscripts*. London.

Bovon, F. 1988. 'Les Actes de Philippe'. *ANRW* 2.25.6, 4431–527.

Bovon, F., and C. Matthews. 2012. *The Acts of Philip: A New Translation*. Waco.

Bowie, E. L. 1994. 'The readership of the Greek novels in the ancient world', in J. Tatum, ed., *The Search for the Ancient Novel*. Baltimore. 435–59.

Boyce, G. K. 1942. 'Significance of the serpents on Pompeian house shrines'. *AJA* 46, 14–22.

Bracht, K. 2020. 'The appropriation of the book of Jonah in 4th century Christianity by Theodore of Mopsuestia and Jerome of Stridon', in V. Gasparini et al., eds, *Lived Religion in the Ancient Mediterranean World*. Berlin. 531–52.

Braeger, P. C. 1986. 'Connotations of (*earm*)*sceapen*: Beowulf ll. 2228–9 and the shape-shifting dragon'. *Essays in Literature* 13, 327–30.

Brakke, D. 2001. 'Ethiopian demons: male sexuality, the black-skinned other, and the monastic self'. *Journal of the History of Sexuality* 10, 501–35.

Brakke, D. 2006. *Demons and the Making of the Monk: Spiritual Combat in Early Christianity*. Cambridge, MA.

Brednich, R. W. 1975–. 'Schlangenkönig', in K. Ranke et al., eds, *Enzyklopädie des Märchens. Handwörterbuch zur historischen und vergleichenden Erzählforschung*. 13+ vols. Berlin. xii, coll. 54–6.

Breiner, L. 1979. 'The career of the cockatrice'. *Isis* 70, 30–47.

Bremmer, J. N., ed. 1996. *The Apocryphal Acts of John*. Kampen.

Bremmer, J. N. 1998. 'The novel and the apocryphal Acts: place, time and readership', in H. Hofmann and M. Zimmerman, eds, *Groningen Colloquia on the Novel* ix. Groningen. 157–80.

Bremmer, J. N., ed. 2000. *The Apocryphal Acts of Andrew*. Leuven.

Bremmer, J. N., ed. 2001a. *The Apocryphal Acts of Thomas*. Leuven.

Bremmer, J. N. 2001b. 'The *Acts of Thomas*: place, date and women', in Bremmer 2001a, 74–90.

Bremmer, J. N. 2001c. 'The apocryphal Acts: authors, place, time and readership', in Bremmer 2001a, 149–70.

Bremmer, J. N. 2008. *Greek Religion and Culture, the Bible and the Ancient Near East*. Leiden.

Bremmer, J. N. 2017a. 'Paganism in the hagiography of Asia Minor', in W. Ameling, ed., *Die Christianisierung Kleinasiens in der Spätantike. Asia Minor Studien* 87. 33–48.

Bremmer, J. N. 2017b. *Maidens, Magic and Martyrs in Early Christianity*. Tübingen.

Bremmer, J. N. 2018. 'The long Latin version of the vision of Ezra: date, place and tour of hell', in J. N. Bremmer, V. Hirschberger, and T. Nicklas, eds, *Figures of Ezra*. Leuven. 162–84.

Bremmer, J. N., and M. Formisano, eds. 2012. *Perpetua's Passions: Multidisciplinary Approaches to the* Passio Perpetuae et Felicitatis. Oxford.

Brenk, F. E. 1986. 'In the light of the moon: demonology in the early imperial period'. *ANRW* ii.16.3, 2068–145.

Brereton, J., and S. W. Jamison, eds. 2014. *The Rigveda: The Earliest Religious Poetry of India*. Oxford.

Brewer, J. S., J. F. Dimock, and G. F. Warner, eds, 1861–9. *Giraldus Cambrensis: Works*. 8 vols. London.

Brock, S. P. 2011. 'Syriac hagiography', in Efthymiadis 2011–14. i.259–84.

Brodeur, A. G. 1916. *The Prose Edda*. New York.

Brøgger, A. W., and H. Shetelig. 1951. *The Viking Ships: Their Ancestry and Evolution*. Oslo. Reissued with different pagination, London, 1971.

Brown, A. K. 1980. 'The firedrake in *Beowulf*. *Neophilologus* 64, 439–60.

Brown, A. L. 1984. 'Eumenides in Greek tragedy'. *CQ* 34, 260–81.

Brown, C. G. 1991. 'Empousa, Dionysus, and the Mysteries: Aristophanes, *Frogs* 285ff'. *CQ* 41, 41–50.

Brown, T. 1964. 'The folklore of Devon'. *Folklore* 75, 145–60.

Bruce-Mitford, R. L. S. 1975–83. *The Sutton Hoo Ship-Burial*. 3 vols. London.

Brunning, S. 2015. '"(Swinger of) the Serpent of Wounds": swords and snakes in the Viking mind', in M. Bintley and T. Williams, eds, *Representing Beasts in Early Medieval England and Scandinavia*. Woodbridge. 53–72.

Brynteson. W. E. 1982. '*Beowulf*, monsters and manuscripts: classical associations'. *Res Publica Literarum* 5, 41–57.

Budge, E. A. W. 1889. *The History of Alexander the Great, Being the Syriac Version of the Pseudo-Callisthenes*. Cambridge.

Budge, E. A. W. 1899. *The History of the Blessed Virgin Mary and the History of the Likeness of Christ which the Jews of Tiberias Made to Mock At*. 2 vols. London.

Budge, E. A. W. 1910. *Facsimiles of Egyptian Hieratic Papyri in the British Museum*. London.

Budge, E. A. W. 1927. *The Book of the Cave of Treasures: A History of the Patriarchs and the Kings, their Successors, from the Creation to the Crucifixion of Christ*. London.

Buitron-Oliver, D. 1992. *The Odyssey and Ancient Art*. Exhibition catalogue. Annandale.

Bulgakov, M. 1925. *Роковые яйца*. Moscow. Trans. (R. Cockrell) as *The Fatal Eggs*, Richmond, Surrey, 2011.

Burkert, W. 1987. 'Oriental and Greek mythology: the meeting of parallels', in J. N. Bremmer, ed., *Interpretations of Greek Mythology*. London. 10–40. [Reprinted at Burkert 2001–11: ii.48–72.]

Burkert, W. 1992. *The Orientalizing Revolution*. Cambridge, MA.

Burkert, W. 2001–11. *Kleine Schriften*. 8 vols. Göttingen.

Byock, J. L., trans. 1990a. *The Saga of the Volsungs*. Berkeley.

Byock, J. L. 1990b. 'Sigurðr Fáfnisbani: an eddic hero carved on Norwegian stave churches', in T. Pàroli, ed., *Poetry in the Scandinavian Middle Ages*. Spoleto. 619–28.

Byock, J. L., trans. 1998. *The Saga of King Hrolf Kraki*. London.

Byock, J. L., trans. 2009. *Grettir's Saga*. Oxford.

Byock, J. L., and R. Poole, trans. 2005. *Snorri Sturluson: The Prose Edda*. London.

Cahier, C. 1867. *Caractéristiques des saints dans l'art populaire*. 2 vols. Paris. Reprint, Brussels, 1966.

Cameron, A. 2004. *Greek Mythography in the Roman World*. Oxford.

Cameron, A., and S. Hall, trans. 1999. *Eusebius, Life of Constantine*. Oxford.

Canella, T. 2006. *Gli Actus Silvestri*. Spoleto.

Canivet, P., and A. Leroy-Molinghen. 1979. *Théodoret de Cyr. L'histoire des moines de Syrie*. Sources chrétiennes 234. Paris.

Caquot, A., M. Sznycer, and A. Herdner. 1974. *Textes ougaritiques*, Vol. 1: *Mythes et légendes*. Paris.

Cardew, P. 2000. *A translation of* Þorskfirðinga (Gull-Þóris) saga. Lewiston and Lampeter.

Carlson, S. M. 1967. 'The monsters of *Beowulf*: creations of literary scholars'. *Journal of American Folklore* 80, 357–64.

Cassuto, U. 1961. *A Commentary on the Book of Genesis*. Jerusalem.

Castellana, M. 2000. 'Le regard du dragon dans la légende de saint Georges', in Privat 2000, 159–72.

Castriota, D. 1995. *The Ara Pacis Augustae and the Imagery of Abundance in Later Greek and Early Roman Imperial Art*. Princeton.

Catalogus codicum hagiographicorum Bibliothecae regiae Bruxellensis. 1886–9. i. Brussels.

Catalogus codicum hagiographicorum latinorum antiquiorum saeculo xvi qui asservantur in Bibliotheca Nationali Parisiensi. 1889–93. 4 vols. Brussels.

Cavanaugh, T. A. 2018. *Hippocrates' Oath and Asclepius' Snake: The Birth of the Medical Profession*. New York.

Cazzaniga, I. 1957. 'L'episodo dei serpi libici in Lucano e la tradizione dei *Theriaca* Nicandrei'. *Acme* 10: 27–41.

Cederschiöld, G., ed. 1884. *Fornsögur Suðurlanda*. Lund.

Chadwick, N. K. 1946. 'Norse ghosts: a study in the *draugr* and the *haugbúi*'. *Folklore* 57, 50–65 and 106–27.

Chadwick, N. K. 1959. 'The monsters and *Beowulf*', in B. Dickins hon., P. A. M. Clemoes, ed., *The Anglo-Saxons: Studies in some Aspects of their History and Culture Presented to Bruce Dickins*. London. 171–203.

Chappel, A. H., ed., and trans. 1972. *Saga af Viktor ok Blavus: A Fifteenth Century Icelandic Lygisaga. An English Edition and Translation*. Janua linguarum, series practica, 88. The Hague.

Charcot, J. M., and P. Richer. 1984. *Les Démoniaques dans l'art*. Paris.

Charlesworth, J. H. 2010. *The Good and Evil Serpent: How a Universal Symbol Became Christianized*. New Haven.

Chase, C., ed. 1981. *The Dating of Beowulf*. Toronto.

Chazan, M. 2000. 'Le dragon dans la légende de le saint Clément, premier évêque de Metz', in Privat 2000, 17–35.

Chrestou, P. K. 1992. Γρηγορίου τοῦ Παλαμᾶ συγγράμματα. v. Thessaloniki.

Christensen, A. E. 1995. 'Ship Graffiti', in O. Crumlin-Pedersen and B. Munch Thye, eds, *The Ship as Symbol in Prehistoric and Medieval Scandinavia*. Copenhagen. 180–5.

Clarke, W. K. L. 1918. *The Lausiac History of Palladius*. London.

Classen, E., and F. E. Harmer, eds, 1926. *An Anglo-Saxon Chronicle from British Museum Cotton MS., Tiberius B. iv*. Manchester.

Clayton, M., and H. Magennis. 1994. *The Old English Lives of St Margaret*. Cambridge.

Cleasby, R., and G. Vigfusson. 1874. *An Icelandic–English Dictionary*. Oxford.

Clunies Ross, M. 2000. 'The conservation and reinterpretation of myth in medieval Icelandic writings', in M. Clunies Ross, ed., *Old Icelandic Literature and Society*. Cambridge. 116–39.

Coens, M. 1930. 'La vie ancienne de S. Front de Périgueux'. *Analecta Bollandiana* 48, 324–60.

Coens, M. 1957. 'La "Scriptum de Sancto Fronto nova" attribuée au chorévêque Gauzbert'. *Analecta Bollandiana* 75, 340–65.

Coens, M., ed. 1963. 'Otloh of St Emmeram, *Vita S. Magni confessoris*'. *Analecta Bollandiana* 81, 184–227.

Colgrave, B., ed., and trans. 1940. *Two Lives of Saint Cuthbert: A Life by an Anonymous Monk of Lindisfarne and Bede's Prose Life: Texts, Translation, and Notes*. Cambridge.

Colgrave, B., ed., and trans. 1956. *Felix's Life of Saint Guthlac*. Cambridge.

Collins, N. L. 2000. *The Library at Alexandria and the Bible in Greek*. Leiden.

Colpe, C., et al. 1976. 'Geister (Dämonen)'. *RAC* 10, 546–797.

Conybeare, F. C. 1898. 'The Testament of Solomon'. *Jewish Quarterly Review* 11, 1–45.

Coogan, M. D. 1978. *Stories from Ancient Canaan*. Louisville.

Cook, R., trans. 2001. *Njal's Saga*. London.

Cornell, T. J., ed. 2013. *The Fragments of the Roman Historians*. 3 vols. Oxford.

Corpus inscriptionum Latinarum. 1863–. Berlin.

Coulet, N. 1995. 'Dévotions communales: Marseille entre Saint Victor, Saint Lazare et Saint Louis (XIIIe–XVe siècle)', *Actes du colloque organisé par le Centre de recherche 'Histoire sociale et culturelle de l'Occident, XIIᵉ–XVIIIᵉ siècle' de l'Université de Paris X-Nanterre et l'Institut universitaire de France (Nanterre, 21–23 juin 1993)*. Publications de l'École Française de Rome. 119–33.

Coulston, J. C. N. 1991. 'The "*draco*" standard'. *Journal of Roman Military Equipment Studies* 2, 101–14.

Craigie, W. A. 1880. 'The *Acts of Xanthippe and Polyxena*', in Menzies 1880, 203–17.

Creaghan, J. S., and A. E. Raubitschek. 1947. 'Early Christian epitaphs from Athens'. *Hesperia* 16, 1–52.

Cross, J. E. 1986. 'An unpublished story of Michael the Archangel and its connections', in A. Groos, ed., *Magister Regis: Studies in Honour of Robert Earl Kaske*. New York. 23–35.

Cross, J. E., and C. J. Tuplin. 1980. 'An unrecorded variant of the *Passio S. Christinae* and the *Old English Martyrology*'. *Traditio* 36, 161–236.

Czachesz, I. 2001. 'The bride of the demon: narrative strategies of self-definition in the *Acts of Thomas*', in Bremmer 2001a, 36–52.

Dalley, S., trans. 2000. *Myths from Mesopotamia*. Oxford World's Classics. Revised ed. Oxford.

d'Andria, F. 2011–12. 'Il santuario e la tomba dell'apostolo Filippo a Hierapolis de Frigia'. *Rendiconti della pontificia accademia romana di archeologia* 84, 1–52.

d'Andria, F. 2016–17. '"Hierapolis alma Philippum": nuovi scavi, ricerche e restauri nel Santuario dell'Apostolo'. *Rendiconti della pontificia accademia romana di archeologia* 89, 129–202.

Darmesteter, J., and L. H. Mills. 1880–7. *The Zend-Avesta*. 3 vols. The Sacred Books of the East, vols. 4, 23, 31. Oxford.

Davidson, H. R. E. 1950. 'The hill of the dragon: Anglo-Saxon burial mounds in literature and archaeology'. *Folklore* 6, 169–85.

Davidson, H. R. E. 1964. *Gods and Myths of Northern Europe*. London.

Davidson, H. R. E., and P. Fisher. 1979–80. *Saxo Grammaticus: The History of the Danes, Books i–ix*. 2 vols. Cambridge. Reissued in a single volume, 1996.

Davies, M., ed. 1991. *Sophocles: Trachiniae*. Oxford.

Davies, M., and P. Finglass. 2014. *Stesichorus: The Poems*. Cambridge.

Davis, S. J. 2000. 'Jonah in early Christian art: allegorical exegesis and the Roman funerary context'. *Australian Religion Studies Review* 13, 72–83.

Dawkins, R. M. 1953. *Modern Greek Folktales*. Oxford.

Day, J. 1977. *God's Conflict with the Dragon and the Sea: Echoes of a Canaanite Myth in the Old Testament*. University of Cambridge Oriental Publications 5. Cambridge.

de Abrahamse, D. F. 1982. 'Magic and sorcery in the hagiography of the Middle Byzantine Period'. *Byzantinische Forschungen* 7, 3–17.

de Angfeli, S. 1988. '[Demeter/] Ceres'. *LIMC* iv.1, 893–908. [NB out of sequence in *LIMC*]

de Beauvais, V. 1473. *Speculum historiale*. Strasbourg.

de Cerny, E. 1861. *Saint-Suliac et ses traditions: contes et légendes d'Ille-et-Vilaine*. Dinan. [Page references are supplied from the 2014 Rue des Scribes reprint.]

Deckers, E. 1995. *Clavis patrum Latinorum*. 3rd ed. Turnhout.

de Jerphanion, G. 1925–42. *Une nouvelle province de l'art byzantine: les églises rupestres de Cappadoce*. 5 vols. Paris.

de la Borderie, A., ed. 1887. *Histoire de Bretagne: critique des sources des trois vies anciennes de Saint Tudual*. Paris.

de la Borderie, A., ed. 1891. '*Vita S. Euflami confessoris*'. *Annales de Bretagne* 7, 282–96.

Delcor, M. 1977. 'Les monstres du chaos primitif', in L. Monloubou, ed., *Apocalypses et théologie de l'espérance*. Paris. 143–77.

Delehaye, H., ed. 1902. *Synaxarium ecclesiae Constantinopolitanae e codice Sirmondiano nunc Berolinensi*. Propylaeum ad Acta sanctorum Novembris. Brussels. Repr. 1985.

Delehaye, H. 1909. *Les Légendes grecques des saints militaires*. Paris.

Delehaye, H. 1955. *Les Légends hagiographiques*. 4th ed. Subsidia hagiographica 18. Brussels.

Delehaye, H., et al., eds, 1883. '*Passio S. Victoriae*'. *Analecta Bollandiana* 2, 157–60.

Dench, E. 1995. *From Barbarians to New Men: Greek, Roman and Modern Perceptions of Peoples from the Central Apennines*. Oxford.

de Ridder, A. 1911. *Collection de Clercq: Catalogue*, Vol. 7.2: *Les pierres gravées*. Paris.

des Guerrois, C. 1920. *Lucien ou de la décadence*. Paris.

de Smedt., C., W. Van Hoof, J. de Backer, eds, 1882. '*Passio SS. Nicasii episcopi, Quirini presbyteri, Scuviculi diaconi*'. *Analecta Bollandiana* 1, 628–32.

de Stefano, F. 2013. 'Hierapolis (Frigia), la tomba di Filippo', in A. Carandini, ed., *Su questa pietra: Gesù, Pietro e la nascita della Chiesa*. Rome. 175–9.

de Visser, M. W. 1913. *The Dragon in China and Japan*. Amsterdam.

Devlin, J. D. 1848. *The Mordiford Dragon and Other Subjects*. London.

de Vogüé, A., and P. Antin. 1979. *Grégoire le Grand: Dialogues. Tome ii (Livres i–iii)*. Paris.

de Vries, J. 1956. *Altgermanische Religionsgeschichte*. 2 vols. Berlin.

Dickens, C. 1863. 'La Guivre'. *All the Year Round* 10, 318–19.

Didi-Huberman, G., R. Garbetta, and M. Morgaine. 1994. *Saint Georges et le dragon: versions d' une légende*. Paris.

Diény, J.-P. 1987. *Le Symbolisme du dragon dans la Chine antique*. Paris.

Dietrich, M., O. Loretz, and J. Sanmartín. 1995. *The Cuneiform Alphabetic Texts from Ugarit, Ras Ibn Hani and Other Places*. 2nd ed. Münster [= *KTU*: abbreviation derives from title of 1st ed., *Die keilalphabetischen Texte aus Ugarit*, Bd. 1. Neukirchen-Vluyn, 1976.]

Djurslev, C. T., and D. Ogden. 2018. 'Alexander, *Agathoi Daimones*, Argives and Armenians'. *Karanos* 1, 11–21.

Dobbie, E. v. K., ed. 1942. *The Anglo-Saxon Minor Poems*. New York.

Donington, R. 1990. *Wagner's Ring and its Symbols*. London.

Douglas, E. M. 1913. 'Iuno Sospita of Lanuvium'. *Journal of Roman Studies* 3, 60–72.

Doutreleau, L., and P. Nautin, eds, 1976–8. *Didyme l'Aveugle: Sur la Genèse*. 2 vols. Sources chrétiennes 233–4. Paris.

Drake, M., and W. Drake. 1916. *Saints and their Emblems*. London. Reprint Detroit, 1971.

Dresken-Weiland, J. 2010. *Bild, Grab und Wort: Untersuchungen zu Jenseitsvorstellungen von Christen des 3. und 4. Jahrhunderts*. Regensburg.

Dresvina, J. 2012. 'The significance of the demonic episode in the legend of St. Margaret of Antioch'. *Medium Ævum* 81, 189–209.

Dresvina, J. 2016. *A Maid with a Dragon: The Cult of St Margaret of Antioch in Medieval England*. Oxford.

Dronke, U. 1969. 'Beowulf and Ragnarok'. *Saga-Book* 17, 302–25.

Dronke, U., ed., and trans. 1969–2011. *The Poetic Edda*. 3 vols. Oxford.

DuBois, A. E. 1957. 'The dragon in Beowulf'. *Proceedings of the Modern Language Association* 72, 819–22.

Duchemin, J. 1995. *Mythes grecs et sources orientales*. Paris.

Duchesne, L., ed. 1892. *Le Liber pontificalis*. 4 vols. Paris.

Duchesne, L. 1897. 'S. Maria Antiqua: notes sur la topographie de Rome au moyen-âge'. *Mélanges d'archéologie et d'histoire* 17, 13–37.

Duine, F. 1904–5. 'Saint Armel'. *Annales de Bretagne* 20, 136–45, 431–71.

Duling, D. C. 1983. 'The *Testament of Solomon*', in J. H. Charlesworth, ed., *The Old Testament Pseudepigrapha*. 2 vols. New York. i.935–87.

Dumas, A., ed. 1981. *Liber sacramentorum Gellonensis: Textus*. CCSL 159-159a. 2 vols. Turnhout.

Dumont, L. 1951. *La Tarasque: essai de description d'un fait local d'un point de vue ethnographique*. Paris.

Dunand, F. 1969. 'Les representations de l'Agathodémon; à propos de quelques bas-reliefs du Musée d'Alexandrie'. *Bulletin de l'Institut français d'archéologie orientale* 67, 9–48.

Dunbabin, K. 1989. '*Baiarum grata voluptas*: pleasures and dangers of the baths'. *Papers of the British School at Rome* 57, 6–46.

Düwel, K. 1988. 'On the Sigurd representations in Great Britain and Scandinavia', in M. A. Jazayery and W. Winter, eds, *Language and Culture: Studies in Honor of Edgar C. Polomé*. Berlin. 133–56.

Dyssel, A. 2019. 'Jonah's *dāg gādôl*, a sea-monster associated with the primeval sea?' *Journal for Semitics* 28, 1–18.

Easterling, P. E., ed. 1982. *Sophocles: Trachiniae*. Cambridge.

Ebner, M., H. Gzella, H.-G. Nesselrath, and E. Ribbat. 2001. *Lukian:* Die Lügenfreunde. Scripta antiquitatis posterioris ad ethicam religionemque pertinentia (SAPERE) 3. Darmstadt.

Edelstein, E. J., and L. Edelstein. 1945. *Asclepius: A Collection and Interpretation of the Testimonies.* 2 vols. Baltimore; reprinted in 1998 with a new introduction.

Edwards, C. 2007. *German Romance III: Iwein, or The Knight with the Lion.* Martlesham.

Edwards, M. J. 1989. 'Three exorcisms in the New Testament world'. *Eranos* 87, 117–26.

Efthymiadis, S. 2011. 'Hagiography from the "Dark Age" to the age of Symeon Metaphrastes (eighth–tenth centuries)', in Efthymiadis 2011–14, i.95–142.

Efthymiadis, S., ed. 2011–14. *The Ashgate Research Companion to Byzantine Hagiography.* 2 vols. Farnham.

Efthymiadis, S., and V. Déroche. 2011. 'Greek hagiography in late antiquity (fourth–seventh centuries)', in Efthymiadis 2011–14, i. 35–94.

Ehrman, B. D. 2003. *The Apostolic Fathers.* Vol. 2. Loeb Classical Library. Cambridge, MA.

Eighteen-Bisang, R., and E. Miller. 2013. *Bram Stoker's Notes for* Dracula: *A Facsimile Edition.* Jefferson, NC.

Elderkin, G. W. 1937. 'Two curse inscriptions'. *Hesperia* 6, 382–95.

Eldevik, R. 1987. 'The Dares Phrygius Version of *Trójumanna saga*: A Case Study in the Cross-cultural Mutation of Narrative'. PhD diss., Harvard University.

Elliot, J. K., trans. 1993. *The Apocryphal New Testament.* 2nd ed. Oxford.

Ellis, H. R. [= H. R. E. Davidson]. 1942a. 'Sigurd in the art of the Viking age'. *Antiquity* 16, 216–36.

Ellis, H. R. 1942b. 'The hoard of the Nibelungs'. *Modern Language Review* 37, 466–79.

Ellis, H. R. 1943. *The Road to Hel.* Cambridge.

Elm, E., and N. Hartmann, eds. 2020. *Demons in Late Antiquity: Their Perception and Transformation in Different Literary Genres.* Berlin.

Elton, O., trans. 1894. *The First Nine Books of the* Danish History *of Saxo Grammaticus.* London.

Eppinger, A. 2015. *Hercules in der Spätantike: Die Rolle des Heros im Spannungsfeld von Heidentum und Christentum.* Philippika 89. Wiesbaden.

Ettmüller, L. 1850. *Engla and Seaxna Scôpas and Bôceras.* Quedlinburg.

Evans, J. D. 1984. 'A Semiotic of the Old English Dragon'. PhD. diss. Indiana University.

Evans, J. D. 1985. 'Semiotics and traditional lore: the medieval dragon tradition'. *Journal of Folklore Research* 22, 85–112.

Evans, J. D. 1998. 'Medieval dragon-lore in Middle-Earth'. *Journal of the Fantastic in the Arts* 9, 175–91.

Evans, J. D. 2000. 'The Heynesbók dragon: an Old Icelandic maxim in its legal-historical context'. *Journal of English and Germanic Philology* 99, 461–91.

Evans, J. D. 2005. ' "As rare as they are dire": Old Norse dragons, *Beowulf,* and the *Deutsche Mythologie*', in T. Shippey, ed., *The Shadow-Walkers: Jacob Grimm's Mythology of the Monstrous.* Tempe. 207–69.

Evans, J. G., and J. Rhys, eds, 1893. *The Text of the Book of Llan Dâv.* Old Welsh Texts 4. Oxford.

Fabricius, J. A., ed. 1719. *Codex apocryphus Novi Testamenti.* 2nd ed. 2 vols. Hamburg.

Falk, H. 2010. 'Libation trays from Gandhara'. *Bulletin of the Asia Institute* 24, 89–113.

Fallon, F. T., and R. Cameron. 1988. 'The Gospel of Thomas: a Forschungsbericht and analysis'. *ANRW* 2.25.6, 4195–251.

Faraone, C. A. 1992. *Talismans and Trojan Horses: Guardian Statues in Ancient Greek Myth and Ritual.* New York.

Farber, W. 1983. 'Lamaštu'. *Reallexikon der Assyriologie* 6, 439–46.

Faulkes, A. 1998. *Edda by Snorri Sturluson:* Skáldskaparmál. 2 vols. London.

Fauth, W. 1999. 'Der christliche Reiterheilige des Sisinnios-Typs in Kampf gegen eine viel-namige Dämonin'. *Vigiliae Christianae* 53, 401–25.

Felton, D. 2013. 'Apuleius' Cupid considered as a Lamia (*Metamorphoses* 5.17–18)'. *Illinois Classical Studies* 38, 229–24.

Fernández Marcos, N. 2000. *The Septuagint in Context: Introduction to the Greek Versions of the Bible*. Leiden.

Ferrari, F. 1613. *Catalogus sanctorum Italiae in menses duodecim distributus*. Milan.

Festugière, A.-J., ed. 1971. *Historia monachorum in Aegypto*. Brussels.

Finch, R. G., ed., and trans. 1965. *The Saga of the Volsungs*. Edinburgh.

Finlay, A., trans. 2000. *The Saga of Bjorn, Champion of the Men of Hitardale*. Enfield Lock.

Fischer, H. 1975–. 'Georg, Hl', in K. Ranke et al., eds, *Enzyklopädie des Märchens: Handwörterbuch zur historischen und vergleichenden Erzählforschung*. 13+ vols. Berlin. v, 1030–9.

Flobert, P., ed. 1997. *La Vie ancienne de Saint Samson de Dol*. Paris.

Floquet, A. 1833. *Histoire du privilége de Saint Romain*. 2 vols. Rouen.

Flower, H. I. 2017. *The Dancing Lares and the Serpent in the Garden: Religion at the Roman Street Corner*. Princeton.

Foerster, W. 1935. 'Δράκων', in C. Kittel and G. Friedrich, eds, *Theologisches Wörterbuch zum Neuen Testament*. Stuttgart. ii, 284–6.

Foerster, W., J. Grether, and J. Fichtner. 1957. 'ὄφις', in C. Kittel and G. Friedrich, eds, *Theologisches Wörterbuch zum Neuen Testament*. Stuttgart. v, 566–82.

Fontenrose, J. 1959. *Python: A Study of the Delphic Myth and its Origins*. Berkeley.

Fontenrose, J. 1983. Review of Mundkur 1983. *Asian Folklore Studies* 2, 292–4.

Forsyth, N. 1987. *The Old Enemy: Satan and the Combat Myth*. Princeton.

Foster, B. R., trans. 2005. *Before the Muses: An Anthology of Akkadian Literature*. 3rd ed. 2 vols. Bethesda, MD.

Fowler, R. L. 2000–13. *Early Greek Mythography*. 2 vols. Oxford.

Fox, P. 1990. *The Book of Kells*. 2 vols. Lucerne.

Franchi de' Cavalieri, P. 1908. *Hagiographica*. Studi e Testi 19. Rome.

Frangoulidis, S. 2008. *Witches, Isis and Narrative*. Berlin.

Frantz, A. 1965. 'From paganism to Christianity in the temples of Athens'. *Dumbarton Oaks Papers* 19, 187–205.

Fraser, P. M. 1972. *Ptolemaic Alexandria*. 3 vols. Oxford.

Friedman, J. B. 1988. 'Bald Jonah and the exegesis of 4 Kings 2:23'. *Traditio* 44, 125–44.

Friis-Jensen, K., ed., and P. Fisher, trans. 2015. *The History of the Danes: Saxo Grammaticus, Gesta Danorum*. 2 vols. Oxford.

Frost, P. 1991. 'Attitudes towards blacks in the early Christian era'. *Second Century* 8, 1–11.

Fry, D. K., ed. 1974. *The Fight at Finnsburg: Finnsburh Fragment and Episode*. London.

Fulk, R. D. 1992. *A History of Old English Meter*. Philadelphia.

Fulk, R. D., ed., and trans. 2010. *The Beowulf Manuscript: Complete Texts and The Fight at Finnsburg*. Dumbarton Oaks Medieval Library. Cambridge, MA.

Gager, J. G. 1992. *Curse Tablets and Binding Spells from the Ancient World*. New York.

Gambari, S. 2017. *La grotta dei serpenti: tra medicina e folclore*. Rome.

Ganschinietz/Ganszyniec, R. 1918. 'Agathodaimon'. *RE Supplementband* 3, 37–59.

Gantz, T. 1993. *Early Greek Myth: A Guide to Literary and Artistic Sources*. Baltimore.

Garitte, G. 1956. 'La passion géorgienne de sainte Golindouch'. *Analecta Bollandiana* 74, 405–40.

Gathercole, S. 2012. *The Composition of the Gospel of Thomas: Original Language and Influences*. Cambridge.

Gayrard, P. J. 2001. *Un dragon provençal: la légende de saint Hermentaire*. Arles.

Geldner, K.-F. 1886–96. *Avesta: The Sacred Books of the Parsis*. Stuttgart.

Gerard, E. 1885. 'Transylvanian superstitions'. *Nineteenth Century* (July 1885), 128–44.

Gero, S. 1971. 'The *Infancy Gospel of Thomas*: a study of the textual and literary problems'. *Novum Testamentum* 13, 46–80.

Gibson, J. C. L. 1978. *Canaanite Myths and Legends*. Edinburgh.

Glauser, J. 1993. '2. Draugr and aptrganga', in Pulsiano 1993, 623–4.

Godding, R. 2000. 'De Perpétue à Caluppan: les premières apparitions du dragon dans l'hagiographie', in Privat 2000, 145–57.

Goetz, O. 2000. 'Le théâtre du monstre', in Privat 2000, 53–78.

Gold, B. K. 2018. *Perpetua, Athlete of God*. Women in Antiquity. New York.

Goldsmith, M. E. 1963. 'The Christian perspective in *Beowulf*', in A. G. Brodeur hon. and S. B. Greenfield, ed., *Studies in Old English Literature in Honor of Arthur G. Brodeur*. Eugene, OR. 71–90.

Goldsmith, M. E. 1970. *The Mode and Meaning of Beowulf*. London.

Gooding, D. W. 1963. 'Aristeas and Septuagint origins: a review of recent articles'. *Vetus Testamentum* 13, 357–79.

Goodman, M. J., ed. 2012. *The Apocrypha*. Oxford.

Goslin, O. 2010. 'Hesiod's Typhonomachy and the ordering of sound'. *TAPA* 140, 351–73.

Goullet, M. ed. and trans. 1999. *Hrotsvita. Dramata*. Paris.

Gourmelen, L. 2004. *Kékrops, le roi-serpent: imaginaire athénien, représentations de l'humain et de l'animalité en Grèce ancienne*. Paris.

Gow, A. S. F., and A. F. Scholfield. 1953. *Nicander*. Cambridge.

Grabar, A. 1936. *L'Empereur dans l'art byzantin: recherches sur l'art officiel de l'empire d'Orient*. Paris.

Grabow, E. 1998. *Schlangenbilder in der griechischen schwartzfigurigen Vasenkunst*. Münster.

Graesse, J. G. T., ed. 1850. *Jacobus de Voragine: Legenda aurea*. Leipzig.

Gregory, T. E. 1986. 'The survival of paganism in Christian Greece'. *American Journal of Philology* 107, 229–42.

Grimm, Brüder. 1986. *Kinder- und Hausmärchen, gesammelt durch die Brüder Grimm*. 3 vols. Göttingen. [The standard edition of the originally 1812–15 work.]

Grindberg, M. 2013. 'Representation of angels in Byzantine art: interpretation of corporeality', in I. Moga, ed., *Angels, Demons and Representations of Afterlife in Jewish, Pagan and Christian Imagery*. Iasi, Romania. 373–84.

Grosjean, P., ed. 1956a. 'Vies et miracles de S. Petroc i'. *Analecta Bollandiana* 74, 145–65.

Grosjean, P. 1956b. 'Vies et miracles de S. Petroc ii'. *Analecta Bollandiana* 74, 487–96.

Guðmundsdóttir, A. 2012. 'Gunnarr and the snake pit in medieval art and legend'. *Speculum* 87, 1015–49.

Guralnick, E. 1974. 'The Chrysapha relief and its connections with Egyptian art'. *Journal of Egyptian Archaeology* 60, 175–88.

Gutch, Mrs. 1952. 'Saint Martha and the Dragon'. *Folklore* 63, 193–203.

Habermehl, P. 1992. *Perpetua und der Ägypter*. Berlin.

Hahn, K. A., and F. Norman. 1965. *Ulrich von Zatzikhoven. Lanzelet: eine Erzählung*. Berlin.

Haider, P. W. 2005. 'Von Baal Zaphon zu Zeus und Typhon', in R. Rollinger, ed., *Von Sumer bis Homer*. Münster. 303–37.

Haldon, J., trans. 2016. *A Tale of Two Saints: The Martyrdoms and Miracles of Saints Theodore 'the Recruit' and 'the General'*. Liverpool.

Halkin, F., ed. 1957. *Bibliotheca hagiographica Graeca*. 3rd ed. 3 vols. Subsidia Hagiographica 8a. Brussels.

Halkin, F. 1962. 'Un opscule inconnu du Magister Ouranos (la *Vie de Thédore le conscript*, *BHG* 1762m)'. *Analecta Bollandiana* 80, 308–24.

Halkin, F. 1966. 'La Passion de Sainte Parascève par Jean d'Eubée', in *Corpus der griechischen Urkunden des Mittelalters und der neueren Zeit. Reihe D: Beihefte, Forschungen zur griechischen Diplomatik und Geschichte*, Bd. 1. [Reprinted in F. Halkin, *Recherches et documents d'hagiographie byzantine* (= Subs. hag. 51). Brussels, 1971. 270–81.]

Halkin, F. 1973. 'Sainte Élisabeth d'Héraclée, abbesse à Constantinople'. *Analecta Bollandiana* 91, 249–64; corrections to text by W. Lackner at *Analecta Bollandiana* 92 (1974), 287–8.

Halkin, F. 1974. *Martyrs grecs, ii–viii siècles*. London.

Halkin, F., and A.-J. Festugière. 1984. 'Vie de s. Artémon (*BHG* 2047)', in F. Halkin, ed., *Dix textes inédits tirés du ménologe impérial de Koutloumous*. Geneva. 112–17.

Hall, A., S. D. P. Richardson, and H. Þorgeirsson. 2012–13. 'Sigrgarðs saga frækna: a normalised text, translation and introduction'. *Scandinavian-Canadian Studies/Études Scandinaves au Canada* 21, 81–155.

Hall, J. R. C. 1940. *Beowulf and the Finnsburg Fragment*. 2nd ed. London.

Hamilton, W., and J. H. W. Tischbein. 1791–5. *Collection of Engravings from Ancient Vases*. 4 vols. Naples.

Hansen, W. F. 2002. *Ariadne's Thread: A Guide to International Tales found in Classical Literature*. Ithaca.

Harder, A. 2012. *Callimachus: Aetia*. 2 vols. Oxford.

Harkins, A. K. 2020. 'Looking at the *Shepherd of Hermas* through the experience of lived religion', in V. Gasparini et al., eds, *Lived Religion in the Ancient Mediterranean World*. Berlin. 49–70.

Harrison, J. 1899. 'Delphika'. *JHS* 19, 205–51.

Harrison, J. 1922. *Prolegomena to the Study of Greek Religion*. 3rd ed. Cambridge.

Hartland, E. S. 1894–6. *The Legend of Perseus: A Study of Tradition in Story, Custom and Belief*. 3 vols. London.

Hartranft, C. D., trans. 1890. 'Sozomen *Church History*', in P. Schaff and H. Wace, eds, *Nicene and Post-Nicene Fathers*. Second Series. Vol. 2. Buffalo, NY. 448–952.

Hatto, A. T., trans. 1960. *Gottfried von Strassburg: Tristan*. London.

Hatto, A. T., trans. 1965. *The Niebelungenlied*. London.

Haubrichs, W. 1979. *Georgslied und Georgslegende im frühen Mittelalter: Text und Rekonstruktion*. Königstein.

Haustein-Bartsch, E., ed. 2016. *Von Drachenkämpfern und anderen Helden: Kriegerheilige auf Ikonen*. Recklinghausen.

Hay, J. 1994. 'The persistent dragon (*lung*)', in W. J. Petersen, A. Plaks, and Yü Ying-shi, eds, *The Power of Culture: Studies in Chinese Cultural History*. Hong Kong. 119–49.

Hayashi, T. 1992. *Bedeutung und Wandel des Triptolemos-Bildes vom 6.–4. Jh. v. Chr. Religionshistorische und typologische Untersuchungen*. Würzburg.

Haymes, E. R., trans. 1988. *The Saga of Thidrek of Bern*. London.

Headlam, W. 1922. *Herodas*. Cambridge.

Heckenbach, J. 1912. 'Hekate'. *RE* vii, 2769–82.

Heffernan, T. J. 2012. *The Passion of Perpetua and Felicity*. Oxford.

Heinzle, J. 1978. *Mittelhochdeutsche Dietrichepik: Unterschungen zur Tradierungsweise, Überlieferungskritik und Gattungsgeschichte später Heldendichtung*. Zürich.

Heinzle, J. 1999. *Einführung in die mittelhochdeutsche Dietrichepik*. Berlin.

Helgason, J., ed. 1924. *Heiðreks saga*. Copenhagen.

Helgason, J. 1950. *Biskupa sǫgur: MS Perg. fol. No. 5 in the Royal Library of Stockholm*. Copenhagen.

Hengstenberg, W. 1912. 'Der Drachenkampf des heiligen Theodor'. *Oriens Christianus* 2, 78–106 and 241–80.

Henken, E. R. 1991. *The Welsh Saints: A Study in Patterned Lives*. Cambridge.

Henrichs, A. 1994. 'Anonymity and polarity: unknown gods and nameless altars at the Areopagus'. *ICS* 19, 27–58.

Herdner, A. 1963. *Corpus de tablettes cunéiformes alphabétiques*. Mission de Ras Shamra, 10. Paris.

Herrick, S. K. 2010. 'Studying apostolic hagiography: the case of Fronto of Périgueux, disciple of Christ'. *Speculum* 85, 235–70.

Herter, H. 1950. 'Böse Dämonen im frühgriechischen Volksglauben'. *Rheinisches Jahrbuch für Volkskunde* 1, 112–43.

Heyman, A. 2013. 'Sirens chanting in Auvergne-Velay: a story of exegetical pilgrimage on the Via Podiensis'. *Ad Limina* 4, 69–115.

Hill, J., trans. 1977. 'Saga af Tristram ok Ísodd', in J. Hill, ed., *The Tristan Legend: Texts from Northern and Eastern Europe in Modern English Translation*. Leeds. 6–28.

Hinterberger, M. 2014. 'The Byzantine hagiographer and his text', in Efthymiadis 2011–14, ii.211–46.

Hoffner, H. A. 1998. *Hittite Myths*. 2nd ed. Atlanta.

Höfler, O. 1961. *Siegfried, Arminius und die Symbolik*. Heidelberg.

Höfler, O. 1978. *Siegfried, Arminius und der Nibelungenhort*. Sitzungsberichte, Österreichische Akademie der Wissenschaften. Philosophisch-historische Klasse 332. Vienna.

Hohler, E. B. 1999. *Norwegian Stave Church Sculpture*. 2 vols. Oslo.

Hollander, L. M., trans. 1949. *The Sagas of Kormák and the Sworn Brothers*. Princeton.

Honegger, T. 2017. 'The sea-dragon—in search of an elusive creature', in G. Huber-Rebenich, C. Rohr, and M. Stolz, eds, *Wasser in der mittelalterlichen Kultur/Water in Medieval Culture: Gebrauch—Wahrnehmung—Symbolik/Uses, Perceptions, and Symbolism*. Das Mittelalter 4. Berlin. 521–31.

Hopfner, T. 1921–4. *Griechisch-ägyptischer Offenbarungszauber*. Studien zur Paläographie und Papyruskunde. 2 vols. Frankfurt.

Hopman, M. G. 2013. *Scylla: Myth, Metaphor, Paradox*. Cambridge.

Hornblower, S. 2015. *Lykophron: Alexandra*. Oxford.

Hreinsson, V., ed. 1997. *The Complete Sagas of Icelanders, Including 49 Tales*. 5 vols. Reykjavik.

Hume, K. 1980. 'From saga to romance: the use of monsters in Old Norse literature'. *Studies in Philology* 77, 1–25.

Hunter, R. 2017. 'Serpents in the soul: the "Libyan myth" of Dio', in G. Hawes, ed., *Myths on the Map: The Storied Landscapes of Ancient Greece*. Oxford. 281–98.

Huttner, U. 2013. *Early Christianity in the Lycus Valley*. Leiden.

Huxley, G. 1974. 'Antecedents and context of *Digenes Akrites*'. *GRBS* 15, 217–38.

Icard-Gianolio, N. 1997. 'Hippokampos'. *LIMC* viii.1, 634–7.

Ingemark, C. A., and D. Ingemark. 2013. 'More than scapegoating: the therapeutic potential of stories of child-killing demons in ancient Greece and Rome', in C. A. Ingemark, ed., *Therapeutic Uses of Storytelling: An Interdisciplinary Approach to Narration as Therapy*. Lund. 75–84.

Inscriptiones Graecae. 1903–. Berlin.

Inscriptiones Graecae ad res Romanas pertinentes. 1906–27. Paris.

Irvine, S., ed. 2004. *The Anglo-Saxon Chronicle: A Collaborative Edition*. vii. *MS E*. Cambridge.

Irving, E. B., Jr. 1997. 'Christian and pagan elements', in Bjork and Niles 1997, 175–94.

Jacobsen, T. 1987. *The Harps That Once... Sumerian Poetry in Translation.* New Haven.

Jacoby, F., et al., eds, 1923–. *Die Fragmente der griechischen Historiker.* Multiple vols. and parts. Leiden.

Jacques, J.-M. 2002. *Nicandre: Oeuvres.* ii. Paris.

Jakobsson, Á. 2009. 'Talk to the dragon: Tolkien as translator'. *Tolkien Studies* 6, 27–39.

Jakobsson, Á. 2010. 'Enter the dragon: legendary saga courage and the birth of the hero', in M. Arnold and A. Finlay, eds, *Making History: Essays on the* Fornaldarsögur. London. 33–52.

Jakobsson, Á. 2011. 'Vampires and watchmen: categorizing the medieval Icelandic undead'. *Journal of English and Germanic Philology* 110, 281–300.

James, E., trans. 1991. *Gregory of Tours: Life of the Fathers.* Liverpool.

James, M. R. 1893–7. *Apocrypha anecdota.* 2 vols. Cambridge.

James, M. R. 1921. *A Peterborough Psalter and Bestiary of the Fourteenth Century.* Roxburghe Club editions 178. Oxford.

James, M. R. 1924. *The Apocryphal New Testament.* Oxford.

Janin, R. 1964. *Constantinople byzantine.* 2nd ed. Paris.

Jensen, B. 2017. 'Skull-cups and snake-pits: men's revenge and women's revenge in Viking Age Scandinavia', in U. Matić and B. Jensen, eds, *Archaeologies of Gender and Violence.* Oxford. 197–222.

Jensen, R. M. 2000. 'Art', in P. F. Esler, ed., *The Early Christian World.* 2 vols. London.

Jensen, S. R. 1993. *Beowulf and the Swedish Dragon.* Sidney.

Jentel, M.-O. 1997. 'Skylla I', *LIMC* viii.1, 1137–45.

Johnston, S. I. 1990. *Hekate Soteira: A Study of Hekate's Roles in the Chaldean Oracles and Related Literature.* American Classical Studies 21. Atlanta, GA.

Johnston, S. I. 1995. 'Defining the dreadful: remarks on the Greek child-killing demon', in M. Meyer and P. Mirecki, eds, *Ancient Magic and Ritual Power.* Leiden. 361–87.

Johnston, S. I. 1999. *Restless Dead: Encounters between the Living and the Dead in Ancient Greece.* Berkeley.

Joines, K. R. 1974. *Serpent Symbolism in the Old Testament: A Linguistic, Archaeological, and Literary Study.* Haddonfield, NJ.

Joines, K. R. 1975. 'The serpent in Gen. 3'. *Zeitschrift für die Alttestamentliche Wissenschaft* 87, 1–11.

Jones, D. E. 2000. *An Instinct for Dragons.* London.

Jones, G., trans. 1961. *Eirik the Red and Other Icelandic Sagas.* Oxford.

Jones, G. 1972. *Kings, Beasts and Heroes.* London.

Jónsson, F., ed. 1904. *Hrólfs saga kraka og Bjarkarímur.* Copenhagen.

Jónsson, F., ed. 1931. *Edda Snorra Sturlusonar.* Copenhagen.

Jónsson, F., ed. 1932a. *Morkinskinna.* Copenhagen.

Jónsson, F., ed. 1932b. *Saga Óláfs Tryggvasonar af Oddr Snorrason munk.* Copenhagen.

Jónsson, G., ed. 1935. *Edda Snorra Sturlusonar: með skáldatali.* Reykjavík.

Jónsson, G., ed. 1936. *Grettis saga Ásmundarsonar.* Reykjavik.

Jónsson, G., ed. 1954a. *Fornaldar sögur Norðurlanda.* 4 vols. Akureyri.

Jónsson, G., ed. 1954b. *Thiðreks saga af Bern.* 2 vols. Reykjavík.

Jónsson, G., ed. 1986. *Islendinga sögur.* 13 vols. Reykjavík.

Jordan, D. R. 1980. 'Hekatika'. *Glotta* 83, 62–5.

Jordan, D. R. 1985. 'A survey of Greek defixiones not included in the special corpora'. *Greek, Roman and Byzantine Studies* 26, 151–97.

Jorgensen, P., ed. and trans. 1999. 'Tristrams saga ok Ísöndar', in M. E. Kalinke, ed., *Norse Romance.* 3 vols. Cambridge. i, 23–226.

Junge, M. 1983. *Untersuchungen zur Ikonographie der Erinys in der griechischen Kunst.* Kiel.

Junod, E., and Kaestli, J.-D., eds. *Acta Johannis*. 2 vols. Turnhout.

Justi, F. 1868. *Der Bundehesh*. Leipzig.

Kaestli, J.-D. 1988. 'Où en est l'étude de l' "Évangile de Barthélemy"?' *Rev. Bib.* 95, 5–33.

Kahil, L., et al., eds, 1981–99. *Lexicon iconographicum mythologiae classicae*. 9 vols in 18 parts, with supplements. Zurich and Munich.

Kalinke, M. E. 1981. *King Arthur North-by-Northwest: The Matière de Bretagne in Old Norse-Icelandic Romances*. Copenhagen.

Kalleres, D. S. 2015. *City of Demons: Violence, Ritual, and Christian Power in Late Antiquity*. Berkeley.

Kålund, K., ed. 1898. *Gull-Þóris saga eller Þorskfirðinga saga*. Copenhagen.

Kandler, P. 1847. *Pel fausto ingresso di Monsignore illustrissimo e reverendissimo D. Bartolomeo Legat vescovo di Trieste e Capodistria nella sua chiesa di Trieste il dì XVIII Aprile MDCCCXLVII*. iv. Trieste. [Unpaginated]

Kapteyn, J. M. N., ed. 1926. *Wigalois, der Ritter mit dem Rade, von Wirnt von Gravenberc*. Rheinische Beiträge und Hülfsbücher zur germanischen Philologie und Volkskunde 9. Bonn.

Karras, V., trans. 1996. 'The Life of St Elisabeth the Wonderworker', in A.-M. Talbot, ed., *Holy Women of Byzantium: Ten Saints' Lives in English Translation*. Washington DC. 117–35.

Karttunen, K. 1989. *India in Early Greek Literature*. Helsinki.

Karttunen, K. 1997. *India and the Hellenistic World*. Helsinki.

Kassel, R., and C. Austin. 1983–2001. *Poetae comici Graeci*. 8 vols. Berlin.

Katz, J. 1998. 'How to be a dragon in Indo-European: Hittite *illuyankaš* and its linguistic and cultural congeners in Latin, Greek and Germanic', in J. Jasanoff, H. C. Melchert, and L. Oliver, eds, *Mir Curad: Studies in Honor of Calvert Watkins*. Innsbrucker Beiträge zur Sprachwissenschaft 92. Innsbruck. 317–34.

Keil, G., and T. Heirich, eds, 1857–80. *Grammatici latini*. 8 vols. Leipzig.

Keklidze, K. 1955. *Etiudebi jveli kʿartʿuli literaturis istoriidan*. iii. Tiflis.

Kelly, H. A. 1972. 'The metamorphoses of the Eden serpent during the Middle Ages and Renaissance'. *Viator* 2, 301–32.

Kermode, P. M. C. 1907. *Manx Crosses*. Angus.

Kershaw, N., trans. 1921. *Stories and Ballads of the Far Past*. Cambridge.

Kerth, T., K. G. T. Webster, and R. S. Loomis, trans. 2004. *Ulrich von Zatzikhoven: Lanzelet*. New York.

Khalifa-Gueta, S. 2018. 'The evolution of the western dragon'. *Athens Journal of Mediterranean Studies* 4, 265–90.

Kiessling, N. 1970. 'Antecedents of the medieval dragon in sacred history'. *Journal of Biblical Literature* 89, 167–77.

King, K. C., ed. 1958. *Das Lied vom hürnen Seyfrid*. Manchester.

Kircher, A. 1678. *Mundus subterraneus*. 3rd ed. 2 vols. Amsterdam.

Kirschbaum, E., et al., eds, 1968. *Lexikon der christlichen Ikonographie*. 8 vols. Freiburg im Breisgau.

Kißel, W. 1990. *Aules Persius Flaccus. Satiren*. Heidelberg.

Kittel, R., K. Elliger, and W. Rudolph, eds, 1997. *Biblia Hebraica Stuttgartensia*. Stuttgart.

Klaeber, F. 1911–12. 'Die christlichen Elemente im *Beowulf*. *Anglia* vol. 35, pp. 111–36, 249–70, 453–82; and vol. 36, pp. 169–99. English trans. (P. Battles) *The Christian Elements in Beowulf*. Old English Newsletter Subsidia 24. Kalamazoo, 1996.

Klaeber, F., et al. 2008. [*Klaeber's*] *Beowulf and The Fight at Finnsburg*. 4th ed. Toronto.

Klijn, A. F. J. 2001. 'The *Acts of Thomas* revisited', in Bremmer 2001, 1–10.

Klijn, A. F. J. 2003. *The Acts of Thomas: Introduction, Text, Commentary*. 2nd ed. Leiden. [1st ed. 1962.]

Klingshirn, W., trans. 1994. *Caesarius of Arles: Life, Testament, Letters.* Translated Texts for Historians 19. Liverpool.

Kneebone, E. 2020. *Oppian's* Halieutica: *Charting a Didactic Epic.* Cambridge.

Knös, B. 1962. 'Qui est l'auteur du roman de Callimache et Chrysorrhoe?' Ἑλληνικά 17, 274–95.

Koch, M. 2004. *Drachenkampf und Sonnenfrau: Zur Funktion des Mythischen in der Johannesapokalypse am Beispeil von Apk 12.* Tübingen.

Krappe, A. H. 1933. 'La légende de Persée'. *Neuphilologische Mitteilungen* 34, 225–323.

Krappe, A. H. 1941a. 'Irish earth'. *Folklore* 52, 229–36.

Krappe, A. H. 1941b. 'Sur un épisode de la saga de Ragnar Lodbrók'. *Acta Philologica Scandinavica* 15, 326–38.

Krappe, A. H. 1947. 'St Patrick and the snakes'. *Traditio* 5, 323–30.

Kraus, T. 1960. *Hekate: Studien zu Wesen und Bild der Göttin in Kleinasien und Griechenland.* Heidelberg.

Kreutzer, G. 1998. 'Die Saga von König Flores und seinen Söhnen', in J. Glauser, G. Kreutzer, and H. Wäckerlin, eds, *Isländische Märchensagas.* i. Munich. 77–112.

Kriaras, D. 1955. Βυζαντινὰ ἱπποτικὰ μυθιστορήματα. Βασικὴ Βιβλιοθήκη 2. Athens.

Krohn, R. 1980. *Gottfried von Strassburg.* 3 vols. Stuttgart.

Kroll, J. 1932. *Gott und Hölle: der Mythos vom Descensuskampfe.* Leipzig.

Krusch, B., and W. Levison, eds, 1951. *Gregorii episcopi Turonensis. Libri Historiarum X. MGH Scriptores rerum Merovingicarum* i.1. 2nd ed. Hannover.

Kuehn, S. 2011. *The Dragon in Medieval East Christian and Islamic Art.* Leiden.

Kunckel, H. 1974. *Der römische Genius.* Heidelberg.

Küster, E. 1913. *Die Schlange in der griechischen Kunst und Religion.* RVV 13.2. Giessen.

Lagerholm, Å., ed. 1927. *Drei Lygisögur.* Altnordische Sagabibliothek 17. Halle. 121–77.

Lai, W. 1992. 'From folklore to literate theater: unpacking "Madame White Snake"'. *Asian Folklore Studies* 51, 51–66.

Laing, S., trans. 1844. *The Heimskringla or The Sagas of the Norse Kings from the Icelandic of Snorre Sturluson.* New York.

Lalonde, G. V. 2006. Horos Dios: *An Athenian Shrine and Cult.* Leiden.

Lambert, W. G., and S. B. Parker. 1966. Enuma Eliš: *The Babylonian Epic of Creation: The Cuneiform Text.* Oxford.

Lamer, H. 1913. 'Hippokampos'. *RE* viii.2, 1748–72.

Lane, A. 1933–4. 'Laconian vase painting'. *ABSA* 34, 88–189.

Lane Fox, R. 2008. *Travelling Heroes: Greeks and their Myths in the Epic Age of Homer.* London.

Lanzillotta, L. R. 2015. 'A Syriac original for the *Acts of Thomas*? The hypothesis of Syriac priority revisited', in I. Ramelli and J. Perkins, eds, *Early Christian and Jewish Narrative: The Role of Religion in Shaping Narrative Forms.* Tübingen. 105–34.

Lapidge, M., and J. L. Rosier, trans. 1985. *Aldhelm: The Poetic Works.* Dover, NH.

Lapidge, M., and M. W. Herren, trans. 2009. *Aldhelm: The Prose Works.* Woodbridge.

Laporte, J., et al. 1965–72. *Millénaire monastique du Mont Saint-Michel.* 6 vols. Paris.

Laroche, E. 1971. *Catalogue des textes hittites.* Paris.

Larrington, C., trans. 1996. *The Poetic Edda.* Oxford World's Classics. Oxford.

Larrington, C. 2010. 'Þóra and Áslaug in *Ragnars saga lóðbrokar*: women, dragons and destiny', in M. Arnold and A. Finlay, eds, *Making History: Essays on the* Fornaldarsögur. London. 53–68.

Larson, J. 2016. *Understanding Greek Religion.* London.

Laufner, R., and P. K. Klein. 1974–5. *Trierer Apokalypse: Vollständige Faksimile-Ausgabe im Originalformat des Codex 31 der Stadtbibliothek Trier.* 2 vols. Graz.

Lausberg, M. 1990. 'Epos und Lehrgedicht: Ein Gattungsvergleich am Beispiel von Lucans Schlangenkatalog'. *Würzburger Jahrbücher für die Altertumswissenschaft* 16, 173–203.

Lautwein, T. 2009. *Hekate: Die dunkle Göttin*. Rudolstadt.

La Velue, légende sarthoise. 1813. Le Mans. [Anonymous pamphlet.]

Lawrence, W. W. 1918. 'The dragon and his lair in *Beowulf*. *Publications of the Modern Language Association of America* 33, 547–83.

Lawson, J. C. 1910. *Modern Greek Folklore and Ancient Greek Religion*. Cambridge.

le Bon, L. 2001. 'The "Bryggen shipstick": a challenge in art and ship technology', in I. Øye, A. Christensson, and E. Mundahl, eds, *Ships and Commodities. The Bryggen Papers*, Supplementary Series 7. Bergen. 9–34.

Leclerc, P., E. M. Morales, and A. de Vogüé. 2007. *Jérôme: Trois vies des moines (Paul, Malchus, Hilarion)*. Paris.

Lecouteux, C. 1979. 'Der Drache'. *Zeitschrift für deutsches Altertum und deutsche Literatur* 108, 13–31.

Lecouteux, C. 1995. *La Légende de Siegfried d'après la Chanson de Seyfried à la peau de corne et la Saga de Thidrek de Vérone*. Paris.

le Goff, J. 1980. *Time, Work, and Culture in the Middle Ages*. Chicago.

Leinweber, D. W. 1994. 'Witchcraft and lamiae in *The Golden Ass*'. *Folklore* 105, 77–82.

Leitz, C. 1997. *Die Schlangennamen in den ägyptischen und griechischen Giftbüchern*. Abhandlungen der Akademie der Wissenschaften und der Literatur 6. Stuttgart.

Lent, F. 1915. 'The Life of St. Simeon Stylites: a translation of the Syriac text in Bedjan's *Acta martyrum et sanctorum*, vol. iv'. *Journal of the American Oriental Society* 35, 103–98.

Lestón Mayo, A. 2014. 'Tracing the Dragon: A Study of the Origin and Evolution of the Dragon Myth in the History and Literature of the British Isles'. Diss. Santiago de Compostela.

Letta, C. 1972. *I Marsi e il Fucino nell'antichità*. Milan.

Leutsch, E. L., and F. G. Schneidewin. 1839–51. *Corpus paroemiographorum Graecorum*. 2 vols. Göttingen.

Levack, B. P. 2013. *The Devil Within: Possession and Exorcism in the Christian West*. New Haven.

Leventopoulou, M. 1997. 'Gryps'. *LIMC* viii.1, 609–11.

Lichtheim, M. 1973–80. *Ancient Egyptian Literature*. 3 vols. Berkeley.

LiDonnici, L. R. 1995. *The Epidaurian Miracle Inscriptions: Text, Translation and Commentary*. Atlanta.

Lillywhite, H. B. 2014. *How Snakes Work: Structure, Function and Behavior of the World's Snakes*. New York.

Lindholm, D., and W. Roggenkamp. 1968. *Stabkirchen in Norwegen: Drachenmythos und Christentum in der altnorwegischen Baukunst*. Stuttgart. Trans. as *Stave Churches in Norway: Dragon Myth and Christianity in Old Norwegian Architecture*. London, 1969.

Lionarons, J. T. 1993. 'The sign of a hero: dragon-slaying in Þiðreks saga af Bern'. *Proceedings of the Medieval Association of the Midwest* 2, 47–57.

Lionarons, J. T. 1998. *The Medieval Dragon: The Nature of the Beast in Germanic Literature*. Enfield Lock.

Lionarons, J. T. 2000. 'Sometimes the dragon wins: unsuccessful dragon-fighters in medieval literature', in R. P. Tripp, Jr., hon., L. C. Gruber, ed., *Essays on Old, Middle, Modern English and Old Icelandic in Honor of Raymond P. Tripp Jr.* Lewiston, ME. 301–16.

Lipsett, B. D. 2011. *Desiring Conversion: Hermas, Thecla, Aseneth*. Oxford.

Lipsius, R. A., and M. Bonnet, eds, 1891–1903. *Acta apostolorum apocrypha*. 2 vols. Leipzig.

Litavrin, G. G. 2003. *Кекавмен, Советы и Рассказы*. 2nd ed. Moscow.

Lloyd, A. B. 1976. *Herodotus. Book II. Commentary 1–98*. Leiden.

Lloyd-Jones, H. 1990. 'Erinyes, Semnai Theai, Eumenides', in E. M. Craik, ed., *Owls to Athens: Essays on Classical Subjects Presented to Sir Kenneth Dover*. Oxford. 203–11.

Loenertz, R. J. 1975. 'Actus Silvestri, genèse d'une légende'. *Revue d'histoire ecclésiastique* 70, 426–39.

López-Ruiz, C. 2006. 'Some oriental elements in Hesiod and the Orphic cosmogonies'. *Journal of Ancient Near Eastern Religions* 6, 71–104.

López-Ruiz, C. 2010. *When the Gods Were Born: Greek Cosmogonies and the Near East*. Cambridge.

López-Ruiz, C. 2018. *Gods, Heroes and Monsters: A Sourcebook of Greek, Roman and Near Eastern Myths in Translation*. 2nd ed. New York.

Loth, A., ed. 1962–5. *Late Medieval Icelandic Romances*. 5 vols. Copenhagen.

Loth, J., ed. 1893–4. '*Vita S. Teliavi*'. *Annales de Bretagne* 9, 81–5, 277–86, 438–46.

Loth, J., ed. 1894–5. '*Vita S. Teliavi*'. *Analecta Bollandiana* 10, 66–77.

Louden, B. 2011. *Homer's* Odyssey *and the Near East*. Cambridge.

Louis-Jensen, J., ed. 1981. *Trójumanna saga: The Dares Phrygius Version*. Copenhagen.

Lundberg, M. 1981. *Studier i anglabildens utformning och funktion under den kristna kyrkans forsta irtusende*. Uppsala.

Lunn-Rockliffe, S. 2012. 'Visualising the demonic: the Gadarene exorcism in early Christian art and literature', in R. Raiswell and P. Dendle, eds, *The Devil in Society in Premodern Europe*. Toronto. 439–58.

Macchioro, R. 2019. *Le redazioni latine della 'Passio Tryphonis martyris': Traduzioni e riscritture di una leggenda bizantina*. Quaderni di 'hagiographica' 16. Florence.

McCown, C. C. 1922. *The Testament of Solomon*. Untersuchungen zum Neuen Testament 9. Leipzig.

McCreless, P. 1982. *Wagner's* Siegfried: *Its Drama, History and Music*. Ann Arbor.

Mackensen, L. 1930. 'Drache', in H. Bächtold-Stäubli and E. Hoffmann-Krayer, eds, *Handwörterbuch des deutschen Aberglaubens*. 10 vols. Berlin. ii, coll. 364–405.

McTurk, R. 1991. *Studies in* Ragnars saga Loðbrókar *and its Major Scandinavian Analogues*. Oxford.

Malbon, E. S. 1990. *The Iconography of the Sarcophagus of Junius Bassus*. Princeton.

Mango, C. 1959. *The Brazen House: A Study of the Vestibule of the Imperial Palace of Constantinople*. Copenhagen.

Mango, C. 1983. 'The two Lives of St. Ioannikios and the Bulgarians', in *Okeanos: Essays Presented to Ihor Ševčenko on his Sixtieth Birthday by his Colleagues and Students*. Harvard Ukrainian Studies 7, 393–404.

Männlein-Robert, I., ed. 2019. *Über das Glück: Marinos, Das Leben des Proklos*. Tübingen.

Manteghi, H. 2018. *Alexander the Great in the Persian Tradition: History, Myth and Legend in Medieval Iran*. Library of Medieval Studies Book 8. London.

Maraval, P., ed. 1990. *La Passion inédite de S. Athénogène de Pédachthoé en Cappadoce (BHG 197b)*. Subsidia Hagiographica 75. Brussels.

Marchant, J., and J. Petit, eds, 1511. *Magni Honorati vita*. Paris.

Margeson, S. 1980. 'The Völsung legend in medieval art', in F. G. Andersen et al., *Medieval Iconography and Narrative: A Symposium*. Odense. 183–211.

Marinatos, S. 1926. 'Μινωικὴ καὶ Ὁμηρικὴ Σκύλλα'. Ἀρχαιολογικὸν Δελτίον 10, 51–62.

Martin, T. 2001. 'The development of winged angels in early Christian art'. *Espacio, Tiempo y Forma. Serie vii. Historia del Arte* 14, 11–29.

Martin-Hisard, B. 2011. 'Georgian hagiography', in Efthymiadis 2011–14, i.285–98.

Marwick, E. W. 1975. *The Folklore of Orkney and Shetland*. London.

Massman, H. F. 1857. *Ulfilas. Die heiligen Schriften alten und neuen Bundes in gothischer Sprache*. Stuttgart.

Mastrocinque, A. 2011. *Kronos, Shiva, and Asklepios: Studies in Magical Gems and Religions of the Roman Empire*. Philadelphia.

Mayor, A. 2000. *The First Fossil Hunters: Palaeontology in Greek and Roman Times*. Princeton.

Megas, G. A. 1970. *Folktales of Greece*. Chicago.

Merkelbach, R. 1959. 'Drache'. *RAC* iv, 226–50.

Michaux, L. 2000. 'Le Graouilly, entre histoire et l'imaginaire', in Privat 2000, 37–52.

Michel, F. X. 1836–40. *Chroniques anglo-normandes*. 3 vols. Rouen.

Michel, S. 2001. *Die magischen Gemmen im Britischen Museum*. 2 vols.

Migne, J.-P., ed. 1857–1904. *Patrologiae cursus completus: Series Graeca*. Paris.

Migne, J.-P., ed. 1884–1904. *Patrologiae cursus completus: Series Latina*. Paris.

Miller, A. M. 1986. *From Delos to Delphi: A Literary Study of the Homeric Hymn to Apollo*. Leiden.

Miller, M. C. 2000. 'The myth of Bousiris: ethnicity and art', in B. Cohen, eds, *Not the Classical Ideal: Athens and the Construction of the Other in Greek Art*. Leiden. 413–42.

Millington, B. 2011. '*Der Ring des Niebelungen*: conception and interpretation', in T. S. Grey, ed., *The Cambridge Companion to Wagner*. Cambridge. 74–84.

Minard, A. 2007. 'Colorful monsters: the afanc in medieval Welsh narrative', in J. F. Nagy, ed., *Myth in Celtic Literatures*. CSANA Yearbook 6. Dublin. 120–31.

Mitchell, B. 1963. 'Until the dragon comes…: some thoughts on *Beowulf*. *Neophilologus* 47, 126–38.

Mitropoulou, E. 1977. *Deities and Heroes in the Form of Snakes*, 2nd ed. Athens.

Möbius, T., ed. 1855. *Blómsstrvalla saga*. Leipzig.

Mombritius, B. 1910. *Sanctuarium sive vitae sanctorum*. 2nd ed. 2 vols. Paris. [1st ed. Milan, *c*.1480.]

Momma, H. 2016. 'Worm: a lexical approach to the *Beowulf* manuscript', in R. D. Fulk hon., L. Niedorf, R. J. Pascual, and T. A. Shippey, eds, *Old English Philology: Studies in Honor of R. D. Fulk*. Anglo-Saxon Studies 31. Cambridge. 200–14.

Monumenta Germaniae historica. 1826–. Hannover.

Moortgat, A. 1967. *The Art of Ancient Mesopotamia: The Classical Art of the Near East*. London.

Moretus, H. 1907. 'La légende de Saint Béat, apôtre de Suisse'. *Analecta Bollandiana* 26, 423–53.

Moricca, U. 1921–2. 'Un nuovo testo dell' "Evangelo di Bartolomeo"'. *Revue biblique* 30 (1921), 489–516; and 31 (1922), 20–30.

Morin, G., ed. 1937–42. *Sancti Caesarii episcopi Arelatensis opera omnia: nunc primum in unum collecta*. 2 vols. Bruges.

Morris, P., and D. Sawyer, eds, 1992. *A Walk in the Garden: Biblical, Iconographical and Literary Images of Eden*. Journal for the Study of the Old Testament Supplement Series 136. Sheffield.

Morris, W. 1876. *The Story of Sigurd the Volsung and the Fall of the Niblungs*. London.

Muguet, P., trans. 1900. *La Vie de Ste. Françoise Romaine*. Paris.

Müllenhoff, K. 1849. 'Der Mythus von Beovulf'. *Zeitschrift für deutsches Altertum* 7, 419–41.

Munch, P. A., ed. 1853. *Saga Olafs konungs Tryggvasunar: Kong Olaf Truggvesöns Saga.* Christiania (Oslo).

Mundkur, B. 1983. *Cult of the Serpent: An Interdisciplinary Survey of its Manifestations and Origins.* New York.

Murray, P., and L. Murray, eds, 1996. *The Oxford Companion to Christian Art and Architecture.* Oxford.

Mycoff, D., trans. 1989. *The Legend of Mary Magdalene and of her Sister Martha.* Kalamazoo.

Mylona, D. 2013. 'Dealing with the unexpected: unusual animals in an early Roman cistern fill in the sanctuary of Poseidon at Kalauria, Poros', in G. Ekroth and J. Wallenstein, eds, *Bones, Behaviour and Belief: The Zooarchaeological Evidence as a Source for Ritual Practice in Ancient Greece and Beyond.* Stockholm. 150–66.

Nagy, J., ed. (forthcoming). *Comparing Dragons, Ancient, Medieval, and Modern.* Turnhout.

Narkiss, B. 1979. 'The sign of Jonah'. *Gesta* 18, 63–76.

Nauck, J. A. 1889. *Tragicorum Graecorum fragmenta.* 2nd ed. Leipzig.

Nawotka, H. 2017. *The Alexander Romance by Ps.-Callisthenes.* Leiden.

Neckel, G. 1920. 'Sigmund's Drachenkampf'. *Edda* 13, 122–40 and 204–29.

Neidorf, L., ed. 2014. *The Dating of Beowulf: A Reassessment.* Cambridge.

Neidorf, L. 2017. *The Transmission of Beowulf: Language, Culture, and Scribal Behavior.* Ithaca.

Neils, J. 1990. 'Iason'. *LIMC* v.1, 629–38.

Neubauer, Ł. 2019. 'Quid Sigurthus cum Christo? An examination of Sigurd's Christian potential in medieval Scandinavia', in J. Morawiec, A. Jochymek, and G. Bartusik, eds, *Social Norms in Medieval Scandinavia.* Leeds. 155–72.

New English Bible. 1961. Oxford and Cambridge.

Nielsen, P. O. 2016. *The National Museum: Danish Prehistory.* Copenhagen.

Noegel, S. B. 2015. 'Jonah and Leviathan: inner-biblical allusions and the problem with dragons'. *Hen* 37, 236–60.

Nordal, S., ed. 1944–5. *Flateyjarbók.* 4 vols. Akranes.

Nordal, S., and G. Jónsson, eds, 1938. *Íslensk fornrit.* Vol. 3. Reykjavík.

North, R. 2006. *The Orgins of Beowulf: From Vergil to Wiglaf.* Oxford.

Nouveau-Piobb, M. F. 1961. *Hécate, la déesse magique des âmes.* Paris.

Oesterreich, T. K. 1930. *Possession, Demonical and Other: Among Primitive Races in Antiquity, the Middle Ages and Modern Times.* London. Trans. of *Die Besessenheit* (Langsalza, Germany, 1921).

Ogden, D. 1999. 'Binding spells', in V. Flint, R. L. Gordon, G. Luck, and D. Ogden, *Witchcraft and Magic in Europe.* Vol. 2. London. 1–90.

Ogden, D. 2007. *In Search of the Sorcerer's Apprentice: The Traditional Tales of Lucian's Lover of Lies.* Swansea.

Ogden, D. 2009a. *Magic, Witchcraft and Ghosts in the Greek and Roman Worlds: A Sourcebook.* 2nd ed. New York.

Ogden, D. 2009b. 'Lucianus, Glycon and the two Alexanders', in M. Çevik, ed., *International Symposium on Lucianus of Samosata.* Adiyaman. 279–300.

Ogden, D. 2010. *Alexander the Great: Myth, Genesis and Sexuality.* Exeter.

Ogden, D. 2013a. *Drakōn: Dragon Myth and Serpent Cult in the Greek and Roman Worlds.* Oxford.

Ogden, D. 2013b. *Dragons, Serpents and Slayers in the Classical and Early Christian Worlds: A Sourcebook.* New York.

Ogden, D. 2013c. 'The Alexandrian foundation myth: Alexander, Ptolemy, the *agathoi daimones* and the *argolaoi*', in V. Alonso Troncoso and E. Anson, eds, *After Alexander: The Time of the Diadochoi*. Oxford. 241–52.

Ogden, D. 2015. '*Katabasis* and the Serpent'. *Les Études classiques* 83, 193–210.

Ogden, D. 2017. *The Legend of Seleucus*. Cambridge.

Ogden, D. 2018a. 'Introduction', in R. J. Evans, ed., *Prophets and Profits: Ancient Divination and its Reception*. London. 1–15.

Ogden, D. 2018b. 'Dragonscapes and dread', in D. Felton, ed., *Landscapes of Dread in Classical Antiquity: Negative Emotion in Natural and Constructed Spaces*. London. 165–84.

Ogden, D. 2019a. 'The function of dragon episodes in early hagiography', in I. Schaaf, ed., *Animal Kingdom of Heaven: Anthropozoological Aspects in the Late Antique World*. Berlin. 35–58.

Ogden, D. 2019b. 'Lies too good to lay to rest: the survival of pagan ghost stories in early Christian literature', in D. Romero-González, I. Muñoz-Gallarte, and G. Laguna-Mariscal, eds, *Visitors from beyond the Grave: Ghosts in World Literature*. Coimbra. 65–80.

Ogden, D. 2021. *The Werewolf in the Ancient World*. Oxford.

Ogden, D. (forthcoming a). 'A snake and something more: the dragon in classical antiquity and the early medieval West', in Nagy (forthcoming). ch. 6.

Ogden, D. (forthcoming b). 'The serpent sire of Alexander the Great: a palinode', in F. Pownall, S. Müller, and S. Asirvatham, eds, *The Courts of Philip II and Alexander the Great: Monarchy and Power in Ancient Macedonia*. Berlin.

O'Hear, N., and A. O'Hear. 2015. *Picturing the Apocalypse: The Book of Revelation in the Arts over Two Millennia*. Oxford.

Olrik, J., and H. Raeder. 1931. *Saxonis* Gesta Danorum. Haunia.

Olsen, M. 1906–8. *Völsunga saga ok Ragnars saga loðbrókar*. 2 vols. Copenhagen.

Orchard, A. 1995. *Pride and Prodigies: Studies in the Monsters of the* Beowulf-*Manuscript*. Cambridge.

Orchard, A. 2003. *A Critical Companion to* Beowulf. Cambridge.

Otero Pereira, E. 2014. 'La evolución de la leyenda de san Frontón de Périgueux hasta Juan Gil de Zamora a propósito de la nueva edición de sus *Legende Sanctorum*'. *Studia Zamorensia* 13, 125–30.

Otto, W. F. 1910. 'Genius'. *RE* vii, 1155–70.

Overduin, F. 2005. 'Hellenistische slangen: De *Theriaka* van Nikander van Kolophon'. *Hermeneus* 77, 222–30.

Overduin, F. 2012. 'Snake poetry in ancient Greek: Nicander's *Theriaca*/Oudgriekse slangenpoëzie: de *Theriaca* van Nicander' [bilingual article]. *Litteratura Serpentium. Journal of the European Snake Society* 32, 78–92.

Overduin, F. 2014. 'The anti-bucolic world of Nicander's *Theriaca*'. *CQ* 64, 623–41.

Overduin, F. 2015. *Nicander of Colophon's* Theriaca: *A Literary Commentary*. Leiden.

Pailler, J.-M. 1997. 'La vierge et le serpent: de la trivalence à l'ambiguïté'. *Mélanges de l'École française de Rome. Antiquité* 109, 513–75.

Palli, E. L. 1968. 'Drache'. *LCI* i, 516–24.

Palmer, B. D. 1992. 'The inhabitants of hell: devils', in C. Davidson and T. H. Seiler, eds, *The Iconography of Hell*. Kalamazoo, MI. 20–40.

Palmer, K. 1976. *The Folklore of Somerset*. London.

Pálsson, H. 1980. *Göngu-Hrolfs Saga*. Toronto.

Pálsson, H., and P. Edwards, trans. 1985. *Seven Viking Romances*. London.

Pálsson, H., and P. Edwards, trans. 1989. *Vikings in Russia: 'Yngvar's saga' and 'Eymund's Saga'*. Edinburgh.

Pancaroğlu, O. 2004. 'The itinerant dragon-slayer: forging paths of image and identity in medieval Anatolia'. *Gesta* 43, 151–64.

Pankenier, D. W. 2013. *Astrology and Cosmology in Early China: Conforming Earth to Heaven*. Cambridge.

Papadopoulos, J. K. 2016. 'The natural history of a Caeretan hydria'. *Bulletin Antieke Beschaving* 91, 69–85.

Papadopoulos-Kerameus, A., ed. 1897–98. Ἀνάλεκτα Ἱεροσολυμιτικῆς σταχυολογίας. Vols 4–5. St. Petersburg. [Reprint Brussels, 1963.]

Paradiso, A. 2012-. 'Xanthos (765)', in Worthington 2012-.

Paschini, P. 1925. 'Richeche agiografiche: S. Cristina di Bolsena'. *Rivista di archeologia Cristiana*, 167–94.

Patera, M. 2015. *Figures grecques de l'épouvante de l'antiquité au présent: peurs enfantines et adultes*. Mnemosyne Suppl. 376. Leiden.

Paul, J. 1968. 'Jonas'. *LCI* ii, 414–21.

Pauly, A., G. Wissowa, and W. Kroll, eds, 1893-. *Realencyclopädie der klassischen Altertumswissenschaft*. Multiple volumes and parts. Munich.

Pedersen, C. W. 2019. 'The cursed and the committed: a study in literary representations of "involuntary" shapeshifting in early medieval Irish and Old Norse narrative traditions', in S. Barreiro and L. Cordo Russo, eds, *Shapeshifters in Medieval North Atlantic Literature*. Amsterdam. 107–26.

Peeters, P. 1910. *Bibliotheca hagiographica orientalis*. Subsidia hagiographica 10. Brussels.

Peeters, P. 1944. 'Sainte Golinduch, martyre perse († 13 juillet 591)'. *Analecta Bollandiana* 62, 74–125.

Penglase, C. 1994. *Greek Myths and Mesopotamia: Parallels and Influence in the Homeric Hymns and Hesiod*. London.

Perriam, W. 1989. *Devils, for a Change*. London.

Perry, B. E. 1967. *The Ancient Romances*. Berkeley.

Peters, D. E. 1997. 'The *Life* of Martha of Bethany by Pseudo-Marcilia'. *Theological Studies* 58, 441–60.

Peterson, E. 1954. 'Die Begegnung mit dem Ungeheuer: Hermas, Visio IV'. *Vigiliae Christianae* 8, 52–71.

Petroff, E. A. 1994. *Body and Soul: Essays on Medieval Women and Mysticism*. New York.

Petrus de Natalibus. 1493. *Catalogus sanctorum et gestorum eorum*. Vicenza.

Phillips, O. 1995. 'Singing away snakebite: Lucan's magical cures', in M. Meyer and P. Mirecki, eds, *Ancient Magic and Ritual Power*. Leiden. 391–400.

Piccalugia, G. 1976. 'I Marsi e gli Hirpi', in R. Garosi, hon., *Magia: Studi di Storia delle Religioni in Memoria di Rafaela Garosi*. Rome. 207–31.

Pichard, M., ed. 1956. *Le Roman de Callimaque et de Chrysorrhoé*. Paris.

Pietersma, A., and B. C. Wright. 2007. *A New English Translation of the Septuagint*. New York.

Pillion, L. 1903. 'Deux "vies" d'évèques sculptées à la cathédrale de Rouen'. *Gazette des Beaux-arts* 30, 441–54.

Plaine, F., ed. 1882. 'Vita S. Pauli Aureliani episcopi Leonensis in Britannia minori*, auctore Wormonoco'. *Analecta Bollandiana* 1, 208–58.

Plaine, F., ed. 1884. 'Vita S. Mevenni'. *Analecta Bollandiana* 3, 142–56.

Plaine, F., ed. 1887. 'Vita ii S. Samsonis'. *Analecta Bollandiana* 6, 77–150.

Ploss, E. 1966. *Siegfried-Sigurd, der Drachenkämpfer: Untersuchungen zur germanisch-deutschen Heldensage. Zugleich ein Beitrag zur Entwicklungsgeschichte des alteuropäischen Erzählgutes*. Cologne.

Pohlkamp, W. 1983. 'Tradition und Topographie: Papst Silvester I. (314–335) und der Drache vom Forum Romanum'. *Römisch Quartalschrift für christliche Altertumskunde und Kirchengeschichte* 78, 1–100.

Polo de Beaulieu, M.-A. 1991. *La Scala coeli de Jean Gobi*. Paris.

Poncelet, A. 1910. *Catalogus codicum hagiographicorum latinorum Bibliothecae Vaticanae*. Brussels.

Pons, J. 2011. 'From Gandahāran trays to Gandahāran Buddhist art: the persistence of Hellenistic motifs from the second century BC and beyond', in A. Kouremenos, S. Chandrasekaran, and R. Rossi, eds, *From Pella to Gandhara: Hybridisation and Identity in the Art and Architecture of the Hellenistic East*. Oxford. 153–75.

Porck, T., and S. Stolk. 2017. 'Marking boundaries in *Beowulf*: Æschere's head, Grendel's arm and the dragon's corpse'. *Amsterdamer Beiträge zur älteren Germanistik* 77, 521–40.

Porter, J., trans. 1991. *Beowulf: Text and Translation*. Hockwold-cum-Wilton.

Preisendanz, K., and A. Henrichs. 1973–4. *Papyri Graecae magicae: Die griechischen Zauberpapyri*. 2nd ed. 2 vols. Stuttgart. [Major classical libraries hold photocopies of the unpublished index volume.]

Price, R. M., trans. 1985. *Theodoret: A History of the Monks of Syria*. Ann Arbor.

Prieur, J.-M., ed. 1989. *Acta Andreae*. Corpus Christianorum, Series Apocryphorum 6. 2 vols. Turnhout. [Continuous pagination.]

Pritchard, J. B., ed. 1969. *Ancient Near Eastern Texts Relating to the Old Testament*. 3rd ed. Princeton.

Privalova, E. L. 1977. *Pavnisi*. Tbilisi.

Privat, J.-M., ed. 2000. *Dans la Gueule du dragon: histoire—ethnologie—literature*. Sarreguemines.

Provera, M. 1973. *Il vangelo arabo dell' infanzia*. Jerusalem.

Pulsiano, P., ed. 1993. *Medieval Scandinavia: An Encyclopedia*. New York.

P'yankov, I. V. 2006. 'Scythian genealogical legend in "Rustamiada" ', in M. Compareti, P. Raffetta, and G. Scarcia, eds, *Ērān ud Anērān: Studies Presented to Boris Il'ič Maršak on the Occasion of his 70th Birthday*. Venice. 505–12.

Quacquarelli, A. 1975. *Il leone e il drago nella simbolica dell' età patristica*. Bari.

Quasten, J. 1949–60. *Patrology*. 3 vols. [The fourth volume that subsequently appeared under the name of Quasten is by other hands.]

Quispel, G. 1957. 'The Gospel of Thomas and the New Testament'. *Vigiliae Christianae* 11, 189–207.

Radermacher, L. 1927. *Griechische Quellen zur Faustsage: Der Zauberer Cyprianus. Die Erzählung des Helladius. Theophilus*. Sitzungberichte der Akademie der Wissenschaft in Wien 206.4. Vienna.

Raison du Cleuziou, J., and R. Couffon. 1966. 'Le dragon dans l'art et l'hagiographie en Bretagne'. *Bulletin et mémoires de la Société d'émulation des Côtes-du-Nord* 94, 1–47.

Rajak, T. 2011. *Translation and Survival: The Greek Bible of the Ancient Jewish Diaspora*. Oxford.

Ranke, K. 1934. *Die zwei Brüder: Eine Studie zur vegleichenden Märchenforschung*. FFC 114. Helsinki.

Raschle, C. R. 2001. *Pestes Harenae. Die Schlangenepisode in Lucans Pharsalia (IX 587–949): Einleitung, Text, Übersetzung, Kommentar*. Frankfurt am Main.

Rauer, C. 2000. *Beowulf and the Dragon*. Cambridge.

Rawson, J. 1984. *Chinese Ornament. The Lotus and the Dragon*. London.

Reallexikon für Antike und Christentum. 1950–. Stuttgart.

Rebschloe, T. 2014. *Der Drache in der mittelalterlichen Literatur Europas*. Heidelberg.

Rees, W. J., ed. 1853. *Lives of the Cambro-British Saints*. Landovery.

Regnault, L. 1977. *Les Sentences des pères du désert. Nouveau recueil: Apophtegmes inédits ou peu connus.* 2nd ed. Sablé-sur-Sarthe.

Reichert, H. 2005. *Das Nibelungenlied.* Berlin.

Renberg, G. H. 2017. *Where Dreams May Come: Incubation Sanctuaries in the Greco-Roman World.* 2 vols Leiden. [Continuous pagination]

Resnick, I. M., and K. F. Kitchell, Jr. 2007. '"The sweepings of Lamia": transformations of the myths of Lilith and Lamia', in A. Cuffel and B. Britt, eds, *Religion, Gender, and Culture in the Pre-modern World.* Basingstoke. 77–104.

Riaño Rufilanchas, D. 1999. 'Δράκων', in C. Serrano, hon., *Τῆς φιλίης τάδε δῶρα: Miscelánea léxica en memoria de Conchita Serrano.* Madrid. 171–86.

Riches, S. J. E. 2003. 'Encountering the monstrous: saints and dragons in medieval thought', in B. Bildhauer and R. Mills, eds, *The Monstrous Middle Ages.* Cardiff. 196–218.

Riethmüller, J. W. 2005. *Asklepios: Heiligtümer und Kulte.* 2 vols. Heidelberg.

Rigault, N. 1609. *Vita S. Romani, episcopi Rotomagensis, e vetere martyrologio nunc primum edita.* Paris.

Robert, C. 1919. *Die antiken Sarkophag-Reliefs.* 3 vols. Berlin.

Roberts, A., J. Donaldson, and A. C. Coxe, trans. 1886. 'The Arabic gospel of the infancy of the Saviour', in A. C. Coxe, ed., *The Ante-Nicene Fathers* viii. Edinburgh. 405–15.

Rodríguez Pérez, D. 2008. *Serpientes, dioses y héroes: el combate contra el monstruo en el arte y la literatura griega antigua.* León: Universidad de León.

Rohde, E. 1925. *Psyche.* London. Translated from the 8th German ed.

Ropartz, M. S. 1864. *Notice sur la ville de Ploërmel.* Paris.

Rutherford, I. 2001. *Pindar's Paeans: A Reading of the Fragments with a Survey of the Genre.* Oxford.

Rutherford, I. 2007. 'Trouble in Snake-Town: interpreting an oracle from Hierapolis-Pammukale', in S. Swain, S. Harrison, and J. Elsner, eds, *Severan Culture.* Cambridge. 449–57.

Ryan, W. G. 1993. *Jacobus de Voragine. The Golden Legend. Readings on the Saints.* 2 vols. Princeton.

Salapata, G. 2009. 'Female triads on Laconian terracotta plaques'. *ABSA* 104, 325–40.

Salapata, G. 2021. 'Labor XI: the Apples of the Hesperides', in D. Ogden, ed., *The Oxford Handbook of Heracles.* New York. 149–64.

Sammer, M. 1999. 'Basilisk-regulus: Eine bedeutungsgeschichtliche Skizze', in U. Müller and W. Wunderlich, eds, *Dämonen, Monster, Fabelwesen.* Mittelalter Mythen. Band 2. St Gallen. 135–60.

Sancassano, M. L. 1997. *Il serpente e le sue immagini: il motivo del serpente nel poesia greca dall'Iliade all'Orestea.* Bibliotheca di Athenaeum 36. Como.

Sanjana, P. B., ed. 1874–1928. *The Dinkard.* 19 vols. Bombay.

Sarian, H. 1986. 'Erinys'. *LIMC* iii.1, 825–43.

Sarian, H. 1992. 'Hekate'. *LIMC* vi.1, 985–1018. [NB out of alphabetic sequence in *LIMC*.]

Sauerland, H., ed. 1896. *Sancti Clementis primi episcopi Mettensis vita, translatio ac miracula.* Trèves.

Sauzeau, P. 2000. 'Hékatè, archère, magicienne et empoisonneuse', in A. Moreau and J.-C. Turpin, eds, *La Magie.* 4 vols. Montpellier. ii, 199–222.

Sävborg, D. 2014. 'Búi the Dragon: some intertexts of *Jómsvíkinga saga'. Scripta Islandica* 64, 101–18.

Scarborough, J. 1977. 'Nicander's toxicology i: snakes'. *Pharmacy in History* 19, 3–23. Reprinted (with same pagination) in J. Scarborough, *Pharmacy and Drug Lore in Antiquity: Greece, Rome, Byzantium.* London, 2009.

Schade, H. 1968a. 'Adam und Eva'. *LCI* i, 42–70.

Schade, H. 1968b. 'Dämonen'. *LCI* i, 465–8.

Schermann, T. 1907. *Prophetarum vitae fabulosae*. Leipzig.

Schichler, R. L. 1986. 'Heorot and the dragon-slaying in *Beowulf*. *Proceedings of the PMR Conference* 11, 159–75.

Schiller, G. 1966. *Iconography of Christian Art*. 2 vols. London. Trans. of *Ikonographie der christlichen Kunst*. 5 vols. Gütersloh, 1966.

Schmerber, H. 1905. *Die Schlange des Paradieses*. Zur Kunstgeschichte des Auslandes 31. Strassburg.

Schmidt, M. 1992. 'Medeia'. *LIMC* vi.1, 386–98.

Schmidt, S. 1975–. 'Schlangenkrone, -stein', in K. Ranke et al., eds, *Enzyklopädie des Märchens: Handwörterbuch zur historischen und vergleichenden Erzählforschung*. 13+ vols. Berlin. xii, coll. 56–63.

Schneemelcher, W., ed. 1991–2. *New Testament Apocrypha*. rev. ed., 2 vols. Cambridge.

Scholl, O. H. F., ed. 1852. *Diu Crône von Heinrich von dem Türlin*. Stuttgart.

Schouten, J. 1967. *The Rod and Serpent of Asklepios*. Amsterdam.

Schröder, F. R., ed. 1917. *Hálfdanar saga Eysteinssonar*. Altnordische Sagabibliothek 15. Halle.

Schuchman, A. M. 2000. 'Politics and prophecy in the *Life* of Umiliana dei Cerchi'. *Florilegium* 17, 101–14.

Schwartz, G. 1987. *Triptolemos. Ikonographie einer Agrar- und Mysteriengottheit*. Horn.

Schwartz, G. 1997. 'Triptolemos'. *LIMC* viii.1, 56–68.

Schwemer, A. M. 1995. *Studien zu den frühjüdischen Prophetenlegenden. Vitae prophetarum Bd. I: Die Viten der großen Propheten Jesaja, Jeremia, Ezechiel und Daniel. Einleitung, Übersetzung und Kommentar*. Tübingen.

Schwenn, F. 1924. 'Lamia'. *RE* xii.1, 544–6.

Scobie, A. 1977. 'An ancient Greek *drakos*-tale in Apuleius' *Metamorphoses* viii, 19–21'. *Journal of American Folklore* 90, 339–43.

Scobie, A. 1983. *Apuleius and Folklore: Toward a History of ML3045, AaTh567, 449A*. London.

Scully, S. 2015. *Hesiod's Theogony: From Near Eastern Creation Myths to Paradise Lost*. Oxford.

Seaford, R. A. S. 1996. *Euripides: Bacchae*. Warminster.

Shanzer, D., and I. N. Wood. 2002. *Avitus of Vienne: Letters and Selected Prose*. Liverpool.

Shepard, K. 1940. *The Fish-Tailed Monster in Greek and Etruscan Art*. New York.

Shilton, H. 1997. 'The nature of Beowulf's dragon'. *Bulletin of the John Rylands Library* 73, 67–77.

Shouquan, S. 1989. *Dragon Tales: A Collection of Chinese Stories*. Beijing.

Sichtermann, H. 1983. 'Der Jonaszyklus', in Beck and Bol 1983, 241–8.

Siegelova, J. 1971. *Appu-Märchen und Hedammu-Mythos*. Wiesbaden.

Simon, E. 1957. *Die Portlandvase*. Mainz.

Simon, M. 1955. *Hercule et le Christianisme*. Paris.

Simpson, J. 1973. *The Folklore of Sussex*. London.

Simpson, J. 1978. 'Fifty British dragon tales: an analysis'. *Folklore* 89, 79–93.

Simpson, J. 1980. *British Dragons*. London.

Sineux, P. 2007. *Amphiaraos, guerrier, devin et guérisseur*. Paris.

Sisam, K. 1953. *Studies in the History of Old English Literature*. Oxford.

Sisam, K. 1958. 'Beowulf's fight with the dragon'. *Review of English Studies* 9, 129–40.

Skórzewska, J. 2011. *Constructing a Cult: The Life and Veneration of Guðmundr Arason (1161–1237) in the Icelandic Written Sources*. Leiden.

Skuse, M. 2015. 'The Reception of Egypt in the Archaic Period'. PhD diss., University of Exeter. Exeter.

Smith, G. 2008. 'How thin is a demon?' *Journal of Early Christian Studies* 16, 479–512.

Smith, M. S. 1994. *The Ugaritic Baal Cycle*. Vetus Testamentum Supplement 55. Leiden.

Smithers, G. V. 1961. 'The Making of *Beowulf*. Inaugural lecture, University of Durham. Durham.

Snell, B., R. Kannicht, and S. Radt. 1971–2004. *Tragicorum Graecorum fragmenta*. 5 vols. Göttingen.

Sorrell, P. 1994. 'The approach to the dragon fight in Beowulf, Aldhelm and the *Traditions folkloriques* of Jacques Le Goff'. *Parergon* n.s. 12, 57–87.

Sourvinou-Inwood, C. 1987. 'Myth as history: the previous owners of the Delphic oracle', in J. N. Bremmer, ed., *Interpretations of Greek Mythology*. London. 215–41.

Spaltenstein, F. 1986. *Commentaire des* Punica *de Silius Italicus*. 2 vols. Paris.

Speiser, J.-M. 1976. 'La christianisation des sanctuaires paiens en Grèce', in U. Jantzen, ed., *Neue Forschungen in griechischen Heiligtumern*. Tübingen. 309–20.

Spier, J. 2007. *Picturing the Bible: The Earliest Christian Art*. New Haven.

Stannish, S. M., and C. M. Doran. 2013. 'Magic and vampirism in Philostratus's *Life of Apollonius of Tyana* and Bram Stoker's *Dracula*'. *Preternature* 2, 113–38.

Steffen, U. 1963. *Das Mysterium von Tod und Auferstehung: Formen und Wandlungen des Jona-Motivs*. Göttingen.

Steffen, U. 1984. *Drachenkampf: Der Mythos vom Bösen*. Stuttgart.

Stephenson, P. 2016. *The Serpent Column: A Cultural Biography*. New York.

St John, C. 1923. *The Plays of Roswitha*. London.

Stoker, B. 1897. *Dracula*. London.

Stoker, B. 1911. *The Lair of the White Worm*. London.

Stokes, W., ed., and trans. 1890. *Lives of Saints from the Book of Lismore*. Oxford.

Stoneman, R., ed. 2007–. *Il Romanzo de Alessandro*. 3 vols. Milan.

Stordalen, T. 2000. *Echoes of Eden: Genesis 2–3 and the Symbolism of the Eden Garden in Biblical Hebrew Literature*. Leuven.

Studniczka, F. 1906. ' "Skylla" in der mykenischen Kunst'. *MDAI* 31, 50–2.

Supplementum epigraphicum Graecum. 1923–. Leiden.

Susi, E. 1995. 'La "Vita beati Mauri Syri abbatis et felicis eius filii apud vallem Narci prope Naris ripam" del Codice Alessandrino 89'. *Hagiographica* 2, 93–136.

Sveinsson, E. Ó., ed. 1939. *Vatnsdœla saga*. Íslenzk fornrit 8. Reykjavík.

Sveinsson, E. Ó., ed. 1954. *Brennu-Njáls saga*. Íslenzk fornrit 12. Reykjavík.

Swanton, M. 1996. *The Anglo-Saxon Chronicles*. London.

Symons, V. 2015. 'Wreoþenhilt ond wyrmfah: confronting serpents in *Beowulf* and beyond', in M. Bintley and T. J. T. Williams, eds, *Representing Beasts in Early Medieval England and Scandinavia*. Woodbridge. 73–93.

Talbot, A. 1983. 'Sigemund the dragon-slayer'. *Folklore* 94, 153–62.

Tally, J. 1983. 'The Dragon's Progress: The Significance of the Dragon in *Beowulf*, the *Bolunga Saga*, *Das Nibelungenlied*, and *Der Ring des Nibelungen*'. PhD diss. Denver.

Talon, P., ed., and trans. 2005. *The Standard Babylonian Creation Myth*: Enûma Elish. *Introduction, Cuneiform Text, Transliteration and Sign List with a Translation and Glossary in French*. Helsinki.

Taylor, J. H., ed. 1982. *Augustine: The Literal Meaning of Genesis*. 2 vols. Ancient Christian Writers 41 and 42. New York.

Taylor, T. 1925. *The Life of St Samson of Dol*. London.

Thiele, J. M. 1843. *Danmarks Folkesagn*. 2 vols. Copenhagen.

Thierry, N. 1963. *Nouvelles églises rupestres de Cappadoce: région du Hasan Daği*. Paris.

Thomas, A. M., and J. M. Abgrall, eds, 1901. *Albert le Grande, Les Vies des saints de la Bretagne armorique*. Quimper.

Thomas, J. W., trans. 1977. *Wigalois, the Knight of Fortune's Wheel*. Lincoln, NE.

Thomas, J. W., trans. 1986. *Ortnit and Wolfdietrich: Two Medieval Romances*. Columbia, SC.

Thomas, J. W., trans. 1989 *Heinrich von dem Türlin: The Crown, A Tale of Sir Gawein and King Arthur's Court*. Lincoln, NE.

Thorpe, L., trans. 1974. *Gregory of Tours: History of the Franks*. London.

Thorpe, R. S., W. Wüster, and A. Malhorta, eds, 1997. *Venomous Snakes: Ecology, Evolution, and Snakebite*. Oxford.

Thorsson, Ö. 1985. *Völsunga saga: og, Ragnars saga loðbrókar*. Reykjavik.

Thraede, K. 1967. 'Exorzismus'. *RAC* 7, 44–117.

Ting, N. 1966. 'The holy man and the snake woman: a study of a Lamia story in Asian and European literature'. *Fabula* 8, 145–91.

Tischendorf, C. 1876. *Evangelia apocrypha*. 2nd ed. Leipzig.

Tolkien, J. R. R. 1936. 'Beowulf: the monsters and the critics'. *Proceedings of the British Academy* 22, 245–95. Reprinted in J. R. R. Tolkien, *The Monsters and the Critics*. London, 1983. 5–48.

Tolkien, J. R. R. 1937. *The Hobbit, or There and Back Again*. London.

Tolkien, J. R. R. 1954–5. *The Lord of the Rings*. London.

Tomlin, R. S. O. 1988. 'The curse tablets', in B. Cunliffe, ed., *The Temple of Sulis Minerva at Bath*. ii. Oxford University Committee for Archaeology monographs 16. Oxford. 59–277.

Topper, K. 2007. 'Perseus, the maiden Medusa, and the imagery of abduction'. *Hesperia* 76, 73–105.

Trapp, E. 1972. '*Digenes Akrites*, Epos oder Roman?', in *Studi classici in onore di Quintino Cataudella*. 3 vols. Catania. ii.637–43.

Trautmann, R., and R. Klostermann. 1934. 'Das Martyrium von Paulus und Iuliana'. *Zeitschrift für slavische Philologie* 11, 2–21.

Travlos, I. N. 1939–41. *Ἡ παλαιὰ Χριστιανικὴ βασιλικὴ τοῦ Ἀσκληπιείου τῶν Ἀθηνῶν*. *Αρχαιολογική Εφημερίς* [no serial no.], 34–68.

Tripp, R. P., Jr. 1983. *More about the Fight with the Dragon: Beowulf 2208b–3182. Commentary, Edition and Translation*. Lanham, MD.

Tunstall, P., trans. 2003. *The Saga of Hrolf Kraki and his Champions*. London.

Tupet, A.-M. 1976. *La Magie dans la poésie latine*, Vol. 1: *Des origines à la fin du règne d'Auguste*. Paris.

Turville-Petre, G. 1956. *Hervarar saga ok Heiðreks*. London.

Twelftree, G. 1986. '*Ei de ego ekballo ta daimonia...*', in D. Wenham and C. Blomberg, eds, *Gospel Perspectives: The Miracles of Jesus*. Sheffield. 361–400.

Twelftree, G. 1993. *Jesus the Exorcist: A Contribution to the Study of the Historical Jesus*. Tübingen.

Twelftree, G. 2007a. *In the Name of Jesus: Exorcism among Early Christians*. Grand Rapids, MI.

Twelftree, G. 2007b. 'Jesus the exorcist and ancient magic', in M. Labahn and B. Jan Lietaert Peerbolte, eds, *A Kind of Magic: Understanding Magic in the New Testament and its Religious Environment*. London and New York. 57–86.

Unger, C. R., ed. 1877. *Heilagra manna søgur, Fortællinger og Legender om hellige Mænd og Kvinder*. 2 vols. Christiania (Oslo).

Uro, R. 2003. *Thomas: Seeking the Historical Context of the Gospel of Thomas*. London.

Usener, H., ed. 1886. *Acta S. Marinae et S. Christophori. Festschrift zur fünften Säcularfeier der Carl-Ruprechts-Universität zu Heidelberg, überreicht von Rector und Senat der Rheinischen Friedrich-Wilhelms-Universität*. Bonn.

Ustinova, Y. 2005. 'Snake-limbed and tendril-limbed goddesses in the art and mythology of the Mediterranean and the Black Sea', in D. Braund, ed., *Scythians and Greeks:*

Cultural Interactions in Scythia, Athens and the Early Roman Empire (Sixth Century BC–First Century AD). Exeter. 64–79.

Uther, H.-J. 2004. *The Types of International Folktales: A Classification and Bibliography*. 3 vols. FFC 284–6. Helsinki.

Valantasis, R. 1997. *The Gospel of Thomas*. London.

van den Gheyn, J. 1904. Review of Pillion 1903 (Bulletin no. 86). *Analecta Bollandiana* 23, 337–8.

van Dijk, J. 1983. *LUGAL UD ME-LAM-BI NIR-GAL*. Leiden.

van Dyke, C. 2003. *Ragnars Saga Loðbrókar*. Denver.

van Henten, J. W. 1999. 'Dragon, Δράκων', in K. van der Toorn, B. Becking, and P. W. van der Horst, eds, *Dictionary of Deities and Demons in the Bible*. 2nd ed., Leiden. 265–7.

van Hooff, G. 1883. 'Acta graeca S. Theodori Ducis martyris'. *Analecta Bollandiana* 2, 359–67.

van Nooten, B. A., and G. B. Holland. 1994. *Rig Veda: A Metrically Restored Text with Introduction and Notes*. Cambridge, MA.

van Thiel, H. 1971–2. *Der Eselroman*. Zetemata: Monographien zur klassischen Altertumswissenschaft 54. 2 vols. Munich.

Vassis, I. 2002. *Leon Magistros Choirosphaktes: Chiliostichos Theologia. Editio princeps. Einleitung, kritischer Text, Übersetzung, Kommentar, Indices*. Supplementa Byzantina 6. Berlin and New York.

Verbanck-Piérard, A., and E. Gilis. 1998. 'Héraclès, pourfendeur de dragons', in C. Bonnet, C. Jourdan-Annequin, and V. Pirenne-Delforge, eds, *Le bestiaire d'Héraclès: III*ᵉ *rencontre Héracléenne*. Kernos Suppl. 7. Liège. 37–60.

Verkerk, D. 2001. 'Black servant, black demon: color ideology in the Ashburnham Pentateuch'. *Journal of Medieval and Early Modern Studies* 31, 57–78.

Vermeule, E. 1977. 'Heracles brings a tribute', in F. Brommer, hon., U. Höckmann, and A. Krug, eds, *Festschrift für Frank Brommer*. Mainz. 295–301.

Vigfusson, G. 1886. 'Sigfred Arminius', in G. Vigfussen and F. York Powell, eds, *Sigfred Arminius and Other Papers*. Oxford. 5–21.

Vigfusson, G., and J. Sigurdsson. 1858–78. *Biskupa sögur*. 2 vols. Kaupmannahöfn.

Vikan, G. 1991–2. 'Two Byzantine amuletic armbands and the group to which they belong'. *Journal of the Walters Art Gallery* 49/50, 35–9.

Vilhjálmsson, B., ed. 1949–54. *Riddarasögur*. 6 vols. Reykjavík. vi, 85–145.

Vilmundarson, T., and B. Vilhjálmsson, eds, 1991. *Harðar saga*. Reykjavik.

Viltanioti, I. F. 2012. 'La Démone Yellô dans la Grèce ancienne, byzantine et moderne', in J. Ries and H. Limet, eds, *Anges et démons*. Louvain-la-Neuve. 173–89.

Vinogradov, A. 2013. 'St Parasceve of Iconium and her lost Greek *Acts*'. *Analecta Bollandiana* 131, 276–9.

Visintin, M. 2000. 'Echidna, Skythes e l'arco di Herakles: figure della marginalità nella versione greca delle origini degli Sciti, Herodot. 4, 8–10'. *Materiali e discussioni per l'analisi dei testi classici* 45, 43–81.

Vogels, W. 2011. '"And God created the great tanninim" (Gn 1:21)'. *Science et esprit* 63, 349–65.

Vos, N., and W. Otten, eds. 2011. *Demons and the Devil in Early and Medieval Christianity*. Leiden.

Waddell, H. 1934. *Beasts and Saints*. London.

Wade-Evans, A. W. 1944. *Vitae sanctorum Britanniae et genealogiae*. Cardiff.

Wagner, P.-E. 2000. 'Le Graouilly, chronique d'une folkorisation', in Privat 2000, 79–98.

Walcot, P. 1966. *Hesiod and the Near East*. Cardiff.

Walter, C. 1989a. 'The cycle of St George in the Monastery of Dečani', in V. J. Đuric, ed., *Децани и византијска уметност средином XIV века /Dečani et l'art byzantine au milieu du XIVe siècle*. Belgrade. 347–57.

Walter, C. 1989b. 'The Thracian horseman: ancestor of the warrior saints?' *Byzantinische Forschungen* 14, 659–73.

Walter, C. 1989–90. 'The intaglio of Solomon in the Benaki museum and the origins of the iconography of the warrior saints'. Δελτίον Χριστιανικῆς Ἀρχαιολογικῆς Ἑταιρείας 15, 33–42; reprinted in his *Pictures as Language: How the Byzantines Exploited Them. Collected Articles*. London, 2000. No. xxiii.

Walter, C. 1995. 'The origins of the cult of St George'. *Revue des études byzantines* 53, 295–326.

Walter, C. 1999. 'Theodore, archetype of the warrior saint'. *Revue des études byzantines* 57, 163–210.

Walter, C. 2003a. *The Warrior Saints in Byzantine Art and Tradition*. Aldershot.

Walter, C. 2003b. 'Saint Theodore and the dragon', in C. Entwistle ed. and D. Buckton, hon., *Through a Glass Brightly: Studies in Byzantine and Medieval Art and Archaeology Presented to David Buckton*. Oxford. 95–106.

Walz, D., ed. 1989. *Auf den Spuren der Meister: Die Vita des heiligen Magnus von Füssen*. Sigmaringen. 102–95.

Waser, O. 1905. 'Empusa'. *RE* 5, 2540–3.

Wathelet, P. 1998. 'Héraklès, le monstre de Poseidon et les chevaux de Tros', in C. Bonnet, C. Jourdan-Annequin, and V. Pirenne-Delforge, eds, *Le Bestiaire d'Héraclès. IIIe rencontre Héracléenne*. Kernos Suppl. 7. Liège. 61–74.

Watkins, C. 1995. *How to Kill a Dragon: Aspects of Indo-European Poetics*. New York.

Waugh, A. 1961. 'The folklore of the whale'. *Folklore* 72, 361–71.

Wellman, M. 1908. *Philumeni De venenatis animalibus eorumque remediis*. Leipzig.

Welti, F. E., ed. 1925. *Die Pilgerfahrt des Hans von Waltheym im Jahre 1474*. Bern.

West, D. R. 1995. *Some Cults of the Greek Goddesses and Female Daemons of Oriental Origin*. Alter Orient und Altes Testament 233. Neukirchen-Vlyun.

West, M. L. 1966. *Hesiod: Theogony*. Oxford.

West, M. L. 1997. *The East Face of Helicon*. Oxford.

West, M. L. 2003. *Homeric Hymns, Homeric Apocrypha, Lives of Homer*. LCL. Cambridge, MA.

West, M. L. 2007. *Indo-European Poetry and Myth*. Oxford.

Whatley, E. G., A. B. Thompson, and R. K. Upchurch, eds. 2004. *Saints' Lives in Middle English Collections*. Kalamazoo.

White, M. 2008. 'The rise of the dragon in Middle Byzantine hagiography'. *Byzantine and Modern Greek Studies* 32, 149–67.

White, M. 2013. *Military Saints in Byzantium and Rus 900–1200*. Cambridge.

White, T. H. 1954. *The Book of Beasts: Being a Translation from a Latin Bestiary of the Twelfth Century*. New York.

Whitehill, W. M., ed. 1944. *Liber sancti Jacobi. Codex Calixtinus*. 3 vols. Santiago de Compostela.

Whitney, K. W. 2006. *Two Strange Beasts: Leviathan and Behemoth in Second Temple and Early Rabbinic Judaism*. Harvard Semitic Monographs 63. Winona Lake, IN.

Whittaker, M., ed. 1967. *Die apostolischen Väter*, Vol. 1: *Der Hirt des Hermas*. 2nd ed. Berlin.

Wick, C. 2009. '"*Veros dracones putares*": Schlangenkunde in der antiken Fachliteratur und Poesie', in M. A. Harder, R. F. Regtuit, and G. Wakker, eds, *Nature and Science in Hellenistic Poetry: Proceedings of the Eighth Groningen Workshop on Hellenistic Poetry*. Leuven. 277–94.

Wilberforce Clarke, H. 1881. *The Sikandar Nama, e Bara*. London.

Wild, F. 1962. *Drachen im* Beowulf *und andere Drachen. Mit einem Anhang: Drachenfeldzeichen, Drachenwappen und St. Georg*. Vienna.

Wilson, D. M. 1970. 'Manx memorial stones of the Viking period'. *Saga-Book of the Viking Society* 18.1, 1–18.

Wilson, D. M. 1985. *The Bayeux Tapestry*. London.

Wilson, K. trans. 1998. *Hrotsvit of Gandersheim: A Florilegium of her Works*. Library of Medieval Women. Cambridge.

Winkelmann, F., ed. 1975. *Eusebius Werke*, Band 1.1: *Über das Leben des Kaisers Konstantin*. Berlin.

Winkler, J. J. 1980. 'Lollianos and the desperadoes'. *Journal of Hellenic Studies* 100, 155–81.

Wissowa, G. 1912. *Religion und Kultus der Römer*. Munich.

Wolohojian, A. M., trans. 1969. *The Romance of Alexander the Great by Pseudo-Callisthenes*. Trans. from the Armenian version. New York.

Wood, I. N. 2001. 'Avitus of Vienne, the Augustinian poet', in R. W. Mathisen and D. Shanzer, eds, *Society and Culture in Late Antique Gaul: Revisiting the Sources*. Aldershot. 263–77.

Woods, D. 2009. 'The origin of the cult of St. George', in D. V. Twomey and M. Humphries, eds, *The Great Persecution*. Dublin. 141–58.

Worthington, I., ed. 2012–. *Brill's New Jacoby*. Leiden. [Online resource.]

Yasumura, N. 2014. *Challenges to the Power of Zeus in Early Greek Poetry*. Bristol.

Yerkes, D., ed. 1984. *The Old English Life of Machutus*. Toronto Old English Series 9. Toronto.

Young, F. 2016. *A History of Exorcism in Catholic Christianity*. London.

Zimmerman, O. J., trans. 1959. *Gregory the Great: Dialogues*. The Fathers of the Church: A New Translation 39. Washington, DC.

Ziolkowski, J. 1984. 'Folklore and learned lore in Letaldus' whale poem'. *Viator* 15, 107–18.

Zitzelsberger, O. 1980. 'Konráðs saga keisarasonar'. *Seminar for Germanic Philology Yearbook* [no serial no.], 38–67.

Zitzelsberger, O., ed. 1988. *Konráðs saga keisarasonar*. New York.

Zoëga, G. T. 1910. *A Concise Dictionary of Old Icelandic*. Oxford.

Index